McGraw-Hill Ryerson
Foundations for College Mathematics 11

Authors

Wayne Erdman
B.Math., B.Ed.
Toronto District School Board

Steve Etienne
B.Sc., B.Admin., Ed.Cert.
District School Board of Niagara

John Ferguson
B.Sc., B.Ed.
Lambton Kent District School Board

Roland W. Meisel
B.Sc., B.Ed., M.Sc.
Port Colborne, Ontario

David Petro
B.Sc. (Hons.), B.Ed., M.Sc.
Windsor Essex Catholic District
School Board

John Santarelli
B.Sc., B.Ed.
Hamilton-Wentworth Catholic
District School Board

Ken Stewart
B.Sc. (Hons.), B.Ed.
York Region District School Board

Contributing Authors

Lynda M. Ferneyhough
B.Math, M.Ed.
Peel District School Board

Kirsten Boucher
B.Math., B.Ed.
Durham District School Board

Assessment Consultant

Lynda M. Ferneyhough
B.Math., M.Ed.
Peel District School Board

Differentiated Instruction Consultant

Barb Vukets
B.Ed., M.Ed.
Waterloo District School Board

Literacy Consultant

Steve Bibla
B.Sc. (Hons.), B.Ed.
Toronto District School Board

Pedagogy Consultant

Lynda M. Ferneyhough
B.Math., M.Ed.
Peel District School Board

Jacqueline Hill
B.Sc., B.Ed.
Durham District School Board

David Lovisa
B.A., B.Ed.
York Region District School
Board

Technology Consultant

Roland W. Meisel
B.Sc., B.Ed., M.Sc.
Port Colborne, Ontario

Advisors

Derrick Driscoll
B.Sc., B.Ed.
Thames Valley District School
Board

Carol Miron
B.Sc., B.Ed.
Toronto District School Board

Colleen Morgulis
B.Math. (Hons.), B.Ed.
Durham Catholic District School
Board

Terry Paradellis
B.A., B.Ed., M.A., M.Ed.
Toronto District School Board

Larry Romano
B.A. (Hons.), B.Ed.
Toronto Catholic District School
Board

Carol Shiffman
B.Math. (Hons.), B.Ed.
Peel District School Board

Sunil Singh
B.Sc., B.Ed.
Toronto District School Board

Susan Siskind
B.A. (Hons), Professional Ed.
Program
Toronto, Ontario

McGraw-Hill Ryerson

Toronto   Montréal   Boston   Burr Ridge, IL   Dubuque, IA   Madison, WI   New York
San Francisco   St. Louis   Bangkok   Bogotá   Caracas   Kuala Lumpur   Lisbon   London
Madrid   Mexico City   Milan   New Delhi   Santiago   Seoul   Singapore   Sydney   Taipei

COPIES OF THIS BOOK MAY BE OBTAINED BY CONTACTING:
McGraw-Hill Ryerson Ltd.

WEB SITE:
www.mcgrawhill.ca

E-MAIL:
orders@mcgrawhill.ca

TOLL-FREE FAX:
1-800-463-5885

TOLL-FREE CALL:
1-800-565-5758

OR BY MAILING YOUR ORDER TO:
McGraw-Hill Ryerson
Order Department
300 Water Street
Whitby, ON L1N 9B6

Please quote the ISBN and title when placing your order.

Student Text ISBN:
978-0-07-078084-2

The McGraw·Hill Companies

McGraw-Hill Ryerson
Foundations for College Mathematics 11

ISBN-13: 978-0-07-078084-2
ISBN-10: 0-07-078084-6

www.mcgrawhill.ca

4 5 6 7 8 9 10   TCP   0 9

Printed and bound in Canada

Care has been taken to trace ownership of copyright material contained in this text. The publishers will gladly accept any information that will enable them to rectify any reference or credit in subsequent printings.

CBR™ is a trademark of Texas Instruments.

Fathom Dynamic Statistics™ *Software* and *The Geometer's Sketchpad*®, Key Curriculum Press, 1150 65th Street, Emeryville, CA 94608, 1-800-995-MATH.

Microsoft® *Excel* is a registered trademark of Microsoft Corporation in the United States and/or other countries.

Statistics Canada information is used with the permission of Statistics Canada. Users are forbidden to copy the data and redisseminate them, in an original or modified form, for commercial purposes, without permission from Statistics Canada. Information on the availability of the wide range of data from Statistics Canada can be obtained from Statistics Canada's Regional Offices, its World Wide Web site at http://www.statcan.ca, and its toll-free access number 1-800-263-1136.

PUBLISHER: Linda Allison
ASSOCIATE PUBLISHER: Kristi Clark
PROJECT MANAGEMENT: First Folio Resource Group, Inc.: Eileen Jung,
                                    Maggie Cheverie
DEVELOPMENTAL EDITORS: Ingrid d'Silva, Susan Lishman
MANAGER, EDITORIAL SERVICES: Crystal Shortt
SUPERVISING EDITOR: Janie Deneau
COPY EDITORS: Laurel Sparrow, Loretta Johnson
PHOTO RESEARCH: Maria De Cambra
PERMISSIONS: Maria De Cambra
EDITORIAL ASSISTANT: Erin Hartley
REVIEW COORDINATOR: Jennifer Keay
MANAGER, PRODUCTION SERVICES: Yolanda Pigden
PRODUCTION CO-ORDINATOR: Jennifer Wilkie
COVER DESIGN: Liz Harasymczuk
INTERIOR DESIGN: Pronk&Associates
ART DIRECTION: First Folio Resource Group, Inc.: Tom Dart
ELECTRONIC PAGE MAKE-UP: First Folio Resource Group, Inc.: Tom Dart,
                                    Kim Hutchinson, Adam Wood
COVER IMAGE: Courtesy of Getty Images

Acknowledgements

Reviewers of Foundations of Mathematics 11

The publishers, authors, and editors of *McGraw-Hill Ryerson Foundations For College Mathematics 11*, wish to extend their sincere thanks to the students, teachers, consultants, and reviewers who contributed their time, energy, and expertise to the creation of this textbook. We are grateful for their thoughtful comments and suggestions. This feedback has been invaluable in ensuring that the text and related teacher's resource meet the needs of students and teachers.

Rachel Abraham
Ottawa-Carleton Catholic District School Board

Kirsten Boucher
Durham District School Board

Joe Cammara
Toronto Catholic District School Board

Dave Caraher
Lambton Kent District School Board

Angela Chan
Toronto District School Board

Dan Ciarmoli
Hamilton-Wentworth District School Board

Andrea Clarke
Ottawa-Carleton District School Board

Emidio DiAntonio
Dufferin-Peel Catholic District School Board

Roxanne Evans
Algonquin and Lakeshore Catholic District School Board

Karen Frazer
Ottawa-Carleton District School Board

Robert R. Gleeson
Bluewater District School Board

Magdalena Grzesiuk
Dufferin-Peel Catholic District School Board

Raymond Ho
Durham District School Board

Murray Johnston
Halton District School Board

John Kreisz
Kawartha Pine Ridge District School Board

Alison Lane
Ottawa-Carleton District School Board

Janine LeBlanc
Toronto District School Board

Donna Manning-Currie
Simcoe County District School Board

Paul Marchildon
Ottawa-Carleton District School Board

Steve Martinello
Peel District School Board

Janet Moir
Toronto Catholic District School Board

Donald Mountain
Thames Valley District School Board

Natalie O'Byrne
Ottawa-Carleton Catholic District School Board

Michael Ralphs
Halton Catholic District School Board

Julie Sheremeto
Ottawa-Carleton District School Board

Carolyn Sproule
Ottawa-Carleton District School Board

Tony Stancati
Toronto Catholic District School Board

Maria Stewart
Dufferin-Peel Catholic District School Board

Henry Tam
Toronto District School Board

Nancy Tsiobanos
Dufferin-Peel Catholic District School Board

Anne Walton
Ottawa-Carleton District School Board

David Young
Peel District School Board

Contents

A Tour of Your Textbook   vi

Chapter 1

Trigonometry   2
Prerequisite Skills   4
1.1 Revisit the Primary Trigonometric Ratios   6
1.2 Solve Problems Using Trigonometric Ratios   16
1.3 The Sine Law   24
1.4 The Cosine Law   34
1.5 Make Decisions Using Trigonometry   42
Chapter 1 Review   52
Chapter 1 Practice Test   54

Chapter 2

Probability   56
Prerequisite Skills   58
2.1 Probability Experiments   60
2.2 Theoretical Probability   68
2.3 Compare Experimental and Theoretical Probabilities   76
2.4 Interpret Information Involving Probability   86
Chapter 2 Review   94
Chapter 2 Practice Test   96

Chapter 3

One Variable Statistics   98
Prerequisite Skills   100
3.1 Sampling Techniques   102
3.2 Collect and Analyse Data   110
3.3 Display Data   118
3.4 Measures of Central Tendency   130
3.5 Measures of Spread   140
3.6 Common Distributions   148
Chapter 3 Review   156
Chapter 3 Practice Test   158
Chapters 1 to 3 Review   160
Task: Road to the Stanley Cup   162

Chapter 4

Quadratic Relations I   164
Prerequisite Skills   166
4.1 Modelling With Quadratic Relations   168
4.2 The Quadratic Relation $y = ax^2 + k$ 180
4.3 The Quadratic Relation $y = a(x - h)^2$ 194
4.4 The Quadratic Relation $y = a(x - h)^2 + k$ 204
4.5 Interpret Graphs of Quadratic Relations   218
Chapter 4 Review   226
Chapter 4 Practice Test   228

Chapter 5

Quadratic Relations II   230
Prerequisite Skills   232
5.1 Expand Binomials   234
5.2 Change Quadratic Relations From Vertex Form to Standard Form   242
5.3 Factor Trinomials of the Form $x^2 + bx + c$ 248
5.4 Factor Trinomials of the Form $ax^2 + bx + c$ 256
5.5 The x-Intercepts of a Quadratic Relation   264
5.6 Solve Problems Involving Quadratic Relations   276
Chapter 5 Review   286
Chapter 5 Practice Test   288
Task: Design a Soccer Field   290

Chapter 6

Geometry in Design	**292**
Prerequisite Skills	**294**
6.1 Investigate Geometric Shapes and Figures	**296**
6.2 Perspective and Orthographic Drawings	**306**
6.3 Create Nets, Plans, and Patterns	**318**
Use Technology	
Use *The Geometer's Sketchpad*® to Draw Plans With Dynamic Measurements	**325**
6.4 Scale Models	**327**
6.5 Solve Problems With Given Constraints	**335**
Use Technology	
Use *The Geometer's Sketchpad*® to Create Tessellations Using Rotations	**344**
Chapter 6 Review	**346**
Chapter 6 Practice Test	**348**
Chapters 4 to 6 Review	**350**

Chapter 7

Exponents	**352**
Prerequisite Skills	**354**
7.1 Exponent Rules	**356**
7.2 Zero and Negative Exponents	**364**
7.3 Investigate Exponential Relationships	**372**
7.4 Exponential Relations	**382**
7.5 Modelling Exponential Growth and Decay	**395**
7.6 Solve Problems Involving Exponential Growth and Decay	**406**
Chapter 7 Review	**414**
Chapter 7 Practice Test	**416**

Chapter 8

Compound Interest	**418**
Prerequisite Skills	**420**
8.1 Simple and Compound Interest	**422**
8.2 Compound Interest	**430**
8.3 Present Value	**436**
8.4 The TVM Solver	**442**
8.5 Effects of Changing the Conditions on Investments and Loans	**446**
Chapter 8 Review	**454**
Chapter 8 Practice Test	**456**

Chapter 9

Personal Finance	**458**
Prerequisite Skills	**460**
9.1 Savings Alternatives	**462**
9.2 Investment Alternatives	**468**
9.3 Manage Credit Cards	**476**
9.4 Obtain a Vehicle	**482**
9.5 Operate a Vehicle	**489**
Chapter 9 Review	**496**
Chapter 9 Practice Test	**498**
Chapters 7 to 9 Review	**500**
Task: Organise Your Personal Finances	**502**
Chapter 1 to 9 Review	**504**
Technology Appendix	**514**
Answers	**550**
Glossary	**588**
Index	**595**
Credits	**599**

A Tour of Your Textbook

Chapter Opener

- This two-page spread introduces the concepts you will learn about in the chapter.
- The specific curriculum expectations that the chapter covers are listed.
- Key Terms lists the mathematical terms that are introduced and defined in the chapter.

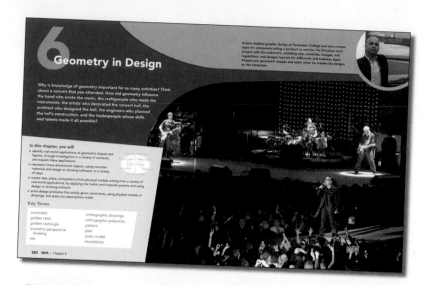

Prerequisite Skills

- Questions review key skills from previous mathematics courses that are needed for success with the new concepts of the chapter.
- The chapter problem is introduced. Questions related to the chapter problem occur in the Apply sections of the exercises throughout the chapter and are identified by a **Chapter Problem** descriptor.

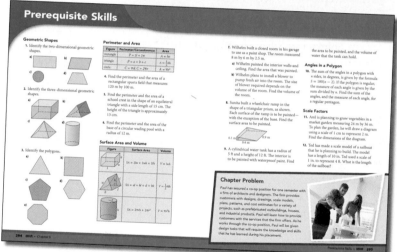

Numbered Sections

Lesson Opener

Lessons start with a photograph and short description of a real-world setting to which the mathematical concepts relate.

Investigate

These are step-by-step activities, leading you to build your own understanding of the new concepts of the lesson. Many of these activities can best be done by working in pairs or small groups to share ideas.

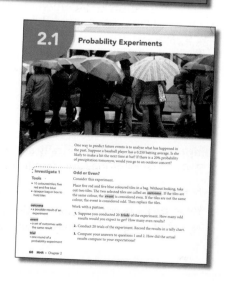

Examples

- Worked Examples provide model solutions that show how the new concepts are used.
- The Examples and their worked Solutions include several tools to help you understand the work.
  - Side notes help you think through the steps.
  - Sometimes different methods of solving the same problem are shown. One method may make more sense to you than the other.
  - Calculator key strokes for scientific, Direct Algebraic Logic (DAL), and graphing calculators are provided. Sample graphing calculator screens are shown.

Key Concepts

- This feature summarizes the concepts learned in the lesson.
- You can refer to this summary when you are studying or doing homework.

Discuss the Concepts

These questions allow you to reflect on the concepts of the section. By discussing these questions in a group, you can see whether you understand the main points and are ready to start the exercises.

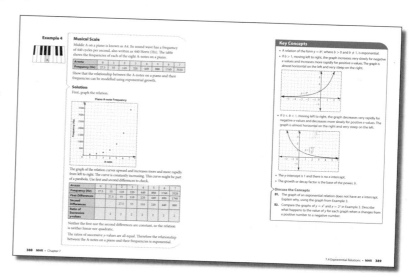

Exercises

Practise (A)

- These questions provide an opportunity to practise your knowledge and understanding of the new concept.
- To help you, questions are referenced to the worked Examples.

Apply (B)

- These questions allow you to use what you learned to solve problems and make connections among concepts. In answering these questions you will be integrating many of the math processes.
- Some questions are specifically designed to help you improve your literacy skills. These questions are identified with a **Literacy Connect** descriptor.

Extend (C)

- These are more challenging and thought-provoking questions.
- Some Extend questions may require integration of skills from other areas.

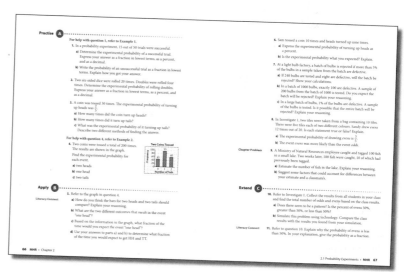

A Tour of Your Textbook

Technology

Scientific calculators are useful for many sections. Key-stroke sequences are provided for techniques that may be new to you.

- A TI-83 Plus or TI-84 Plus graphing calculator is useful for some sections, particularly for data analysis and for graphing relations.

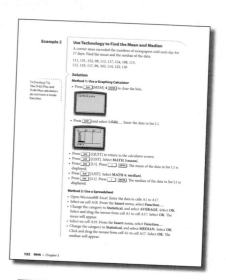

- *The Geometer's Sketchpad®* is used in several sections for investigating concepts related to measurement and geometry. Alternative steps for doing investigations using pencil and paper are provided for those who may not have access to this computer software.
- Spreadsheet software and *Fathom*™ are used in the Statistics chapter.

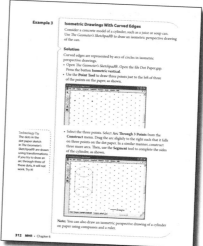

- The Technology Appendix, on pages 514–549, provides detailed instructions for some basic functions of the technology tools used in the text. The Appendix will be helpful to anyone who has not used these tools before.

Technology Tip

This margin feature provides helpful hints or alternative strategies for working with the specific tools shown in a solution.

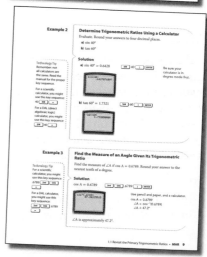

Assessment

Discuss the Concepts

- These questions provide an opportunity to assess your understanding of the key concepts before proceeding to use your skills in the Practise, Apply, and Extend questions.
- Through this discussion you can identify any concepts or areas you need to study further.

Special Apply questions:

- Questions with the **Chapter Problem** descriptor are related to the Chapter Problem.
- The last Apply question of some sections provides an opportunity to demonstrate your knowledge and understanding, and your ability to apply, think, and communicate what you have learned. **Achievement Check** questions occur every two or three sections and are designed to assess learning of the key concepts of those few sections.

Practice Test

Each chapter ends with a Practice Test. Most tests include some multiple-choice questions. Practising this type of question will help you prepare for college entrance tests.

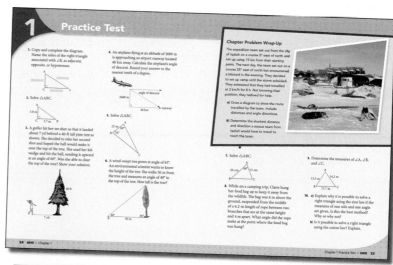

Chapter Problem Wrap-Up

This summary problem occurs at the end of the Practice Test. The Chapter Problem Wrap-Up may be assigned as a project.

Tasks

Tasks are presented at the end of chapters 3, 5, and 9. These are more involved problems that require you to use several concepts from the preceding chapters. Each task has multi-part questions and will take at least 20 min to complete.

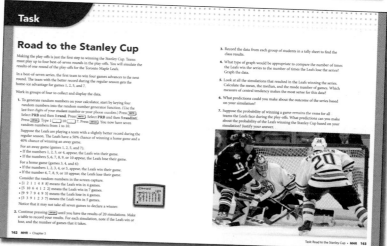

A Tour of Your Textbook

Chapter Review

- This feature appears at the end of each chapter.
- By working through these questions, you will identify areas where you may need more review or study before doing the Practice Test.

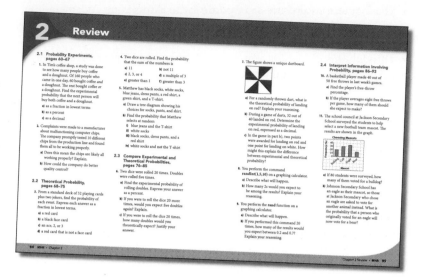

Cumulative Review

- A cumulative review occurs at the end of chapters 3, 6, and 9. These questions allow you to review concepts you learned in the chapters since the last cumulative review.
- A course review follows chapter 9. You can use this to help prepare for a final examination.

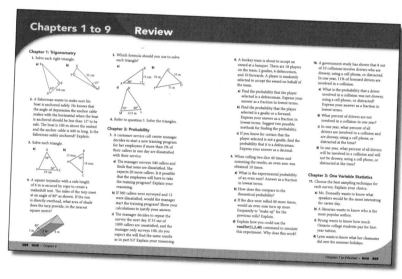

Other Features

The Mathematical Process

Seven mathematical processes that are integral to learning mathematics:

- problem solving
- reasoning and proving
- reflecting
- selecting tools and computational strategies
- connecting
- representing
- communicating

The processes are interconnected and are used throughout the course. Some exercises are flagged with a mathematical processes graphic to remind you which of the processes are involved in solving the problem.

Math Connect

This margin feature points out connections among topics in the course or provides extra information related to an example.

Math Connect

1 knot = 1.852 km/h

Literacy Connect

This margin feature provides tips to help you read and interpret problems.

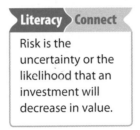

Literacy Connect

Risk is the uncertainty or the likelihood that an investment will decrease in value.

Internet Links

In some questions, it is suggested that you use the Internet to help solve the problem or to research or collect information. Some direct links are provided via our Web site *www.mcgrawhill.ca/links/foundations11*.

Back Matter

Answers

Complete answers are provided on pages 550–587 for all questions in each Prerequisite Skills, numbered section, Chapter Review, Practice Test, and cumulative review. Answers for the Investigate, Discuss the Concepts, and Achievement Check questions are provided in *Foundations for College Mathematics 11 Teacher's Resource*.

Glossary

A complete illustrated glossary is included on pages 588–594. It includes all the key terms of the text, as well as other mathematical terms.

Index

A general index is included on pages 595–597.

1 Trigonometry

How do pilots navigate a plane safely to their destination? How do surveyors determine the distance through an inaccessible area to make way for a road? How do carpenters determine the angle to cut for the rafters to support a roof truss? These careers require a knowledge of trigonometry. To do their jobs, these individuals need to understand the relationship between ratios of sides and their related angles. In this chapter, you will investigate and practise the use of trigonometry as it relates to real-world situations.

In this chapter, you will

- solve problems, including those that arise from real-world applications, by determining the measures of the sides and angles of right triangles using the primary trigonometric ratios
- verify, through investigation using technology, the sine law and the cosine law
- describe conditions that guide when it is appropriate to use the sine law or the cosine law, and use these laws to calculate sides and angles in acute triangles
- solve problems that arise from real-world applications involving metric and imperial measurements and that require the use of the sine law or the cosine law in acute triangles

Reasoning and Proving

Representing | Selecting Tools

Problem Solving

Connecting | Reflecting

Communicating

Key Terms

adjacent	cosine law
angle of depression	hypotenuse
angle of elevation	opposite
angle of inclination	sine law
complementary	

Demar completed a two-year geomatics diploma at Fleming College. Now, he is training to be a licensed surveyor. Demar works under the supervision of an experienced surveyor and uses trigonometry and computerized instruments to take exact measurements of the land and its features. He uses these measurements to establish official land, air, and water boundaries.

Prerequisite Skills

Solve Equations

1. Solve.

a) $x^2 = 36$

b) $x^2 - 6 = 19$

c) $x^2 = 64 + 36$

d) $x^2 = 5^2 + 12^2$

e) $7^2 + x^2 = 25^2$

The Pythagorean Theorem

2. Find the measure of the unknown side.

a)

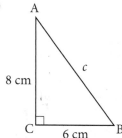

b)

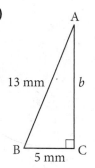

c)

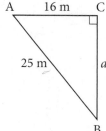

3. A 12-m ladder leans against the wall of a house. The top of the ladder reaches a window 10.5 m above the ground. Calculate the distance from the base of the ladder to the wall of the house.

Ratios

4. Express each ratio in lowest terms.

a) 4:8

b) 15:35

c) 20:50

5. The ratio between the selling price and the purchase price of a computer chip is 18:7. If the computer chip sells for $27, determine the purchase price of the chip.

Proportions

6. Solve for each unknown.

a) $\dfrac{x}{13} = \dfrac{9}{39}$

b) $\dfrac{15}{1} = \dfrac{45}{x}$

c) $\dfrac{x}{25} = \dfrac{y}{5} = \dfrac{8}{10}$

7. The scale on a Canadian road map is 1:700 000.

a) What does this scale represent?

b) Determine the actual distance between two cities, in kilometres, if the distance on the map is 12 cm.

c) Determine the distance on the map, in centimetres, if the actual distance between two cities is 40 km.

Rounding

8. Round each value to two decimal places.

   a) 3.4576

   b) 19.832

   c) 9015.982 36

9. Evaluate each answer to one decimal place.

   a) $\sqrt{59}$

   b) $\sqrt{723}$

   c) $\sqrt{0.85}$

Angle Sum of a Triangle

10. Determine the measure of the missing angles.

a)

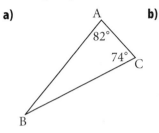

b)

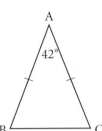

c)

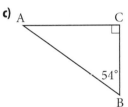

Chapter Problem

An expedition team decides to trek 400 km to the North Pole from a drop point in the Arctic. The team plans to travel 40 km per day. By the end of the third day, they have unknowingly wandered seven degrees off course to the east. At the end of the sixth day, the team navigator makes the discovery and finds that they are now three more degrees off course to the east. Can you determine the correct angle that they must turn to reach the North Pole? Can you calculate how many kilometres they must travel each day for the remainder of their journey?

1.1 Revisit the Primary Trigonometric Ratios

Carpenters use trigonometry to determine the length of roof rafters. They often use a tool called a square to measure accurately. The slope of a roof is described in terms of its pitch. The pitch of the roof can be associated with the angle of the roof. Do you know what a "7–12 pitch" roof is?

Investigate

Tools

- *The Geometer's Sketchpad*®
- computer

Optional
- pencil and paper
- ruler
- protractor

SOH–CAH–TOA?

You will investigate the ratios between pairs of sides associated with an acute angle in a right triangle.

1. Copy the table.

Triangle	AB (cm)	AC (cm)	BC (cm)	∠A (°)	$\frac{BC}{AB}$	sin A	$\frac{AC}{AB}$	cos A	$\frac{BC}{AC}$	tan A
ABC#1										
ABC#2										

2. Construct a right triangle with sides of 3 cm, 4 cm, and 5 cm, using *The Geometer's Sketchpad*®.
- Open *The Geometer's Sketchpad*®.
- From the **Edit** menu, choose **Preferences**. Click on the **Text** tab, and check the box **For All New Points**. This will label points as you draw them. Click on the **Units** tab. Set the precision for Angle to units, and Distance to tenths.
- From the **Graph** menu, choose **Show Grid**. Drag the origin to the lower left corner of the workspace. From the **Graph** menu, choose **Snap Points**.

- Use the **Straightedge Tool** to draw a right triangle. Select the three sides of the triangle. From the **Measure** menu, choose **Length**. Move each measurement beside the correct side.
- To measure ∠A, select points B, A, and C, in that order. From the **Measure** menu, choose **Angle**. Move the measurement beside ∠A. Repeat this process for the measures of ∠B and ∠C.

3. Ensure that ∠C = 90°.

4. Identify the sides associated with ∠A.

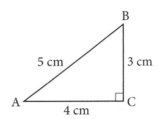

opposite
- in right △DEF, side DE is the side opposite ∠F

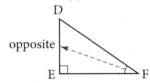

adjacent
- in right △DEF, side EF is the side adjacent to ∠F that is not the hypotenuse

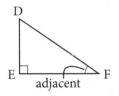

hypotenuse
- the longest side of a right triangle

a) Label the sides associated with ∠A. Side BC is **opposite** ∠A. Side AC is **adjacent** to ∠A. Side AB is the **hypotenuse**.

b) Calculate the ratios between the following pair of sides for △ABC.
$$\frac{\text{opposite}}{\text{hypotenuse}}, \frac{\text{adjacent}}{\text{hypotenuse}}, \frac{\text{opposite}}{\text{adjacent}}$$
Add the information to your table.

c) Calculate the angle measure for ∠A.

d) Calculate the following for ∠A.
sin A, cos A, tan A

e) Construct a triangle that has sides three times longer than △ABC.

f) Repeat steps a) to d) for this new △ABC. Complete the table.

5. Compare ∠A in the two triangles that you constructed. Did the measure of ∠A change? Explain.

6. a) Compare the ratios between the same pairs of sides in both triangles and the trigonometric ratios. What do you notice?

b) Name the sides associated with ∠B. Write the ratios for sin B, cos B, and tan B. Make sure to write the ratio of the side measurements as a fraction.

7. Reflect Recall how to find the slope of a line segment. How is the slope of the hypotenuse AB associated with tan A?

8. Reflect You can associate the sides of a right triangle using the Pythagorean theorem: $c^2 = a^2 + b^2$. How can you associate the sides of a right triangle to a given angle? Use a diagram to help you explain.

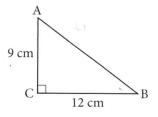

$$\sin A = \frac{\text{opposite}}{\text{hypotenuse}} = \frac{BC}{AB} \qquad \sin B = \frac{\text{opposite}}{\text{hypotenuse}} = \frac{AC}{AB}$$

$$\cos A = \frac{\text{adjacent}}{\text{hypotenuse}} = \frac{AC}{AB} \qquad \cos B = \frac{\text{adjacent}}{\text{hypotenuse}} = \frac{BC}{AB}$$

$$\tan A = \frac{\text{opposite}}{\text{adjacent}} = \frac{BC}{AC} \qquad \tan B = \frac{\text{opposite}}{\text{adjacent}} = \frac{AC}{BC}$$

Example 1

Write the Trigonometric Ratios for an Angle

Write the trigonometric ratios for sin A, cos A, and tan A.
Express each answer as a fraction in lowest terms.

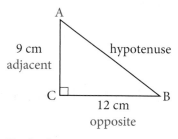

Solution

Write the names of the sides associated with ∠A.

To find sin A, you need to know the length of the hypotenuse.

Use the Pythagorean theorem.

$$c^2 = 9^2 + 12^2$$
$$c^2 = 81 + 144$$
$$c = \sqrt{225}$$
$$c = 15$$

$$\sin A = \frac{\text{opposite}}{\text{hypotenuse}} \qquad \cos A = \frac{\text{adjacent}}{\text{hypotenuse}} \qquad \tan A = \frac{\text{opposite}}{\text{adjacent}}$$

$$= \frac{12}{15} \qquad\qquad = \frac{9}{15} \qquad\qquad = \frac{12}{9}$$

$$= \frac{4}{5} \qquad\qquad = \frac{3}{5} \qquad\qquad = \frac{4}{3}$$

Example 2

Determine Trigonometric Ratios Using a Calculator

Evaluate. Round your answers to four decimal places.

a) sin 40°

b) tan 60°

Solution

a) sin 40° = 0.6428

SIN 40 **)** **ENTER**

Be sure your calculator is in degree mode first.

b) tan 60° = 1.7321

TAN 60 **)** **ENTER**

Technology Tip

Remember: not all calculators are the same. Read the manual for the proper key sequence.

For a scientific calculator, you might use this key sequence:

40 **SIN** **=**

For a DAL (direct algebraic logic) calculator, you might use this key sequence:

SIN 40 **=**

Example 3

Find the Measure of an Angle Given Its Trigonometric Ratio

Find the measure of ∠A if cos A = 0.6789. Round your answer to the nearest tenth of a degree.

Solution

cos A = 0.6789

2nd **COS** .6789 **)** **ENTER**

Use pencil and paper, and a calculator.

cos A = 0.6789

∠A = cos^{-1}(0.6789)

∠A ≐ 47.2°

∠A is approximately 47.2°.

Technology Tip

For a scientific calculator, you might use this key sequence:

.6789 **2nd** **COS** **=**

For a DAL calculator, you might use this key sequence:

2nd **COS** .6789 **=**

Example 4

Find the Length of a Side

Find the length of side *a*. Round your answer to one decimal place.

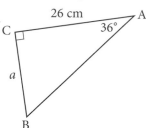

Sides opposite an angle can be labelled with a lower case letter associated with the angle. Side *a* is opposite ∠A.

Solution

The measure of ∠A and the side adjacent to the angle are known.

Side *a* is opposite ∠A. AC = 26 cm and is adjacent to ∠A.

With the given information, you can use the tangent ratio to find the measure of side *a*.

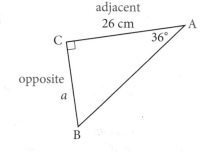

$$\tan A = \frac{\text{opposite}}{\text{adjacent}}$$

$$\tan 36° = \frac{a}{26}$$

$$26 \, (\tan 36°) = a$$

$$a = 26 \, (\tan 36°)$$

$$a \doteq 18.9$$

How would the solution change if the unknown side were represented in the denominator?

Side *a* is approximately 18.9 cm.

Technology Tip

For a scientific calculator, you might use this key sequence:

26 [×] 36 [TAN]
[=]

For a DAL calculator, you might use this key sequence:

26 [TAN] 36 [=]

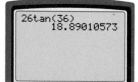

26tan(36)
          18.89010573

26 [TAN] 36 [ )] [ENTER]

Example 5

Find an Angle Given the Length of Two Sides

Find the measure of ∠A to the nearest tenth of a degree.

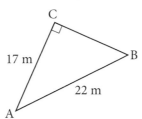

Solution

Identify the known sides of the triangle with respect to ∠A.

$$\cos A = \frac{\text{adjacent}}{\text{hypotenuse}}$$

$$\cos A = \frac{17}{22}$$

$$\angle A = \cos^{-1}\left(\frac{17}{22}\right)$$

$$\angle A \doteq 39.4°$$

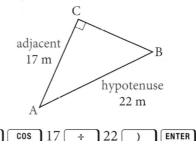

Technology Tip

For a scientific calculator, you might use this key sequence:

For a DAL calculator, you might use this key sequence:

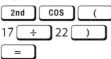

∠A is approximately 39.4°.

Example 6

Solve a Right Triangle

Solve the triangle. Round your answers to two decimal places, where necessary.

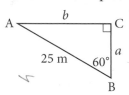

"Solve the triangle." means "Determine the measures of any angles and sides of the triangle that were not given."

Solution

Find the measure of ∠A.

$$\angle A = 180° - 90° - 60°$$
$$= 30°$$

The sum of the interior angles of a triangle is 180°. One angle in a right triangle is always 90°. The sum of the other two angles must equal 90°. These angles are complementary.

Check: $60° + 30° = 90°$

complementary
• angles whose sum is 90°

Find the measure of side *a*.

Method 1: Use cos 60°

$$\frac{a}{25} = \cos 60°$$
$$a = 25 \times \cos 60°$$
$$a = 12.5$$

Method 2: Use sin 30°

$$\frac{a}{25} = \sin 30°$$
$$a = 25 \times \sin 30°$$
$$a = 12.5$$

Side *a* is 12.5 m.

Find the measure of side *b*.

Method 1: Use sin 60°

$$\frac{b}{25} = \sin 60°$$
$$b = 25 \times \sin 60°$$
$$b \doteq 21.65$$

Method 2: Use cos 30°

$$\frac{b}{25} = \cos 30°$$
$$b = 25 \times \cos 30°$$
$$b \doteq 21.65$$

Method 3: Use the Pythagorean Theorem

Once you have found the measure of side *a*, you can find the measure of side *b*.

$$b^2 = 25^2 - 12.5^2$$
$$b^2 = 468.75$$
$$b = \sqrt{468.75}$$
$$b \doteq 21.65$$

You can also solve for *a* using the Pythagorean theorem, if you solve for *b* first.

$$a^2 = 25^2 - 21.65^2$$
$$a^2 = 156.2775$$
$$a = \sqrt{156.2775}$$
$$a \doteq 12.50$$

Side *b* is approximately 21.65 m.

Key Concepts

- You can use the primary trigonometric ratios to find the measures of sides and angles of a right triangle.

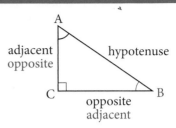

$$\sin A = \frac{\text{opposite}}{\text{hypotenuse}} = \frac{BC}{AB} \qquad \sin B = \frac{\text{opposite}}{\text{hypotenuse}} = \frac{AC}{AB}$$

$$\cos A = \frac{\text{adjacent}}{\text{hypotenuse}} = \frac{AC}{AB} \qquad \cos B = \frac{\text{adjacent}}{\text{hypotenuse}} = \frac{BC}{AB}$$

$$\tan A = \frac{\text{opposite}}{\text{adjacent}} = \frac{BC}{AC} \qquad \tan B = \frac{\text{opposite}}{\text{adjacent}} = \frac{AC}{BC}$$

- Use the acronym **SOH–CAH–TOA** to help you remember the trigonometric ratios.

Discuss the Concepts

D1. Explain to a classmate what SOH–CAH–TOA stands for.

D2. Is it possible to solve a right triangle given just one side measure? Explain.

D3. In Example 6, you were shown two methods for finding the measure of side *a*. Look closely at the two methods. What change was made? Is the following true: sin 40° = cos 50°? Explain.

Practise Ⓐ ....

For help with question 1, refer to Example 1.

1. Name the opposite, adjacent, and hypotenuse sides associated with ∠B, ∠F, and ∠Z.

a)
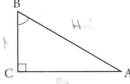

b)

c)

For help with question 2, refer to Example 2.

2. Evaluate. Round your answers to four decimal places.

   a) sin 30°   **b)** cos 45°   **c)** tan 60°

For help with question 3, refer to Example 3.

3. Find the measure of each angle to the nearest tenth of a degree.

   a) sin A = 0.2345   **b)** cos B = 0.8765   **c)** tan C = 1.2345

For help with question 4, refer to Example 4.

4. **a)** Find the measure of side a to the nearest metre.

   b) Find the measure of side c to the nearest metre.

   c) Find the measure of ∠A.

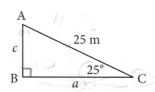

For help with question 5, refer to Example 5.

5. **a)** Find the measure of ∠A to the nearest tenth of a degree.

   b) Find the measure of ∠B to the nearest tenth of a degree.

   c) Find the measure of side b to the nearest centimetre.

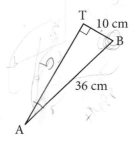

Apply **B** ·

Where necessary, round answers to the nearest tenth.

For help with questions 6 to 13, refer to Example 6.

6. **a)** Find the measure of the hypotenuse.

   b) Find the measure of side a.

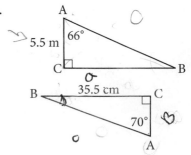

7. **a)** Find the measure of side b.

   b) Find the measure of side c.

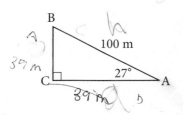

8. **a)** Find the measure of side a.

   b) Find the measure of side b.

9. Solve △ABC.

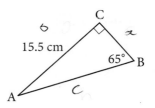

10. Find the measure of side AD.

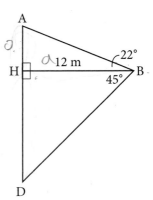

11. Find the measure of side BC.

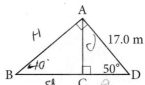

12. Find the measure of side AD.

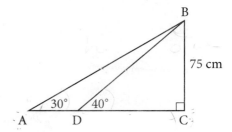

Extend C •

13. Find the measure
of side AD to the
nearest millimetre.

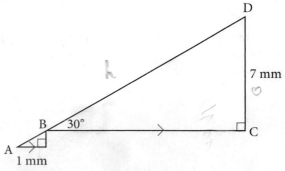

14. Find the area of the trapezoid
to the nearest square centimetre.

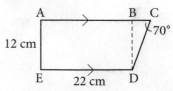

1.2 Solve Problems Using Trigonometric Ratios

The heights of some structures are best determined using trigonometry rather than a measuring tape. For example, a person could stand a certain distance from the base of the CN Tower and use a clinometer to determine the angle of elevation to the top of the tower. Then, using trigonometry, she could find the height of the tower.

A clinometer measures the angle of a line of sight above or below the horizontal. It is used by construction workers to measure grade angles, by forestry workers to measure the heights of trees, and by movie directors to measure the sun's elevation. It is also used by satellite antenna installers to locate satellites.

Investigate

Tools

- BLM Make Your Own Clinometer
- metre stick
- measuring tape

Angle of Elevation

Work with a partner.

Part A: Vary the Adjacent Side

1. Copy the table. Use it to record your results.

Distance From Wall (m)	Height to Eye Level (m)	Angle of Elevation, θ (°)	tan θ	Height of Wall (m)
2.0	0.9			
2.5	0.9			
3.0	0.9			

2. Use a hand-made clinometer and stand 2.0 m from the wall of your classroom.

angle of elevation

- the angle between the horizontal and the sight line from the observer's eye to some object above eye level

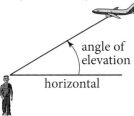

angle of elevation

horizontal

3. Hold the clinometer along the edge of a metre stick at the 90 cm (0.9 m) mark. Look through the straw of the clinometer to where the ceiling meets the wall. Have your partner record the **angle of elevation** (or incline) to where the ceiling meets the wall.

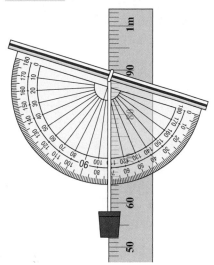

4. Repeat steps 1 to 3 at distances of 2.5 m and 3.0 m from the wall.

5. Copy the diagram that models the situation. Use the data from your table to complete the diagram with additional labels.

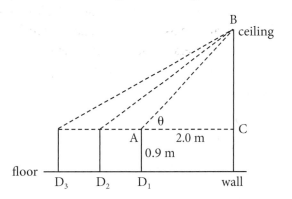

The symbol θ represents the angle of elevation.

Part B: Vary the Opposite Side

6. Copy the table.

Distance From Wall (m)	Height to Eye Level (m)	Angle of Elevation, θ (°)	tan θ	Height of the Wall (m)
2.0	0.8			
2.0	0.9			
2.0	1.0			

7. Stand 2.0 m from the wall. Hold the clinometer along an edge of a metre stick at the 80 cm (0.8 m) mark. Look through the straw of the clinometer to where the ceiling meets the wall. Have your partner record the angle of elevation to where the ceiling meets the wall.

8. Raise the clinometer 10 cm along the edge of the metre stick to 90 cm (0.9 m). Record the angle of elevation. Make sure your clinometer is level.

9. Repeat step 8 at the 1 m mark.

10. Copy the diagram. Use the data from your table to complete the diagram with additional labels.

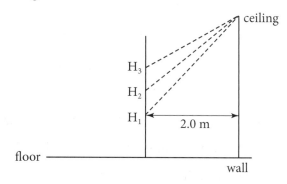

H_1, H_2, and H_3 are different heights of the clinometer.

11. How did the angle of elevation change in Part A?

12. Use a measuring tape to find the exact height of the wall.

13. Did your results appear to be close to the height in both parts of the Investigate? How close? If there are discrepancies between the heights, what are possible reasons for the differences?

Example 1

Example 1

angle of depression
• the angle between the horizontal and the sight line from the observer's eye to a point below eye level

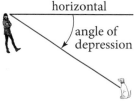

Calculate Distances

From the top of the Niagara Escarpment, Juan sees a car below at an **angle of depression** (or descent) of 40°. Juan is approximately 100 m above the car. How far is the car from the base of the escarpment? Round your answer to the nearest metre.

Solution

What do I know?	What do I need to know?
• angle of depression: 40° • height: 100 m	• distance from the base of the escarpment

Obtain information from the problem.
Use a right triangle to model the problem.

Draw a horizontal line from Juan so that it is parallel to the base of the triangle. The angle made with the line of sight and the distance from the base of the escarpment is equal to the angle of depression. These are alternate angles.

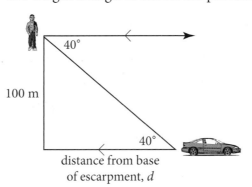

100 m

distance from base
of escarpment, d

Draw and label the triangle with the information provided.

Solve for the unknown side or angle. In this case, find side d.

Use the given information. Write an appropriate trigonometric ratio.

$$\tan 40° = \frac{100}{d}$$

$$d \times \tan 40° = 100$$

$$\frac{d \times \tan 40°}{\tan 40°} = \frac{100}{\tan 40°}$$

$$d \doteq 119$$

100 [÷] [TAN] 40 [)] [ENTER]

Technology Tip
For a scientific calculator, you might use this key sequence:

100 [÷] 40 [TAN]
[=]

For a DAL calculator, you might use this key sequence:

100 [÷] [TAN] 40
[=]

Write a concluding sentence.

The car is approximately 119 m from the base of the escarpment.

Example 2

Calculate the Measure of an Angle

In construction, the pitch of a roof may be given as "7–12" in feet. This means the maximum height of the roof is 7 ft and the distance from the midpoint of the base of the roof to the outer wall is 12 ft.

Calculate the roof's **angle of inclination**. Round your answer to the nearest degree.

angle of inclination
• another name for the angle of elevation

Solution

Model the problem.

$\angle A$ is the angle of inclination.

$$\tan A = \frac{\text{opposite}}{\text{adjacent}}$$

$$\tan A = \frac{7}{12}$$

$$\angle A = \tan^{-1}\left(\frac{7}{12}\right)$$

$$\angle A \doteq 30°$$

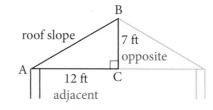

Technology Tip
For a scientific calculator, you might use this key sequence:

(7 ÷ 12
) 2nd TAN
=

For a DAL calculator, you might use this key sequence:

2nd TAN (
7 ÷ 12)
=

tan⁻¹(7/12)
30.25643716

2nd TAN 7 ÷ 12) ENTER

The roof's angle of inclination is approximately 30°.

Key Concepts

• The angle of elevation, or angle of inclination, is the angle made between the horizontal and the upward line of sight.

• The angle of depression is the angle made between the horizontal and the downward line of sight.

• Use these steps to solve problems using trigonometric ratios.
  – Identify what needs to be calculated. Is it a side or an angle?
  – Model the problem using a right triangle. Label the sides associated with the unknown angle (i.e., opposite, adjacent, hypotenuse).
  – Write an equation using a trigonometric ratio. Substitute the given values.
  – Solve for the unknown measure.
  – Write a concluding sentence that answers the question.

> **Discuss the Concepts**

D1. Is it possible to solve a problem involving right triangles given only the measure of one side? Explain.

D2. Work in pairs. One partner explains to the other how to solve the following problem using trigonometric ratios. (Do *not* actually solve the problem.)

A 10-m ladder is leaning against a wall. The top of the ladder rests against the wall 9.3 m above the ground. What angle does the base of the ladder make with the ground?

Practise

For questions 1 to 15, round your answers to the nearest unit of measurement.

1. A wheelchair ramp is needed at the entrance of a restaurant. The ramp is to be 6.10 m long and have a rise of 0.45 m. Calculate the angle of inclination of the ramp.

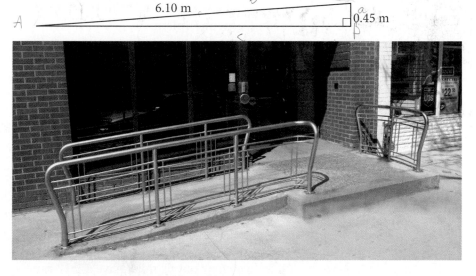

For help with question 2, refer to Example 1.

2. From the top of a bridge over the Burlington Canal, Maria looks down at a sailboat at an angle of depression of 15°. The bridge is 18 m above the water. Calculate the horizontal distance from the bridge to the sailboat.

For help with question 3, refer to Example 2.

3. A 7.6-m flagpole is 4.6 m away from a pedestrian. What is the angle of elevation from where the pedestrian is standing to the top of the flagpole?

For help with question 4, refer to Example 2.

4. A garage floor is made of poured concrete. The length of the garage is 6.7 m and the grade (the rise of the floor from the front to the back) is 9.1 cm. Calculate the angle of inclination of the garage floor.

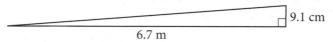

5. A rafter makes an angle of 22.5° with the roof joist, as shown. How tall is the board supporting the middle of the roof?

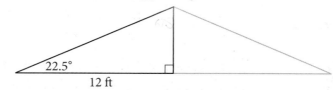

6. Safety by-laws state that for a ladder to be stable, the angle the base of the ladder makes with the ground should be between 70° and 80°. A safety inspector at a construction site notices a painter on a 10-m ladder that is leaning against a wall. The base of the ladder is 1.5 m away from the wall. Does the inspector have cause to be concerned? Explain.

7. Solve the problem from question D2 in Discuss the Concepts. Is the ladder stable? Explain.

8. A rescue helicopter sights a boat in distress at an angle of 40° from the horizontal. The helicopter is hovering 400 m above the water. What is the horizontal distance between the helicopter and the boat?

Chapter Problem

9. The expedition team decided to have a practice run prior to their North Pole trek. One team member started to walk due north. The other three travelled 65° east of north at a pace of 3 km/h. How far off the first team member's course were they after 2 h?

Literacy Connect

10. Wheelchair ramps must have a 1:12 ratio of vertical height to horizontal length to meet safety standards. The safety standards for other types of ramps are different. What are the safety standards for building a skateboard ramp at a skateboard park? Investigate the ramps at a skateboard park and provide measurements of one of the ramps. Determine the angle of inclination. Include a diagram.

11. The CN Tower is 553.33 m high. Lina looks up at the top of the tower at a 15° angle of elevation. She calculates the distance, d, from the base of the tower as follows:

$$\frac{d}{553.33} = \tan 15°$$
$$d = 553.33 \times \tan 15°$$
$$d \doteq 149$$

Explain why Lina's solution is incorrect. Write a correct solution.

12. Two buildings are 20 m apart. The angle from the top of the shorter building to the top of the taller building is 20°. The angle from the top of the shorter building to the base of the taller building is 45°. What is the height of the taller building?

13. The shuttle *Enterprise* lifts off from Cape Canaveral. Calculate the angle of elevation of the shuttle, from an observer located 8 km away, when the shuttle reaches a height of 3500 m.

14. The Instrument Landing System (ILS) common to most major airports uses radio beams to bring an aircraft down a 3° glide slope. A pilot noted that his height above the ground was 200 m. How far would the pilot have to travel before landing on the runway?

Extend **C**

15. From the top of a 200-m high cliff, the angles of depression of two boats on the water are 20° and 25°. How far apart are the boats? What assumptions must you make?

16. The high end of a 22-ft-long roof rafter is nailed to a 7-ft vertical support, which is located at the middle of the roof. Calculate the height of the first support piece to be nailed 16 in. from the middle support piece to the nearest tenth of a foot.

1.3 The Sine Law

sine law
- the relationship between the length of the sides and their opposite angles in any triangle

Some situations are modelled by non-right triangles. The Leaning Tower of Pisa, for example, leans from its vertical and does not form a right angle with the ground. The height of the tower must be determined using other tools of trigonometry, such as the **sine law**. How can you use the sine law to calculate the height of the tower?

Investigate

Tools

- *The Geometer's Sketchpad®*
- computer

The Sine Law

1. Construct a right triangle using *The Geometer's Sketchpad®*. Measure the lengths of the sides and the angles.
   - Open *The Geometer's Sketchpad®*.
   - From the **Edit** menu, choose **Preferences**. Click on the **Text** tab, and check the box **For All New Points**. This will label points as you draw them.
   - From the **Graph** menu, choose **Show Grid**. Drag the origin to the lower left corner of the workspace. From the **Graph** menu, choose **Snap Points**.

Technology Tip
Hold the Shift key down
while drawing a vertical
or horizontal line.

- Use the **Straightedge Tool** to draw a right triangle. Select the three sides of the triangle. From the **Measure** menu, choose **Length**. Drag each measurement beside the correct side.
- Right-click on each measurement in turn. Choose **Label Distance Measurement**. Enter the label *a* for BC, *b* for AC, and *c* for AB.
- Select the points B, A, and C, in that order. From the **Measure** menu, choose **Angle**. Move the measurement beside ∠A. Repeat this process for the measures of ∠B and ∠C.

2. Calculate the ratio of the sine of an angle and the length of the opposite side.

From the **Measure** menu, choose **Calculate**. A calculator box will appear. Click on the **Functions** button, and choose **sin**. Click on the measure of ∠A. Press the ÷ button. Click on the measurement of the side opposite ∠A. Click on **OK**. Repeat this process to calculate the corresponding ratios for ∠B and ∠C.

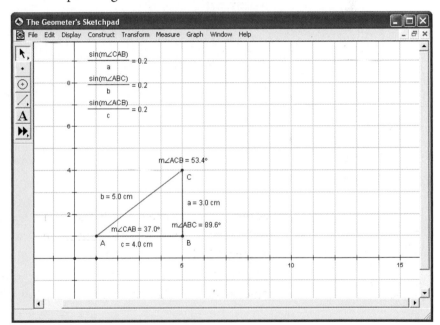

3. **Reflect** What do you notice about the three ratios?

4. Drag point B so that the triangle is no longer a right triangle. How are the ratios affected?

5. Drag point A, and then point C. How are the ratios affected?

6. **Reflect** Are these ratios equal for any triangle? Explain.

7. **Reflect** Evaluate sin 90°. What is its value? Is there a relation between using the sine law and using the sine ratio for a right triangle?

The Sine Law $\dfrac{a}{\sin A} = \dfrac{b}{\sin B} = \dfrac{c}{\sin C}$

or

$\dfrac{\sin A}{a} = \dfrac{\sin B}{b} = \dfrac{\sin C}{c}$

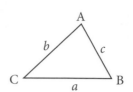

Example 1

Find the Measure of a Side

Find the measure of side c to the nearest centimetre.

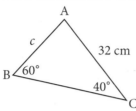

Solution

Solve for c.

$$\dfrac{c}{\sin 40°} = \dfrac{32}{\sin 60°}$$

$$c = \dfrac{32 \times \sin 40°}{\sin 60°}$$

$$c \doteq 24$$

Use the proportion in the form $\dfrac{a}{\sin A} = \dfrac{b}{\sin B} = \dfrac{c}{\sin C}$ to find the measure of a side. Note that any two ratios can be used at one time.

To make your calculation easier, start with the unknown as the numerator on the left.

$$32 \boxed{\times} \boxed{\text{SIN}} 40 \boxed{)} \boxed{\div} \sin 60 \boxed{)} \boxed{\text{ENTER}}$$

Side c is approximately 24 cm.

Technology Tip

For a scientific calculator, you might use this key sequence:

For a DAL calculator, you might use this key sequence:

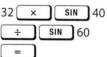

Example 2

Find the Measure of an Angle

Find the measure of ∠C to the nearest tenth of a degree.

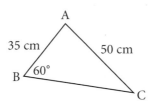

Solution

$$\frac{\sin C}{c} = \frac{\sin B}{b}$$

$$\frac{\sin C}{35} = \frac{\sin 60°}{50}$$

$$\sin C = \frac{35 \times \sin 60°}{50}$$

$$\angle C = \sin^{-1}\left(\frac{35 \times \sin 60°}{50}\right)$$

$$\angle C \doteq 37.3°$$

Use the proportion in the form

$$\frac{\sin A}{a} = \frac{\sin B}{b} = \frac{\sin C}{c}$$

to find the measure of an angle.

Check that, for all triangles, the largest angle is opposite the longest side. The smallest angle is opposite the shortest side.

The measure of ∠C is approximately 37.3°.

Example 3

Solve Triangles

Solve the following triangles. Round your answers to the nearest unit of measurement.

a)

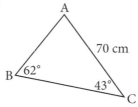

b) For a triangle XYZ, $\angle X = 65°$, $x = 14$ cm, and $y = 9$ cm.

Solution

a) $\angle A = 180° - 62° - 43°$ Find the measure of $\angle A$ first.
    $= 75°$

$$\frac{c}{\sin 43°} = \frac{70}{\sin 62°}$$

Next find the measure of the shortest side. In this case, find c. The shortest side is opposite the smallest angle.

$$c = \frac{70 \times \sin 43°}{\sin 62°}$$

$$c \doteq 54$$

70 ⨯ SIN 43) ÷ SIN 62
) ENTER

Side c is approximately 54 cm.

$$\frac{a}{\sin 75°} = \frac{70}{\sin 62°}$$

Now find the measure of the longest side. The longest side is opposite the largest angle.

$$a = \frac{70 \times \sin 75°}{\sin 62°}$$

$$a \doteq 77$$

70 ⨯ SIN 75) ÷ SIN 62
) ENTER

Side a is approximately 77 cm.

b) Sketch the triangle.

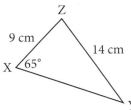

$$\frac{\sin Y}{9} = \frac{\sin 65°}{14}$$

$$\sin Y = \frac{9 \times \sin 65°}{14}$$

$$Y = \sin^{-1}\left(\frac{9 \times \sin 65°}{14}\right)$$

$$\angle Y \doteq 36°$$

Find the smaller angle measure first. In this case, it is $\angle Y$.

Use the proportion in the form $\frac{\sin A}{a} = \frac{\sin B}{b} = \frac{\sin C}{c}$ to find the measure of an angle.

$$\angle Z = 180° - 65° - 36°$$
$$= 79°$$

Next find the measure of the third angle.

$$\frac{z}{\sin 79°} = \frac{14}{\sin 65°}$$

$$z = \frac{14 \times \sin 79°}{\sin 65°}$$

$$z \doteq 15$$

Use the proportion in the form $\frac{a}{\sin A} = \frac{b}{\sin B} = \frac{c}{\sin C}$ to find the unknown side, z.

Side z is approximately 15 cm.

Example 4

Solve Problems Using the Sine Law

Two ships are located 15 nautical miles apart. *Alpha*'s angle to the entrance of the port is 55° with respect to *Beta*. *Beta*'s angle to the entrance to the port is 45° with respect to *Alpha*. Which ship is closer to the port entrance? How far is the ship from port? Round your answer to the nearest tenth.

Solution

Draw the triangle to model the problem.

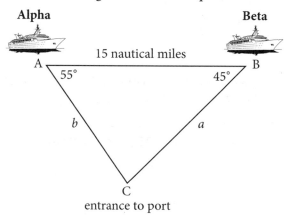

Literacy **Connect**

The nautical mile is used around the world for maritime and aviation measures.
1 nautical mile
= 1.852 km

Remember that the shortest side is opposite the smallest angle.

$\angle C = 180° - 55° - 45°$
$\qquad = 80°$

Side b is the shortest side. Find its measure.

$$\frac{b}{\sin B} = \frac{c}{\sin C}$$

$$\frac{b}{\sin 45°} = \frac{15}{\sin 80°}$$

$$b = \frac{15 \times \sin 45°}{\sin 80°}$$

$$b \doteq 10.8$$

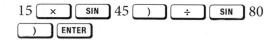

Alpha is closer to port. It is approximately 10.8 nautical miles from the port entrance.

Key Concepts

- An acute triangle, ABC, can be solved using the sine law if you know:
  - two angle measures and one side measure
  - an angle measure and two side measures, provided one of the sides is opposite the given angle
- The measure of a side of a triangle can be calculated using a proportion made of two of the ratios from the sine law: $\frac{a}{\sin A} = \frac{b}{\sin B} = \frac{c}{\sin C}$.
- The measure of an angle of a triangle can be calculated using a proportion made of two of the ratios from the sine law:

$$\frac{\sin A}{a} = \frac{\sin B}{b} = \frac{\sin C}{c}.$$

> **Discuss the Concepts**

D1. Is it possible to solve △ABC given the measures of all three sides using the sine law? Explain.

D2. Work in pairs. Explain to your partner how to solve △ABC, where ∠A = 65°, ∠B = 75°, and a = 8 cm.

Practise Ⓐ •••

In questions 1 to 4, round your answers to the nearest tenth.

For help with question 1, refer to Example 1.

1. Find the measure of the indicated side in each triangle.

a)
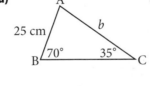

b)
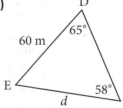

c)
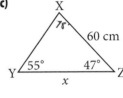

For help with question 2, refer to Example 2.

2. Find the measure of the unknown angle as indicated.

a)
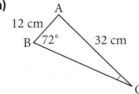

b)
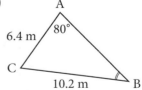

For help with questions 3 and 4, refer to Example 3.

3. Solve each triangle.

a)

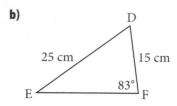

b)

4. a) Solve △ABC, given ∠B = 39°, ∠C = 79°, and a = 24 cm.

b) Solve △DEF, given ∠D = 75°, d = 25 m, and e = 10 m.

Apply **B** •

For help with question 5, refer to Example 4.

5. A communication tower is built on the slope of a hill. A surveyor, 50 m uphill from the base of the tower, measures an angle of 50° between the ground and the top of the tower. The angle from the top of the tower to the surveyor is 60°. Calculate the height of the tower to the nearest metre.

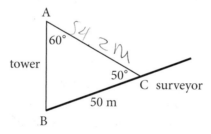

Chapter Problem

6. The expedition team decides to have another practice run. Two team members head due north at a pace of 4 km/h. The second pair decide to head 60° west of north travelling at the same pace. How far from the first pair is the second pair after 2 h?

Literacy Connect

7. You are asked to solve a triangle with two known sides using the sine law. Explain to a classmate what additional information you need to know about the triangle.

8. A shed is 8 ft wide. One rafter makes an angle of 30° with the horizontal on one side of the roof. A rafter on the other side makes an angle of 70° with the horizontal. Calculate the length of the shorter rafter to the nearest foot.

9. Three islands—Fogo, Twillingate, and Moreton's Harbour—form a triangular pattern in the ocean. Fogo and Twillingate are 15 nautical miles apart. The angle between Twillingate and Moreton's Harbour from Fogo is 45°. The angle between Moreton's Harbour and Fogo from Twillingate is 65°. How far is Moreton's Harbour from the other two islands to the nearest nautical mile?

Achievement Check

10. A house is 7 m wide and 20 m long. The roof slopes at an angle of 35° as shown. The two rectangular parts on top of the roof are to be shingled at a cost of $25/m². Calculate the total cost, to the nearest dollar.

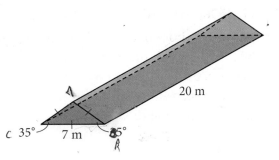

Extend C

11. The Leaning Tower of Pisa leans 5.5° from its vertical. Suppose that the sun is directly overhead. A surveyor notices that the distance from the base of the tower to the tip of its shadow is 5.35 m. What is the height of the tower on the lower side to the nearest tenth of a metre?

12. Search the Internet for an image of the Leaning Tower of Pisa. Cut and paste the image into *The Geometer's Sketchpad*®. Determine the angle that the tower makes with the vertical.

13. Find the length of side *x* to the nearest tenth of a centimetre.

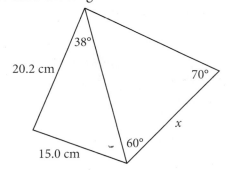

1.4 The Cosine Law

cosine law

- the relationship between the lengths of the three sides and the cosine of an angle in any triangle

The Channel Tunnel that links England and France, is 51.5 km long with 37.5 km under the English Channel. Construction started on both sides of the Channel. When the two crews met, the walls of the two tunnels were only a few millimetres off. Trigonometry had something to do with this amazing feat! In this lesson you learn about the **cosine law**.

Investigate

Tools

- *The Geometer's Sketchpad*®
- computer

The Cosine Law

1. Construct a right triangle using *The Geometer's Sketchpad*®. Measure the lengths of the sides, and the angles.
   - Open *The Geometer's Sketchpad*®.
   - From the **Edit** menu, choose **Preferences**. Click on the **Text** tab, and check the box **For All New Points**. This will label points as you draw them.
   - From the **Graph** menu, choose **Show Grid**. Drag the origin to the lower left corner of the workspace. From the **Graph** menu, choose **Snap Points**.
   - Use the **Straightedge Tool** to draw a right triangle. Select the three sides of the triangle. From the **Measure** menu, choose **Length**. Drag each measurement beside the correct side.

- Right-click on each measurement in turn. Choose **Label Distance Measurement**. Enter the label *a* for BC, *b* for AC, and *c* for AB.
- To measure ∠A, select points B, A, and C, in that order. From the **Measure** menu, choose **Angle**. Move the measurement beside ∠A. Repeat this process for the measures of ∠B and ∠C.

2. Calculate the value of a^2 and of the expression $b^2 + c^2 - 2bc \cos A$.
   - Choose **Calculate** from the **Measure** menu. A calculator box will appear. Click on the measure of length *a*, then click the ∧ button and the 2 button. Click on **OK**.
   - Click on the measure of length *b*, then click the ∧ button and the 2 button. Click on the + button. Enter the remaining terms. Click on **OK**.

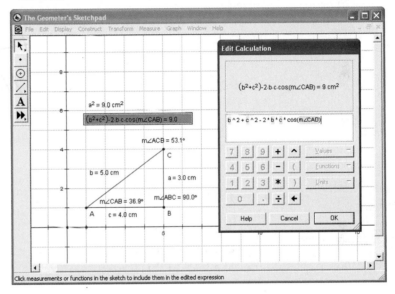

3. **Reflect** How does the value of a^2 compare to the value of the expression $b^2 + c^2 - 2bc \cos A$?

4. Drag point B so that the triangle is no longer a right triangle. How does the value of a^2 compare to the value of the expression?

5. Drag point A, and then point C. How does the value of a^2 compare to the value of the expression?

6. **Reflect** The relationship $a^2 = b^2 + c^2 - 2bc \cos A$ in △ABC is known as the cosine law. What is the value of cos 90°? What do you call the equation in this case?

7. **Reflect** How can you rearrange the cosine law to get an equation for cos A?

The Cosine Law $a^2 = b^2 + c^2 - 2bc \cos A$

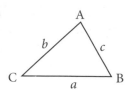

Example 1

Find the Measure of a Side Given Two Sides and the Contained Angle

Find the measure of the unknown side to the nearest tenth of a centimetre.

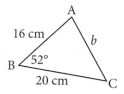

Solution

Use the cosine law.   The sine law cannot be used here. Why?

Write the equation to find the measure of the unknown side.

$b^2 = a^2 + c^2 - 2ac \cos B$
$b^2 = 20^2 + 16^2 - 2(20)(16) \cos 52°$
$b^2 = 400 + 256 - 640 \cos 52°$
$b^2 = 656 - 640 \cos 52°$
$b = \sqrt{656 - 640 \cos 52°}$ Length is a positive value. Find
$b \doteq 16.2$ the positive square root.

[2nd] [x^2] 656 [–] 640 [COS] 52 [ )]
[ )] [ENTER]

Side b is approximately 16.2 cm.

Example 2

Find the Measure of an Angle Given Three Side Lengths

Find the measure of $\angle A$ to the nearest degree.

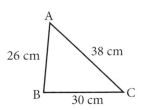

Solution

Use the cosine law.

Write the equation to find the measure of $\angle A$.

$$a^2 = b^2 + c^2 - 2bc \cos A$$

Rearrange the equation to isolate the term containing A.

$$2bc \cos A = b^2 + c^2 - a^2$$
$$2(38)(26)\cos A = 38^2 + 26^2 - 30^2$$
$$1976 \cos A = 1444 + 676 - 900$$
$$1976 \cos A = 1220$$
$$\cos A = \frac{1220}{1976}$$
$$\angle A = \cos^{-1}\left(\frac{1220}{1976}\right)$$
$$\angle A \doteq 52°$$

[2nd] [COS] 1220 [÷] 1976 [ )] [ENTER]

The measure of $\angle A$ is 52°, to the nearest degree.

Example 3

Math **Connect**

The Bruce Trail is the oldest and longest continuous footpath in Canada. It runs along the Niagara Escarpment from Niagara to Tobermory, spanning more than 850 km of main trail and 250 km of side trails.

Solve a Problem Using the Cosine Law

Two hikers set out in different directions from a marked tree on the Bruce Trail. The angle formed between their paths measures 50°. After 2 h, one hiker is 6 km from the starting point and the other is 9 km from the starting point. How far apart are the hikers, to the nearest tenth of a kilometre?

Solution

Draw a diagram to model the problem.

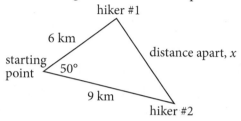

Let x represent the distance apart, in kilometres.

Use the cosine law.

You are given the measures of two sides and a contained angle.

$$x^2 = 6^2 + 9^2 - 2(6)(9) \cos 50°$$
$$x^2 = 36 + 81 - 108 \cos 50°$$
$$x^2 = 117 - 108 \cos 50°$$
$$x = \sqrt{117 - 108 \cos 50°}$$
$$x \doteq 6.9$$

Technology Tip

For a scientific calculator, you might use this key sequence:

117 [–] 108 [×]
50 [COS] [=]
[√] [=]

For a DAL calculator, you might use this key sequence:

[√] [( ] 117
[–] 108 [COS] 50
[ )] [=]

[2nd] [x^2] 117 [–] 108 [COS] 50
[ )] [ )] [ENTER]

The hikers are approximately 6.9 km apart.

Key Concepts

- For △ABC, to find the measure of any side, given two sides and the contained angle, the cosine law can be written as follows:

$$a^2 = b^2 + c^2 - 2bc \cos A$$
$$b^2 = a^2 + c^2 - 2ac \cos B$$
$$c^2 = a^2 + b^2 - 2ab \cos C$$

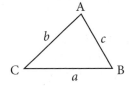

- The cosine law can also be used to find the measure of an unknown angle, given three sides.

$$\cos A = \frac{b^2 + c^2 - a^2}{2bc}, \cos B = \frac{a^2 + c^2 - b^2}{2ac}, \cos C = \frac{a^2 + b^2 - c^2}{2ab}$$

Discuss the Concepts

D1. Explain to a classmate what information about a triangle is necessary to use the cosine law to find the measure of an unknown side.

D2. Explain when you would use the sine law and when you would use the cosine law.

Practise A

In questions 1 and 2, round your answers to the nearest tenth.

For help with question 1, refer to Example 1.

1. Find the measure of the unknown side.

a)

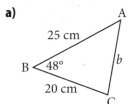

b)

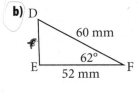

c)

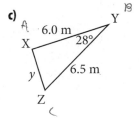

For help with question 2, refer to Example 2.

2. Find the measure of the unknown angle as indicated.

a) Find ∠A.

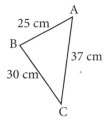

b) Find ∠D.

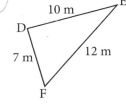

c) Find ∠X.

3. Find the measures of the unknown sides and angles in △ABC, given ∠A = 32°, $b = 25.5$ m, and $c = 22.5$ m. Round side lengths to the nearest tenth of a metre and angles to the nearest degree.

4. Find the measures of the unknown angles in △ABC, given $a = 14$ m, $b = 15$ m, and $c = 8$ m. Round angles to the nearest degree.

Chapter Problem

5. The expedition team plan a final practice run to test the range of their communication equipment. One member travels a distance of 12 km due north. Another team member heads 50° east of north and travels a distance of 10 km. How far apart are the two team members? Round your answer to the nearest tenth of a kilometre.

Literacy Connect

6. What information about a triangle do you need to know to use the cosine law? Provide examples to help you explain.

For help with question 7, refer to Example 2.

7. A motocross ramp is to be built for an upcoming race. The measures for the sides of the ramp are as shown. Calculate the angle of inclination of the ramp to the nearest degree.

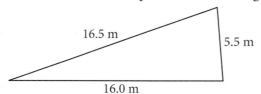

16.5 m   5.5 m

16.0 m

For help with question 8, refer to Example 3.

8. Dahliwal is an engineer. For his latest contract, he has to determine the length of a tunnel that is to be built through a mountain. He chooses a point facing the mountain. He measures a distance of 840 m from one end of the tunnel to the point and a distance of 760 m from the other end of the tunnel to the point. The angle at the point to both ends of the tunnel is 62°. Calculate the length of the proposed tunnel to the nearest metre.

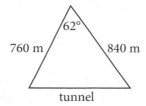

760 m   62°   840 m

tunnel

9. An intersection between two country roads makes an angle of 68°. Along one road, 5 km from the intersection, is a dairy farm. Along the other road, 7 km from the intersection, is a poultry farm. How far apart are the two farms? Round your answer to the nearest tenth of a kilometre.

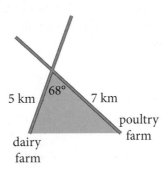

10. A flock of Canada geese are flying in a V-formation that forms an angle of 68°. The lead goose is 12.8 m from the last goose on the left and 13.5 m from the last goose on the right. How far apart are the last two geese in the V-formation? Round your answer to the nearest tenth of a metre.

Extend **C** ·····································

11. Solve for x to the nearest tenth of a metre.

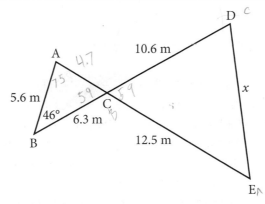

12. **a)** A triangle is built using three poles with lengths of 170 cm, 152 cm, and 88 cm. What are the angles between adjacent poles?

   b) Could you still build a triangle if the 152-cm pole was replaced by a pole half as long?

Math **Connect**

1 knot = 1 nautical mile per hour

13. Two ships set sail from port. *Alpha* is sailing at 12 knots and *Beta* is sailing at 10 knots. After 3 h, the ships are 24 nautical miles apart. Calculate the angle between the ships at the time they sailed from port. Round your answer to the nearest degree.

1.5 Make Decisions Using Trigonometry

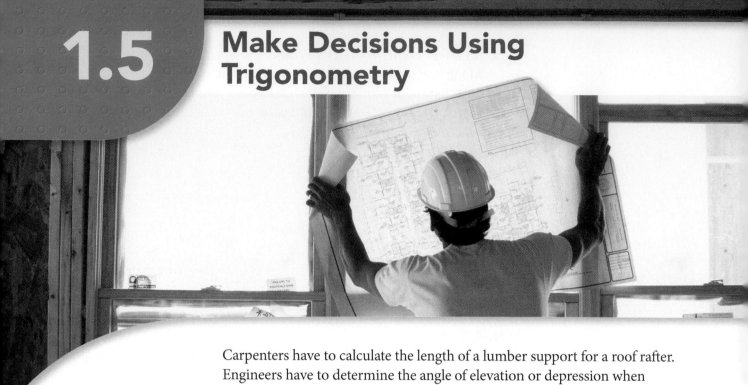

Carpenters have to calculate the length of a lumber support for a roof rafter. Engineers have to determine the angle of elevation or depression when calculating the height of a structure. Pilots use trigonometry to navigate aircraft, and to correct for wind effects. Ships' captains do the same for ocean currents. To calculate unknown measurements, these professionals first need to decide which trigonometric tool or formula to use.

Investigate 1

Tools

- BLM Match Me Up cards
  – 6 triangle cards
  – 3 formula/tool cards

Decision, Decision, Decision: You Be the Judge

Work with a partner.

In the game *Match Me Up*, you start with six triangle cards, each showing a triangle and its associated measures.

You also get three tool cards. The tools are:
- primary trigonometric ratios
- sine law
- cosine law

You have to decide which trigonometric formula or tool you should use to solve each triangle.

Taking turns, one player turns over a triangle card and the other player has to select the correct tool to solve the triangle. If you find the correct tool and answer, you get three points. If you only choose the correct tool, you get one point. If you only answer the question correctly, you get two points.

Play continues until each player's six cards have been played.

The player with the greatest score is the winner.

Trigonometry Problems

Work in pairs.

Three problems are given below.

Each partner decides which formula to use to solve the problem.

Each partner takes turns explaining how to solve the problem.

Check your solutions with the teacher.

Problems

1. Chi is flying his kite. The kite string is 40 m long. The angle of elevation the string makes with the horizontal is 26°. What is the height of the kite?

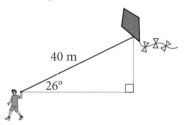

2. Three lights are located in a park along three different paths. The distance between the first light and the second light is 15 m. The distance between the second light and the third light is 19 m. The distance between the first light and the third light is 17 m. Calculate the angles between the lights.

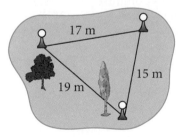

Math **Connect**

1 knot = 1.852 km/h

3. Two ships leave port at exactly the same time. *Doria* heads north at 10 knots and *Stockholm* heads 32° west of north at 12 knots. Calculate how far apart the two ships are after 2 h.

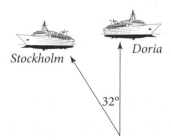

Example 1

Use the Primary Trigonometric Ratios

A 10-m ladder leans against a wall. The top of the ladder is 9 m above the ground. Safety standards call for the angle between the base of the ladder and the ground to be between 70° and 80°. Is the ladder safe to climb?

Solution

Draw a diagram to model the problem. Label it with the given information.

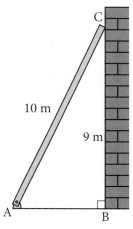

This is a right triangle and you have to find the angle the base of the ladder makes with the ground.

Determine the formula to use.

The problem involves a right triangle. Use the primary trigonometric ratios.

Locate the angle and label it A. The wall is opposite the angle and the ladder forms the hypotenuse of the triangle.

Write a ratio using the sides associated with the unknown angle.

$$\sin A = \frac{\text{opposite}}{\text{hypotenuse}}$$

$$\sin A = \frac{9}{10}$$

Substitute the known values into the ratio.

$$\angle A = \sin^{-1}\left(\frac{9}{10}\right)$$

Solve for the angle.

$$\angle A \doteq 64°$$

The base of the ladder makes an angle with the ground that is less than 70°. The ladder is not safe to climb.

Example 2

Use the Sine Law

A cable car stops part of the way across an 86-m wide gorge. The cable holding the car makes an angle of depression of 57° at one end and an angle of depression of 40° at the other end. How long is the cable that holds the car? Round your answer to the nearest metre.

Solution

Draw a diagram to model the problem. Label the diagram with the given information.

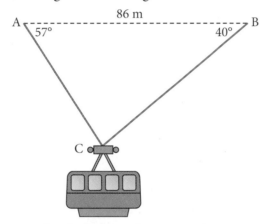

Decide which formula to use. This is not a right triangle, so primary trigonometric ratios cannot be used.

You are given the measures of two angles and one side of the triangle, so use the sine law.

$$\angle C = 180° - 57° - 40°$$
$$= 83°$$

Write a proportion to find an unknown side.

$$\frac{AC}{\sin B} = \frac{AB}{\sin C}$$

$$\frac{AC}{\sin 40°} = \frac{86}{\sin 83°}$$

$$AC = \frac{86 \times \sin 40°}{\sin 83°}$$

$$AC \doteq 55.7$$

You have to find the lengths of AC and BC, which are the length of the cable.

86 [×] [SIN] 40 [ )] [÷] [SIN] 83 [ )] [ENTER]

$$\frac{BC}{\sin A} = \frac{86}{\sin C}$$

$$\frac{BC}{\sin 57°} = \frac{86}{\sin 83°}$$

$$BC = \frac{86 \times \sin 57°}{\sin 83°}$$

$$BC \doteq 72.7$$

86 [×] [SIN] 57 [ )] [÷] [SIN] 83
[ )] [ENTER]

Cable length = 55.7 + 72.7
            = 128.4

The length of the cable is approximately 128 m.

Example 3

Use the Cosine Law

A sewer pipe for a new subdivision has to be laid underground. A connection is made to the main service pipe at either end of the 4.8-km stretch of road. One pipe, 2.5 km long, makes an angle of 72° at one end of the road.

a) Calculate the length of the second pipe that will connect the first pipe to the other end of the road.

b) What is the measure of the angle made by connecting the two pipes?

Solution

a) Draw and label a diagram that models the problem.

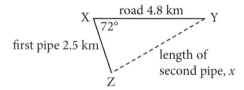

Decide which tool or formula to use. This is not a right triangle, so primary trigonometric ratios cannot be used.
The measures of two sides and a contained angle are given. Use the cosine law.

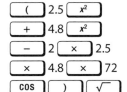

Technology Tip

For a scientific calculator, you might use this key sequence:

(2.5 x^2

+ 4.8 x^2

− 2 × 2.5

× 4.8 × 72

COS) √

For a DAL calculator, you might use this key sequence:

√ (2.5

x^2 + 4.8

x^2 − 2

× 2.5 ×

4.8 COS 72)

=

$$x^2 = 2.5^2 + 4.8^2 - 2(2.5)(4.8)\cos 72°$$
$$x = \sqrt{2.5^2 + 4.8^2 - 2(2.5)(4.8)\cos 72°}$$

$$x \doteq 4.67$$

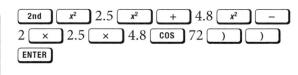

The length of the second pipe will be approximately 4.7 km.

b) $\dfrac{\sin Y}{2.5} = \dfrac{\sin 72°}{3.8}$

$\sin Y = \dfrac{2.5 \times \sin 72°}{3.8}$

$\angle Y \doteq 38.73°$

Calculate the measure of the smallest angle first using the sine law. The smallest angle is $\angle Y$.

The angle made between the road and the second pipe is about 39°.

The angle at the connection of the two pipes is:
$\angle Z \doteq 180° - 52° - 39°$
$\quad \doteq 89°$

The angle made between the connecting pipes is approximately 89°.

Key Concepts

- Decide which formula or tool to use based on the type of triangle the situation presents.
- If the problem is modelled by a right triangle, use the primary trigonometric ratios.
- If the problem is modelled by an acute triangle
    - with two angles and a given side or two sides and an opposite angle, use the sine law
    - with two sides and a contained angle or three sides, use the cosine law

Discuss the Concepts

D1. Is it possible to use any of the formulas to solve a right triangle given only the measure of one side? Explain.

D2. Is it possible to find an angle measure in a triangle given the measures of one angle and one side? Explain.

Practise (A) •

Round your answers to the nearest tenth, where necessary.

1. Work in pairs. One partner chooses a triangle. The other partner decides which formula to use to solve it.

   a)
   10 cm
   26°

   b)
   25 m   29 m
   32 m

   c)
   6.5 m
   70°
   80°

   d)
   26 mm   13 mm

   e)
   45 m
   52°
   60 m

   f)
   17.5 cm   70°
   80°

2. Refer to question 1. Solve each triangle.

For help with questions 3 and 4, refer to Example 1.

3. Lorie Kane, one of Canada's great female golfers, hits a tee shot short of a water hazard (a pond). A second shot to the centre of the green will give her a chance for an eagle. However, she can lay up directly in front for 120 yd, avoiding the hazard, and then take a third shot to the green. She decides to go for the green on her second shot using a four-iron, which has a maximum distance of 200 yd. She estimates the angle between the fairway and the shot to the green to be 52°. Did she make the right decision? Explain. What assumptions are you making?

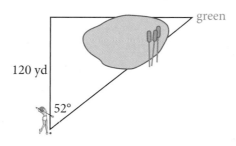

4. A golfer is faced with a shot that has to pass over some trees. The trees are 33 ft tall. The golfer finds himself 7 yd behind these trees, which obstruct him from the green. He decides to go for the green by using a 60° lob wedge. This club will allow the ball an angle of elevation of 60°. Did he make the right choice? Explain. What assumptions are you making? Hint: 1 yd = 3 ft

Literacy Connect

5. Golf is one sport in which skills in trigonometry are useful. What other sports use trigonometry to help a player be more skillful? Provide examples of the types of plays that might use trigonometry.

For help with question 6, refer to Example 2.

6. Two tracking stations, 5 km apart, track a weather balloon floating between them. The tracking station to the west tracks the balloon at an angle of elevation of 52°, and the station to the east tracks the balloon at an angle of elevation of 60°. How far is the balloon from the closest tracking station?

7. Three cell phone towers form a triangle. The distance between the first tower and the second tower is 16 km. The distance between the second tower and the third tower is 19 km. The distance between the first tower and the third tower is 19 km. Calculate the angles between the cell phone towers.

8. A triangular garden is to be enclosed by a fence. How much fencing will be required?

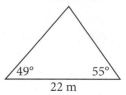

9. Complete the information needed to solve each triangle. Draw the triangle to help you explain.

   a) a right triangle, given one side and ▪

   b) an acute triangle, given two sides and ▪

   c) an acute triangle, given one angle and ▪

10. Three roads join Hometown, Mytown, and Ourtown.

   a) What is the distance from Hometown to Ourtown?

   b) What angles do the roads make at Hometown and at Ourtown?

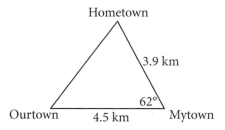

Achievement Check

11. The three stages of a triathlon involve swimming, cycling, and running, in that order. The distances for each stage can vary. For a triathlon held in Hawaii each year, competitors swim across an ocean bay, cycle 180.2 km, and run 42.2 km. In the diagram, S is the start of the swim and F is the finish of the swim. A surveyor, at point P, used the dimensions shown to calculate the length of SF across the ocean bay.

   a) Find the distance the athletes swim in the Hawaiian triathlon.

   b) What is the total distance of the race?

   c) What assumptions have you made?

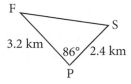

Reasoning and Proving

Representing   Selecting Tools

Problem Solving

Connecting   Reflecting

Communicating

12. David Beckham, one of professional soccer's most talented players, can bend his kicks but sometimes misses his target. Beckham gets ready for a free kick from 35 m away. He is located directly in front of the goalkeeper, who is 5 m from the right goal post. The net is 7.32 m wide and 2.44 m high. Once Beckham kicks the ball, the ball's angle of elevation of 4° takes a turn to the right at 9°. The goalie has no chance of making the save because the ball is heading toward the upper right corner of the net. Will Beckham score? Explain.

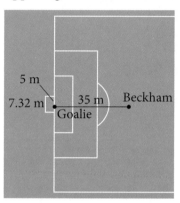

13. Find the measure of ∠CED to the nearest degree.

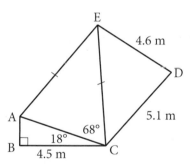

14. Murray is a forest ranger in a lookout tower 52 m above the ground. Directly south of him, at an angle of depression of 2.2° is a ranger station. The station has just radioed Murray to ask if he can spot a group of lost hikers. Murray spots the hikers camped out 60° east of south and at an angle of depression of 1.5° from the tower.

   a) How far is the lookout tower from the ranger station?

   b) How far is the lookout tower from the hikers?

   c) How far are the hikers from the ranger station?

   d) In which direction, to the nearest degree, should the rescue team leave the ranger station to reach the hikers?

1.1 Primary Trigonometric Ratios, pages 6–15

Where necessary, round answers to the nearest tenth.

1. Solve the right triangles.

a)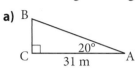

b)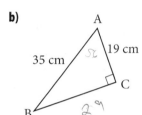

2. Solve △ABC where ∠C = 90°, $a = 15$ cm, and $b = 7$ cm.

3. Is it possible to solve △ABC, given ∠C = 90° and $c = 35$ cm? Explain. If not, what additional information is necessary?

1.2 Solve Problems Using Trigonometric Ratios, pages 16-23

4. A communication tower casts a shadow of 55 m when the sun is at an angle of elevation of 72°. What is the height of the tower to the nearest metre?

5. A person walks 5 km north, turns east, and then walks another 6 km. At what angle, east of north, did the person stop?

1.3 The Sine Law, pages 24-33

6. Is it possible to solve the triangle using the sine law? Explain. If not, what information is required?

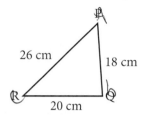

7. Solve the triangle.

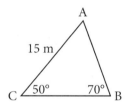

8. A sailboat is 5 nautical miles east of its starting point. At the start of its journey, it made an angle of 60° with a buoy on the right side of its path. After 45 min, it made an angle of 40° with the buoy as shown. How far is the sailboat from the buoy after 45 min?

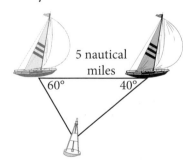

1.4 The Cosine Law, pages 34-41

9. Find the length of the unknown side, d.

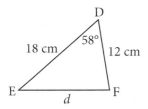

10. What information must be known about a triangle to use the cosine law? Provide examples with diagrams to help you explain.

11. Create a question with a triangle that can be solved using the cosine law. Trade problems with a classmate and solve each other's questions.

12. Two cyclists leave from the same location with an angle of 63° between their paths. Johal cycles at a speed of 35 km/h and Julio at a speed of 40 km/h. How far apart are they after 3 h?

13. Solve △KLM using the cosine law.

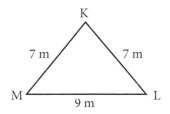

1.5 Make Decisions Using Trigonometry, pages 42-51

14. The pitch of a roof is 45°. The rise of the roof is 12 ft. A carpenter decided to cut a roof rafter 20 ft long to allow for a 1-ft overhang. Did the carpenter cut the correct length for the rafter? Explain. Draw a diagram and show your work. Include the formulas that you use.

15. The posts of a hockey goal are 2.0 m apart. Leah is 3.8 m from one post and 4.2 m from the other post. Within what angle must she shoot the puck to score a goal?

16. Determine the radius of the cone.

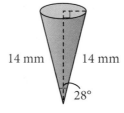

17. How can you solve the triangle in question 6 if it is not possible to solve it using the sine law? Solve it.

1. Copy and complete the diagram. Name the sides of the right triangle associated with ∠B, as adjacent, opposite, or hypotenuse.

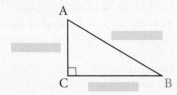

2. Solve △ABC.

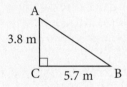

3. A golfer hit her tee shot so that it landed about 7 yd behind a 40-ft tall pine tree as shown. She decided to take her second shot and hoped the ball would make it over the top of the tree. She used her lob wedge and hit the ball, sending it upward at an angle of 60°. Was she able to clear the top of the tree? Show your solution.

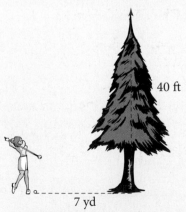

40 ft

7 yd

4. An airplane flying at an altitude of 2600 m is approaching an airport runway located 48 km away. Calculate the airplane's angle of descent. Round your answer to the nearest tenth of a degree.

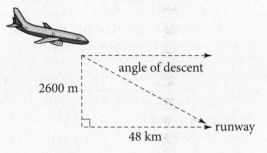

5. Solve △ABC.

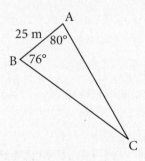

6. A wind-swept tree grows at angle of 85°. An environmental scientist wants to know the height of the tree. She walks 50 m from the tree and measures an angle of 40° to the top of the tree. How tall is the tree?

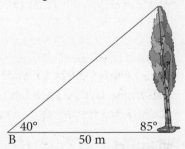

Chapter Problem Wrap-Up

The expedition team set out from the city of Iqaluit on a course 5° east of north and set up camp 15 km from their starting point. The next day, the team set out on a course 25° east of north but encountered a blizzard in the evening. They decided to set up camp until the storm subsided. They estimated that they had travelled at 2 km/h for 8 h. Not knowing their position, they radioed for help.

a) Draw a diagram to show the route travelled by the team. Include distances and angle directions.

b) Determine the shortest distance and direction a rescue team from Iqaluit would have to travel to reach the team.

---

7. Solve △ABC.

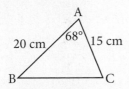

8. While on a camping trip, Claire hung her food bag up to keep it away from the wildlife. The bag was 6 m above the ground, suspended from the middle of a 6.2-m length of rope between two branches that are at the same height and 4 m apart. What angle did the rope make at the point where the food bag was hung?

9. Determine the measures of ∠A, ∠B, and ∠C.

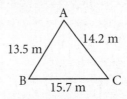

10. a) Explain why it is possible to solve a right triangle using the sine law if the measures of one side and one angle are given. Is this the best method? Why or why not?

b) Is it possible to solve a right triangle using the cosine law? Explain.

2 Probability

What would happen if people could predict details of the future? Farmers would know exactly when to plant and harvest their crops. Doctors could identify those at risk of contracting a disease. Businesses would know which products to develop and how to market them. Fortunes would be made in the stock market.

In this chapter, you will learn how probability is used to predict the likelihood that an event will happen.

In this chapter, you will

- identify examples of the use of probability in the media and various ways in which probability is represented
- determine the theoretical probability of an event, and represent the probability in a variety of ways
- perform a probability experiment, represent the results using a frequency distribution, and use the distribution to determine the experimental probability of an event
- compare, through investigation, the theoretical probability of an event with the experimental probability, and explain why they might differ
- determine, through investigation using class-generated data and technology-based simulation models, the tendency of experimental probability to approach theoretical probability as the number of trials in an experiment increases
- interpret information involving the use of probability and statistics in the media, and make connections between probability and statistics

Reasoning and Proving

Representing | Selecting Tools

Problem Solving

Connecting | Reflecting

Communicating

Key Terms

data	statistics
event	theoretical probability
experimental probability	trial
outcome	

Rabia completed the two-year fish and wildlife technician course at Sault College. She works as a park conservation officer, protecting wildlife and the environment. Rabia applies her skills in probability and statistics to provide reliable data on fish and wildlife populations.

Prerequisite Skills

Fractions, Decimals, and Percents

1. Express each fraction as a decimal without the use of a calculator.

   a) $\frac{97}{100}$ b) $\frac{2}{5}$

   c) $\frac{3}{20}$ d) $\frac{5}{8}$

2. Use a calculator to express each fraction as a decimal. Round your answers to four decimal places, if necessary.

   a) $\frac{17}{40}$ b) $\frac{4}{13}$

   c) $\frac{5}{6}$ d) $\frac{4}{9}$

3. Express each decimal as a fraction in lowest terms.

   a) 0.75   b) 0.16

   c) 0.65   d) 0.125

   e) 0.3333…   f) 0.001

4. Express each percent as a fraction in lowest terms.

   a) 30%   b) 25%

   c) 80%   d) 45%

   e) $66.\overline{6}\%$ f) 100%

5. Evaluate without the use of a calculator. Express answers as a fraction in lowest terms.

   a) $1 - \frac{1}{4}$ b) $\frac{1}{2} - \frac{1}{6}$

   c) $\frac{1}{5}$ of 80   d) $\frac{3}{13} \times \frac{1}{6}$

6. Use a calculator to evaluate each expression in question 5. If your calculator has a fraction button, answer as a fraction.

Interpreting Data

7. The table shows the results of rolling a six-sided die several times.

Result	Frequency
1	3
2	4
3	3
4	5
5	2
6	1

   a) What was the total number of rolls?

   b) What percent of the total number of rolls resulted in a 4?

   c) What fraction of the total number of rolls resulted in an even number?

   d) For the number of rolls that resulted in an even number, what percent resulted in a 2?

8. Consider the following graph.

   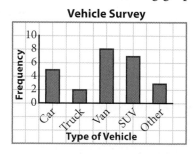

   a) What type of graph is this?

   b) How many vehicles were seen?

   c) What was the most popular vehicle?

   d) What fraction of the vehicles were cars?

   e) What percent of the vehicles were trucks?

9. Two hundred people were surveyed. The results are shown in the graph.

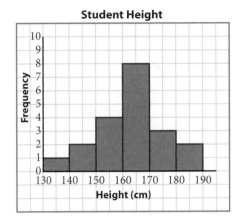

Favourite Teams

Boston Red Sox 10%

New York Yankees 30%

Toronto Blue Jays 40%

Detroit Tigers 20%

a) Of the people surveyed, how many prefer the Boston Red Sox?

b) What fraction of the people surveyed prefer the Toronto Blue Jays?

c) What percent of the people surveyed prefer the Blue Jays or the New York Yankees?

10. The histogram shows the heights of the students in Mr. Lee's math class.

Student Height

a) How many students are in the class?

b) How many students are between 160 cm and 170 cm tall?

c) What percent of students are shorter than 160 cm?

d) What fraction of students are taller than 150 cm?

Chapter Problem

Every five years, Statistics Canada conducts a census to collect information about the residents of Canada.

Suggest reasons why it is not possible to conduct a census on wildlife populations. What groups of people would be interested in this kind of information?

Many people rely directly or indirectly on the fishing industry. Sport fishing is very popular throughout Ontario and is important to tourism. How can probability and statistics be used to provide reliable data on fish populations?

2.1 Probability Experiments

One way to predict future events is to analyse what has happened in the past. Suppose a baseball player has a 0.250 batting average. Is she likely to make a hit the next time at bat? If there is a 20% probability of precipitation tomorrow, would you go to an outdoor concert?

Investigate 1

Tools

- 10 coloured tiles; five red and five blue
- opaque bag or box to hold tiles

outcome
- a possible result of an experiment

event
- a set of outcomes with the same result

trial
- one round of a probability experiment

Odd or Even?

Consider this experiment.

Place five red and five blue coloured tiles in a bag. Without looking, take out two tiles. The two selected tiles are called an **outcome**. If the tiles are the same colour, the **event** is considered even. If the tiles are not the same colour, the event is considered odd. Then replace the tiles.

Work with a partner.

1. Suppose you conducted 20 **trials** of the experiment. How many odd results would you expect to get? How many even results?

2. Conduct 20 trials of the experiment. Record the results in a tally chart.

3. Compare your answers to questions 1 and 2. How did the actual results compare to your expectations?

4. Combine your results with those of nine other pairs of students. How do the combined results compare to your expectations?

5. Reflect Suppose you were to predict the number of odd events from five trials of the experiment. Which results would you use to make your prediction, your results from question 2, or the combined results from question 4? Explain your choice.

In the Investigate you conducted a probability experiment. The experiment consisted of 20 trials. In each trial, two tiles were drawn. Each trial had two possible events: odd or even.

Gone Fishing

The Ministry of Natural Resources wants to know the ratio of bass to carp to catfish in a lake. The ministry has asked registered anglers to keep track of the number of each type of fish they catch. You will use coloured tiles to simulate this method of analysing fish populations.

1. Put the 15 tiles in a bag. The yellow tiles will represent the number of bass in the lake, the red tiles will represent the number of carp, and the blue tiles will represent the number of catfish.

2. Without looking, draw one tile from the bag. Record the results in a tally chart. Replace the tile.

3. Suppose you repeated this experiment 30 times. What fraction of the events do you expect to be bass? What fraction do you expect to be carp?

4. Conduct 30 trials of this experiment. Record the results in a tally chart.

5. Use the data from your tally chart. Draw a bar graph showing the number of each type of fish.

6. a) Write your experimental results as a ratio, bass : carp : catfish.

  b) How does this ratio compare to the ratio of the colours of tiles in the bag?

  c) Does the simulation give a reasonable estimate of the ratio of the colours of tiles in the bag? Explain.

7. Reflect If you performed 100 trials instead of 30, would the estimate likely be more or less accurate? Explain.

8. Reflect Do you think the number of each type of fish caught is an accurate indicator of the actual ratio of fish in the lake? Explain.

Example 1

Roll a Single Die

The results of rolling a six-sided die are displayed in the graph.

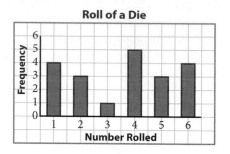

a) How many times was a 5 rolled?

b) Find the **experimental probability** of rolling a 6. Express your answer as a fraction in lowest terms, as a decimal, and as a percent.

c) Find the experimental probability of **not** rolling a 6. How is this related to the probability of rolling a 6?

d) How would you expect the heights of the bars to relate to each other? Explain.

Solution

a) From the graph, a 5 was rolled three times.

b) Add the frequencies to determine the total number of rolls.
$4 + 3 + 1 + 5 + 3 + 4 = 20$

The number 6 was rolled four times.

$$P(\text{rolling } 6) = \frac{\text{number of successful trials}}{\text{total number of trials}}$$

$$= \frac{\text{number of times 6 was rolled}}{\text{total number of trials}}$$

$$= \frac{4}{20}$$

$$= \frac{1}{5}$$

Express $\dfrac{1}{5}$ as a decimal.

$\dfrac{1}{5} = 0.2$

Express $\dfrac{1}{5}$ as a percent.

$\dfrac{1}{5} = 20\%$

The probability of rolling a 6 is $\dfrac{1}{5}$, or 0.2, or 20%.

c) From part b), the total number of rolls is 20. The number 6 was rolled four times. So, a different number turned up 16 times.

$$P(\text{not rolling 6}) = \frac{\text{number of successful trials}}{\text{total number of trials}}$$

$$= \frac{\text{number of times a number other than 6 was rolled}}{\text{total number of trials}}$$

$$= \frac{16}{20}$$

$$= \frac{4}{5}$$

$$P(\text{rolling a 6}) + P(\text{not rolling a 6}) = \frac{1}{5} + \frac{4}{5}$$
$$= 1$$

It is certain the number rolled will be either a 6 or a number other than 6. So, the sum of the probabilities is 1.

d) Because each number is equally likely, you would expect 1, 2, 3, 4, 5, and 6 to turn up an equal number of times. The bar graph would have all bars of equal height. Since one roll of the die does not depend on the previous rolls, the likelihood of getting a particular number on each roll is the same. In 20 rolls of the die, it is possible to get all 6s. Experimental probability is a measure of what actually happened, not what is expected to happen.

It is possible to have zero successful trials, which gives a probability of 0. For example, the probability of rolling a 7 with a single die is 0.

The number of successful trials can equal the total number of trials. In this case, the probability is 1. For example, the probability of rolling a 1, 2, 3, 4, 5, or 6 is 1.

Probability always has a value between 0 (certain not to happen) and 1 (certain to happen).

Example 2

How Many Females?

A probability experiment was designed to find the expected number of females in a family of six children. To simulate the genders of the six children, a coin was tossed six times. Heads represented a male; tails represented a female. The experiment was repeated a number of times. The results are shown in the graph.

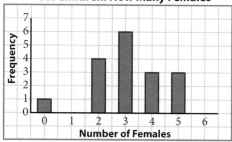

Six Children: How Many Females

a) How many trials were performed?

b) What is the experimental probability of having two females in a family of six children?

c) According to this experiment, what is the average number of females in a family with six children?

Solution

a) The height of each bar indicates the number of times a trial predicted a given number of children. For example, the event "zero females" occurred one time. The numbers of occurrences were 1, 0, 4, 6, 3, 3, and 0 respectively.

Their sum is: $1 + 0 + 4 + 6 + 3 + 3 + 0 = 17$.
There were 17 trials.

b) From the graph, the event "two females" occurred four times.

$$P(2 \text{ females}) = \frac{\text{number of successful trials}}{\text{total number of trials}}$$

$$= \frac{\text{number of trials with 2 females}}{\text{total number of trials}}$$

$$= \frac{4}{17}$$

c) The average number of females per family of six will be the total number of females from the experiment divided by the total number of trials.

The total number of females can be shown in a table.

Number of Females Per Family	Occurrences	Total Number of Females
0	1	$0 \times 1 = 0$
1	0	$1 \times 0 = 0$
2	4	$2 \times 4 = 8$
3	6	$3 \times 6 = 18$
4	3	$4 \times 3 = 12$
5	3	$5 \times 3 = 15$
6	0	$6 \times 0 = 0$

Total number of females $= 8 + 18 + 12 + 15$
$$= 53$$

Average number of females per family $= \dfrac{\text{total number of females}}{\text{total number of trials}}$
$$= \frac{53}{17}$$
$$\doteq 3.1$$

From this experiment, the average number of females in a family with six children is 3.1.

Key Concepts

- Probability is a measure of the likelihood that a specific event will occur.
- Probability experiments can be used to estimate the probability of an event.
- Experimental probability $= \dfrac{\text{number of successful trials}}{\text{total number of trials}}$.
- Probability is always a value between 0 and 1.

Discuss the Concepts

D1. Does experimental probability always give an accurate prediction of the likelihood that an event will occur? Explain.

D2. Which would you consider to be more accurate: a probability experiment with five trials, or one with 100 trials? Explain.

D3. In a probability experiment, you toss a fair coin 10 times. Is it possible that heads will turn up 10 times? Explain.

Practise **A** •••

For help with question 1, refer to Example 1.

1. In a probability experiment, 15 out of 50 trials were successful.

   a) Determine the experimental probability of a successful trial. Express your answer as a fraction in lowest terms, as a percent, and as a decimal.

   b) Write the probability of an unsuccessful trial as a fraction in lowest terms. Explain how you got your answer.

2. Two six-sided dice were rolled 20 times. Doubles were rolled four times. Determine the experimental probability of rolling doubles. Express your answer as a fraction in lowest terms, as a percent, and as a decimal.

3. A coin was tossed 30 times. The experimental probability of turning up heads was $\frac{2}{5}$.

   a) How many times did the coin turn up heads?

   b) How many times did it turn up tails?

   c) What was the experimental probability of it turning up tails? Describe two different methods of finding the answer.

For help with question 4, refer to Example 2.

4. Two coins were tossed a total of 200 times. The results are shown in the graph.

   Find the experimental probability for each event.

   a) two heads

   b) one head

   c) two tails

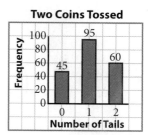

Apply **B** •••

5. Refer to the graph in question 4.

Literacy Connect

   a) How do you think the bars for two heads and two tails should compare? Explain your reasoning.

   b) What are the two different outcomes that result in the event "one head"?

   c) Based on the information in the graph, what fraction of the time would you expect the event "one head"?

   d) Use your answers to parts a) and c) to determine what fraction of the time you would expect to get HH and TT.

6. Sam tossed a coin 10 times and heads turned up nine times.

   a) Express the experimental probability of turning up heads as a percent.

   b) Is the experimental probability what you expected? Explain.

7. At a light bulb factory, a batch of bulbs is rejected if more than 5% of the bulbs in a sample taken from the batch are defective.

   a) If 240 bulbs are tested and eight are defective, will the batch be rejected? Show your calculations.

   b) In a batch of 1000 bulbs, exactly 100 are defective. A sample of 200 bulbs from the batch of 1000 is tested. Do you expect the batch will be rejected? Explain your reasoning.

   c) In a large batch of bulbs, 1% of the bulbs are defective. A sample of the bulbs is tested. Is it possible that the entire batch will be rejected? Explain your reasoning.

8. In Investigate 1, two tiles were taken from a bag containing 10 tiles. There were five tiles each of two different colours. Sandy drew *evens* 12 times out of 20. Is each statement true or false? Explain.

   a) The experimental probability of drawing *evens* is $\frac{3}{5}$.

   b) The event *evens* was more likely than the event *odds*.

Chapter Problem

9. A Ministry of Natural Resources employee caught and tagged 100 fish in a small lake. Two weeks later, 100 fish were caught, 10 of which had previously been tagged.

   a) Estimate the number of fish in the lake. Explain your reasoning.

   b) Suggest some factors that could account for differences between your estimate and a classmate's.

Extend

10. Refer to Investigate 1. Collect the results from all students in your class and find the total number of odds and evens based on the class results.

   a) Does there seem to be a pattern? Is the percent of evens 50%, greater than 50%, or less than 50%?

   b) Simulate this problem using technology. Compare the class results with the results you found from your simulation.

Literacy Connect

11. Refer to question 10. Explain why the probability of evens is less than 50%. In your explanation, give the probability as a fraction.

Theoretical Probability

Consider the following situation.

In a TV game show based on a popular board game, Janna is trying to win money for a charity of her choice. She has to choose between two options:
• automatically win $500 for her charity
• win $5000 for her charity if she rolls doubles with two six-sided dice

What would you do?

Investigate 1

Building on Probability

1. Copy and complete each statement. Express the probability as a fraction.

   a) When tossing a coin, the probability of it turning up heads is ■.

   b) When rolling a single die, the probability of turning up 4 is ■.

   c) When drawing a card from a regular deck of playing cards, the probability of it being an ace is ■.

   d) A radio station held a contest; 100 people qualified. There will be 10 winners. For the 100 contestants, the probability of winning is ■.

2. **Reflect** Refer to question 1. For each situation, explain the meaning of the numerator and the denominator in your answer.

3. **Reflect** Refer to your answer to question 2. Describe how you can calculate the probability of an event.

$$\text{Experimental probability} = \frac{\text{number of successful trials}}{\text{total number of trials}}$$

theoretical probability
• the number of successful outcomes as a fraction of the total number of possible outcomes

Theoretical probability is another measure of the likelihood of an event. It is the ratio of the number of successful outcomes and the total number of possible outcomes.

$$\text{Theoretical probability} = \frac{\text{number of successful outcomes}}{\text{total number of possible outcomes}}$$

To calculate the theoretical probability, all outcomes must be equally likely.

"Equally likely" means the same chance of occurring because the conditions are fair.

For example, in the toss of a fair coin, the chances of getting heads or tails are equally likely.

Investigate 2

Who Gets What?

Jason, Tony, and Lisa have each won a video game from Ace Video Games. Inc. as part of an advertising promotion. The video games, Xtreme Racing, Golf Legends, and Hoops will be randomly assigned to the three winners. What is the probability Jason will receive Golf Legends?

1. Draw a table with three columns, as shown. Label them with the names Jason, Tony, and Lisa.

Jason	Tony	Lisa

2. Use X, G, and H to represent the games. In your table record all the different possible ways the games can be given to the three people.

3. Reflect

   a) In how many different ways can the three games be arranged?

   b) In how many of these arrangements does Jason receive Golf Legends?

   c) Assume that all the arrangements are equally likely. What is the theoretical probability that Jason receives Golf Legends?

4. Reflect Another way to approach the problem is to consider the number of different games and the fact that there is an equal chance of getting each of them. Explain how this approach will lead to the same result as when we considered the arrangements.

Example 1

Draw!

A standard deck of playing cards has 52 cards, 13 of each suit.

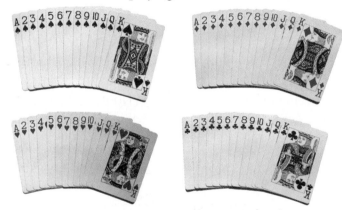

If one card is drawn from the deck, find the probability of each event.

   a) a heart

   b) an ace

   c) a heart, a club, or a jack

   d) a black diamond

   e) a heart, a club, a spade, or a diamond

Solution

a) $P(\text{heart}) = \dfrac{\text{number of successful outcomes}}{\text{total number of possible outcomes}}$

$= \dfrac{\text{number of hearts}}{\text{total number of cards}}$

$= \dfrac{13}{52}$

$= \dfrac{1}{4}$

b) $P(\text{ace}) = \dfrac{\text{number of successful outcomes}}{\text{total number of possible outcomes}}$

$= \dfrac{\text{number of aces}}{\text{total number of cards}}$

$= \dfrac{4}{52}$

$= \dfrac{1}{13}$

c) $P(\text{heart, club, or jack}) = \dfrac{\text{number of successful outcomes}}{\text{total number of possible outcomes}}$

$= \dfrac{\text{number of hearts, clubs, or jacks}}{\text{total number of cards}}$

$= \dfrac{13 + 13 + 2}{52}$

$= \dfrac{28}{52}$

$= \dfrac{7}{13}$

Be careful not to count the jacks twice; two are already included in the hearts and clubs.

d) $P(\text{black diamond}) = \dfrac{\text{number of successful outcomes}}{\text{total number of possible outcomes}}$

$= \dfrac{\text{number of black diamonds}}{\text{total number of cards}}$

$= \dfrac{0}{52}$

$= 0$

There are no black diamonds, so it is impossible to draw.

e) $P(\text{heart, club, spade, or diamond})$

$= \dfrac{\text{number of successful outcomes}}{\text{total number of possible outcomes}}$

$= \dfrac{\text{number of hearts, clubs, spades, diamonds}}{\text{total number of cards}}$

$= \dfrac{13 + 13 + 13 + 13}{52}$

$= \dfrac{52}{52}$

$= 1$

You are certain to draw a heart, club, spade, or diamond.

| | **Example 2** | **Roll the Dice** |

Example 2

Roll the Dice

Recall Janna's dilemma from the introduction.

What is the probability of rolling doubles with a pair of dice?

Solution

Method 1: Draw a Tree Diagram or Table

Draw a tree with six branches representing the six outcomes from rolling the first die.

From each branch, draw six more branches representing the six outcomes from rolling the second die. The tree will have a total of 36 branches, representing all possible rolls of the two dice.

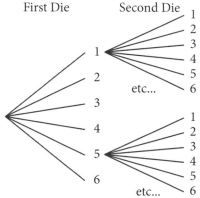

There are six outcomes that result in doubles.

$$P(\text{rolling doubles}) = \frac{\text{number of ways of rolling doubles}}{\text{total number of possible rolls}}$$
$$= \frac{6}{36}$$
$$= \frac{1}{6}$$

Another way to show all possible outcomes is to use a table.

	1	**2**	**3**	**4**	**5**	**6**
1	1, 1	1, 2	1, 3	1, 4	1, 5	1, 6
2	2, 1	2, 2	2, 3	2, 4	2, 5	2, 6
3	3, 1	3, 2	3, 3	3, 4	3, 5	3, 6
4	4, 1	4, 2	4, 3	4, 4	4, 5	4, 6
5	5, 1	5, 2	5, 3	5, 4	5, 5	5, 6
6	6, 1	6, 2	6, 3	6, 4	6, 5	6, 6

Method 2: Work With a Simpler Problem

Assume one die has been rolled. There are six possible outcomes for the second roll, one of which will match the results of rolling the first die, giving doubles.

$$P(\text{rolling doubles}) = P(\text{second die will match the first die})$$
$$= \frac{1}{6}$$

The probability of rolling the same number as on the first die is $\frac{1}{6}$.

Key Concepts

- Theoretical probability $= \dfrac{\text{number of successful outcomes}}{\text{total possible number of outcomes}}$, where all outcomes are equally likely.

- The probability of an event is a value between 0 and 1.

Discuss the Concepts

D1. Use the formula for theoretical probability to explain why the value must be between 0 and 1.

D2. Give an example of an event that has a 0 probability of happening. Explain why the probability is 0.

Practise ●

For help with questions 1 and 2, refer to Example 1.

1. A card is randomly selected from a standard deck of cards. Write the theoretical probability of each event as a fraction in lowest terms.

   a) a spade

   b) a face card (jack, queen, or king)

   c) not a face card

   d) a black jack

   e) a red or black card

   f) a red face card

2. Queen's Slipper playing cards are popular in Australia. In addition to the standard 52 cards, a deck contains the 11, 12, and 13 of each suit. When drawing a card from such a deck, find the theoretical probability of drawing

   a) an 11

   b) an 11, 12, or 13

3. Britt rolls a regular six-sided die. Find the theoretical probability of each event. Express your answer as a fraction in lowest terms.

   a) rolling a 6

   b) rolling a number greater than 3

   c) rolling an 8

   d) rolling an even number

4. A pet store has 10 cats, 12 dogs, and 3 turtles. If Bobby randomly selects a pet to take home, find the theoretical probability of getting

   a) a cat

   b) a turtle

   c) a dog or a turtle

For help with question 5, refer to Example 2.

5. Suppose you roll two six-sided dice. Find the theoretical probability of rolling each sum. Express each answer as a fraction in lowest terms.

   a) 2   **b)** 11   **c)** a sum greater than 5

   d) 7   **e)** not 7

Apply **B** •••

6. During a game of musical chairs, 10 people walk around eight chairs waiting for the music to stop. Find the probability of a person not getting a chair.

7. Twelve charms representing the 12 months of the year are attached, in order, onto a chain bracelet. Find the probability that the clasp is between the charms for June and July. Include a diagram with your solution.

8. Suppose you roll two six-sided dice.

   a) Explain why the probability of rolling a sum of 14 is 0.

   b) Explain why the probability of rolling a sum from 2 to 12 is 1.

9. Ronald's Restaurant offers this sandwich menu.

   > **Sandwiches $3.95***
   >
   > • tuna   *Your choice of*
   > • egg   *whole wheat*
   > • ham   *or white bread.*

   a) How many different types of sandwiches are possible?

   b) Suppose you like all sandwich fillings and both types of bread. If you randomly selected a sandwich, what is the probability of each sandwich being

      i) tuna on white bread?

      ii) egg salad or ham on whole wheat bread?

      iii) ham?

      iv) egg salad on white or whole wheat bread?

Literacy Connect

10. The complement of an event is *all other events*. For example, when rolling a die, the complement of rolling a 1 is rolling a 2, 3, 4, 5, or 6; the complement of rolling an odd number is rolling an even number.

a) Use the tree diagram or the table from Example 2 to find the probability of not rolling doubles.

b) Explain how you can use the thinking from Method 2 to find the probability of not rolling doubles.

c) P(rolling doubles) + P(not rolling doubles) = 1. Explain why this makes sense.

11. The radius of the entire dartboard is 40 cm, while the radius of the red circle is 20 cm.

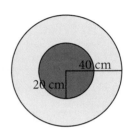

a) If a dart is thrown at random, find the probability that it will land in the red circle. Justify your answer.

b) What assumption have you made?

Chapter Problem

12. A fisheries employee caught a number of bass, carp, and catfish and is preparing to tag them for tracking purposes. There are a total of 60 fish: 20 bass, 25 carp, and 15 catfish. A fish is randomly selected to be tagged.

a) Find the probability that the fish selected is a catfish. Express your answer as a fraction in lowest terms.

b) Find the probability that the fish selected is a bass or a carp. Suggest two possible methods for doing this.

c) If you know for certain that the fish selected is not a bass, find the probability that it is a carp. Express your answer as a decimal.

Extend

13. Ann, Bob, and Cathy are posing for a group photograph.

a) What is the probability that Ann will not be standing between Bob and Cathy?

b) What is the probability that Bob and Cathy will be standing beside each other?

c) Are the probabilities for parts a) and b) related? Explain.

14. A cylindrical drum contains clear plastic pellets to be sent to a factory. By accident, a red pellet has contaminated the container of clear pellets. The pellets from the drum are poured into a cone-shaped container of the same height and radius as the cylinder. What is the probability of the red pellet remaining in the drum? Justify your answer.

The theoretical probability of rolling a 2 with a die is $\frac{1}{6}$. However, if you try it, do you suppose you will roll one 2 in every six trials?

If you toss a coin, will the result be tails exactly half of the time? If you toss a coin 100 times or 1000 times, will the experimental probability eventually reach 50%?

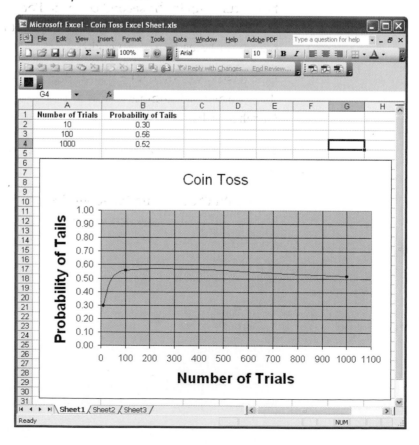

Tools

- coins
- grid paper

Optional

- spreadsheet software
- random number generator

Toss Coins

1. If you toss a coin 10 times, how many times do you expect to turn up heads? Explain your reasoning.

2. Copy the table for one to 10 trials.

Trial Number	Number of Heads	Average Number of Heads
1		
2		
3		
. . .		
10		

3. Toss a coin 10 times. In row 1, record the number of times that heads turns up in the second column. The 10 tosses represent one trial. For this row, the average number of heads will be the same as the number of heads.

4. Repeat the experiment. In row 2, record the number of times that heads turns up in the second column. For this row, the average number of heads will be the sum of the first two values in the Number of Heads column divided by 2, the number of trials.

5. Repeat step 4 until you have completed 10 rows of the table. For each row, the average number of heads will be the sum of the values in the Number of Heads column, divided by the number of trials.

6. Draw a scatter plot of Number of Trials versus Average Number of Heads.

7. **Reflect** What do you notice about the graph as the number of trials increases? Why do you suppose this is the case? Do you think this is always the case? Explain.

Investigate 2

Tools

- graphing calculator
- grid paper

How Many Girls?

When a child is born, there is a 50% chance it will be a girl. You will use a graphing calculator to find the probability that two out of three children in a family are girls.

1. Use a graphing calculator. Enter the month and day of your birthday, followed by the street number of your home, using all digits. Press [STO▸]. Press [MATH]. Use the arrow keys to highlight **PRB**. Press [ENTER] twice.

2. Press [MATH]. Use the arrow keys to highlight **PRB**. Select **5:randInt**. Type **0** [,] **1** [,] **3** [ )].

To simulate rolling two dice, you would use **randInt(1,6,2)**.

The program will generate 0s and 1s, in sets of three to represent the genders of the three children. Assume a 0 represents a male and a 1 represents a female.

3. Press [ENTER] to simulate one family of three children. Copy and complete the table for 1 to 25 trials.

Trial Number	Number of Girls
1	

Each time you press [ENTER], another set of three "children" will be generated.

4. **Reflect** Of the 25 trials, how many times were there two girls? Is this what you expected? Explain.

5. **Reflect** Without calculating, what do you expect is the probability of having two boys out of three children? Explain.

Example 1

Will It Rain?

During the month of April 2006, at least some rainfall was recorded on 12 different days at the Sarnia Airport weather station.

a) Suppose one day in April 2006 is selected at random. What is the probability of choosing a day on which it rained?

b) Refer to the probability of precipitation you calculated in part a). Describe how to make a spinner to simulate the situation for part a).

c) On a graphing calculator, press $\boxed{\text{MATH}}$, select **PRB** and then **1:rand**. Press $\boxed{\text{ENTER}}$ several times. Describe what occurs and how this method can be used in place of the spinner in part b).

Solution

a) There are 30 days in April and it rained on 12 of those days.

$$P(\text{rain on selected day}) = \frac{\text{number of days of rain}}{\text{total number of days}}$$
$$= \frac{12}{30}$$
$$= \frac{2}{5}$$
$$= 0.4 \text{ or } 40\%$$

The probability of choosing a day in April 2006 on which it rained is 40%.

b) To make a spinner to model rain 40% of the time, create a sector angle whose measure represents 40% of the entire circle.

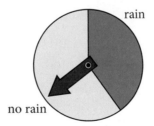

One full revolution is 360°.
40% of 360° = 0.40 × 360°
$\qquad\qquad\quad$ = 144°

The sector angle representing rain should have a measure of 144°.

c) The **rand** command on a graphing calculator generates a random decimal between 0 and 1. You can decide that if it gives a result less than or equal to 0.4, then it will represent a rainy day. A result greater than 0.4 will represent a dry day.

Example 2

Math ⟩ **Connect**

Mark the branches that represent a successful outcome. The total numbers of outcomes is the total number of branches on the right side of the tree.

How Many Girls?

Suppose a couple would like to have three children.

a) Determine the theoretical probability of having two girls and one boy.

b) Explain how your answer in part a) can help determine the theoretical probability of having two boys and one girl.

c) Determine the theoretical probability of having at least one girl.

Solution

a) Draw a tree diagram with three levels, each level representing one child.

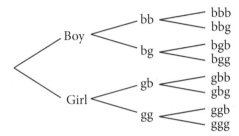

There are a total of eight branches. Three branches represent two girls and one boy.

$$P(\text{2 girls, 1 boy}) = \frac{\text{number of outcomes with 2 girls}}{\text{total number of outcomes}}$$

$$= \frac{3}{8}$$

The probability of having two girls and one boy in a family with three children is $\frac{3}{8}$.

b) The theoretical probability of having two boys and one girl would be the same as having two girls and one boy.

c) Method 1: Use a Tree Diagram

Having at least one girl means the couple can have one, two, or three girls. Examine the branches of the tree diagram. There are: three branches with one girl; three branches with two girls; and one branch with three girls.

$$P(\text{at least 1 girl}) = P(\text{1 girl, 2 girls, or 3 girls})$$

$$= \frac{\text{number of branches with at least 1 girl}}{\text{total number of branches}}$$

$$= \frac{3 + 3 + 1}{8}$$

$$= \frac{7}{8}$$

Method 2: Use the Complement

If there are three children, there must be zero, one, two, or three girls. The complement of "at least one girl" is "no girls."

$$P(\text{no girls}) = \frac{\text{number of branches with 0 girls}}{\text{total number of branches}}$$

$$= \frac{1}{8}$$

Finding the probability of the complement

$$P(\text{0 girls}) + P(\text{at least one girl}) = 1$$

$$\frac{1}{8} + P(\text{at least one girl}) = 1$$

$$P(\text{at least one girl}) = 1 - \frac{1}{8}$$

$$P(\text{at least one girl}) = \frac{7}{8}$$

Therefore the theoretical probability of having at least one girl in three children is $\frac{7}{8}$.

Key Concepts

- Real-life situations can be simulated by probability experiments.
- Computers and graphing calculators have random number generators that can simulate probability experiments.
- The theoretical probability and experimental probability of an event are not necessarily the same. As the number of trials increases, the experimental probability usually gets closer to the theoretical probability.

Discuss the Concepts

D1. How can a spinner be used to simulate rolling a six-sided die?

D2. If you perform a probability experiment, does the reliability increase or decrease when you increase the number of trials? Explain your reasoning.

D3. If you toss a coin 10 times, is it possible to obtain 10 heads? How many heads do you expect? Would your answer change if you used a graphing calculator to simulate the situation instead of tossing a real coin? Explain.

1. Consider the spinner shown.

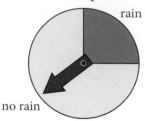

rain

no rain

a) What is the theoretical probability of the spinner landing on rain?

b) If the spinner lands on no rain 13 times in 15 trials, what would be the experimental probability of a day having no rain?

2. You toss a coin 10 times. It turns up heads eight times.

a) What is the experimental probability of turning up heads?

b) What is the theoretical probability of turning up heads?

c) If you tossed the coin several more times, would you expect the experimental probability to increase or decrease? Explain.

3. In a bag, there are 14 yellow marbles and six blue marbles. A marble is removed, the colour is recorded, and then it is put back into the bag. This is repeated for a total of 20 times. The results are displayed on the bar graph.

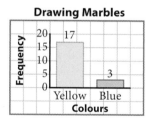

a) What is the experimental probability of drawing a yellow marble? Express your answer as a percent.

b) What is the theoretical probability of drawing a yellow marble? Express your answer as a percent.

4. A random number generator is used to simulate the results of rolling a die 30 times. The results are shown in the table.

Outcome	Frequency
1	4
2	6
3	7
4	5
5	6
6	2

a) Determine the probability of each outcome.

b) Is each probability in part a) theoretical or experimental? Explain your reasoning.

5. A die was rolled six times. The number 3 was rolled twice, and the number 2 was rolled four times.

a) Find the experimental probability of the following:
  i) rolling a 3   **ii)** rolling a 2   **iii)** rolling a 6

b) What is wrong with this experiment as a predictor of experimental probability?

6. When rolling two dice 60 times, doubles turned up a total of 15 times.

a) What is the experimental probability of doubles? Answer as a fraction in lowest terms.

b) What is the theoretical probability of rolling doubles?

c) Do you think the dice are fair? Explain your reasoning.

d) If the dice were rolled 60 more times, would doubles turn up less frequently to "make up" for the previous rolls? Explain.

7. Refer to question 1. Describe how you could use a graphing calculator to simulate the same situation

a) by using the **rand** command

b) by using the **randInt(** command

8. A multiple-choice test has 10 questions. Each question has four possible answers.

a) If a student randomly guesses at each of the 10 questions, how many would you expect to be correct? Explain your reasoning.

b) Explain how you can use the **randInt(1,4,10)** command on a graphing calculator to simulate guessing at 10 questions on a multiple-choice test.

Reasoning and Proving
Representing | Selecting Tools
Problem Solving
Connecting | Reflecting
Communicating

9. Refer to question 8. Chris used the **randInt(** command in his simulation, 20 times. The results are shown in the following table.

Trial Number	1	2	3	4	5	6	7	8	9	10	11	12	13	14	15	16	17	18	19	20
Number Correct	4	3	2	4	2	2	2	4	3	2	6	2	6	1	1	3	3	1	1	2
Average Number Correct																				

a) According to these results, what is the experimental probability of passing a 10-question test by guessing? Assume each question is multiple choice with four possible answers.

b) Is the result from part a) greater than you expected? Explain. Try this yourself and compare your results to the ones in the table.

10. Enter the data from the table in question 9 into a spreadsheet.
   - Enter the titles in cells A1 to A3.
   - In B3, enter the following formula: =AVERAGE(B2:B2).
   - Copy the formula and fill the remaining 19 cells in row 3. Hint: Click and drag the lower right corner of cell B3 to extend it to the cell U3.
   - Create a scatter plot of Average Number Correct versus Trial Number.

   a) Examine the formula in row 3. What is it calculating? In the formula, why does the first B2 stay the same while the second cell reference changes to C2, D2, and so on?

   b) Describe what you see in the scatter plot. Do a rough sketch of it on paper. If you performed more than 20 trials, how would the graph change? Explain your reasoning.

11. The area of a red circle in the centre of the dart board has one-quarter of the area of the entire dart board. This means there is a 25% theoretical probability of a dart hitting the red circle. During a game of darts, a shot landing in the red is worth two points, while a shot landing in the yellow scores only one point. In one game, 16 shots landed in red, while 24 landed in yellow.

   a) Find the experimental probability of landing in red. Express your answer as a decimal.

   b) How does your answer in part a) compare to the theoretical probability?

   c) What factor might explain this difference?

Chapter Problem **12.** In a small lake, it has been determined that bass, carp, and catfish are present in the ratio 3:5:2. However, in one sample, the three species have been caught in the ratio 3:3:2.

   a) What is the theoretical probability of catching a bass?

   b) What is the experimental probability of catching a bass?

   c) Suggest reasons why there is a difference between the experimental and theoretical probabilities in this situation.

13. The graph shows the percent frequency for the possible outcomes when a die was rolled. The results are shown for 12, 30, and 120 trials.

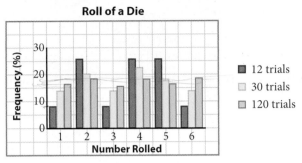

a) For 12 trials, in approximately what percent of the results was a 2 rolled?

b) For 12 trials, exactly how many times was a 3 rolled? Justify your answer.

c) What is happening to the heights of the bars as you progress from 12 to 30 then to 120 trials?

d) If you had data for 1000 trials, and included this on a multiple bar graph, describe what you would expect to see. Explain your reasoning.

Extend **C**

14. A game of chance involves the rolling of two dice. You win $5 if you roll doubles, otherwise you have to pay $1. If you played this game repeatedly, would you expect to win or lose money? Justify your answer.

15. You and a partner each toss a coin. If both are heads, your partner gives you three marbles. If both are tails, your partner gives you one marble. If one is heads and the other is tails, you give your partner two marbles.

a) Is this a fair game, or does the game favour one of the players? Explain.

b) Work with a partner. Record the results from 10 plays.

c) Use technology to simulate the results from 1000 plays.

d) Was your answer to part a) correct? Explain.

16. Sandor used a graphing calculator to find **randInt(2,12,10)**. He claimed that this will model the rolling of sums from 2 to 12 with a pair of dice 10 times. Marucia says that this procedure is not correct. Conduct several trials and record the results. Who is right? Explain.

Interpret Information Involving Probability

statistics
- the collection and analysis of numerical information

data
- facts or pieces of information

If you read a newspaper, listen to the radio, or watch television, you have encountered statistics about a number of different topics. **Statistics** are closely related to probability; people use them to make predictions about future events. Probability experiments involve simulating real-life events and using the results to make predictions. Statistics involve gathering **data** from real-life events in order to make predictions about future events.

Investigate 1

Tools
- graphing calculator
- grid paper

Optional
- spreadsheet software
- random number generator

Opinion Polls

A public opinion poll is a survey asking people about issues. Before an election, people were asked whom they planned to vote for: the Yays or the Nays. The results are shown.

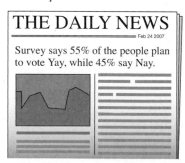

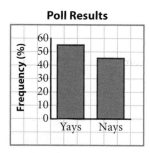

1. Use a graphing calculator. Press [MATH]. Use the arrow keys to highlight **PRB**.

2. Select **1:rand** and press [ENTER].

3. On the screen, you should now see **rand**. Press [ENTER] a few times and see what happens.

4. For this activity, a random number less than 0.55 will be considered a vote for the Yays. A number greater than or equal to 0.55 will be considered a vote for the Nays.

5. **Reflect** Explain how the statements in step 4 are related to the results of the poll.

6. On paper, create a tally chart with columns for the Yays and Nays.

7. Perform the **rand** command by pressing ENTER. Record the result in your tally chart.

8. Repeat step 7 until you have performed 100 trials.

9. Find the totals for each of the two parties and display the data using a bar graph.

10. **Reflect** How do the results of your 100 trials compare to the original 55% and 45% values?

11. **Reflect** Is it possible for the Nays to win your "mini-election"? Explain your reasoning.

12. Compare your results to those of classmates. Did the Nays win for any of your classmates?

Investigate 2

Tools

- graphing calculator

Optional

- spreadsheet software with random number generator application
- appropriate spinner to simulate the problem

Key Saves

After 813 regular season games, goalie Martin Brodeur of the New Jersey Devils had compiled a 0.912 save percentage (SPCT). This means that out of every 1000 shots, he made 912 saves. SPCT is calculated by dividing the total number of saves by the total number of shots.

Brodeur and the New Jersey Devils have faced the Toronto Maple Leafs several times in the playoffs. If the Leafs average 25 shots per game, how many goals can they expect to score in a game?

1. Three different options are suggested to simulate 25 shots on goal.

   Option 1: Perform the **rand** command 25 times on a graphing calculator. Describe which results will represent a goal.

   Option 2: Perform the command **randInt(0,1000,25)** on a graphing calculator. Describe what this command does and what determines a goal.

   Option 3: Create a spinner for which 0.912 of the spinner is shaded to represent a save, while the remainder represents a goal.

2. Use one of the three methods to simulate 25 shots on goal. Record the number of goals. Assume the Leafs allow two goals each game. State whether this would be a win for the Leafs or for the Devils.

3. Repeat step 2 until one of the teams has won four games.

4. **Reflect** How realistic is this simulation? What assumptions have been made? Explain why this might not make an accurate prediction about the result of a playoff series.

5. **Reflect** The term *save percentage* is somewhat incorrect. Explain why.

Example

Favourite Music

A local radio station surveyed 200 students from one high school to determine their favourite music.

The results are shown in the table.

Music	Percent of Students
rock	45
rap	35
country	20

a) Express each percent as a decimal, and as a fraction in lowest terms.

b) If there are 4000 high school students in the city, how many of them would you expect to like rock? rap? country?

c) Is it possible that the poll might not be accurate? What factors could have influenced the responses?

Solution

a) Rock

$$45\% = \frac{45}{100}$$
$$= 0.45$$
$$\frac{45}{100} = \frac{9}{20}$$

Rap

$$35\% = \frac{35}{100}$$
$$= 0.35$$
$$\frac{35}{100} = \frac{7}{20}$$

Country

$$20\% = \frac{20}{100}$$
$$= 0.20$$
$$\frac{20}{100} = \frac{1}{5}$$

Check: The total number of students should be 4000, the original number of students.

b) Rock
45% of 4000
= 0.45 × 4000
= 1800

Rap
35% of 4000
= 0.35 × 4000
= 1400

Country
20% of 4000
= 0.20 × 4000
= 800

c) Yes, it is possible that the results are not accurate.
Some factors that could have influenced the responses are
• the type of music normally played by the radio station conducting the survey
• popular music teachers or bands within the school

Key Concepts

• Probability and statistics are presented through the media in a variety of contexts.
• Statistics are collected from real-life events or studies.
• Statistics, like probability, help predict the result of future events.

Discuss the Concepts

D1. Explain the similarities and differences between statistics and experimental probability.

D2. Why might you question some of the statistics you see in the media?

D3. Describe how you use statistics in your life.

Practise A

For help with question 1, refer to the Example.

1. All students in a high school were asked if they like rock, rap, both rock and rap, or neither. The results are displayed on the graph. A student from this same high school was chosen as the winner of a contest. Determine the probability that this student likes

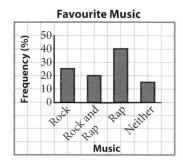

a) rock but not rap

b) either rock or rap, but not both

c) rock or rap or both

2. A football quarterback has completed 125 passes in 200 attempts so far this season.

   a) What percent of his passes has he completed?

   b) If he attempts 30 passes in the next game, how many would you expect him to complete?

   c) Suggest some factors that might affect your estimate.

3. After 12 games, the Toronto Maple Leafs have five wins, four losses, and three overtime losses. Teams are awarded two points for a win, one point for an overtime loss, and no points for a loss.

   a) How many points do the Leafs have after 12 games?

   b) Predict how many points the Leafs will have if the regular season has 82 games.

4. Your high school's girls' volleyball team has the following record: seven wins, four losses, and two ties. A win is worth three points, a loss is worth zero points, and tie is worth one point.

   a) How many points does the team have after 13 games?

   b) Predict how many points the volleyball team will have if the regular season has 20 games.

5. After half a season, a major league baseball player has a 0.300 batting average.

   a) In your own words, describe what this means. If necessary, work with a partner who is knowledgeable about baseball.

   b) If this player gets to bat 40 times in the next 10 games, how many hits would you expect him to get? For simplicity, assume he either gets a hit or makes an out.

   c) Is it possible that your prediction in part b) is not accurate? Explain.

6. A study by Health Canada has shown that, by age 14, one in four teenagers have tried smoking. Of those who try smoking, 36% become smokers.

   a) What is the probability that a person has not tried smoking by age 14?

   b) What percent of people who have tried smoking do not become smokers?

   c) What percent of the population have tried smoking by age 14, but not become smokers?

   d) How many Canadians do you estimate have tried or will try smoking by age 14, and become smokers? Assume the Canadian population is approximately 33 million people.

7. Canadian researchers have found that the number of women with multiple sclerosis (MS) has risen compared to the number of men who have the disease. For those born in the 1930s, there were 1.9 females with MS for every male. However, for those born in the 1980s, there are now 3.2 women who have MS for every man who has it.

   a) For Canadians born in the 1930s, what percent of those who have MS are female?

   b) For Canadians born in the 1980s, what percent of those who have MS are female?

   c) Divide your answer in part b) by your answer from part a). Now divide 3.2 by 1.9. Which of these calculations appears to indicate a greater increase? Justify your response.

   d) Why do you suppose the statistics were presented using the numbers 1.9 and 3.2 instead of using percents?

8. The horizontal bar graph shows the countries of origin for immigrants in Canada in 2001.

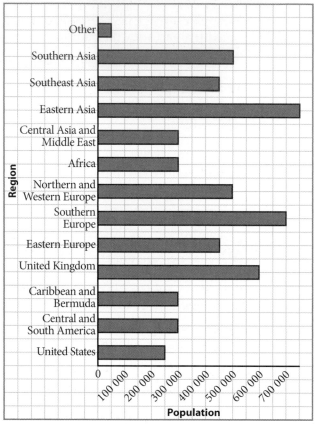

Immigrant Population by Place of Birth

Adapted from Statistics Canada, http://www40.statcan.ca/l01/cst01/demo34a.htm, Feb 14, 2007.

a) What percent of immigrants were from Eastern Asia (mainly from China) or Southern Asia (mainly from India)?

b) Why do you suppose China and India are two large sources of immigrants to Canada?

c) You know that an immigrant is from the United States, Eastern Europe, or the United Kingdom. What is the probability the person is from the United States?

Reasoning and Proving

Representing   Selecting Tools

Problem Solving

Connecting   Reflecting

Communicating

Achievement Check

9. In a recent article about the effects of playing loud music on MP3 players, it was suggested that one in eight students who have MP3 players may have already suffered irreparable hearing loss.

  a) In a survey of 30 students who have MP3 players, how many would you expect to have hearing loss?

  b) How do you suppose the researcher arrived at the ratio of one in eight?

  c) Search the Internet to find more information about the research on this topic. Create a question related to probability or statistics based on your findings.

Extend

10. The Canadian Radio-television and Telecommunications Commission (CRTC) controls the amount of Canadian content on both radio and television in Canada. Find its Web site and answer the following questions.

  a) How much Canadian content is required for radio and television? Is it the same for both media?

  b) Can radio and TV stations play the Canadian shows during the night when people are asleep? Explain.

  c) If a TV show hires a Canadian actor to stand in the background, will this make the CRTC consider the show to be Canadian? Give details.

  d) Create a question involving probability using information from the CRTC Web site.

11. A local radio station has predicted a 30% probability of precipitation (P.O.P.) for each of the next two days.

  a) Describe how you can model a 30% P.O.P. using the **rand** command on a graphing calculator.

  b) Perform an experiment that will allow you to predict the probability of having no rain for the next two days.

  c) Find the theoretical probability of having two days with no rain, given a P.O.P. of 30%.

2.1 Probability Experiments, pages 60–67

1. In Tim's coffee shop, a study was done to see how many people buy coffee and a doughnut. Of 160 people who came in one day, 60 bought coffee *and* a doughnut. The rest bought coffee *or* a doughnut. Find the experimental probability that the next person will buy both coffee and a doughnut.

a) as a fraction in lowest terms

b) as a percent

c) as a decimal

2. Complaints were made to a manufacturer about malfunctioning computer chips. The company promptly tested 10 different chips from the production line and found them all to be working properly.

a) Does this mean the chips are likely all working properly? Explain.

b) How could the company do better quality control?

2.2 Theoretical Probability, pages 68–75

3. From a standard deck of 52 playing cards plus two jokers, find the probability of each event. Express each answer as a fraction in lowest terms.

a) a red card

b) a black face card

c) an ace, 2, or 3

d) a red card that is not a face card

4. Two dice are rolled. Find the probability that the sum of the numbers is

a) 11
b) not 11

c) 2, 3, or 4
d) a multiple of 3

e) greater than 1
f) greater than 3

5. Matthew has black socks, white socks, blue jeans, dress pants, a red shirt, a green shirt, and a T-shirt.

a) Draw a tree diagram showing his choices for socks, pants, and shirt.

b) Find the probability that Matthew selects at random
i) blue jeans and the T-shirt
ii) white socks
iii) black socks, dress pants, and a red shirt
iv) white socks and not the T-shirt

2.3 Compare Experimental and Theoretical Probabilities, pages 76–85

6. Two dice were rolled 20 times. Doubles were rolled five times.

a) Find the experimental probability of rolling doubles. Express your answer as a percent.

b) If you were to roll the dice 20 more times, would you expect five doubles again? Explain.

c) If you were to roll the dice 20 times, how many doubles would you theoretically expect? Justify your answer.

7. The figure shows a unique dartboard.

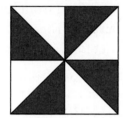

a) For a randomly thrown dart, what is the theoretical probability of landing on red? Explain your reasoning.

b) During a game of darts, 32 out of 40 landed on red. Determine the experimental probability of landing on red, expressed as a decimal.

c) In the game in part b), two points were awarded for landing on red and one point for landing on white. How might this explain the difference between experimental and theoretical probability?

8. You perform the command **randInt(1,5,10)** on a graphing calculator.

a) Describe what will happen.

b) How many 2s would you expect to be among the results? Explain your reasoning.

9. You perform the **rand** function on a graphing calculator.

a) Describe what will happen.

b) If you performed this command 20 times, how many of the results would you expect between 0.2 and 0.7? Explain your reasoning.

2.4 Interpret Information Involving Probability, pages 86–93

10. A basketball player made 40 out of 50 free throws in last week's games.

a) Find the player's free-throw percentage.

b) If the player averages eight free throws per game, how many of them should she expect to make?

11. The school council at Jackson Secondary School surveyed the students to help select a new football team mascot. The results are shown in the graph.

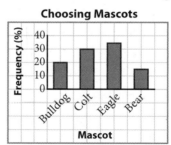

a) If 80 students were surveyed, how many of them voted for a bulldog?

b) Johnson Secondary School has an eagle as their mascot, so those at Jackson Secondary who chose an eagle are asked to vote for another animal instead. What is the probability that a person who originally voted for an eagle will now vote for a bear?

For questions 1 to 3, choose the best answer.

1. During a probability experiment, a die was rolled 18 times. The results are shown in the bar graph.

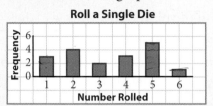

Roll a Single Die

The experimental probability of rolling a 2 is

A $\frac{1}{6}$ B $\frac{2}{18}$ C $\frac{2}{9}$ D 16.7%

2. The theoretical probability of rolling a 6 is

A $\frac{1}{6}$ B $\frac{1}{18}$ C $\frac{1}{3}$ D 0

3. To simulate guessing on 10 multiple-choice questions, each with four possible answers, it would be appropriate to use:

   A 10 spins on a spinner divided into quarters, each quarter of a different colour

   B **randInt(1,4,10)** on a graphing calculator

   C drawing and replacing 10 playing cards from a standard deck of cards

   D any of these methods

4. True or false?

   When rolling two dice, the sums 2 through 11 are all equally likely.

5. Richie Rich has a limousine, a sports car, and a motorcycle for travelling from his condominium to the airport. There, he has a helicopter and a jet for flying to his favourite golf courses.

   a) Draw a tree diagram, showing his choices for the two stages of his trip to play golf.

   b) Find the probability that he randomly:
     i) takes the sports car then his helicopter
     ii) does not take his limousine
     iii) takes the sports car or motorcycle and the jet

6. Immigrants come to Canada for a variety of reasons. A report from Citizenship and Immigration Canada divides the reasons into three categories: business/economic, family, and protected persons. In 2005, there were 256 246 new immigrants.

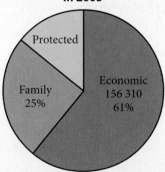

Immigrants to Canada in 2005

Protected

Family 25%

Economic 156 310 61%

   a) Find the number of people in the "family" and "protected" categories.

   b) If an immigrant to Canada does not fall into the "protected" category, find the probability, as a percent, that he or she came to Canada for business/economic reasons.

Chapter Problem Wrap-Up

The government and anglers have a keen interest in protecting Ontario's waterways and fish stocks. Sometimes, species are endangered due to overfishing or to the introduction of invasive species. Search the media or the Internet to find statistics on declining fish stocks or increasing invasive species in Ontario (or Canadian) waters. Write a brief report on your findings.

Write a concluding statement that uses probability to describe the future of a particular fish stock or effects on the fishing industry.

7. If a farmer waits one week to sell his corn, there is a 50% chance that he will earn an extra $10 000. However, there is a 10% chance that he will lose $30 000. Should he sell now, or wait one week?

a) Describe how you could use a spinner to perform a probability experiment to simulate this situation.

b) Describe how you could use the **rand** command on a graphing calculator to perform the same probability experiment.

c) Use either a spinner or a graphing calculator for 25 trials. Each time, record whether the farmer gained $10 000, lost $30 000, or neither. Calculate the average amount the farmer will lose or gain if he waits one week to sell his corn.

8. A spinner is designed for three outcomes. The blue outcome is twice as likely as the red, while the yellow is three times as likely as the blue.

a) Find the measures of the three angles required to make this spinner.

b) For this spinner, find the theoretical probability of
i) landing on red
ii) not landing on red

c) Describe how the command **randInt(1,9,1)** can simulate spinning red, yellow, or blue.

d) Perform the **randInt(1,9,1)** command 20 times, each time recording whether it indicates red, blue, or yellow. How many times did red occur twice in a row? How many times did yellow occur twice in a row?

e) Find the theoretical probability of yellow occurring twice in a row. Hint: Part d) will provide an estimate, which can be improved upon if you perform more than 20 trials. You might also try drawing a tree diagram.

3 One Variable Statistics

Statistics is the process of collecting, displaying, and analysing data. Data can be gathered by conducting an experiment or a survey. In this chapter you will look at survey design, ways of displaying data, and the measures used to analyse data.

In this chapter, you will

- identify situations involving one variable data, and design questionnaires or experiments for gathering one variable data
- collect one variable data from secondary sources, organize and store the data using a variety of tools, and solve problems by analysing the data
- explain the distinction between the terms *population* and *sample,* describe the characteristics of a good sample, and explain why sampling is necessary
- describe and compare sampling techniques, collect one variable data from primary sources, and organize and store the data
- identify different types of one variable data and represent the data, with and without technology, in appropriate graphical forms
- identify and describe properties associated with common distributions of data
- calculate and interpret measures of central tendency and spread; use these measures to compare sets of one variable data
- explain the appropriate use of measures of central tendency and measures of spread

Reasoning and Proving
Representing | Selecting Tools
Problem Solving
Connecting | Reflecting
Communicating

Key Terms

bias	mean	quartiles
bimodal distribution	median	range
box-and-whisker plot	mode	sample
categorical data	normal distribution	secondary source
continuous data	outlier	skewed distribution
discrete data	population	standard deviation
interquartile range	primary source	variance

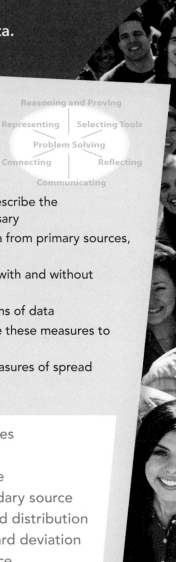

Craig completed the three-year manufacturing technology program at Sheridan College. He now works as an industrial engineering technologist. Craig analyses the production process to improve factory efficiency. He decides the number of workers needed on the production line, where to place the workers, and how to organize their work.

Prerequisite Skills

Numeracy Skills

1. Order the numbers in each set from least to greatest.
   a) 5, 4, 11, 9, 15, 7, 8, 1, 5, 19, 4, 9
   b) 3, 3, 5, 7, 1, 3, 5, 6, 9,
      11, 12, 6, 4, 2, 2, 1
   c) 5, 8, 1, −3, 0, 12, −11,
      4, 5, 1, 7, −3, −5
   d) $\dfrac{1}{2}, \dfrac{5}{8}, \dfrac{1}{4}, \dfrac{3}{16}$

2. Evaluate. Round your answer to two decimal places, if necessary.
   a) $\dfrac{14 + 16 + 22 + 75 + 85 + 35}{6}$
   b) $\dfrac{5 + 11 + 4 + 7 + 15 + 12 + 22 + 8}{8}$
   c) $\dfrac{77 + 54 + 71 + 51 + 64 + 88 + 90}{7}$
   d) $\dfrac{38 + 45 + 56 + 76 + 83}{5}$
   e) $\dfrac{2.2 + 2.4 + 3.7 + 7.1 + 4.5 + 5.9 + 7.7 + 1.3}{8}$

3. Evaluate. Round your answer to two decimal places, if necessary.
   a) $\sqrt{121}$
   b) $\sqrt{47}$
   c) $\sqrt{3^2 + 4^2}$
   d) $\sqrt{1^2 + 2^2 + 3^2}$

Interpret Graphs

4. The graph shows the favourite sports of students in Minh's physical education class.

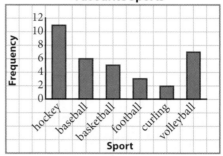

Favourite Sports

   a) Identify the type of graph.
   b) Which sport is the most popular?
   c) Which sport is the least popular?
   d) Does "least popular" mean the same as "not popular"? Explain.

5. The circle graph shows Jyoti's spending pattern over the last three months.

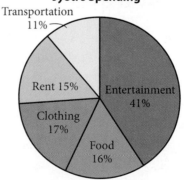

Jyoti's Spending

   a) What was Jyoti's greatest expense?
   b) If Jyoti earned $1220 over the last three months, how much did she spend on clothing?

6. The graph shows the average weekly temperature at a Caribbean island resort for four months. The average for the ninth week is missing.

Resort Temperature

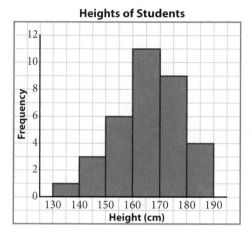

a) Identify the type of graph.

b) Estimate the average weekly temperature for the ninth week.

c) The graph ends on the sixteenth week. Predict the average weekly temperature for the seventeenth week. Justify your answer.

d) What information would you need to check your answer in part c)?

7. The graph shows the heights of the students in a club.

Heights of Students

a) Identify the type of graph.

b) How many students are in the club?

Chapter Problem

Andrew is very interested in statistics, so he took a co-op placement at a market research company to learn more about the field. Throughout this chapter, you will see how Andrew uses mathematics in his job as a market researcher.

3.1 Sampling Techniques

When conducting a survey, it is important to choose the right questions to ask and to select the appropriate group to survey.

Before a market research department designs a survey, the target group for the survey needs to be identified.

Use a Random Number Generator

There are 300 students taking mathematics this semester at Royal Secondary School. The table shows the number of mathematics students in each grade.

Grade	Number of Mathematics Students
9	100
10	80
11	75
12	45

Mrs. Barron, the principal, wishes to survey a total of 60 mathematics students. She has chosen 20 grade 9s, 16 grade 10s, 15 grade 11s, and 9 grade 12s.

1. Calculate the percent of the population that each grade represents.

The percent for grade 9 is done for you.

$$\frac{100}{300} \times 100 = 33.\overline{3}\%$$

2. Calculate the percent of the sample that each of Mrs. Barron's choices represents.

The percent for grade 9 is done for you. $\frac{20}{60} \times 100 = 33.\overline{3}\%$

How does the proportion of students from each grade in the group Mrs. Barron selected compare to the proportion of mathematics students in each grade? Explain.

3. Mrs. Barron decides to select each student for the sample using a random number generator on her graphing calculator. Help her select the grade 9 students.

- Clear the lists on the graphing calculator. Press [2nd] [MEM] **4**, then [ENTER].
- Press [STAT], and select **1:Edit...**.
- Use the arrow keys to highlight L1.
- Type the month and day of your birthday, followed by the street number of your home, using all digits. Press [STO▸]. Press [MATH] and cursor over to **PRB**. Press [ENTER] twice. Press [MATH] and cursor over to **PRB**. Select **5:randInt(** and press [ENTER].
- Type 1 [,] 100 [,] 20 [ )] [ENTER].
- The calculator will generate 20 random integers between 1 and 100 and display them in list L1.

4. Reflect Mrs. Barron could have numbered all 300 mathematics students and then used the formula **randInt(1,300,60)** to choose her sample. What are some difficulties that Mrs. Barron might have encountered using this method?

It is usually impractical to survey every member of a target group or **population** , so only a **sample** of the population is surveyed.

There are a number of different ways to choose a sample.
- **Simple Random Sample** Each member of the population has an equal chance of being selected.
- **Stratified Random Sample** The population is divided into subgroups (for example, by gender, age, nationality) and a random sample is selected from each subgroup in proportion to its size in the population.
- **Voluntary-Response Sample** The sample contains those members of the population who have chosen to respond to the survey.
- **Cluster Sample** The population is divided into clusters and a certain number of clusters are chosen. Every member of these clusters is part of the sample.
- **Convenience Sample** The sample contains those members of the population from which data are most easily collected.
- **Systematic Sample** Every *n*th member of the population is selected.

population
- all individuals or items that belong to a group being studied

sample
- a group of individuals or items that are representative of the population from which they are taken

Example 1

Population and Sample

Meena wants to know which band Ontario high school students think is the best. Meena's friend Cindy goes to a different school, so they each survey students at their own school. Meena uses the completed surveys from both schools to draw conclusions.

a) Identify the population and the sample.

b) Is the sample representative of the population? If it is representative, explain why. If it is not, suggest how the sample could be improved.

Solution

a) The population is all Ontario high school students. Meena's sample of the population is the students surveyed in both her school and her friend's school.

b) The students Meena and Cindy surveyed might be a representative sample of the population of the two schools, but there are approximately 5000 schools in Ontario. The sample size from the two schools is too small to draw conclusions about students in the entire province. Meena should include more schools from different areas of the province to make her sample more representative.

bias
- a survey contains bias if it does not reflect the population
- may be caused by an unrepresentative sample, the wording of the survey questions, and/or the interpretation and presentation of the results

When the results of a survey do not reflect the population, the survey is said to contain **bias**.

Bias may be introduced by selecting a sample that is not representative of the population, by the wording of the survey question, or by the presentation of the results of the survey.

Example 2

Choose a Sampling Technique

Determine the best sampling technique for each survey. Describe one method of selecting the sample. Identify any problems with using the sampling technique.

a) The school newspaper wants to determine which presidential candidate in the upcoming student council elections is supported by the majority of students.

b) A light bulb manufacturer wants to determine the lifespan of a certain type of light bulb, in hours.

c) The Parent–Teacher Association wants to determine the average number of hours per week that students spend on homework.

d) The producers of "Rock Idol" want to determine which of the two remaining candidates should be the next rock idol.

Solution

a) All students can vote in the elections, so use a sampling technique that represents the entire student population. Choose simple random sampling. Use a computer or graphing calculator to randomly select about 20% of the school's population for the sample. This sampling technique might be inaccurate if students in certain grades are unlikely to vote in the actual election.

b) Light bulbs are identical (unless there are manufacturing flaws), so the sampling technique does not need to be random. Choose systematic sampling. Select every hundredth light bulb for the sample. This sampling technique might be inaccurate if the manufacturing process is not standardized.

c) Students in different grades have different amounts of homework, so use a sampling technique that represents all of the grades. Choose stratified random sampling. Select a random sample of students from each grade for the sample. This sampling technique might be inaccurate if the randomly selected students spend more (or less) time on homework than their peers, or if certain classes have more (or less) homework than other classes in the same grade.

d) While the producers of "Rock Idol" know the number of people who watch the show, it would be very difficult to contact a representative sample of viewers, so use a sampling technique in which the viewers contact the producers. Choose voluntary-response sampling. Viewers who call a toll-free number with their opinion make up the sample. This sampling technique is likely to introduce bias because viewers can call more than once and some viewers might not respond.

Math Connect

When the population of a study is very large, it takes a large organization (such as Statistics Canada) or a large company (such as Ipsos Reid) to find a representative sample and conduct the survey.

Practise **A**

1. You are stopped in the mall and asked to participate in a survey. Which sampling technique is being used?

2. Mr. Rush's grade 5 students want to play soccer. Mr. Rush splits the class into girls and boys, numbers each group from 1 to 10, and then forms two teams: one with even-numbered students and one with odd-numbered students.

   a) Explain the sampling technique Mr. Rush used to create the teams.

   b) Is this a fair way of choosing teams? Explain why or why not.

   c) Suggest an improvement to the sampling technique Mr. Rush used.

3. Choose the best sampling technique for each survey. Explain your choice.

   a) Umar wants to know at which festivals his dance company would like to perform.

   b) Sherry wants to find out which Canadian actress is most popular with Ontario teens.

   c) Laurel wants to know which actor her classmates think is the best performer.

   d) Bruno wants to know which search engine is used most often by Ontario high school students.

4. In each situation, identify the sample and the population.

   a) Zoe noticed that most teenagers at the local library were reading murder mysteries. She suggested to the student council at her school that they organize a school murder mystery read-a-thon.

   b) Enrica and her friends call the "Canadian Idol" show several times a week to vote for the same performer.

   c) The Canadian Dental Association surveys several outlets of a popular drug store chain to collect information on the most popular toothpaste.

   d) Tony is working for a political party. He stands at a busy street corner asking people whom they plan to vote for in the upcoming election.

   e) Angelo is the manager of a gym. He asks members who are at the gym on Wednesday night if he should have a party for gym members.

   f) Maya surveyed her science class to identify the rock group most listened to by the students in her grade.

Apply **B** •

5. The Canadian government conducts a country-wide survey called a census every five years. The survey is designed to collect information on every Canadian.

   a) Which Canadians will not be included in this census?

   Literacy Connect

   b) Use the terms *population*, *representative sample*, and *sampling technique* to explain why the government does not conduct a census every year.

   c) If 3% of the population were not included in the survey, can the government still make valid statements regarding the population? Explain.

6. Mykele used a random number generator to select numbers from 1 to 10. The first three numbers she recorded were 7, 7, 7. Derek thinks Mykele made a mistake. Is Derek correct? Explain.

7. Andrew has his first assignment at the market research company. He is helping to conduct a survey on what Ontario high school students do after finishing high school.

a) Identify the population of the survey.

b) Why is it impractical to survey everyone in the population?

c) If the whole population were surveyed, how could this be done effectively?

d) What sampling technique could Andrew suggest that the company use for the survey? Explain how this sample could be chosen.

8. Jeff works as a quality control officer at a bolt manufacturing plant. Each day, he randomly selects and tests 100 bolts. On Monday, Jeff finds that 11 of the 100 bolts are defective. On Tuesday, he finds that 4 of the 100 bolts are defective. For the rest of the week, he finds no defective bolts in his samples.

a) What type of sampling technique is Jeff using?

b) Jeff finds varying numbers of defective bolts over the week. Does this mean that his sampling technique is not effective? Explain.

c) How could Jeff improve the information that he will get from his data?

9. Alice wants to know if the students at her school are in favour of a school uniform. She surveys 30 students from grade 9, 25 students from grade 10, 25 students from grade 11, and 20 students from grade 12. The table shows the numbers of students in each grade at Alice's school.

Grade	Number of Students
9	307
10	242
11	230
12	212

a) Is the sample representative of the population? Justify your answer.

b) Is the sampling method appropriate for the situation? Explain.

10. You want to know which types of music students at your school prefer.

    a) Explain how to obtain a sample of students using each sampling technique.

       i) random sampling

       ii) cluster sampling

       iii) stratified random sampling

       iv) convenience sampling

    b) Which technique would be best for this situation? Justify your answer.

Extend

11. Keira works for the Canada Customs and Revenue Agency at a busy border crossing. She needs to search 10 randomly selected vehicles over a 10-h period. To choose the vehicles, she randomly selects a time from 2 P.M. to midnight. She does this 10 times. For each time, she randomly selects one of 20 gates. The vehicle at that gate and time will be searched.

    a) What type of sampling is Keira using? Justify your answer.

    b) Use technology to make a table of random times and gates.

    c) How likely is it that the same time and gate will occur twice? Explain.

12. A school board wants to select 200 elementary students to test a new mathematics home study program for grades 4 to 7. The board numbers the elementary schools from 1 to 35 then uses a random number generator to choose two schools. Each school selects 100 students. Students are randomly selected from each grade by applying the percent of students in each grade to the number who will use the program.

    a) Identify the sample and the population in the study.

    b) The first school has chosen 100 students: 20% are grade 4s, 25% are grade 5s, 30% are grade 6s, and the rest are grade 7s. How many students from each grade will participate in the study?

    c) The second school has 500 students in grades 4 to 7. If there are 100 grade 4s, 100 grade 5s, 150 grade 6s, and the rest are grade 7s, how many students from each grade will be chosen for the study?

    d) Explain a method to determine which students at each school will participate in the study.

Collect and Analyse Data

Market research is often conducted at shopping malls or over the telephone. At the mall, researchers ask passers-by if they are willing to take part in a survey.

Investigate 1   Design a Survey Question

Design a one-question survey. Choose a topic from the list below or a topic of your own interest (with your teacher's approval).

- favourite band or singer
- favourite television show
- favourite sport
- favourite dinner
- favourite snack

1. What is the population for your survey?

2. How will you select a sample of the population?

3. Write a survey question to find data about your topic.

4. Exchange survey questions with a partner. Comment on your partner's survey design and return it to your partner.

5. Use the suggestions made by your partner to refine your survey question.

6. Reflect People sometimes might not answer a survey question according to their own viewpoint if the nature of the question, or the way the question is asked, influences their opinion. This response bias produces inaccurate survey results. Study your own question and your partner's question. Discuss the way each question is written and decide if the question may result in response bias.

primary source
- a person who collects data for their own use

secondary source
- a database or research collected by someone else

When you conduct a survey or perform an experiment, you are the **primary source** of the data. When you work with data from the Internet, published materials, or Statistics Canada, you are using a **secondary source**.

Investigate 2   Data Gathered From Secondary Sources

In this investigation, you will be looking at the Statistics Canada Web site for data collected and summarized by the Canadian government.

1. To access the Statscan Web site, go to *www.mcgrawhill.ca/links/ foundations11* and follow the links.

2. Select English.

3. From the left sidebar, select the Summary tables.

4. From the left sidebar, select Tables by… • subject.

5. Select a subject that interests you. Then, select a subtopic to access a data table. For example, you might choose "Population and demography," then "Population by ethnic origin" or by province and territory (2001 Census).

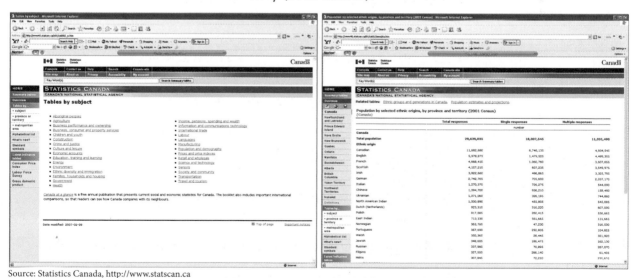

Source: Statistics Canada, http://www.statscan.ca

6. Write a brief summary of your findings.

7. Share your findings with a partner.

8. **Reflect** What are some advantages of using secondary sources? What are some disadvantages?

Example 1

Response Bias

A parent council survey is conducted to learn if an after-school music program should be offered. The survey question reads: *Early musical training helps develop brain areas involved in language and reasoning. Should the school offer an after-school music program?*

a) Explain why this question may result in response bias.

b) Rewrite the question to eliminate possible response bias.

Solution

a) By stating an opinion about music training in the first sentence, before asking the question, the survey makes it clear that the parent council wants a positive answer.

b) A possible question might be: *Would you enrol your child in an after-school music program*?

Example 2

Measurement Bias

Andre wrote this survey question: *Who do you think is the best female tennis player of all time?*

a) *Martina Navratilova*

b) *Chris Evert*

c) *Billie Jean King*

d) *Serena Williams*

e) *Other:* _____

Identify any weaknesses in this survey question.

Solution

By naming specific players, the survey influences the respondents' answers. Respondents might not take the time to fill in the "Other" selection and might randomly select a player or simply choose a name they recognise. This measurement bias might cause an exaggeration or an underestimation of the results for the population.

Example 3

Non-Response Bias

At a new restaurant, wait staff ask every fifth customer to answer a questionnaire about food quality and service once they have finished their meal. About 30% of customers surveyed fill out the questionnaire. The majority of customers who fill out the questionnaire complain about poor service. The restaurant manager concludes that the wait staff need more training. Is her conclusion reasonable?

Solution

The conclusion is not reasonable because only 30% of those surveyed answered the questionnaire. Customers who did respond might have done so because they were unhappy with the service. Those who were happy with the service might have simply ignored the questionnaire because the service did not need to be improved. This non-response bias leads to inaccurate results because only a small number of people in the sample respond.

Key Concepts

- Someone who collects data for their own use is a primary source.
- A database or research collected by someone else is a secondary source.
- Bias is an intentional or unintentional distortion of the data collected in a survey. A survey should be as free of bias as possible.

Discuss the Concepts

D1. Discuss the bias that will result from each situation. Suggest ways to remove the bias.

  a) Residents of a community are asked this survey question:
  Building a garbage incineration power plant in the neighbourhood will increase jobs and encourage government funding of other programs beneficial to our community. Would you be in favour of this much needed venture?

  b) A group of professional football players are asked if they have ever taken banned performance enhancing substances.

  c) The members of an elite golf club are asked if they will approve the construction of a subsidized housing complex on the land adjacent to their golf course.

D2. Discuss the advantages and disadvantages of using primary and secondary data sources. Give examples of when each type of data source should be used.

1. Dharma wants to know what the best-selling lunch item in the cafeteria is. She records what she sees on the students' trays as they pass by the cashier after paying for their lunch. Her school has two lunch periods. When she has completed a survey during her lunch period, she asks the cafeteria staff to keep track of the items they sell during the other lunch period. She collects the information after school.

   a) Which data are primary data? Which data are secondary data? Justify your answers.

   b) For this survey, is one data source more accurate than the other? Explain.

2. A political candidate wants to know how the members of his riding feel about a major issue in the upcoming election. He and his team send surveys to every even-numbered address in the riding that has the word *Street* in the address. Each survey contains a self-addressed stamped envelope for returns. Two weeks later, 56% of the surveys have been returned.

   a) What type of sampling technique was used?

   b) Do you think the sampling technique is effective? Explain.

   c) How could the candidate increase the survey return rate?

   d) Do you think the candidate will have enough data to draw accurate conclusions? Explain.

3. Identify the bias in each survey. Suggest how it might be removed.

   a) A Canadian Football League (CFL) team hands out a survey at a home game. The survey asks: *Should the provincial and federal governments help build a new stadium and save the team from being relocated?*

   b) A radio talk show host asks listeners to phone in and express their opinions on an issue.

   c) A market research company mails surveys to 1000 households and 200 are returned. The company feels that 200 is a good return and that the opinions expressed can represent the sample of 1000.

   d) Shoppers at a mall are asked: *Are you against the poor decision made by a developer to close this mall in order to build a subdivision, making the traffic in the area even more congested?*

4. The student council is planning events for Spirit Week. They send out this survey question: *Which of the following events would you like to participate in during Spirit Week?*

- *carnival day*
  - *read-a-thon*
  - *music at lunch*
  - *after-school sports*

a) Which type of bias does this survey illustrate?

b) How can the bias be removed? Give examples.

Apply B

· ·

5. Your student council wants to know how the $2000 raised in the last fundraiser should be spent. They ask you to survey the students in the school. Write a survey question that is free from bias. Describe how you would conduct the survey and collect the results.

Literacy Connect

6. There are many bestseller lists for fiction and non-fiction books. Find a bestseller list in a newspaper or on the Internet.

a) How often is the list updated?

b) Describe how the list is presented.

c) Suggest another way to present the information in the list.

7. A community radio station asks its listeners to call in and vote on building a new swimming pool in town. The survey begins just after the 8 A.M. news. By noon, about 50 people have responded, with 30% in favour and 70% opposed. The station reports these interim results at the end of the noon news.

By 4 P.M., when the phone-in ends, the numbers have shifted to 60% in favour and 40% opposed.

a) Could reporting the interim results have affected the outcome of the survey? Explain.

b) Suppose you were in favour of the pool and heard the results at noon. What action would you have taken?

8. Air traffic control services in Canada were privatized a number of years ago. Transport Canada has invited pilots to anonymously report on their experiences with the privatized service. Since reporting is anonymous, can Transport Canada conclude that reports will be unbiased? Justify your answer.

9. **a)** "Who is the most popular act in the music industry today?" Suggest one way to collect primary data to answer the question. Suggest one way to collect secondary data to answer the question.

    b) Which type of data would be most reliable? Explain.

10. Spyware is software that secretly sends information about your Internet surfing habits to a Web site. This statistical data is often collected without the knowledge or consent of the user.

    a) Why would companies want to obtain data on Internet surfing habits without the users' knowledge?

    b) Is data collected using spyware biased? Justify your answer.

    c) With a classmate, discuss other forms of data collection that invade a person's privacy. List them.

Chapter Problem

11. Andrew is helping to conduct a second survey. The survey question asks: *What is your favourite sport?* Describe any problems associated with the survey question.

12. The student council wants to know the type of music that should be played at the next school dance. Terence and Linda are asked to collect information.
    - Terence uses the Internet to find the top 10 songs on 15 radio stations. He assigns 10 points to the number one song on each list, 9 points for the second place song, 8 points for the third, and so on. He determines the point rating for each song and uses the ratings to develop his playlist.
    - Linda decides to survey the school population. She creates a questionnaire asking students to list their top 5 songs. The homeroom teachers distribute the questionnaire and give students 5 min to complete it. Linda collects the questionnaires and ranks the songs according to the results to develop her playlist.

    a) Identify the type of data source each student used.

    b) Outline the strengths and weaknesses of each person's sampling technique.

    c) How could Terrence and Lisa improve their results?

13. A marketing company gave four dentists two brands of toothpaste to try. Proteeth has ingredients that provide protection against cavities, gingivitis, and plaque. Freshie simply freshens breath. The dentists were asked which toothpaste they prefer: Proteeth or Freshie. All preferred Proteeth to Freshie. The marketing company ran an advertisement stating: *Four out of four dentists prefer Proteeth.*

a) Is the marketing claim true? Explain.

b) Why might the marketing company have conducted the survey in this way?

c) How could you redesign the survey to determine if four out of four dentists truly prefer Proteeth?

Achievement Check

14. For each survey, suggest an unbiased method of collecting the data. Write two survey questions for each scenario.

a) a survey that will ask individuals in a community if a new community centre should be built beside the local mall

b) a survey on ways in which a public transit system can be improved

c) a survey that will decide which courses a high school will offer in the following school year

d) a survey that will assess the ability of the current provincial government to make important decisions and follow its election platform

Extend

15. Work with a partner. Design a poster or summary page that displays information in a misleading way that will cause the reader to form an incorrect conclusion. Explain how you have made the information misleading.

16. Find a newspaper article that quotes a survey or statistics. Research the survey or statistics in detail on the Internet and decide if there was any bias in the survey. Write a report on your findings.

3.3 Display Data

You have heard the saying "a picture is worth a thousand words." The same can be said about a graph. A graph is a visual representation of data that displays the relationship among the variables. Graphs can summarize data, and present data more clearly and concisely than a table or written text.

Investigate 1

Bar Graph and Circle Graph

Jong has a part-time job at a music store. The table shows Jong's expenses last month.

Expense	Amount ($)
entertainment	100
clothing	225
cell phone	50
lunch	75
transportation	80
rent	150

Tools

- calculator
- protractor
- compass
- grid paper
- coloured pencils or markers
- ruler

Method 1: Create Graphs by Hand

1. Create a bar graph to represent the data. Include a title for the graph and label both axes.

2. Copy and complete the table. Calculate the percent and angle measure for each expense. Create a circle graph to represent the data. Include a title for the graph and label the sectors.

Expense	Amount ($)	Percent (%)	Measure of Angle (°)
entertainment	100	$\frac{100}{680} \times 100 \doteq 14.7$	$\frac{14.7}{100} \times 360 \doteq 52.9$
clothing	225		
cell phone	50		
lunch	75		
transportation	80		
rent	150		
TOTAL	**680**		

3. Reflect Which graph best displays Jong's expenses? Justify your answer.

4. When is a bar graph the best choice to display data? When is a circle graph the best choice? Give examples for both.

Method 2: Create Graphs Using Technology

Use the table of Jong's expenses.

1. Follow these steps to create a bar graph using Microsoft® *Excel*.
- Open Microsoft® *Excel*. Enter the expense categories in column A. Enter the amounts in column B.
- Click and drag the mouse from cell A1 to cell B6.
- From the **Insert** menu, choose **Chart ....**
- Under **Chart type**, choose **Column**. Select **Next** twice.
- Enter a chart title (such as "Jong's Expenses"). Enter "Expense" for the Category (X) axis, and "Amount ($)" for the Value (Y) axis. Select **Next**.
- Select **Finish**.
- If the labels are not all visible, click and drag a corner of the chart to make the chart larger.

Tools
- computer
- Microsoft® *Excel*

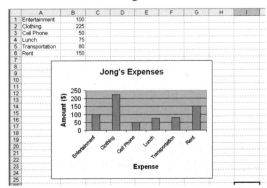

2. Follow these steps to create a circle graph using Microsoft® *Excel*.
   • Open a new spreadsheet. Enter the expense categories in column A. Enter the amounts in column B.
   • Click and drag the mouse from cell A1 to cell B6.
   • From the **Insert** menu, choose **Chart …**.
   • Under **Chart type**, choose **Pie**. Select **Next** twice.
   • Enter a chart title (such as "Jong's Expenses"). Select the **Data Labels** tab. Check the boxes **Category Name** and **Percentage**. Select **Next**.
   • Select **Finish**.
   • If the labels are not all visible, click and drag a corner of the chart to make it larger.

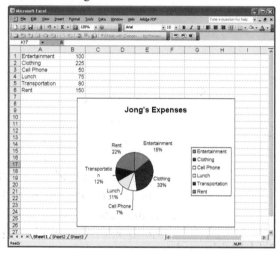

3. **Reflect** List some advantages and disadvantages of using a spreadsheet to graph data.

categorical data
• data that are types rather than numbers; for example: colours, types of snack foods

continuous data
• data that can have any numerical value within a finite or infinite interval; for example: the heights of students in your class

discrete data
• data that are distinct and can be counted; for example: the number of students who like rice

The data relating to Jong's expenses are **categorical data**. The entries in the first column of the table are non-numerical—they are categories.

There are two types of data. Data that can have any numerical value are **continuous data**. Data that can only have certain values within a given range are **discrete data**.

You can use a histogram to display continuous data.

Create a Histogram

William measured the heights of students in his mathematics class. The heights are rounded to the nearest centimetre.

154, 175, 166, 138, 161, 171, 165, 188, 139, 137, 144, 154, 186, 191, 177, 173, 164, 154, 186, 173, 151, 164, 174, 154, 138, 156, 146, 176, 194, 151

Height can have any numerical value, so this is continuous data.

Tools

• calculator
• grid paper

Method 1: Create a Histogram by Hand

1. Copy and complete the table. Record the number of students in each interval, and then determine each frequency.

Interval	Tally	Frequency
[130–140)	||||	4
[140–150)		
[150–160)	|||| ||	7
[160–170)		
[170–180)		
[180–190)		
[190–200)		

A square bracket is used to indicate that a value is included in the interval. A round bracket is used to indicate that a value is not included in the interval. The interval [130–140) includes all heights from 130 cm up to, but not including, 140 cm.

2. Graph the data with Interval on the horizontal axis and Frequency on the vertical axis. Include a title for the graph and label the axes.

Method 2: Create a Histogram Using a Graphing Calculator

Tools

• graphing calculator

Use the heights of the students in William's class.

1. Press [2nd] [MEM] 4 [ENTER] to clear the lists.

2. Press [STAT] and select **1:Edit…**. Enter the student heights in list L1.

3. Press [Y=]. Use the [CLEAR] key to erase any equations in the list.

4. Press [2nd] [STAT PLOT]. Select **4:PlotsOff**. Press [ENTER].

5. Press [2nd] [STAT PLOT]. Select **1:Plot1**. Set the plot to On, the graph style to Histogram, and the XList to L1.

6. Press ⎡ZOOM⎤ and select **9:ZoomStat**. The histogram will appear.

7. Use the window settings shown. The histogram will begin at 130, with a bin width of 10. Then press ⎡GRAPH⎤.

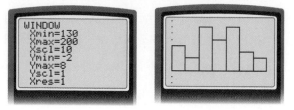

Method 3: Create a Histogram Using *Fathom*™

1. Start *Fathom*™. From the **Object** menu, choose **New** then **Case Table**.

2. Enter the heading "Height_cm" in the second column. Enter the student heights in this column.

3. Double-click on the heading "Collection 1". In the **Rename Collection** dialogue box, enter the title "Student Heights". Select **OK**.

4. From the **Object** menu, choose **New** then **Graph**. In the case table, select the heading "Height_cm", hold the mouse button, and drag the heading to the horizontal axis of the graph.

5. Select the pop-up menu at the top right of the graph. Change the graph type to **Histogram**.

6. Select the graph. From the **Object** menu, choose **Inspect Graph**. Click on the **Properties** tab. Set **binAlignmentPosition** to 120, **binWidth** to 10, and **yLower** to 0. You may need to adjust the value for **yUpper**. Close the dialogue box.

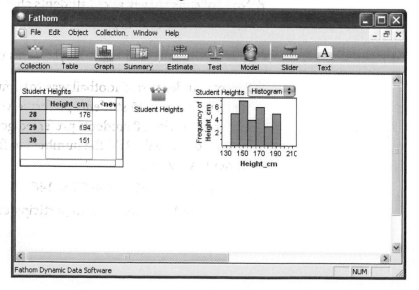

Example 1

Interpret a Bar Graph

Colleen surveyed the students at her school about their favourite sports. She chose a bar graph to display her results. Use the bar graph to answer each question.

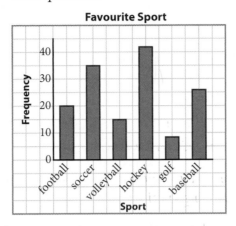

a) Which sport is the most popular?

b) Which sport is the least popular?

c) Does your answer to part b) mean that students do not like this sport? Explain.

d) How many students said that volleyball was their favourite sport?

e) How many students participated in Colleen's survey?

Solution

a) The tallest bar is for hockey. Hockey is the most popular sport.

b) The shortest bar is for golf. Golf is the least popular sport.

c) No. Colleen's survey asked students about the sports they liked, not the sports they disliked.

d) Fifteen students said that volleyball was their favourite sport.

e) Twenty students said football was their favourite sport, 35 students preferred soccer, 15 students preferred volleyball, 42 students preferred hockey, 8 students preferred golf, and 26 students preferred baseball. Add the numbers to find the total number of students surveyed.

$20 + 35 + 15 + 42 + 8 + 26 = 146$

There were 146 students who participated in Colleen's survey.

Example 2

Analyse Continuous Data

The histogram shows the masses of a sample of patients at a hospital.

a) How many patients have a mass of at least 85 kg but less than 90 kg?

b) How many patients have a mass of at least 100 kg?

c) How many patients are in the sample?

d) Find the percent of patients who have a mass of at least 100 kg.

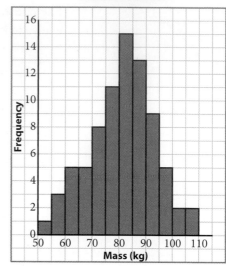

Patients' Masses

Solution

a) The bar with left side 85 and right side 90 represents the number of patients who have a mass in the interval [85–90).

90 kg is included in the next interval.

The height of the bar is 13; therefore, 13 patients have a mass of at least 85 kg but less than 90 kg.

b) Two patients have a mass in the interval [100–105) and two patients have a mass in the interval [105–110). So, four patients have a mass of at least 100 kg.

c) Add the frequencies to find the number of patients in the sample.

$$1 + 3 + 5 + 5 + 8 + 11 + 15 + 13 + 9 + 5 + 2 + 2 = 79$$

There are 79 patients in the sample.

d) $\frac{4}{79} \times 100 = 5.1\%$

In the sample, 5.1% of the patients have a mass of at least 100 kg.

Key Concepts

- Data can be numerical or categorical.
- Continuous data can have any numerical value, finite or infinite. For example, think of the time required to run 1 km. A histogram or a line graph may be used to display continuous data.
- Discrete data are distinct and can be counted. For example, think of the number of employees at each coffee shop in a city. A bar graph or a circle graph may be used to represent discrete data.

Discuss the Concepts

D1. Describe the similarities and the differences between a bar graph and a histogram. Give an example of data that you would display in a bar graph. Give an example of data that you would display in a histogram.

D2. **a)** Can a set of numerical data be discrete? Explain.
b) Can a set of categorical data be continuous? Explain.

Practise

1. Classify each set of data as either discrete or continuous.

   a) the number of blue cars in a parking lot recorded every day at 5 P.M. for a month

   b) the temperature outside at noon measured each day for a week

   c) barometric pressure collected each hour for a month

   d) the number of students in each Ontario high school mathematics classroom

2. Which type of graph would best suit each situation? Explain your choice.

   a) the number of students in each homeroom of your school

   b) the time it takes your classmates to travel to school each day

   c) your monthly spending habits

   d) the daily sales of fruit drinks at a variety store

   e) the heights of trees in a forest

   f) a hockey team's budget for players' salaries, based on the players' positions

3. Examine the bar graph and the histogram.

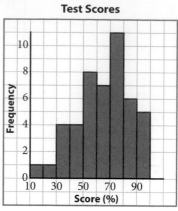

Snowfall in December

Test Scores

a) Could a bar graph have been used to display the data in the histogram? Explain.

b) Could a histogram have been used to display the data in the bar graph? Explain.

4. Which graph displays discrete data and which graph displays continuous data? Explain how you know.

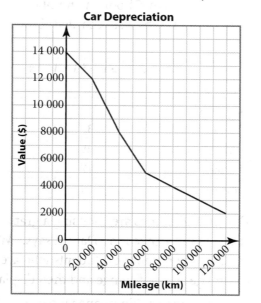

Car Depreciation

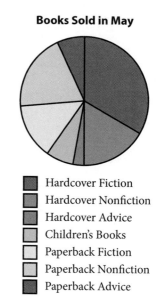

Books Sold in May

- Hardcover Fiction
- Hardcover Nonfiction
- Hardcover Advice
- Children's Books
- Paperback Fiction
- Paperback Nonfiction
- Paperback Advice

5. Students in a mathematics class scored the following marks out of 100 on the last test.

71, 54, 64, 81, 77, 75, 63, 74, 54, 79, 83, 92,
83, 65, 37, 48, 36, 85, 88, 61, 77, 70, 66, 52

a) Copy and complete the table.

Score Interval	Tally	Frequency
[30, 40)		
[40, 50)		
[50, 60)		
[60, 70)		
[70, 80)		
[80, 90)		
[90, 100]		

b) Create a histogram to display the data. If you are using a graphing calculator or computer software, print or sketch a copy of your histogram. Add a title to your graph and label the axes.

6. At the local high school, the number of students participating in six school clubs was recorded. Construct a bar graph to display the data.

Club	Number of Students
Environment	40
Debating	52
Drama	38
SADD	28
Wellness	17
Yearbook	25

7. Darren and Tomas are choosing a graph to display the heights of students in their school. Darren says: "We should use a bar graph. We can find the number of students who are in the 4-ft range, 5-ft range, 6-ft range, and 7-ft range and then display the frequencies as bars."

Tomas disagrees. "Someone who is 5 ft 11 in. might report their height to be 6 ft, which would skew the results. The data is continuous, so a bar graph is not the best display."

Who is correct? Justify your answer.

8. Use newspapers or the Internet to find an example of each type of data. Graph the data using an appropriate display. Justify your choice of graph.

   a) categorical data   **b)** discrete data   **c)** continuous data

9. Give an example for which a bar graph would be a good choice to display data. Give an example for which a bar graph would not be appropriate for the data. Explain your reasons.

Literacy Connect

10. Find an article or advertisement in a newspaper or magazine that shows information using a graph.

    a) What is the source of the data?

    b) How was the data collected?

    c) Who collected the data?

    d) Is the graph chosen the best type of graph to display the information? Why or why not?

    e) What other type of graph could be used to display the information? Justify your answer.

Chapter Problem

11. For another market research project, Andrew is analysing several sets of data collected at a local fall fair. Classify each set of data as discrete or continuous. Choose a graph to display each set of data. Justify your choice.

    a) daily receipts at the front gate of the fair over the 10 days

    b) daily attendance at the fair

    c) winning mass of the largest pumpkin over the last 100 years at the fair

    d) the numbers of each item sold at the snack stand

    e) the most popular carnival game at the fair

Achievement Check

12. Chantal conducted a survey to determine the favourite snack food of students at her school. The data is shown in the table. Display the data using an appropriate graph. Justify your choice of graph.

Favourite Snack Food	Tally
tortilla chips	‖‖ ‖‖ ‖‖ ‖‖
fruit bar	‖‖ ‖‖ ‖‖ ‖‖ ‖
muffin	‖‖ ‖
fruit	‖‖ ‖‖
crackers and cheese	‖‖ ‖
granola bar	‖‖ ‖‖ ‖

13. Use the Internet to find the heights or masses of players on your favourite sports team. Display the data using an appropriate graph. Justify your choice of graph.

14. A line graph can be used to show a trend in data that changes over time, such as how a company's stock price changes over time. The table shows the weekly closing stock price of a share in a small mining company.

Week Number	Stock Price ($)
1	92.50
2	100.00
3	91.30
4	98.60
5	112.60
6	104.50
7	111.70
8	108.10
9	104.30
10	121.30
11	101.40
12	119.50

a) Draw a set of axes. Number the horizontal axis from 0 to 12 and the vertical axis from 90 to 125 in increments of 5. Graph the data. Add a title to your graph and label the axes.

b) A volatile stock is one whose price changes dramatically. Examine your graph from part a). Does the stock appear to be a volatile stock?

c) Draw another set of axes. Number the horizontal axis from 0 to 12 and the vertical axis from 0 to 130 in increments of 10. Graph the data. Add a title to your graph and label the axes.

d) Examine your graph from part c). Does the stock seem to be more or less volatile than in the graph from part a)?

e) Suppose you are an investor looking to purchase stable stock in a company. The marketing manager from the mining company sends you a report on the company's stock performance. Which graph would the manager most likely send you? Why? Why would the manager not send the other graph?

3.4 Measures of Central Tendency

In the last three sections, you explored methods of collecting and displaying data. In the next three sections, you will calculate statistics that can be used to analyse a set of data. Measures of central tendency provide information on the centre of a set of data.

Tools

• calculator

mean

• the sum of values in a set of data divided by the number of values in the set of data

median

• the middle value when data is ordered from least to greatest

mode

• the value or attribute that occurs most often in the set of data

Measures of Central Tendency

Sam works for a company that maintains a career and employment Web site. The Web site provides information on positions and salaries at various companies. The table shows data from one of the companies, Cabinets-R-Us, a small kitchen cabinetry company.

Position	Number of Employees	Annual Salary ($)
cabinet maker	8	43 000
secretary	2	38 000
sales representative	2	48 000
president	1	100 000

1. How many employees work at Cabinets-R-Us?

2. Calculate the **mean** salary.

3. Calculate the **median** salary.

4. What is the **mode** salary?

5. Reflect Which measure of central tendency best describes a typical employee salary at Cabinets-R-Us? Justify your answer.

Example 1

Calculate Mean, Median, and Mode

Consider these test scores, all out of 100.

61, 76, 89, 72, 65, 71, 61, 83, 45, 68, 62, 59, 71, 68, 69, 86

a) Find the mean score.

b) Find the median score.

c) Find the mode score.

Solution

a) $\text{Mean} = \dfrac{\text{sum of all values}}{\text{number of values}}$

$= \dfrac{61+76+89+72+65+71+61+83+45+68+62+59+71+68+69+86}{16}$

$= \dfrac{1106}{16}$

$= 69.125$

The mean score is 69.125.

b) Order the data from least to greatest.

45, 59, 61, 61, 62, 65, 68, **68, 69**, 71, 71, 72, 76, 83, 86, 89

The middle values are 68 and 69. The median is the mean of the middle values.

$\dfrac{68 + 69}{2} = 68.5$

The median score is 68.5.

c) Each of the scores 61, 68, and 71 occur twice. No other scores are repeated.

There are three mode scores: 61, 68, and 71. The data are trimodal.

Example 2

Use Technology to Find the Mean and Median

A corner store recorded the numbers of newspapers sold each day for 17 days. Find the mean and the median of the data.

111, 131, 152, 98, 112, 117, 124, 108, 113,
112, 119, 117, 99, 103, 114, 122, 130

Solution

Method 1: Use a Graphing Calculator

- Press [2nd] [MEM] **4** [ENTER] to clear the lists.

- Press [STAT] and select **1:Edit…**. Enter the data in list L1.

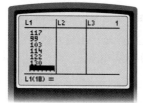

- Press [2nd] [QUIT] to return to the calculator screen.
- Press [2nd] [LIST]. Select **MATH 3:mean(**.
- Press [2nd] [L1]. Press [ )] [ENTER]. The mean of the data in list L1 is displayed.
- Press [2nd] [LIST]. Select **MATH 4: median(**.
- Press [2nd] [L1]. Press [ )] [ENTER]. The median of the data in list L1 is displayed.

Method 2: Use a Spreadsheet

- Open Microsoft® *Excel*. Enter the data in cells A1 to A17.
- Select cell A18. From the **Insert** menu, select **Function…**.
- Change the category to **Statistical**, and select **AVERAGE**. Select **OK**. Select and drag the mouse from cell A1 to cell A17. Select **OK**. The mean will appear.
- Select cell A19. From the **Insert** menu, select **Function…**.
- Change the category to **Statistical**, and select **MEDIAN**. Select **OK**. Click and drag the mouse from cell A1 to cell A17. Select **OK**. The median will appear.

Technology Tip
The TI-83 Plus and TI-84 Plus calculators do not have a mode function.

Technology Tip
You can see a list of
available functions by
clicking on the + icon
next to Functions in
the calculator window.

Method 3: Use *Fathom*™

- Start *Fathom*™. From the **Object** menu, choose **New** then **Case Table**.
- Enter the heading "Data" in the second column. Enter the data in this column.
- Double-click on the heading "Collection 1". In the **Rename Collection** dialogue box, enter the title "Measures of Central Tendency". Select **OK**.
- From the **Object** menu, choose **New** then **Graph**. In the case table, select the heading "Data", hold the mouse button, and drag the heading to the horizontal axis of the graph.
- Select the graph. From the **Graph** menu, choose **Plot Value**. Type "mean(data)" then select **OK**. The mean will appear on the graph and below the graph.
- Select the graph. From the **Graph** menu, choose **Plot Value**. Type "median(data)" then select **OK**. The median will appear on the graph and below the graph.

Example 3

Best Measure of Central Tendency

Find the mean, the median, and the mode of each set of data. Which measure of central tendency best describes the data? Explain.

a) Erika recorded the masses, in grams, of bags of cashews sold on Monday at her bulk food store.

58, 37, 37, 38, 42, 41, 46, 43, 41, 37, 38, 37

b) The scores on a mathematics quiz, out of 100, are shown.

63, 71, 40, 99, 52, 94, 83, 67, 94, 89, 14, 76, 68

c) The table shows the number of prizes and the value of each prize in a charity fundraiser.

Prize Value ($)	Number of Prizes
5000	1
1000	4
500	8
10	80

Solution

a) Mean

$$\text{Mean} = \frac{\text{sum of all values}}{\text{number of values}}$$

$$= \frac{58+37+37+38+42+41+46+43+41+37+38+37}{12}$$

$$= \frac{495}{12}$$

$$= 41.25$$

The mean mass is 41.25 g.

Median

37, 37, 37, 37, 38, **38, 41**, 41, 42, 43, 46, 58

$$\text{Median} = \frac{38 + 41}{2}$$

$$= 39.5$$

The median mass is 39.5 g.

Since there is an even number of values, the median value is the average of the two middle values.

Mode

The value 37 occurs most frequently; it appears four times. Therefore, the mode mass is 37 g.

For this set of data, the mean is a good choice for the measure of central tendency. Most of the values are close to the mean.

The median could also be used since it is close to the mean. Notice that this median is not a value in the set of data.

The only measure of central tendency that is a value in the set of data is the mode. However, the mode is the least value in the set of data, making it a poor choice as the best measure of central tendency.

b) Mean

$$\text{Mean} = \frac{\text{sum of all values}}{\text{number of values}}$$

$$= \frac{63+71+40+99+52+94+83+67+94+89+14+76+68}{13}$$

$$= \frac{910}{13}$$

$$= 70$$

The mean score is 70.

Median

14, 40, 52, 63, 67, 68, **71**, 76, 83, 89, 94, 94, 99

There are six values before and after the median. The median score is 71.

Since there are 13 values, the median is the seventh value.

Mode

The number 94 occurs twice. No other score is repeated. Therefore, the mode score is 94.

For this set of data, the median is the best measure of central tendency. The median is not affected by **outliers** . The median value occurs in the set of data.

outlier
• an extreme value in a set of data
• a value "far away" from the other values in a set of data

c) Mean

$$\text{Mean} = \frac{\text{sum of all values}}{\text{number of values}}$$

$$= \frac{1 \times 5000 + 4 \times 1000 + 8 \times 500 + 80 \times 10}{93}$$

$$= \frac{13\ 800}{93}$$

The mean prize value is $148.39.

Median

There are 93 prizes, of which 80 have a value of $10.
Therefore, the median prize value is $10.

Mode

The value $10 occurs 80 times.
Therefore, the mode prize value is $10.

For this set of data, the median and the mode are the same. Due to the frequency of the $10 prize, the mode is the best measure of central tendency.

Key Concepts

- The mean, the median, and the mode are measures of central tendency of a set of data.
- The mean is calculated by adding the data and dividing the total by the number of data values.
- The median is found by listing the data in order from least to greatest and finding the middle value. If there is an even number of values, the median is the mean of the two middle values.
- The mode is found by finding the most frequently occurring value. A set of data can have more than one mode or no mode.

Discuss the Concepts

D1. Is it possible for a set of data to have the same mean, median, and mode? Explain, using an example.

D2. Which measure of central tendency is usually the least representative of a set of data?

D3. Which measure(s) of central tendency can be used for categorical data? Explain, using an example.

For help with question 1, refer to Example 1.

1. Find the mean (to one decimal place), the median, and the mode of each set of data.

a) the number of litres of gasoline purchased by customers in one hour at a gas station:
25, 21, 38, 29, 32, 44, 38, 21, 16

b) the number of points scored by a basketball team at home games:
44, 36, 82, 53, 71, 74, 38, 81, 94, 58

For help with questions 2 to 4, refer to Example 3.

2. The table shows the prizes awarded in Jason's school fundraiser.

Prize Value ($)	Number of Prizes
100	2
50	4
10	10

Find the mean (to one decimal place), the median, and the mode prize value.

3. Find the mean, the median, and the mode of each set of data. Which measure of central tendency best describes the data? Explain.

a) the wages earned by Alisa each month:
214, 333, 197, 310, 622, 410, 520, 285, 540, 383, 427, 345

b) the at-bats of 15 Toronto Blue Jays for one season:
87, 461, 611, 260, 466, 581, 433, 546,
348, 450, 437, 540, 290, 296, 251

4. The table shows the heights of grade 11 students at Sacha's school.

Height (cm)	Frequency
[155–160)	2
[160–165)	6
[165–170)	12
[170–175)	11
[175–180)	6
[180–185)	4
[185–190)	2

a) Find the median, the mode, and the range of heights.

b) Which measure of central tendency best describes the data? Explain.

5. Give an example of when the mode is the best measure of central tendency of a set of data.

Literacy Connect

6. Some schools report trends in class marks using the median. Why do you think this measure is preferred over the mean? Explain.

7. Veronica conducted a survey to find the average shoe size of the female students in two grade 11 classes. She displayed the information in a bar graph.

Grade 11 Girls' Shoe Sizes

a) Find the mean (to the nearest shoe size), the median, and the mode shoe size.

b) Which measure of central tendency is easiest to find from the graph? Explain.

c) Which measure of central tendency best describes the data? Explain.

Chapter Problem

8. As part of his final project in his co-op placement, Andrew found the attendance for the local fair over the past 20 years. He recorded the attendance in thousands of people.

23, 31, 44, 27, 32, 41, 35, 42, 37, 41,
43, 39, 36, 37, 43, 27, 36, 42, 41, 43

a) Find the mean, the median, and the mode attendance.

b) Which measure of central tendency best describes the attendance per year?

c) Why might the attendance vary so greatly from year to year?

9. Lionel and Jeffrey are trying out for the final spot on the school archery team. The coach has invited both boys to a shootout. Based on the results, she will make her choice. Here are their results after ten flights (rounds) of three arrows.

Flight	1	2	3	4	5	6	7	8	9	10
Lionel	18	12	22	22	29	22	14	28	26	20
Jeffrey	20	22	22	19	21	21	21	21	22	20

a) Find the mean, the median, and the mode score for each archer.

b) Which measure of central tendency best represents each archer's performance? Explain.

c) Which archer should the coach choose? Justify your choice.

10. The batting average for a baseball player is found by dividing the player's total hits by the player's total at-bats. The value is rounded to three decimal places. The table shows the number of hits and at-bats for a girls' baseball team.

Position	Hits	At-Bats	Batting Average
1st base	26	71	0.366
2nd base	38	84	
3rd base	25	62	
shortstop	31	67	
catcher	28	70	
pitcher	12	39	
left field	41	88	
centre field	52	88	
right field	47	88	

a) Copy and complete the table.

b) Find the mean batting average.

c) Find the team's batting average.

d) Compare your answers for parts b) and c). What do the two results mean in relation to each other? Why are the two results not the same?

e) Find the mean batting average for the three fielders.

f) Add the number of hits for the three fielders and divide this value by their total number of at-bats. Find the fielders' batting average.

g) Compare your results from parts e) and f). Why are the two results the same?

11. A company employs 15 people at a weekly salary of $250 each, 4 people at a weekly salary of $500 each, and 3 people at a weekly salary of $1200 each.

   a) Find the mean, the median, and the mode salary.

   b) Which measure of central tendency best represents salaries at the company? Explain.

Extend

12. Search the Internet for the salaries of players on a professional sports team.

   a) Find the mean, the median, and the mode salary.

   b) Which measure of central tendency best describes the data?

   c) Compare results with several classmates who have chosen different teams or different sports.

   d) Do the measures of central tendency for each team correspond to the team's current year performance? Explain. List any assumptions you have made.

13. Given the set of numbers 11, 8, 14, 14, x, consider each situation.

   a) The mean of the numbers is 13. Find the value of x.

   b) The median of the numbers is 14. What do you know about x?

   c) There are two modes. What do you know about x?

14. Annette has a mean bowling score of 150 after six games. What score must she get in the seventh game to raise her mean score to 152?

3.5 Measures of Spread

Measures of central tendency are values around which a set of data tends to cluster. However, to analyse a set of data, it is useful to know how spread out the data are. Measures of spread describe how the values in a set of data are distributed.

Investigate 1

Tools

- graphing calculator

Use a Graphing Calculator to Analyse Data

There are two first-year mathematics classes at Caldwell College. The tables show the midterm marks for the two classes.

Class 1	59	79	89	49	71	68	67	48	69	67	75
	82	80	59	58	74	66	90	73	81	59	

Class 2	91	88	50	44	42	88	79	92	83	77	43
	62	98	52	67	84	70	55	89	48		

1. Use these steps to graph the data for each class.

- Press [Y=] and clear any equations.
- Press [STAT] and select **1:Edit…**.
  Enter the data for Class 1 in list L1.
  Enter the data for Class 2 in list L2.
- Press [2nd] then [STATPLOT] to access **PLOT1**. Turn Plot1 On.
- Cursor down to Type. Turn the second type of Box Plot On as shown. Enter L1 for Xlist.

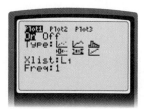

• Press [2nd] then [STATPLOT] to access **PLOT2**. Turn Plot2 On.
• Cursor down to Type. Turn the second type of Box Plot On. Enter L2 for Xlist.
• Press [ZOOM] **9:Zoomstat** to see both plots.
• Press [TRACE]. Use the cursor to see the five values for each plot: the minimum, Q1, the median, Q3, and the maximum. Q1 and Q3 are the first and third **quartiles**, the median is the second quartile.

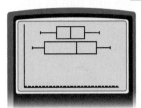

2. Compare the median score for each class. Which class has the better performance?

3. Calculate the **range** for each class. What does the range tell you?

4. **Reflect** This type of graph is called a **box-and-whisker plot**. Refer to the box-and-whisker plots. Which class performed better? How does this compare to your answer to question 2? Explain.

Variance and **standard deviation** are measures of the spread of the values in a distribution. The greater the standard deviation and the greater the variance, the greater the distance of the values from the mean.

$$\text{Variance} = \frac{(x_1-\text{mean})^2 + (x_2-\text{mean})^2 + (x_3-\text{mean})^2 + \ldots + (x_n-\text{mean})^2}{n}$$

where $x_1, x_2, x_3, \ldots$ are values in the set of data, and n is the number of values in the set of data.

$$\text{Standard deviation} = \sqrt{\text{variance}}$$

Example 1

Determine Quartiles and the Interquartile Ranges

Iris works part-time selling cell phones. She recorded the numbers of cell phones she sold each month for the last 12 months.

51, 17, 25, 39, 7, 49, 62, 41, 20, 6, 43, 13

a) Find the median, the first quartile (Q1), and the third quartile (Q3).

b) Display the data in a box-and-whisker plot.

Solution

a) Order the data from least to greatest.

6, 7, 13, 17, 20, **25**, **39**, 41, 43, 49, 51, 62

$$\text{Median} = \frac{25 + 39}{2}$$

$$= 32$$

> The median is the mean of the two middle values.

The median indicates that half of Iris's monthly sales were more than 32 phones and half were fewer than 32 phones.

To determine the first quartile, find the median of the lower half of the data.

6, 7, **13**, **17**, 20, 25

$$Q1 = \frac{13 + 17}{2}$$

$$= 15$$

> There is an even number of values, so find the mean of the two middle values.

The first quartile is 15 phones. The first quartile indicates that for one-quarter of the months, Iris sold fewer than 15 phones and for three-quarters of the months, she sold more than 15 phones.

To determine the third quartile, find the median of the upper half of the data.

39, 41, **43**, **49**, 51, 62

$$Q3 = \frac{43 + 49}{2}$$

$$= 46$$

> There is an even number of values, so find the mean of the two middle values.

The third quartile is 46 phones. The third quartile indicates that for three-quarters of the months, Iris sold fewer than 46 phones and for one-quarter of the months, she sold more than 46 phones.

The first and third quartiles are the boundaries for the central half of the data. They show that half of Iris's monthly sales were between 15 and 46 phones. The difference between the third quartile, 46, and the first quartile, 15, is the **interquartile range**. The interquartile range is 31.

b) Draw a number line with values from 0 to 70.
- The minimum value is 6 and the maximum value is 62. Draw a horizontal line segment from 6 to 62.
- Draw a vertical line segment at the first quartile, 15, the median, 32, and the third quartile, 46. Join the vertical segments to form a box.

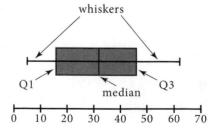

interquartile range
- the range of the central half of a set of data when the data are arranged from least to greatest
- a measure of how closely data clusters around its mean

Example 2

Calculate Range, Variance, and Standard Deviation

Carmella's monthly gasoline expenses, in dollars, for the past year are shown.

61, 83, 77, 88, 67, 71, 65, 72, 67, 84, 90, 80

Calculate the range, the mean, the variance, and the standard deviation. Round your answers to the nearest dollar.

Solution

Range = greatest value − least value
$$= 90 - 61$$
$$= 29$$

The range of the expenses is $29.

$$\text{Mean} = \frac{61 + 83 + 77 + 88 + 67 + 71 + 65 + 72 + 67 + 84 + 90 + 80}{12}$$
$$\doteq 75.42$$

The mean expense is approximately $75.

Calculate the variance and the standard deviation.
- Subtract the mean from each data value and square the result.
- Add the squared numbers.
- Divide this sum by the number of data values.
- Calculate the square root of the quotient.

Amount ($)	Amount − Mean ($)	(Difference From Mean)^2
61	61 − 75 = −14	196
83	83 − 75 = 8	64
77	77 − 75 = 2	4
88	88 − 75 = 13	169
67	67 − 75 = −8	64
71	71 − 75 = −4	16
65	65 − 75 = −10	100
72	72 − 75 = −3	9
67	67 − 75 = −8	64
84	84 − 75 = 9	81
90	90 − 75 = 15	225
80	80 − 75 = 5	25
Total		1017

$$\text{Variance} \doteq \frac{1017}{12}$$
$$\doteq 85$$

The variance is approximately $85.

$$\text{Standard deviation} \doteq \sqrt{85}$$
$$\doteq 9$$

The standard deviation is approximately $9.

Example 3

Compare Measures of Spread in Two Set of Data

Not all manufactured items will be identical in size or shape. Usually companies have guidelines as to how much an item can vary from the specified measurements. The decision to accept or reject an item depends on whether the item falls within the specified limits of variation.

A company needs bolts for its heavy machinery. The company must choose between two bolt manufacturers: CanInco and QualiTek. Both manufacturers produce bolts with a mean length of 72 mm. According to quality control records, bolts from CanInco have a standard deviation of 2 mm while bolts from QualiTek have a standard deviation of 0.1 mm. Which manufacturer should the company choose?

Solution

Although both manufacturers produce bolts with the same mean length, the bolts from CanInco have a greater standard deviation. This suggests that there is greater variety in the length of bolts from CanInco. If the company wants a consistently uniform bolt size, it should choose QualiTek, assuming the prices for both manufacturers are similar.

Key Concepts

- Several quantities can be used to measure the spread in a set of data.
- The range is the difference between the greatest and least values in a set of data. To calculate the range, subtract the least value from the greatest value.
- The variance is a measure of how spread out the values in a set of data are from the mean. The greater the variance, the greater the spread of the data values.

$$\text{Variance} = \frac{(x_1 - \text{mean})^2 + (x_2 - \text{mean})^2 + (x_3 - \text{mean})^2 + \ldots + (x_n - \text{mean})^2}{n},$$

  where $x_1, x_2, x_3, \ldots$ are values in the set of data, and n is the number of values in the set of data.
- The standard deviation is another measure of how spread out the values in a set of data are from the mean. The greater the standard deviation, the greater the spread of the data values.

  Standard deviation $= \sqrt{\text{variance}}$
- Quartiles are three values that divide a set of data into four intervals with equal numbers of data.
- The interquartile range measures how closely data clusters around the median.

Practise

For help with question 1, refer to Example 1.

1. This set of data shows the numbers of customers who made purchases at a coffee shop each day in one month.

   114, 142, 59, 122, 111, 128, 158, 79, 88, 107, 133, 131, 113, 152, 149, 99, 84, 112, 104, 109, 122, 131, 144, 155, 139, 142, 119, 80, 127, 140, 135

   a) Find the median for the set of data.

   b) Find the first and third quartiles.

   c) What is the interquartile range?

For help with questions 2 to 7, refer to Example 2.

2. Find the range for each set of data.

   a) the number of hours worked by restaurant staff in a given week:
   11, 4, 55, 42, 41, 36, 50, 6, 8, 44, 39

   b) Alex's monthly earnings, in dollars:
   100, 115, 112, 125, 104, 101, 117, 121, 98, 100, 95, 102

   c) the number of songs Matilda downloaded each month:
   12, 11, 9, 12, 13, 15, 14, 11, 11, 8, 6, 7

   d) the masses of students in a club, in kilograms:
   65, 45, 71, 85, 37, 91, 88, 74, 76, 68, 65

3. A set of data has a range of 30. The least value in the set of data is 22. What is the greatest value in the set of data?

4. A set of data has a range of 14. The greatest value in the set is 116. What is the least value in the set of data?

5. Each measurement is the variance for a set of data. Find the standard deviation for each set of data. Round your answer to one decimal place, if necessary.

   a) 154 g

   b) 36 m

   c) 80 cm

   d) 18 L

6. Each measurement is the standard deviation for a set of data. Find the variance for each set of data.

   a) 14.1 cm

   b) 3.5 kg

   c) $22

   d) 6.7 mL

7. Calculate the variance and the standard deviation for each set of data.

   a) the age of members of a book club:
      24, 35, 45, 41, 22, 51, 46, 40

   b) the number of double-faults per game for a tennis player:
      5, 4, 7, 11, 1, 6, 6, 7, 7

   c) the points scored at home games by the varsity boys' basketball team:
      100, 105, 101, 103, 100, 99, 102, 98

   d) the number of pizzas made per day at a pizzeria:
      56, 57, 54, 51, 58, 59, 51, 50, 53, 51

Apply B

8. The players on two basketball teams have the same mean height of 200 cm. The standard deviation of the heights of the players on Team One is 15 cm and on Team Two is 20 cm. What can be said about the players on each team, given the difference in the standard deviation of their heights? Explain.

9. The mathematics test scores, out of 100, for 13 students are shown. Display the data in a box-and-whisker plot.

   80, 75, 90, 95, 65, 65, 80, 57, 85, 70, 74, 100, 84

Literacy Connect **10.** A bowling team needs one more person. Eileen and Ingrid are being considered for the spot. They both have the same mean score, but Ingrid's scores have a lower standard deviation than Eileen's scores. Which person should be chosen? Explain your answer.

Reasoning and Proving

Representing | Selecting Tools

Problem Solving

Connecting | Reflecting

Communicating

11. The manufacturing process allows for slight differences in the width of a piston in a cylinder. Slightly smaller or larger piston diameters mean the gaskets used to provide a tight seal will be slightly more or less compressed by the piston on the cylinder walls. In a quality control test, 10 pistons were chosen at random and measured. The table shows the results.

Piston	Diameter (cm)
1	12.85
2	12.77
3	12.91
4	12.87
5	12.81
6	12.90
7	12.78
8	12.80
9	12.92
10	12.99

a) Calculate the standard deviation of the diameters.

b) An item is defective if its diameter is more than two standard deviations from the mean. How many of the tested pistons are defective?

c) What percent of pistons sampled are defective?

d) Does your answer to part c) represent the expected failure rate of pistons made at this manufacturing plant? Explain why or why not.

Chapter Problem

12. Andrew is still working with the attendance figures, in thousands of people, for the fall fair over the past 20 years. Find the range, the variance, and the standard deviation for the data.

23, 31, 44, 27, 32, 41, 35, 42, 37, 41, 43, 39, 36, 37, 43, 27, 39, 42, 41, 43

Achievement Check

13. Joanna's mathematics test scores have a mean of 81% and a standard deviation of 5%. Adam's mathematics test scores have a mean of 84% with a standard deviation of 10%. Whose test scores are more consistent? What do these measures of central tendency and spread tell you about each student?

Extend **C** ●

14. Select a National Basketball Association (NBA) or Women's National Basketball Association (WNBA) team.

a) Use the Internet to find the heights of players on your chosen team.

b) Convert these heights to centimetres. Find the mean height, the range, and the standard deviation.

c) Compare results with several classmates who researched different teams in the same league.

d) Is there a relationship between the heights of the players on the teams and their scoring records? Explain.

3.6 Common Distributions

Frequency distributions show the frequency of each outcome in a given situation. The range in values and the frequency of specific values are important measures in data analysis.

Investigate 1

Normal Distribution

Tools
- calculator
- grid paper
- ruler

Alice recorded the heights of people who walked into a hockey arena over a two-hour period.

Class Intervals of Heights (cm)	Tally	Frequency
[100–110)	‖‖	
[110–120)	‖‖ ‖‖	
[120–130)	‖‖ ‖‖ ‖‖ ‖	
[130–140)	‖‖ ‖‖ ‖‖ ‖‖ ‖‖	
[140–150)	‖‖ ‖‖ ‖‖ ‖‖ ‖‖ ‖‖ ‖‖	
[150–160)	‖‖ ‖‖ ‖‖ ‖‖ ‖‖ ‖‖ ‖‖ ‖‖ ‖	
[160–170)	‖‖ ‖‖ ‖‖ ‖‖ ‖‖ ‖‖ ‖‖ ‖‖	
[170–180)	‖‖ ‖‖ ‖‖ ‖‖ ‖‖	
[180–190)	‖‖ ‖‖ ‖‖	
[190–200)	‖‖ ‖‖	
[200–210)	‖	

Method 1: Graph a Normal Distribution By Hand

1. Copy and complete the table.

2. Display the data using a histogram.

3. Place a point at the centre of the top of each bar in your histogram. Join the points with a smooth curve.

normal distribution

• a bell-shaped distribution that is symmetrical about the mean

4. The data approximates a **normal distribution**. Describe the shape of a normal distribution in your own words.

5. Alice calculated the mean height as 154 cm, the median height as 152 cm, and the mode height as 157 cm. How do these measures of central tendency relate to the curve in the normal distribution?

6. **Reflect** What does the shape of the curve tell you about the heights of the people at the game?

Method 2: Graph a Normal Distribution Using Technology

Tools

• graphing calculator

Use the data from the frequency table.

1. Follow these steps to create a histogram using a graphing calculator.
   • Press [2nd] [MEM] **4** [ENTER] to clear the lists.
   • Press [STAT] and select **1:Edit…**. Enter the median value of each interval in list L1. For example, for the interval [100–110), enter 105. Enter the frequencies in list L2.

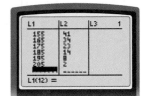

   • Press [Y=]. Clear any equations in the list.
   • Press [2nd] [STATPLOT]. Select **4:PlotsOff**. Press [ENTER].
   • Press [2nd] [STATPLOT] again. Select **1:Plot1**. Set the plot to On, the graph style to Histogram, the XList to L1, and the frequency to L2.
   • Press [ZOOM]. Select **9:ZoomStat**.
   • Adjust the window settings as shown. The histogram will begin at 100, with a bin width of 10. Press [GRAPH].

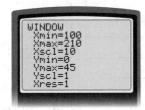 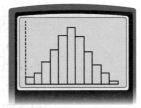

2. Print or sketch the histogram.

3. Place a point at the centre of the top of each bar in your histogram. Join the points with a smooth curve.

4. The data approximates a normal distribution. Describe the shape of a normal distribution.

5. Alice calculated the mean height as 154 cm, the median height as 152 cm, and the mode height as 157 cm. How do these measures of central tendency relate to the curve in the normal distribution?

6. **Reflect** What does the shape of the curve tell you about the heights of the people at the game?

Example 1

Bimodal Distribution

Frank recorded the heights of the peewee and senior girls' Falcon soccer teams.

Height (cm)	[100–110)	[110–120)	[120–130)	[130–140)	[140–150)	[150–160)
Frequency	4	8	3	4	8	2

a) Display the data using a histogram. Place a point at the centre of the top of each bar in your histogram. Join the points with a smooth curve.

b) Describe the shape of the curve.

c) What does the shape of the curve tell you about the heights of the players?

Solution

a)

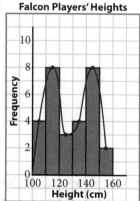

b) The curve represents a **bimodal distribution**. It has two peaks representing the two modes and is symmetrical about the centres.

c) Most of the players fall into two subgroups: players with heights between 110 cm and 130 cm, and players with heights between 130 cm and 150 cm. Measures of central tendency may not be good indicators of this data.

bimodal distribution

• a distribution that contains two equally likely measures of central tendency within the data

Example 2

Skewed Distribution

Students in the French club recorded their final marks, out of 100, for grade 9 French.

Interval	[50–60)	[60–70)	[70–80)	[80–90)	[90–100]
Frequency	0	1	2	6	3

a) Display the data using a histogram. Place a point at the centre of the top of each bar in your histogram. Join the points with a smooth curve.

b) Describe the shape of the curve.

c) What does the shape of the curve tell you about the students?

Solution

a)

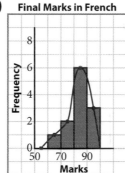

Final Marks in French

skewed distribution
• a non-symmetrical distribution of data

b) The curve represents a **skewed distribution**. It has a greater cluster of data on the right side than on the left.

c) Most marks are clustered between 80 and 90. This means that most of the French club members are doing well in French. Since the data are skewed, measures of central tendency may not be good indicators of this data.

Example 3

Identify the Type of Distribution

In each case, predict the shape of the data distribution. Give a reason for your prediction.

a) the heights of members of the Toronto Raptors basketball team

b) the cost of 1 L of gas in a city in Ontario

c) the masses of players on the Canadian Olympic men's and women's hockey teams

Solution

a) NBA basketball players are tall, so the heights of the members of the basketball team should be skewed to the right when compared to rest of the population.

b) Since the price of gas is fairly standard in a city, with few differences between self-serve or full service stations, the data should be normally distributed.

c) Most male players will have a greater mass than most female players, so the distribution should be bimodal.

Key Concepts

- In a normal distribution, the data are distributed symmetrically about the mean. The mean, the median, and the mode are close in value and are located at the centre of the distribution.

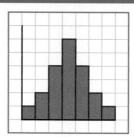

- A skewed distribution has the appearance of a normal distribution that has been pushed to one side of the mean. The result is an asymmetrical or lopsided distribution.

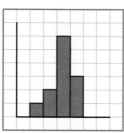

- A bimodal distribution has two peaks. It is symmetrical, with frequencies clustering around two sub-groups.

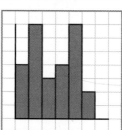

Discuss the Concepts

D1. What is the difference between a skewed distribution and a normal distribution? Explain, using examples.

D2. Can skewed, normal, and bimodal distributions have the same range? Explain.

Practise A

For help with questions 1 to 3, refer to Examples 1 and 2.

1. Classify each distribution as normal, skewed, or bimodal.

a)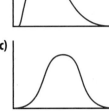

b)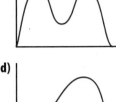

c)

d)

2. Give an example of a set of data that has each distribution.

a) normal distribution

b) skewed distribution

c) bimodal distribution

Apply B

3. The histogram shows the reading scores for a grade 4 class.

Reading Scores

a) What type of distribution is this?

b) What might cause this type of distribution in the reading scores in this class?

Literacy Connect

4. a) Why would a clothing manufacturer monitor the mean dress size for women who shop at stores carrying its clothing?

b) Would the manufacturer be interested in the standard deviation of dress sizes? Explain.

5. The graph shows the ages of homeowners in a subdivision.

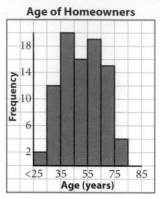

Age of Homeowners

a) What does the distribution tell you about the population?

b) Why might a mayoral candidate be interested in this information? Explain.

c) Approximate the mean and the median age.

6. The graph shows the salaries of employees at a large company.

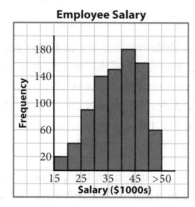

Employee Salary

a) What conclusions can you draw about the salaries at the company? Explain.

b) Suppose you were a recruiter, trying to entice people to work for the company. Which measure of central tendency would you use? Explain.

c) Suppose you have to report salaries to head office and want to convey that salary expenditure is low. Which measure of central tendency would you use? Explain.

7. Scores out of 100 on a college entrance examination are shown.

Mark Interval	Tally	Frequency
[30–40)	⊞⊞ ⊞⊞	
[40–50)	⊞⊞ ⊞⊞ ⊞⊞ ||	
[50–60)	⊞⊞ ⊞⊞ ⊞⊞ ⊞⊞ ⊞⊞		
[60–70)	⊞⊞ ⊞⊞ ⊞⊞ ⊞⊞ ⊞⊞ ⊞⊞ ⊞⊞	
[70–80)	⊞⊞ ⊞⊞ ⊞⊞ ⊞⊞ ⊞⊞ ⊞⊞ ⊞⊞ ⊞⊞ |||	
[80–90)	⊞⊞ ⊞⊞ ⊞⊞ ⊞⊞ ⊞⊞ ⊞⊞		
[90–100]	⊞⊞ ⊞⊞ ⊞⊞ ||||	

a) Copy and complete the table. Display the data using a histogram.

b) Place a point at the centre of the top of each bar in your histogram. Join the points with a smooth curve.

c) What type of distribution does the curve represent? Explain.

Extend •

8. In a normal distribution, about 68% of all values are within 1 standard deviation of the mean. A run of juice cans at a canning factory were found to contain a mean of 760 mL of juice per can. The standard deviation was 20 mL and the values formed a normal distribution. Out of 2000 cans, about how many cans contain between 740 mL and 780 mL of juice?

9. Search for information on the properties of a population that can be represented in a normal distribution. Research what the mean value is for the property, and find information on its standard deviation. Write a report on your findings.

3.1 Sampling Techniques, pages 102–109

1. In each situation, identify the sampling technique.

a) Kuljit went to the local music store to ask what people thought of the "Canadian Idol" winner's debut CD.

b) The school council has set up a booth at the front of the school on Parents' Night to ask about changing the school uniform.

c) Sherry asks 20 girls and 20 boys on the school sports teams if the sports council should spend the fundraising money on new football equipment.

2. Cary plans to survey 100 people. Describe how Cary can choose a stratified sample if her survey population contains 1200 people, and 60% are female.

3. Describe how a graphing calculator can be used to choose a random sample of 15 people from a population of 200 people.

3.2 Collect and Analyse Data, pages 110–117

4. Rewrite the survey question so that it does not contain bias.

Most schools hold a carnival during their Spirit Week, which is usually a great success. Do you think that having a carnival would be a good idea for this year's Spirit Week?

5. Identify the type of bias in each survey.

a) A survey to determine the effectiveness of a government's social services is conducted at a homeless shelter.

b) A survey sent via the Internet asks people to answer a questionnaire and email it to a central processing station.

c) When asked to circle their favourite candidate in the student council, the choices were:
The President
The secretary
The treasurer
Other: _____

6. Randy decides to hand out a survey to every fifth person entering the school. He asks them to fill it out and hand it in at the office when they are done.

a) What type of sampling technique is Randy using?

b) How could this sampling technique lead to inaccurate results?

3.3 Display Data, pages 118–129

7. The table shows the approximate amount of time Le Hing spent on various activities in one week.

Activity	Time (h)
doing homework	8.0
watching television	6.0
making phone calls and text messaging	8.0
playing volleyball	3.0
practising guitar	6.0

a) Which two types of graphs could Le Hing use to display the information?

b) Display the data using each type of graph.

8. The histogram shows the birth masses, in kilograms, of babies born at a hospital in one week.

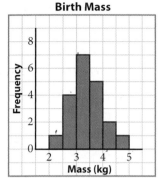

Birth Mass

a) How many babies were born with a mass of at least 4.0 kg?

b) What percent of the babies born were at least 2.0 kg but less than 3.5 kg?

c) Explain why birth mass can be displayed in a histogram.

3.4 Measures of Central Tendency, pages 130–139

9. Find the mean, the median, and the mode for each set of data.

a) 21, 45, 53, 47, 82, 21, 64, 77, 54, 92, 91, 72

b) 4, 7, 11, 8, 6, 6, 5, 3, 5, 7, 8, 14, 17, 18, 6, 4, 2, 2

c) 77, 78, 67, 54, 82, 91, 71, 73, 64, 68, 53, 87, 79

10. A gallery has these items for sale.
- 12 bronze statues for $500 each
- 50 paintings for $100 each
- 100 hand-painted tiles for $25 each

a) Find the mean, the median, and the mode of the prices.

b) Which measure of central tendency best represents the price of an item at the gallery? Explain.

3.5 Measures of Spread, pages 140–147

11. Find the range, the variance, and the standard deviation for each set of data.

a) 28, 51, 91, 47, 56, 77, 64, 52, 71, 63

b) 202, 205, 213, 197, 200, 190, 198, 195

12. If you were the general manager for an NBA basketball team, would you prefer a larger or smaller standard deviation for player heights on your team? Explain.

3.6 Common Distributions, pages 148–155

13. Describe the characteristics of each distribution and give an example of each.

a) a skewed distribution

b) a bimodal distribution

c) a normal distribution

14. The table shows the results of a test out of 100.

Mark Interval	Tally	Frequency
[30–40)	|	
[40–50)	||||	
[50–60)	⫟⫟ |	
[60–70)	⫟⫟ ⫟⫟	
[70–80)	⫟⫟ ||	
[80–90)	|||	
[90–100]	|	

a) Copy and complete the table. Use the data to create a histogram.

b) Do the data appear to be normally distributed? Explain.

For questions 1 to 3, choose the best answer.

1. The mean value of a set of data is found by:

   A adding the values and dividing by the number of values in the set

   B putting the values in order and finding the one located in the middle

   C finding the value that occurs most often

   D subtracting the least value from the greatest value

2. Any survey that asks people to return their completed questionnaires by mail is subject to:

   A response bias   **B** non-response bias

   C sampling bias   **D** no bias at all

3. A population is split into groups. Members of each group are selected randomly in proportion to their number in the population. The sampling technique used was:

   A cluster sampling

   B voluntary-response sampling

   C stratified random sampling

   D simple random sampling

4. Classify the data as coming from a primary or a secondary source.

   a) a survey of your friends

   b) an Internet search to find information

   c) a phone poll conducted by a radio station

   d) data given to you that a friend collected

5. Identify the bias in each survey question.

   a) *The government has been underfunding our transit system for years. Should we turn to private-sector investment to finally solve our transit problems?*

   b) *Please select your favourite type of television show.*
   A Sports
   B Reality show
   C Crime drama
   D Other: _____

6. Rewrite each survey question in question 5 to remove the bias.

7. A nut and a washer are to fit onto the end of a bolt. The centre of the washer must have a mean diameter of 1.5 cm. The variance of the washers is 0.01 cm. The centre of the nut must have a diameter of 1.15 cm, with a standard deviation of 0.01 cm. Assume the diameters are distributed normally.

   a) What is the standard deviation of the washers?

   b) Give the range of centre diameters necessary for the washers to be within two standard deviations of the mean.

   c) Give the range of centre diameters necessary for the nuts to be within two standard deviations of the mean.

   d) Why do the nuts and the washers have different standard deviations? Explain.

Chapter Problem Wrap-Up

In each section, you followed Andrew during his co-op placement at a marketing research company as he learned about and applied statistics. As part of his final project, Andrew studied the attendance at the local fall fair over the last 20 years. Write a report of this data for Andrew. Include a graph of the data and explain your choice of graph. Use your graph to analyse the data's distribution.

8. A large doughnut chain recorded the opening week sales for eight new shops

$37 500, $42 300, $58 000, $31 300, $41 800, $37 100, $63 200, $58 000

 a) Find the range, the mean, the median, and the mode for the data.

 b) Are sales at the new shops likely to increase or decrease after the opening week? Explain.

9. A manufacturer of rechargeable batteries tests 10 batteries at random and records the time it takes, in minutes, to drain each battery after a full charge has been applied.

195, 203, 177, 186, 191, 225, 216, 202, 197, 218

Find the range, the variance, and the standard deviation of the data.

10. The graph shows the shoe sizes of a sample of men.

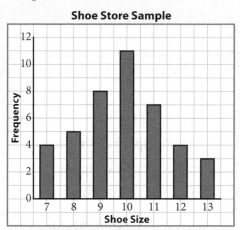

 a) Identify the type of graph.

 b) Identify the type of distribution.

Chapter 1 Trigonometry

1. Write the three trigonometric ratios for angle A. Express each answer as a fraction in lowest terms.

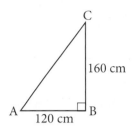

2. Botanists want to confirm the height of the world's tallest redwood tree. They walk 10 m from the base of the tree and measure the angle of elevation to the top to be 85.05°. How tall is the tree, to the nearest metre?

3. Solve each triangle.

a)

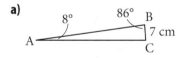

b)

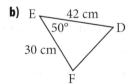

4. Solve for *e*.

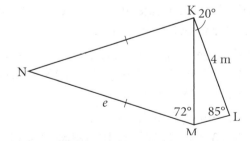

Chapter 2: Probability

5. Three dice were rolled 48 times. Their sum was greater than 8 a total of 36 times. Determine the experimental probability of rolling a sum greater than 8.

6. Suppose two ten-sided dice, with the numbers 1 to 10 on the faces, were rolled. Find the probability of rolling each sum. Express each answer as a fraction in lowest terms.

a) 3   **b)** 11

c) not 11   **d)** 18 or less

e) a sum that is divisible by 10

7. In a bag, there are 11 green marbles, 18 purple marbles, and 1 red marble. A marble is removed, the colour is recorded, and then it is put back into the bag. This is repeated for a total of 30 times. The results are displayed on the bar graph.

a) What is the experimental probability of drawing each colour marble? Express your answers as a percent.

b) What is the theoretical probability of drawing each colour marble? Express your answers as a percent.

8. A baseball player has 60 hits out of 300 at-bats so far this season.

   a) What percent of at-bats has he obtained a hit?

   b) If he has 60 more at-bats this season, how many hits would you expect him to get?

   c) Suggest some factors that might affect your estimate.

Chapter 3: One Variable Statistics

9. In each situation, identify the sample and the population.

   a) Ken filled out the survey in the back of his cycling magazine and mailed it to the publisher.

   b) Chinedu went door to door in his neighbourhood to ask people for which mayoral candidate they planned to vote.

10. Identify the bias in each survey. Suggest how it might be removed.

   a) At the end of the week, there are five entries in the cafeteria suggestion box, and they all say "No more meatloaf!"

   b) Nobody in the biology class raised their hand when the teacher asked who had not started their term project yet.

   c) The student council asks two people from each homeroom: *Do you think it's fair that the principal is planning to ban cell phones in the hallways and cafeteria, even though they don't cause any problems?*

11. Mr. Lowery collected the votes from a mock election his history classes held for the new local MPP.

Candidate	Number of Votes
Raj Pateel	44
Bernice Kryzinsky	37
Evelyn Cho	22
Jacob Mueller	5
Spoiled ballots	8

   a) Graph the data.

   b) List three facts you can gather from the graph.

12. The table shows the number of times a coin was tossed before getting heads and tails at least once.

Number of Flips	Frequency
2	23
3	11
4	6
5	4
6	1

   a) Find the mean, the median, and the mode of the data.

   b) Which measure of central tendency best describes the data? Explain.

13. Calculate the range, the variance, and the standard deviation for each set of data.

   a) the ages of people at a family reunion: 2, 3, 7, 10, 16, 17, 39, 42, 44, 45, 49, 50, 51, 56, 68, 70, 77

   b) number of tracks on CDs: 8, 13, 15, 11, 16, 13, 10, 11, 11, 14, 12

14. Draw a box-and-whisker plot for the data in question 13, part a).

Task

Road to the Stanley Cup

Making the play-offs is just the first step to winning the Stanley Cup. Teams must play up to four best-of-seven rounds in the play-offs. You will simulate the results of one round of the play-offs for the Toronto Maple Leafs.

In a best-of-seven series, the first team to win four games advances to the next round. The team with the better record during the regular season gets the home-ice advantage for games 1, 2, 5, and 7.

Work in groups of four to collect and display the data.

1. To generate random numbers on your calculator, start by keying four random numbers into the random number generator function. (Use the last four digits of your student number or your phone number.) Press MATH. Select **PRB** and then **1:rand**. Press MATH. Select **PRB** and then **5:randInt(**. Press ENTER. Type 1 [,] 10 [,] 7. Press ENTER. You now have seven random numbers from 1 to 10.

   Suppose the Leafs are playing a team with a slightly better record during the regular season. The Leafs have a 50% chance of winning a home game and a 40% chance of winning an away game.

   For an away game (games 1, 2, 5, and 7):
   • If the numbers 1, 2, 3, or 4, appear, the Leafs win their game.
   • If the numbers 5, 6, 7, 8, 9, or 10 appear, the Leafs lose their game.

   For a home game (games 3, 4, and 6):
   • If the numbers 1, 2, 3, 4, or 5, appear, the Leafs win their game.
   • If the number 6, 7, 8, 9, or 10 appear, the Leafs lose their game.

   Consider the random numbers in the screen capture.
   • {1 2 1 1 4 8 8} means the Leafs win in 4 games.
   • {5 10 6 4 1 2 2} means the Leafs win in 7 games.
   • {9 9 7 9 4 9 5} means the Leafs lose in 4 games.
   • {3 3 9 1 2 3 7} means the Leafs win in 5 games.

   Notice that it may not take all seven games to declare a winner.

2. Continue pressing ENTER until you have the results of 20 simulations. Make a table to record your results. For each simulation, note if the Leafs win or lose, and the number of games that it takes.

3. Record the data from each group of students in a tally sheet to find the class results.

4. What type of graph would be appropriate to compare the number of times the Leafs win the series to the number of times the Leafs lose the series? Graph the data.

5. Look at all the simulations that resulted in the Leafs winning the series. Calculate the mean, the median, and the mode number of games. Which measure of central tendency makes the most sense for this data?

6. What predictions could you make about the outcome of the series based on your simulation?

7. Suppose the probability of winning a game remains the same for all teams the Leafs face during the play-offs. What predictions can you make about the probability of the Leafs winning the Stanley Cup based on your simulation? Justify your answer.

4 Quadratic Relations I

Gaming software designers use mathematics and physics to make figures and vehicles move realistically. Often, the motion can be modelled by a quadratic relation.

In this chapter you will extend your knowledge of quadratic relations by connecting their equations and graphs in real world settings.

In this chapter, you will

- construct tables of values and graph quadratic relations arising from real-world applications
- determine and interpret meaningful values of the variables, given a graph of a quadratic relation arising from a real-world application
- determine, through investigation using technology, and describe the roles of a, h, and k in quadratic relations of the form $y = a(x - h)^2 + k$ in terms of transformations on the graph of $y = x^2$
- sketch graphs of quadratic relations represented by the equation $y = a(x - h)^2 + k$

Reasoning and Proving

Representing | Selecting Tools

Problem Solving

Connecting | Reflecting

Communicating

Key Terms

mathematical model	parabola
maximum	vertex
minimum	vertex form

P1: Sam
P2: Russ

Min is an industrial furniture designer. A four-year course at the Ontario College of Art and Design gave her the skills to create products that perform well, look good, and meet the economic needs of her clients. She uses her skills in mathematics to design and produce her furniture and also to calculate her designs' marketability and cost.

Prerequisite Skills

Number Skills

1. Add.

    a) $3.4 + 9.7$ **b)** $1.3 + (-3)$

    c) $-11.3 + 3.6$ **d)** $-4.8 + (-12.3)$

2. Subtract.

    a) $8.8 - 15.3$ **b)** $17.5 - (-8.6)$

    c) $-4.5 - 6.0$ **d)** $-10 - (-3.3)$

3. Multiply.

    a) $(4.5)(9.2)$ **b)** $(6.3)(-4)$

    c) $(-10)(13)$ **d)** $(-7.1)(-1.5)$

Algebraic Expressions

4. Simplify.

    a) $3x + (-5x)$

    b) $9x^2 - (-10) + 3x - 2x^2$

    c) $3x^2 - 4x + 2x + 5x^2$

    d) $-5x^2 + 2x - (3x^2 - 2)$

5. Find the value of y when $x = 0$.

    a) $y = 3x^2$

    b) $y = -9x^2 + 6$

    c) $y = 6(x + 4)^2$

    d) $y = -3(x + 8)^2 - 10$

6. Find the value of y when $x = 3$.

    a) $y = -2x^2$ **b)** $y = 5x^2 + 2$

    c) $y = -4(x - 8)^2$ **d)** $y = (x + 9)^2 + 7$

7. Find the value of y when $x = -4$.

    a) $y = 12x^2$

    b) $y = -11x^2 - 7$

    c) $y = -3(x + 15)^2$

    d) $y = 9(x - 12)^2 - 20$

Linear Relations

8. Copy and complete each table of values.

    a) $y = 3x - 4$ **b)** $y = -0.5x + 21$

x	y
−2	
−1	
0	
1	
2	

x	y
8	
12	
16	
20	
24	

9. Refer to question 8.

    a) Graph each relation.

    b) Identify the slope and the y-intercept for each graph.

10. Copy and complete each table. Find the first differences for each set of data.

a)

x	y	First Differences
3	8	
4	15	
5	23	
6	31	
7	39	

b)

x	y	First Differences
13	0	
14	1	
15	4	
16	9	
17	16	

c)

x	y	First Differences
−5	3	
−4	3	
−3	3	
−2	3	
−1	3	

11. Identify the slope and the *y*-intercept of each line.

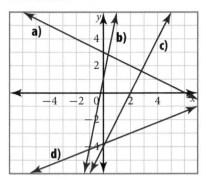

Transformations

12. Describe a transformation that would move each red figure onto its image.

a)

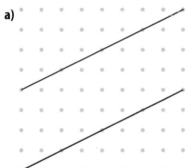

b)

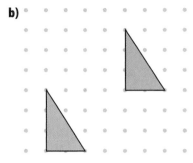

c)

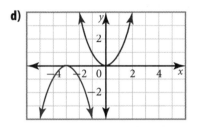

d)

Chapter Problem

You have just been hired by Gamerz Inc. to develop a new extreme sports simulation game. Which extreme sports would you include in your game? What types of motion will you need to model?

4.1 Modelling With Quadratic Relations

Quadratic relations can be used to represent the shape of a suspension bridge or the path of water from a fountain. The ancient Babylonians (3000 B.C.E.) studied quadratic relations in the context of farming. Quadratic relations were the subject of a debate in the House of Commons in London, England, in 2003. Why do you think the British Parliament would discuss quadratic relations?

Investigate

Tools

• calculator

Math **Connect**

1 ha = 10 000 m²

Develop a Mathematical Model

Several farmers have square fields of different sizes. They want to know how much fertilizer to buy given that six bags of fertilizer cover one hectare (ha).

1. Copy and complete the table.

Side Length of Square Farm (m)	Area of Farm (ha)	Bags of Fertilizer Needed
100	1	6
200		
300		
400		
500		
600		

mathematical model
- a mathematical description of a real situation
- can be a diagram, a graph, a table of values, a relation, a formula, a physical model, or a computer model

parabola
- a symmetrical U-shaped curve
- the graph of a quadratic relation

2. Draw a graph comparing the bags of fertilizer needed to the area of the fields. Describe the shape of the graph.

3. a) Draw a graph comparing the bags of fertilizer needed to the side length of the fields. Describe the shape of the graph.

   b) How many bags of fertilizer are needed for a square field with a side length of 1200 m?

   c) Describe how you could find the number of bags of fertilizer needed for a field with side length n.

4. Reflect Refer to the table and your graphs from questions 1 to 3. How can you use the table to determine if the relation is linear or non-linear?

In the Investigate, you used a **mathematical model** to represent the relationship between the side length of the field and the number of bags of fertilizer needed. On a graph, this model is represented by half of a **parabola**. Since negative side lengths for fields do not make sense, the graph does not show the other half of the parabola, on the left side of the vertical axis.

Example 1

Use a Graph to Identify a Quadratic Relation

The table shows a soccer ball's height above the ground over time after it was kicked in the air.

Time (s)	Height (m)
0	0.10
0.5	7.80
1.0	12.00
1.5	13.80
2.0	13.00
2.5	9.75
3.0	4.00

a) Graph the data. Draw a smooth curve through the points.

b) Describe the shape of the graph.

c) What was the ball's maximum height?

d) For about how many seconds was the ball in the air?

Solution

a) Time is the independent variable, so plot it on the horizontal axis.

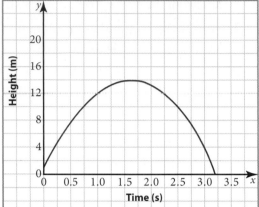

Height of Ball Over Time

b) The graph is a parabola that opens downward.

c) The ball reached a maximum height of about 13.80 m.

d) The ball was in the air for about 3 s.

vertex
- the lowest point on a parabola that opens upward, or the highest point on a parabola that opens downward

minimum
- on an *x*–*y* plane, the *y*-coordinate of the lowest point on a parabola that opens upward
- the *y*-coordinate of the vertex

maximum
- on an *x*–*y* plane, the *y*-coordinate of the highest point on a parabola that opens downward
- the *y*-coordinate of the vertex

The **vertex** of a parabola is the highest point if the parabola opens downward. The vertex is the lowest point if the parabola opens upward. In general, it is the point at which the graph changes from decreasing to increasing or from increasing to decreasing. A parabola always has a **minimum** or a **maximum**.

Example 2

Use Patterns to Identify a Quadratic Relation

The table shows how two variables, *x* and *y*, are related.

x	y
0	1
1	6
2	9
3	10
4	9
5	6
6	1

a) Calculate the first and second differences.

b) Is the relation linear or quadratic? Explain.

Solution

a)

x	y	First Differences	Second Differences
0	1		
		$6 - 1 = 5$	
1	6		$3 - 5 = -2$
		$9 - 6 = 3$	
2	9		$1 - 3 = -2$
		$10 - 9 = 1$	
3	10		$-1 - 1 = -2$
		$9 - 10 = -1$	
4	9		$-3 - (-1) = -2$
		$6 - 9 = -3$	
5	6		$-5 - (-3) = -2$
		$1 - 6 = -5$	
6	1		

Remember, for any quadratic relation, second differences are constant.

b) First differences are not constant, so the relation is not linear. Second differences are constant, so the relation is quadratic.

Example 3

Use Algebra to Identify a Quadratic Relation

a) Graph each relation.

  i) $y = 3x + 4$

  ii) $y = 2x^2 - 5x + 3$

  iii) $y = -4x^2 + 3x - 4$

  iv) $y = -0.5x^2 - 2$

b) Which of the relations are quadratic?

c) Look at the graphs that are parabolas. What do the equations of these relations have in common?

Solution

a) Method 1: Use Pencil and Paper

- Create a table of values for each relation. Use the same x-values for each relation.
- Plot the points. Draw a line or a smooth curve through the points.

i) $y = 3x + 4$

x	y
-2	-2
-1	1
0	4
1	7
2	10

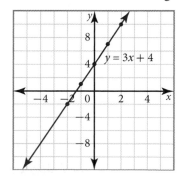

ii) $y = 2x^2 - 5x + 3$

x	y
−2	21
−1	10
0	3
1	0
2	1

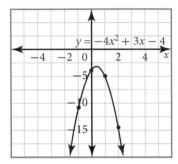

iii) $y = -4x^2 + 3x - 4$

x	y
−2	−26
−1	−11
0	−4
1	−5
2	−14

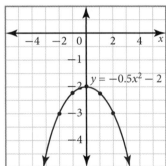

iv) $y = -0.5x^2 - 2$

x	y
−2	−4
−1	−2.5
0	−2
1	−2.5
2	−4

Method 2: Use a Graphing Calculator

Clear all equations from the [Y=] window and turn off any stat plots.
- Press [2nd] [STATPLOT] **4:PlotsOff** [ENTER].
- Press [Y=]. Enter the first equation in Y1. Press [ZOOM] **6:Standard** to graph the first relation. For the other relations, just press [GRAPH].
- Sketch each graph in your notes and label it with its relation.

i)

ii)

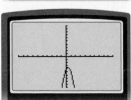

iii)

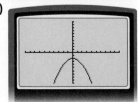

iv)

Technology Tip

^ means "raised to the exponent"

Method 3: Use *The Geometer's Sketchpad®*

- Open a **New Sketch**. From the **Graph** menu, choose **Plot New Function**.
- In the **New Function** window, type $3x + 4$. Select **OK**.
- From the **Display** menu, choose **Color**. Select a unique colour for that graph and relation. Deselect the relation and the graph.
- Repeat these steps to graph the other relations.

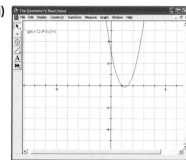

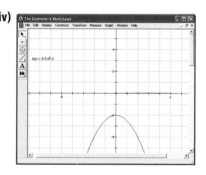

b) $y = 2x^2 - 5x + 3$, $y = -4x^2 + 3x - 4$, and $y = -0.5x^2 - 2$ result in parabolas when graphed. These are quadratic relations.

c) Each equation that results in a parabola has an x^2-term.

Key Concepts

- The graph of a quadratic relation is a parabola.
- For any quadratic relation, second differences are constant.
- Every quadratic relation has an x^2-term; the degree of the polynomial is 2.

Discuss the Concepts

D1. How can you use the table of values for a relation to determine if the relation is linear or quadratic?

D2. Write two different quadratic relations. Explain why they are quadratic.

For help with question 1, refer to Example 1.

1. Graph each relation. Determine if the relation is linear, quadratic, or neither.

a)
x	y
−3	−32
−1	−12
1	0
3	4
5	0
7	−12
9	−32

b)
x	y
0	−3
1	5
2	13
3	21
4	29
5	37
6	45

c)
x	y
5	−18
6	−11
7	−10
8	−9
9	−2
10	17
11	54

d)
x	y
2	73
4	97
6	97
8	73
10	25
12	−47
14	−143

e)
x	y
−2	0
−1	−15
0	−16
1	−9
2	0
3	5
4	0

f)
x	y
0	0
1	1
4	2
9	3
16	4
25	5
36	6

For help with question 2, refer to Example 2.

2. Which of these relations are quadratic? How do you know?

a)
x	y
−30	250
−29	241
−28	232
−27	223
−26	214
−25	205
−24	196

b)
x	y
18	0
20	3
22	4
24	4
26	0
28	−5
30	−12

c)
x	y
3	128
6	200
9	288
12	392
15	512
18	648
21	800

d)
x	y
1	2
2	4
3	8
4	16
5	32
6	64
7	128

For help with question 3, refer to Example 3.

3. a) Predict which relations are quadratic. Explain your reasoning.

   i) $y = 14x^2 - 5x + 7$ **ii)** $y = -8x + 5$

   iii) $y = 3x^2 + 2$ **iv)** $y = 2^x$

   v) $y = 3 + 2x - 15x^2$ **vi)** $y = 4 + x$

   b) Check your predictions by graphing each relation.

4. Does each graph have a maximum or minimum value? Use the graph to estimate the maximum or minimum.

a) Bridge Cable Height vs Distance

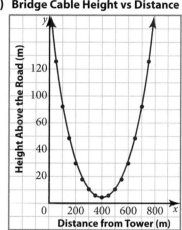

b) Bungee Jump

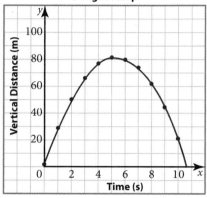

c) Braking Distances

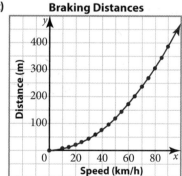

Apply B

5. Bonita and Carl ran a race. They used a CBR™ to measure their distance over time.

Time (s)	0	1	2	3	4	5
Bonita's Distance (m)	0.00	2.50	5.00	7.50	10.00	12.50
Carl's Distance (m)	0.00	0.75	3.00	6.75	12.00	18.75

a) Graph the data for Bonita and Carl on the same set of axes.

b) Which runner's distance–time relationship is quadratic? Explain.

6. A cannonball is shot horizontally from the top of a cliff. Its path can be modelled by the relation $h = 150 - 4.9t^2$, where h is the cannonball's height above the ground, in metres, and t is the time, in seconds.

a) Copy and complete the table.

b) Is the relation quadratic? How do you know?

c) Graph the relation.

Time (s)	Height (m)
0	
1	
2	
3	
4	
5	

7. Two balls are thrown upward at 15 m/s: one on Earth, near sea level, and one on the moon. The path of the ball on Earth is given by the relation $h = -4.9t^2 + 15t$, where h is the ball's height above the ground, in metres, and t is the time, in seconds. The path of the ball on the moon is given by the relation $h = -0.8t^2 + 15t$.

a) Create a table of values for each relation.

b) Refer to the graphing calculator screen shown below. Which curve models each relation? Justify your answer.

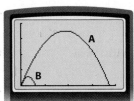

Literacy Connect

8. These words contain the prefix "quad."
- Quadrilateral: a polygon with four sides
- Quadriceps: a muscle divided into four parts that unite in a single tendon at the knee
- Quadruped: a four-legged animal

a) What does the prefix "quad" mean?

b) Explain how the word *quadratic* relates to the relation $y = ax^2 + bx + c$.

9. A farmer wants to use 100 m of fencing to build a small rectangular pen for his llamas. He would like the pen to have the greatest possible area.

a) Copy and complete the table. Provide six possible sets of dimensions for the pen.

Length (m)	Width (m)	Perimeter (m)
40	10	$2(40) + 2(10) = 100$

b) Add a fourth column to the table. Calculate the area of each pen.

c) Draw a graph to compare length and area.

d) Use the graph to determine the dimensions of the pen with the greatest possible area.

Chapter Problem

10. For part of a new extreme sports video game, you have to model the path of a snowboarder jumping off a ledge. The mathematical model developed from a video clip is $h = -0.05d^2 + 11.25$ where h is the snowboarder's height above the base of the cliff and d is the snowboarder's horizontal distance from the base of the cliff, both in metres.

a) Create a table of values for the relation. Choose consecutive d-values.

b) Graph the relation.

c) At what horizontal distance from the cliff will the snowboarder land?

Achievement Check

11. Toothpicks can be arranged to create equilateral triangles, where n is the number of toothpicks on one side.

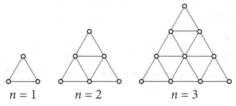

$n = 1$ $n = 2$ $n = 3$

a) Draw triangles that have 4, 5, and 6 toothpicks on one side.

b) Copy and complete the table. Graph the relation between side length and total number of toothpicks.

Side length, n	Total number of toothpicks, T	First Differences	Second Differences
0	0		
1			
2			
3			
4			
5			

c) Use first and second differences to determine if the relationship between the side length of a triangle and the total number of toothpicks is quadratic. Explain how your graph supports your answer.

d) How many toothpicks are needed to build a triangle with a side length of 20 toothpicks?

e) What is the side length of the largest triangle that can be made with 200 toothpicks?

12. A police officer is parked on the side of the road. She sees a speeding car. The distance between the speeding car and the spot where the police car was parked is given by the relation $d = 20t$, where d is the distance, in metres, and t is the time, in seconds. The officer accelerates to catch the speeding car. Her distance from the spot where she was parked is given by the relation $d = 1.5t^2$. When will the officer catch up with the speeder? How far will she be from the spot where she was parked?

13. Suzy challenges Oliver to a 100-m race. Suzy runs and Oliver rides his bicycle. Suzy's speed is modelled by the relation $d = 3t$ and Oliver's speed is modelled by the relation $d = 0.1t^2$. For both, d is the distance, in metres, and t is the time, in seconds. Use a graph to determine who will win the race.

14. **a)** For the relation $y = x^3$, make a table of values and graph the relation. Is this relation quadratic? Explain why or why not.

     b) For the relation $y = x^4$, make a table of values and graph the relation. Is the relation quadratic? Explain why or why not.

Literacy Connect

15. Many people think that the St. Louis Gateway Arch in St. Louis, Missouri, is in the shape of a parabola. However, it is actually in the shape of a catenary [ka-*tee*-na-ree]. Research the characteristics of a catenary and find other examples of this shape.

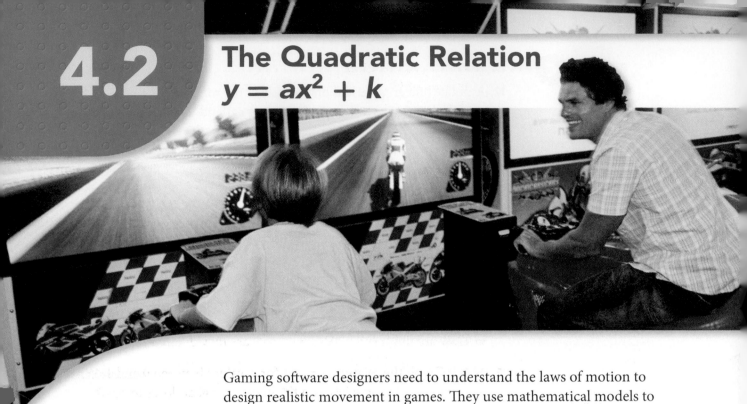

4.2

The Quadratic Relation $y = ax^2 + k$

Gaming software designers need to understand the laws of motion to design realistic movement in games. They use mathematical models to represent situations such as a daredevil cyclist jumping off a cliff.

Investigate

Graphs of $y = ax^2 + k$

Tools

- graphing calculator

Method 1: Use a Graphing Calculator

Clear any equations in the [Y=] window and turn off any stat plots.

1. Start by graphing $y = x^2$.
   - Press [Y=] and enter x^2 for Y1.
   - Use the left arrow key and move the cursor as far left as it will go. Change the graph's appearance by repeatedly pressing [ENTER] until a dotted line appears.
   - Press [ZOOM] **6:ZStandard** to graph the relation in the standard window.
   - As you add new relations, keep the graph of $y = x^2$ for comparison.

Part A: The Effect of Changing a

2. **a)** Graph each relation.

   i) $y = 4x^2$

   ii) $y = 0.5x^2$

   iii) $y = 12x^2$

   b) How are the graphs the same? How are they different?

   c) Press [2nd][TABLE]. Compare the y-values for corresponding x-values. What do you notice?

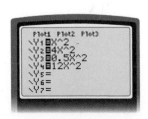

3. a) Graph each relation.

    i) $y = -3x^2$

    ii) $y = -0.2x^2$

    iii) $y = -10x^2$

b) How are the graphs the same? How are they different?

4. Write an equation for a parabola that

    a) opens downward

    b) opens upward

5. a) Graph each relation.

    i) $y = 0.1x^2$

    ii) $y = 0.05x^2$

    iii) $y = 0.6x^2$

b) How are the graphs the same? How are they different?

6. Reflect Graph the relation $y = ax^2$ for a-values between 0 and 1. What effect does changing a have on the graph as a gets closer to zero?

7. a) Graph each relation.

    i) $y = 2x^2$

    ii) $y = 5x^2$

    iii) $y = 8.2x^2$

b) How are the graphs the same? How are they different?

8. Reflect Graph the relation $y = ax^2$ for a-values greater than 1. What effect does changing a have on the graph as a increases?

9. Compare the graphs of $y = x^2$ and $y = ax^2$. For what values of a is the graph of $y = ax^2$

    a) narrower than the graph of $y = x^2$?

    b) wider than the graph of $y = x^2$?

10. When the shape of a parabola is described, it is often compared to the graph of $y = x^2$, using terms such as "vertically stretched" (narrower) or "vertically compressed" (wider). Write an equation for a parabola that is

    a) vertically stretched and opens upward

    b) vertically stretched and opens downward

    c) vertically compressed and opens upward

    d) vertically compressed and opens downward

Part B: The Effect of Changing k

Clear all relations except $y = x^2$.

11. a) Graph the relation $y = x^2 + 1$.

    b) How does the graph of $y = x^2 + 1$ compare to the graph of $y = x^2$?

12. The relation $y = x^2 + 1$ is in the form of $y = x^2 + k$. What happens to the graph if the value of k increases? Graph the relation using different positive values of k.

13. Reflect Graph the relation using different negative values of k. How does the graph change as the value of k decreases?

14. Describe the position of the graph of $y = x^2 + k$ relative to the x-axis when the value of k is

    a) positive

    b) negative

    c) zero

15. One way to describe the position of the graph of $y = x^2 + k$ is to say that its vertex is translated upward or translated downward relative to the x-axis. Write an equation for a parabola with a vertex

    a) translated above the x-axis

    b) translated below the x-axis

    c) at the origin

> **Math** **Connect**
>
> A translation is one type of transformation. It is a slide. Other transformations include reflections and rotations.

Part C: The Effects of Changing a and k

The effects of changing a and k can be seen in a new equation $y = ax^2 + k$.

16. Write an equation for each parabola. Graph each relation.

    a) vertically stretched, opens upward, vertex is 4 units below the x-axis

    b) vertically compressed, opens downward, vertex is 2 units above the x-axis

    c) vertically stretched, opens downward, vertex is at the origin

17. Reflect You are given a graph of a parabola and must write its equation in the form $y = ax^2 + k$. Which value is easier to determine, a or k? Explain.

Method 2: Use *The Geometer's Sketchpad*®

Tools

- computer
- *The Geometer's Sketchpad*®
- 4.2 Investigation.gsp

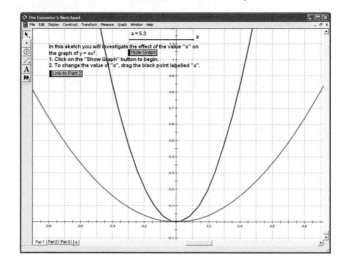

Go to *www.mcgrawhill.ca/links/foundations11* and follow the links to 4.2. Download the file **4.2 Investigation.gsp**. Open the sketch.

Part A: The Effect of Changing *a*

1. Select **Show Graph** and drag point *a*. How does changing the value of *a* affect the shape of the blue parabola?

2. **Reflect** Compare the blue parabola to the graph of $y = x^2$ when *a* is

   a) positive   **b)** negative

3. Write an equation for a parabola that

   a) opens downward   **b)** opens upward

4. **Reflect** Compare the blue parabola to the graph of $y = x^2$ when *a* is

   a) greater than 0 but less than 1

   b) greater than 1

   c) less than 0 but greater than -1

   d) less than -1

5. When the shape of a parabola is described, it is often compared to the graph of $y = x^2$, using terms such as "vertically stretched" (narrower) or "vertically compressed" (wider). Write an equation for a parabola that is

   a) vertically stretched and opens upward

   b) vertically stretched and opens downward

   c) vertically compressed and opens upward

   d) vertically compressed and opens downward

Part B: The Effect of Changing *k*

Select **Link to Part 2**.

6. Select **Show Graph** and drag point *k*. How does changing the value of *k* affect the position of the blue parabola?

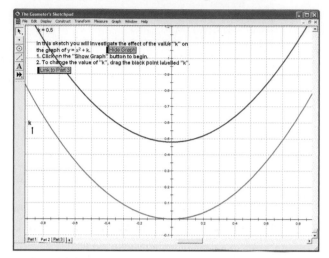

7. Reflect Describe the position of the blue parabola relative to the *x*-axis when *k* is

a) positive

b) negative

c) zero

8. One way to describe the position of the blue parabola is to say that its vertex is translated upward or translated downward relative to the *x*-axis. The equation for the blue parabola is $y = x^2 + k$. Write an equation for a parabola with a vertex

a) translated above the *x*-axis

b) translated below the *x*-axis

c) on the *x*-axis

Part C: The Effects of Changing *a* and *k*

The effects of changing the values of *a* and *k* can be combined in a new relation $y = ax^2 + k$.

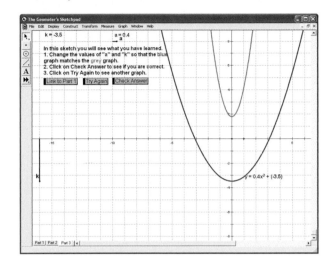

9. Select **Link to Part 3**. Find the equation for the grey parabola by changing the values of *a* and *k* in the blue parabola until it matches the grey parabola. Select **Try Again** to input different values of *a* and *k*. When you are satisfied with your solution, select **Check Answer** to see the equation for the grey parabola. A solution that is within one or two tenths is considered correct.

10. **Reflect** When matching the blue parabola to the grey parabola, which value was easier to determine, *a* or *k*? Explain.

Example 1

Identify Transformations of a Parabola

Describe the transformations that would be applied to the graph of $y = x^2$ to obtain the graph of each relation. Identify the vertex of the new graph. Sketch the graph.

a) $y = 3x^2 - 5$

b) $y = 0.4x^2 - 10$

c) $y = -11x^2 + 8$

Solution

Each time, sketch the graph of $y = x^2$. Plot the points (0, 0), (1, 1), (−1, 1), (2, 4), and (−2, 4) and draw a smooth curve through the points. To sketch the graph of the transformed equation, find the coordinates of the vertex for the graph of the new equation. Then adjust the shape of $y = x^2$ if necessary, starting at the new vertex.

a) The parabola is translated 5 units downward, so the vertex is at (0, −5).
Since $a > 1$, the parabola opens upward and is vertically stretched.

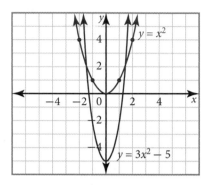

b) The parabola is translated 10 units downward, so the vertex is at (0, −10).
Since $0 < a < 1$, the parabola opens upward and is vertically compressed.

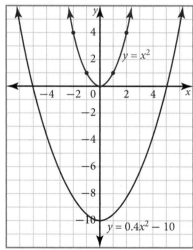

c) The parabola is translated 8 units upward, so the vertex is at (0, 8).
Since $a < -1$, the parabola opens downward and is vertically stretched.

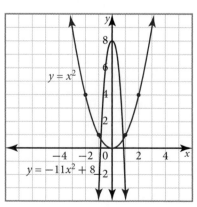

Example 2

Describe the Shape of a Parabola

In each standard viewing window, the graph of $y = x^2$ is shown as a dotted parabola. Describe the shape and position of each solid parabola relative to the graph of $y = x^2$ in terms of a and k.

a) 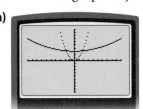 **b)** 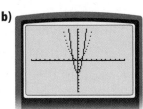 **c)**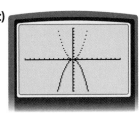

Solution

For each parabola, start with the vertex.

a) The vertex has been translated 3 units above the x-axis, so $k = 3$. The coordinates of the vertex are $(0, 3)$.

The parabola opens upward, so a is positive.

The graph is vertically compressed relative to the graph of $y = x^2$, so $0 < a < 1$.

b) The vertex has been translated 4 units below the x-axis, so $k = -4$. The coordinates of the vertex are $(0, -4)$.

The parabola opens upward, so a is positive.

The graph is vertically stretched relative to the graph of $y = x^2$, so $a > 1$.

c) The vertex is on the x-axis, so $k = 0$. The coordinates of the vertex are $(0, 0)$.

The parabola has been reflected in the x-axis.
The parabola opens downward, so a is negative.

The parabola appears to have the same shape as the graph of $y = x^2$, so a is approximately -1.

Example 3

Predict the Equation of a Parabola Without Using Technology

During filming of the *Lord of the Rings* trilogy, Andy Serkis, the actor who played the character Gollum, wore a motion capture suit. The motion of the dots on the suit was analysed by computer to model the motion of the computer-generated image of Gollum.

Suppose it makes sense to have negative time values. The graph shows Gollum's height above the ground over time as he jumped from one rock to another.

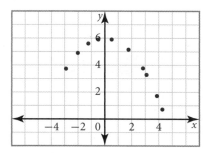

Write a relation in the form $y = ax^2 + k$ to represent Gollum's jump.

Solution

The vertex is 6 units above the x-axis, so $k = 6$. The coordinates of the vertex are $(0, 6)$.

The parabola is reflected in the x-axis. The parabola opens downward, so a is negative.

To estimate the value of a, graph $y = -x^2 + 6$ on the same set of axes as the parabola that represents Gollum's jump. Here $a = -1$, so the orientations of the parabolas are the same.

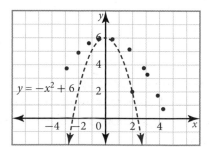

The parabola that represents Gollum's jump is vertically compressed relative to the graph of $y = -x^2 + 6$, so $-1 < a < 0$.

Use systematic trial to find the value of a. Test a point, such as $x = 2$.

Value of a	Equation	Calculation	Point	Does it match Gollum's graph?
$a = -0.5$ $x = 2$	$y = -0.5x^2 + 6$	$y = -0.5(2)^2 + 6$ $= -2 + 6$ $= 4$	$(2, 4)$	The point is below the parabola that represents Gollum's jump. The graph of $y = -0.5x^2 + 6$ needs to be vertically compressed.
$a = -0.1$ $x = 2$	$y = -0.1x^2 + 6$	$y = -0.1(2)^2 + 6$ $= -0.4 + 6$ $= 5.6$	$(2, 5.6)$	The point is above the parabola that represents Gollum's jump. The graph of $y = -0.1x^2 + 6$ needs to be vertically stretched.
$a = -0.3$ $x = 2$	$y = -0.3x^2 + 6$	$y = -0.3(2)^2 + 6$ $= -1.2 + 6$ $= 4.8$	$(2, 4.8)$	The point appears to lie on the parabola that represents Gollum's jump.

Choosing $a = 0.5$ is a good way to start since it is halfway between 0 and 1.

Try a value greater than -0.5, but less than -0.1.

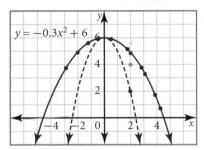

$y = -0.3x^2 + 6$

Gollum's jump can be modelled by the relation $y = -0.3x^2 + 6$.

Key Concepts

For any quadratic relation of the form $y = ax^2 + k$:

- The value of a determines the orientation and shape of the parabola.
  - If $a > 0$, the parabola opens upward.
  - If $a < 0$, the parabola is reflected in the x-axis; it opens downward.
  - If $-1 < a < 1$, the parabola is vertically compressed relative to the graph of $y = x^2$.
  - If $a > 1$ or $a < -1$, the parabola is vertically stretched relative to the graph of $y = x^2$.
- The value of k determines the vertical position of the parabola.
  - If $k > 0$, the vertex of the parabola is k units above the x-axis.
  - If $k < 0$, the vertex of the parabola is k units below the x-axis.
- The coordinates of the vertex are $(0, k)$.

D1. You are generating a table of values for a relation of the form $y = ax^2 + k$. Why are the coordinates of the vertex the easiest points to determine?

D2. Compare each parabola labelled $y = ax^2 + k$ to the graph of $y = x^2$. Describe what you know about the values of a and k.

a)

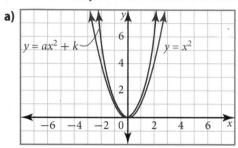

b)

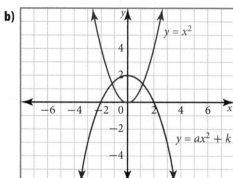

Practise **A** •

For help with questions 1 to 4, refer to Example 1.

1. In each standard viewing window, the graph of $y = x^2$ is shown as a dotted parabola and the graph of a relation of the form $y = ax^2$ is shown as a solid parabola. For each solid parabola, is a less than -1, between 0 and -1, between 0 and 1, or greater than 1? Explain.

a)

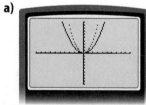

b)

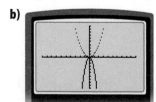

c)

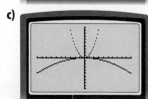

d)

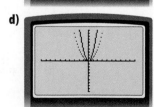

2. In each standard viewing window, the graph of $y = x^2$ is shown as a dotted parabola and the graph of a relation of the form $y = ax^2 + k$ is shown as a solid parabola. For each solid parabola, is k positive or negative? Explain.

a)

b)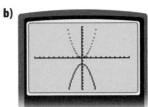

c)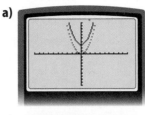

d)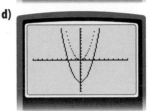

3. For each solid parabola in question 2, identify the value of k and the coordinates of the vertex.

4. Describe the shape and position of each parabola relative to the graph of $y = x^2$. Sketch each graph.

   a) $y = 3x^2$
   b) $y = x^2 + 3$
   c) $y = -0.5x^2$
   d) $y = x^2 - 12$
   e) $y = 0.15x^2 + 13$
   f) $y = -7x^2 + 6$
   g) $y = -0.3x^2 - 5$
   h) $y = 10x^2 - 9$

For help with question 5, refer to Example 2.

5. In each standard viewing window, the graph of $y = x^2$ is shown as a dotted parabola. Describe the shape and position of each solid parabola relative to the graph of $y = x^2$ in terms of a and k.

a)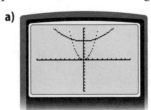

b)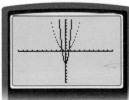

c)

d)

For help with question 6, refer to Example 3.

6. Graph each relation. Then, represent the relation with an equation of the form $y = ax^2 + k$.

a)

x	y
−0.5	−5.0
0.0	−6.0
0.5	−5.0
1.0	−2.0
1.5	3.0
2.0	10.0

b)

x	y
−10	1
−5	4
0	5
5	4
10	1
15	−4

c)

x	y
−9	−48
−6	−23
−3	−8
0	−3
3	−8
6	−23

Apply **B** •

7. Suppose each pair of relations were graphed on the same set of axes.
   - Which parabola would be the widest (most vertically compressed)?
   - Which parabola would have its vertex farther from the x-axis?
   Justify your answers.

   a) $y = 0.2x^2$ $\qquad\qquad$ $y = 5x^2 + 6$

   b) $y = 3x^2 + 9$ $\qquad\qquad$ $y = -0.4x^2 - 8$

   c) $y = 5x^2 + 7$ $\qquad\qquad$ $y = 2x^2 - 5$

   d) $y = 0.1x^2$ $\qquad\qquad$ $y = 0.25x^2 + 11$

   e) $y = -0.2x^2 - 1$ $\qquad\qquad$ $y = 0.03x^2 + 2$

   f) $y = x^2 - 6$ $\qquad\qquad$ $y = 0.9x^2 + 6$

Chapter Problem

8. You are creating a computer model of a skateboarder jumping off a ramp for the next part of your game. The path of the skateboarder is modelled by the relation $h = -0.85t^2 + 2$, where h is the skateboarder's height above the ground, in metres, and t is the time, in seconds.

   a) How far from the ground will the skateboarder be after 0.5 s? After 1 s?

   b) For how long will the skateboarder be in the air?

9. The stopping distance of a particular car can be modelled by the relation $d = 0.006s^2$, where d is the distance, in metres, and s is the speed in kilometres per hour.

   a) Graph the relation.

   b) Determine the stopping distance for the car if it is travelling at
      i) 50 km/h ii) 60 km/h iii) 100 km/h iv) 110 km/h

c) The speed limit on city roads is 50 km/h, while the speed limit on highways is 100 km/h. Use your answers to part b) to calculate the extra stopping distance needed for a car travelling 10 km/h over the speed limit in the city. Compare this to the extra stopping distance needed for a car travelling 10 km/h over the speed limit on the highway.

10. The path of water from this fountain can be modelled by a relation of the form $y = ax^2 + k$.

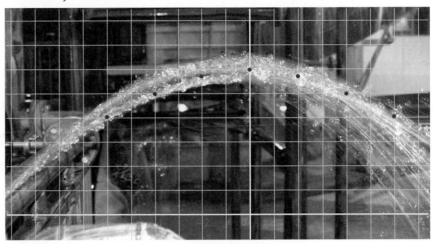

a) What are the coordinates of the vertex of this parabola?

b) Determine the approximate value of a.

c) Write an equation to model the parabola.

Extend ·

11. In January 2006, Jamie Pierre set a new world record with a cliff jump of more than 77 m into deep snow. His jump from the top of the cliff can be modelled by the relation $d = 4.9t^2$, where d is his distance from below the top of the cliff, in metres, and t is the time, in seconds.

a) How much farther did Jamie fall in the third second of his jump compared to the first second?

b) How long did it take Jamie to make the 77-m jump?

12. The path of a cannonball shot horizontally off a cliff can be modelled by the relation $h = 25 - \dfrac{4.9d^2}{V_0^2}$, where h is the cannonball's height above the ground, in metres, d is the cannonball's horizontal distance from the base of the cliff, in metres, and V_0 is the initial velocity of the cannonball, in metres per second. How much farther will a cannonball travel before hitting the ground if it is shot at an initial velocity of 50 m/s compared to an initial velocity of 35 m/s?

4.3

The Quadratic Relation $y = a(x - h)^2$

Karry-Anne is an engineer. She is designing a bridge. She has to determine a relation that models the shape of the cables that support the road deck. In her model, Karry-Anne must consider the shape, orientation, and position of the cables. Each of these factors will contribute to the formula, as you will learn in your investigation of graphs in this section.

Investigate

Graphs of $y = a(x - h)^2$

Tools

- graphing calculator

Method 1: Use a Graphing Calculator

Clear all equations from the equation window.

1. Start by graphing $y = x^2$.
   - Press ⸤ Y= ⸥ and enter x^2 for Y1.
   - Use the left arrow key to move the cursor as far left as it will go. Press ⸤ ENTER ⸥ repeatedly to change the line style to the dotted line.
   - Press ⸤ ZOOM ⸥ **6:ZStandard**.
   - As you add new relations, keep the graph of $y = x^2$ for comparison.

Part A: The Effect of Changing h

2. **a)** Graph each relation.

   i) $y = (x + 2)^2$ **ii)** $y = (x + 4)^2$

   b) How does the shape of each graph compare to the shape of $y = x^2$?

   c) What is similar about the positions of all three graphs?

   d) Each relation in part a) has a constant term inside the brackets. How does this constant term relate to the position of the graph?

3. a) Graph each relation.

i) $y = (x - 3)^2$ **ii)** $y = (x - 6)^2$

b) What is similar about the positions of these graphs and the position of $y = x^2$?

c) Each relation in part a) has a constant term inside the brackets. How does the constant term relate to the position of the graph?

4. A quadratic relation is in the form $y = (x - h)^2$. Describe the position of the graph of $y = (x - h)^2$ relative to the y-axis when h is

a) positive **b)** negative **c)** zero

5. A quadratic relation is in the form $y = (x - h)^2$. Substitute a value for h to write an equation for a parabola with a vertex

a) translated to the right of the y-axis

b) translated to the left of the y-axis

c) on the y-axis

Part B: The Effects of Changing *a* and *h*

The effects of a and h can be combined in a new relation $y = a(x - h)^2$.

6. Write an equation for each parabola. Use a graphing calculator to check your answers.

a) vertically compressed, opens upward, vertex at $(5, 0)$

b) vertically stretched, opens downward, vertex is $(-3, 0)$

c) vertically stretched, opens upward, vertex is on the y-axis

7. Reflect Suppose you are to write a relation in the form $y = a(x - h)^2$ given the graph of a parabola. Which value is easier to determine, a or h? Explain.

Tools

- computers
- *The Geometer's Sketchpad®*
- 4.3 Investigation.gsp

Method 2: Use *The Geometer's Sketchpad®*

Go to *www.mcgrawhill.ca/links/foundations11* and follow the links to 4.3. Download the file **4.3 Investigation.gsp**. Open the sketch.

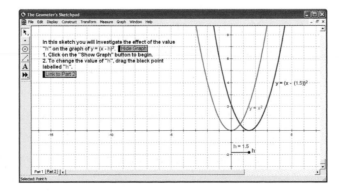

Part A: The Effect of Changing *h*

1. Select **Show Graph** and drag point *h*. How does changing the value of *h* affect the position of the blue parabola?

2. Describe the position of the blue parabola relative to the *y*-axis when *h* is

   a) positive   **b)** negative   **c)** zero

3. The blue parabola can be represented by a relation of the form $y = (x - h)^2$. Substitute a value for *h* to write an equation for a parabola with a vertex

   a) translated to the right of the *y*-axis

   b) translated to the left of the *y*-axis

   c) on the *y*-axis

Part B: The Effects of Changing *a* and *h*

The effects of *a* and *h* can be combined in a new relation $y = a(x - h)^2$.

4. Select **Link to Part 2**. Find an equation for the grey parabola by changing the values of *a* and *h* in the blue parabola until it matches the grey parabola. Select **Try Again** to input different values of *a* and *h*. When you are satisfied with your solution, select **Check Answer** to see the equation for the grey parabola. A solution that is within one or two tenths is considered correct.

5. **Reflect** You are given the graph of a parabola and must write the equation of the parabola in the form $y = a(x - h)^2$. Which value is easier to determine, *a* or *h*? Explain.

Notice the negative sign in the equation $y = a(x - h)^2$.

When *h* is positive, the number after the subtraction symbol is positive.

For example,
$y = 3(x - \boxed{8})^2$ $y = a(x - \boxed{h})^2$ The 8 replaces the *h* and the subtraction symbol does not change.
$h = +8$

When *h* is negative, the number after the subtraction symbol is negative.

For example,
$y = 4(x + 6)^2$ becomes
$y = 4(x - (\boxed{-6}))^2$ $y = a(x - \boxed{h})^2$
$h = -6$

Example 1

Identify Transformations of a Parabola

Describe the transformations that would be applied to the graph of $y = x^2$ to obtain the graph of each relation. Identify the vertex of the new graph. Sketch the graph.

a) $y = -0.1(x - 6)^2$

b) $y = 4(x + 7)^2$

c) $y = 0.9(x + 3)^2$

Solution

Each time, sketch the graph of $y = x^2$. Plot the points $(0, 0)$, $(1, 1)$, $(-1, 1)$, $(2, 4)$, and $(-2, 4)$ and draw a smooth curve through the points. To sketch the graph of the transformed equation, find the coordinates of the vertex for the graph of the new equation. Then adjust the shape of $y = x^2$ if necessary.

a) The parabola is translated 6 units to the right, so the vertex is at $(6, 0)$.
Since $-1 < a < 0$, the parabola is reflected in the x-axis (it opens downward) and is vertically compressed.

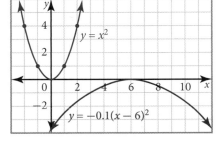

b) The parabola is translated 7 units to the left, so the vertex is at $(-7, 0)$.
Since $a > 1$, the parabola is vertically stretched and opens upward.

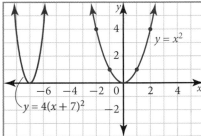

c) The parabola is translated 3 units to the left, so the vertex is at $(-3, 0)$.
Since $0 < a < 1$, the parabola is vertically compressed and opens upward.

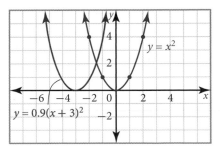

Example 2

Describe the Shape of a Parabola

In each standard viewing window, the graph of $y = x^2$ is shown as a dotted parabola. Describe the shape and position of each solid parabola relative to the graph of $y = x^2$ in terms of a and h.

a) **b)** **c)**

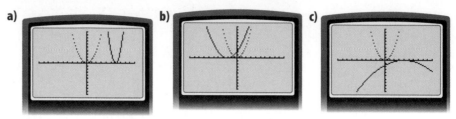

Solution

For each graph, start with the vertex.

a) The vertex has been translated 6 units to the right of the y-axis, so $h = 6$. The coordinates of the vertex are $(6, 0)$.

The parabola opens upward, so a is positive.

The parabola is vertically stretched relative to the graph of $y = x^2$, so $a > 1$.

b) The vertex has been translated 2 units to the left of the y-axis, so $h = -2$. The coordinates of the vertex are $(-2, 0)$.

The parabola opens upward, so a is positive.

The parabola is vertically compressed relative to the graph of $y = x^2$, so $0 < a < 1$.

c) The vertex has been translated 4 units to the right of the y-axis, so $h = 4$. The coordinates of the vertex are $(4, 0)$.

The parabola has been reflected in the x-axis. The parabola opens downward, so a is negative.

The parabola is vertically compressed relative to the graph of $y = x^2$, so $-1 < a < 0$.

Key Concepts

For any quadratic relation of the form $y = a(x - h)^2$:

- The value of a determines the orientation and shape of the parabola.
  - If $a > 0$, the parabola opens upward.
  - If $a < 0$, the parabola opens downward.
  - If $-1 < a < 1$, the parabola is vertically compressed relative to the graph of $y = x^2$.
  - If $a > 1$ or $a < -1$, the parabola is vertically stretched relative to the graph of $y = x^2$.
- The value of h determines the horizontal position of the parabola.
  - If $h > 0$, the vertex of the parabola is h units to the right of the y-axis.
  - If $h < 0$, the vertex of the parabola is h units to the left of the y-axis.
- The coordinates of the vertex are $(h, 0)$.

Discuss the Concepts

D1. You are given a graph of a parabola and must write its equation in the form $y = a(x - h)^2$. Which value is easier to determine, a or h? Explain.

D2. Compare each parabola labelled $y = a(x - h)^2$ to the graph of $y = x^2$. Describe what you know about the values of a and h.

a)

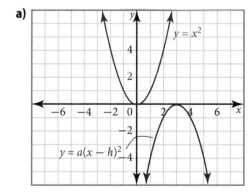

b)

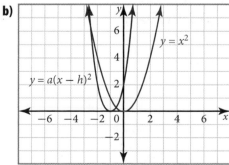

For help with questions 1 and 2, refer to Example 1.

1. In each standard viewing window, the graph of $y = x^2$ is shown as a dotted parabola and the graph of a relation of the form $y = a(x - h)^2$ is shown as a solid parabola.

For each solid parabola, identify the value of h and the coordinates of the vertex.

a)
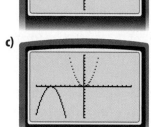

b)
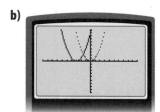

c)
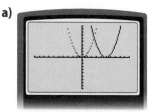

d)
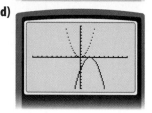

2. Describe the graph of each parabola relative to the graph of $y = x^2$ in terms of a and h. Sketch each graph.

a) $y = (x - 7)^2$

b) $y = -(x + 3)^2$

c) $y = 1.5(x + 8)^2$

d) $y = -0.8(x - 2)^2$

e) $y = 0.1(x - 5)^2$

f) $y = 2(x + 1)^2$

g) $y = -2(x - 8)^2$

h) $y = 0.3(x + 14)^2$

For help with question 3, refer to Example 2.

3. In each standard viewing window, the graph of $y = x^2$ is shown as a dotted parabola. Describe the shape and position of each solid parabola relative to the graph of $y = x^2$ in terms of a and h.

a)
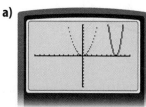

b)
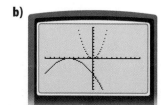

c)
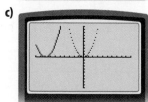

d)
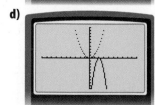

4. Graph each relation. Then, write a relation in the form of $y = a(x - h)^2$ that models each parabola.

a)

x	y
0	-32
1	-18
2	-8
3	-2
4	0
5	-2

b)

x	y
-7.0	2.0
-6.0	0.5
-5.0	0.0
-4.0	0.5
-3.0	2.0
-2.0	4.5

Apply **B** •

5. Suppose each pair of relations were graphed on one set of axes. Which parabola would have its vertex farther from the y-axis? Justify your answers.

a) $y = 2(x + 3)^2$ $y = 0.1(x + 1)^2$

b) $y = 9(x - 3)^2$ $y = -0.2(x - 8)^2$

c) $y = 0.001(x + 3)^2$ $y = 32(x - 10)^2$

d) $y = -15(x - 2)^2$ $y = 0.85(x + 9)^2$

Literacy Connect

6. Why do you think the general equation for a quadratic relation is written as $y = a(x - h)^2$ instead of $y = a(x + h)^2$?

7. The top view of a car headlight shows that the back part of the headlight is parabolic. For the headlight shown, the shape of the parabolic part can be modelled by the relation $d = 0.08(w - 7)^2$, where d is the depth of the parabola and w is the width of the headlight from edge to edge.

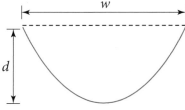

a) Draw a graph to represent the shape of the back part of the headlight.

b) How wide is the headlight when the parabola is 4 cm deep?

Gary Allan High School – Halton Hills
96 Guelph Street
Georgetown, ON. L7G 3Z5

8. In another part of the video game, you are modelling a mountain biker performing a stunt. The mountain biker is speeding along the edge of a mesa toward a cliff, marked *P*. A rock ramp begins 10 m before, and 10 m below, *P*. The mountain biker must judge when to jump off the mesa to land safely on the ramp. The mountain biker's path through the air (shown with the dotted line) can be modelled using the relation $y = -\dfrac{5}{v^2}(x - h)^2$, where *v* is the mountain biker's speed, in metres per second, *y* is the mountain biker's height above the top of the mesa, in metres, and *x* is the mountain biker's horizontal distance from the cliff, *P*, in metres.

a) The value of *h* is the distance from the cliff at which the mountain biker must jump to land safely on the ramp, for a given speed. Suppose the mountain biker's speed is 5 m/s. Find the value of *h*.

b) If the mountain biker's speed increases, will the value of *h* from part a) increase, decrease, or remain the same? Explain your reasoning.

c) Check your answer to part b) by calculating a value of *h* for a speed of 10 m/s.

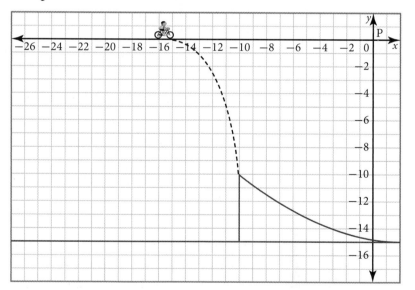

9. The curve formed by the cables on a suspension bridge can be modelled by the relation $y = a(x - h)^2$, where y is the height above the bridge deck and x is the horizontal distance from one support tower, both in metres.

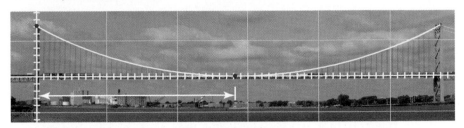

a) What are the coordinates of the vertex of this parabola?

b) Determine the approximate value of a.

c) Write an equation for the quadratic relation that models the parabola.

d) Based on your equation, at what height above the deck are the cables attached to the support tower?

Extend   •••

10. a) Copy and complete the table.

x	$y = (x - 3)^2$	$y = 3 + \sqrt{x}$	$y = 3 - \sqrt{x}$
0			
1			
2			
3			
4			
5			
6			
7			

b) Graph the three relations on the same set of axes.

c) Compare the second and third graphs to the first graph. How are the graphs similar? How are they different?

4.4 The Quadratic Relation $y = a(x - h)^2 + k$

Human immunodeficiency virus (HIV), the virus that causes AIDS, is a global concern. In an effort to combat the spread of HIV in the United States, the Department of Health developed a prevention program. The table shows the number of infants with HIV born each year from 1985, the year the program began, to 1998.

Prenatal HIV Transmission

Year	Years Since 1985	Number of Cases
1985	0	210
1986	1	380
1987	2	500
1990	5	780
1993	8	770
1994	9	680
1996	11	460
1998	13	300

The relationship between the number of infants with HIV and the number of years since the start of the program appears to be quadratic.

Graphs of $y = a(x - h)^2 + k$

Method 1: Use a Graphing Calculator

Clear all equations from the [Y=] window and turn off any stat plots.

1. Start by graphing $y = 2(x - 3)^2 - 5$.
   • Press ⬚Y=⬚ and enter $2(x - 3)^2 - 5$ for Y1.
   • Press ⬚ZOOM⬚ **6:ZStandard** to graph the relation in the standard window.

Technology Tip
If you do not see the cursor, it might be off screen. Look at the coordinates at the bottom of the screen to locate the cursor. Use the arrow keys to move the cursor into the visible screen area.

2. Find the minimum value for the graph.
   • Press ⬚2nd⬚[CALC] **3:minimum**.
   • Use the arrow keys to move the cursor to the left of the minimum point and press ⬚ENTER⬚.
   • Use the arrow keys to move the cursor to the right of the minimum point and press ⬚ENTER⬚ twice.
   • The minimum value will be displayed. Record the equation and the coordinates of the vertex.

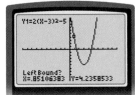

3. Graph each relation. Find the minimum value for each graph. Record each equation and the coordinates of the vertex.

   a) $y = 0.2(x - 5)^2 + 7$

   b) $y = 10(x - 8)^2 - 9$

4. For these relations, a is negative, so the y-coordinate of the vertex represents a maximum. Graph each equation. Find the maximum value for each graph. Record each relation and the coordinates of the vertex.

   a) $y = -4(x + 7)^2 + 2$

   b) $y = -0.5(x - 8)^2 + 1$

   c) $y = -9(x + 4)^2 - 6$

5. Refer to your answers to questions 2 to 4. For each set of vertex coordinates, how does the minimum or maximum value relate to the relation?

6. **Reflect** If you are given the coordinates of the vertex of a parabola, do you have enough information to write an equation for the parabola? Explain why or why not.

Method 2: Use *The Geometer's Sketchpad®*.

Go to *www.mcgrawhill.ca/links/foundations11* and follow the links to 4.4. Download the file **4.4 Investigation.gsp**. Open the sketch.

1. Change the values of a, k, and h to create new parabolas. Which of the coefficients relate directly to the coordinates of the vertex?

2. Record the equation and the coordinates of the vertex for three different parabolas that
   a) open upward
   b) open downward

3. Refer to your answers to question 2. For each set of vertex coordinates, how does the minimum or maximum value relate to the equation?

   The effects of the values of a, h, and k can be combined in a new equation, $y = a(x - h)^2 + k$.

4. Select **Link to Part 2**. Find the equation for the grey parabola by changing the values of a, h, and k in the blue parabola until it matches the grey parabola. Select **Try Again** to input different values of a, h, and k. When you are satisfied with your solution, select **Check Answer** to see the equation for the grey parabola. A solution that is within one or two tenths is considered correct.

5. **Reflect** In question 4, did it matter in which order you changed the values of a, h, and k? Was there an order that helped you find the solution more easily?

vertex form
- a quadratic relation of the form $y = a(x - h)^2 + k$
- the coordinates of the vertex are (h, k)

The equation $y = a(x - h)^2 + k$ is the **vertex form** of a quadratic relation.

Example 1

Sketch Graphs of $y = a(x - h)^2 + k$

Describe the graph of each relation, and identify the coordinates of the vertex. Sketch each graph.

a) $y = 15(x + 5)^2 + 7$
b) $y = 0.5(x - 1)^2 + 9$
c) $y = -4(x + 6)^2 - 8$

Solution

To sketch the graph of $y = x^2$, plot the points $(1, 1)$, $(-1, 1)$, $(0, 0)$, $(2, 4)$, and $(-2, 4)$ and draw a smooth curve through the points. To sketch the graph of the transformed equation, find the coordinates of the vertex for the graph of the new equation.

a) The coordinates of the vertex are $(-5, 7)$.

Since $a > 1$, the parabola opens upward and is vertically stretched.

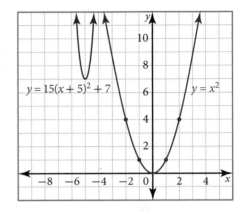

b) The coordinates of the vertex are $(1, 9)$.

Since $0 < a < 1$, the parabola opens upward and is vertically compressed.

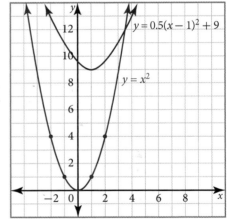

c) The coordinates of the vertex are $(-6, -8)$.

Since $a < -1$, the parabola opens downward and is vertically stretched.

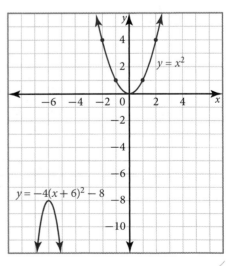

Example 2

Use Points to Sketch Graphs of $y = a(x - h)^2 + k$

For each relation:

i) Identify the coordinates of the vertex.

ii) Determine the x-coordinate of a point
  - 2 units to the left of the vertex
  - 2 units to the right of the vertex

iii) Use the x-values from part ii) to find two points on the parabola. Plot the two points and the vertex on the same set of axes.

iv) Sketch the parabola by drawing a smooth curve through the points.

a) $y = 2(x - 6)^2 + 3$

b) $y = -0.5(x + 9)^2 - 2$

Solution

a) $y = 2(x - 6)^2 + 3$

  i) vertex: $(6, 3)$

  ii) 2 units left: $x = 6 - 2$ 2 units right: $x = 6 + 2$

                 $= 4$ $= 8$

  iii) When $x = 4$,   When $x = 8$,

       $y = 2(4 - 6)^2 + 3$ $y = 2(8 - 6)^2 + 3$

          $= 2(-2)^2 + 3$ $= 2(2)^2 + 3$

          $= 11$ $= 11$

  The first point is $(4, 11)$.   The second point is $(8, 11)$.

  iv)
  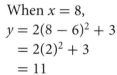

  Check: a is positive, so the parabola opens upward.
  $a > 1$, so the parabola is vertically stretched relative to the graph of $y = x^2$.

b) $y = -0.5(x + 9)^2 - 2$

      $= -0.5(x - (-9))^2 + (-2)$

  i) vertex: $(-9, -2)$

  ii) 2 units left: $x = -9 - 2$ 2 units right: $x = -9 + 2$

                  $= -11$ $= -7$

iii) When $x = -11$,   When $x = -7$,
$$y = -0.5(-11 + 9)^2 - 2 \qquad y = -0.5(-7 + 9)^2 - 2$$
$$= -0.5(-2)^2 - 2 \qquad\qquad = -0.5(2)^2 - 2$$
$$= -4 \qquad\qquad\qquad\qquad = -4$$

The first point is $(-11, -4)$. The second point is $(-7, -4)$.

iv)

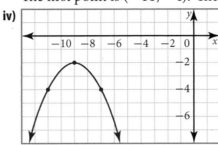

Check: a is negative, so the parabola opens downward.

$-1 < a < 1$, so the parabola is vertically compressed relative to the graph of $y = x^2$.

Due to the symmetry of a parabola, only the vertex and one other point are needed to sketch a parabola. For the non-vertex point, there is a corresponding point that is equidistant from the line of symmetry, $x = h$.

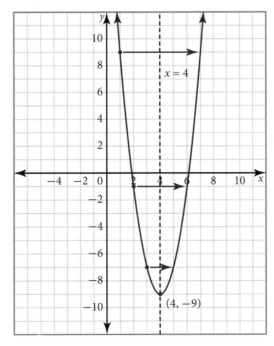

Example 3

Use Points to Determine the Value of *a*

Consider this parabola.

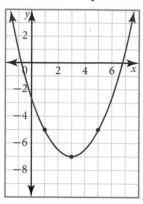

a) Find the coordinates of the vertex, and the values of h and k.

b) Identify the coordinates of the two other points shown.

c) Find the value of a by substituting the coordinates of the vertex and one of the other two points into the relation $y = a(x - h)^2 + k$.

d) Write an equation for the parabola.

Solution

a) The vertex is $(3, -7)$, so $h = 3$ and $k = -7$.

b) The coordinates of the other two points are $(1, -5)$ and $(5, -5)$.

c) Use $(x, y) = (1, -5)$ and $(h, k) = (3, -7)$ to solve for a.

$$y = a(x - h)^2 + k$$
$$-5 = a(1 - 3)^2 + (-7)$$
$$-5 = a(-2)^2 - 7 \qquad \text{Evaluate the expression in brackets,}$$
$$-5 = a(4) - 7 \qquad \text{then simplify.}$$
$$-5 + 7 = 4a - 7 + 7 \qquad \text{Add 7 to both sides.}$$
$$2 = 4a$$
$$\frac{2}{4} = \frac{4a}{4} \qquad \text{Divide both sides by 4.}$$
$$0.5 = a$$

d) An equation for the parabola is $y = 0.5(x - 3)^2 - 7$.

Key Concepts

- For any quadratic relation of the form $y = a(x - h)^2 + k$:
  - The value of a determines the orientation and shape of the parabola relative to the graph of $y = x^2$.
  - The coordinates of the vertex of the parabola are (h, k).
- To sketch a given quadratic relation, plot the vertex and two other points, one on either side of the vertex. Then, draw a smooth curve through the points.
- To determine the equation for a quadratic relation from a graph, use the vertex and another point to solve for a. Then, write the relation using the vertex and the value of a.

Discuss the Concepts

D1. There are two methods for graphing a quadratic relation:

  A determine the values of a, h, and k in the relation $y = a(x - h)^2 + k$ and sketch the graph

  B determine three points that satisfy the relation, plot the points, and join the points with a smooth curve

  a) Which method do you think is easier? Why?

  b) Which method do you think is more accurate? Why?

D2. Match each relation with its graph.

  a) $y = -(x + 1)^2 + 4$

  b) $y = 0.5(x - 1)^2 - 4$

  c) $y = (x - 1)^2 + 4$

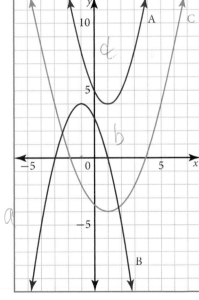

D3. Refer to Example 2, part iii). When you calculated the coordinates for the points two units to the right and the left of the vertex, what similarities did you notice in the calculations? How might these change if you found the coordinates of points three units to the right and the left of the vertex?

For help with questions 1 and 2, refer to Example 1.

1. For each parabola
    i) identify the coordinates of the vertex
    ii) determine whether *a* is positive or negative

a)

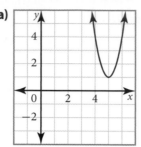

b)

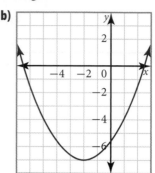

c)

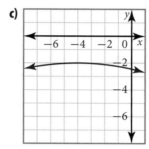

d)

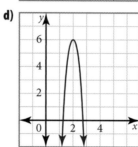

e)

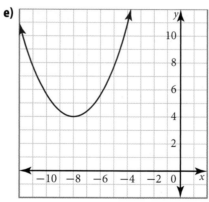

f)

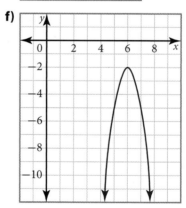

g)

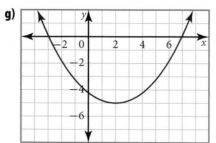

h)

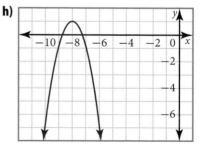

2. For each quadratic relation

   i) identify the coordinates of the vertex

   ii) determine if the parabola opens upward or downward

   iii) determine if the parabola is vertically stretched or vertically compressed

   iv) sketch the graph

   a) $y = 2(x - 3)^2 + 12$ **b)** $y = -0.5(x - 10)^2 - 1$

   c) $y = -7(x + 4)^2 - 8$ **d)** $y = -(x + 20)^2 - 5$

   e) $y = 0.5(x - 11)^2 - 3$ **f)** $y = 8(x + 2)^2 + 9$

   g) $y = -0.5(x + 6)^2 + 7$ **h)** $y = 2(x - 8)^2 + 2$

   i) $y = 7.5(x + 2)^2 - 1$ **j)** $y = -0.8(x - 4)^2 + 6$

For help with question 3, refer to Example 2.

3. Graph each quadratic relation by plotting the vertex and two other points. Then, draw a smooth curve through the points.

   a) $y = 4(x - 6)^2 + 10$ **b)** $y = -0.25(x + 4)^2 - 2$

   c) $y = 0.8(x + 1)^2 + 9$ **d)** $y = -2.5(x - 9)^2 - 5$

   e) $y = 0.2(x - 3)^2 - 7$ **f)** $y = 5(x + 7)^2 + 3$

   g) $y = 6(x + 2)^2 - 1$ **h)** $y = -0.5(x - 10)^2 + 6$

For help with questions 4 and 5, refer to Example 3.

4. Identify the coordinates of the vertex of each parabola. Then, write an equation for the relation in the form $y = a(x - h)^2 + k$.

a)

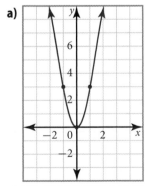

b)

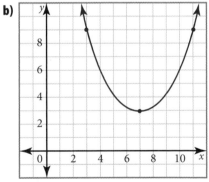

c)

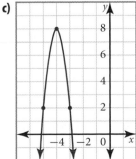

d)

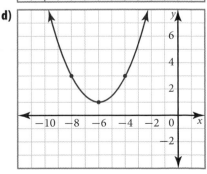

5. Write an equation for each parabola in the form $y = a(x - h)^2 + k$.

a)
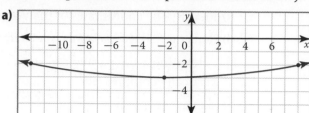

b)
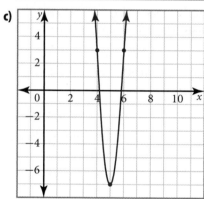

c)

d)
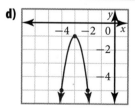

Apply **B** ·

6. A football was kicked. Its path can be modelled by the relation $h = -0.1(d - 8.7)^2 + 7.6$ where h is the football's height above the ground and d is the horizontal distance from where the football was kicked, both in metres.

a) What is the vertex of the parabola?

b) What is the football's initial height?

c) Sketch a graph of the football's path.

d) What does the vertex represent in terms of the football's path?

Solution

a) Use the *The Geometer's Sketchpad*®
to graph the relation.
- Open a new sketch.
- From the **Graph** menu, choose **Plot New Function**.
- Enter the relation with x as the variable instead of t.
- Select **OK**.
- From the **Graph** menu, choose **Grid Form>Rectangular Grid**.
  Stretch or shrink each scale by dragging the scale points at $(1, 0)$
  and $(0, 1)$.

The relation can also be
graphed by hand or using
a graphing calculator.

Technology Tip
The [^] key (shift 6)
is the symbol for an
exponent.

Technology Tip
To rescale the axes,
slide the points on the
x- and y-axes.

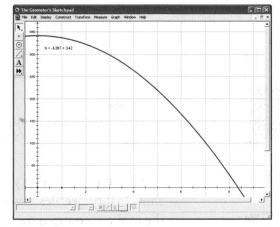

The graph is a parabola that opens downward.
$a = -4.9$, so the parabola is vertically stretched relative to
the graph of $y = x^2$.
$h = 0$ and $k = 342$, so the vertex is $(0, 342)$.

b) Method 1: Use the Equation

When the wrench was dropped, $t = 0$, so substitute 0 for t in the
relation:
$$h = -4.9t^2 + 342$$
$$= -4.9(0)^2 + 342$$
$$= 342$$

The wrench was 342 m above the ground when it was dropped.

Method 2: Use the Vertex

The vertex is a maximum, so $k = 342$ gives the wrench's maximum
distance from the ground. The wrench was 342 m above the ground
when it was dropped.

c) The relation will give a more accurate answer than the graph. To find the distance the wrench has fallen after 5 s, first calculate how far the wrench is above ground when $t = 5$.

$$h = -4.9t^2 + 342$$
$$= -4.9(5)^2 + 342$$
$$= -4.9(25) + 342$$
$$= -122.5 + 342$$
$$= 219.5$$

The wrench is 219.5 m above the ground. To find the distance the wrench has fallen, subtract 219.5 m from the wrench's initial height above the ground.

$$\text{Distance fallen} = 342 - 219.5$$
$$= 122.5$$

The wrench has fallen 122.5 m after 5 s.

d) To calculate the wrench's height above the ground after 10 s, substitute $t = 10$.

$$h = -4.9t^2 + 342$$
$$= -4.9(10)^2 + 342$$
$$= -4.9(100) + 342$$
$$= -490 + 342$$
$$= -148$$

The value of -148 does not make sense in this situation because it would mean that the wrench was 148 m below the ground after 10 s. The answer could make sense if the wrench fell down a well or into a lake, which would allow for a depth below ground level.

e) When the wrench hits the ground, $h = 0$.

$$h = -4.9t^2 + 342$$
$$0 = -4.9t^2 + 342$$
$$0 + 4.9t^2 = -4.9t^2 + 342 + 4.9t^2 \qquad \text{Add } 4.9t^2 \text{ to both sides.}$$
$$4.9t^2 = 342$$
$$\frac{4.9t^2}{4.9} = \frac{342}{4.9} \qquad \text{Divide both sides by 4.9.}$$
$$t^2 \doteq 69.80$$
$$\sqrt{t^2} \doteq \sqrt{69.80} \qquad \text{Find the square root of both sides.}$$
$$t \doteq 8.35$$

The wrench hits the ground after approximately 8.4 s.

Example 2

Quadratic Model for the Path of a Football

A football player kicks a football held 0.5 m above the ground. The football reaches a maximum height of 30 m at a horizontal distance of 18 m from the player.

a) Determine a quadratic relation that models the path of the football.

b) At what horizontal distance from the player does the football hit the ground?

Solution

a) Let y represent the height above the ground and x represent the horizontal distance from the player, both in metres.

The football reaches its maximum height of 30 m at a horizontal distance of 18 m, so the vertex is at (18, 30).

$$y = a(x - 18)^2 + 30$$

Substitute the coordinates of the vertex into the relation $y = a(x - h)^2 + k$.

$$0.5 = a(0 - 18)^2 + 30$$

$$-29.5 = 324a$$

$$\frac{-29.5}{324} = \frac{324a}{324}$$

$$-0.091 \doteq a$$

The initial position of the football is (0, 0.5). Substitute the coordinates of this point and solve for a.

The path of the football can be modelled by the relation $y = -0.091(x - 18)^2 + 30$.

Graph to check that the parabola passes through the points (0, 0.5) and (18, 30).

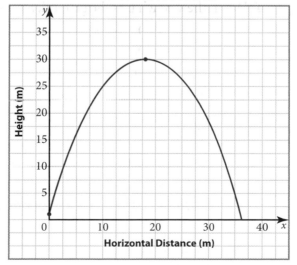

Path of Kicked Football

b) To calculate the football's horizontal distance from the player when it hits the ground, let $y = 0$ and solve for x.

$$y = -0.091(x - 18)^2 + 30$$
$$0 = -0.091(x - 18)^2 + 30$$
$$-30 = -0.091(x - 18)^2 \qquad \text{Subtract 30 from both sides.}$$
$$\frac{-30}{-0.091} = \frac{-0.091(x - 18)^2}{-0.091} \qquad \text{Divide both sides by } -0.091.$$
$$329.67 \doteq (x - 18)^2$$
$$\sqrt{329.67} \doteq \sqrt{(x - 18)^2} \qquad \text{Find the square root of both sides.}$$
$$18.16 \doteq x - 18 \qquad \text{Add 18 to both sides.}$$
$$36.16 \doteq x$$

The football lands about 36.2 m from the player.

Key Concepts

- When modelling a quadratic relation, choose a convenient location for the origin.
- A quadratic relation can be represented by a table, a graph, or an equation.
- To determine the equation for a quadratic relation from a graph, use the vertex and another point to solve for a. Then, write the equation using the vertex and the value of a.

Discuss the Concepts

D1. Describe how to write a quadratic relation from its graph.

D2. What information do you need to have about a parabola to write its equation?

Practise

For help with questions 1 and 2, refer to Example 1.

1. Find the y-intercept for each relation.

a) $y = -15x^2 + 25x - 7$ **b)** $y = 0.45x^2 - 0.17x + 20$

c) $y = 20(x - 12)^2 + 15$ **d)** $y = -0.5(x + 1.5)^2 + 4.5$

e) $y = 10x^2 + 8x - 3$ **f)** $y = 0.2(x - 3.4)^2 + 1$

g) $y = -0.1x^2 - 0.4x - 1.8$ **h)** $y = -3(x + 2)^2 - 9$

2. For each parabola, identify
- the x-intercepts
- the y-intercept
- the maximum or minimum value
- the coordinates of the vertex

a)

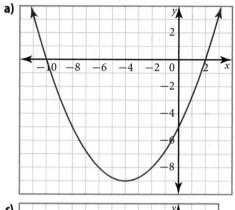

b)

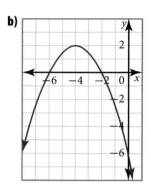

c)

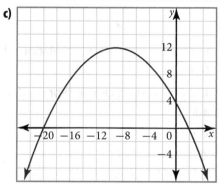

d)

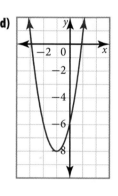

e)

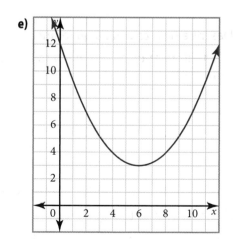

f)

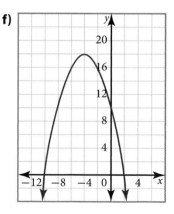

For help with question 3, refer to Example 2.

3. Sketch each parabola. Start each one at the vertical axis. Then, determine its equation.

 a) The parabola is 6 cm wide and 27 cm deep.

 b) The parabola starts at its highest point of 24.5 m. It drops to zero 7 m to the right of the highest point.

 c) The parabola has a width of 20 and a height of 10.

 d) The parabola starts at a minimum. It reaches a height of 9375 units at a point 25 units to the right.

Apply B ···

4. The Windsor–Detroit International Freedom Festival hosts one of the largest fireworks displays in the world. The fireworks are set off over the Detroit River. The path of a particular firework rocket is modelled by the relation $h = -4.9(t - 2)^2 + 169.6$, where h is the rocket's height above the water, in metres, and t is the time, in seconds.

 a) How long will the rocket take to reach its maximum height? What is the maximum height?

 b) A firework rocket will stay lit for an average of 5 s. What will the height of a rocket be 5 s after it is launched?

Literacy Connect

5. Car manufacturers have invented some unique car designs to help drivers cope with rising fuel costs. The Smart Car Fortwo is a very small, fuel-efficient vehicle. The distance it travels when accelerating from rest can be modelled by the relation $d = 1.4t^2$. The Tesla Roadster is an electric car with a top speed of over 200 km/h. The distance it travels when accelerating from rest can be modelled by the relation $d = 6.9t^2$. In both cases, d is the distance, in metres, and t is the time, in seconds.

 a) Construct a table of values for each relation, using t-values from 0 to 5. Graph the data on the same set of axes.

 b) In 5 s, how much farther will the Tesla travel relative to the Smart Car? What parts of the relations indicate the results that you found?

 c) How far will each car travel in the first second? In the fourth second? What do your answers tell you about the speeds of the cars during each time period?

6. The shape of a satellite dish is parabolic. The dish is 5 cm deep and 40 cm wide. Write a relation of the form $y = a(x - h)^2 + k$ that models the shape of this dish. What assumption are you making?

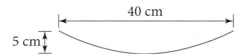

40 cm

5 cm

7. A projectile is fired straight up from the ground. It reaches a maximum height of 101.25 m after 4.5 s. Then, it falls to the ground 4.5 s later.

   a) Write a relation that models this situation.

   b) What is the height of the projectile after 3 s? Is there another time when the projectile is at the same height above the ground? Explain.

Chapter Problem

8. When studying ballistics, Galileo Galilei found that by changing the angle between a cannon and the ground, a cannonball could be fired different distances using the same amount of explosive.

The same method is used by video game designers when determining the angle of a ramp in a ski jump game. For each relation in the table, h is the ski jumper's height above the ground and d is the ski jumper's horizontal distance from the ramp, both in metres.

Ramp Angle	Quadratic Relation
25°	$h = -0.018d^2 + 0.47d + 2$
35°	$h = -0.022d^2 + 0.70d + 2$
45°	$h = -0.029d^2 + 1.00d + 2$
55°	$h = -0.044d^2 + 1.43d + 2$
65°	$h = -0.081d^2 + 2.15d + 2$
75°	$h = -0.216d^2 + 3.73d + 2$

   a) Use a graphing calculator or graphing software to graph each relation in the table on the same set of axes.

   b) Which angle gives the greatest horizontal distance?

   c) Which angle gives the greatest height?

   d) What is the meaning of the constant 2 in each relation?

Extend **C** •

9. Refer to question 5. The Smart Car starts a race at 0 s. At what time should the Tesla start so that both cars are at the same point after 5 s of the race? Justify your answer.

4.1 Modelling With Quadratic Relations, pages 168–179

1. Is each relation quadratic? How do you know?

   a) $y = 3x - 15$

   b) $y = 4x^2 - 2x + 8$

   c)

x	y
−5	1
0	4
5	16
10	64
15	256

2. A baseball is thrown upward. The path of the ball is modelled by the relation $h = -4.9t^2 + 15t + 2$, where h is the baseball's height above the ground, in metres, and t is the time, in seconds.

   a) Copy and complete the table.

Time (s)	Height (m)
0.0	
0.5	
1.0	
1.5	
2.0	
2.5	
3.0	

   b) How long will it take the baseball to reach its maximum height?

   c) After how many seconds will the baseball land?

   d) How can you tell that this relationship is quadratic? List as many reasons as possible.

4.2 The Quadratic Relation $y = ax^2 + k$, pages 180–193

3. Describe the shape and position of each parabola relative to the graph of $y = x^2$.

   a) $y = x^2 - 3.4$

   b) $y = -0.35x^2$

   c) $y = 0.005x^2 + 15$

   d) $y = 6.5x^2 - 3.4$

4. Sketch the graph of each relation in question 3.

5. Write a relation that models each table of values.

   a)

x	y
−1	−88
0	−100
1	−88
2	−52
3	8
4	92

   b)

x	y
−5.0	19.5
0.0	20.0
5.0	19.5
10.0	18.0
15.0	15.5
20.0	12.0

4.3 The Quadratic Relation $y = a(x - h)^2$, pages 194–203

6. Write a relation that models each table of values.

   a)

x	y
8	−32
10	0
12	−32
14	−128
16	−288
18	−512

   b)

x	y
−26	60
−16	15
−6	0
4	15
14	60
24	135

4.4 The Quadratic Relation $y = a(x - h)^2 + k$, pages 204–217

7. Describe the shape and position of each parabola relative to the graph of $y = x^2$.

   a) $y = -0.004(x - 18)^2 + 15$

   b) $y = 7(x + 1)^2 - 2$

   c) $y = -80(x + 9)^2 + 10.8$

   d) $y = 0.6(x - 40)^2$

8. Sketch the graph of each relation in question 7.

9. A computer repair technician is deciding what hourly rate to charge for her services. She knows that if she charges $60/h, she will get 30 h of work per week. She also knows that for every $5 increase in her hourly rate, she will lose 4 h of work per week.

   a) Copy and complete the table.

Hourly Rate ($)	Expected Number of Hours per Week	Weekly Revenue ($)
45		
50		
55		
60	30	(60)(30) = $1800
65	26	
70		

   b) Graph the relation between hourly rate and weekly revenue.

   c) Write a relation in the form $y = a(x - h)^2 + k$ to represent the graph.

d) What hourly rate should the technician charge to earn the maximum weekly revenue?

10. Sketch the graph of each parabola. Then, determine its equation.

   a) opens upward, vertex is $(3, -5)$, passes through point $(13, 20)$

   b) opens downward, vertex is $(-4, 7)$, passes through point $(0, -39)$

4.5 Interpret Graphs of Quadratic Relations, pages 218–225

11. One of the largest solar furnaces in the world is in Odeillo, France. The parabolic mirror is 54 m wide and 10 m deep. Write a relation to model the parabolic shape of the mirror.

12. A water balloon is thrown upwards. The balloon follows a path modelled by the relation $h = -2.6d^2 + 7.8d + 2.15$, where h is the balloon's height above the ground and d is the balloon's horizontal distance from the release point, both in metres.

   a) Copy and complete the table. Graph the relation.

d	0.0	0.5	1.0	1.5	2.0	2.5	3.0
h							

   b) What was the balloon's initial height above the ground?

   c) Write a relation in the form $y = a(x - h)^2 + k$ to model the balloon's path.

For questions 1 to 6, choose the best answer.

1. Which of these relations is quadratic?

   A $y = 0.5x - 7$

   B $y = 5.8x + 3x^2 - 9$

   C $y = 4x^3 + 2x^2 - 5x + 1$

   D $3x + 2y + 10 = 0$

2. Which of these relations is not quadratic?

   A the path of a ball thrown in the air

   B the distance a car travels when it is accelerating

   C the distance travelled when running at a constant speed

   D the shape of a satellite dish

3. Which parabola has its vertex 3 units above the x-axis?

   A $y = 3(x - 5)^2 + 4$

   B $y = 5(x + 4)^2 - 3$

   C $y = 0.1(x - 15)^2 + 3$

   D $y = 0.3(x + 3)^2 - 10$

4. Which parabola has its vertex farthest from the y-axis?

   A $y = 3(x - 5)^2 + 4$

   B $y = 5(x + 4)^2 - 3$

   C $y = 0.1(x - 15)^2 + 3$

   D $y = 0.3(x + 0.8)^2 - 10$

5. Which parabola is the most vertically stretched?

   A $y = 3(x - 5)^2 + 4$

   B $y = 5(x + 4)^2 - 3$

   C $y = 0.1(x - 15)^2 + 3$

   D $y = 0.3(x + 0.8)^2 - 10$

6. The parabola represented by the relation $y = -8(x + 15)^2 + 12$ has which vertex?

   A $(-8, 15)$

   B $(-15, 12)$

   C $(-15, -12)$

   D $(-8, -12)$

7. What is always true about the first and second differences of a quadratic relation?

8. Describe the shape and position of each parabola relative to the graph of $y = x^2$. Sketch a graph of each parabola.

   a) $y = 0.5(x + 8)^2$

   b) $y = -8x^2 - 14$

   c) $y = -10(x - 7)^2 - 13$

   d) $y = 0.002(x + 20)^2 + 16$

9. A soccer ball is kicked from ground level. When it has travelled 35 m horizontally, it reaches its maximum height of 25 m. The soccer ball lands on the ground 70 m from where it was kicked.

   a) Model this situation with a relation in the form $y = a(x - h)^2 + k$.

   b) What is the soccer ball's height when it is 50 m from where it was kicked?

Chapter Problem Wrap-Up

Throughout this chapter you have developed relations to model the paths of a snowboarder, a skateboarder, a mountain biker, a motocross biker, and a ski jumper. There are many more extreme sports that involve flying through the air. Think of a different sport and develop a relation that can model the sport's motion to complete your video game.

10. Pennies are stacked in a triangular pattern.

a) Continue the pattern. Copy and complete the table for the first ten layers of pennies.

Number of Layers	Total Number of Pennies
1	1
2	3
3	6
4	
5	

b) Describe the relationship between the number of layers and the total number of pennies.

c) How many layers are in a triangle made of 105 pennies?

d) How many pennies are needed for a triangle with 50 layers? Explain how you found your answer.

11. A basketball was thrown upward. The basketball's path is given by the relation $h = -0.2(d - 2.5)^2 + 4.25$, where h is the basketball's height above the ground and d is the basketball's horizontal distance from where it was thrown, both in metres.

a) What was the basketball's initial height above the ground?

b) What was the basketball's greatest height above the ground? What was the basketball's horizontal distance at this point?

c) The basketball was thrown toward a net 6 m away and 3 m above the ground. Will the basketball go through the net? Justify your answer.

5 Quadratic Relations II

Many fountains are more than just decorative; they are attractions unto themselves. The streams of water follow a path in the shape of a parabola. Understanding these paths allows designers to combine several fountains to create beautiful patterns.

In this chapter, you will

- expand and simplify quadratic expressions in one variable involving multiplying binomials or squaring a binomial, using a variety of tools
- express the equation of a quadratic relation in the standard form $y = ax^2 + bx + c$, given the vertex form $y = a(x - h)^2 + k$, and verify, using graphing technology, that these forms are equivalent representations
- factor trinomials of the form $ax^2 + bx + c$, where $a = 1$ or where a is the common factor, by various methods
- determine, through investigation, and describe the connection between the factors of a quadratic expression and the x-intercepts of the graph of the corresponding quadratic relation
- solve problems, using an appropriate strategy, given equations of quadratic relations, including those that arise from real-world applications

Reasoning and Proving

Representing | Selecting Tools

Problem Solving

Connecting | Reflecting

Communicating

Key Terms

axis of symmetry	perfect square trinomial
difference of squares	standard form
intercept form	zeros

Yao attended a two-year program at Mohawk College to become an architectural technician. In his job, Yao helps architects prepare blueprints and build models of proposed buildings. Mathematics is the key to successful construction of the architect's design. Mathematical shapes, such as parabolas, make the finished structure a work of art.

Prerequisite Skills

Polynomials

1. Simplify.

   a) $6(3x)$ **b)** $-9(-15x)$

   c) $11(-8x)$ **d)** $1.5(3x)$

2. Simplify.

   a) $4x^2 - 3x + 9x^2 + 7x$

   b) $3x + 2 - 5x + 15$

   c) $10x^2 - 12x - 7x + 9$

   d) $5x^2 - 3x + 5 - 7x^2 + 4x - 10$

3. Expand and simplify.

   a) $4(x + 16)$ **b)** $3x(17 + 2x)$

   c) $-7x(12x - 3)$ **d)** $10x(4x - 5)$

Area

4. Use algebra tiles to model each rectangle.
Then, find an expression, in simplified
form, for the area.

   a) $x + 2$ **b)** $3x$

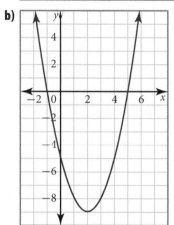

Draw and Interpret Graphs

5. Graph each linear relation.

   a) $y = x + 4$ **b)** $x + 4y - 3 = 0$

   c) $y = -\dfrac{1}{4}x + 3$ **d)** $x - y + 4 = 0$

6. Which of the equations from question 5
represent the same relation?

7. Find the x- and y-intercepts of each
relation.

   a)

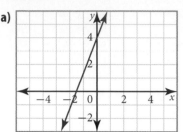

   b)

   c)

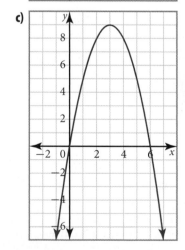

Algebraic Expressions

8. Use algebra tiles to model each expression.

a) $x^2 - 6x$ **b)** $x^2 - x - 2$

c) $3x^2 + 5x - 2$ **d)** $-2x^2 - 7x + 15$

9. Refer to question 8. Evaluate each expression for $x = -4$.

Number Skills

10. List the factors of each number.

a) 24 **b)** 81

c) 30 **d)** -18

11. Find two integers with each product and sum.

	Product	Sum
a)	21	10
b)	12	8
c)	20	12
d)	32	18
e)	50	27
f)	-20	1
g)	-64	0
h)	-64	-12

Solve Equations

12. Solve for x.

a) $3x = 15$ **b)** $17 = x + 4$

c) $x - 15 = 22$ **d)** $-5x = 65$

e) $4x - 7 = 21$ **f)** $-9x + 22 = -50$

g) $5x + 15 = 2x$ **h)** $-9x = 6x + 30$

Factor Polynomials

13. Find the greatest common factor, then factor each expression.

a) $3x + 9$ **b)** $5x + 20$

c) $7x - 35$ **d)** $-8x - 48$

e) $x^2 - 4x$ **f)** $4x^2 + 24x$

g) $-15x^2 + 27x$ **h)** $20x^2 - 55$

14. Factor each trinomial.

a) $x^2 + 3x + 2$ **b)** $x^2 + x - 6$

c) $x^2 - 8x + 12$ **d)** $x^2 + 9x + 14$

e) $x^2 - 3x - 10$ **f)** $x^2 - 2x + 1$

Chapter Problem

You have been hired to design a fountain that will be the main attraction for a new park. What should you consider when designing the fountain? How can you use your understanding of quadratic relations to make an attractive design?

5.1 Expand Binomials

The area of a rectangular surface can be found by multiplying the length and the width of the figure. The dimensions of a junior high basketball court are approximately 23 m by 13 m. The dimensions of senior high and university/college courts differ. Binomial expressions can be used to represent the dimensions of any basketball court.

The product of two numbers can be rewritten as the product of two sums. For example:

$$42 \times 64 = (40 + 2) \times (60 + 4)$$
$$= 40 \times 60 + 40 \times 4 + 2 \times 60 + 2 \times 4$$
$$= 2400 + 160 + 120 + 8$$
$$= 2688$$

The product of two numbers can also be rewritten as the product of a sum and a difference or the product of two differences. For example:

$$28 \times 75 = (30 - 2) \times (70 + 5)$$
$$= 30 \times 70 + 30 \times 5 - 2 \times 70 - 2 \times 5$$
$$= 2100 + 150 - 140 - 10$$
$$= 2100$$

In this section, you will apply this method to multiply algebraic expressions.

Model the Product of Binomials

1. The diagram shows a rectangle made of algebra tiles.

   a) Write an expression to represent each of the dimensions of the rectangle.

   b) Write an expression to represent the area of the rectangle.

2. Copy this diagram.

   a) Write an expression to represent the area of each small rectangle.

   b) Write an expression to represent the area of the large rectangle.

3. Reflect Compare the expression that represents the area of the large rectangle to the expressions that represent its dimensions. How are they related? Explain.

Example 1

Multiply Two Binomials

Expand and simplify.

$(2x + 1)(x + 4)$

Solution

Method 1: Use Algebra Tiles

Draw a multiplication frame. Use algebra tiles to model each binomial.

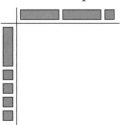

Fill in the rectangle using algebra tiles.

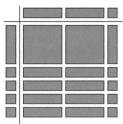

There are two x^2-tiles, nine x-tiles, and four unit tiles.

So, $(2x + 1)(x + 4) = 2x^2 + 9x + 4$.

Method 2: Use an Area Model

Draw a large rectangle with length $2x + 1$ and width $x + 4$. Divide the large rectangle into smaller rectangles. Find the area of each small rectangle.

Multiply the length and the width:
- $2x \times x = 2x^2$
- $1 \times x = x$
- $2x \times 4 = 8x$
- $1 \times 4 = 4$

The sum of the areas of the small rectangles gives the area of the large rectangle.

$$(2x + 1)(x + 4) = 2x^2 + x + 8x + 4$$
$$= 2x^2 + 9x + 4$$

Method 3: Use the Distributive Property

$$(2x + 1)(x + 4) = \boxed{(2x + 1)}(x + 4)$$
$$= (2x + 1)(x) + (2x + 1)(4)$$
$$= (2x + 1)(x) + (2x + 1)(4)$$
$$= 2x^2 + x + 8x + 4$$
$$= 2x^2 + 9x + 4$$

Method 4: Use a Multiplication Pattern

Math Connect

This method is often referred to by the acronym **FOIL**. Multiply the **F**irst terms, the **O**utside terms, the **I**nside terms, and the **L**ast terms.

When multiplying polynomials, each term in one binomial must be multiplied by each term in the other binomial. Think of it as two pairs of people who meet at a party. Each person in one pair will shake hands with each person in the other pair.

$$(2x + 1)(x + 4) = (2x + 1)(x + 4)$$
$$= (2x)(x) + (2x)(4) + (1)(x) + (1)(4)$$
$$= 2x^2 + 8x + x + 4$$
$$= 2x^2 + 9x + 4$$

Method 5: Use a Computer Algebra System (CAS)

From the home screen,
press ⌊ F2 ⌋ 3:expand(.

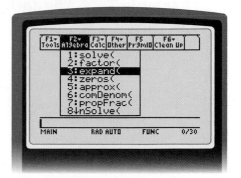

Press ⌊ (⌋ 2 ⌊ x ⌋ ⌊ + ⌋ 1 ⌊) ⌋
⌊ (⌋ ⌊ x ⌋ ⌊ + ⌋ 4 ⌊) ⌋ ⌊) ⌋
⌊ ENTER ⌋.

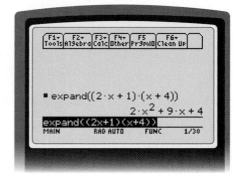

$(2x + 1)(x + 4) = 2x^2 + 9x + 4$

Example 2

Find the Product of Two Binomials

Find each product, then simplify.

a) $(2x - 7)(4x + 9)$

b) $(3x - 5)(3x + 5)$

Solution

a) $(2x - 7)(4x + 9) = (2x - 7)(4x + 9)$

$$= 8x^2 + 18x - 28x - 63$$
$$= 8x^2 - 10x - 63$$

b) $(3x - 5)(3x + 5) = (3x - 5)(3x + 5)$

$$= 9x^2 + 15x - 15x - 25$$
$$= 9x^2 - 25$$

Example 3

Square a Binomial

Expand and simplify.
$(2x + 3)^2$

Solution

$(2x + 3)^2 = (2x + 3)(2x + 3)$

$= 4x^2 + 6x + 6x + 9$

$= 4x^2 + 12x + 9$

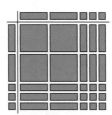

Check: Use algebra tiles.

When you use algebra tiles to square a binomial, the tiles that represent the product form a square.

Key Concepts

• To find the product of two binomials, each term in one binomial is multiplied by each term in the other binomial.

Discuss the Concepts

D1. Which method do you prefer to use when expanding binomials? Give reasons for your answer.

D2. How is expanding a binomial using an area model related to expanding a binomial using a multiplication pattern? Explain.

Practise

For help with questions 1 to 6, refer to Examples 1 and 2.

1. Write an expression for each dimension of each large rectangle.

a)   b) c)   d)

2. For each large rectangle in question 1, write a simplified algebraic expression to represent its area.

3. Expand and simplify.

   a) $x(x + 8)$ **b)** $(x + 7)(x + 1)$

   c) $(x + 3)(x + 4)$ **d)** $(2x + 1)(x + 3)$

   e) $(4x + 5)(6x + 2)$ **f)** $(3x + 2)(3x + 2)$

4. Expand and simplify.

   a) $(3x + 5)(4x + 7)$ **b)** $(6x - 11)(x + 4)$

   c) $(9x - 6)(2x + 10)$ **d)** $(7x + 2)(5x - 8)$

   e) $(3 - 8x)(3 + 8x)$ **f)** $(4x + 9)(4x + 9)$

5. Expand and simplify.

   a) $(2x + 3)(x + 10)$ **b)** $(3x + 10)(x + 5)$

   c) $(x - 12)(3x + 11)$ **d)** $(5 - 10x)(15 + 2x)$

   e) $(4x - 9)(x - 15)$ **f)** $(16x + 9)(16x + 9)$

6. Expand and simplify.

   a) $(x - 5)(x + 5)$ **b)** $(x - 10)(x + 10)$

   c) $(3x + 7)(3x - 7)$ **d)** $(8x - 5)(8x + 5)$

   e) $(7x - 7)(7x + 7)$ **f)** $(12x + 9)(12x - 9)$

For help with question 7, refer to Example 3.

7. Expand and simplify.

   a) $(x + 6)(x + 6)$ **b)** $(x - 8)(x - 8)$

   c) $(4x + 15)^2$ **d)** $(9x - 2)^2$

   e) $(5x - 3)^2$ **f)** $(6x + 12)^2$

Apply   B

8. Refer to your answers to questions 6 and 7. Compare the factors with the products. Describe any patterns you see.

9. a) Write a simplified expression for the area of each rectangle.

   i) $3x + 7$ **ii)** $x - 2$ **iii)** $2x - 11$

   $2x - 2$ $6x + 5$

   $5x - 3$

   b) Determine each area if $x = 12$ cm.

10. Dania's yard has dimensions $s + 6$ by $2s - 5$.

    a) Write an expression, in simplified form, for the area of Dania's yard.

    b) If $s = 10$ m, find the area of Dania's yard.

11. Write an expression, in simplified form, for the area of this shape.

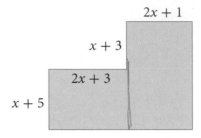

2x + 1

x + 3

2x + 3

x + 5

Chapter Problem

12. The city planners have not confirmed the exact size of the fountain but you know that the base of the fountain will be rectangular. You have determined expressions for the dimensions of the base, in metres, as shown.

3x + 5

2x + 3

    a) Write an expression, in simplified form, to represent the area of the base of the fountain.

    b) When $x = 0$, the base of the fountain will be 5 m by 3 m, the minimum dimensions requested by the planners. The planners do not want the fountain to be too large, so you have designed it to have a maximum size when $x = 3$. How much greater in area is the base of the largest fountain than the base of the smallest fountain?

    c) The projected cost for the base, including labour and materials, is $900/m^2$. What are the projected costs for the bases of the smallest and largest fountains?

Literacy Connect

13. A rectangle in which the ratio of the length to the width is approximately 1.618:1 is called a golden rectangle. The ancient Greeks frequently used this proportion in their architecture and art.

    a) Refer to question 12. What is the value of x if the base of the fountain is a golden rectangle?

    b) This ratio is more formally called phi. Research the accurate value of phi. Determine where else this ratio occurs in nature, architecture, and art. Write a report of your findings.

14. Write an expression, in simplified form, for the area of this shape.

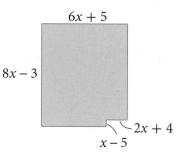

15. A box with a rectangular base and no lid can be created from a cardboard template as shown. The height of the box, x, is variable.

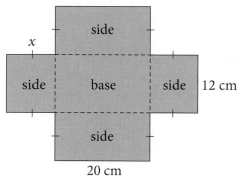

a) Find an expression for the area of the cardboard.

b) Calculate the total area of the cardboard for boxes with heights of 3 cm, 5 cm, and 10 cm.

c) If the cardboard costs 5¢/100 cm^2, how much will each box in part b) cost?

16. When multiplying two polynomials, each term in the first polynomial is multiplied by each term in the second polynomial. Expand and simplify.

a) $(3x + 2)(x^2 + 4x + 9)$

b) $(2x - 5)(7x^2 - 2x + 8)$

c) $(x^2 + 10x + 1)(x^2 - 3x + 11)$

17. Write each expression as the product of two binomials. Use the patterns that you found in question 8 to help you.

a) $x^2 + 10x + 25$ **b)** $x^2 - 18x + 81$

c) $x^2 + 24x + 144$ **d)** $x^2 - 36$

e) $x^2 - 64$ **f)** $x^2 - 121$

Change Quadratic Relations From Vertex Form to Standard Form

You have already learned about quadratic relations in vertex form, $y = a(x - h)^2 + k$. In this section, you will use a different form to represent quadratic relations.

:Investigate

Tools

• graphing calculator

Different Forms of a Quadratic Relation

1. Graph each pair of relations in the same window. Use the standard viewing window. What do you notice?

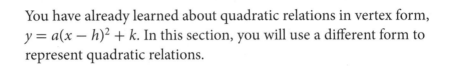

a) $y = (x - 2)^2 + 1$ $y = x^2 - 4x + 5$

b) $y = (x + 5)^2 + 3$ $y = x^2 + 10x + 28$

c) $y = -(x + 1)^2 - 4$ $y = -x^2 - 2x - 5$

d) $y = 0.5(x - 4)^2 + 3$ $y = 0.5x^2 - 4x + 11$

2. Refer to question 1. Expand and simplify the first relation in each pair. How does the result compare to the second relation in each pair?

3. For each pair of relations in question 1, find the coordinates of the vertex and the y-intercept. Compare the coordinates of the vertex and the y-intercept to the relations. What do you notice?

standard form
• a quadratic relation of the form $y = ax^2 + bx + c$
• the constant, c, represents the y-intercept of the relation

4. The quadratic relation $y = ax^2 + bx + c$ is in **standard form**. The relation $y = a(x - h)^2 + k$ is in vertex form. Which relations in question 1 are written in standard form? Which are written in vertex form?

5. Reflect Without graphing, what do you know about a parabola given the relation in standard form? in vertex form? Use examples to explain.

Example 1

Write Quadratic Relations in Standard Form

Each relation is in vertex form. Write each relation in standard form.

a) $y = (x + 6)^2$

b) $y = -2(x - 7)^2$

c) $y = 3(x - 5)^2 - 8$

Solution

a) $y = (x + 6)^2$
$= (x + 6)(x + 6)$
$= x^2 + 6x + 6x + 36$
$= x^2 + 12x + 36$

The relation $y = (x + 6)^2$ in standard form is $y = x^2 + 12x + 36$.

b) $y = -2(x - 7)^2$
$= -2(x - 7)(x - 7)$
$= -2(x^2 - 7x - 7x + 49)$
$= -2(x^2 - 14x + 49)$
$= -2x^2 + 28x - 98$

The relation $y = -2(x - 7)^2$ in standard form is
$y = -2x^2 + 28x - 98$.

c) $y = 3(x - 5)^2 - 8$
$= 3(x - 5)(x - 5) - 8$
$= 3(x^2 - 5x - 5x + 25) - 8$
$= 3(x^2 - 10x + 25) - 8$
$= 3x^2 - 30x + 75 - 8$
$= 3x^2 - 30x + 67$

The relation $y = 3(x - 5)^2 - 8$ in standard form is
$y = 3x^2 - 30x + 67$.

Example 2

Projectile Motion

The path of a projectile can be modelled by the relation
$y = -4.9t^2 + vt + h$, where t is the time, in seconds, since launching;
y is the projectile's height, in metres; h is the projectile's initial height,
in metres; and v is the projectile's initial velocity, in metres per second.
Find the initial velocity and the initial height of a projectile that reaches
a maximum height of 50 m after 3 s.

Solution

The maximum height of 50 m is reached after 3 s. So, the vertex is (3, 50).

Use the coordinates of the vertex and the given value of a, -4.9, to write
the quadratic relation in vertex form. Then, convert the relation
to standard form.

$$
\begin{aligned}
y &= -4.9(t - 3)^2 + 50 \\
&= -4.9(t - 3)(t - 3) + 50 \\
&= -4.9(t^2 - 3t - 3t + 9) + 50 \\
&= -4.9(t^2 - 6t + 9) + 50 \\
&= -4.9t^2 + 29.4t - 44.1 + 50 \\
&= -4.9t^2 + 29.4t + 5.9
\end{aligned}
$$

For a given quadratic relation, the vertex form and the standard form have the same a-value.

The initial velocity, v, is the coefficient of t. The projectile's initial
velocity is 29.4 m/s.

The initial height, h, is the y-intercept. The projectile's initial height is 5.9 m.

Key Concepts

- A quadratic relation can be written in vertex form, $y = a(x - h)^2 + k$,
  or in standard form, $y = ax^2 + bx + c$.
- Expand and simplify the vertex form to write the quadratic relation in
  standard form.
- Given a quadratic relation in vertex form, $y = a(x - h)^2 + k$, the
  coordinates of the vertex are (h, k).
- Given a quadratic relation in standard form, $y = ax^2 + bx + c$, the
  y-intercept is c.

Discuss the Concepts

D1. A quadratic relation may be written in standard form or vertex form.
What information does each form give about the parabola?

D2. Explain how you would convert the relation $y = -6(x - 10)^2 + 15$
to standard form.

Practise **A** •

For help with questions 1 to 4, refer to Example 1.

1. Write each relation in standard form.

a) $y = (x + 6)^2$

b) $y = (x - 4)^2$

c) $y = (x - 15)^2$

d) $y = (x - 2)^2$

e) $y = (x + 9)^2$

f) $y = (x - 1)^2$

2. Write each relation in standard form.

a) $y = 3(x + 9)^2$

b) $y = -2(x + 7)^2$

c) $y = -8(x - 5)^2$

d) $y = 0.5(x + 2)^2$

e) $y = -0.25(x + 8)^2$

f) $y = 9.8(x - 3.2)^2$

3. Write each relation in standard form.

a) $y = (x - 8)^2 + 3$

b) $y = (x + 5)^2 + 10$

c) $y = (x + 1)^2 - 13$

d) $y = (x - 3)^2 + 1$

e) $y = (x + 6)^2 - 7$

f) $y = (x - 5)^2 - 3$

4. Write each relation in standard form.

a) $y = 5(x - 4)^2 + 12$

b) $y = -6(x + 9)^2 - 7$

c) $y = -2(x + 7)^2 - 10$

d) $y = -8(x - 5)^2 + 6$

e) $y = 2.4(x - 5.1)^2 + 3$

f) $y = -1.9(x + 2.7)^2 - 5.1$

For help with question 5, refer to the Investigate.

5. Graph each relation. Which relations are the same?

a) $y = 10(x - 7)^2 - 4$

b) $y = -2x^2 - 8x - 2$

c) $y = -2(x - 1)^2 + 5$

d) $y = -2(x + 2)^2 + 6$

e) $y = 10x^2 - 140x + 486$

f) $y = 10(x + 5)^2 + 3$

g) $y = -2x^2 + 4x + 3$

h) $y = 10x^2 + 100x + 253$

For help with questions 6 and 7, refer to Example 2.

6. For each quadratic relation, write an equation in standard form.

a) $a = 5$, vertex at $(1, 7)$

b) $y = -3x^2 + bx + c$, vertex at $(-5, 6)$

c) $a = -8$, maximum of 17 when $x = 10$

d) $y = 12x^2 + bx + c$, minimum of 3 when $x = -1$

7. Determine the y-intercept for each relation.

a) $y = 3(x + 12)^2 + 15$

b) $y = 10x^2 - 15x + 7$

c) $y = -7(x - 5)^2 - 6$

d) $y = 9x^2 - 20$

e) $y = 4x^2 + 5x - 1$

f) $y = 1.5(x - 2.4)^2 + 6.4$

8. The strategy for long-distance rollerblading is to find the best speed that can be maintained for a long time. A racer's performance can be modelled by the quadratic relation $d = -2(v - 6)^2 + 50$, where d is the racer's maximum distance travelled, in kilometres, at a speed, v, in metres per second.

a) Find the v-coordinate of the vertex. What does this value represent?

b) Find the d-coordinate of the vertex. What does this value represent?

c) Write the quadratic relation in standard form.

d) Use technology to graph both forms of the relation. Verify the coordinates of the vertex.

Literacy Connect

9. Explain the advantages and disadvantages of each form of a quadratic relation.

a) standard form, $y = ax^2 + bx + c$

b) vertex form, $y = a(x - h)^2 + k$

10. The curve of a suspension cable on the Golden Gate Bridge in San Francisco, California, can be modelled by the quadratic relation $h = 0.000\,549x^2 + bx + c$, where h is the cable's height above the ground, and x is the horizontal distance from one tower, both in metres. The centre of the cable is 640 m from the tower and 227 m above the ground.

a) Write the quadratic relation that models the curve of the cable in vertex form.

b) Write the quadratic relation in standard form.

c) At what height does a cable attach to a tower?

d) Graph the relations from parts a) and b) on the same set of axes.

Chapter Problem

11. Water from the main fountain for your project must reach a maximum height of 20 m after 2 s. The water's path can be modelled by the quadratic relation $y = -4.9t^2 + vt + h$, where y is the water's height, in metres, h is the fountain's height above the ground, in metres, and v is the initial velocity of the water, in metres per second.

a) Write the quadratic relation that models the path of the water in vertex form.

b) Write the quadratic relation in standard form.

c) What is the initial velocity of the water?

d) What is the maximum height reached by the water?

Achievement Check

12. The distributive property can be used to square whole numbers close to 50, without using a calculator. Consider these examples:

$$53^2 = (53)(53)$$
$$= (50 + 3)(50 + 3)$$
$$= 2500 + 100n + n^2$$
$$= 2500 + 300 + 9$$
$$= 2809$$

$$46^2 = (46)(46)$$
$$= (50 - 4)(50 - 4)$$
$$= 2500 + 100n + n^2$$
$$= 2500 - 400 + 16$$
$$= 2116$$

a) Use the distributive property to calculate 56^2 and 48^2.

b) Explain how to calculate the square of a number that is x units away from 50. Write a statement similar to the examples above to illustrate your explanation.

c) Test this method using whole numbers close to 20. Does the pattern work for any value or only for values close to 50? Explain your reasoning.

Extend **C**

13. Step-Up is a new extreme sport in which a motorcycle rider uses a steep ramp to jump a high bar, as in the high jump or pole vault. The path of the rider can be modelled by the quadratic relation

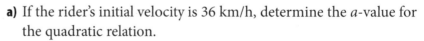

$y = -\dfrac{2106}{v^2}x^2 + 5.85x + h$, where y

is the height of the rider above the ground, x is the rider's horizontal distance from the ramp, and h is the height of the ramp, all in metres, and v is the rider's initial velocity, in kilometres per hour.

a) If the rider's initial velocity is 36 km/h, determine the a-value for the quadratic relation.

b) A rider is 1.8 m from the ramp when the maximum height of 8.0 m is reached. Write this relation in vertex form.

c) What is the height of the ramp?

14. A quadratic relation can be represented by an equation of the form $y = a(x - s)(x - t)$.

a) Show that $y = 3(x - 1)^2 - 48$ represents the same quadratic relation as $y = 3(x + 3)(x - 5)$.

b) Graph both relations on the same set of axes.

c) Compare the relation $y = 3(x + 3)(x - 5)$ to the graph. What connections do you see between the graph and the relation?

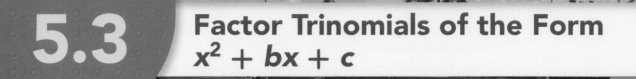

5.3

Factor Trinomials of the Form $x^2 + bx + c$

In mathematics, opposite operations are used to undo operations. For addition, the opposite operation is subtraction. For multiplication, the opposite operation is division. For expanding, the opposite operation is factoring.

You can find the dimensions of a rectangular surface if you know its area. The surface area of a tennis court is approximately 264 m². If the width of the court is 11 m, what is the length?

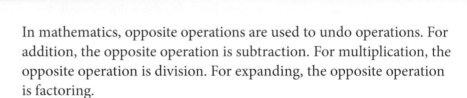

Investigate

The Pattern in the Product of Two Binomials

1. Expand and simplify.

    a) $(x + 6)(x + 1)$

    b) $(x + 5)(x + 5)$

    c) $(x + 2)(x + 3)$

    d) $(x + 4)(x - 7)$

    e) $(x - 1)(x + 4)$

    f) $(x - 2)(x - 8)$

2. Refer to your answers to question 1.

    a) Compare the constant terms in each pair of binomial factors to the constant term in the trinomial. What do you notice?

    b) Compare the constant terms in each pair of binomial factors to the coefficient of x in the trinomial. What do you notice?

    c) Compare the signs of the constant terms in each pair of binomial factors to the signs of the coefficient of x and the constant term in the trinomial. What do you notice?

3. Predict the coefficient of x and the constant term of the trinomial produced by each pair of binomial factors. Record your prediction. Then, expand to check your prediction.

a) $(x + 1)(x + 4)$

b) $(x + 6)(x + 2)$

c) $(x + 8)(x - 1)$

d) $(x - 3)(x - 5)$

e) $(x - 10)(x + 4)$

f) $(x - 5)(x - 1)$

4. **Reflect** For the trinomial $x^2 + 7x + 12$, how could you identify the constant terms in the binomial factors $(x + \blacksquare)(x + \blacksquare)$?

Example 1

Use Algebra Tiles to Factor a Trinomial

a) Factor $x^2 + 8x + 12$ using algebra tiles.

b) Check your answer by expanding, using the distributive property.

Solution

a) Use algebra tiles to model $x^2 + 8x + 12$.
   Arrange the tiles to form a rectangle.

The dimensions of the rectangle represent the factors of the trinomial.

$$x^2 + 8x + 12 = (x + 6)(x + 2)$$

b) $(x + 6)(x + 2) = x^2 + 2x + 6x + 12$
   $ = x^2 + 8x + 12$

By expanding, the original trinomial is obtained.

Example 2

Factor Trinomials

Find the binomial factors of each trinomial.

 a) $x^2 + 15x + 36$

 b) $x^2 + 7x - 18$

 c) $x^2 - 10x + 25$

Solution

Find two numbers:
- whose product equals the constant term of the trinomial
- whose sum equals the coefficient of the x-term of the trinomial

a) $x^2 + 15x + 36$

List pairs of numbers whose product is 36.
Choose the pair of numbers whose sum is 15.

Product of 36		Sum
1	36	37
2	18	20
3	12	15
4	9	13
6	6	12

Since the product, 36, and the sum, 15, are both positive, the numbers are both positive.

The numbers are 3 and 12, so $x^2 + 15x + 36 = (x + 3)(x + 12)$.

b) $x^2 + 7x - 18$

List pairs of numbers whose product is -18.
Choose the pair of numbers whose sum is 7.

Product of −18		Sum
1	−18	−17
−1	18	17
2	−9	−7
−2	9	7
3	−6	−3
−3	6	3

Since the product, −18, is negative, the numbers have opposite signs.

The numbers are -2 and 9, so $x^2 + 7x - 18 = (x - 2)(x + 9)$.

c) $x^2 - 10x + 25$

List pairs of numbers whose product is 25.

Choose the pair of numbers whose sum is -10.

Product of 25		Sum
1	25	26
-1	-25	-26
5	5	10
-5	-5	-10

Since the product, 25, is positive and the sum, -10, is negative, both numbers are negative.

The numbers are -5 and -5.

So, $x^2 - 10x + 25 = (x - 5)(x - 5)$
$$= (x - 5)^2$$

The trinomial $x^2 - 10x + 25$ is an example of a **perfect square trinomial**.

perfect square trinomial
- a trinomial with identical binomial factors
- the result of squaring a binomial

Example 3

Factor $x^2 + bx$

Factor.

a) $x^2 + 5x$ **b)** $x^2 - 7x$

Solution

Method 1: Rewrite as a Polynomial of the Form $x^2 + bx + c$

a) $x^2 + 5x$ can be rewritten as $x^2 + 5x + 0$.

$x^2 + 5x = x^2 + 5x + 0$ Find pairs of numbers whose product is 0. For a product of 0, at least one factor must be 0 Choose the pair of numbers whose sum is 5.

$$= (x + 0)(x + 5)$$
$$= x(x + 5)$$

b) $x^2 - 7x = x^2 - 7x + 0$
$$= (x + 0)(x - 7)$$
$$= x(x - 7)$$

Method 2: Find the Greatest Common Factor (GCF)

a) The GCF of $x^2 + 5x$ is x.

So, $x^2 + 5x = x(x + 5)$

b) The GCF of $x^2 - 7x$ is x.

So, $x^2 - 7x = x(x - 7)$

Example 4

> ### Factor a Difference of Squares
>
> Factor. Describe any patterns you see in the answers.
>
> **a)** $x^2 - 25$ **b)** $x^2 - 81$
>
> ### Solution
>
> **a)** $x^2 - 25$ can be rewritten as $x^2 + 0x - 25$.
>
> $\begin{aligned} x^2 - 25 &= x^2 + 0x - 25 \qquad -5 \times 5 = -25,\ -5 + 5 = 0 \\ &= (x - 5)(x + 5) \end{aligned}$
>
> **b)** $x^2 - 81$ can be rewritten as $x^2 + 0x - 81$.
>
> $\begin{aligned} x^2 - 81 &= x^2 + 0x - 81 \qquad -9 \times 9 = -81,\ -9 + 9 = 0 \\ &= (x - 9)(x + 9) \end{aligned}$
>
> In both answers, the binomial factors are almost the same, but with opposite signs.

difference of squares
- a binomial of the form $x^2 - r^2$
- the factors of a difference of squares are $(x - r)(x + r)$

In Example 4, each polynomial is a difference of two perfect squares. The first term in each binomial factor is the square root of the first term in the polynomial. The second terms in the binomial factors are the positive and negative square roots of the second term of the polynomial. This type of polynomial is called a **difference of squares**.

Example 5

> ### Difference of Areas
>
> Find an expression, in factored form, for the shaded area of this figure.
>
>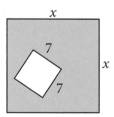
>
> ### Solution
>
> The area of the large square is x^2. The area of the small square is 49 square units. The shaded area is the difference between the areas of the large square and the small square.
>
> $\begin{aligned} A &= x^2 - 49 \\ &= (x + 7)(x - 7) \end{aligned}$ This is a difference of squares. The second terms of the binomial factors are the positive and negative square roots of 49.

Key Concepts

- Factoring is the opposite of expanding.
- To factor $x^2 + bx + c$, find two numbers whose product is equal to c and whose sum is equal to b.
- To factor $x^2 + bx$, rewrite as $x^2 + bx + 0$ or find the greatest common factor.
- A polynomial in the form $x^2 - r^2$ is a difference of squares. The factors are $(x + r)(x - r)$.
- Check the factors by expanding.

Discuss the Concepts

D1. Explain the steps needed to factor the expression $x^2 + 6x + 8$, using algebra tiles.

D2. Explain how to factor $x^2 + 6x + 8$ algebraically.

D3. What are the factors of $x^2 - 9$? Explain.

Practise

For help with questions 1 to 3, refer to Example 2.

1. Find two numbers that have the given product and sum.

	Product	Sum
a)	25	10
b)	32	12
c)	24	−14
d)	36	−20
e)	−30	1
f)	−42	−11
g)	−50	23
h)	−64	0

2. Factor. Check your answers by expanding.

a) $x^2 + 15x + 36$ b) $x^2 + 8x + 16$

c) $x^2 + 12x + 20$ d) $x^2 + 13x + 40$

3. Factor each trinomial.

a) $x^2 - 13x + 22$ b) $x^2 - 14x + 49$

c) $x^2 - 11x + 28$ d) $x^2 - 20x + 100$

e) $x^2 + 14x - 32$ f) $x^2 + 13x - 48$

g) $x^2 - x - 20$ h) $x^2 - 18x - 63$

For help with questions 4 and 5, refer to Example 1.

4. Model each expression using algebra tiles. Then, factor the expression.

   a) $x^2 + 3x + 2$ b) $x^2 + 7x + 6$

   c) $x^2 + 8x + 12$ d) $x^2 + 6x + 8$

5. For each rectangle, write a trinomial expression for its area. Then, write an expression for each of its dimensions.

   a)   b)

   c)   d)

For help with question 6, refer to Example 3.

6. Factor.

   a) $x^2 + 5x$ b) $x^2 + 22x$ c) $x^2 - 19x$

   d) $x^2 - 15x$ e) $x^2 - 9.8x$ f) $x^2 + 33.5x$

For help with question 7, refer to Example 4.

7. Factor, then check by expanding.

   a) $x^2 - 25$ b) $x^2 - 100$ c) $x^2 - 121$

   d) $x^2 - 1$ e) $x^2 - 49$ f) $x^2 - 144$

8. Factor.

   a) $x^2 + 25x$ b) $x^2 + 16x + 28$

   c) $x^2 - x - 42$ d) $x^2 - 64$

   e) $x^2 + 13x + 36$ f) $x^2 - 12x + 36$

   g) $x^2 - 4$ h) $x^2 - 32x$

Apply B ●

9. Factor each trinomial, if possible.

   a) $x^2 + 4x + 3$ b) $x^2 + 3x + 3$

   c) $x^2 + 3x + 4$ d) $x^2 + 3x + 2$

   e) $x^2 - 4x + 3$ f) $x^2 + 2x - 3$

Literacy Connect   10. Refer to the trinomials in question 9 that you could not factor. Explain why you could not factor each of these trinomials.

11. Find an expression, in factored form, for the area of the shaded region of each figure.

a)

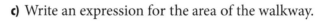

b)

12. A circular garden with radius 5 m is surrounded by a walkway with radius x.

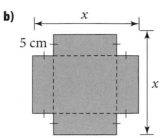

   a) Write an expression for the total area of the garden and the walkway.

   b) Write an expression for the area of the garden. Do not evaluate the expression.

   c) Write an expression for the area of the walkway.

   d) Factor the expression from part c).

Chapter Problem

13. City planners now wish to have a fountain with a square base. They want a 2-m square platform, which will remain dry, centred on the base. The area of the base not covered by the platform will have water on it.

   a) The base of the fountain has side length x. Write an expression for the area that will have water on it.

   b) The area of the base not covered by the platform will be tiled. The cost of the tile is $50/m^2$. How much will it cost to tile this area if the base of the fountain has side length 10 m?

14. The area of a rectangular garden can be represented by the expression $x^2 + 7x + 10$.

   a) Find expressions for the length and width of the garden.

   b) If the area is 40 m^2, find the length and width.

Extend **C** •

15. Some trinomials do not appear to be quadratic, but can be rewritten as quadratic expressions. For each trinomial, substitute $x^2 = s$ and $x^4 = s^2$, factor the trinomial that results, then substitute $s = x^2$.

   a) $x^4 - 26x^2 + 25$

   b) $x^4 - 53x^2 + 196$

   c) $x^4 - 45x^2 + 324$

Sometimes the most complex systems can be disrupted by something very simple. The power blackout in August 2003 that affected much of northeastern North America was caused by trees that hung over the power lines in the Ohio service area. The blackout might have been avoided by simply trimming the trees.

In mathematics, an incorrect solution can often be corrected by making a minor change, such as using the correct sign for a number or fixing a simple calculation error.

Investigate

Factor Trinomials of the Form $ax^2 + bx + c$

1. a) Copy and complete the table. Factor each trinomial by finding the greatest common factor. Then, write the trinomial factor as a product of its binomial factors.

Trinomial	Common Factored Form	Fully Factored Form
$3x^2 + 21x + 36$		
$2x^2 + 2x - 12$		
$5x^2 - 30x + 40$		
$-7x^2 - 21x - 14$		

b) Check your answers by expanding.

2. Refer to your answers to question 1. Use a similar method to factor each trinomial fully.

a) $4x^2 + 8x + 4$
b) $5x^2 - 5x - 30$
c) $-2x^2 - 6x + 20$
d) $-x^2 + 5x - 4$

3. Factor each trinomial.

    a) $3x^2 - 3x + 18$ **b)** $2x^2 - 18x + 28$

4. Compare the trinomials and your answers from questions 2 and 3. Explain any similarities or differences.

5. Factor each trinomial, if possible.

    a) $3x^2 + 13x - 10$ **b)** $12x^2 + 11x + 2$

6. Compare the trinomials and your answers from questions 2 and 5. Explain any similarities or differences.

7. Reflect Describe a method you could use to factor a trinomial of the form $ax^2 + bx + c$ where $a \neq 1$. Will this method always work? Use examples to explain.

Example 1

Factor $ax^2 + bx + c$

Factor the trinomial $4x^2 - 8x - 60$.

Solution

$$4x^2 - 8x - 60$$
$$= 4[x^2 - 2x - 15] \quad \text{Divide each term by 4 to find the other factor.}$$
$$= 4(x + 3)(x - 5) \quad \text{Factor the simplified trinomial. Find two numbers}$$
$$\text{whose product is } -15 \text{ and whose sum is } -2.$$

Example 2

Factor a Polynomial

Factor each polynomial.

    a) $2x^2 - 50$ **b)** $-4.9t^2 + 19.6t$

Solution

a) $2x^2 - 50$
$$= 2[x^2 - 25] \quad \text{Factor out the GCF, 2.}$$
$$= 2(x + 5)(x - 5) \quad \text{The second factor, } x^2 - 25, \text{ is a difference of squares.}$$

b) $-4.9t^2 + 19.6t$
$$= -4.9t(t - 4) \quad \text{Factor out the GCF, } -4.9t.$$
$$\text{The expression } t - 4 \text{ cannot be factored further.}$$

In part b) of Example 2, it may not have been obvious that -4.9 was a common factor. When there is a coefficient on the x^2-term, always check to see if it is a common factor. Not all trinomials of the form $ax^2 + bx + c$ can be factored. For example, $2x^2 + 5x + 7$ becomes $2(x^2 + 2.5x + 3.5)$. The trinomial factor cannot be factored further since there is no pair of numbers whose sum is 2.5 and whose product is 3.5.

Example 3

Simplify Formulas by Factoring

The surface area of a cylinder is given by the formula S.A. $= 2\pi r^2 + 2\pi rh$.

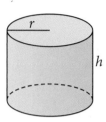

a) Factor the expression for the surface area.

b) A cylinder has radius 3 cm and height 10 cm. Use both the original expression and the factored expression to find the surface area of this cylinder to the nearest square centimetre.

c) Describe a situation in which the factored form of the formula would be more useful than the original form.

Solution

a) Look for common factors in each term. Both terms have 2, π, and r as factors. So, $2\pi r$ is the greatest common factor.

$$\begin{aligned} \text{S.A.} &= 2\pi r^2 + 2\pi rh \\ &= 2\pi r(r + h) \qquad \text{Factor out the GCF, } 2\pi r. \end{aligned}$$

b) $$\begin{aligned} \text{S.A.} &= 2\pi r^2 + 2\pi rh \\ &= 2\pi(3)^2 + 2\pi(3)(10) \\ &\doteq 245.044 \end{aligned}$$

$$\begin{aligned} \text{S.A.} &= 2\pi r(r + h) \\ &= 2\pi(3)(3 + 10) \\ &= 6\pi(13) \\ &\doteq 245.044 \end{aligned}$$

The surface area of this cylinder is about 245 cm². Both methods gave the same result.

Math Connect

Your answer may be slightly different depending on the number of decimal places used for π. For example, if $\pi \doteq 3.14$ was used, the calculated surface area would be 244.92 cm².

c) If you had to find the surface area for several cylinders, the factored form would be more useful. Fewer keystrokes are required for the factored form, so there is less chance of making a calculation error.

Key Concepts

- To factor a trinomial of the form $ax^2 + bx + c$, where $a \neq 1$, first use common factoring to factor a out of each term. Then, express the trinomial factor as a product of binomial factors.
- When working with formulas, it is often useful to factor the expression to simplify calculations.

Discuss the Concepts

D1. Factor the trinomial $0.5x^2 + 4x + 6$ fully. How does the method you used to factor this trinomial, in which $a < 1$, compare to the method used in Example 1, in which $a > 1$? Explain.

D2. Describe a situation in which it is useful to factor an expression of a formula before using it to calculate measures.

Practise   A

For help with questions 1 to 3, refer to Example 1.

1. Factor the common factor from each trinomial. Then, factor the trinomial factor. Expand to check.

   a) $2x^2 + 16x + 30$ **b)** $4x^2 + 20x - 24$

   c) $3x^2 + 18x + 15$ **d)** $2x^2 + 2x - 24$

   e) $5x^2 + 5x - 10$ **f)** $3x^2 - 12x + 12$

2. Factor each trinomial fully. Expand to check.

   a) $7x^2 - 77x + 210$ **b)** $6x^2 - 60x + 126$

   c) $-3x^2 - 30x - 72$ **d)** $10x^2 - 140x - 320$

   e) $-5x^2 + 50x - 105$ **f)** $-2x^2 + 4x + 96$

3. Factor each trinomial fully. Check your work.

   a) $1.2x^2 - 8.4x - 36$ **b)** $-2.5x^2 - 30x - 80$

   c) $3.4x^2 - 37.4x + 95.2$ **d)** $-4.6x^2 - 55.2x - 165.6$

For help with questions 4 to 6, refer to Example 2.

4. Factor each polynomial fully. Expand to check.

   a) $5x^2 + 20x$ **b)** $3x^2 - 21x$ **c)** $-7x^2 + 49x$

   d) $-15x^2 - 75x$ **e)** $8.2x^2 + 65.6x$ **f)** $-4.9x^2 + 44.1x$

5. Factor fully. Then, check your work.

   a) $3x^2 - 27$ **b)** $6x^2 - 96$ **c)** $-3x^2 + 48$

   d) $-8x^2 + 648$ **e)** $1.2x^2 - 30$ **f)** $-4.5x^2 + 162$

6. Factor fully. Then, check your work.
   a) $6x^2 + 48x + 96$
   b) $5x^2 - 45$
   c) $9x^2 - 27x$
   d) $10x^2 - 50x - 240$
   e) $-4x^2 + 196$
   f) $-2x^2 + 18x$
   g) $1.5x^2 + 4.5x - 27$
   h) $-6.2x^2 + 396.8$

7. Which pairs contain equivalent expressions? How do you know?
   a) $3x^2 + 30x + 75$ $3(x + 5)(x + 5)$
   b) $5x^2 + 3x + 2$ $5(x + 2)(x + 1)$
   c) $4x^2 - 10x + 24$ $4(x - 6)(x - 4)$
   d) $-2x^2 - 22x - 40$ $-2(x + 4)(x + 5)$

Apply B ●

For help with questions 8 and 9, refer to Example 3.

8. George is a designer for ZupperWare, a manufacturer of resealable tin containers with plastic lids. His latest design is a set of cylindrical containers that fit inside each other for easy storage.

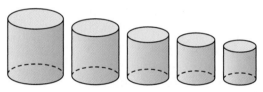

The dimensions of the five containers are given in the table. The surface area of the tin portion of a container is given by the formula S.A. $= 2\pi rh + \pi r^2$.

Height (cm)	Radius (cm)
20	10
18	9
16	8
14	7
12	6

a) Factor the expression for the surface area.

b) The exteriors of the containers are to be painted. Calculate the total surface area of the five containers.

c) The height of each container is double its radius. Explain how you could use this fact to further simplify the expression for the surface area from part a).

9. The surface area of a cone is given by the formula S.A. $= \pi r^2 + \pi r s$.

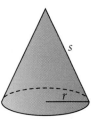

a) Factor the expression for the surface area.

b) Five cones all have a radius of 20 cm. Their slant height, s, is given in the table. Find the surface area of each cone.

Slant Height (cm)
40
45
50
55
60

c) A cone has a slant height that is three times its radius. Use your answer to part a) to write a simpler form of the expression for the surface area for this cone.

10. The makers of the Gateway Geyser in St. Louis, Missouri, claim that water is shot out of the fountain at 76 m/s and reaches heights of over 183 m. Ignoring air resistance, the height, h, in metres, of the water can be modelled by the relation $h = -4.9t^2 + 76t$, where t is the time, in seconds.

a) Factor the expression for the height of the water.

b) Make a table of values for times from 0 s to 10 s, in increments of 1 s. What is the approximate maximum height of the water (neglecting air resistance)?

c) Due to air resistance, the water only reaches about 65% of the predicted height. Is the manufacturer's claim regarding the maximum height of the fountain reasonable? Explain.

11. The fountain you are designing will use a pump that shoots water vertically out of the main fountain at 19.6 m/s and out of the smaller fountains at 14.7 m/s.

a) Write a relation for the height of the water, *h*, for each type of fountain using the general relation $h = -4.9t^2 + v_0t$, where v_0 is the initial velocity of the water and *t* is the time, in seconds.

b) Factor each expression from part a).

c) Find the approximate maximum height of the water from the main fountain and from the smaller fountains.

Achievement Check

12. Consider this pattern.

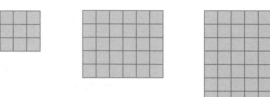

Diagram 1   **Diagram 2**   **Diagram 3**   **Diagram 4**

a) Count the number of unit squares in each diagram. Copy and complete the table.

Diagram	Number of Squares
1	
2	
3	
4	

b) The pattern continues. How many squares will be in Diagram 5?

c) Use first and second differences to determine if the relationship between the diagram number and the number of squares is quadratic.

d) Use a graphing calculator. Find an expression to represent the number of squares in a diagram.

e) Factor the expression from part d).

f) How do the factors of your expression relate to the side lengths of the rectangles?

13. Expand and simplify each expression. Describe any patterns.

a) $(3x - 5)(3x + 5)$ **b)** $(4x + 7)(4x - 7)$ **c)** $(5x + 2)(5x - 2)$

14. Refer to your answer to question 13. Factor each expression.

i) $64x^2 - 9$ **ii)** $49x^2 - 36$ **iii)** $100x^2 - 9$

15. For a trinomial of the form $ax^2 + bx + c$ in which a is not a common factor, you can use the decomposition method to factor the trinomial. This method is shown below, using $6x^2 + 23x + 20$.

- Find two numbers whose product is ac and whose sum is b.

$$ac = 6 \times 20 \qquad\qquad b = 23$$
$$= 120$$
$$15 \times 8 = 120 \qquad 15 + 8 = 23$$

- Use the two numbers to "decompose" the middle term.

$$6x^2 + 23x + 20$$
$$= 6x^2 + 15x + 8x + 20$$

- Factor the first and second pairs of terms. The two binomial factors should be the same.

$$= 3x(2x + 5) + 4(2x + 5)$$

- Factor out the common binomial factor.

$$= (2x + 5)(3x + 4)$$

Factor each trinomial by decomposition. Expand to check.

a) $2x^2 + 19x + 24$

b) $10x^2 + 27x + 5$

c) $12x^2 + 13x + 3$

16. The quadratic relations in Group 1 have expressions that can be factored. Those in Group 2 have expressions that cannot be factored.

Group 1	Group 2
$y = x^2 + 5x + 4$	$y = x^2 + x + 1$
$y = 3x^2 - 27x + 54$	$y = -4x^2 - 10x - 8$
$y = -0.5x^2 + 3x + 8$	$y = 1.5x^2 - 5x + 8$

a) Graph each relation.

b) How are the graphs of the relations in Group 1 similar?

c) How are the graphs of the relations in Group 2 similar?

d) Compare the graphs of the relations in Group 1 to the graphs of the relations in Group 2. What do you notice? Explain.

5.5 The *x*-Intercepts of a Quadratic Relation

In the James Bond film, *The Man with the Golden Gun*, a complicated spiral car jump was filmed in only one take. The exact speed of the car had been determined by a computer, so the stunt could be performed precisely as planned. For stunts like this and others, it is important for a stunt coordinator to model not only where a car will begin to spiral and its general path, but also where it will land.

Investigate

Compare the Equation of a Quadratic Relation to Its Graph

Tools

• graphing calculator

1. a) Graph the quadratic relation $y = x^2 + 10x + 16$. What are the *x*-intercepts?

b) Factor the expression on the right side of the relation.

c) Compare the *x*-intercepts to the constant terms in the binomial factors of the factored form of the relation. What do you notice?

d) Graph the factored relation in the same window. What do you notice?

2. Copy and complete the table. Find the *x*-intercepts without graphing.

Relation	Factored Relation	x-Intercepts
$y = x^2 + 10x + 21$		
$y = x^2 - 8x + 15$		
$y = x^2 + 2x - 24$		
$y = x^2 - 49$		

3. Graph each factored relation from question 2. Use the graph to find the x-intercepts. How do these x-intercepts compare to those you found in question 2?

4. Reflect Given a quadratic relation in the form $y = x^2 + bx + c$, how can you find the x-intercepts without graphing?

intercept form
- a quadratic relation of the form $y = a(x - r)(x - s)$
- the constants, r and s, represent the x-intercepts of the relation

zeros
- the x-coordinates of the points where the graph of a relation crosses the x-axis
- the x-intercepts of a relation
- the values of x for which $y = 0$

The relation $y = x^2 + 5x + 6$ can be expressed as $y = (x + 2)(x + 3)$. This is the **intercept form** of the quadratic relation. The x-intercepts are -2 and -3.

In general, to find the x-intercepts of a quadratic relation $y = ax^2 + bx + c$, first write the relation in intercept form, $y = a(x - r)(x - s)$. The x-intercepts are at $x = r$ and $x = s$. Since $y = 0$ at the points where the graph crosses the x-axis, the x-intercepts are also called the **zeros** of a quadratic relation.

Example 1

Factor to Find the Zeros of a Quadratic Relation

Factor each quadratic relation. Use the factors to find the zeros. Then, sketch the graph using the zeros and the y-intercept. Refer to the a-value to decide if the parabola opens upward or downward.

a) $y = 4x^2 + 4x - 168$

b) $y = -3x^2 + 24x - 48$

c) $y = x^2 - 8x$

d) $y = x^2 + 3x + 20$

Solution

a) $y = 4x^2 + 4x - 168$
$ = 4[x^2 + x - 42]$ Factor out the greatest common factor, 4.
$ = 4(x + 7)(x - 6)$ Factor the resulting trinomial.

The zeros are at $x = -7$ and $x = 6$.

From the original relation, the y-intercept is -168. To sketch the graph of the relation, plot the zeros and the y-intercept. Since $a > 0$, the graph opens upward.

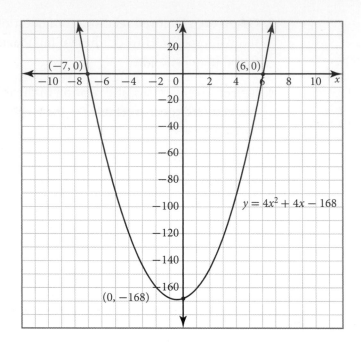

b) $y = -3x^2 + 24x - 48$

$\quad = -3[x^2 - 8x + 16]$ Factor out the greatest common factor, -3.

$\quad = -3(x - 4)(x - 4)$

$\quad = -3(x - 4)^2$

Since both factors are the same, there is only one zero at $x = 4$.

The intercept form of this relation is the same as the vertex form. The vertex is $(4, 0)$; this is also the x-intercept of the graph. From the original relation, the y-intercept is -48. Since $a < 0$, the graph opens downward.

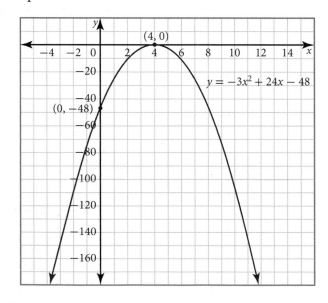

c) $y = x^2 - 8x$

$\quad = x(x - 8)$ The greatest common factor is x.

$\quad = (x + 0)(x - 8)$ You can also write the factors this way.

The zeros of this relation are at $x = 0$ and $x = 8$.

From the original relation, the y-intercept is 0. Since $a > 0$, the graph opens upward.

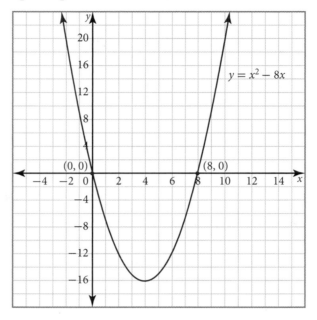

d) $y = x^2 + 3x + 20$

To factor this relation, try to find two values whose product is 20 and whose sum is 3.

There are no such values. There are two possible reasons for this:
• the relation has zeros that are not integers
• the relation has no zeros

Graph the relation to determine which reason applies to the relation.

The graph of $y = x^2 + 3x + 20$ does not cross the x-axis, so the relation has no zeros.

Example 2

Different Forms of a Quadratic Relation

Consider the quadratic relation $y = 3(x + 4)^2 - 108$.

a) What do you know about the graph of the given relation? Graph this relation.

b) Write the relation in standard form. What do you know about the graph of the relation from the standard form? Graph the relation.

c) Write the relation in intercept form. What do you know about the graph of the relation given the intercept form? Graph the relation.

d) Compare the graphs of each form of the relation. Check your graphs using technology.

Solution

a) From the given relation, the vertex is at $(-4, -108)$.
Since $a = 3$, the graph opens upward.

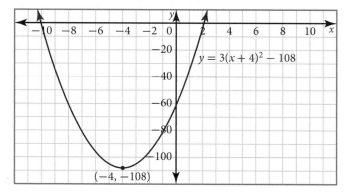

b) $y = 3(x + 4)^2 - 108$
$\quad = 3(x + 4)(x + 4) - 108$
$\quad = 3[x^2 + 4x + 4x + 16] - 108$
$\quad = 3x^2 + 12x + 12x + 48 - 108$
$\quad = 3x^2 + 24x - 60$

From the standard form, the y-intercept is -60.

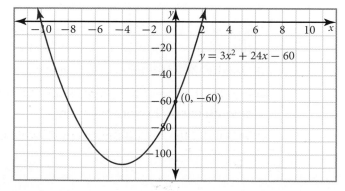

c) $y = 3x^2 + 24x - 60$
$= 3[x^2 + 8x - 20]$
$= 3(x - 2)(x + 10)$

From the intercept form, the zeros, or x-intercepts, are at $x = 2$ and $x = -10$.

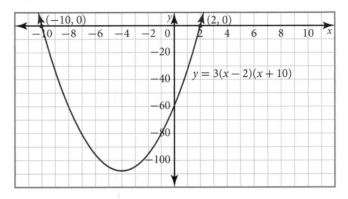

d) The graphs are identical for all forms of the relation. Use a graphing calculator to check.

 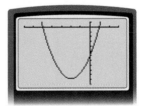

Example 3

Projectile Motion

A football is kicked from ground level. Its path is given by the relation $h = -4.9t^2 + 22.54t$, where h is the ball's height above the ground, in metres, and t is the time, in seconds.

a) Write the relation in intercept form.

b) Use the intercept form of the relation. Make a table of values with times from 0.5 s to 3.5 s, in increments of 0.5 s.

c) Use the intercept form of the relation to find the zeros.

d) Plot the zeros and the points from the table of values. Draw a smooth curve through the points.

e) When did the ball hit the ground? Explain how you found your answer.

Solution

a) There is no constant term. Factor out $-4.9t$.

$$h = -4.9t^2 + 22.54t$$
$$= -4.9t(t - 4.6)$$

b)

Time (s)	Height (m)
0.5	10.045
1.0	17.640
1.5	22.785
2.0	25.480
2.5	25.725
3.0	23.520
3.5	18.865

c) The intercept form is $h = -4.9t(t - 4.6)$. The zeros are at $t = 0$ and $t = 4.6$.

d)

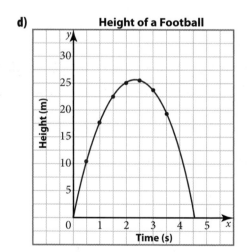

Height of a Football

e) The zeros represent the times when the ball was on the ground. One of the zeros is at $t = 0$, which is when the ball was kicked. The other zero is at $t = 4.6$, which is when the ball landed.
The ball hit the ground at 4.6 s.

Key Concepts

- Given a quadratic relation in intercept form, $y = a(x - r)(x - s)$, the zeros, or x-intercepts, are r and s.
- The vertex, standard, and intercept forms of a quadratic relation give the same parabola when graphed.

Discuss the Concepts

D1. What do you know about the graph given each form of a quadratic relation?

    a) vertex form, $y = a(x - h)^2 + k$

    b) standard form, $y = ax^2 + bx + c$

    c) intercept form, $y = a(x - r)(x - s)$

D2. The x-intercepts of a quadratic relation are at $x = -3$ and $x = 5$, and $a = 5$. Explain how you would find the standard form of the quadratic relation.

Practise A

For help with questions 1 to 5, refer to Example 1.

1. Find the x-intercepts of each quadratic relation.

    a)

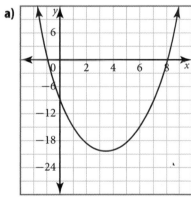

    b)

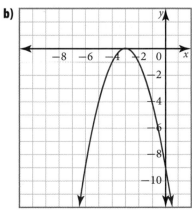

2. Find the zeros of each quadratic relation.

a)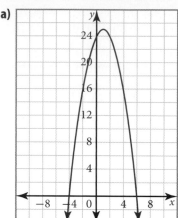

b)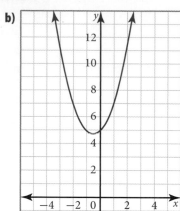

3. Find the zeros of each quadratic relation.

a) $y = (x - 5)(x + 3)$

b) $y = (x - 4)(x - 1)$

c) $y = 5(x - 9)(x - 9)$

d) $y = 3(x - 7)(x + 6)$

e) $y = -2(x + 8)(x + 2)$

f) $y = -3x(x + 5)$

4. Find the zeros by factoring. Check by graphing the intercept form and the standard form of each relation.

a) $y = x^2 + 10x + 16$

b) $y = x^2 - 2x - 35$

c) $y = x^2 - 6x - 7$

d) $y = 5x^2 - 125$

e) $y = 3x^2 + 39x + 108$

f) $y = 2x^2 - 28x + 98$

5. Find the zeros by factoring. Check by graphing the intercept form and the standard form of each relation.

a) $y = 4x^2 - 16x$

b) $y = 5x^2 - 125x$

c) $y = -5x^2 + 5x + 360$

d) $y = -x^2 - 18x - 81$

e) $y = -3.9x^2 + 19.5x$

f) $y = 7.5x^2 + 90x + 270$

For help with questions 6 and 7, refer to Example 2.

6. Which relations have more than one zero? Explain how you know.

a) $y = 3(x - 15)^2 + 2$

b) $y = -5(x + 2)^2 + 9$

c) $y = -(x - 8)^2 - 6$

d) $y = 9(x + 3)^2 - 10$

7. Given each quadratic relation in vertex form, express the relation in standard form and in intercept form. Then, check your answers by graphing all three forms.

a) $y = (x + 5)^2 - 4$

b) $y = (x - 3)^2 - 36$

c) $y = -2(x + 4)^2 + 8$

d) $y = 6(x + 2)^2 - 6$

e) $y = 3(x - 4)^2 - 48$

f) $y = -4(x - 5)^2 + 100$

8. A skateboarder jumps a gap that is 1.3 m wide. Her path can be modelled by the relation $h = -1.25d^2 + 1.875d$, where h is her height above the ground and d is her horizontal distance from the edge of the gap, both in metres.

a) Write the relation in intercept form.

b) Determine the zeros of the relation. Will the skateboarder make it across the gap? Explain.

c) Copy and complete the table.

Horizontal Distance (m)	Height (m)
0	
0.25	
0.50	
0.75	
1.00	
1.25	
1.50	

d) Estimate the maximum height the skateboarder reached during her jump.

e) Graph the relation.

9. A second skateboarder jumps off a ledge. His path is modelled by the relation $h = -0.8d^2 + 0.8d + 1.6$, where h is his height above the ground and d is his horizontal distance from the ledge, both in metres.

a) What is the height of the ledge?

b) Factor to find the zeros of the relation.

c) At what point will the skateboarder land on the ground?

d) Graph the relation.

10. In a target game at an amusement park, players launch a beanbag toward a bucket using a mallet and a small seesaw. The path of a beanbag that lands directly in the bucket can be modelled by the relation $h = -0.65d^2 + 1.625d$, where h is the beanbag's height above the table and d is the beanbag's distance from the seesaw, both in metres.

a) Find the zeros of the relation.

b) How far is the bucket from the seesaw?

c) Find the beanbag's maximum height above the table to the nearest tenth of a metre.

11. The path of a stunt car can be modelled by the relation $h = -0.1d^2 + 0.5d + 3.6$ where h is the car's height above the ground and d is the car's horizontal distance from the edge of the ramp, both in metres.

a) Find the zeros of the relation.

b) How far from the ramp will the car land?

c) Suppose the stunt is done inside a sound studio with a ceiling height of 10 m. Will the car hit the ceiling? Explain your reasoning.

12. A quadratic relation of the form $y = ax^2 + bx + c$ that cannot be factored might still have zeros. Another method for finding the zeros of a quadratic relation is to use the quadratic formula:

$$x = \frac{-b \pm \sqrt{b^2 - 4ac}}{2a}$$

Use the quadratic formula to find the zeros of each relation.

a) $y = 3x^2 + 21x + 30$

b) $y = 16x^2 - 40x - 75$

c) $y = 2x^2 + 5x - 6$

13. A quadratic relation of the form $y = ax^2 + bx + c$ has zeros if the expression $b^2 - 4ac$ in the quadratic formula $x = \dfrac{-b \pm \sqrt{b^2 - 4ac}}{2a}$ is greater than or equal to zero. Determine if each relation has zeros.

a) $y = 5x^2 + 3x + 15$

b) $y = 25x^2 + 60x + 36$

c) $y = 7x^2 - 10x + 5$

14. A cannonball is shot from ground level with an initial velocity of 20 m/s. Ignoring air resistance, its path can be modelled by the relation $h = -\dfrac{0.0125}{(\cos \theta)^2} d^2 + (\tan \theta)d$, where h is the cannonball's height above the ground, in metres, d is the horizontal distance from the cannon, in metres, and θ is the cannon's angle of elevation, in degrees. What angle of elevation will allow the cannonball to travel the greatest distance?

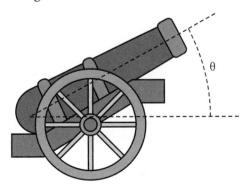

5.6 Solve Problems Involving Quadratic Relations

A company that produces fireworks displays must be sure that the sparks are no longer burning when they reach the ground. The path of a firework rocket can be modelled by a quadratic relation. By analysing the relation and understanding the characteristics of projectile motion, the company can ensure that their fireworks displays are safe.

Example 1

Use the Zeros to Find the Maximum

Consider the quadratic relation $y = 4x^2 - 72x + 260$.

a) Does this relation have a maximum or minimum? How do you know?

b) Find the zeros of the relation.

c) Determine the x-coordinate of the maximum or minimum point.

d) Find the maximum or minimum.

e) Write the relation in vertex form.

Solution

a) Since a is positive, the parabola opens upward. It has a minimum.

b) To find the zeros, factor the expression.
$$y = 4x^2 - 72x + 260$$
$$= 4(x^2 - 18x + 65)$$
$$= 4(x - 5)(x - 13)$$
The zeros are at $x = 5$ and $x = 13$.

c) The minimum point occurs at the vertex. The x-coordinate of the vertex is midway between the zeros. It is the mean of the zeros.

$$\frac{5 + 13}{2} = 9$$

To find the mean of two numbers, add the numbers and divide the sum by 2.

The x-coordinate of the minimum point is 9.

d) Substitute $x = 9$.

$$\begin{aligned} y &= 4x^2 - 72x + 260 \\ &= 4(9)^2 - 72(9) + 260 \\ &= 324 - 648 + 260 \\ &= -64 \end{aligned}$$

The minimum is -64.

e) The minimum value, -64, occurs when $x = 9$. The coordinates of the vertex are $(9, -64)$. From the original relation, $a = 4$. Substitute the a-value and the coordinates of the vertex into $y = a(x - h)^2 + k$.

$$y = 4(x - 9)^2 - 64$$

The relation in vertex form is $y = 4(x - 9)^2 - 64$.

---

axis of symmetry
- a vertical line through the vertex of a parabola
- the x-intercept of the vertical line is halfway between the zeros

The graph of a quadratic relation is symmetrical. The maximum or minimum lies halfway between the zeros, on the **axis of symmetry**, which is a vertical line through the vertex. The x-intercept of the axis of symmetry is midway between the zeros.

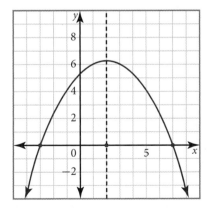

The zeros are at $x = -3$ and $x = 7$.
The equation for the axis of symmetry is $x = 2$.

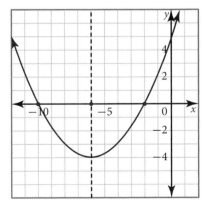

The zeros are at $x = -10$ and $x = -2$.
The equation for the axis of symmetry is $x = -6$.

| Example 2 | ## Find the Width of a Walkway |

A rectangular garden with dimensions 12 m by 8 m is surrounded by a walkway of uniform width, x. The total area of the garden and the walkway is 252 m².

a) Write expressions for the total length and the total width of the garden and walkway.

b) Write an expression for the total area of the garden and walkway.

c) Find the width of the walkway.

d) Check your answer to part c).

Solution

a) Draw and label a diagram to represent the situation.

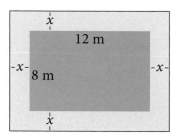

$$\text{Length} = x + 12 + x$$
$$= 12 + 2x$$

$$\text{Width} = x + 8 + x$$
$$= 8 + 2x$$

The total length of the garden and the walkway is $12 + 2x$. The total width of the garden and the walkway is $8 + 2x$.

b) $\text{Area} = \text{length} \times \text{width}$
$$= (12 + 2x)(8 + 2x)$$
$$= 96 + 24x + 16x + 4x^2$$
$$= 4x^2 + 40x + 96$$

An expression for the total area of the garden and walkway is $4x^2 + 40x + 96$.

c) Substitute 252 for the area and find the zeros.

$$252 = 4x^2 + 40x + 96$$
$$252 - 252 = 4x^2 + 40x + 96 - 252 \qquad \text{To make the left side equal zero,}$$
$$\text{subtract 252 from both sides.}$$
$$0 = 4x^2 + 40x - 156$$
$$0 = 4(x^2 + 10x - 39)$$
$$0 = 4(x - 3)(x + 13)$$

From the factored form, the zeros are 3 and -13. Only the positive answer, 3, is realistic given the question. The walkway is 3 m wide.

d) You can check your answer to part c) two ways.

Substitute $x = 3$ into the expressions for length and width, then find the area.

$$\begin{aligned}
\text{Length} &= 12 + 2x & \text{Width} &= 8 + 2x \\
&= 12 + 2(3) & &= 8 + 2(3) \\
&= 18 & &= 14
\end{aligned}$$

$$\begin{aligned}
\text{Area} &= \text{length} \times \text{width} \\
&= (18)(14) \\
&= 252
\end{aligned}$$

Substitute $x = 3$ into the expression for the total area.

$$\begin{aligned}
\text{Area} &= 4x^2 + 40x + 96 \\
&= 4(3)^2 + 40(3) + 96 \\
&= 252
\end{aligned}$$

Example 3

Write the Equation of a Quadratic Relation

a) Graph each quadratic relation on the same set of axes.

i) $y = 0.15x(x - 12)$ **ii)** $y = -0.2x(x - 12)$ **iii)** $y = -0.4x(x - 12)$

b) What is the same about the graphs and their relations? What is different?

c) Write the equation for a parabola that has the same zeros but passes through point (4, 8).

Solution

a)

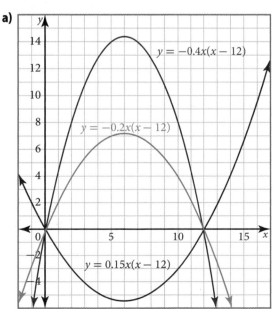

b) From the graphs, the parabolas have the same zeros: 0 and 12. Each parabola has a different vertical stretch or compression, and a different vertex. Two of the parabolas open downward and one opens upward. Each relation contains the expression $x(x - 12)$. The a-values of the relations are different.

c) Each relation has the form $y = ax(x - 12)$. Substitute the coordinates of the point that is to lie on the parabola.

Substitute $x = 4$ and $y = 8$.

$y = ax(x - 12)$
$8 = a(4)(4 - 12)$
$8 = a(4)(-8)$
$8 = -32a$
$a = -0.25$

The relation is $y = -0.25x(x - 12)$. The graph of this relation is the light blue parabola.

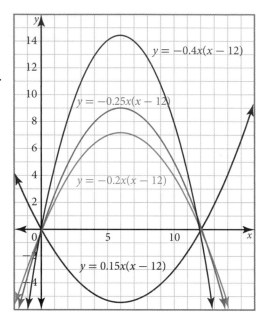

$y = -0.4x(x - 12)$
$y = -0.25x(x - 12)$
$y = -0.2x(x - 12)$
$y = 0.15x(x - 12)$

Key Concepts

- The maximum or minimum point of a parabola is halfway between the zeros of the parabola.

- The axis of symmetry is a vertical line through the vertex and a point on the x-axis halfway between the zeros.

Discuss the Concepts

D1. You have learned about three forms of quadratic relations:
  - standard form, $y = ax^2 + bx + c$
  - vertex form, $y = a(x - h)^2 + k$
  - intercept form, $y = a(x - r)(x - s)$

  What information about the parabola can you obtain from each form?

D2. Is it always possible to find the maximum or minimum of a quadratic relation using the zeros of the relation? Use examples to explain.

1. Find the zeros of each quadratic relation.

    a) $y = (x + 4)(x - 5)$ **b)** $y = (x + 9)(x + 15)$

    c) $y = 8(x + 3)(x + 19)$ **d)** $y = 5(x - 8)(x + 10)$

2. Express each quadratic relation in intercept form.

    a) $y = x^2 + 7x + 12$ **b)** $y = x^2 + 11x + 28$

    c) $y = 3x^2 + 39x + 120$ **d)** $y = -2x^2 + 10x + 132$

3. Find the zeros of each quadratic relation.

    a) $y = x^2 + 3x - 28$ **b)** $y = x^2 - 16$

    c) $y = 2x^2 - 2x - 112$ **d)** $y = 3x^2 + 21x - 294$

    e) $y = 5x^2 - 280$ **f)** $y = -2x^2 + 18$

    g) $y = -4.9x^2 + 24.5x + 245$ **h)** $y = 2.5x^2 + 50x - 560$

For help with questions 4 to 6, refer to Example 1.

4. What is the equation of the axis of symmetry for each parabola?

a)
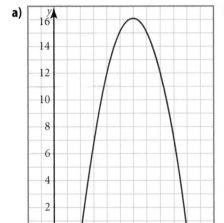

b)
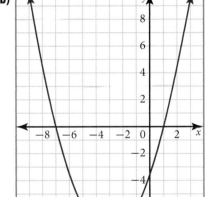

c)
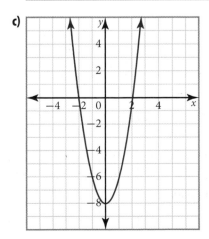

d)
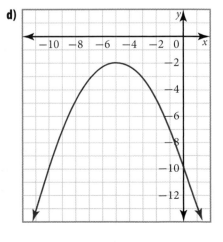

5. Find the equation of the axis of symmetry for each quadratic relation.

   a) $y = (x + 4)(x + 12)$ **b)** $y = (x - 7)(x - 1)$

   c) $y = 8(x - 5)(x + 9)$ **d)** $y = -5(x + 12)(x - 4)$

   e) $y = 6x(x + 10)$ **f)** $y = -3x(x - 8)$

6. Refer to question 5. Write each relation in standard form and in vertex form. Check your answers by graphing.

Apply **B** • ·

For help with question 7, refer to Example 2.

7. A rectangular pool is 6 m wide and 10 m long. A concrete deck of uniform width is to surround the pool.

   a) Sketch and label a diagram to represent the pool and the concrete deck.

   b) Write an expression for the total width and the total length of the pool and deck.

   c) Write a relation, in standard form, for the total area of the pool and deck.

   d) If the total area of the pool and deck cannot exceed 320 m², what is the greatest possible width of the deck?

8. A square-based box with an open top is to be made from a square piece of cardboard that has side length 100 cm. The sides of the box are formed when four congruent square corner pieces are removed. The height of the box to be formed is represented by the value x.

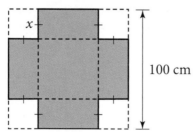

   a) Determine an expression for the area of cardboard used to make the box.

   b) If the surface area of the box is to be 6400 cm², find the height of the box.

9. a) Write an expression for the area of this rectangle.

8x – 16

2x + 6

b) For what value of x will the rectangle have area 576 m^2?

For help with question 10, refer to Example 3.

10. a) Write three different quadratic relations, in standard form, for parabolas with zeros at $x = 1$ and $x = -5$.

b) Graph each relation.

c) Determine the quadratic relation for a parabola with the same zeros that passes through $(-3, -20)$.

11. A pattern of rectangles is made with unit squares. The relationship between the total number of unit squares, T, and the diagram number, d, is given by the relation $T = d^2 + d$.

Diagram 1   Diagram 2   Diagram 3   Diagram 4

a) How many unit squares are needed for Diagram 8?

b) What diagram number would you expect to contain 110 unit squares?

12. Logs are stacked in a triangular pattern as shown. The relationship between the total number of logs, T, and the number of layers, L, is given by the relation $T = 0.5L^2 + 0.5L$.

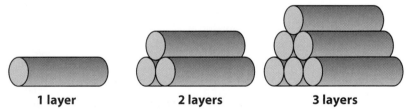

1 layer   2 layers   3 layers

a) How many logs would be in 7 layers?

b) How many layers would there be for 120 logs?

c) Would a pile of 160 logs fit the triangular pattern? Explain.

13. A fireworks company is testing a new firework rocket. Once it explodes in the air, its path can be modelled by the relation $h = -4.9t^2 + 44.1t$, where h is the rocket's height, in metres, and t is the time, in seconds.

  a) When will the rocket hit the ground?

  b) What is the rocket's maximum height?

  c) If the rocket continues to glow for 2.5 s after it begins to fall, will it be glowing when it hits the ground? Explain.

14. The speed of a turbine aircraft engine is controlled by a power setting, x. The length of time, t, in hours, that the engine will run on a given amount of fuel at power setting x is given by the relation $t = -0.2x^2 + 3.2x - 5.6$.

  a) Find the zeros of the relation.

  b) Find the coordinates of the vertex. What do the coordinates of the vertex represent in terms of this situation?

  c) Check your answers to parts a) and b) by graphing the relation, using technology.

15. In July 2005, professional skateboarder Danny Way jumped over the Great Wall of China. His path can be modelled by the relation $h = -0.05d^2 + 1.15d$, where h is his height above the Great Wall and d is his horizontal distance from the take-off ramp, both in metres.

  a) Factor the relation.

  b) Use the factored relation to determine the distance between Danny's take-off and landing.

  c) What was Danny's maximum height above the Great Wall?

Chapter Problem

16. The fountain will have two identical jets of water side-by-side. The horizontal distance between the streams of water is 3 m. The path of the water from the jet on the left is modelled by the relation $h = -1.5(d - 1)^2 + 1.5$, where h is the height of the water and d is the horizontal distance from the nozzle, both in metres.

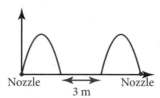

Nozzle   3 m   Nozzle

a) Find the horizontal distance from the left nozzle to where the water hits the ground.

b) Determine the horizontal distance between the nozzles for the two jets.

Reasoning and Proving

Representing | Selecting Tools

Problem Solving

Connecting | Reflecting

Communicating

Achievement Check

17. A football player kicks a ball into the air. The ball's path can be modelled by the relation $h = -0.04(d - 19)^2 + 14.44$, where h is the ball's height and d is the ball's distance from the kicker, both in metres.

a) What is the ball's maximum height reached by the ball?

b) Express the relation in standard form and in intercept form.

c) What horizontal distance will the ball travel before it lands?

d) The goalposts are 35 m away and the crossbar is approximately 3 m high. Will the ball clear the crossbar?

Extend **C**

18. Ignoring air resistance, the path of a cannonball shot from ground level is modelled by the relation $h = -\dfrac{5}{(v_0 \cos \theta)^2} d^2 + (\tan \theta)d$,

where h is the cannonball's height above the ground, in metres, d is the cannonball's horizontal distance from the cannon, in metres, v_0 is the cannonball's initial velocity, in metres per second, and θ is the cannon's angle of elevation, in degrees. If θ is 45°, what initial velocity should be used to hit a target 90 m from the cannon?

5 Review

5.1 Expand Binomials, pages 234–241

1. Expand and simplify.

a) $(x + 5)(x + 8)$

b) $(2x + 9)(7x - 10)$

c) $(x + 13)^2$

d) $(x - 7)(x + 7)$

2. Write a simplified expression for the area of the rectangle.

$8x - 2$

$2x + 1$

5.2 Change Quadratic Relations From Vertex Form to Standard Form, pages 242–247

3. Write each relation in standard form.

a) $y = 5(x + 10)^2 + 7$

b) $y = -0.5(x + 8)^2 + 4$

c) $y = 9(x - 8)^2 - 4$

d) $y = 2(x + 1)^2 - 6$

4. Find the y-intercept for each relation in question 3.

5. A ball is kicked straight up. Its path is modelled by the relation $h = -4.9t^2 + v_0t + h_0$, where h is the ball's height in metres, h_0 is the ball's initial height, in metres, t is the time in seconds, and v_0 is the ball's initial velocity, in metres per second. The ball reaches a maximum height of 45 m after 3 s. Determine the ball's initial velocity and initial height.

5.3 Factor Trinomials of the Form $x^2 + bx + c$, pages 248–255

6. Factor.

a) $x^2 + 15x$

b) $x^2 + 13x + 40$

c) $x^2 + 10x + 25$

d) $x^2 - 81$

e) $x^2 + 2x - 24$

f) $x^2 - 12x + 35$

g) $x^2 - 100$

h) $x^2 - 11x - 12$

7. a) Write a factored expression for the area of the shaded region of this figure.

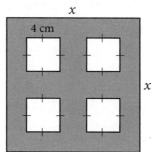

b) Calculate the area of the shaded region when $x = 30$ cm.

5.4 Factor Trinomials of the Form $ax^2 + bx + c$, pages 256–263

8. Factor fully.

a) $4x^2 + 72x + 308$

b) $12x^2 + 96x$

c) $3x^2 - 12x - 135$

d) $-2x^2 - 24x - 72$

e) $-8x^2 + 200$

f) $10x^2 - 80x - 200$

9. a) Write a factored expression for the area of the shaded region of this figure.

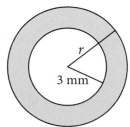

3 mm

b) Suppose $r = 15$ mm. Find the area of the shaded region.

5.5 The *x*-Intercepts of a Quadratic Relation, pages 264–275

10. Find the zeros of each quadratic relation.

a) $y = x^2 - 16x$

b) $y = x^2 - 16$

c) $y = 6x^2 + 24x - 192$

11. Write each quadratic relation in standard form, then find the zeros.

a) $y = 3(x - 1)^2 - 147$

b) $y = -4(x + 6)^2 + 36$

12. The path of a soccer ball can be modelled by the relation $h = -0.1d^2 + 0.5d + 0.6$, where h is the ball's height and d is the horizontal distance from the kicker.

a) Find the zeros of the relation.

b) What do the zeros mean in this context?

5.6 Solve Problems Involving Quadratic Relations, pages 276–285

13. For each quadratic relation, find the zeros and the maximum or minimum.

a) $y = x^2 + 16x + 39$

b) $y = 5x^2 - 50x - 120$

c) $y = -2x^2 - 28x + 64$

d) $y = 6x^2 + 36x - 42$

14. A garden is to be surrounded by a paved border of uniform width.

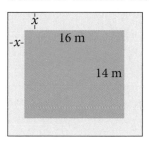

a) Write a simplified expression for the area of the border.

b) The border is to have an area of 216 m². Find the width of the border.

15. A rider on a mountain bike jumps off a ledge. Her path is modelled by the relation $h = -0.3d^2 + 1.2d + 1.5$, where h is her height above the ground and d is her horizontal distance from the ledge, both in metres.

a) What is the height of the ledge?

b) How far was the rider from the ledge when she landed?

5 Practice Test

For questions 1 to 6, choose the best answer.

1. Which expression is equivalent to $(2x + 9)(2x + 9)$?

   A $4x^2 + 81$

   B $4x^2 - 81$

   C $4x^2 + 18x + 81$

   D $4x^2 + 36x + 81$

2. Which expression is the result of expanding and simplifying $(5x - 7)(3x + 5)$?

   A $15x^2 + 46x + 35$

   B $15x^2 + 4x - 35$

   C $8x^2 + 20x + 13$

   D $8x^2 - 13$

3. Which relation represents the same parabola as $y = 5(x - 6)^2 - 20$?

   A $y = 5x^2 - 6x - 20$

   B $y = 5x^2 - 12x + 16$

   C $y = 5x^2 - 60x + 160$

   D $y = 5x^2 - 12x + 160$

4. Which expression is the factored form of $x^2 - 8x - 20$?

   A $(x - 8)(x - 20)$

   B $(x - 10)(x + 2)$

   C $(x + 8)(x + 20)$

   D $(x - 2)(x + 10)$

5. Which is the equation of the axis of symmetry for the quadratic relation $y = (x - 7)(x + 17)$?

   A $x = -5$ **B** $x = 7$

   C $x = 12$ **D** $x = 17$

6. Which are the zeros for the quadratic relation $y = 5x^2 - 1125$?

   A $x = 0$

   B $x = 5, x = 15$

   C $x = -15, x = 5$

   D $x = -15, x = 15$

7. Which expression is the factored form of $4x^2 - 44x - 240$?

   A $4(x - 44)(x - 240)$

   B $4(x - 4)(x - 60)$

   C $4(x - 15)(x + 4)$

   D $4(x - 11)(x - 60)$

8. **a)** Write an expression, in simplified form, for the area of the rectangle.

   $6x + 8$

   $3x - 10$ [rectangle]

   b) Find the area of the rectangle when $x = 5$ cm.

9. Write each quadratic relation in standard form.

   a) $y = 13(x + 7)^2 + 11$

   b) $y = -4(x - 3)^2 + 16$

   c) $y = 5.6(x - 1.2)^2 - 8.2$

10. Find the zeros of each quadratic relation.

    a) $y = x^2 - 2x - 35$

    b) $y = 3x^2 + 12x - 96$

    c) $y = -2.5x^2 - 40x - 70$

Chapter Problem Wrap-Up

Throughout this chapter, you looked at many aspects of designing and building a fountain. Now, you will design your own fountain. Describe how you would use quadratic relations in the design. Besides the jets of water, what other aspects of the fountain must you consider?

11. The curve of a cable on a suspension bridge can be modelled by the relation $h = 0.0025(d - 100)^2 + 25$ where h is the cable's height above the ground and d is the horizontal distance from the tower, both in metres.

a) At what height does the cable meet the tower?

b) What is the least height of the cable above the ground?

12. A circus acrobat jumps off a raised platform. He lands on a trampoline at stage level below. His path can be modelled by the relation $h = -0.7d^2 + 0.7d + 4.2$, where h is his height above the stage and d is his horizontal distance from the edge of a platform, both in metres.

a) What is the height of the platform?

b) How far from the edge of the platform did the acrobat land?

c) What was the acrobat's maximum height above the stage?

Design a Soccer Field

Have you ever walked on a new football or soccer field? If so, you probably noticed that the field was slightly arched, not flat. These fields are highest in the centre, permitting rainwater to drain away quickly.

1. The graph shows the profile of the width of a soccer field, viewed from one end. Assume that the cross-section is parabolic. Write a quadratic relation that models the profile of the soccer field. Let h represent the height, in metres, above the sidelines, and d represent the horizontal distance, in metres, from the left sideline.

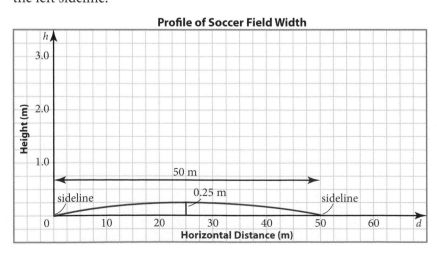

Profile of Soccer Field Width

2. When viewed lengthwise, the cross-section of the soccer field has the same parabolic shape and the same 0.25 m rise in the middle of the field, but the goal lines are 100 m apart. Write a quadratic relation that models this profile of the soccer field.

3. The spot where penalty kicks are taken is 11 m in front of the goal line. How high above the goal line is the penalty spot, to the nearest tenth of a centimetre?

4. A sprinkler system is to be installed in the field. Precise positioning of the piping and sprinkler heads is necessary so the heads are flush with the ground. How far from the sidelines should a sprinkler head along the halfway line be placed so that it is flush with the ground 0.16 m above the side?

5. The centre circle in the middle of the field has a radius of 9.15 m. What are the minimum and maximum heights above the sideline along the centre circle, to the nearest tenth of a centimetre?

6 Geometry in Design

Why is knowledge of geometry important for so many activities? Think about a concert that you attended. How did geometry influence the band who wrote the music, the craftspeople who made the instruments, the artists who decorated the concert hall, the architect who designed the hall, the engineers who planned the hall's construction, and the tradespeople whose skills and talents made it all possible?

In this chapter, you will

- identify real-world applications of geometric shapes and figures, through investigation in a variety of contexts, and explain these applications
- represent three-dimensional objects, using concrete materials and design or drawing software, in a variety of ways
- create nets, plans, and patterns from physical models arising from a variety of real-world applications, by applying the metric and imperial systems and using design or drawing software
- solve design problems that satisfy given constraints, using physical models or drawings, and state any assumptions made

Reasoning and Proving

Representing | Selecting Tools

Problem Solving

Connecting | Reflecting

Communicating

Key Terms

constraint

golden ratio

golden rectangle

isometric perspective drawing

net

orthographic drawings

orthographic projection

pattern

plan

scale model

tessellation

Arqum studied graphic design at Fanshawe College and now creates signs for companies selling a product or service. He discusses each project with his customers, including size, materials, budget, and regulations, and designs layouts for billboards and business signs. Arqum uses geometric shapes and scale when he creates his designs on the computer.

Prerequisite Skills

Geometric Shapes

1. Identify the two-dimensional geometric shapes.

a)

b)

c)

d)

2. Identify the three-dimensional geometric shapes.

a)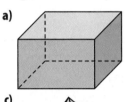

b)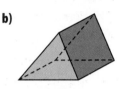

c)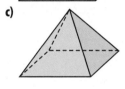

d)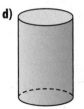

3. Identify the polygons.

a)

b)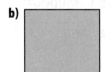

c)

d)

e)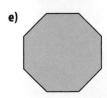

Perimeter and Area

Figure	Perimeter/Circumference	Area
rectangle	$P = 2l + 2w$	$A = lw$
triangle	$P = a + b + c$	$A = \frac{1}{2}bh$
circle	$C = \pi d$, $C = 2\pi r$	$A = \pi r^2$

4. Find the perimeter and the area of a rectangular sports field that measures 120 m by 100 m.

5. Find the perimeter and the area of a school crest in the shape of an equilateral triangle with a side length of 15 cm. The height of the triangle is approximately 13 cm.

6. Find the perimeter and the area of the base of a circular wading pool with a radius of 12 m.

Surface Area and Volume

Figure	Surface Area	Volume
cube/rectangular prism with dimensions l, w, h	$SA = 2lw + 2wh + 2lh$	$V = lwh$
triangular prism with a, b, c, h, l	$SA = al + bl + cl + bh$	$V = \frac{1}{2}blh$
cylinder with r, h	$SA = 2\pi rh + 2\pi r^2$	$V = \pi r^2 h$

7. Wilhelm built a closed room in his garage to use as a paint shop. The room measured 8 m by 6 m by 2.5 m.

   a) Wilhelm painted the interior walls and ceiling. Find the area that was painted.

   b) Wilhelm plans to install a blower to pump fresh air into the room. The size of blower required depends on the volume of the room. Find the volume of the room.

8. Sunita built a wheelchair ramp in the shape of a triangular prism, as shown. Each surface of the ramp is to be painted—with the exception of the base. Find the surface area to be painted.

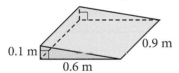

0.1 m

0.9 m

0.6 m

9. A cylindrical water tank has a radius of 5 ft and a height of 12 ft. The interior is to be painted with waterproof paint. Find the area to be painted, and the volume of water that the tank can hold.

Angles in a Polygon

10. The sum of the angles in a polygon with n sides, in degrees, is given by the formula $S = 180(n - 2)$. If the polygon is regular, the measure of each angle is given by the sum divided by n. Find the sum of the angles, and the measure of each angle, for a regular pentagon.

Scale Factors

11. Anil is planning to grow vegetables in a market garden measuring 24 m by 36 m. To plan the garden, he will draw a diagram using a scale of 1 cm to represent 2 m. Find the dimensions of the diagram.

12. Ted has made a scale model of a sailboat that he is planning to build. The model has a length of 10 in. Ted used a scale of 1 in. to represent 4 ft. What is the length of the sailboat?

Chapter Problem

Paul has secured a co-op position for one semester with a firm of architects and designers. The firm provides customers with designs, drawings, scale models, plans, patterns, and cost estimates for a variety of projects, such as prefabricated outbuildings, houses, and industrial products. Paul will learn how to provide customers with the services that the firm offers. As he works through the co-op position, Paul will be given design tasks that will require the knowledge and skills that he has learned during his placement.

Investigate Geometric Shapes and Figures

What is the link between the cells that make up a cell phone network and a tesselation pattern? How are the *Mona Lisa* and the Great Pyramid of Cheops in Egypt related? What is the connection between music and geometry?

In this section, you will investigate some of these relations, and begin to learn how to use geometric principles in art, architecture, and fashion.

Investigate 1

Tools

- copy of Leonardo da Vinci's painting *Mona Lisa*
- ruler

or

- computer
- *The Geometer's Sketchpad®*

Technology Tip

If the picture appears too large or too small, you can resize it using any drawing program, such as Microsoft® Paint.

The *Mona Lisa*

Uncover one of the secrets of the *Mona Lisa*.

1. Draw a rectangle that encloses the face of the *Mona Lisa*.

   Method 1: Use Pencil and Paper

   Use your ruler and pencil to draw the rectangle. Measure the length and width of the rectangle. Divide the length by the width.

   Method 2: Use *The Geometer's Sketchpad®*

   Open *The Geometer's Sketchpad®*. Search the Internet for a picture of the *Mona Lisa*. Right-click on the picture, and select **Copy**. Return to *The Geometer's Sketchpad®*. Select **Paste Picture** from the **Edit** menu. Draw a rectangle around the face of the *Mona Lisa*. Measure the length and width of the rectangle. Divide the length by the width.

golden ratio
- the ratio of two lengths is approximately 1.618:1

golden rectangle
- a rectangle that is pleasing to the eye
- the ratio of the length to the width is approximately 1.618:1

2. The ratio of the length to the width on the actual painting is 1.618:1. This is known as the **golden ratio**. A rectangle that is drawn using the golden ratio is known as a **golden rectangle**. The proportions of golden rectangles are pleasing to the eye. The golden ratio is often used in art and architecture.

3. Reflect Think about windows that you have seen on buildings in your neighbourhood. Which windows appear to be golden rectangles?

To learn more about the golden ratio in art and architecture, go to *www.mcgrawhill.ca/links/foundations11* and follow the links.

Investigate 2

Tools
- centimetre grid paper
- coloured pencils or markers
- pattern block template or pattern blocks

tessellation
- a pattern that covers a plane without overlapping or leaving gaps
- also called a tiling pattern

Tessellations

Certain shapes can be used to fill a plane completely, with no gaps. This is known as a **tessellation**, or "tiling the plane." As you can see from a piece of grid paper, a square is one of these shapes. Clothing is often made from fabrics with a checkerboard pattern. If colours are carefully chosen and placed, the pattern becomes more attractive.

Method 1: Use Pencil and Paper

1. Draw a square. Then, draw additional squares identical to the first square such that they form a tessellation. Use at least four different colours to make a pleasing pattern for clothing.

2. Triangles can also be used to form tessellations. Draw a triangle. Then, draw additional triangles identical to the first triangle such that they form a tessellation. Colour the triangles to create a pleasing pattern.

3. Reflect Can you use any triangle to tile the plane? Try several examples.

4. You can use a combination of triangles and rectangles to form a tessellation. Find a combination of a rectangle and several triangles that can be used to tile the plane. Draw your tessellation. Colour your pattern to create a pleasing design.

5. You can also use other regular geometric shapes to construct tessellations. Pattern blocks include many different regular geometric shapes. Use the blocks to experiment with different shapes that can tile the plane. Examine a vertex that is common to several polygons. What is the measure of the angle around the vertex?

Tools

- computer
- *The Geometer's Sketchpad®*
- pattern block applet

Technology Tip

Once you have a basic pattern, you can select all elements of the pattern. Then, use the **Copy** command from the **Edit** menu, and **Paste** it repeatedly. This is a fast way of tiling the plane.

Method 2: Use Computer Software

1. Open *The Geometer's Sketchpad®*. From the **Graph** menu, choose **Show Grid**. Select both axes, the origin, and the unit point. Choose **Hide Objects** from the **Display** menu.

2. Start in the upper left corner, and draw four points to enclose one of the squares. Select the four points in order. From the **Construct** menu, choose **Quadrilateral Interior**. Select the four points, and the interior. From the **Edit** menu, choose **Copy**, and then **Paste**. Drag the image to another square.

3. Right-click on one of the interiors. Choose **Color**, and change the colour of the square. You can continue this process to tile the screen with different coloured squares. Use at least four different colours to design a tessellation that would make a pleasing pattern for clothing.

4. Triangles can also be used to form tessellations. Start a new sketch. Draw a triangle. Then, draw additional triangles identical to the first triangle such that they form a tessellation. Colour the triangles to form a pleasing pattern.

5. **Reflect** Can you use any triangle to tile the plane? Try several examples.

6. You can use a combination of triangles and rectangles to form a tessellation. Start with a grid of squares. Find a combination of a rectangle and several triangles that can be used to tile the plane. Draw your tesselation. Colour your pattern to form a pleasing design.

7. You can also use other regular geometric shapes to construct tessellations. Go to *www.mcgrawhill.ca/links/foundations11* and follow the links to the Pattern Block Applet. Use the applet to experiment with different shapes that can tile the plane. Examine a vertex that is common to several polygons. What is the measure of the angle around the vertex?

The only regular polygons (triangle, square, pentagon, and so on) that can tile the plane are those whose interior angles divide evenly into 360°. These are the triangle (60°), the square (90°), and the hexagon (120°). A pentagon, for example, will not tile a plane because its interior angles (108°) do not divide evenly into 360°.

To learn more about tessellations, go to *www.mcgrawhill.ca/links/foundations11* and follow the links.

Investigate 3

Cell Phone Tower Networks

Cell phones are really small radios that communicate with towers connected to the telephone system. The towers in an urban area must be placed close together because cell phones are low-powered, typically about 3 W, and have a limited range. Also, each tower only offers a limited number of frequencies (about 800), restricting the number of calls that a tower can handle at one time.

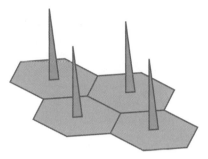

In an urban area, towers are placed about 5 km apart. Each tower is thought of as the centre of a hexagonal cell, as shown. Consider an urban area that measures 20 km on a side. Draw a tessellation using hexagons, and show how many towers are needed to service the cell phone network.

Tools

- ruler
- grid paper

Method 1: Use Pencil and Paper

1. Let 1 cm represent 1 km. Draw a square to represent an area 20 km by 20 km.

2. Lightly draw a hexagon, with a dot in the centre to represent the tower. Draw another hexagon next to the first one, leaving no gaps. Measure the distance between the two towers. If it is not close to 5 cm, adjust your hexagons. Once you think you have the correct size of hexagon, continue your diagram to cover the entire area.

3. How many towers are required to service the urban area?

4. **Reflect** What are the similarities between tiling the plane with triangles, designing a pattern for clothing, and ensuring that cell phone users have good service?

Technology Tip

Do not worry if your hexagons look a bit irregular. You will learn how to draw regular geometric shapes accurately later in this chapter.

Method 2: Use *The Geometer's Sketchpad*®

1. Open *The Geometer's Sketchpad*®. From the **Graph** menu, choose **Show Grid**. Drag the unit point on the horizontal axis until you can see +10 and −10 on your screen, on both the horizontal and vertical axes. Use the **Segment Tool** to draw a rectangle measuring 20 squares by 20 squares. This will represent an area 20 km by 20 km.

2. Use the **Segment Tool** to construct a hexagon in the upper left hand corner of the 20 km by 20 km grid. Draw a point in the centre of your hexagon to represent the tower.

3. Draw another hexagon next to the first one, leaving no gaps. Determine the distance between the two towers. If it is not close to 5 km, adjust your hexagons by dragging vertices. Once you think you have the correct size of hexagon, continue your diagram to cover the entire area.

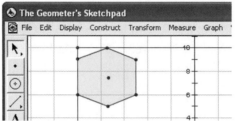

4. How many towers are required to service the urban area?

5. **Reflect** What are the similarities between tiling the plane with triangles, designing a pattern for clothing, and ensuring that cell phone users have good service?

To learn more about cell phones and how they work, go to *www.mcgrawhill.ca/links/foundations11* and follow the links.

Example

The Golden Ratio in Ancient Architecture

A cross-section of the Great Pyramid of Cheops on the Giza plateau in Egypt is shown. Find the ratio of the slant height *s* to half of the base. Express your answer to three decimal places.

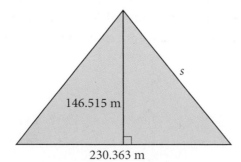

Solution

Half of the base $= 230.363 \div 2$
$$\doteq 115.182$$

Use the Pythagorean theorem to find the slant height.
$$s^2 \doteq (115.182)^2 + (146.515)^2$$
$$s^2 \doteq 34\,733.538$$
$$s \doteq \sqrt{34\,733.538}$$
$$s \doteq 186.369$$

The slant height is approximately 186.369 m.

Slant height:half of the base $\doteq 186.369:115.182$
$$\doteq 1.618:1$$

Math **Connect**

The number given for the golden ratio, 1.618, is an approximation. The exact value is $\dfrac{1 + \sqrt{5}}{2}$. Use a calculator to verify that this expression gives the correct approximation.

The ratio in the Example is the golden ratio once again. The golden ratio is a connection between the Mona Lisa and the Great Pyramid. A triangle that has this property, such as the cross-section of the Pyramid of Cheops, is known as an Egyptian triangle.

To learn more about the Pyramids, go to *www.mcgrawhill.ca/links/ foundations11* and follow the links.

Key Concepts

- Geometric shapes are used in architecture, art, and fashion. These shapes often use the golden ratio, which is approximately 1.618:1. The golden ratio is used in design because its proportions are pleasing to the eye.

- Some geometric shapes can be used to "tile a plane" such that there are no spaces. These tiling patterns are known as tessellations. Some polygons that tile a plane are squares, rectangles, equilateral triangles, and regular hexagons. Combinations of regular polygons can also tile a plane.

Discuss the Concepts

D1. How are geometric shapes used in the construction of your school? Make a list of the shapes that you notice, and where they are used.

D2. Can the shape shown be used to tile the plane? Use a sketch to explain.

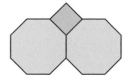

1. Which of these regular polygons cannot be used to tile a plane?

A triangle   **B** square

C hexagon   **D** octagon

2. Sandor claims that the screen on his new HD television is a golden rectangle. It measures 32 in. by 18 in. Is he correct? Justify your answer.

3. Look at the buildings in your neighbourhood. Identify geometric shapes that you see in the construction of these buildings. In particular, describe the use of shapes other than squares or rectangles.

4. Think about musical instruments that you have seen. Geometric shapes are present in the design of many musical instruments. List several instruments, and identify the geometric figures used in their design.

5. The old railroad station in Petrolia, ON, is now the public library. Identify the different two-dimensional and three-dimensional geometric figures that were used in its design.

Apply **B** •

Literacy Connect

6. Uploading personal digital pictures to the Internet is a popular activity. If you do this, and identify people in your pictures, the software that operates the posting site can "learn" to identify faces. It uses measurements and ratios similar to those you found for the *Mona Lisa* in Investigate 1. Once a face is in the database, other users can employ the software to identify individuals in other pictures. Write a short paragraph discussing the advantages and disadvantages of having such a software tool freely available on the Internet.

For help with questions 7 and 8, refer to Investigate A.

7. Sports such as soccer or lacrosse are often played on rectangular fields. Investigate the dimensions of several sports fields. Find the dimensions of an Olympic swimming pool. Are any dimensions close to a golden rectangle?

Technology Tip
You can search for images directly using most search engines, rather than searching for web sites and then looking for images.

8. Use the Internet to find a picture of each of these famous buildings. Copy each picture into *The Geometer's Sketchpad*®, and use the software to identify any golden rectangles that were used in the design.

   a) The Parthenon, in Athens, Greece. Use a front view.

   b) The Taj Mahal, in Agra, India. Use a front view, taken down the reflecting pool.

   c) The United Nations building in New York, NY. Use a view from the river.

   d) The Buddhist Temple in Niagara Falls, ON. Use a front view.

9. The actor Drew Barrymore is considered as a classic example of a "round face," while actor Fred Gwynne (who played a Frankenstein-like character on a popular television show) is considered to be an example of a "long face." Search for pictures of each actor. Use pencil and paper or *The Geometer's Sketchpad*® to determine how the actors' faces compare to the golden ratio.

10. The faces of some animals appear to have a greater width than height. One example is a house cat. Use pencil and paper or *The Geometer's Sketchpad*® to determine the facial ratio of a typical cat.

11. Paul has been reading about the history of architecture. Ancient Egyptian builders often needed to lay out large right angles for their constructions. They did this using a "12-knot rope." Obtain a piece of string about 1 m long. Tie 12 knots in the string such that the knots are 5 cm apart. Tie the ends of the string together such that you have 12 equal sections. Arrange the string to form a triangle with sides of 3, 4, and 5 sections.

    a) Measure the angle opposite the longest side.

    b) Write a short explanation of the mathematics behind this method.

12. Where is the geometry in music? The first few bars of the classic hard rock piece "In-A-Gadda-Da-Vida" by Iron Butterfly, widely acknowledged as the first heavy metal band, are shown.

    a) Notice the groupings of four notes. Draw lines joining adjacent notes in each group, and then a single line returning to the first note. The first triangle has been drawn for you. Describe the kinds of triangles that are formed.

    b) Triangles are often present in music composition. Find two three-note congruent triangles in this short excerpt from the popular holiday song "O Tannenbaum."

13. A stained glass panel contains several rectangles. Which rectangle is a golden rectangle or close to being a golden rectangle? Explain how you know.

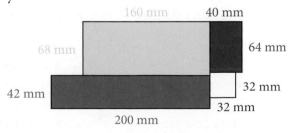

160 mm   40 mm
68 mm   64 mm
42 mm   32 mm
       32 mm
200 mm

14. Anwar claims that a hexagon does not need to be regular to tile the plane. He says that any hexagon that has opposite sides equal will work.

    a) Draw a hexagon with opposite sides equal. Be sure to use three different lengths in your drawing.

    b) Determine whether your hexagon can be used to tile the plane. If it can, show how it can be done. If it cannot, explain why not.

Extend

15. An architect is designing a window using the golden ratio.

    a) The longer side measures 2.5 m. To the nearest thousandth of a metre, what should be the length of the shorter side?

    b) Draw a sketch of the window. Cut a square out of the window, starting at the top, with a side length that is equal to the width. Compare the ratios the sides of the remaining rectangle. What do you notice?

16. Many countries use international paper sizes, such as ISO A4. A sheet of A4 paper measures 29.7 cm by 21.0 cm. This size is sold in Canada at office supply stores. Obtain a piece of A4 paper, or make one from a larger piece of paper.

    a) Find the ratio of the length to the width, and record it.

    b) Fold the paper in half across a line joining the midpoints of the lengths. Measure the length and width of the folded paper. Find the ratio of the length to the width.

    c) Fold the paper again. Find the ratio of the length to the width of the folded piece. What do you notice?

    d) The ratio of length to width for the ISO standard is always $\sqrt{2} : 1$. Use a calculator to compare this ratio to the ratios that you found.

17. Use pencil and paper or software, such as *The Geometer's Sketchpad®*, to design fabric with a tessellation print. The fabric should appeal to a person with a particular career or hobby, such as a musician, a golfer, a pilot, a nurse, etc. Be sure to use basic geometric shapes to form a more complex shape. Be creative in your selection of colours.

6.2 Perspective and Orthographic Drawings

scale model
- a model that is an enlargement of a small object or a reduction of a large object

isometric perspective drawing
- visual representation of three-dimensional objects in two dimensions

orthographic projection
- a set of drawings that show up to six views of an object
- usually front, side, and top views are given

orthographic drawing
- a drawing that uses orthographic projection

Habitat 67 is an apartment complex in Montreal. It was designed by Canadian architect Moshe Safdie for Expo '67, as an experiment in building apartments that allowed urban dwellers to enjoy both privacy and outdoor space. A **scale model** was used to represent what the complex would look like when finished.

Another means of representing three-dimensional objects is an **isometric perspective drawing**, which creates the illusion of three dimensions on a two-dimensional plane. A third representation is a series of **orthographic projections**, which illustrate front, side, and top views of the object.

How could you draw the isometric perspective and the orthographic representations of Habitat 67? How can drawing software be used to create these representations?

To learn more about Habitat 67, go to *www.mcgrawhill.ca/links/foundations11* and follow the links.

Investigate 1

Perspective Drawings of Cubes and Rectangular Prisms

Use a single linking cube or a model of a cube. Turn the cube until an edge is facing you. Then, tip the cube downwards. This is the perspective that you will draw.

Tools

- isometric dot paper
- linking cubes or other physical models of cubes
- ruler
- coloured pencils

Method 1: Use Pencil and Paper

1. **a)** Inspect the isometric dot paper. Find the lines of dots that are vertical. Draw a short vertical line segment in blue.

    b) Find the lines of dots that slope down to the right at 30°. Draw a short line segment sloping down to the right at 30° in red.

    c) Find the lines of dots that slope down to the left at 30°. Draw a short line segment sloping down to the left at 30° in green.

    d) Use the dot pattern to draw the isometric perspective, as shown.

2. **Reflect** Compare the isometric perspective drawing with the view of the cube. On an isometric perspective drawing, the lengths on the drawing are the same as the lengths on the real cube. Check that the sides of the cube on the drawing are of equal length.

3. Use linking cubes to construct a model of a rectangular prism that measures 1 cube by 2 cubes by 3 cubes. Draw an isometric perspective drawing of the prism.

Math Connect

The word "isometric" comes from the Greek words "iso," meaning "the same," and "metric," meaning "measure."

Tools

- computer
- *The Geometer's Sketchpad*®

Method 2: Use *The Geometer's Sketchpad*®

1. Open *The Geometer's Sketchpad*®. Choose **Open** from the **File** menu. Navigate to the directory that stores *The Geometer's Sketchpad*® files on your computer. This will likely be called **Sketchpad**, and be located in the **Program Files** directory. Choose **Samples**, then **Sketches**, and then **Geometry**. Select and open the file Dot Paper.gsp. Select the button **Isometric vertical**.

2. Inspect the isometric vertical dot pattern. Find the lines of dots that are vertical. Find the lines of dots that slope down to the right at 30°. Find the lines of dots that slope down to the left at 30°. Use the dot pattern to create the isometric perspective drawing of the cube, as shown.

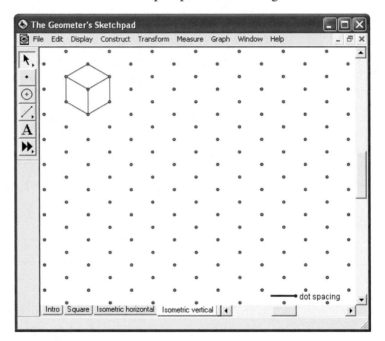

3. **Reflect** Compare the isometric perspective drawing with the view of the cube. On an isometric perspective drawing, the lengths on the drawing are the same as the lengths on the real cube. Check that the sides of the cube on the drawing are of equal length.

4. Use linking cubes to construct a model of a rectangular prism that measures 1 cube by 2 cubes by 3 cubes. Draw an isometric perspective drawing of the prism.

Orthographic Drawings of Cubes and Rectangular Prisms

Tools

- square dot paper
- linking cubes or other physical models of cubes
- ruler

Method 1: Use Pencil and Paper

1. Use a single linking cube or a model of the cube. Turn the cube until the front is facing you. Draw the front of the cube. Label the drawing.

Front View

2. Turn the cube until the right side is facing you. Draw and label the side view. Similarly, draw and label the top view.

3. **Reflect** What do you notice about the three orthographic drawings of the cube? A cube is a simple shape. However, the same method can be used to represent more complex shapes.

4. Use linking cubes to construct a model of a rectangular prism that measures 1 cube by 2 cubes by 3 cubes. Create three orthographic drawings of the prism: front view, side view, and top view.

Method 2: *Use The Geometer's Sketchpad®*

1. Open *The Geometer's Sketchpad®*. Open the file Dot Paper.gsp. Select the button **Square dot paper**.

2. Use a single linking cube or a model of a cube. Turn the cube until the front is facing you. Draw the front of the cube. Label the drawing.

3. Turn the cube until the side is facing you. Draw and label the side view. Similarly, draw and label the top view. Refer to the diagrams in Method 1.

4. **Reflect** What do you notice about the three orthographic drawings of the cube? A cube is a simple shape. However, the same method can be used to represent more complex shapes.

5. Use linking cubes to construct a model of a rectangular prism that measures 1 cube by 2 cubes by 3 cubes. Create three orthographic drawings of the prism: front view, side view, and top view.

You have been using *The Geometer's Sketchpad®* to draw perspective diagrams. Technical designers use more sophisticated programs, such as *AutoCAD®*. The science-fiction television series *Babylon 5* was created using *AutoCAD®* to render three-dimensional spaceships, space stations, and even some aliens. Amateur filmmakers often use commonly available drawing and design software to create inexpensive special effects for their productions.

To learn more about drawing software, go to *www.mcgrawhill.ca/links/ foundations11* and follow the links.

Example 1

Modelling a Flight of Stairs

a) Use linking cubes to create a model for a flight of stairs. There are three steps. The steps are 30 cm deep and 120 cm wide. Each riser measures 30 cm. Let the side of a cube represent 30 cm.

b) Draw an isometric perspective drawing of the model.

c) Sketch a set of orthographic drawings of the model.

Solution

a) The side of a cube represents 30 cm. The stairs will be 4 cubes wide, and 3 cubes deep at the bottom layer.

b) Use isometric dot paper or *The Geometer's Sketchpad*® to create the isometric perspective drawing of the stairs.

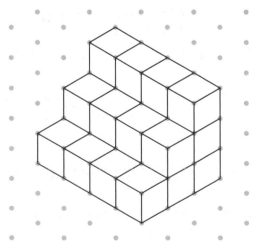

c) Use square dot paper or *The Geometer's Sketchpad*® to draw the orthographic drawings for the stairs.

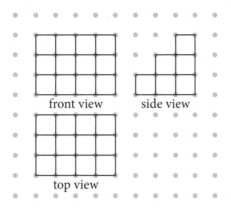

front view   side view

top view

Example 2

Isometric Drawing of a Square-Based Pyramid

Construct a model of a square-based pyramid using drinking straws and masking tape or other materials. Use isometric dot paper or *The Geometer's Sketchpad*® to draw an isometric perspective drawing of the pyramid.

Solution

First, draw the base. The base will appear as a diamond shape. Select a point in line with two opposite vertices to be the apex of the pyramid. Complete the pyramid by drawing the sides.

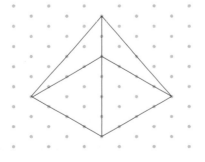

Example 3

Isometric Drawings With Curved Edges

Consider a concrete model of a cylinder, such as a juice or soup can. Use *The Geometer's Sketchpad®* to draw an isometric perspective drawing of the can.

Solution

Curved edges are represented by arcs of circles in isometric perspective drawings.
- Open *The Geometer's Sketchpad®*. Open the file Dot Paper.gsp. Press the button **Isometric vertical**.
- Use the **Point Tool** to draw three points just to the left of three of the points on the paper, as shown.

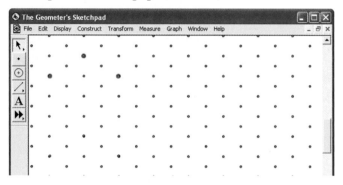

- Select the three points. Select **Arc Through 3 Points** from the **Construct** menu. Drag the arc slightly to the right such that it falls on three points on the dot paper. In a similar manner, construct three more arcs. Then, use the **Segment** tool to complete the sides of the cylinder, as shown.

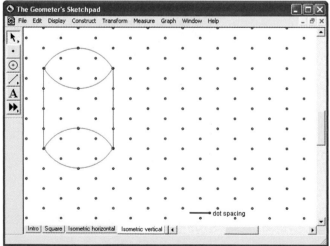

Note: You can also draw an isometric perspective drawing of a cylinder on paper using compasses and a ruler.

Key Concepts

- A three-dimensional object can be represented in three ways.
  - as a scale model using concrete materials
  - as an isometric perspective drawing
  - as a set of orthographic drawings (usually the front view, side view, and top view)

Discuss the Concepts

D1. Consider the isometric perspective drawing shown. Indira claims that all three orthographic drawings of this object will look the same. Laszlo says that only the front and the side will look the same. Soon-Tek says that all three will be different. Who is correct? Give reasons.

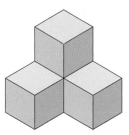

D2. Consider the isometric perspective drawing shown. Discuss whether the drawing could represent a real object. Give reasons for your answer.

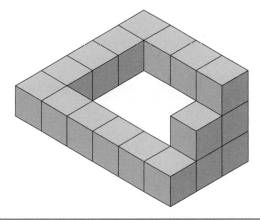

1. Which of these representations is not suitable for representing a three-dimensional object? Explain why.

   A a scale model

   B an isometric perspective drawing

   C a blueprint showing front and side views

   D a set of orthographic drawings

2. Marcie is building a scale model of an office building using linking cubes. The building is a rectangular prism with a length of 49 m, a width of 35 m, and a height of 56 m. Suggest a suitable scale, and calculate the dimensions for the model.

3. Farmer Jacques is building a new silo in the shape of a cylinder. To maximize the storage volume, he is planning to make the diameter the same as the height. Which of these diagrams matches the side view?

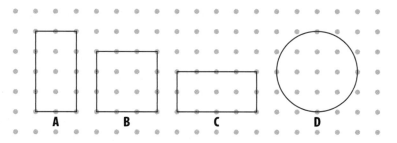

A   B   C   D

4. Ivanka is using linking cubes to make a scale model of the isometric perspective drawing shown. Describe the physical model in terms of length, width, and height.

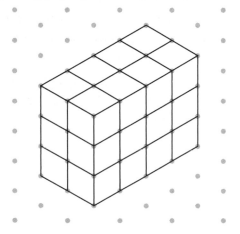

5. Study the isometric perspective drawing shown. Write a short paragraph explaining why this drawing cannot represent a real object.

For help with question 6, refer to Example 1.

6. Central courtyards are featured in the architecture of many cultures. The Romans often built their houses, or villas, with a central open space surrounded by the rooms of the house.

  a) Use linking cubes or other concrete materials to build a scale model of a Roman villa. Include a set of rooms surrounding a central open space.

  b) Use isometric dot paper or *The Geometer's Sketchpad*® to create an isometric perspective drawing of the model.

  c) Use isometric dot paper or *The Geometer's Sketchpad*® to create a set of orthographic drawings for the model.

For help with question 7, refer to Examples 2 and 3.

7. Salvatore needs an isometric perspective drawing of a cone such that the height of the cone appears equal to the diameter.

  a) Use isometric dot paper or *The Geometer's Sketchpad*® to create an isometric perspective drawing of a cone that closely matches Salvatore's requirements.

  b) Is it possible to match the height to the diameter exactly, if the diameter and the tip of the cone must land on one of the dots? Explain.

8. The artist M. C. Escher often used false perspective in his drawings to depict impossible situations. Study the Escher work *Convex and Concave* carefully to see how the illusions work. Consider the "stairway" at the centre right of the drawing.

a) Approximate the stairway with a triangluar prism (i.e., do not show the individual steps). Create a set of orthographic drawings in which you see this as a stairway going up.

b) Create a set of orthographic drawings in which you see this as the bottom support of an arch.

c) Describe the triangles that occur in your orthographic drawings.

Chapter Problem

9. Paul has been given a set of orthographic drawings for an inn, to be built near a tropical beach. The design incorporates open spaces throughout the building for air circulation. Paul's task is to create a scale model and an isometric perspective drawing of the inn.

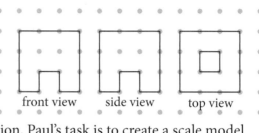

front view   side view   top view

a) Use the orthographic drawings to construct a scale model using linking cubes or other concrete materials.

b) Use isometric dot paper or *The Geometer's Sketchpad*® to make an isometric perspective drawing of the inn.

Reasoning and Proving

Representing | *Selecting Tools*

Problem Solving

Connecting | *Reflecting*

Communicating

10. Sara used linking cubes to build the structure shown in isometric perspective. Which drawing is a possible orthographic projection of the top view of the structure? Explain.

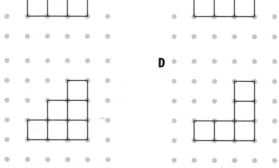

11. Use isometric dot paper or *The Geometer's Sketchpad*® to create an "impossible" isometric perspective drawing different from the ones in question D2 and question 5.

12. In isometric perspective drawings the lengths in the drawing of a cube match the side lengths of the real cube. In real life, the apparent size of an object decreases as the object moves farther away from an observer. Artists use the concept of a "vanishing point" to achieve the effect of perspective in their art.

To see how this works, draw a square using square dot paper or *The Geometer's Sketchpad*®. Select a point far away from the square, as shown. Join the vertices of the square to this "vanishing point."

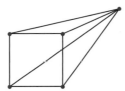

Use these lines to draw the rest of the cube in perspective. Then, hide or erase the parts of the lines that extend outside of the cube.

13. Advertisements for buildings that have not yet been constructed often make use of two-point perspective. In the example shown, each street leads to a vanishing point. The left side view of the building uses the left vanishing point, while the right side view uses the right vanishing point.

Use square dot paper or *The Geometer's Sketchpad*® to make a two-point perspective drawing of the model in question 4.

6.3 Create Nets, Plans, and Patterns

net
- a two-dimensional diagram that can be cut out, and folded to form a three-dimensional object

plan
- a scale drawing of a structure or object
- a design or arrangement scheme

pattern
- a form, template, or model from which an object can be created

Commercial products are packaged in various shapes of containers. These containers are often manufactured as a two-dimensional **net** and then folded or bent into a three-dimensional shape. One example is a cereal box, which is a rectangular prism.

Other three-dimensional objects, such as houses or items of furniture, are constructed from a **plan**. Plans are usually parts of nets, drawn to scale, that give enough information to construct the three-dimensional object.

Clothing is made by using a **pattern** to cut the cloth. The cloth pieces are then sewn together to make the clothing item. A pattern is usually a net that is drawn in separate pieces.

Investigate 1

Tools

- empty cereal box
- scissors
- ruler
- tape

Design a Box

Many products are packaged in rectangular prisms.

1. Measure and record the dimensions of the cereal box.

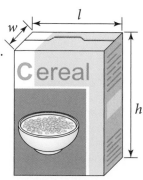

2. Find the edge on the cereal box that was used to join the cardboard. Cut along this edge. Cut any other joins that you find.

3. Unfold the cereal box to form a net. Measure the edges of the net. Identify each edge as one of the dimensions of the box.

4. Reflect Compare the measures of the net to the measures of the cereal box. How are the dimensions of the net found to produce a box of the desired shape and size?

5. Sketch a net for a box that will measure 4 cm by 3 cm by 2 cm. Label the edges. Test your net by cutting it out and folding it into a box. Tape the box together. Measure the dimensions to check that the box matches the dimensions given. Suggest a product that would be suitable for a package of this size.

Investigate 2

Tools

- empty tissue roll
- ruler
- tape

Design a Cylinder

Some products are packaged in cylindrical containers.

1. Measure and record the height and diameter of the tissue roll.

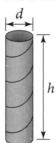

2. Cut the roll along its height, and spread it into a rectangle. Trace the rectangle onto a piece of paper. Measure the dimensions of the rectangle. Which dimension is equal to the height of the roll? What is the name of the other dimension in relation to the cylinder? Divide the other dimension by the diameter of the tissue roll. What do you notice?

3. To draw two congruent circles for the top and bottom of the cylinder, what dimension do you need to consider? Draw two circles for the top and bottom using this dimension. Cut out the net, and bend it to form a cylinder with a top and a bottom.

4. Reflect Compare the measures of the net to the measures of the cylinder. How are the dimensions of the net related to the height and diameter of the cylinder?

5. Sketch a net that can be bent into a cylinder with a diameter of 6 cm and a height of 10 cm. Test your net by cutting it out and bending it into a cylinder with a top and a bottom. Tape the model together.

Patterns

Patterns for clothing are nets that are used to cut cloth. The pieces of cloth are sewn to form the three-dimensional garment.

1. Identify the seams on the article of clothing. Use scissors to carefully cut the threads along each seam. Lay out the pieces.

2. Sketch the pattern on newsprint.

3. **Reflect** How can clothing manufacturers use a pattern to cut out hundreds of pieces at one time? Research clothing manufacturing on the Internet to help you explain.

4. Sketch a pattern that could be used to cut out the pieces for a bucket hat.

Example

Cabin Plan

a) Draw a floor plan for a vacation cabin. The cabin will measure 8 m along the side by 6 m across the front. There will be two congruent square bunkrooms at the back, with side length 3 m. There will be a bathroom measuring 2 m by 3 m along the front wall. The remaining space will be living area. Label the measurements on your plan.

b) The cabin will be of the A-frame type, measuring 5 m tall.

Sketch orthographic drawings of the cabin. Label all measurements.

Solution

a) Select a suitable scale. For example, let 1 cm represent 1 m. Draw a rectangle to represent the floor of the cabin. Draw walls for the two bunkrooms and the bathroom. Label all dimensions.

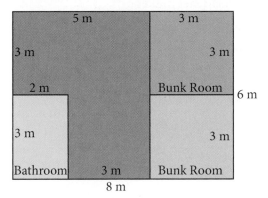

b) Draw the front, side, and top views of the cabin.

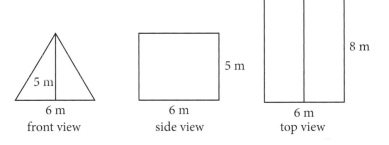

Key Concepts

- A three-dimensional object can be constructed by folding or bending a two-dimensional net.
- Parts of a net drawn to scale can be used as a plan to construct a three-dimensional object.
- A net can be separated into pieces to form a pattern. The pattern can be used to make pieces of a three-dimensional object, which can be assembled into the object.

Discuss the Concepts

D1. Sketch a net for a cube. Explain how it must be folded to make the cube.

D2. A hobby club builds and flies model airplanes. To make such an airplane, would you use a net, a plan, or a pattern? Discuss the advantages and disadvantages of each representation.

1. Consider the net shown. The distance between two dots represents 5 cm. When folded, what three-dimensional object will the net make?

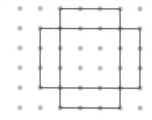

   A an open box 5 cm high, with a square base with side length 15 cm

   B a closed box 5 cm high, with a square base with side length 15 cm

   C an open box 15 cm high, with a square base with side length 5 cm

2. Draw a net that can be used to make a cube-shaped box with an open top.

3. Sketch a pattern that could be used to make a mitten.

4. Woodworking magazines often include diagrams in their articles about building furniture. If you were writing an article about building a bookcase, would you include a net, a plan, or a pattern? Explain.

For help with question 5, refer to Investigate 1.

Literacy Connect

5. Neela submitted an alternative net for a cube, as shown.

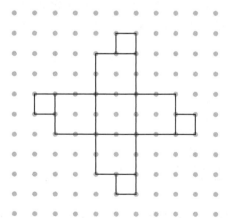

   a) Write a short paragraph explaining why Neela's net will not work.

   b) Explain how the net can be modified so it will work.

For help with question 6, refer to Investigate 2.

6. A bakery needs a new cylindrical package for their oatmeal cookies. Each cookie is 1 cm thick and has a diameter of 8 cm. Each package should hold a dozen cookies.

   a) Draw a net that can be used to make a model of the package.

   b) Cut out your net, and bend it to form the package. Tape the model together.

   c) Check the dimensions of the model by measuring. Do they meet the requirements?

7. An imported cheese is sold in the shape of a triangular prism. The ends of the prism are congruent equilateral triangles. Each triangle has a side length of 4 cm, and the prism is 12 cm long.

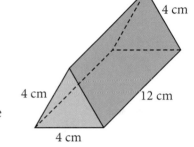

   a) Draw a net that can be used to make a model of the package.

   b) Cut out your net, and fold it to form the model. Tape the model together.

   c) Check the dimensions of the model by measuring. Do they meet the requirements?

Chapter Problem

8. Paul's company has been asked to design a grain storage shed that will be exported to developing countries. The shed will be made of galvanized sheet metal with four congruent square walls, with side length 3 m. The roof will be four congruent equilateral triangles with side length 3 m. The bottom will be left open so that the shed can be attached to a poured concrete base. The sheds will be shipped as nets to conserve shipping space. Paul's task is to design the net for the shed, and to estimate the cost of the metal required.

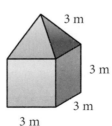

   a) Draw a net that can be used to make a model of the shed.

   b) Find the total area of sheet metal required.

   c) Sheet metal costs $6.50/m². Find the cost of the metal for the shed.

9. The owner of a garden centre needs a pedestal for displaying a prize-winning flowering plant. The pedestal is to be made of painted sheet metal, with dimensions as shown. The bottom of the pedestal will be left open. Draw a net that could be used to make the pedestal. Show all measurements.

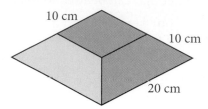

10. Refer to question 9. The pedestal will be modified. Now, the top will have a circular hole to accommodate a 10-cm diameter metal cylinder. The height of the cylinder will be 30 cm. Draw the net for the modified pedestal, and the net for the cylinder. Show all measurements.

Extend

11. A regular tetrahedron is a three-dimensional shape with four congruent equilateral triangular faces. Consider a tetrahedron made of equilateral triangles with side length 3 cm.

   a) Draw a net that can be used to make the tetrahedron.

   b) Cut out your net, and fold it into a tetrahedron. Tape the tetrahedron together.

12. Lydia made a square shape using eight linking cubes, leaving the centre space empty. Draw a net that could be used to make a paper model of the shape. If you think it is not possible to make a net, explain why.

13. A regular octahedron has eight congruent equilateral triangular faces. It looks like two square-based pyramids glued together at their bases. Draw a net that can be used to make a regular octahedron. Cut out your net, and fold it into an octahedron. Tape the octahedron together.

Use Technology

Use *The Geometer's Sketchpad®* to Draw Plans With Dynamic Measurements

Use *The Geometer's Sketchpad®* to draw a scale floor plan for the vacation cabin in the Example in section 6.3. The cabin will measure 8 m along the side by 6 m across the front. There will be two congruent square bunk rooms at the back, with side length 3 m. There will be a bathroom measuring 2 m by 3 m along the front wall. The remaining space will be living area.

1. Start by constructing the fixed boundaries of the cabin. Open *The Geometer's Sketchpad®*. Choose **Preferences** from the **Edit** menu, and then the **Units** tab. Choose **Show Grid** from the **Graph** menu. Drag the origin to the lower left area of the workspace. If necessary, adjust the unit point until you can see at least 10 gridlines horizontally and 8 gridlines vertically.

2. Choose **Plot Points** from the **Graph** menu. Plot the point (8, 6). In the same way, plot the points (0, 6) and (8, 0). Select the origin and the three plotted points, moving clockwise. Choose **Segments** from the **Construct** menu. You now have a rectangle that represents the boundaries of the cabin. Try to move one of the corners. What happens?

3. Use the **Segment Tool** to sketch the bunk rooms and the bathroom. Select the endpoints of the width of a bunk room. Choose **Coordinate Distance** from the **Graph** menu. Move the measurement to a convenient location. Measure and label dimensions for the remaining rooms. Include the outside dimensions of the cabin. Hide the axes and the grid.

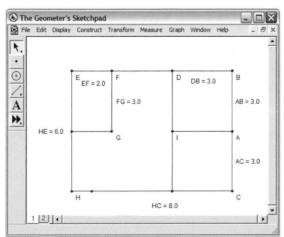

4. Reflect Select the line segment that forms the wall between the bunk rooms. Move it up and down. Note how the measurements change as you move the line segment. Try changing the dimensions of the other rooms.

5. Calculate the area of each room. Choose **Calculate** from the **Measure** menu. A calculator will appear. Select the length of one bunk room. Press the ***** button. Select the width of the bunk room. Move the area measurement to a convenient location. Change the label to Bunk Room #1. Measure the areas of the other rooms. To find the living area, calculate the area of the entire cabin, and subtract the areas of the rooms.

6. Reflect Change the dimensions of one room by dragging a wall. Notice how the measurements, including the areas, change.

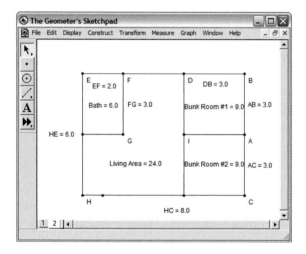

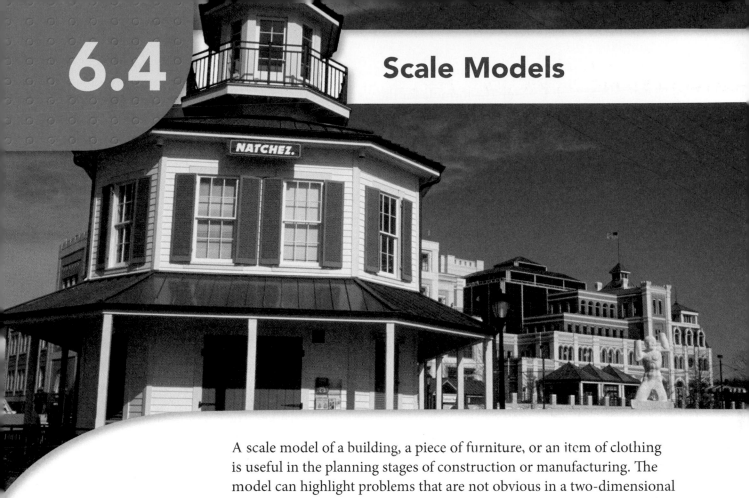

6.4 Scale Models

A scale model of a building, a piece of furniture, or an item of clothing is useful in the planning stages of construction or manufacturing. The model can highlight problems that are not obvious in a two-dimensional representation. The model can also demonstrate improvements to a plan. Fixing the plan before production can save materials, resources, and time.

Example 1

Design a Cylindrical Tank

An engineer is designing a cylindrical tank for a tanker truck that will hold about 800 ft³ of liquid. The length of the cylinder should be twice the diameter and should be a whole number of feet.

a) Use the formula for the volume of a cylinder to determine the dimensions of the tank required.

b) Select a suitable scale, and draw a net for a paper model of the tank.

c) Cut out your net, and bend it into the cylindrical shape. Tape the model together.

Solution

a) The formula for the volume of a cylinder is $V = \pi r^2 h$. In this case h is twice the diameter, or four times the radius.

The volume formula becomes
$$V = \pi r^2 (4r)$$
$$ = 4\pi r^3$$

Try different values for the radius.

Radius (ft)	Volume (ft³)
1	12.6
2	100.5
3	339.3
4	804.2
5	1570.8

A radius of 4 ft gives a volume of just over 800 ft³. Using a radius of 4 ft, the diameter is 2×4 ft, or 8 ft, and the length is 2×8 ft, or 16 ft.

b) One dimension of the rectangle for the net is the length of the cylinder, or 16 ft. The other dimension is the circumference of the cylinder.

$$C = \pi d$$
$$ = \pi(8)$$
$$ \doteq 25.1$$

The circumference is approximately 25.1 ft.

Select a suitable scale (for example, 1 in. represents 4 ft). Draw the rectangle for the curved side. Add two circles, each diameter of 2 in., for the ends.

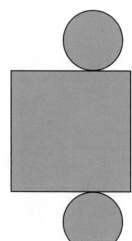

c)

Example 2

Design a Pentagonal House

An architect has designed a house in the shape of a regular pentagonal prism. The floor forms a pentagon with a side length of 6 m. The five walls are congruent squares. The peaked roof is made of five congruent equilateral triangles. Select a suitable scale. Draw a net that can be used to make a scale model of this house. Then, cut out your net and fold it into a model of the house. Tape the model together.

Solution

Method 1: Use Pencil and Paper

- Choose an appropriate scale. For example, 1 cm represents 1 m. Draw a regular pentagon. A regular pentagon consists of five congruent isosceles triangles whose apexes meet at the centre of the pentagon. The apex angle for each triangle is 360° ÷ 5 = 72°. Draw a dot for the centre, and a horizontal line segment to the first vertex. Draw an angle of 72° from the horizontal line segment. Use compasses to help you create an isosceles triangle that includes the second vertex. Continue this process until you have 5 vertices. Join the vertices.
- Use a ruler and compasses to draw a square on each side of the pentagon. Then, draw an equilateral triangle on each square.
- Use your net to make a scale model of the house.

Method 2: Use *The Geometer's Sketchpad*®

- Draw the pentagonal base. Turn on automatic labelling of points. Sketch a horizontal line segment AB. Select point A, and choose **Mark Center** from the **Transform** menu. Select the segment and point B. Choose **Rotate** from the **Transform** menu. Change the fixed angle to 72°. Select **Rotate**. Continue until you have five vertices. Join the vertices.
- Draw the square walls. Select one endpoint of a side. Choose **Mark Center** from the **Transform** menu. Select the segment and the other endpoint. Choose **Rotate** from the **Transform** menu. Change the fixed angle to 90°. Select **Rotate**. Repeat for each side. Then, use the other

endpoint of the side as the centre, and rotate through an angle of 270°. Complete the five squares.

- Draw the triangular roof faces. Select one outside corner of a square. Choose **Mark Center** from the **Transform** menu. Select the outside segment and the other endpoint. Choose **Rotate** from the **Transform** menu. Change the fixed angle to 60°. Select **Rotate**. Repeat for the other squares. Complete the five triangles. Hide the points and labels.
- Print your net, and use it to make a scale model of the house.

Example 3

Design a Tent

An outfitting company plans to manufacture a new tent. Orthographic drawings for the tent are shown. The distance between pairs of horizontal or vertical dots represents 1 m.

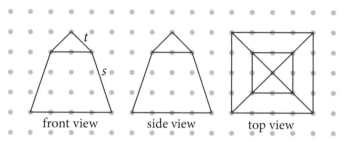

front view   side view   top view

Use paper or drinking straws and masking tape to construct a scale model of the tent. Select a suitable scale. Make any necessary calculations.

Solution

Let s represent the slant length of the side of the tent and t represent the slant length of the roof. Use the Pythagorean theorem to find the lengths of s and t.

$s^2 = 3^2 + 1^2$
$s^2 = 10$
$s = \sqrt{10}$
$s \doteq 3.2$

The side slant length is approximately 3.2 m.

$t^2 = 1^2 + 1^2$
$t^2 = 2$
$t = \sqrt{2}$
$t \doteq 1.4$

The top slant length is approximately 1.4 m.

Select a scale that is suitable for your materials. For example, let 4 cm represent 1 m. The base of the model will measure 4×4 cm, or 16 cm. The side slant length will measure 4×3.2 cm, or 12.8 cm. The top slant length will measure 4×1.4 cm, or 5.6 cm.

Key Concepts

- Scale models can be constructed using nets, orthographic drawings, or isometric perspective drawings.
- Models are useful in the planning stages of a project.
- Models can identify problems in a plan, or suggest improvements.

Discuss the Concepts

D1. Can a model of any three-dimensional object be constructed using a net? Explain.

D2. To obtain a building permit for a house, the owner must submit a set of orthographic drawings, known as elevations. Suggest reasons why orthographic drawing are required rather than a scale model or an isometric perspective drawing.

Practise

1. Maria is building a scale model of a garden shed. She will let 1 in. represent 2 ft. If the base of the shed measures 10 ft by 12 ft, what measurements will Maria need for the model?

2. The most famous Canadian-designed and -built aircraft was the Avro CF-105 Arrow. A number of $\frac{1}{8}$ scale models were made for testing in a wind tunnel. The length of the model was 10 ft 8 in. What was the length of the full-size aircraft?

3. The town of Port Colborne is planning to construct a new recreational centre, including a skating arena and a swimming pool. Suggest reasons why an architect bidding on the contract would provide a scale model in addition to drawings.

4. Freda is planning a new silo for her farm, made of a cylinder topped with a hemisphere. The height of the cylinder will form a golden ratio with its diameter. Freda would like to make a scale model of the silo to see if her design works. Describe a procedure and suggest materials that Freda could use to make the scale model.

5. Suleiman plans to construct a "minimalist" chair as shown in the isometric perspective drawing. He will use three pieces of 1-in.-thick plywood. The distance between a pair of dots represents 1 ft. Draw plans that show the pieces of wood required, with measurements.

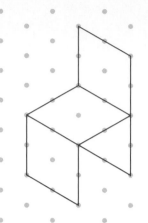

Apply B ••

Literacy Connect

6. A standard golf ball has a diameter of 1.68 in. You have been contracted to design a package to hold 12 golf balls. Sketch a set of orthographic drawings for your chosen package. Write a brief explanation of why you selected this design.

7. Draw an isometric perspective drawing for the tent in Example 3.

8. A local artist wants to include a rectangular prism in her newest sculpture. The prism should have a length of 1 m, a width of 2 m, and a height of 3 m.

   a) Select a suitable scale. Use pencil and paper or *The Geometer's Sketchpad*® to draw a net that can be used to make a scale model of the prism.

   b) Cut out your net and fold it to make the model. Tape the model together.

   c) The artist has decided to paint all of the sides of the prism except one, which will be placed on the ground. She has not, however, decided which side will be placed on the ground. If paint costs $2/m^2$, what are the possible costs for painting the prism?

For help with question 9, refer to Example 1.

9. A new soup can must hold at least 500 mL of soup. Its height must be equal to its diameter. The height and the diameter must be whole numbers of centimetres.

   a) Determine the minimum height and width of the can.

   b) Select a suitable scale. Draw a net that can be used to make a scale model of the can.

   c) Cut out your net and bend it to make a scale model of the can. Tape the model together.

Reasoning and Proving

Representing | Selecting Tools

Problem Solving

Connecting | Reflecting

Communicating

10. A band council has decided to commission a new community centre to be used for various events such as the annual pow-wow. The centre will be in the shape of a regular hexagon with each side measuring 10 m. Each congruent rectangular wall will be 3 m high. The building will have a flat roof.

a) Select a suitable scale. Choose measurements that ensure you have a regular hexagon. Use pencil and paper or *The Geometer's Sketchpad*® to draw a net that can be used to make a scale model of the centre.

b) Cut out your net and fold it to make the model. Tape the model together.

c) The base of the centre will be poured concrete, 10 cm thick. Take measurements from your net to find the area of the hexagonal base. Multiply the area by the thickness to determine how many cubic metres of concrete will be needed.

d) Concrete costs \$75/m³, delivered to the site. Estimate the cost of the concrete for the base.

11. After studying the scale model in question 10, the band council decided to change the flat roof to one made of six congruent isosceles triangles. This will ensure that snow and rain will not accumulate on the roof. It will also make the building more attractive. The central peak of the roof will be 5 m above the floor.

a) How will this change affect your net? Explain.

b) How will this change affect the cost of concrete for the base? Explain.

Chapter Problem

12. A customer has seen the post office in Gorrie, ON, and would like a similar building for his business. He has supplied Paul's company with sample orthographic drawings, as shown. The distance between pairs of horizontal or vertical dots represents 2 m.

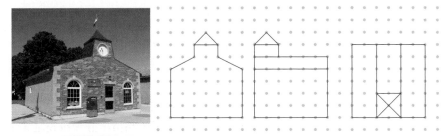

a) Draw a net that can be used to make a scale model of the building.

b) Cut out the net, and construct the model. Tape the model together.

c) The cost of the building is estimated to be \$1200/m² of floor area. Estimate the cost of the building.

13. A propane storage tank is to be built from the orthographic drawings shown. The distance between pairs of horizontal or vertical dots represents 1 m.

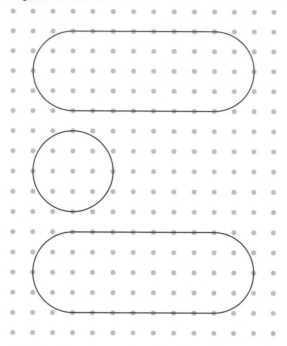

Which description best fits the propane tank? Explain.

A A cylinder 11 m long, with a hemisphere of radius 2 m at each end.

B A cylinder 7 m long, with a hemisphere of radius 2 m at each end.

C A cylinder 11 m long, with a hemisphere of radius 4 m at each end.

D A cylinder 7 m long, with a hemisphere of radius 4 m at each end.

Extend

14. How can you make a net for a cone? Roll a piece of notebook paper to form a horn. Cut the horn to form a cone. Continue cutting until you have the minimum amount of paper necessary to form the cone. Unroll the paper, and sketch the net.

15. Use trial and error to make a net for a cone with a radius of 5 cm and a height of 3 cm. Cut out your net and use it to make the cone. Measure the dimensions to check that they are correct.

6.5 Solve Problems With Given Constraints

constraint
• a condition that limits the acceptable range of values for a variable

Designers such as architects, engineers, or fashion designers often must ensure their designs satisfy given **constraints**. Examples of constraints include a maximum cost, a minimum or maximum size, or regulations governing safety, energy efficiency, or performance.

Example 1	**Modular House**

Orthographic drawings for a modular house are shown.

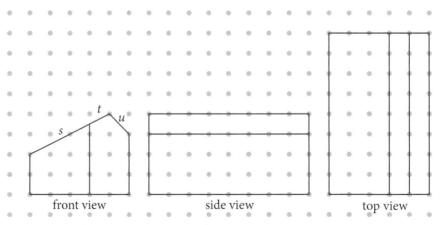

front view   side view   top view

The distance between pairs of vertical or horizontal dots represents 5 ft. The house will be built in two sections and then transported to the building site for assembly. Highway traffic rules limit the width of each section to 15 ft or less. The centre wall will be located 15 ft from the left front wall. It will be doubly thick, so that each half of the house will have four walls during transport.

a) Select a suitable scale. Draw a net for each section of the house.

b) Cut out your nets, and make scale models for the two sections of the house. Tape your models together. Ensure that the models fit together properly for assembly.

Solution

a) From the orthographic drawings, the centre wall is 17.5 ft high. Use the Pythagorean theorem to determine the slant lengths of the roof.

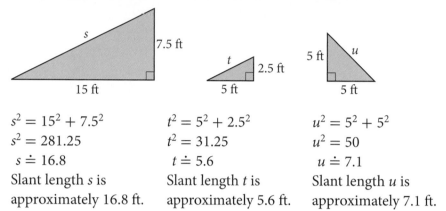

$s^2 = 15^2 + 7.5^2$
$s^2 = 281.25$
$s \doteq 16.8$

Slant length s is approximately 16.8 ft.

$t^2 = 5^2 + 2.5^2$
$t^2 = 31.25$
$t \doteq 5.6$

Slant length t is approximately 5.6 ft.

$u^2 = 5^2 + 5^2$
$u^2 = 50$
$u \doteq 7.1$

Slant length u is approximately 7.1 ft.

Let the distance between pair of horizontal or vertical dots represent 5 ft. Calculate the measures for the scale drawing by dividing each actual measure by 5.

The net for the left side of the house.

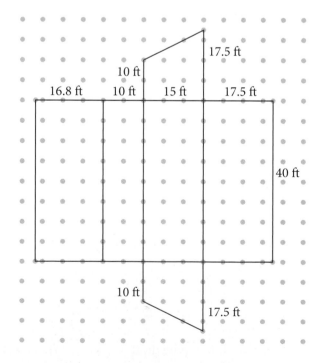

The net for the right side of the house.

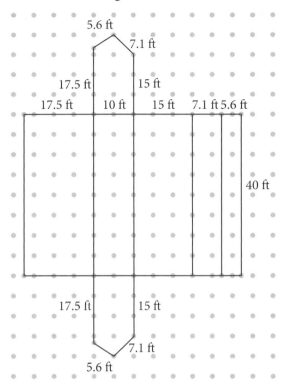

b) Use the nets to make scale models of the two halves of the house.

To learn more about modular homes, go to *www.mcgrawhill.ca/links/ foundations11* and follow the links.

Example 2

Oil Tank

Sometimes, basic safety considerations depend on understanding nets and volumes. Consider an engineer who needs to design a square-based berm, a shallow container to prevent the spread of oil from a leaking oil tank. The cylindrical oil tank is 20 m in diameter, and has a height of 20 m. The berm must have a height of 5 m.

a) Make appropriate calculations, and find the minimum dimensions of the berm.

b) Select a suitable scale. Draw a net for the berm and a net for the oil tank. Use your nets to construct a scale model of the arrangement required.

Solution

a) Start by calculating the maximum volume of oil that must be contained if the tank is full.

$$V = \pi r^2 h$$
$$= \pi \times 10^2 \times 20$$
$$\doteq 6283$$

The berm must be able to hold 6283 m³ of oil.

Let the side length of the square base of the berm be represented by s.

Volume of berm = area of base × height
$$= s^2 \times 5$$
$$= 5s^2$$

$$5s^2 = 6283$$
$$s^2 = \frac{6283}{5}$$
$$s^2 = 1256.6$$
$$s = \sqrt{1256.6}$$
$$s \doteq 35.4$$

It is safer to overestimate. Round 35.4 m up to 40 m. Suitable dimensions for the berm would be 40 m by 40 m by 5 m.

b) Draw a net for the berm. Let the space between pairs of horizontal or vertical dots represent 5 m. The base of the berm measures 8 dots by 8 dots, and the height measures 1 dot.

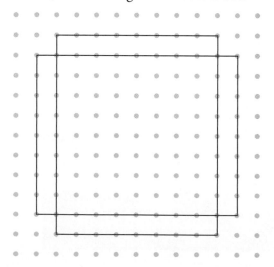

> **Math Connect**
>
> A square-based berm has the shortest side lengths required to contain a given volume. Minimizing the berm's perimeter cuts down on the cost of materials.

Draw a net for the oil tank. The net consists of two circles of diameter 20 m for the top and bottom, plus a rectangle for the wall of the cylinder. One dimension of the rectangle is the same as the height of the tank, or 20 m. The other dimension is the same as the circumference of the tank.

$$C = \pi d$$
$$= \pi \times 20$$
$$\doteq 63$$

The circumference is approximately 63 m.

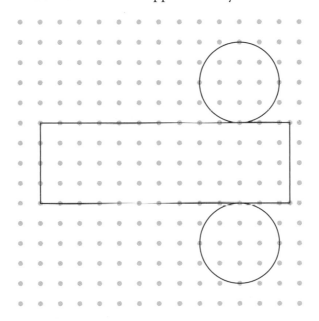

Use the nets to construct the scale models for the berm and the oil tank.

Key Concepts

- Design problems are often subject to constraints or conditions.
- Constraints may include cost considerations, safety regulations, maximum or minimum sizes, or performance requirements.

Discuss the Concepts

D1. A fashion designer is to design a new line of sunglasses to complement a clothing line. Discuss some of the constraints that she might face during the design stage.

D2. The highest mountain in Africa is Mt. Kilimanjaro in Tanzania. On the Marangu hiking route to the top, climbers spend the night in huts designed by Norwegian architects. There is no road. The trail is the only route to the huts.

Discuss some of the constraints that the architects faced when designing the huts.

Practise

1. A new laundry detergent will be sold in a cubical box. The box holds 1 L of detergent. Find the side length of the box.

2. A factory temporarily stores liquid wastes in a circular cement-lined pond that has a base area of 500 m². Find the length of berm needed to enclose the pond.

3. Santo's Pizzeria is introducing a new giant-size pizza with a diameter of 24 in. Give possible reasons why the pizza will be packaged in an octagonal box rather than a square box.

4. Prefabricated housing for developing countries with warm climates is often made of galvanized sheet metal. Discuss some of the constraints that might affect the designers of this type of housing.

5. A one-story bungalow is to be designed for a small lot. The floor plan of the house must fit into a rectangle measuring 30 ft by 40 ft. The buyer has made the following specifications.

Room	Minimum Floor Area (ft²)
bedroom #1	200
bedroom #2	150
bedroom #3	100
bathroom	100
eat-in kitchen	200
living room	300

There must be a clear path to all rooms. Use pencil and paper or drawing software to design such a house. **Design Tip:** Lay out the rooms such that you minimize the area required for hallways.

6. A flexible floating pipe is used to contain an oil spill. The pipe can contain a depth of 50 cm of oil. It is placed around a leaking tanker carrying 200 000 m³ of oil. The pipe is laid such that it forms a circle around the leaking tanker. What length of pipe is needed to contain all of the oil?

7. Build a boat using one piece of water-resistant cardboard or plastic the same size as notebook paper, up to six popsicle sticks, glue as required, and enough tape to join the edges. The boat must hold the maximum load possible without sinking. Test the boat using standard weights, coins, or other materials. Record your plan.

Math **Connect**

Many bridges use triangles in their construction. Triangles are rigid and add to the strength of the bridge.

8. Build a bridge using 12 plastic drinking straws, one sheet of notebook paper, and duct tape to join the straws. The bridge must span 15 cm and hold the maximum load possible. **Note:** The duct tape may be used only to join the straws. It may not be used to reinforce the bridge. Place the bridge over a gap of 15 cm, and test it with standard weights, coins, or other materials. Record your plan.

9. Farmer Macdonald sketched an isometric perspective drawing of a new chicken coop that he would like to build. The space between pairs of dots represents 1 m.

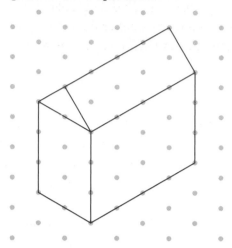

a) Draw a set of orthographic drawings for the coop.

b) Draw a net that can be used to make a scale model of the coop. Cut out the net, and construct the model. Tape the model together.

c) All sides of the coop except the floor will be made of sheet metal, which sells for $15/m². Estimate the cost of buying the sheet metal for the coop.

Chapter Problem

10. The uranium fuel for a nuclear reactor is placed in a cylinder. The cylinder lies horizontally on its side with a diameter of 8 m and a length of 6 m. It must be surrounded by a containment building in the shape of a vertical cylinder. Paul has been given the task of designing the building and estimating the cost of the buildings concrete exterior.

a) Use pencil and paper or drawing software to determine the minimum dimensions of the containment building required.

b) Find the area of the walls and roof of the building. The concrete exterior must be 80 cm thick. Multiply the area by the thickness to determine the approximate volume of concrete required, in cubic metres.

c) Concrete can be delivered to the site and poured for $90/m³. Estimate the cost of the concrete for the building.

Achievement Check

11. Refer to the oil tank problem from Example 2. Hartmut suggests using a circular berm that is also 5 m high. He says that the circular berm would be smaller than the square berm. Is he correct? Show calculations to support your answer.

Extend C •

12. The inside of a new high-pressure scuba tank has a volume of 1 ft^3. The walls, top, and bottom must be 0.5 in. thick to withstand the pressure. The ratio of height to diameter will be 3:1. Model the tank using a cylinder. Use a calculator or other technology to find the dimensions required, in feet, correct to two decimal places. Prepare a set of orthographic drawings for the tank.

13. An electric furnace can produce a maximum of 12 000 W of heat. A concrete building requires a heat source of 10 W/m^2 on its exterior walls and roof.

   a) Design a small office building in the shape of a rectangular prism that could be heated by this furnace, running at maximum. **Note:** For multiple storeys, the building code requires that each storey be a minimum of 3 m in height.

   b) Construct a scale model of your building.

14. The layout for a new terminal at the international airport will use the "snowflake" design. Passengers will arrive through one face of a square-based reception building. Once they have checked in,

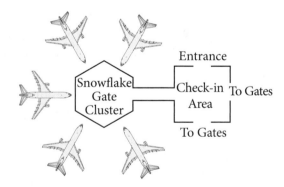

they will follow a passageway through one of the other faces to a hexagonal "snowflake" gate cluster. Five of the faces will be gates for aircraft, while the sixth will house the passageway. The aircraft using these gates need a clear, square area with a side length of at least 50 m in front of the gate.

Use pencil and paper or drawing software to design the terminal. The passageways should be kept as short as possible to minimize the distance that passengers need to walk to get from one "snowflake" to another.

Use Technology

Use *The Geometer's Sketchpad®* to Create Tessellations Using Rotations

Tools

- computer
- *The Geometer's Sketchpad®*

Use *The Geometer's Sketchpad®* to draw a complex tessellation using rotations. Begin with a regular hexagon. Then, alter the interior of the hexagon using the **Transform** menu.

1. Open *The Geometer's Sketchpad®*. Use the method shown in Section 6.4, Example 2, Method 2, to draw a regular hexagon. All the angles in each triangle will be 60°. Draw a point approximately in the centre of one of the triangles that make up the hexagon. Select this point, as well as the centre and a vertex of the hexagon, as shown. Choose **Arc Through 3 Points** from the **Construct** menu.

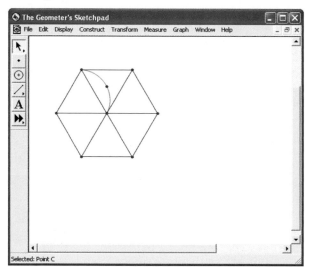

2. Select the centre of the hexagon. Choose **Mark Center** from the **Transform** menu. Select the arc. Choose **Rotate** from the **Transform** menu. Adjust the angle of rotation to 60°. Repeat the rotation until you have six arcs, one in each triangle.

3. Select the six vertices of the hexagon. Choose **Hexagon Interior** from the **Construct** menu. You can change the colour by choosing **Color** from the **Display** menu. Select one of the arcs. Choose **Arc Interior** from the **Construct** menu. Then, choose **Arc Segment**. While the arc interior is selected, change the colour by choosing **Color** from the **Display** menu. Repeat this procedure until you have six arc segments of different colours.

4. Hide the lines, the points, and the arcs.

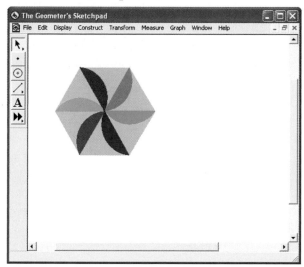

5. Select the hexagonal pattern, and then choose **Copy** from the **Edit** menu. Choose **Paste** from the **Edit** menu. Move the copy beside the original pattern. Continue pasting copies until you have formed a tessellation.

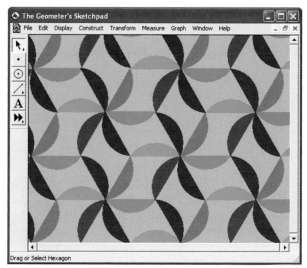

6. Reflect Think of other ways to use rotations. For example, you can use a polygon in place of an arc. Consider other colour variations. What other regular polygons can be used for tessellations? What combinations of polygons can be used?

6.1 Investigate Geometric Shapes and Figures, pages 296–305

1. After using the "12-knot rope" to lay out a square or rectangle on the ground, ancient builders then measured the two diagonals. Why did they do this? Why does this method work?

2. Basiruddin has sewn a blanket for his sister's new baby. It measures 130 cm by 80 cm. Basiruddin claims that the blanket is a golden rectangle, and that, if it is folded in half, the half-rectangle is also a golden rectangle. Use calculations to check his claims.

6.2 Perspective and Orthographic Drawings, pages 306–317

3. Shawna is designing an unusual seven-room house for a client. Each room will have the shape of a cube. Shawna has represented the basic plan as an isometric perspective drawing, as shown.

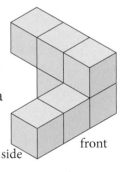

a) Use linking cubes or other materials to build a scale model of the house.

b) Draw a set of orthographic drawings for the house.

4. Jorge drew orthographic drawings of his family home in Spain, as shown. The distance between horizontal or vertical pairs of dots represents 2 m. Draw an isometric perspective drawing of the house.

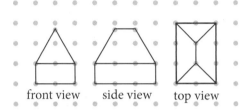

front view   side view   top view

6.3 Create Nets, Plans, and Patterns, pages 318–326

5. You are designing a rondaval, a circular hut. The hut will have a diameter of 24 ft. In the centre will be a square washroom block with side length 8 ft. The hut's diameter will divide the washroom block and the hut into two units, each with a washroom and a bedroom. Select a suitable scale, and draw a floor plan for the rondaval. Include all measurements.

6. A new line of bath crystals will be marketed in a decorative cylindrical container with a diameter of 6 cm and a height of 18 cm. A cork will be used to seal the container, so no top is required.

Draw a net that could be used to make a model of the container. Cut out your net and construct the container. Check the dimensions of the model by measuring.

7. David is building an airplane. The frame is made of welded steel tubing, and will be covered with fabric. Each wing is in the shape of a rectangle measuring 5 m long by 1 m wide, with a semicircle at one end. The wing will be covered with fabric. Sketch a pattern that could be used to sew an envelope to slip over the wing frame. Show all measurements.

6.4 Scale Models, pages 327–334

8. Model airplane kits are commonly sold in $\frac{1}{72}$ scale. A Boeing 777 airliner has a wingspan of 60.9 m and a length of 73.9 m. Find the wingspan and length of a $\frac{1}{72}$ model of the Boeing 777.

9. Quonset huts are often used for storage of farm machinery, aircraft, or other large machines.

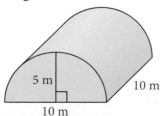

Sandrine is planning to build a Quonset hut to shelter the ultralight aircraft that she is building. It will have a square floor with side length 10 m. The curved roof will have a maximum height of 5 m. Draw a net that can be used to make a scale model of the Quonset hut. Cut out your net, and construct the scale model.

10. A new office building will have a square base with side length 40 m. It will be 60 m high. A revolving restaurant in the shape of a cylinder with a diameter of 80 m and a height of 4 m will be built on top. Draw nets that can be used to make scale models of the building and the restaurant. Cut out your nets, and construct the models.

6.5 Solve Problems With Given Constraints, pages 335–345

11. Martin is designing a hexagonal bunkhouse containing six triangular rooms that meet at the centre. The base of the bunkhouse will be poured concrete 10 cm thick. Concrete can be delivered to the site for \$75/m³. The budget for the concrete base is a maximum of \$600. The walls will be congruent squares, and the roof will be flat. The cost of wood for the walls and the roof is \$20/m².

a) Design the base such that the hexagon is as large as possible without exceeding the cost constraint.

b) Continue the design for the walls and roof. Estimate the total cost of materials for the base, walls, and roof.

For questions 1 to 3, choose the best answer.

1. Which rectangle is closest to being a golden rectangle?

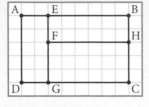

   A ABCD

   B AEGD

   C EBHF

   D FHCG

2. The measures of the interior angles of several regular polygons are shown. Which of these polygons can be used to tile the plane?

   A 108° pentagon

   B 120° hexagon

   C 135° octagon

   D all of them

3. An ornament is a square-based pyramid with a sphere on top. The pyramid has a base of side length 4 cm and a height of 6 cm. The diameter of the sphere is 5 cm. Which of these represents the top view of the ornament?

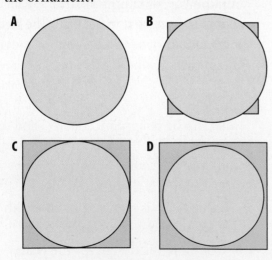

4. A new specialty fruit and nut bar is being made. The bar has a diamond cross-section made up of two congruent equilateral triangles with side length 12 cm. The bar is 24 cm long. Draw a set of orthographic drawings for the bar. Include all measurements.

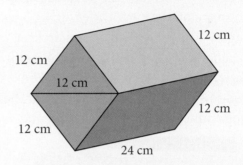

5. Select a suitable scale, and draw a net that could be used to make a scale model of a package for the fruit and nut bar in question 4.

6. Yasmini received a pet budgie in a cylindrical cage with a diameter of 60 cm and a height of 50 cm. Yasmini needs a night cover for the cage. The cover requires a top and sides, but no bottom. Select a suitable scale, and draw a pattern that could be used to cut the pieces of cloth needed to make the cover.

Chapter Problem Wrap-Up

Paul has learned a lot about geometry and architecture during his co-op placement. Choose a design project of your own, similar to the projects you have worked on throughout this chapter. It could be a building or structure, a package, or an item of clothing.

a) Write a plan for your project. Include at least four geometric elements in the design. Describe the constraints on your project and how you can meet them.

b) Draw an isometric perspective drawing or a set of orthographic drawings for your project.

c) Calculate the project's dimensions. Draw a pattern or a net. Build a scale model of your project.

d) Write a summary of your project. Include your drawings and model. Show all your calculations and measurements.

---

7. An isometric perspective drawing for a new building is shown. The distance between pairs of dots represents 5 m. Draw orthographic drawings for the building.

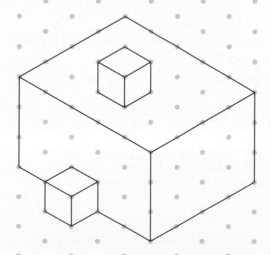

8. A gift box for a travel mug will have a square base with side length 4 in. and a square lid with side length 6 in. The box must be 5 in. high. Select a scale, and draw nets that can be used to make a model of the box and the lid. Show all measurements on the net.

9. A new tomato juice can is being designed such that the ratio of the height to the diameter is equal to the golden ratio. The diameter will be 12 cm.

   a) Select a scale, and draw a net that could be used to make a scale model of the can.

   b) Determine the volume of tomato juice that the can will hold.

Chapters 4 to 6   Review

Chapter 4: Quadratic Relations I

1. **a)** Which of these relations are quadratic? Explain your reasoning.

i)

x	y
0	17
1	13
2	9
3	5
4	1
5	−3
6	−7

ii)

x	y
1	0
3	1
5	3
7	6
9	10
11	15
13	21

    iii) $y = 2x + 1$ **iv)** $y = 12 - 2x^2$

  b) Check your predictions by graphing each relation.

2. Describe the graph of each parabola relative to the graph of $y = x^2$.

  a) $y = (x + 4)^2$ **b)** $y = -(x - 1)^2$

  c) $y = -0.3(x + 7)^2$ **d)** $y = 2(x + 9)^2$

  e) $y = 0.9(x + 32)^2$ **f)** $y = -4(x - 18)^2$

3. For each relation:

  i) identify the coordinates of the vertex

  ii) determine if the parabola opens upward or downward

  iii) determine if the parabola is vertically stretched or vertically compressed

  iv) graph the relation

  a) $y = (x - 1)^2 + 9$ **b)** $y = -2(x + 8)^2 - 5$

  c) $y = 0.1x^2 - 1$ **d)** $y = 9.1x^2$

  e) $y = 0.5(x - 2)^2 + 2$ **f)** $y = 8(x + 1)^2 + 13$

4. A flare is sent up as a distress signal. The path is modelled by the relation $h = -4.9(t - 6)^2 + 177.4$, where h is the flare's height, in metres, and t is the time, in seconds.

  a) How long will the flare take to reach its maximum height? What is the maximum height?

  b) A typical flare will stay lit for 7 s. What will the height of the flare be 7 s after it is launched?

  c) Graph this relation.

  d) After how many seconds will the flare hit the water?

Chapter 5: Quadratic Relations II

5. Expand and simplify.

  a) $(3x + 4)(10x + 1)$ **b)** $(x - 2)(4x + 15)$

  c) $(12x - 8)(2x + 0.5)$ **d)** $(6 + 2x)(6 - 2x)$

6. **a)** Write an expression, in simplified form, for the area of an apartment with dimensions $s - 1$ by $4s - 7$.

  b) If $s = 15$ m, find the actual area of the apartment.

7. Write each relation in standard form.

  a) $y = (x - 4)^2 + 0.5$

  b) $y = (x + 10)^2 - 3$

  c) $y = 8(x + 2)^2 + 27$

  d) $y = -3.2(x - 4)^2 - 0.8$

8. Determine the y-intercept for $y = (7 - 3x)(2x - 6)$.

9. Factor each trinomial.

    a) $x^2 + 11x + 24$ **b)** $x^2 + x - 30$

    c) $x^2 - 8x + 7$ **d)** $x^2 + 8x + 16$

    e) $3x^2 + 39x + 108$ **f)** $-10x^2 - 110x - 100$

10. Which pairs contain equivalent expressions? How do you know?

    a) $x^2 + 4x - 5$ $(5 + x)(x - 1)$

    b) $x^2 + 3.5x + 3$ $(x - 2)(x - 1.5)$

    c) $x^2 + x - 2$ $(x - 1)(x + 2)$

11. Find the zeros by factoring. Check by substituting your answers for x.

    a) $y = x^2 - x - 20$

    b) $y = 10x^2 - 360$

    c) $y = -2x^2 + 4x + 70$

    d) $y = 3.5x^2 + 21x + 31.5$

12. The height of a rectangular prism is 16 cm more than the length of the base. The width of the base if half the length.

    a) Sketch and label a diagram to represent the rectangular prism.

    b) Write an expression for the surface area of the prism.

    c) What is the surface area of the prism if the width of the base is 5 cm?

Chapter 6: Geometry in Design

13. Can the shape shown be used to tile the plane? Provide evidence in the form of a sketch.

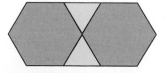

14. a) Use linking cubes to model the capital letter "L". The base of the L should be 10 cm and the height should be 20 cm. The letter should be 10 cm thick. Let the side of a cube represent 5 cm.

    b) Use the model to help you draw an isometric perspective drawing.

    c) Use the model to help you sketch a set of orthographic drawings.

15. A car dealership has ordered a platform to display their newest car models. An isometric perspective drawing for the display platform is shown. The distance between pairs of dots represents 2 m.

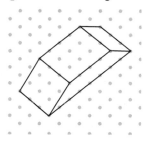

    a) Draw a set of orthographic drawings for the platform.

    b) Draw a net that can be used to make a scale model for the platform. The rectangles that will become the sloped part of the platform should have a length of 3 units and a width of 2.25 units. Cut out the net and construct the model.

    c) The top of the platform is to be made from a special type of thick plywood that sells for \$40/m². Determine how much plywood is needed and the cost of buying it.

7 Exponents

Some relationships are linear, such as how the cost of bananas varies with the mass. Some relationships are quadratic, such as how the height of a space shuttle changes with time. Other relationships—such as how the intensity of sound varies with the distance from the source, and the growth and decay of organisms in nature—are exponential.

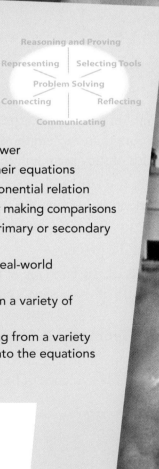

In this chapter, you will

- determine and describe the meaning of negative exponents and of zero as an exponent
- evaluate numerical expressions containing integer exponents and rational bases
- determine the exponent rules for multiplying and dividing numerical expressions involving exponents, and the exponent rule for simplifying numerical expressions involving a power of a power
- graph simple exponential relations, using paper and pencil, given their equations
- make and describe connections between representations of an exponential relation
- distinguish exponential relations from linear and quadratic relations by making comparisons
- collect data that can be modelled as an exponential relation from primary or secondary sources, and graph the data
- describe some characteristics of exponential relations arising from real-world applications by using tables of values and graphs
- pose and solve problems involving exponential relations arising from a variety of real-world applications by using graphs
- solve problems using given equations of exponential relations arising from a variety of real-world applications by substituting values for the exponent into the equations

Reasoning and Proving

Representing | Selecting Tools

Problem Solving

Connecting | Reflecting

Communicating

Key Terms

doubling time	exponential relation
exponential decay	half-life
exponential growth	

Ravi is a medical laboratory technologist. He prepares and analyses medical samples and administers various tests to patients, such as a test for the detection of cancer cells. He uses exponential equations to determine the growth rate of these cells. He trained for this position by taking a three-year course at St. Clair College.

Prerequisite Skills

Powers

1. Write each product as a power.

a) 6×6

b) $7 \times 7 \times 7 \times 7$

c) $(-2) \times (-2) \times (-2)$

d) $(4)(4)(4)(4)(4)(4)(4)(4)$

e) $\frac{1}{4} \times \frac{1}{4} \times \frac{1}{4} \times \frac{1}{4} \times \frac{1}{4}$

f) $\left(-\frac{4}{5}\right)\left(-\frac{4}{5}\right)$

2. Evaluate each power.

a) 5^2

b) 7^3

c) 10^5

d) $(-3)^2$

e) -3^2

f) -12^2

g) $\left(\frac{1}{2}\right)^2$

h) $\left(-\frac{1}{3}\right)^4$

i) $\left(-\frac{1}{5}\right)^3$

Linear Relations

3. Identify the slope and the y-intercept of each linear relation.

a) $y = 2x + 5$

b) $y = 3x - 1$

c) $y = -4x + 3$

d) $y = -\frac{1}{2}x - \frac{2}{3}$

4. Graph each linear relation. Label the y-intercept and any two other points.

a) $y = x - 3$

b) $y = 5x - 7$

c) $y = -2x + 6$

d) $y = \frac{1}{3}x + 2$

5. Ahmed earned \$40 per day plus \$2 per phone call as a marketing representative. Explain why this method of pay can be represented by a linear relation.

Evaluate Formulas

6. Substitute the indicated values. Evaluate for the remaining variable.

a) $A = \pi r^2$, $\quad\quad r = 5$ cm

b) $I = Prt$, $\quad\quad P = \$200, r = 6\%,$ $t = 2$ years

c) $V = s^3$, $\quad\quad s = 5$ m

d) $P = 2(l + w)$, $\quad l = 10$ cm, $w = 7$ cm

Quadratic Relations

7. Describe how each graph differs from the graph of $y = x^2$.

a)

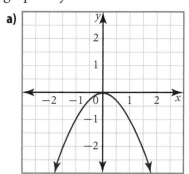

b)

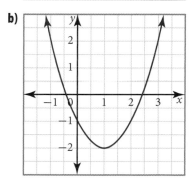

c)

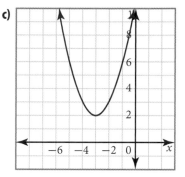

8. Graph each quadratic relation. Label the vertex and at least one other point on either side of the vertex.

a) $y = (x - 1)^2 + 4$

b) $y = 2(x + 3)^2 - 1$

c) $y = -x^2 + 1$

d) $y = -\dfrac{1}{2}(x - 4)^2 + 5$

Chapter Problem

Audiology technicians conduct hearing tests, which include tests for tone, speech reception, speech discrimination, and hearing threshold. Audiology technicians also prescribe and fit hearing aids and offer advice and counselling to patients. Educational requirements for audiology technicians include a 12- to 18-month college program.

Hearing loss can be a serious problem. In this chapter, you will investigate the effects of sound intensities on hearing and the consequences of extended exposure to loud sounds.

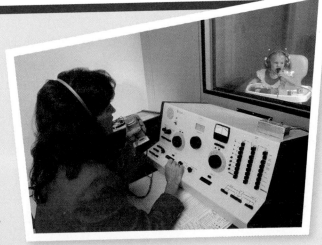

7.1 Exponent Rules

Very large numbers can be awkward to write. Sometimes, they are easier to work with when written in exponential form. For example, the intensity of an earthquake, the population of Earth, and the distance from Earth to the moon can be better expressed using exponents.

Investigate

Tools
• calculator

Patterns With Exponents

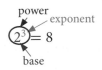

1. Multiply powers with the same base.

a) Copy and complete the table showing the expansion of each product.

Product	Expanded Form	Number of Factors	Single Power
$5^2 \times 5^4$	$(5 \times 5) \times (5 \times 5 \times 5 \times 5)$	6	5^6
$3^5 \times 3^2$			
$(-2)^5 \times (-2)^2$			
$(-3)^4 \times (-3)^3$			
$\left(\frac{1}{2}\right)^3 \times \left(\frac{1}{2}\right)$			

b) Reflect Write a rule for the product of two powers with the same base.

2. Divide powers with the same base.

a) Copy and complete the table. Look for a pattern.

Quotient	Expanded Form	Number of Factors Remaining After Simplifying	Single Power
$\dfrac{5^6}{5^2}$	$\dfrac{5 \times 5 \times 5 \times 5 \times 5 \times 5}{5 \times 5}$	4	5^4
$\dfrac{3^5}{3^3}$			
$\dfrac{(-7)^3}{(-7)^2}$			
$4^7 \div 4^4$			
$\left(\dfrac{2}{3}\right)^4 \div \left(\dfrac{2}{3}\right)^3$			

b) Reflect Compare the single power to the original quotient. Write a rule for the quotient of two powers with the same base.

3. Find the power of a power.

a) Copy and complete the table. Look for a pattern.

Power of a Power	Expanded Form	Number of Factors of Given Base	Single Power
$(5^3)^2$	$(5 \times 5 \times 5)(5 \times 5 \times 5)$		
$(3^2)^4$			
$(2^2)^3$			
$(6^5)^2$			
$(4^3)^3$			

b) Reflect Compare the single power to the original power of a power. Write a rule for simplifying a power of a power.

4. Test your rules by simplifying each expression. Then use a calculator to check your rules.

a) $6^3 \times 6^2$

b) $5^2 \times 5^4$

c) $10^5 \div 10^4$

d) $7^6 \div 7^2$

e) $(10^4)^2$

f) $(5^2)^2$

Example 1

Simplify Expressions Involving Powers

Simplify.

a) $6^2 \times 6^3$ **b)** $\dfrac{7^5}{7^2}$ **c)** $(3^4)^3$ **d)** $\left(\dfrac{1}{2^3}\right)^2$

Solution

Method 1: Use the Exponent Rules

a) $6^2 \times 6^3 = 6^{2+3}$
$$= 6^5$$
$$= 7776$$

b) $\dfrac{7^5}{7^2} = 7^{5-2}$
$$= 7^3$$
$$= 343$$

c) $(3^4)^3 = 3^{4 \times 3}$
$$= 3^{12}$$
$$= 531\ 441$$

d) $\left(\dfrac{1}{2^3}\right)^2 = \dfrac{1^2}{2^{3 \times 2}}$
$$= \dfrac{1}{2^6}$$
$$= \dfrac{1}{64}$$

Method 2: Expand, Then Simplify

$6^2 \times 6^3 = 36 \times 216$
$$= 7776$$

$\dfrac{7^5}{7^2} = \dfrac{16\ 807}{49}$
$$= 343$$

$(3^4)^3 = 81^3$
$$= 531\ 441$$

$\left(\dfrac{1}{2^3}\right)^2 = \left(\dfrac{1}{8}\right)^2$
$$= \dfrac{1}{64}$$

Example 2

Earthquakes

The intensity of an earthquake can range from 1 to 10 000 000. The Richter scale is a base-10 exponential scale used to classify the magnitude of an earthquake. An earthquake with an intensity of 100 000 or 10^5, has a magnitude of 5 as measured on the Richter scale. The chart shows how magnitudes are related.

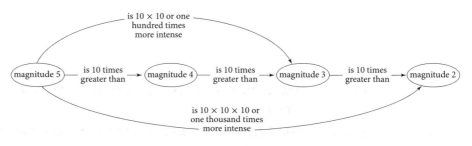

Intensity	Magnitude	Earthquake Effects
Up to $10^{2.5}$	2.5 or less	Usually not felt, but can be recorded by seismograph.
$10^{2.5}$ to $10^{5.4}$	2.5 to 5.4	Often felt, but only causes minor damage.
$10^{5.5}$ to $10^{6.0}$	5.5 to 6.0	Slight damage to buildings and other structures.
$10^{6.1}$ to $10^{6.9}$	6.1 to 6.9	May cause heavy damage in very populated areas.
$10^{7.0}$ to $10^{7.9}$	7.0 to 7.9	Major earthquake. Serious damage.
$10^{8.0}$ and greater	8.0 or greater	Great earthquake. Can totally destroy communities near the epicentre.

An earthquake measuring 2 on the Richter scale can barely be felt, but one measuring 6 often causes damage. An earthquake with magnitude 7 is considered a major earthquake.

a) How much more intense is an earthquake with magnitude 6 than one with magnitude 2?

b) How much more intense is an earthquake with magnitude 7 than one with magnitude 6?

Math **Connect**

The Apollo astronauts discovered disturbances on the moon, now known as moonquakes. They are much weaker than earthquakes. Most are caused by tidal effects from the Earth and the sun. For more information on earthquakes and moonquakes, go to *www.mcgrawhill.ca/links/foundations11* and follow the links.

Solution

Earthquakes are compared by dividing their intensities.

a) An earthquake with magnitude 6 has an intensity of 10^6 and one with magnitude 2 has an intensity of 10^2.

$$\frac{10^6}{10^2} = 10^{6-2}$$
$$= 10^4$$
$$= 10\ 000$$

An earthquake with magnitude 6 is 10 000 times as intense as one with magnitude 2.

b)
$$\frac{10^7}{10^6} = 10^{7-6}$$
$$= 10^1$$
$$= 10$$

An earthquake with magnitude 7 is 10 times as intense as one with magnitude 6.

Key Concepts

- To multiply powers with the same base, keep the base the same and add the exponents.
  $a^p \times a^q = a^{p+q}$
  For example, $3^5 \times 3^3 = 3^8$.

- To divide powers with the same base, keep the base the same and subtract the exponents.
  $a^p \div a^q = a^{p-q}$
  For example, $5^7 \div 5^3 = 5^4$.

- To simplify a power of a power, keep the base the same and multiply the exponents.
  $(a^p)^q = a^{p \times q}$
  For example, $(2^3)^4 = 2^{12}$.

Discuss the Concepts

D1. The magnitudes of most earthquakes are between 0 and 10 on the Richter scale. These magnitudes correspond to intensities of between 1 and 10 000 000 000. Explain how the magnitude of an earthquake, as measured by the Richter scale, is related to its intensity.

D2. Evaluate $\left(\dfrac{1}{81}\right)^3$ and $\left(\dfrac{1}{9}\right)^6$. Use the exponent rules to explain why the answers are the same.

D3. Maggie evaluated the following problem. Her solution is shown.
$2^3 \times 2^2 = 2^6$

Is her solution correct? If not, explain where she went wrong and correct her work.

Practise **A** ·

For help with questions 1 to 5, refer to Example 1.

1. Write each expression as a single power, then evaluate.

   a) $5^2 \times 5^2$ **b)** $2^4 \times 2^3$ **c)** $(-3)^2 \times (-3)^4$

   d) $(-4)^3 \times (-4)^3$ **e)** $\left(\dfrac{1}{4}\right)^2 \times \left(\dfrac{1}{4}\right)^3$ **f)** $\left(-\dfrac{1}{2}\right)^2 \times \left(-\dfrac{1}{2}\right)$

2. Write each expression as a single power, then evaluate.

   a) $6^5 \div 6^4$ **b)** $8^7 \div 8^5$ **c)** $12^8 \div 12^7$

   d) $\dfrac{2^{10}}{2^6}$ **e)** $\dfrac{(-2)^9}{(-2)^6}$ **f)** $\dfrac{(-3)^6}{(-3)^4}$

3. Write the single powers, then evaluate.

a) $(5^2)^3$ b) $(2^3)^3$

c) $[(-4)^3]^2$ d) $\left(\dfrac{1}{7^2}\right)^2$

e) $\left(\dfrac{1}{3^3}\right)^2$ f) $\left(-\dfrac{1}{10^2}\right)^4$

4. Show two ways of evaluating each expression.

a) $6^2 \times 6^3$ b) $7^4 \times 7^2$

c) $9^5 \div 9^3$ d) $\dfrac{(-7)^4}{(-7)^3}$

e) $(5^2)^3$ f) $(10^5)^2$

g) $(-8)^3(-8)$ h) $[(-1)^{11}]^9$

5. Write each expression as a single power, then evaluate.

a) $9^4 \times 9^5$ b) $(7^2)^4$

c) $(-6) \times (-6)^5$ d) $24^6 \div 24^5$

e) $\dfrac{9^7}{9^5}$ f) $\left(\dfrac{3}{4}\right)^5 \times \left(\dfrac{3}{4}\right)^2$

g) $(4^3)^5$ h) $\dfrac{(-8)^9}{(-8)^6}$

i) $\left(-\dfrac{5}{7}\right)^8 \div \left(-\dfrac{5}{7}\right)^4$

For help with questions 6–8, refer to Example 2.

6. Canada's greatest earthquake was recorded in 1949 at the Queen Charlotte Islands in British Columbia. It had a magnitude of about 8. The magnitude of the greatest recorded earthquake in Ontario was about 6. It occurred at the Ontario–Quebec border north of Mattawa in 1935. How much more intense was the earthquake in British Columbia compared to the one in Ontario?

7. The earthquake in the Indian Ocean that caused the devastating tsunami in 2004 measured 9. An earthquake measuring 4 occurred off Vancouver Island in June 2006. How much more intense was the earthquake in the Indian Ocean compared to the one off Vancouver Island?

8. On December 6, 2006 there was an earthquake with magnitude 4.2 near Cochrane, ON. Another earthquake, with magnitude 2.8 occurred on January 29, 2007 near Hawkesbury, ON. In each case, local residents reported feeling the earthquake. Which earthquake was more intense? How much more?

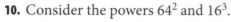
Literacy Connect

9. You can write 3^8 as $3^2 \times 3^6$ using the exponent rules.

  a) Write 3^8 as the product of two powers in three other ways.

  b) Write 2^5 as the quotient of two powers in three ways.

  c) Write 7^{12} as a power of a power in three ways.

Reasoning and Proving

Representing   Selecting Tools

Problem Solving

Connecting   Reflecting

Communicating

10. Consider the powers 64^2 and 16^3.

  a) Are these powers equivalent? Use the exponent rules to explain.

  b) Write a power with a different base that is equivalent to 64^2.

11. The probability of rolling a 5 using a single die is $\frac{1}{6}$. The probability of rolling two 5s using two dice is $\left(\frac{1}{6}\right) \times \left(\frac{1}{6}\right)$ or $\left(\frac{1}{6}\right)^2$.

  a) Evaluate the probability of rolling two 5s. Leave your answer in fraction form.

  b) What would be the probability of rolling three 5s using three dice?

12. The area of a square can be calculated using the formula $A = s^2$, where s is the length of a side. Calculate the area of a square with each side length. Express your answer as a fraction.

a)

$\frac{1}{2}$ in.

b)
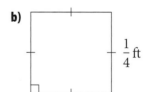
$\frac{1}{4}$ ft

13. There are 12 in. in 1 ft.

  a) Convert your answer in question 12a) to square feet.

  b) Convert your answer in question 12b) to square inches.

14. Copy and complete the table.

Measurement to be Calculated	Formula	Dimensions Given	Calculated Measurement
Area of a Circle	$A = \pi r^2$	$r = \pi$ cm	
Volume of a Cube	$V = s^3$	$s = \dfrac{1}{2}$ in.	
Volume of a Sphere	$V = \dfrac{4}{3}\pi r^3$	$r = \dfrac{1}{8}$ in.	
Volume of a Cylinder	$V = \pi r^2 h$	$r = h = 5$ cm	

15. Rubik's Cube® is a large cube made of small congruent cubes. Each small cube has edges about 2 cm long. The cubes on each face of the Rubik's Cube® are arranged in 3 rows of 3. What is the approximate volume of the Rubik's Cube®?

Extend •

16. Use the exponent rules to simplify each expression. Then use a calculator to evaluate.

a) $10^{3.1} \times 10^{4.2}$

b) $\dfrac{10^{7.9}}{10^{3.1}}$

c) $2^{4.8} \times 2^{1.6}$

d) $\left(\dfrac{1}{2}\right)^{7.8}\left(\dfrac{1}{2}\right)^{1.1}$

17. Use the exponent rules to simplify each expression.

a) $(4x^3)(2x^4)$

b) $\dfrac{-12a^5 b^3}{3a^2 b}$

c) $(m^2 n^3)^5$

d) $\left(\dfrac{k^5 h^2}{k^2}\right)^3$

Zero and Negative Exponents

In Section 7.1, you used exponents to express very large numbers. Exponents can also be used to express very small numbers. The mass of an atom, the length of a bacterium, and the thickness of an eyelash can be expressed using negative exponents.

Investigate

The Meaning of Zero and Negative Exponents

Use patterns to evaluate powers with zero or negative exponents.

1. Copy and complete the statements. Describe each pattern.

a) $2^5 = 32$
$2^4 = 16$
$2^3 = \blacksquare$
$2^2 = \blacksquare$
$2^1 = \blacksquare$
$2^0 = \blacksquare$

b) $3^5 = 243$
$3^4 = \blacksquare$
$3^3 = \blacksquare$
$3^2 = \blacksquare$
$3^1 = \blacksquare$
$3^0 = \blacksquare$

c) $10^5 = 100\ 000$
$10^4 = \blacksquare$
$10^3 = \blacksquare$
$10^2 = \blacksquare$
$10^1 = \blacksquare$
$10^0 = \blacksquare$

2. Reflect For each set of powers, what is true about the values of the powers with zero exponents? Express this as a general rule.

3. Continue your patterns from question 1 to evaluate the powers with negative exponents. Express your answers as whole numbers or fractions.

a) $2^3 = \blacksquare$
$2^2 = \blacksquare$
$2^1 = \blacksquare$
$2^0 = \blacksquare$
$2^{-1} = \blacksquare$
$2^{-2} = \blacksquare$

b) $3^3 = \blacksquare$
$3^2 = \blacksquare$
$3^1 = \blacksquare$
$3^0 = \blacksquare$
$3^{-1} = \blacksquare$
$3^{-2} = \blacksquare$

c) $10^3 = \blacksquare$
$10^2 = \blacksquare$
$10^1 = \blacksquare$
$10^0 = \blacksquare$
$10^{-1} = \blacksquare$
$10^{-2} = \blacksquare$

4. Reflect Explain how to evaluate a power with a negative exponent.

Example 1

Evaluate Powers With Zero or Negative Exponents

Evaluate.

a) 8^{-2}

b) 7^0

c) $(-4)^{-1}$

d) 3^{-2}

Solution

a) $8^{-2} = \dfrac{1}{8^2}$

$\qquad = \dfrac{1}{64}$

b) $7^0 = 1$

c) $(-4)^{-1} = \dfrac{1}{(-4)^1}$ $\qquad \dfrac{1}{-4} = -\dfrac{1}{4}$

$\qquad\qquad = -\dfrac{1}{4}$

d) $3^{-2} = \dfrac{1}{3^2}$

$\qquad\qquad = \dfrac{1}{9}$

Example 2

Simplify Expressions

The rules for positive exponents also work for zero and negative exponents. Use the exponent rules to evaluate.

a) $4^3 \times 4^{-5}$

b) $\dfrac{(-2)^2}{(-2)^{-5}}$

c) $\left(\dfrac{4^2}{4^5}\right)^2$

Solution

a) $4^3 \times 4^{-5} = 4^{3\,+\,(-5)}$

$\qquad\qquad = 4^{-2}$

$\qquad\qquad = \dfrac{1}{4^2}$

$\qquad\qquad = \dfrac{1}{16}$

b) $\dfrac{(-2)^2}{(-2)^{-5}} = (-2)^{2-(-5)}$

$\qquad\qquad = (-2)^7$

$\qquad\qquad = -128$

c) $\left(\dfrac{4^2}{4^5}\right)^2 = (4^{-3})^2$

$\qquad\qquad = 4^{-6}$

$\qquad\qquad = \dfrac{1}{4^6}$

$\qquad\qquad = \dfrac{1}{4096}$

Example 3

Radioactive Decay

Mr. Roberts presented his math class with the following problem involving negative exponents. Every 80 million years, 2^{-1} of the mass of a sample of plutonium-244 decays to a different element. If the original mass of a sample of plutonium-244 was 16 g, determine the mass remaining after

a) 80 million years

b) 240 million years

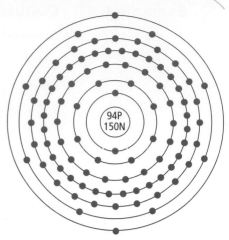
Plutonium-244

Solution

a) Amount remaining $= 16 \times 2^{-1}$

$\qquad\qquad\qquad\quad = 16 \times \dfrac{1}{2}$

$\qquad\qquad\qquad\quad = 8$

After 80 million years, 8 g of plutonium-244 would remain.

b) Number of time units for decay $= 240$ million $\div$ 80 million

$\qquad\qquad\qquad\qquad\qquad\qquad = 3$

Since the decay occurs over 3 units of time,

the amount remaining $= 16 \times (2^{-1})^3$

$\qquad\qquad\qquad\qquad\; = 16 \times (2^{-3})$

$\qquad\qquad\qquad\qquad\; = 16 \times \dfrac{1}{2^3}$

$\qquad\qquad\qquad\qquad\; = 16 \times \dfrac{1}{8}$

$\qquad\qquad\qquad\qquad\; = 2$

After 240 million years, 2 g of plutonium-244 would remain.

Key Concepts

- Any base raised to an exponent of zero equals 1.
  $x^0 = 1$
  For example, $6^0 = 1$.

- Any base raised to a negative exponent is equal to the reciprocal of the base raised to a positive exponent.

  $$x^{-a} = \frac{1}{x^a} \qquad\qquad \frac{1}{x^{-a}} = x^a$$

  For example,

  $$7^{-2} = \frac{1}{7^2} \qquad\qquad \frac{1}{2^{-3}} = 2^3$$
  $$= \frac{1}{49} \qquad\qquad\qquad\quad = 8$$

Discuss the Concepts

D1. Describe the steps you would use to evaluate each power.

    a) 2^{-3}

    b) $\dfrac{1}{3^{-4}}$

D2. Evaluate.

    a) $(-2)^4$ **b)** -2^4 **c)** 2^{-4}

    Explain how the powers are different. Draw and label a number line to help you explain.

D3. Refer to the rules for working with positive exponents. Copy and complete the table. Use examples to show your understanding of the exponent rules involving negative exponents.

Product	Expanded Form	Number of Factors	Single Power

Practise

For help with question 1, refer to the Investigate.

1. a) Write $\dfrac{1}{9^5}$ as a power with base 9.

    b) Write 6^3 as a power with base $\dfrac{1}{6}$.

    c) Write 5^{-2} as a power with base $\dfrac{1}{5}$.

    d) Write $\dfrac{1}{4^{-1}}$ as a power with base 4.

For help with questions 2 to 5, refer to Example 1.

2. Evaluate. Express your answers as whole numbers or fractions.

   a) $5^2, 5^{-2}$
   b) $2^1, 2^{-1}$
   c) $4^4, 4^{-4}$
   d) $10^3, 10^{-3}$
   e) $1^6, 1^{-6}$
   f) $2^9, 2^{-9}$
   g) $(-3)^4, (-3)^{-4}$
   h) $(-8)^1, (-8)^{-1}$

3. Evaluate. Express your answers as whole numbers or fractions.

   a) 12^0
   b) 8^{-1}
   c) 6^{-2}
   d) $100\ 000^0$
   e) 500^{-1}
   f) 5^{-3}
   g) $(-2)^{-8}$
   h) $(-10)^{-3}$
   i) $\left(\dfrac{1}{6}\right)^{-2}$
   j) 3^{-5}
   k) $\left(\dfrac{1}{3}\right)^{-3}$
   l) $(-7)^3$

4. Use a pattern to show that $4^{-3} = \dfrac{1}{4^3}$.

5. Evaluate each of the powers in question 3 using a calculator. Explain the benefits of each form.

6. Simplify each quotient two ways.
   - Write the powers in expanded form and eliminate factors common to the numerator and the denominator.
   - Use the exponent rules.

   Compare the results. How can you use the results from both methods to explain the meaning of a negative exponent?

   a) $\dfrac{8^7}{8^5}$
   b) $\dfrac{5^4}{5^9}$
   c) $\dfrac{7}{7^3}$
   d) $\dfrac{12^5}{12^8}$
   e) $\dfrac{(-4)^7}{(-4)^8}$
   f) $\dfrac{(-3)^2}{(-3)^7}$

7. Simplify each quotient two ways.
   - Write the powers in expanded form and eliminate factors common to the numerator and the denominator.
   - Use the exponent rules.

   Compare the results. How can you use the results from both methods to explain the meaning of a zero exponent?

   a) $\dfrac{6^5}{6^5}$
   b) $\dfrac{8^4}{8^4}$
   c) $\dfrac{16^6}{16^6}$
   d) $\dfrac{2^7}{2^7}$
   e) $\dfrac{(-9)^3}{(-9)^3}$
   f) $\dfrac{(-7)^2}{(-7)^2}$

For help with question 8, refer to Example 2.

8. Rewrite each as a single power, then evaluate. Express your answers as fractions.

   a) $8^3 \times 8^{-1}$

   b) $\dfrac{4^2}{4^{-1}}$

   c) $\dfrac{1}{(2^4)^3}$

   d) $(-3)^3(-3)^{-1}$

   e) $(10^{-2})^3$

   f) $\left(\dfrac{1}{2^4}\right)\left(\dfrac{1}{2^4}\right)$

   g) $6^2 \div 6^5$

   h) $5^{-7} \times 5^4$

   i) $(4^3)^{-2}$

   j) $\left(\dfrac{1}{3}\right)^{-6} \times \left(\dfrac{1}{3}\right)^3$

   k) $\left(\dfrac{1}{9}\right)^{-9} \times \left(\dfrac{1}{9}\right)^7$

   l) $(5^{-2})^3$

For help with question 9, refer to Example 3.

9. A second question on Mr. Roberts' math test is shown.

   Radium-226 is a radioactive element that decays by 2^{-1} of its mass after about 1600 years. Determine the remaining mass of 16 g of radium-226 after

   a) 1600 years

   b) 8000 years

Apply

Literacy Connect

Math ▸ **Connect**

One million seconds is equal to 11.5 days. One billion seconds is equal to 31.7 years!

10. How small is one billionth?

   a) Write one thousand as a power of 10.

   b) Write one thousandth as a fraction, as a power of $\dfrac{1}{10}$, and then as a power of 10.

   c) Write one millionth as a power of 10.

   d) Write one billionth as a power of 10.

   e) Write the ratio of one thousandth to one billionth as a power of 10. How many times larger is one thousandth compared to one billionth?

11. Evaluate the power in each statement. Express your answers as whole numbers or fractions.

   a) One kilobyte is 2^{10} bytes.

   b) One byte is 2^{-10} kilobytes.

   c) One megabyte is $(2^{10})^2$ bytes.

   d) One byte is $(2^{-10})^3$ gigabytes.

   e) One bit is 2^{-3} bytes.

   f) One bit is $2^{-40} \times 2^{-3}$ terabytes.

12. Sound intensity levels are recorded in decibels (dB). The actual intensity is recorded in Watts per square metre (W/m^2). The faintest sound that can be heard by the human ear has an intensity of 10^{-12} W/m^2 and is assigned an intensity level of 0 dB. A sound that is 10 times more intense is assigned a sound level of 10 dB. A sound that is 10×10 or 100 times more intense is assigned a sound level of 20 dB, and so on. To calculate how much more intense sound A is than sound B, divide their intensity levels by 10 to get a and b, then use the ratio $\dfrac{10^a}{10^b}$.

Source	Intensity Level
Threshold of hearing	0 dB
Rustling leaves	10 dB
Whisper	20 dB
Normal conversation	60 dB
Busy street traffic	70 dB
Vacuum cleaner	80 dB
MP3 player at maximum level	100 dB
Front row of seating at a rock concert	110 dB
Threshold of pain	130 dB
Military jet takeoff	140 dB
Instant perforation of eardrum	160 dB

a) How much more intense is the sound from normal conversation compared to the threshold of hearing?

b) How much more intense is sound from the front row of a rock concert compared to the sound from busy street traffic?

c) Some dogs have a threshold of hearing of -5 dB. How much less intense is a dog's threshold of hearing compared to a human's threshold of hearing?

Extend **C** ···

13. Loudness describes the strength of the ear's perception of a sound. The exponent must be increased by a factor of 10 for a sound to sound twice as loud.

a) Refer to the ratio in question 12. What is the corresponding increase in loudness?

b) Write this rule using powers.

c) How many vacuum cleaners would it take to sound twice as loud as one vacuum cleaner? Explain.

14. To estimate how much an item costing T dollars in 2007 would have cost in a given year (after 1914), C, you can use the formula $C = T(1.0323)^{-n}$, where n is the number of years before 2007.

   a) How much would a $150 coat have cost in 1920?
   Hint: Substitute the number of years before 2007 for n.

   b) How much would a $20 000 car have cost in 1970?

   c) How much would a $1.99 bag of dried fruit snacks have cost in 1962?

   d) How much would a $200 000 condominium have cost in 1980?

15. An orange peel may take 1 year to decay to 10^{-1} of its original mass. An aluminum can may take 50 years to decay to 10^{-1} of its original mass.

   a) An orange peel has an original mass of 5 g. What mass will remain after 2 years?

   b) A metal can has an original mass of 16.5 g. What mass will remain after 100 years?

16. Write each numerator and denominator as a power, then use the exponent rules to simplify. Express your answer as a power with a whole number base.

   a) $\dfrac{128}{1024}$

   b) $\dfrac{243}{6561}$

   c) $\dfrac{3125}{625}$

   d) $\dfrac{49}{2401}$

   e) $\dfrac{11}{1331}$

   f) $\dfrac{512}{64}$

   g) $\dfrac{1}{8} \times \dfrac{1}{16}$

   h) $\dfrac{1}{25} \times \dfrac{1}{125}$

17. Suppose $y = 4^2$ and $z = 4^3$. Write each expression as a power with base 4.

   a) $y^{-1}z^2$

   b) $\dfrac{y}{z}$

   c) $\dfrac{z^{-4}}{y}$

   d) y^5z^{-2}

   e) $\dfrac{y^{-2}z^{-4}}{y}$

   f) $\dfrac{yz}{y^2z^{-1}}$

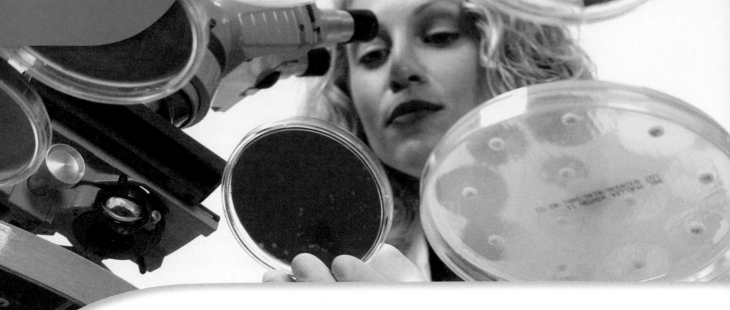

7.3 Investigate Exponential Relationships

Many situations cannot be modelled using linear or quadratic relations. The growth of bacteria, the compound interest earned on an investment, and the rate of decay of radioactive materials, for example, are modelled by exponential relations.

Investigate 1

Tools

- 3 sheets of paper, letter-sized or bigger

Paper Folding

1. a) Copy the table. Add enough rows for seven folds or stages.

Stage	Total Number of Rectangles

b) Take a sheet of paper. Fold the paper about 1 cm in from one edge, as shown. You will create a rectangle that is 1 cm by about 28 cm if using a 21.5 cm by 27.8 cm sheet of paper. Record the number of rectangles for stage 1. Do not count the larger rectangle that is left over.

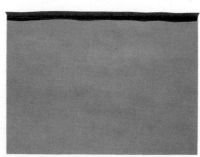

c) Fold the paper again 2 cm from the edge. Record the number of rectangles when there are two folds. Continue folding in a fan-fold manner, for 3 cm from the edge, 4 cm, 5 cm, and so on, as shown. Complete the table.

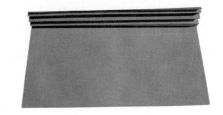

d) Make a scatter plot of the data.

e) Describe the shape of the graph.

2. a) Copy the table. Add enough rows for 5 folds or stages.

Stage	Total Number of Rectangles

b) Take another sheet of paper. Fold the paper about 1 cm in from one edge. Record the number of rectangles for stage 1.

c) Fold the paper as in step 1c), except fold the paper twice while still keeping a 2 cm edge. Record the number of rectangles. Then fold the paper three times keeping a 3 cm edge, four times keeping a 4 cm edge, and so on. Complete the table.

d) Make a scatter plot of the data.

e) Describe the shape of the graph.

3. a) Copy the table. Add enough rows for seven folds or stages.

Stage	Total Number of Rectangles

b) Take a third sheet of paper. Fold it in half across the length of the paper to make two layers, as shown. Record the number of rectangles created.

c) Fold it in half again to make four layers. Record the number of rectangles. Continue until you have made seven folds. Complete the table.

d) Make a scatter plot of the data.

e) Describe the shape of the graph.

4. Reflect In question 1, the data can be represented by a linear relation. In question 2, the data can be represented by a quadratic relation and in question 3, the data can be represented by an **exponential relation**. How are the graphs of these relations similar? different?

exponential relation
- a relation that can be represented by the form $y = a^x$, where a is a positive constant and $a \neq 1$.
- the ratios of consecutive y-values are constant

Tools

- temperature probe
- hot water
- large bowl

Optional:

- thermometer

1. Set up a temperature probe to collect temperature data every 5 min.

2. Place the temperature probe in the bowl of hot water and turn it on immediately. (Alternatively, use a regular thermometer and record the temperature every 5 min.)

3. After 60 min, turn off the probe.

4. Make a scatter plot of the temperature versus time, with time on the horizontal axis.

5. Describe the shape of the graph.

6. Divide each temperature by the previous one in the chart (e.g., divide the temperature after 10 min by the temperature after 5 min).

7. **Reflect** How do the results compare?

In an exponential relation, for equal steps of x, the ratios of consecutive y-values are constant. In the table, dividing each value y by the previous value of y gives a result of 3, so as x increases by 1, y increases by a factor of 3. Because each ratio is constant, the relationship is exponential.

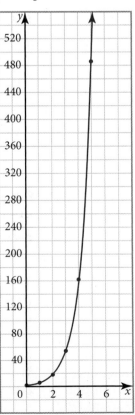

x	y	Ratio of Successive y-values
0	2	
1	6	$6 \div 2 = 3$
2	18	$18 \div 6 = 3$
3	54	$54 \div 18 = 3$
4	162	$162 \div 54 = 3$
5	486	$486 \div 162 = 3$

The graph increases rapidly as you move to the right on the x-axis, and approaches a vertical line.

Example

Pendulum Motion

A large pendulum was set in motion. With each complete swing, the pendulum's maximum distance from its rest position decreased. A motion sensor was used to obtain the data after every 5 swings.

Number of Swings	Maximum Distance (cm)
0	23.5
5	19.9
10	17.0
15	14.6
20	10.4
25	8.7
30	7.6

a) Make a scatter plot of the data. Describe the graph.

b) Calculate the ratio between successive distances. Is the relationship between the number of swings and the maximum distance of the pendulum swing exponential? Explain.

c) Is this relationship an example of **exponential growth** or **exponential decay**?

exponential growth
• non-linear growth represented by an exponential relation and a graph with an upward curve

exponential decay
• non-linear growth represented by an exponential relation and a graph with a downward curve

Solution

a)

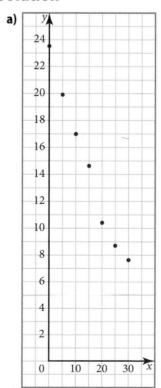

The initial distance was 23.5 cm. The maximum distance declines rapidly at the beginning, but levels off as the number of swings increases. Eventually, the graph will approach a horizontal line.

b)

Number of Swings	Maximum Distance (cm)	Ratio of Successive Distances
0	23.5	
		19.9 ÷ 23.5 = 0.847
5	19.9	
		0.853
10	17.0	
		0.861
15	14.6	
		0.712
20	10.4	
		0.836
25	8.7	
		0.877
30	7.6	

c) The ratio between successive distances is approximately 0.85, indicating a relatively constant rate of change. (The differences in the ratios might be due to measurement error.) Therefore, the relationship between the number of swings and the swing distance is an example of exponential decay.

Key Concepts

- The graph of an exponential relation is a curve that is approximately horizontal at one end and increases or decreases rapidly at the other end.

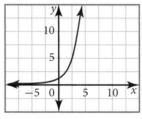
Exponential Growth

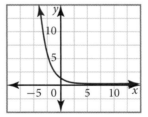
Exponential Decay

- For any exponential relation, the ratio between successive terms is constant.

Discuss the Concepts

A scientific study showed a relationship between the speed of a car and the chance of a collision.

Collision Rates on Various Road Types

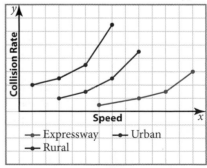

D1. Is the relationship between speed and the chance of a collision exponential? Justify your answer.

D2. On which road type is the chance of a collision the greatest? Suggest reasons why this might be true.

For help with questions 1 to 3, refer to the Example.

1. Show that this relation is exponential.

x	y
1	2
2	4
3	8
4	16
5	32
6	64

2. Which of these graphs could represent an exponential relation? Explain.

a)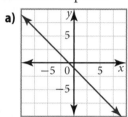

b)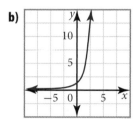

c)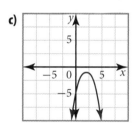

d)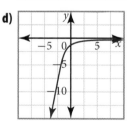

3. In an old story, *The King's Chessboard*, a king rewards a farmer for saving the kingdom. The king gives the farmer 1 grain of rice on the first day, 2 grains of rice on the second day, 4 on the third day, and so on, doubling the number of grains of rice each day, for 64 days.

a) Make a table showing the number of grains of rice the farmer receives each day for the first 7 days.

b) How does this story illustrate exponential growth?

c) How many grains of rice will the farmer receive on the sixteenth day?

d) No matter how rich the king is, he will eventually run out of rice. Explain why.

Reasoning and Proving

Representing | Selecting Tools

Problem Solving

Connecting | Reflecting

Communicating

4. Current radio dials are digital. Look at an older analogue AM or FM radio dial and you will see that the frequencies are not spaced evenly.

   a) Copy and complete the table. Measure the distance, accurate to the nearest tenth of a centimetre, from the left end of the radio dial to each radio frequency on the dial.

Distance (cm)	AM Radio Frequency (kHz)
	540
	600
	700
	900
	1200
	1400
	1600

   b) Make a scatter plot of the data. Let distance be the independent variable.

   c) Is the relationship between the distance and frequency exponential? Justify your answer.

5. On a television game show, the cash prizes were designed to resemble exponential growth.

   The prizes are:

$100	$2000	$64 000
$200	$4000	$125 000
$300	$8000	$250 000
$500	$16 000	$500 000
$1000	$32 000	$1 000 000

   a) Show that these cash prizes do not actually grow exponentially.

   b) Make a new table of 15 cash prizes that do grow exponentially.

   c) Find other examples of cash prizes that seem to—but do not— grow exponentially.

6. The table and graph show the number of bacteria in 1 cm³ of a bacterial culture over a period of hours.

Time (h)	Number of Bacteria (1000s)
2.5	10.07
2.8	13.07
5.4	14.59
6.5	20.70
9.2	27.94
9.5	31.50
11.0	40.04
13.3	49.90
14.6	64.72
16.4	75.57

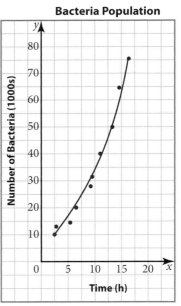

Bacteria Population

a) Describe the shape of the graph.

b) Estimate the number of bacteria present at the beginning of the test. Explain how you got your answer.

c) Estimate the number of bacteria present after 10 h.

d) What is the trend in the bacteria growth?

7. Bacteria tend to grow exponentially, by a common factor over equal time intervals, because each cell divides into two daughter cells. A particular bacteria culture begins with 1000 bacteria. The number of bacteria doubles about every 12 h.

a) Copy and complete the table to show the number of bacteria at the end of every 12 h for one week.

Time (h)	Number of Bacteria (1000s)
12	1000
24	

b) Make a scatter plot of your data, with time as the independent variable.

c) When will the number of bacteria reach 1 000 000 000? Explain how you know.

8. A student in a chemistry laboratory heated a liquid chemical to 120°C and let it cool at room temperature to 60°C. This took 10 min. The graph shows the temperature of the chemical (in degrees Celsius) versus time (in minutes).

Temperature versus Time

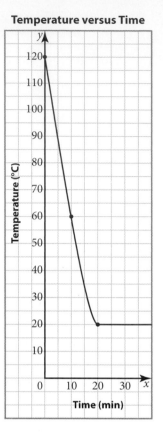

a) Describe the shape of the graph.

b) How long did it take for the chemical to cool to 30°C?

c) The temperature of the chemical will stabilize when it reaches room temperature. What is the temperature in the laboratory?

9. A photocopier is set to reduce an image to 90% of its original size.

a) If you make a copy of the reduced image and reduce it to 90%, what percent of the original is the second image?

b) How many times would you have to reduce the image to 90% for it to be reduced by at least 50% of the original? Explain.

Literacy Connect

10. The graph shows a scatter plot and a curve of best fit of total high-tech exports from China, in hundreds of millions of US dollars, between 1996 and 2003.

Exports of High-Tech Products

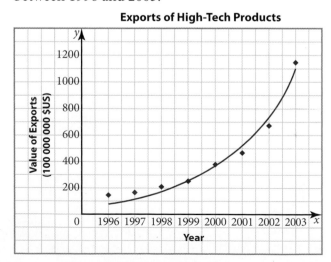

a) Do you think the graph is an example of exponential growth? Explain.

b) Assume the trend continued. What was the value of high-tech exports in 2004? What will it be in 2010?

c) Do you think this trend will continue? Explain.

Achievement Check

11. Mrs. Lynn's math students wanted to know how much homework was expected in her course. She suggested they spend 2 s on homework on the first night then double the time spent on homework every night throughout the course.

a) How much time would have been spent on homework at the end of the first week of classes?

b) How much time would have been spent on homework at the end of the first month of classes? (Assume there are 20 school days in a month.)

c) Estimate when the time spent on homework is 1 h.

d) Estimate when the time spent on homework is one day.

Extend **C**

12. Fractals are geometric figures created by repeatedly applying the same drawing process. Describe how each fractal was created. Explain how these fractals can be considered examples of exponential growth.

a)

b)

7.4 Exponential Relations

How do the graphs of linear, quadratic, and exponential relations compare?

In this section, you will learn how to identify these relations from tables of values and from their graphs.

Graphs of Exponential Relations

Method 1: Use a Graphing Calculator

1. Use a graphing calculator to graph the relations $y = 2^x$ and $y = 4^x$. Use the window settings shown.

2. What points do the graphs have in common?

3. Describe the shape of each graph on the left and the right of the y-axis. How are the graphs similar? How are they different?

4. Predict the shape of each graph and the y-intercept of $y = 5^x$ and $y = 1.5^x$. Check with a graphing calculator.

5. **Reflect** Describe the graph of an exponential relation of the form $y = b^x$, for $b > 1$.

Method 2: Graph by Hand

1. Create a table of values for each relation.
   • $y = 2^x$ • $y = 4^x$
   Use $x = -2, -1, 0, 1, 2$.

2. Plot the data for each relation on the same set of axes. Use a different colour for each data set and join each set of points with a smooth curve.

3. Which points do the graphs have in common?

4. Describe the shape of each graph to the left and the right of the y-axis. How are the graphs similar? How are they different?

5. Predict the shape of each graph and the y-intercept of $y = 5^x$ and $y = 1.5^x$. Check by graphing.

6. **Reflect** Describe the graph of an exponential relation of the form $y = b^x$, for $b > 1$.

Example 1

Exponential Relations

a) Make a table of values and graph each relation.
   i) $y = 2^x$
   ii) $y = 3^x$
   iii) $y = \left(\dfrac{1}{2}\right)^x$

b) Describe the similarities and differences between the graphs.

Solution

a) i)

x	y
−3	$\dfrac{1}{8}$
−2	$\dfrac{1}{4}$
−1	$\dfrac{1}{2}$
0	1
1	2
2	4
3	8
4	16

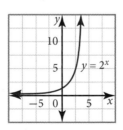

ii)

x	y
−3	$\frac{1}{27}$
−2	$\frac{1}{9}$
−1	$\frac{1}{3}$
0	1
1	3
2	9
3	27
4	81

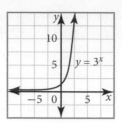

iii)

x	y
−3	8
−2	4
−1	2
0	1
1	$\frac{1}{2}$
2	$\frac{1}{4}$
3	$\frac{1}{8}$
4	$\frac{1}{16}$

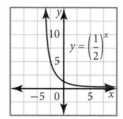

b) The graphs of $y = 2^x$ and $y = 3^x$ are almost horizontal on the left and become steeper toward the right. The graph of $y = \left(\frac{1}{2}\right)^x$ is almost horizontal on the right and becomes steeper toward the left.

All graphs have a y-intercept of 1. None have an x-intercept.

The graphs of $y = 2^x$ and $y = \left(\frac{1}{2}\right)^x$ are reflections of each other in the y-axis.

Example 2

Population Growth

Ontario's population is projected to grow exponentially based on the relation $P = 11\,000\,000(1.0112)^n$, where P is the estimated population and n is the number of years after 1996. The formula is expected to be valid until 2031.

a) Sketch a graph of this relation.

b) What was Ontario's population in 1996? Show this on the graph.

c) What is the projected population for Ontario in 2031?

Solution

a)

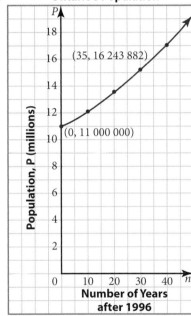

Number of Years After 1996	Population
0	11 000 000
10	12 295 985
20	13 744 657
30	15 364 008
40	17 174 145

b) In the relation, n is the number of years after 1996. So for 1996, $n = 0$.

$$P = 11\,000\,000(1.0112)^0$$
$$= 11\,000\,000 \times 1$$
$$= 11\,000\,000$$

In 1996, the population of Ontario was about 11 000 000 people.

c) The year 2031 is 35 years after 1996, so $n = 35$.

$$P = 11\,000\,000(1.0112)^{35}$$
$$= 11\,000\,000 \times 1.476\,716\,518$$
$$= 16\,243\,881.57$$

The projected population for Ontario in 2031 is 16 243 882 people.

Example 3

Compare Linear, Quadratic, and Exponential Relations

a) Make a table of values for each relation. Use $x = -4, -3, -2, -1, 0,$ $1, 2, 3, 4, 5$. Use first and second differences to determine whether each relation is linear, quadratic, or exponential. Find the ratio of successive y-values for each relation. Compare the results.

i) $y = 2x$ **ii)** $y = x^2$ **iii)** $y = 2^x$

b) Graph each relation on the same set of axes.

c) Describe each graph. Identify the y-intercept and any maximum or minimum point.

Solution

a) i) $y = 2x$

x	y	First Differences	Ratio of Successive y-values
-4	-8		
		2	$\frac{3}{4}$
-3	-6		
		2	$\frac{2}{3}$
-2	-4		
		2	$\frac{1}{2}$
-1	-2		
		2	0
0	0		
		2	undefined
1	2		
		2	2
2	4		
		2	$\frac{3}{2}$
3	6		
		2	$\frac{4}{3}$
4	8		

$\leftarrow \dfrac{-6}{-8} = \dfrac{3}{4}$

• The first differences are constant so this is a linear relation. The ratios of successive y-values are not equal.

ii) $y = x^2$

x	y	First Differences	Second Differences	Ratio of Successive y-values
-4	16			
		-7		$\frac{9}{16}$
-3	9		2	
		-5		$\frac{4}{9}$
-2	4		2	
		-3		$\frac{1}{4}$
-1	1		2	
		-1		0
0	0		2	
		1		undefined
1	1		2	
		3		4
2	4		2	
		5		$\frac{9}{4}$
3	9		2	
		7		$\frac{16}{9}$
4	16			

- The first differences are not constant but the second differences are, so this is a quadratic relation. The ratios of successive y-values are not equal.

iii) $y = 2^x$

x	y	First Differences	Second Differences	Ratio of Successive y-values
-4	$\dfrac{1}{16}$			
		$\dfrac{1}{16}$		2
-3	$\dfrac{1}{8}$		$\dfrac{1}{16}$	
		$\dfrac{1}{8}$		2
-2	$\dfrac{1}{4}$		$\dfrac{1}{8}$	
		$\dfrac{1}{4}$		2
-1	$\dfrac{1}{2}$		$\dfrac{1}{4}$	
		$\dfrac{1}{2}$		2
0	1		$\dfrac{1}{2}$	
		1		2
1	2		1	
		2		2
2	4		2	
		4		2
3	8		4	
		8		2
4	16			

- The first and second differences are not constant, but the ratios of successive y-values are equal. This is an exponential relation.

b)

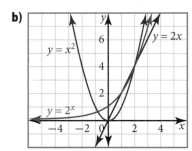

c)
- The graph of $y = 2x$ is a line with a slope of 2 and y-intercept 0. There is no maximum or minimum point.

- The graph of $y = x^2$ is a parabola with y-intercept 0. The minimum point is $(0, 0)$.

- The graph of $y = 2^x$ is a curve that approaches a horizontal line on the left and becomes increasingly steep towards the right. The y-intercept is 1. There is no maximum or minimum point.

Example 4

Musical Scale

Middle A on a piano is known as A4. Its sound wave has a frequency of 440 cycles per second, also written as 440 Hertz (Hz). The table shows the frequencies of each of the eight A-notes on a piano.

A-note	0	1	2	3	4	5	6	7
Frequency (Hz)	27.5	55	110	220	440	880	1760	3520

Show that the relationship between the A-notes on a piano and their frequencies can be modelled using exponential growth.

Solution

First, graph the relation.

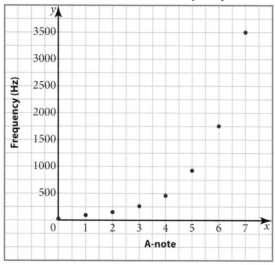

The graph of the relation curves upward and increases more and more rapidly from left to right. The curve is constantly increasing. This curve might be part of a parabola. Use first and second differences to check.

A-note	0	1	2	3	4	5	6	7
Frequency (Hz)	27.5	55	110	220	440	880	1760	3520
First Differences		27.5	55	110	220	440	880	1760
Second Differences			27.5	55	110	220	440	880
Ratio of Successive y-values		2	2	2	2	2	2	2

Neither the first nor the second differences are constant, so the relation is neither linear nor quadratic.

The ratios of successive *y*-values are all equal. Therefore the relationship between the A-notes on a piano and their frequencies is exponential.

Key Concepts

- A relation of the form $y = b^x$, where $b > 0$ and $b \neq 1$, is exponential.

- If $b > 1$, moving left to right, the graph increases very slowly for negative x-values and increases more rapidly for positive x-values. The graph is almost horizontal on the left and very steep on the right.

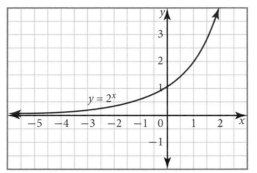

- If $0 < b < 1$, moving left to right, the graph decreases very rapidly for negative x-values and decreases more slowly for positive x-values. The graph is almost horizontal on the right and very steep on the left.

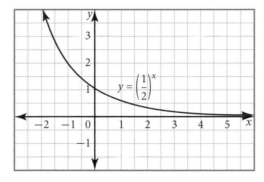

- The y-intercept is 1 and there is no x-intercept.

- The growth or decay factor is the base of the power, b.

Discuss the Concepts

D1. The graph of an exponential relation does not have an x-intercept. Explain why, using the graph from Example 3.

D2. Compare the graphs of $y = x^2$ and $y = 2^x$ in Example 3. Describe what happens to the value of y for each graph when x changes from a positive number to a negative number.

For help with question 1, refer to Example 3.

1. Identify the type of growth (linear, quadratic, exponential) illustrated by each graph. Justify your answers.

a)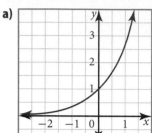

b)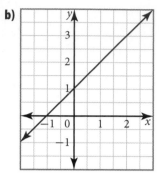

c)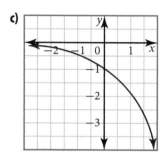

d)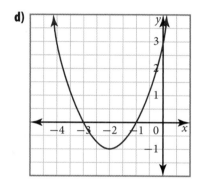

e)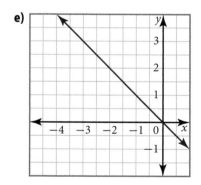

For help with questions 2 to 5, refer to Example 1.

2. Identify which graph represents each relation. Justify your response.

   a) $y = 2^x$

   b) $y = 10^x$

   c) $y = \left(\dfrac{1}{2}\right)^x$

   d) $y = (0.1)^x$

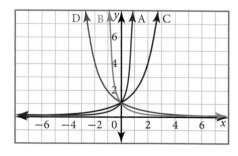

3. a) Sketch each graph. Use a graphing calculator to check.

    i) $y = 2^x$ **ii)** $y = 2(2^x)$

    iii) $y = 3(2^x)$ **iv)** $y = 4(2^x)$

  b) Describe the role of a in $y = a(b^x)$.

4. Make a table of values for each relation. Sketch each pair of relations on the same set of axes. Use a graphing calculator to check.

  a) $y = 3^x$ $y = 2(3^x)$

  b) $y = \left(\dfrac{1}{2}\right)^x$ $y = 2\left(\dfrac{1}{2}\right)^x$

  c) $y = (0.4)^x$ $y = 0.3(0.4)^x$

5. Make a table of values for each relation. Graph each pair of relations on the same set of axes. Use a graphing calculator to check.

  a) $y = 2^x$ $y = 2^{3x}$

  b) $y = 10^x$ $y = 10^{\frac{x}{2}}$

  c) $y = \left(\dfrac{1}{2}\right)^x$ $y = \left(\dfrac{1}{2}\right)^{\frac{x}{4}}$

  d) $y = 2^x$ $y = (3)2^{\frac{x}{5}}$

For help with question 6, refer to Example 2.

6. York Region's population, P, is projected to grow until 2031 based on the relation $P = 610\,000(1.029)^n$, where n is the number of years after 1996.

  a) Sketch a graph of this relation.

  b) What is the P-intercept? What does it represent?

  c) What is the projected population of York Region in

    i) 2015?

    ii) 2031?

7. A pressure reader is used to measure the sound intensity of a bell. The relation $P = 200(0.5)^t$ estimates the sound pressure, P, in pascals, after t seconds.

  a) Sketch a graph of this relation.

  b) What is the P-intercept? What does it represent?

  c) What was the sound pressure after

    i) 1 s?

    ii) 2 s?

8. Between 1996 and 2006, the population of Toronto grew from 2 459 700 to 2 607 600. The population of Peel Region grew from 878 800 to 1 215 300. The populations, P, can be estimated using the relations:

$$P_{Toronto} = 2\ 459\ 700(1.0058)^n \qquad P_{Peel} = 878\ 800(1.033)^n$$

where n is the number of years after 1996.

a) Make a table of values of each population for 10 years after 1996 and sketch a graph for each relation.

b) Compare the growth rates. How do the growth rates affect the graphs?

9. Which model (linear, quadratic, or exponential) would best describe each situation? Why?

a) a car slowing down by $\frac{1}{4}$ of its speed for every second that elapses

b) the height of a stone falling from the top of a cliff

c) a motorcyclist speeding up by 4 km/h each second

d) the number of bacteria doubling every 3 h

e) the path of a basketball when tossed into the air

f) the maximum height of each bounce of a bouncing ball

Chapter Problem

10. The sound pressure, in micropascals, is the air pressure exerted by sound waves on objects such as your ear drums. To convert decibels (dB) to sound pressure (P), you can use the relation $P = 20 \times 10^{\frac{dB}{20}}$.

a) Plot a graph of this relation. Use dB-values from 0 to 160, in steps of 20.

b) Normal conversation measures 60 dB. Sound at a rock concert can reach 120 dB. Compare the sound pressures for these two situations.

c) If the sound level reaches 160 dB, it can perforate your eardrums. What sound pressure will cause this?

11. The sound wave for each note on a piano has a different frequency. A full octave on a piano from note C4 to C5 is shown.

Note	C4	C#	D	D#	E	F	F#
Frequency (Hz)	261.6	277.2	293.7	311.1	329.6	349.2	370.0

Note	G	G	A	A	B	C5
Frequency (Hz)	392.0	415.3	440.0	466.2	493.9	523.2

a) Show that the relationship between the notes in an octave and their frequency can be modelled using exponential growth. How does this compare to the results in Example 4?

b) Graph the relation using a graphing calculator. (Hint: Let C4 represent $x = 1$, C# represent $x = 2$, and so on.) Compare your graph to the graph of a linear relation.

12. The graph shows the population of Canada from 1861 to 2001.

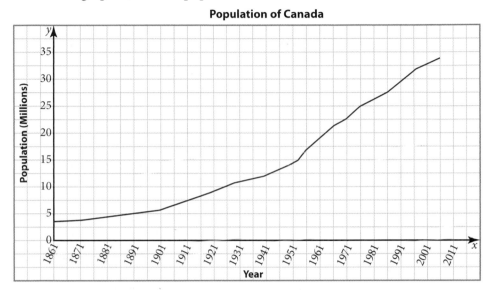

a) What was the approximate annual rate of change in population from 1861 to 1871?

b) What was the approximate annual rate of change in population from 1951 to 1961?

c) What was the approximate annual rate of change in population from 1991 to 2001?

d) What type of relation is represented by this graph? Explain.

e) What was the approximate **doubling time** of Canada's population?

f) Predict when Canada's population will grow to about 64 million people.

doubling time
• time required for a quantity to double in size, number, or mass

Literacy Connect

13. Consider each pattern of diagrams.
i) Describe the pattern.
ii) Continue each pattern for two more diagrams.
iii) What type of relation is represented?

a) Diagram 1   Diagram 2   Diagram 3

b) Diagram 1   Diagram 2   Diagram 3

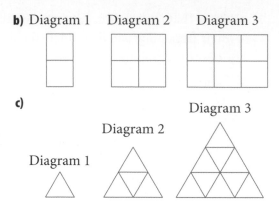

c)

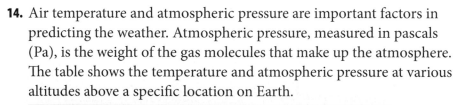

Diagram 1   Diagram 2   Diagram 3

Extend **C** ···

14. Air temperature and atmospheric pressure are important factors in predicting the weather. Atmospheric pressure, measured in pascals (Pa), is the weight of the gas molecules that make up the atmosphere. The table shows the temperature and atmospheric pressure at various altitudes above a specific location on Earth.

Altitude (m)	Temperature (°C)	Atmospheric Pressure (Pa)
0	15.00	10.13
1000	5.16	8.99
2000	−4.68	7.95
3000	−14.52	7.01
4000	−24.36	6.16
5000	−34.20	5.40
6000	−44.04	4.71
7000	−53.88	4.11
8000	−63.72	3.55

   a) Compare the changes in temperature and atmospheric pressure as the altitude increases.

   b) Compare the types of growth for temperature and atmospheric pressure as the altitude increases.

   c) Why does the atmospheric pressure and temperature decrease as the altitude increases?

15. **a)** Explain why $y = 52(0.5)^x$ can be rewritten as $y = 52(0.5)(0.5)^{x-1}$.

   b) Rewrite $y = 52(0.5)(0.5)^{x-1}$ in the form $y = a \times b^{x-1}$.

7.5 Modelling Exponential Growth and Decay

Unchecked exponential growth often leads to problems. Take the improvements in computer chips for example. The processing power of computers doubles every 24 months. Many businesses continually upgrade their computers hoping to achieve greater productivity. This leads to the problem of the disposal of discarded, but often still serviceable, computers.

Investigate 1

Tools

• graphing calculator

Bacterial Growth

You will use linear, quadratic, and exponential regression to find the equation that best represents a given set of data. Each time, you will record the equation and the value of r^2, the coefficient of determination. The value of r^2 measures how well the equation fits the data. The closer r^2 is to 1, the better the equation fits the data.

A biology student is studying the population growth of a bacterial culture. The mass of the culture is measured every hour, but the initial population at time zero is unknown. The table shows the observations for the first 7 h.

Time (h)	0	1	2	3	4	5	6	7
Mass (mg)	■	10	21	43	82	168	320	475

Before starting the activity, clear all lists and equations.

1. a) Enter the data into lists.

- Press STAT . Select **1:Edit**. Enter the time data (from 1 h to 7 h) into list **L1** and the corresponding population data into list **L2**.

b) Make a scatter plot.

- Press 2nd [STATPLOT]. Select **Plot1**. Ensure that it is turned **On**. Set the graph to scatter plot, the **Xlist** to **L1** and the **Ylist** to **L2**.

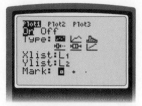

- Press WINDOW . Use the window settings shown.
- Press GRAPH . The scatter plot will appear. Describe the shape of the graph.

c) Perform a linear regression analysis.

- Press 2nd [CATALOG] and scroll down to **Diagnostic On**.
- Press ENTER twice.
- Press STAT . Cursor over to the **CALC** menu then select **4:LinReg(ax+b)**.
- Press 2nd [L1] , [L2] , .
- Press VARS . Cursor over to the **Y-VARS** menu, then select **1:Function**.
- Press ENTER twice. The equation of the line of best fit will be displayed. Record the equation, and the coefficient of determination, r^2, in a table like the one shown.

Method	Equation	Coefficient of Determination, r^2	Mass at Hour 8	Mass at Hour 9
Linear regression				

d) Press Y= to see the equation of the line of best fit in the equation editor.

- Press GRAPH to see the graph of the line of best fit. Explain why this is an unsatisfactory model for this problem.

2. Perform a quadratic regression analysis.

- Press Y= CLEAR .
- Press STAT , then from the **CALC** menu, select **5:QuadReg**.
- Press VARS . Cursor over to the **Y-VARS** menu, then select **1:Function**.
- Press ENTER twice. Add another row to your table for quadratic regression. Record the equation, and the coefficient of determination, r^2.
- Press GRAPH to see the graph of the quadratic equation.

3. **a)** Perform an exponential regression analysis. Record the equation and the coefficient of determination.
   - Press [STAT], then from the **CALC** menu, select **0:ExpReg**.
   - Press [VARS]. Cursor over to the **Y-VARS** menu, then select **1:Function**.
   - Press [ENTER] twice.
   - Press [GRAPH] to see the graph of the exponential equation.

   b) Use this model to estimate the initial mass.

   c) **Reflect** Is the exponential model a better model than those you used in questions 1 and 2? Explain.

4. Which equation fits the data best? worst? Explain how you know.

5. Examine the data for hours 8 and 9 for all three methods. What happens to the accuracy of the linear equation as time progresses?

Investigate 2

Tools
- graphing calculator
- CBR™
- basketball or volleyball

Bouncing Ball

You will work with a partner to determine a model that fits the data for a bouncing ball.

a) Connect a calculator-based ranger (CBR™) to a graphing calculator. Clear all lists.

b) Go to the Ball Bounce application.
   - Press [APPS], select **CBL/CBR**, and press [ENTER]. Then, select **3:Ranger**.
   - Press [ENTER]. Select **3:APPLICATIONS**. Select **1:METERS**, then **3:BALL BOUNCE**.

c) Follow the instructions on the screen. Hold the CBR™ at a height of at least 1.5 m, with the sensor pointing down. Drop the ball from a point about 0.5 m directly below the CBR™. Press the trigger on the CBR™ and allow the ball to bounce at least five times.

d) When the measurements are complete, a graph will appear on the calculator screen. What does the horizontal axis of this graph represent? What does the vertical axis represent?

e) Describe the relationship between the bounce number and height of the bounce. Describe the shapes of the curves. What is the cause of the shape of each curve?

f) Find the maximum height the ball reaches on each bounce.
   - Press [TRACE] and move the cursor to the top of the curve representing each bounce. On a piece of paper, record the coordinates of these points in a table with the headings "Time (s)" and "Bounce Height (m)."

g) Divide each maximum bounce height by the previous one. What is the friction of the floor causing the ball to do?

h) Enter data into lists 3 and 4.
- Press [STAT] and select **1:Edit**, then press [ENTER]. Enter the times into **L3** and the bounce heights into **L4**.

i) Plot these coordinates using **STAT PLOT**.
- Press [2nd] [STATPLOT], then select **2:Plot2**.
- Press [ENTER], and make sure Plot 2 is **On**. Select the line graph icon. Enter **L3** for **XList** and **L4** for **YList**.
- Then, press [GRAPH].

j) Describe the shape of the graph. If you were to extend the graph to the right, what would happen?

k) **Reflect** Is the relationship between time and bounce height exponential? Explain.

Exponential Growth and Decay

Many situations can be modelled with an exponential relation that represents exponential growth or exponential decay. The formula or relation $P = I(b)^t$ can be used to determine the population size, P, after time t, where I is the initial population and b is the growth factor (if $b > 1$) or the decay factor (if $0 < b < 1$).

Example 1

Animal Population

In a national park, a wolf population increased by a growth factor of 1.078 per year over a ten-year period, beginning in 1997. The formula $P = 124(1.078)^n$ modelled the wolf population P after n years.

a) Use technology to graph the relation.

b) What was the wolf population in 1997?

c) What was the wolf population in 2007?

Solution

a) Press [2nd] [STATPLOT]. Select **4:PlotsOff**.
- Press [ENTER].
- Press [Y=]. If necessary, clear all equations.
- Type 124 [×] 1.078 [^], and then press [X,T,θ,n].
- Press [WINDOW]. Use the window settings shown.

• Press GRAPH.

 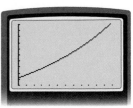

b) Press 2nd [CALC]. Select **1:value**.
  • Press ENTER, then enter 0 for **X=**.
    Press ENTER.
    (Since the values on x-axis begin in 1997, $x = 0$ represents 1997.)

  In 1997, the wolf population was 124 wolves.

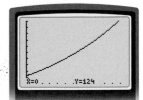

c) Repeat part b) but enter 10 for **X=**.
  (Since the values on the x-axis begin in 1997, $x = 10$ represents 2007.)

  In 2007, the wolf population was 263 wolves.

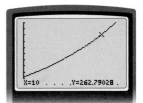

Example 2

Light Intensity

A sheet of translucent glass 1 mm thick reduces the intensity of the light passing through it. Light intensity is further reduced as more sheets of glass are placed together, as shown in the table.

Number of Glass Sheets	0	1	2	3	4	5	6	7	8
Light Intensity (%)	100	89.1	79.4	70.7	63.0	56.1	50.0	44.5	39.7

a) The reduction rate of a sheet of glass is the percent by which the light intensity is reduced by adding a sheet of glass to a viewing panel. What is the light intensity reduction rate of a single sheet of glass? Express your answer as a percent.

b) How many sheets of glass are needed to reduce the light intensity by one half?

c) Use a graphing calculator to graph this relation.

d) Use your graph to determine how many sheets of glass are needed to reduce the light intensity to about 25%.

Solution

a) To find the reduction rate, subtract two successive light intensities and divide by the greater of the two.

$(100 - 89.1) \div 100 \times 100\% = 10.9\%$
$(89.1 - 79.4) \div 89.1 \times 100\% = 10.9\%$
and so on.

The reduction rate of a single sheet of glass is 10.9% of the previous light intensity.

b) From the table, six sheets of glass would reduce the light intensity by 50%.

c) Press [2nd] [MEM] to clear all lists. Then press [ENTER].
- Press [STAT] then select **1:Edit**. Enter the number of glass sheets into list **L1**, and light intensity into list **L2**.
- Press [2nd] [STATPLOT]. Select **Plot1**. Ensure that it is turned **On**. Set the graph to scatter plot, the **XList** to **L1**, and the **YList** to **L2**. Check that **Plot2** and **Plot 3** are turned **Off**.
- Press [WINDOW] and adjust the variables as shown.

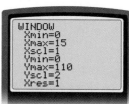

- Press [STAT], then from the **CALC** menu, select **0:ExpReg**.
- Press [VARS]. Cursor over to the **Y-VARS** menu, then select **1:Function**.
- Press [ENTER] twice.
- Press [GRAPH].

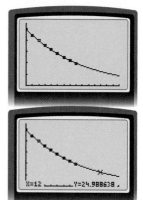

d) Press [TRACE]. Use the cursor keys to move the point shown on the graph until the value of **Y** is as close as possible to 25. The calculator returns the value 12.

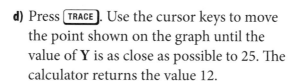

To reduce the intensity to 25%, 12 sheets of glass are needed.

Key Concepts

- Experimental data or data from secondary sources can be graphed as a scatter plot and modelled using technology.
- Exponential regression can be used to generate the equation for an exponential relation.
- The equation $P = I(b)^t$ can be used to model an exponential relation, where P is the current population, I is the initial population, b is the growth factor (if $b > 1$) or decay factor (if $0 < b < 1$), and t is the time.
- The coefficient of determination, r^2, indicates how well an equation fits the data. If r^2 is close to 1, the equation fits the data well.

Discuss the Concepts

D1. Explain why population growth, such as a fox population that grows by 2% per year, represents exponential growth.

D2. Pollution in a lake has reduced the clarity of the water by reducing light intensity by 20%/m of depth. The formula $I = 100(0.8)^d$ can be used to calculate the light intensity, I, at a depth of d metres.

    a) Explain how the formula relates to a 20% reduction in water clarity.

    b) Predict the shape of the graph of this relation. Justify your prediction.

Practise

For help with questions 1 and 2, refer to Example 1.

1. Cells in a culture are growing by a factor of 3.45 per day. The number of cells in the culture, N, can be estimated using the formula $N = 1000(3.45)^d$, where d is the number of days.

    a) Use technology to plot a graph of this relation.

    b) How many cells does this culture begin with?

    c) How many cells would there be after 1 day?

    d) How many cells would there be after 5 days?

2. A deer population is declining by 2.2% per year. The population can be modelled using the formula $P = 240(0.978)^n$, where P is the population after n years.

    a) Use technology to plot a graph of this relation.

    b) What is the current deer population?

    c) What will be the expected deer population after 8 years?

For help with question 3, refer to Example 2.

3. Caffeine is present in coffee, tea, chocolate, and other foods and beverages. This chemical is eliminated from the human body over time. The table shows the mass of caffeine remaining in an average-sized person after drinking a cup of coffee containing 130 mg of caffeine.

Time (h)	0	1	2	3	4	5	6	7
Mass of Caffeine (mg)	130	113.1	98.4	85.6	74.5	64.8	56.4	49.0

a) What percent of the caffeine is eliminated from a person's body per hour?

b) Use a graphing calculator to graph this relation.

c) Use the graph to estimate how long it would take for the mass of caffeine to be reduced to less than 10 mg.

d) Use the graph to estimate how long it would take for the mass of caffeine to be reduced to 0 mg.

Apply B ···

4. A can of cola contains 45.6 mg of caffeine and a typical chocolate bar contains 31 mg of caffeine.

a) Use the rate of change from question 3 a) to make a table of values showing the mass of caffeine remaining in an average-sized person after consuming
   i) a can of cola   ii) a chocolate bar

b) Use a graphing calculator to graph each relation.

c) Use the graph to estimate how long it would take for the mass of caffeine to be reduced to less than 10 mg for each product.

d) Pose and solve a problem relating to this situation.

5. A large number of ice cubes were added to a pitcher of water at room temperature, 22°C. The graph shows the temperature of the water, T, in degrees Celsius, over a period of time, m, in minutes.

a) How long did it take for the temperature to fall to 18°C?

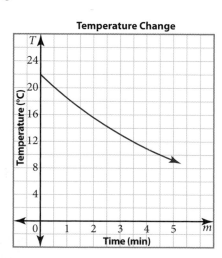

Temperature Change

b) How long did it take for the temperature to fall to 16°C?

c) Is it valid to use this graph to extrapolate past 5 min? Explain.

d) Pose and solve a problem relating to this situation.

Literacy **Connect**

The amplitude of a spring is half the distance between rest and the maximum height it reaches with each oscillation (up and down).

6. A motion detector recorded the amplitude of an oscillating spring. The table shows the results over a 5-min period.

Time (s)	0	30	60	90	120	150	180	210	240	270	300
Amplitude (cm)	9.2	7.2	5.5	4.4	3.4	2.6	2.0	1.6	1.3	1.0	0.7

a) Do the results of this experiment demonstrate exponential decay? Explain.

b) What is the approximate rate of growth or decay?

c) How long would it take for the oscillations to become indiscernible (less than 0.5 cm)?

7. The Mauna Loa Observatory in Hawaii records the level of carbon dioxide (CO_2) in the atmosphere to help study the effects of burning fossil fuels. The April readings, in parts per million (ppm), from 1959 to 2002 are shown.

Year	CO_2 (ppm)	Year	CO_2 (ppm)	Year	CO_2 (ppm)	Year	CO_2 (ppm)
1959	317.71	1970	328.13	1981	342.51	1992	359.15
1960	319.03	1971	327.78	1982	343.56	1993	359.46
1961	319.48	1972	329.72	1983	344.94	1994	361.26
1962	320.58	1973	331.50	1984	347.08	1995	363.45
1963	321.39	1974	332.65	1985	348.35	1996	364.72
1964	322.23	1975	333.31	1986	349.55	1997	366.35
1965	322.13	1976	334.58	1987	350.99	1998	368.61
1966	323.70	1977	336.07	1988	353.59	1999	371.14
1967	324.42	1978	337.76	1989	355.42	2000	371.66
1968	325.02	1979	338.89	1990	356.20	2001	372.87
1969	326.66	1980	340.77	1991	358.60	2002	374.86

Reasoning and Proving

Representing | Selecting Tools

Problem Solving

Connecting | Reflecting

Communicating

a) Describe what is happening to the level of CO_2 in the atmosphere over time.

b) Compare the total and percent increases in CO_2 from 1961 to 1962 with 1981 to 1982 and with 2001 to 2002.

c) Compare the total and percent increases in CO_2 in each of the decades: 1960s, 1970s, 1980s, and 1990s.

d) Which of the answers to parts b) and c) gives a better indication of the exponential growth of CO_2 levels? Explain.

e) Pose a problem relating to this table. Ask a classmate to solve the problem.

8. Many animals and fish show an exponential relationship between length and mass. The table shows the lengths and masses of rainbow trout taken from different rivers in the Muskoka area.

Length (mm)	Mass (g)	Length (mm)	Mass (g)
390	660	305	303
368	581	335	410
385	609	317	335
360	557	351	506
346	433	368	605
438	840	326	353
392	623	270	209
324	387	359	476
360	479	347	432
413	754	259	202
276	235	247	184
334	406	280	248
332	383	265	223
324	353	318	340
337	363	305	303
343	390	335	410
318	340	317	335

a) Use graphing technology to create a scatter plot and an exponential curve of best fit.

b) Is the relationship between fish length and mass exponential? Justify your answer.

c) Estimate the mass of a trout that has a length of 450 mm.

d) How might people use this relationship?

9. Research data on an animal of your choice.

a) Find data on two measures for a sample of animals. Display the data in a table.

b) Use graphing technology to graph the data to create a scatter plot and an exponential curve of best fit.

c) Is the relationship between the two measures exponential? Justify your answer.

d) How might researchers use this relationship?

10. Weather satellites and space probes can be powered by thermoelectric generators. The source of power for these generators is the energy produced by radioactive material that decays. The energy is in the radioisotopes that make up the material. The power output of the radioisotopes is P, in watts, and t is the half-life of the material, in years. Different radioactive materials can be used.

Time, t (years)	Power, P (watts)	Time, t (years)	Power, P (watts)
0	50.0	150	27.4
25	45.2	175	24.8
50	40.9	200	22.4
75	37.0	225	20.3
100	33.5	250	18.4
125	30.3	275	16.6

a) Use graphing technology to create a scatter plot of the data.

b) Find an equation that models the data using an exponential regression.

c) If the equipment in the satellite needs at least 15 W of power to function, for how long can the satellite operate before needing to be recharged?

Extend

11. The projected populations, P, of Metropolis and of Gotham City can be modelled by $P_{\text{Metropolis}} = 117\,000(1.018)^n$ and $P_{\text{Gotham}} = 109\,000(1.028)^n$, where n is number of years after 2006. Use a graphing calculator to determine when the populations will be the same.

12. The world's population in 1980 was about 4.5 billion. Suppose the population increased at a rate of 2% per year since then.

a) Write an exponential relation that models the problem. Explain what each variable represents and how you determined the rate value.

b) What will be the world's population in 2015?

c) What was the population in 1970? What assumptions have you made?

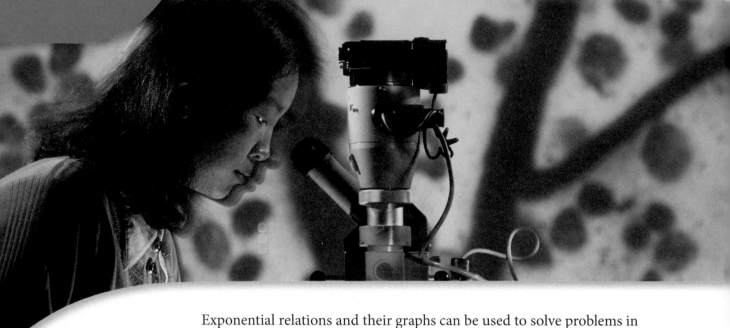

7.6 Solve Problems Involving Exponential Growth and Decay

Exponential relations and their graphs can be used to solve problems in science, medicine, and finance. The ability to analyse data and model it using exponential relations is important for making accurate predictions.

Investigate

Tools

• one die or number cube, or spinner with six equal sections (per student)

Optional:

• random number generator with six outcomes

half-life

• the time it takes for a quantity to decay or be reduced to half its initial amount

Half-Life

Radioactive decay is a process by which a substance made of unstable atomic nuclei changes, or decays, into a different substance. In this process, the core of an original atom or parent nucleus is split into two smaller or daughter nuclei. The time it takes for half of the parent nuclei to decay to daughter nuclei is called the **half-life**.

In this Investigate, your class will simulate radioactive decay. A standing student will represent a parent nucleus. A sitting student will represent a daughter nucleus. Decay is determined by the roll of a die. Each student begins standing. If they roll a 6, the student "decays" to the sitting position. Instead of measuring the time it takes for half of the substance to decay, you will count the number of rolls it takes for half the class to sit down.

Before you begin the activity, predict the number of rolls it will take for half the class to be seated. Record your prediction.

1. On the teacher's prompt, roll your die. If a 6 is rolled, "decay" to the sitting position. Record the number of students who remain standing in a table like the one shown.

Trial	Number of Students in Class	Number of Students Standing After Roll Number										
		1	2	3	4	5	6	7	8	9	10	11
1												
2												
3												
4												

2. Repeat step 1 until only half the students are standing. Record the number of rolls it took for half the students to "decay" to the sitting position in the First Half-Life column in a table like the one shown.

Trial	First Half-Life	Second Half-Life
1		
2		
3		
4		
Average		

3. Remain sitting or standing. Repeat step 1 until half the remaining students are standing, that is, until one quarter of the class are standing. Record the number of students that remain standing after each roll. Record the number of rolls it took for half the students to "decay" to the sitting position in the Second Half-Life column.

4. Repeat steps 1—3 three more times, and record the results.

5. a) Calculate the average for both the first and second half-lives.

   b) The first and second half-lives should be the same. Explain why. They may not be the same for one or more trials. Give an explanation for this.

6. **Reflect** How accurate was the prediction you made before the investigation? What was your thinking?

7. **Reflect** Would the results of this investigation have turned out differently if the number 3 represented a decay? Explain.

Doubling

When the base of an exponential relation is 2, the relation is describing a doubling.

$P = P_0(2)^{\frac{t}{d}}$ is an example of a formula that can be used to determine the population, P, after time t, where d is the doubling time, and P_0 is the initial population.

Half-Life

When the base of an exponential relation is $\frac{1}{2}$, the relation is describing half-life.

$M = M_0\left(\frac{1}{2}\right)^{\frac{t}{h}}$ is an example of a formula that can be used to determine the remaining mass, M, of a decaying substance after time t, where h is the half-life and M_0 is the initial mass.

Example 1

Exponential Growth

A bacterial culture began with 7500 bacteria. Its growth can be modelled using the formula $N = 7500 \times 2^{\frac{t}{36}}$, where N is the number of bacteria after t hours.

a) How many bacteria are present after 36 h?

b) How many bacteria are present after 72 h? How does this relate to the doubling time?

Solution

a) Substitute $t = 36$.
$$N = 7500(2)^{\frac{36}{36}}$$
$$= 7500(2)^1$$
$$= 15\ 000$$
There are 15 000 bacteria present after 36 h.

b) Substitute $t = 72$.
$$N = 7500(2)^{\frac{72}{36}}$$
$$= 7500(2)^2$$
$$= 30\ 000$$
There are 30 000 bacteria after 72 h.

There are two doubling periods in 72 h, so the bacteria have doubled twice in this time.

Example 2

Exponential Decay

All living organisms contain a known concentration of 1 part per trillion parts of carbon-14. Carbon-14 is a radioactive element. It is used to date ancient artefacts because it has a half-life of about 5730 years after the organism dies. The formula $C = \left(\dfrac{1}{2}\right)^{\frac{n}{5730}}$ is used to calculate the concentration, C, in parts per trillion, remaining n years after death.

a) What would be the concentration of carbon-14 in a piece of cloth (made from plant fibres) after 5730 years?

b) What would be the concentration of carbon-14 in an animal bone after 50 000 years? Round your answer to five decimal places.

Math Connect

One trillion is 10^{12}
or
1 000 000 000 000.

Solution

a) Substitute $n = 5730$.

$$C = \left(\frac{1}{2}\right)^{\frac{5730}{5730}}$$
$$= \left(\frac{1}{2}\right)^{1}$$
$$= \frac{1}{2}$$
$$= 0.5$$

After 5730 years, the concentration of carbon-14 would be 0.5 parts per trillion.

b) Substitute $n = 50\ 000$.

$$C = \left(\frac{1}{2}\right)^{\frac{50\ 000}{5730}}$$

$$= 0.002\ 36$$

(1 ÷ 2) y^x (50000 ÷ 5730) = =

(Remember that calculator key sequences may vary depending on your calculator.)

After 50 000 years, the concentration of carbon-14 would be about 0.002 36 parts per trillion.

Key Concepts

- Doubling time is the time it takes for a population to double in size. The relation for doubling is $P = P_0(2)^{\frac{t}{d}}$, where P represents the population, P_0 represents the initial population, t represents time, and d represents the doubling time. The base, 2, indicates doubling.

- Half-life is the time it takes for a quantity to decay to half its original amount.

  The relation for half-life is $M = M_0\left(\frac{1}{2}\right)^{\frac{t}{h}}$, where M represents the final quantity, M_0 represents the initial quantity, t represents time, and h represents the half-life. The base, $\frac{1}{2}$, indicates half-life.

Discuss the Concepts

D1. Refer to the Investigate. If the half-life activity were performed with a fair coin, and tossing heads meant you sit, what would be the half-life of the class?

D2. The relation for doubling uses 2 as the base of the power and the formula for half-life uses $\frac{1}{2}$ as the base. What do you think the base would be if a population is tripling? Explain.

Practise

For help with question 1, refer to Example 1.

1. *E. coli* is a very harmful type of bacteria that can be found in meat that is improperly stored or handled. The relation $N = N_0 \times 2^{\frac{t}{20}}$ estimates the number of *E. coli*, N, of an initial sample of N_0 bacteria after t min, at 37°C (body temperature), under optimal conditions.

   a) What is the doubling time of *E. coli*?

   b) If a sample of *E. coli* contains 5000 bacteria, how many will there be after 1 h?

   c) If a sample of *E. coli* contains 1000 bacteria, how many will there be after 1 day?

2. The intensity of light from a luminating object decays exponentially with the thickness of the material covering it. Stage lights are often covered with gels to colour the light, but they also decrease light intensity. The relation $I = 1200\left(\frac{4}{5}\right)^{n}$ is used to determine the intensity of light, I, in watts per square centimetre, where n is the number of gels used. What is the intensity of light with

   a) 0 gels? b) 1 gel? c) 3 gels? d) 5 gels?

3. Certain types of minor skin wounds heal at a rate modelled by the relation $W = W_0 \left(\frac{1}{2} \right)^{0.36t}$, where W is the area of the wound currently, in square millimetres, W_0 is the initial wound area, and t is the time, in days, after the wound has been dressed. What will be the area of a 25 mm^2 wound after

a) 1 day?   **b)** 4 days?

Apply **B** •

For help with questions 4 and 5, refer to Example 2.

4. The half-life of carbon-14 is 5730 years. The relation $C = \left(\frac{1}{2} \right)^{\frac{n}{5730}}$ is used to calculate the concentration, C, in parts per trillion, remaining n years after death. Determine the carbon-14 concentration in

a) an 11 460-year-old animal bone

b) a 5000-year-old map made from plant fibres

c) a 25 000-year-old fossil

5. A fifteenth-century map (made from plant fibres) indicated that the Vikings settled in Vinland in northern Newfoundland in 970 B.C.E. If this map was made in 1427, what would be the concentration of carbon-14 in the map by 2007?

6. The relation $T = 190 \left(\frac{1}{2} \right)^{\frac{t}{10}}$ can be used to determine the length of time, t, in hours, that milk of a certain fat content will remain fresh. T is the storage temperature, in degrees Celsius.

a) What is the freshness half-life of milk?

b) Graph the relation.

c) How long will milk keep fresh at 22°C? at 4°C?

7. The remaining concentration of a particular drug in a person's bloodstream is modelled by the relation $C = C_0 \left(\frac{1}{2} \right)^{\frac{t}{4}}$, where C is the remaining concentration of drug in the bloodstream in milligrams per millilitre of blood, C_0 is the initial concentration, and t is the time, in hours, that the drug is in the bloodstream.

a) What is the half-life of this drug?

b) A nurse gave a patient this drug. The concentration was 40 mg/mL, at 10:15 A.M. What will the concentration at
i) 3:15 P.M.?   **ii)** 10:00 P.M.?

c) A second dose of the drug needs to be given to this patient when the concentration of drug in the bloodstream is down to 0.5 mg/mL. Estimate after how many hours this would occur.

8. The directions for taking a medication are shown.

> ORAL DOSE: ADULTS: 2 caplets
> every six hours
>
> WARNING: It is hazardous to exceed the
> recommended dose unless
> supervised by a physician.

When you take medication, the amount of drug in your bloodstream rises to a maximum, then decreases over time. The time it takes for half the drug to leave your bloodstream is called the half-life of the medication.

a) How do you think the half-life of a medication relates to the ORAL DOSE instructions that state "every six hours"?

b) Use the words *half-life* and *bloodstream* to explain how someone may receive an **overdose** if more medication is taken before the six-hour recommended period. To learn more about half-life, go to *www.mcgrawhill.ca/links/foundations11* and follow the links.

9. The relation $I = 10^{-12} \times 10^{\frac{dB}{10}}$ is used to calculate the intensity of sound, I, relative to the threshold of human hearing (0 dB), where dB represents the sound being compared. Copy and complete the table.

Sound Source	Intensity Level (dB)	Relative Intensity
Mosquito buzzing	40	$10^{-12} \times 10^{\frac{40}{10}} = 10^{-8} = 0.000\,000\,01$
Rainfall	50	
Quiet alarm clock	65	
Loud alarm clock	80	
Average factory	90	
Large orchestra	98	
Car stereo	125	

10. A general relation between speed and collision rates is "1 km faster results in a 3% increase in the collision rate." On a specific stretch of road, the collision rate is 0.534 collisions per million vehicle kilometres, when vehicles travel at an average speed of 80 km/h.

a) What is meant by "collisions per million vehicle kilometres"?

b) The relation that represents the collision rate for this stretch of road is $R = 0.534(1.03)^s$, where R is the collision rate, in collisions per million vehicle kilometres, and s is the average vehicle speed. What would be the collision rate if the average speed increases to
i) 90 km/h?   **ii)** 120 km/h?

11. Research the growth of the Consumer Price Index since 1914. Go to *www.mcgrawhill.ca/links/foundations11* and follow the links.

   a) Determine the cost of a $10 item in 1914 in subsequent years.

   b) Enter the data into a spreadsheet or a graphing calculator and find the curve of best fit to model the data.

   c) Use your model to predict how much an item costing $10 in 1914 will cost in 2010 and in 2020.

12. Research the world population from 1000 B.C.E. to current times. Go to *www.mcgrawhill.ca/links/foundations11* and follow the links.

   a) Enter the data into a spreadsheet or a graphing calculator and find the curve of best fit to model the data.

   b) Use your model to predict the world's population today. How accurate is your model? Explain any differences.

   c) Use your model to predict the world's population in 2050.

13. In nuclear medicine, very small quantities of a radioactive material are injected into patients. The material is traced so a medical diagnosis can be made. On the label for the material, the supplier indicates the level of radioactivity at a specific date and time. A relation used by the doctor or technician is $A = A_0 \times \left(\frac{1}{2}\right)^{\frac{t}{h}}$, where A is the radioactivity after time t, A_0 is the radioactivity at a specific moment, and h is the half-life of the material. The unit of measure of radioactivity is the Bequerel (Bq), or disintegration per second.

   a) Iodine-131 has a half-life of 8.065 days. The label states that the radioactivity level was 370 MBq (10^6 Bq) at 12:00 P.M. on March 4. What will be the radioactivity level at 12:00 P.M. on March 7? March 16?

   b) Technetium-99 has a half-life of 6.007 h. The label states that the radioactivity level was 284 MBq at 8:20 A.M. on July 7. What will be the radioactivity level at 9:30 P.M. on the same day?

Extend C ....

14. The fox population of a national park was 325 foxes 15 years ago. Today, it is 650 foxes. Assuming the population has experienced exponential growth, write a relation representing the size of the fox population in the park. Use your relation to project the fox population in 20 years.

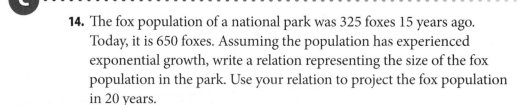

7.1 Exponent Rules, pages 356–364

1. Write as a single power, then evaluate.

   a) $6^2 \times 6^3$

   b) $(-2)^2 \times (-2)^4$

   c) $\dfrac{5^{10}}{5^7}$

   d) $\left(\dfrac{1}{3}\right)^3 \times \left(\dfrac{1}{3}\right)^3$

   e) $(10^4)^2$

   f) $[(-7)^2]^2$

   g) $\dfrac{3^8}{3^5}$

   h) $\left(-\dfrac{1}{2}\right)^2 \times \left(-\dfrac{1}{2}\right)^3$

2. Calculate the area of the square.

$A = s^2$

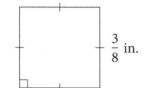

$\dfrac{3}{8}$ in.

7.2 Zero and Negative Exponents, pages 365–371

3. Evaluate. Express your answers as whole numbers or fractions.

   a) 7^0

   b) 5^{-1}

   c) 8^{-3}

   d) $\left(\dfrac{1}{50}\right)^0$

   e) $\left(\dfrac{2}{3}\right)^{-2}$

   f) $4^{-2} \times 4^5$

   g) $\dfrac{7^2}{7^3}$

   h) $[(-3)^2]^{-1}$

   i) $\dfrac{1}{2^{-3}}$

   j) $\dfrac{1}{5^{-1}}$

7.3 Investigate Exponential Relationships, pages 372–381

4. Which graph represents an exponential relationship? Explain.

   a)

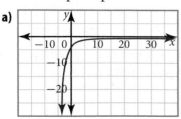

   b)

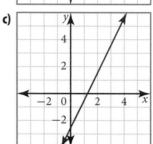

   c)

5. A certain type of bacteria doubles every 8 h. A culture begins with 30 000 bacteria. How many bacteria are there after

   a) 8 h?   **b)** 16 h?   **c)** 4 days?

7.4 Exponential Relations, pages 382–394

6. Compare the graphs of $y = 3^x$, $y = 3x^2$, and $y = 3x$, for values of $x = -4, -3, -2, -1, 0, 1, 2, 3, 4$. How are they similar? different?

7. The measure of the acidity of a solution is called its pH. In wells and swimming pools, the pH level of water needs to be checked regularly for the level of hydrogen. The relation $H = \left(\dfrac{1}{10}\right)^P$ gives an indication of the concentration of hydrogen ions, H, in moles per litre (mol/L), where P represents the pH.

   a) Plot a graph of this relation.

b) Water with a pH of less than 7.0 is acidic. What is the hydrogen concentration for a pH of 7.0?

c) Water in a swimming pool needs to be kept at a pH between 7.0 and 7.6. What is the equivalent range of hydrogen concentration?

d) Rain water has a pH of 5.6. Due to sulphur pollution, acid rain has a pH of less than 5.0. Compare the concentrations of hydrogen in rain and acid rain.

7.5 Modelling Exponential Growth and Decay, pages 395–405

8. A town's raccoon population is growing exponentially. The expected population can be estimated using the relation $P = 1250(1.013)^n$, where P is the population and n is the number of years.

a) Use technology to plot a graph of this relation.

b) What is the current raccoon population?

c) What is the expected population in 5 years?

9. The amplitude of a pendulum over a 60-s period is shown in the table.

Time (s)	0	10	20	30	40	50	60
Amplitude (cm)	80.0	40.0	20.0	10.0	5.0	2.5	1.25

a) Use technology to make a scatter plot.

b) Do the results of this experiment demonstrate exponential growth or decay? Explain.

c) What is the rate of growth or decay, in amplitude?

d) How long would it take for the swings to become unnoticeable (less than 0.2 cm)?

7.6 Solve Problems Involving Exponential Growth and Decay, pages 406–413

10. The remaining mass of a drug in a person's bloodstream is modelled by $M = 500\left(\dfrac{1}{2}\right)^{\frac{t}{2}}$, where M is the remaining mass in milligrams, and t is the time, in hours, that the drug is in the bloodstream.

a) What is the half-life of the drug?

b) What was the dosage of the drug?

c) What will be the concentration of the drug in the bloodstream
  i) after 2 h?
  ii) after 6 h?

11. From 1994 to 2004, average personal incomes grew in Canada according to the relation $I = I_0(1.041)^n$, where I is the resulting income, I_0 is the initial income, and n is the number of years of growth.

a) If a person's income was $34 000 in 1994, what would it be in 2004?

b) If a person's income was $50 000 in 1996, what would it be in 2003?

c) What was the average yearly rate of growth from 1994 to 2004?

1. True or false?

   a) Linear growth shows increases by a constant amount each time period.

   b) Exponential growth shows increases by a constant factor each time period.

   c) Exponential decay shows decreases by a fixed amount each time period.

   d) Quadratic growth is confirmed by unequal first differences and equal second differences.

2. Evaluate. Write your answers as integers or fractions.

   a) $3^3 \times 3^2$

   b) $\dfrac{9^7}{9^5}$

   c) $(2^3)^2$

   d) 6^0

   e) 7^{-2}

   f) $\left(\dfrac{1}{5}\right)^{-3}$

   g) $4^{12} \times 4^{-3} \times 4^{-9}$

   h) $\left(\dfrac{1}{3}\right)^2 \left(\dfrac{1}{3}\right)^{-1}$

3. i) Sketch a graph of each relation.

   ii) Classify each as exponential growth, exponential decay, or neither. Justify your response.

   a) $y = \left(\dfrac{1}{4}\right)^x$

   b) $y = 6x^2$

   c) $y = 5^x$

   d) $y = 3(0.5)^{\frac{x}{4}}$

4. Topsoil is commonly measured in cubic yards (yd^3) and cubic feet (ft^3). A medium-sized dump truck can hold about 9 yd^3 of topsoil. A wheelbarrow can hold about 3 ft^3 of topsoil.

   a) How many cubic feet are in a cubic yard? (1 yd = 3 ft) Express your answer as a power.

   b) Express 9 yd^3 in cubic feet as a power with base 3.

   c) A family ordered 9 yd^3 of topsoil to landscape their yard. How many trips with a wheelbarrow will they need to make in order to move all the topsoil that was delivered?

5. You have investigated graphs of exponential relations of the form $y = b^x$ for $b > 0$. Explain why graphs of this form remain above the x-axis.

6. In 1878, moose were first introduced in Newfoundland with a single bull and a single cow. Today, there are approximately 150 000 moose in Newfoundland.

   a) On the same set of axes, draw a linear, a quadratic, and an exponential graph to represent growth of the moose population.

   b) Which type of growth is most likely? Explain.

Chapter Problem Wrap-Up

The table shows the recommended maximum continuous exposure times to loud sounds.

Sound Intensity	Recommended Maximum Continuous Exposure Time
85 dB	8.0 h
88 dB	4.0 h
91 dB	2 h
94 dB	1.0 h
97 dB	30.0 min
100 dB	15.0 min
103 dB	7.5 min
106 dB	3.75 min
109 dB	1.875 min
112 dB	0.9375 min
115 dB	0.46875 min

a) Consider your answers to the chapter problems in the previous sections. Explain why the relationship between sound intensity and exposure time is exponential.

b) Write a paragraph describing how continued exposure to loud sounds could affect hearing loss. Use the words "exponential relation" and "continuous exposure" in your answer.

7. Atmospheric pressure depends on the altitude above sea level. Altitude is measured in kilopascals (kPa).

Altitude (km)	Atmospheric Pressure (kPa)
0	101.3
1	89.4
2	78.9
3	69.7
4	61.5
5	54.3
6	47.9
7	42.3
8	37.3
9	32.9
10	29.1

a) Use graphing technology to create a scatter plot of the data.

b) Find an equation that models the data using exponential regression.

c) What is the atmospheric pressure at sea level?

d) At how many metres above sea level will a mountain climber experience atmospheric pressure of 89 kPa?

e) What is the atmospheric pressure 4250 m above sea level?

8 Compound Interest

Throughout this chapter, you will learn how to calculate simple and compound interest, and apply these skills to financial situations. These situations include money invested for a period of time and loans made by individuals and businesses.

In this chapter, you will

- determine, through investigation using technology, the compound interest for a given investment, using repeated calculations of simple interest, and compare, using a table of values and graphs, the simple and compound interest earned for a given principal and a fixed interest rate over time

- determine, through investigation, and describe the relationship between compound interest and exponential growth

- solve, using a scientific calculator, problems that involve the calculation of the amount, A, and the principal, P, using the compound interest formula $A = P(1 + i)^n$

- calculate the total interest earned on an investment or paid on a loan by determining the difference between the amount and the principal

- solve problems using a TVM Solver, that involve the calculation of the interest rate per compounding period, i, or the number of compounding periods, n, in the compound interest formula $A = P(1 + i)^n$

- determine, through investigation using technology, the effect on the future value of a compound interest investment or loan of changing the total length of time, the interest rate, or the compounding period

Reasoning and Proving
Representing | Selecting Tools
Problem Solving
Connecting | Reflecting
Communicating

Key Terms

amount	future value
compounding period	growth factor
compound interest	present value
creditor	principal
discount	simple interest

As a self-employed financial planner, Tanisha helps clients achieve their financial goals—starting a business, planning for retirement, or paying for a child's education. To become qualified, Tanisha took four continuing education courses in the certified financial planning program at Centennial College.

Prerequisite Skills

Decimals

1. Use a calculator to evaluate.

    a) 1.2×4.3

    b) 2×1.05

    c) $1000(0.04)(7)$

    d) $350(0.035)(2.5)$

    e) $500 + 500(0.09)(0.5)$

    f) $950 + 950(0.04)\left(\dfrac{7}{12}\right)$

    950 ⬚+⬚ 950 ⬚×⬚ 0.04 ⬚×⬚ ⬚(⬚ 7 ⬚÷⬚ 12 ⬚)⬚ ⬚=⬚

    g) $675[1 + (0.025)(4)]$

    h) $1000\left[1 + (0.038)\left(\dfrac{1}{2}\right)\right]$

2. Evaluate.

    a) $0.04 \div 2$ **b)** $0.05 \div 2$

    c) $0.064 \div 2$ **d)** $0.064 \div 4$

    e) $0.06 \div 12$ **f)** $0.085 \div 4$

    g) $0.03 \div 12$ **h)** $0.095 \div 2$

Percents

3. Convert to a decimal.

    a) 6%   **b)** 4%

    c) 2.5%   **d)** 18%

    e) 18.5%   **f)** 12.25%

    g) 0.5%   **h)** 2.33%

4. Evaluate.

    a) 5% of $400   **b)** 3% of $1000

    c) 5.5% of $2000   **d)** 7% of $350

    e) 6% of $10 000   **f)** 4.5% of $2500

    g) 1.1225% of $200 000

    h) 6.64% of $3500

5. Evaluate. Express your answer as a decimal.

    a) $6\% \div 2$ **b)** $8.4\% \div 2$

    c) $9.3\% \div 12$ **d)** $5.2\% \div 4$

    e) $16\% \div 4$ **f)** $21.6\% \div 12$

    g) $7.5\% \div 4$ **h)** $3.3\% \div 12$

6. Estimate each product.

    a) 4.1% of $1000

    b) 9.9% of $5000

    c) 3.8% of $200

    d) 5.1% of $690

    e) 4% of $329.17

    f) 5% of $236 712

Exponents

7. Use a calculator to evaluate. Round your answers to the nearest hundredth.

    a) 1.03^2

    b) 1.06^8

    c) $200(1.03)^6$

    200 ⬚×⬚ 1.03 ⬚y^x⬚ 6 ⬚=⬚

    d) $5000(1.0225)^{10}$

    e) 2^{-1}

    f) 5^{-2}

    g) 1.03^{-6}

    1.03 ⬚y^x⬚ ⬚±⬚ 6 ⬚=⬚ or

    1.03 ⬚y^x⬚ 6 ⬚±⬚ ⬚=⬚

    h) 1.005^{-12}

Simple Interest

8. Use the formula $I = Prt$ to calculate the simple interest earned on each investment. Recall, t represents the time in years and r is the annual interest rate.

   a) $P = \$500$, $r = 5\%$, $t = 2$ years

   b) $P = \$1200$, $r = 8\%$, $t = \dfrac{1}{2}$ year

   c) $P = \$4000$, $r = 7.5\%$, $t = 9$ months

   d) $P = \$4000$, $r = 7.5\%$, $t = 3$ years, 8 months

9. Calculate the interest earned on each investment.

   a) $\$1000$ invested at 6% per year, simple interest, for 3 years

   b) $\$800$ invested at 7.2% per year, simple interest, for 18 months

   c) $\$1200$ invested at 4.8% per year, simple interest, for 315 days

   d) $\$4000$ invested at 5% per year, simple interest, for 2 years, 3 months

Chapter Problem

An accounting technician may have a career in many business sectors, including manufacturing, merchandising, finance, and government. The work involves managing business-to-business accounts, payroll accounts, companies' assets, and internal auditing. A two-year accounting diploma from a community college is required. Further education is needed to become a certified general accountant or a financial planner, among other careers.

   As people go through their lives, they invest money in different ways, such as guaranteed investment certificates (GICs), term deposits, savings bonds, registered retirement savings plans (RRSPs), and registered education savings plans (RESPs). People also take out loans to buy expensive items (such as a car, furniture, or a house), to pay for education, or to allow their businesses to grow. In this chapter, you will help the Kwan family manage some of their finances as their small business grows and they save money for the expansion of their business.

8.1

Simple and Compound Interest

	A	B	C	D
0		1000	1000	
1		1045	1045	
2		1090	1092.025	
3		1135	1141.16613	
4		1180	1192.5186	
5		1225	1246.18194	
6		1270	1302.26012	
7		1315	1360.86183	
8		1360	1422.10061	
9		1405	1486.09514	
10			1552.96942	
11				

simple interest
- the money paid on a loan or investment
- a percent of the principal

principal
- the value of the initial investment or loan

amount
- the final or future value of an investment, including the principal and the accumulated interest

compound interest
- the interest paid on the principal and its accumulated interest

Banks pay you interest for the use of your money. When you deposit money in a bank account, the bank reinvests your money to make a profit.

Simple interest is calculated on the initial value invested (**principal**), P, at an annual interest rate, r, expressed as a decimal for a period of time, t. The interest is added to the principal at the end of the period.

Interest, $I = Prt$

Amount, $A = P + Prt$

Or in factored form, $A = P(1 + rt)$

Compound interest is calculated on the accumulated value of the investment, which includes the principal and the accumulated interest of prior periods.

Investigate

Compound Interest

Compare the growth of a $1000 investment at 7% per year, simple interest, with another $1000 investment at 7% per year, compounded annually.

Tools

- spreadsheet software
- computer

Method 1: Use a Spreadsheet

1. a) Set up the column headings as shown in cells A1, B1, and C1. Adjust the column widths as required.

YEAR	SIMPLE INTEREST	AMOUNT WITH SIMPLE INTEREST ($)

b) Highlight columns B and C. Under the **Format** menu, choose **Cells…**. Under the **Number** tab, choose **Currency**.

c) In cells A2 to A14, enter the numbers from 0 to 12.

d) In cell B2, enter the formula =1000*0.07*A2, and in cell C2, enter =1000+B2.

e) Highlight cells B2 down to C14. From the **Edit** menu, choose **Fill ▶ Down**. You will see the value of the $1000 investment for each year over the 12 years, at 7% per year, simple interest.

2. a) Use your spreadsheet from question 1. Set up the column headings as shown in cells D1, E1, and F1.

AMOUNT AT START OF YEAR ($)	INTEREST EARNED THIS YEAR	AMOUNT WITH COMPOUND INTEREST ($)

b) Highlight columns D to F. Under the **Format** menu, choose **Cells…**. Under the **Number** tab, choose **Currency**.

c) In cell D2, enter 1000. In cell D3, enter the formula =F2. **Fill ▶ Down** to cell D14.

d) In cell E2, enter the formula =D2*0.07, and in cell F2, enter =E2+D2. Highlight cells E2 down to F14. From the **Edit** menu, choose **Fill ▶ Down**.

3. Look at the entries in the lists. Compare the amounts for simple interest to the amounts for compound interest. Explain the differences in the growth of the two amounts.

4. Graph the amount with simple interest and with compound interest.
- Select the graph icon.
- In the popup window, select **XY (scatter)**. Then **Next >**.
- Click on the **Series** tab. Then click **Add** twice.
- Click on **Series 1**, click in the **X-Values** box. Then highlight cells A2 to A14. Click in the **Y-Values** box and clear any data in the box. Then highlight cells C2 to C14. Name the chart Simple Interest.
- Click on **Series 2**, click in the **X-Values** box. Then highlight cells A2 to A14. Click in the **Y-Values** box and clear any data in the box. Then highlight cells F2 to F14. Name the chart Compound Interest.
- Click **Next > Next > Finish**.

5. How do the graphs compare? Explain the differences in the graphs.

6. Reflect Describe how compound interest grows relative to simple interest.

7. Identify the type of growth (linear, quadratic, or exponential) demonstrated by simple interest and by compound interest. Justify your choices.

Tools

- scientific calculator
- grid paper

Method 2: Use Pencil and Paper

1. Set up a table as shown. Complete the table for 0 to 12 years. Calculate the simple interest on the amount at the start of the year using the formula $I = Prt$.

Year	Simple Interest ($)	Amount ($)
0		

2. Set up a chart as shown. Complete the chart for 0 to 12 years. Calculate the interest, at 7% per year, on the previous value (amount) and add it to the amount before calculating interest for the next year.

Year	Amount at Start of Year ($)	Compound Interest ($)	Amount at End of Year ($)
0	1000	70	1070
1	1070		

3. Look at the entries in the tables. Compare the amounts for simple interest to the amounts for compound interest. Explain the differences in the growth for the two amounts.

4. Sketch a scatter plot of both sets of data on the same set of axes.

5. How do the graphs compare? Explain the differences in the graphs.

6. Reflect Describe how compound interest grows relative to simple interest.

7. Identify the type of growth (linear, quadratic, or exponential) demonstrated by simple interest and by compound interest. Justify your choices.

Tools

- graphing calculator

Technology Tip

Before beginning this investigation, remember to clear all lists and the Y = editor, and make sure all plots have been turned off.

Method 3: Use a Graphing Calculator

1. Enter the numbers from 0 to 12 in list L1 of your graphing calculator. These values represent the times in years.

2. **a)** To generate the values of the $1000 investment each year at 7% per year, simple interest, scroll up to the column heading of list L2. Enter the formula $1000 + 1000 \times 0.07 \times L1$.

   b) Explain what each part of the formula represents.

3. **a)** To generate the value of the $1000 each year at 7% per year, compounded annually, in the first cell of list L3, enter 1000. In each of the subsequent cells of L3, multiply the previous value by 1.07.

   b) Why is each value in list L3 multiplied by 1.07 to generate the next value? Explain.

4. Look at the entries in lists L2 and L3. Compare the results of simple interest to the amounts for compound interest.

5. To graph the results, press ⌈ 2nd ⌉ [STAT PLOT]. In Plot 1, draw a scatter plot comparing L1 and L2. Set up your screen as shown.

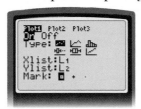

   In Plot 2, draw a scatter plot comparing L1 and L3. Set up your screen as shown.

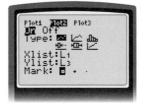

   Press ⌈ ZOOM ⌉ **9:ZoomStat** to fit the window to the data in the graph.

6. How do the graphs compare? Explain the differences in the graphs.

7. **Reflect** Describe how compound interest grows relative to simple interest.

8. Identify the type of growth (linear, quadratic, or exponential) demonstrated by simple interest and by compound interest. Justify your choices.

growth factor
- the number that is multiplied by the principal when calculating its accumulated value

compounding period
- the length of time for which interest is calculated before being accumulated

At the end of each time interval, the simple interest formula is used to calculate the interest, which is then added to the principal or previous amount.

The **growth factor** is $1 + i$, where i is the interest rate per **compounding period**, n.

Example

Compare Simple and Compound Interest

Larry wants to invest $700 for five years. Compare the growth of his investment at 4% per year, simple interest, to the same investment at 4% per year, compounded annually.

Solution

Simple Interest

$P = 700$
$r = 4\%$
$\quad = 0.04$
$t = 5$

$A = P(1 + rt)$
$\quad = 700(1 + (0.04)(5))$
$\quad = 840$

Interest earned $= 840 - 700$
$\qquad\qquad = 140$

If Larry invested $700 at 4% per year, simple interest, the amount would be $840 after five years.

The total interest earned is $140.

Compound Interest

The yearly growth factor is $1 + 0.04 = 1.04$.

Use a chart to show the growth of the investment.

Year	$A = P(1.04)$	Amount ($)
0		700.00
1	700.00(1.04)	728.00
2	728.00(1.04)	757.12
3	757.12(1.04)	787.4048
4	787.4048(1.04)	818.90099
5	818.90099(1.04)	851.65703

If Larry invested $700 at 4% per year, compounded annually, the amount would be $851.66 after five years.

The total interest earned is $151.66, which is $11.66 more than with simple interest.

Key Concepts

- Simple interest is calculated using the formula $I = Prt$.
- Money invested with simple interest grows by adding the interest to the principal, $A = P + Prt$ or $A = P(1 + rt)$.
- The rate of change for simple interest is the interest being added to the principal, so it is linear growth.
- Compound interest occurs when the interest is added to the principal at the end of each compounding period, and is included in further calculations of interest.
- Money invested with compound interest grows by multiplying by the growth factor $1 + i$, so it is exponential growth.

Discuss the Concepts

D1. When investing money with compound interest, when is the growth greater: at the beginning or the end of the term? Why?

D2. Given the same interest rate, does an investment always earn more interest with compound interest than with simple interest? If yes, explain why. If no, give an example to show it is not true.

For help with questions 1 to 3, refer to the Investigate or the Example.

1. Show the growth of a $500 investment, at 6% per year, simple interest, and at 6% per year, compounded annually, for five years, using a table and a graph.

2. Show the growth of an $800 investment, at 8% per year, simple interest, and at 8% per year, compounded annually, for 10 years, using a table and a graph.

3. Shu Ying invested $750 at 5% per year, simple interest. Her sister, Shu Jin, invested $750 at 5% per year, compounded annually. Compare the values of their investments after each year for five years.

4. Determine the value of a $1000 investment after six years, at
   a) 6.5% per year, simple interest
   b) 6.5% per year, compounded annually

5. Using tables and graphs, compare the amounts at the end of each year for three years for $2000 invested at
   a) 4% per year, compounded annually
   b) 5% per year, compounded annually
   c) 6% per year, compounded annually

6. To save for a motorcycle, Abdul deposited $2000 into an account that earned simple interest at 5.4% per year. How much more would the investment earn in three years if it were invested at 5.4% per year, compounded annually? Illustrate your answer using tables and graphs.

7. A bank is offering a new three-year investment. You decide to invest $200.
   a) How much interest would you earn each year if the bank pays 3.8% per year, simple interest?
   b) How much interest would you earn each year if the bank pays 3.8% per year, compounded annually?
   c) Which amount is easier to calculate? Explain your answer.

8. Five years ago, the Kwans invested $20 000 at 4% per year, compounded annually, so they could open a business this year.

  a) Illustrate the growth of their money over the five years using a table and a graph.

  b) Describe how their money grows compared to the same investment at 4% per year, simple interest.

9. The graph shows the growth of a $1000 investment at 4% per year, compounded annually.

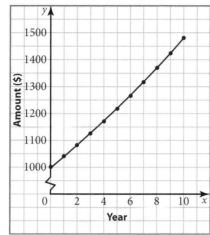

  a) How much is the investment worth after three years?

  b) Estimate the time required for the investment to grow to $1500.

  c) How would the graph change if the interest rate were 5% per year, compounded annually? Justify your response.

Extend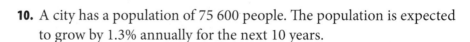

10. A city has a population of 75 600 people. The population is expected to grow by 1.3% annually for the next 10 years.

  a) Use charts and graphs to illustrate the growth of the population over the next 10 years.

  b) Describe how the graph would change if the growth rate were 2% annually.

11. Marcy kept $200 in a savings account paying simple interest at 4% per year for 10 years. Use technology to determine what rate of compound interest would result in the same amount at the end of 10 years.

8.2 Compound Interest

Rather than using a table or a graph to see how the value of an investment grows, you can use a formula.

> **Compound Interest Formula**
> $A = P(1 + i)^n$,
> *P* is the principal, or initial value.
> *A* is the accumulated amount or future value.
> *i* is the interest rate per compounding period.
> *n* is the number of compounding periods.

The table shows how to convert the yearly interest rate and term for various compounding periods.

Compounding Period	Meaning	Interest Rate, *i*	Term, *n*
annually	once per year	unchanged	unchanged
semi-annually	twice per year	divide by 2	multiply by 2
quarterly	four times per year	divide by 4	multiply by 4
monthly	twelve times per year	divide by 12	multiply by 12

Example 1

Interest Compounded Semi-Annually

Determine how much money you will have if $500 is invested for six years, at 4% per year, compounded semi-annually.

Solution

Interest is compounded semi-annually, meaning twice a year, for six years. There are 2 × 6, or 12, compounding periods. This can be illustrated on a timeline.

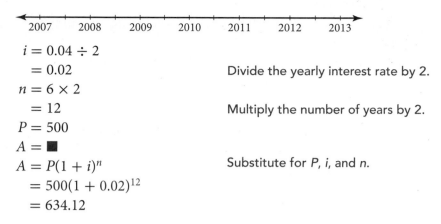

$i = 0.04 \div 2$
$\quad = 0.02$ — Divide the yearly interest rate by 2.
$n = 6 \times 2$
$\quad = 12$ — Multiply the number of years by 2.
$P = 500$
$A = \blacksquare$
$A = P(1 + i)^n$ — Substitute for P, i, and n.
$\quad = 500(1 + 0.02)^{12}$
$\quad = 634.12$

After six years, you will have $634.12.

Example 2

Interest Compounded Monthly

Alice borrowed $5000 to start a small business. The interest rate on the loan was 9% per year, compounded monthly. She is expected to repay the loan in full after four years.

a) How much must Alice repay?

b) How much of the amount Alice repays will be interest?

Solution

a) Interest is compounded monthly, meaning 12 times a year, for four years. There are 12×4, or 48, compounding periods.

$i = 0.09 \div 12$
$\quad = 0.0075$ — Divide the yearly interest rate by 12.
$n = 4 \times 12$
$\quad = 48$ — Multiply the number of years by 12.
$P = 5000$
$A = \blacksquare$
$\quad = P(1 + i)^n$
$\quad = 5000(1 + 0.0075)^{48}$
$\quad = 7157.03$

Alice must repay $7157.03 after four years.

b) Calculate the total interest by subtracting the principal from the amount.
$7157.03 - 5000 = 2157.03$
Alice will pay $2157.03 in interest.

Key Concepts

- Compound interest can be accumulated at various intervals, such as annually, semi-annually, quarterly, and monthly.
- The compound interest formula $A = P(1 + i)^n$ can be used to calculate the future value, or amount.
  - A is the future value or accumulated amount of an investment or loan.
  - P is the principal.
  - i is the interest rate, in decimal form, per interest period.
  - n is the number of compounding periods.

Discuss the Concepts

D1. Draw a timeline to illustrate each situation.

   a) an investment of $1000 at 5% per year, compounded semi-annually, for three years

   b) an investment of $550 at 4% per year, compounded quarterly, for two years

   c) an investment of $700 at 3% per year, compounded monthly, for two years

D2. You can use the same compound interest formula, $A = P(1 + i)^n$, for both debts and investments. Explain why.

Practise

For help with questions 1 to 3, refer to Example 1.

1. Evaluate. Use a scientific calculator and round to two decimal places.

   a) $500(1.02)^3$ **b)** $200(1.03)^7$

   c) $1000(1.06)^4$ **d)** $3500(1.0025)^8$

   e) $1350(1.0375)^{12}$ **f)** $12\,500(1.041)^5$

2. Substitute the values into the formula $A = P(1 + i)^n$. Do not evaluate.

   a) a $2000 investment at 5% per year, compounded annually, for three years

   b) a $1000 loan at 8% per year, compounded semi-annually, for two years

   c) a $50\,000 loan at 12% per year, compounded quarterly, for five years

   d) a $750 investment at 6% per year, compounded monthly, for one year

3. Determine the amount of, and total interest earned on, a $1000 investment at

    a) 4% per year, compounded annually, for five years

    b) 8% per year, compounded semi-annually, for three years

    c) 6.5% per year, compounded quarterly, for two years

    d) 3.6% per year, compounded monthly, for four years

For help with question 4, refer to Example 2.

4. To pay for a vacation, Ming Mei borrowed $900, at 6% per year, compounded quarterly. The loan must be paid in full after two years.

    a) How much must Ming Mei repay?

    b) How much of that amount is interest?

5. Keisha plans to invest $5000 at 6% per year for five years. Calculate the amounts Keisha would have at the end of the five years if the interest is compounded

    a) annually   **b)** semi-annually   **c)** quarterly

    d) monthly   **e)** daily

Apply **B**

6. When Tonya was born, her grandparents invested $10 000 at 5% per year, compounded semi-annually, to pay for her education.

    a) What was the investment worth on Tonya's twelfth birthday?

    b) What was the investment worth on Tonya's eighteenth birthday?

7. A certain investment fund has grown by an average of 13.6% per year, compounded annually, over the past eight years. How much would an investment of $2000 made eight years ago be worth today?

8. A $5000 investment earns interest at 4% per year, compounded quarterly, for 10 years.

    a) What is the value of the investment after one year? two years?

    b) What is the interest earned in the second year?

    c) What is the interest earned in the tenth year?

    d) Explain any differences between your answers in parts b) and c).

9. Wayne invested $2000 at 4.5% per year, compounded semi-annually, and $2500 at 4.2% per year, compounded quarterly. Both investments were for three years.

    a) Which investment earned Wayne more money?

    b) What is the total interest earned on Wayne's investments?

10. To buy a car, Sangar borrowed $8000 at 4.8% per year, compounded monthly, for one year. His brother, Sanjiv, borrowed $8000 for his car, at 3.2% per year, compounded monthly, for one year. How much more interest did Sangar have to pay than Sanjiv?

11. To find current interest rates for car loans at financial institutions across Canada, go to *www.mcgrawhill.ca/links/foundations11* and follow the links.

   a) Which institution charges the lowest interest rate on a 60-month loan? Which institution charges the greatest interest rate?

   b) If interest is compounded monthly on a $15 000 loan, compare the total interest paid on the loan using the two interest rates from part a)?

   c) Select one institution's 48-month loan interest rate. Compare the total interest payable on a $15 000 loan
   i) with simple interest
   ii) with interest compounded monthly

12. Warren needs to borrow $3000. Which loan should he take? Justify your choice.

   A $3000 for five years at 9% per year, compounded semi-annually

   B $3000 for five years at 8.6% per year, compounded quarterly

Literacy **Connect**

A bond is issued by a government or company to raise large sums of money to be repaid after many years. Simple or compound interest is paid to the investors.

13. The town council voted to issue a bond of $3 000 000 to build a new swimming pool. The bond matures in 10 years, with an interest rate of 5% per year, compounded semi-annually. Principal and accumulated interest are due at the end of the term.

   a) Calculate the total amount that the town must pay at the end of the term.

   b) Calculate the total interest paid.

14. The city of Melville has a population of 102 000 and a projected growth rate of 2.3% per year, for the next 10 years. The city of Markton has a population of 97 000 and a projected growth rate of 3.7% per year for the next 10 years. Which city is expected to have the greater population in 10 years? By how many people?

15. The Stereo Warehouse is advertising "No money down and pay no interest for one year!" Peter read the fine print and discovered that, although you pay no interest for one year, interest is calculated at 12% per year, compounded monthly, on the price of the merchandise. What would Peter have to pay for a $1150 stereo after one year?

16. Danielle received an inheritance of $30 000. She wants to split the amount equally among her three children, Robert, David, and Donna.

- Robert plans to buy a house in the near future so he will need the money available. He deposits his portion into a bank account paying interest at 4% per year, compounded quarterly.
- David plans to go to university in a few years. He invests his money in a registered education savings plan (RESP) that pays at 5.5% per year, compounded semi-annually.
- Donna will not need her money for many years. She puts her portion into a trust fund. The fund pays interest at 8% per year, compounded monthly.

a) Find the amounts available to each child after two years. What are the differences between the amounts?

b) What will happen to the differences between the amounts if the money is invested for a longer time?

Extend C

17. Sarah deposited $2000 in an investment fund that earned 12.6% per year, compounded annually. After five years, the proceeds were reinvested in a second investment fund that earned 15.8% per year, compounded semi-annually. If the second fund continues earning at the same rate, how much will Sarah's investment be worth after an additional five years?

18. Determine the yearly interest for each investment.

a) After six months, a $500 investment with interest compounded semi-annually is worth $512.50.

b) After two months, a $2000 investment with interest compounded monthly is worth $2020.05.

c) After six months, a $1000 investment with interest compounded quarterly is worth $1025.16.

19. Bryce bought a savings bond during a recent Ontario Savings Bond campaign. The interest rate increases every year according to the table.

a) How much will Bryce's investment be worth in five years if he invests $500?

b) How much will Bryce's investment be worth in five years if he invests $1500? Use your answer to part a) to determine the value.

Year	Annual Interest Rate (%)
1	3.7
2	3.8
3	3.9
4	4.0
5	4.25

8.3 Present Value

$2399.99
or
$399.99 down
and $2200
after
one year

Suppose you want to buy the TV shown. Interest is 4.2% per year, compounded quarterly. Should you pay the full price for the TV today or make the down payment, leave the rest of the money in the bank, and pay the balance after one year?

Investigate

Growth Factors

1. Consider the sequence 1, 2, 4, 8, ….

   a) Continue the sequence for three more terms.

   b) What is the growth factor?

2. Consider the sequence 8, 12, 18, 27, 40.5, ….

   a) Continue the sequence for three more terms.

   b) What is the growth factor?

3. Consider the sequence 2, 6, 18, ….

   a) What is the growth factor?

   b) One of the later terms in the sequence is 4374. Determine the previous two terms.

   c) Describe how you found your answer in part b).

4. A sequence has a growth factor of 5. One of the terms is 9375.

   a) Describe a method for finding the previous terms.

   b) Determine the previous two terms.

5. An investment paid interest at 4% per year, compounded annually, and so has a growth factor of 1.04. Its value at the end of the term is $4326.75.

   a) Explain why this investment is like a sequence with a growth factor of 1.04.

   b) Describe a method for finding the value of the investment at the end of the previous year.

   c) Calculate the value of the investment at the end of each of the previous two years.

6. Reflect If the final amount of an investment is known, describe a method that could be used to determine all the previous values, including the principal.

To find the amount of an investment, you can use the formula $A = P(1 + i)^n$. The formula can be rearranged to find the principal.

$$A = P(1 + i)^n$$

$$\frac{A}{(1 + i)^n} = \frac{P(1 + i)^n}{(1 + i)^n}$$ To solve for P, divide both sides by $(1 + i)^n$.

$$P = \frac{A}{(1 + i)^n}$$ This formula can also be expressed using a negative exponent.

$$\text{or } P = A(1 + i)^{-n}$$

present value
- the value of an investment or loan on a date before the end of the term

P represents the principal value of a loan or investment. It is also known as the **present value**.

future value
- the value of an investment or loan at the end of the term

A represents the amount of a loan or investment is worth after a period of time. It is also known as the **future value**.

Example 1

Investment

Sam wants to invest enough money today to have $3200 for tuition when he goes to college in two years. If he invests his money at 6% per year, compounded monthly, how much does he need to invest?

Solution

$A = 3200$ The amount needed in two years.

$n = 2 \times 12$

   $= 24$

$i = 0.06 \div 12$

   $= 0.005$

$P = \blacksquare$ P is the unknown quantity.

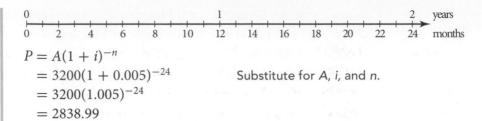

$$P = A(1 + i)^{-n}$$
$$\quad = 3200(1 + 0.005)^{-24} \qquad \text{Substitute for } A, i, \text{ and } n.$$
$$\quad = 3200(1.005)^{-24}$$
$$\quad = 2838.99$$

Sam needs to invest $2838.99 today to have $3200 in two years.

creditor

- a person or organization that lends money

discount

- to sell an investment at a value less than its usual price

Just as you can find the principal value of an investment, you can find the present value of a loan. **Creditors** often sell their loans to other creditors. They **discount** the value of the loan by calculating the present value at current interest rates.

Example 2

Credit Debt

John has a loan for $5000 that is due in four years. He wants to pay off his debt early. The creditor is willing to discount the loan at an interest rate of 8% per year, compounded semi-annually. How much would the creditor be willing to accept today?

Solution

$$A = 5000$$
$$n = 4 \times 2$$
$$\quad = 8$$
$$i = 0.08 \div 2$$
$$\quad = 0.04$$
$$P = \blacksquare$$

January 2007		January 2008		January 2009		January 2010		January 2011
	July 2007		July 2008		July 2009		July 2010	

$$P = A(1 + i)^{-n}$$
$$\quad = 5000(1 + 0.04)^{-8}$$
$$\quad = 5000(1.04)^{-8}$$
$$\quad = 3653.45$$

The creditor would be willing to accept $3653.45 today to pay off the loan.

Key Concepts

- To calculate the amount of an investment or loan, use the formula $A = P(1 + i)^n$.
- To calculate the principal value (present value) of an investment or loan, use the formula $P = A(1 + i)^{-n}$.

> **Discuss the Concepts**

D1. Explain the difference between *amount* and *principal*. Use words, numbers, and/or a diagram.

D2. When calculating the principal value of an amount, which will be the smaller value: the principal or the amount? Why?

D3. Kerry wants to invest enough money today to have $4000 in two years, at 6% per year, compounded quarterly. Describe the appropriate steps and scientific calculator keystrokes needed to solve this problem.

D4. Look at the opening illustration on page 436. What factors would you need to consider when determining which payment plan would be a better deal?

Practise •

For help with questions 1 and 2, refer to Example 1.

1. Evaluate. Round to two decimal places.

a) $2000(1.04)^{-6}$

b) $750(1.005)^{-12}$

c) $500(1.01)^{-10}$

d) $10\,000(1.03)^{-8}$

e) $2450(1.0075)^{-18}$

f) $1500(1.1)^{-3}$

2. Calculate the present value of each amount.

a) $5000 needed in four years, invested at 6% per year, compounded annually

b) $2000 needed in two years, invested at 4% per year, compounded semi-annually

c) $1000 needed in three years, invested at 4.5% per year, compounded monthly

d) $10\,000 needed in five years, invested at 8% per year, compounded quarterly

For help with question 3, refer to Example 2.

3. Calculate the discounted value of each loan today.

   a) a $2000 debt due in three years, discounted at 6% per year, compounded semi-annually

   b) a $5000 debt due in four years, discounted at 5% per year, compounded quarterly

   c) a $100 000 debt due in five years, discounted at 7.5% per year, compounded monthly

   d) a $1000 debt due in three years, discounted at 5% per year, compounded semi-annually

Apply **B** ·

4. Steve borrowed some money at 9% per year, compounded semi-annually. After three years, he paid $2604.52 to pay off the loan. What sum of money did Steve borrow?

5. What principal should be invested today to have $1000 after two years if interest is paid at 4% per year, compounded quarterly?

6. At the birth of their child, how much should a couple invest to have $20 000 on the child's eighteenth birthday, if interest is paid at 8% per year, compounded quarterly? How much interest would be earned?

7. An investment fund pays 6.3% per year, compounded monthly. How much should a 25-year-old woman invest in the fund to have $50 000 by age 35?

8. Jamie took out a $3000 loan, due in four years. If interest is 5.7% per year, compounded semi-annually, how much should Jamie's creditor be willing to accept to pay off the loan today?

Chapter Problem

9. The Kwans will need $50 000 in three years to expand their business. What is the equivalent value today, if inflation is projected to be approximately 3.5% per year, compounded annually?

10. At Giant TV Sales, you can choose between two payment options for a new plasma TV. The first option is to pay $2399.99 now. The second option is to pay a $399.99 down payment plus $2200.00 after one year. If interest is 4.2% per year, compounded quarterly, which option is the better deal?

11. Jenay will invest some money on July 3, her sixteenth birthday, at 4.5% per year, compounded monthly. How much should she invest if she wants to have $10 000 on the November 3 following her eighteenth birthday?

12. Mike lent some money to a relative. The relative will pay back $1000 in one year, $2000 in two years, and $3000 in three years. What is the combined value of the loan today, if interest is calculated at 7.5% per year, compounded semi-annually?

13. Andelko will inherit $30 000 when he turns 21 in six months. He will borrow money today to purchase a new car and will pay off the principal plus interest in a lump sum with his inheritance. The bank offers short-term loans at a rate of 8% per year, compounded monthly.

  a) How much can Andelko borrow today for the new car?

  b) How much of the $30 000 payment will be interest?

Extend **C** ●

14. Interest on a $5000 loan is 4.8% per year, compounded monthly. The loan is due in six years. If the creditor were to sell the loan to another creditor, discounted at 4.2% per year, compounded quarterly,

  a) how much would the new creditor pay?

  b) how much would the original creditor earn on the loan?

15. Emilie borrowed $2700 at 8.6% per year, compounded quarterly. After the first year, she repaid $1000. She is expected to repay the loan in full after three years.

  a) How much must Emilie repay?

  b) Suppose after the second year, Emilie repaid another $1000. How much must she repay now?

  c) Suppose after the first year, Emilie repaid $2000. How much must she repay now?

  d) Determine the total amount Emilie repaid in each situation.

16. For each loan, determine the number of years between the initial loan and repayment. You may need to guess and test.

  a) $1225.04 was repaid for a loan of $1000 at 7% per year, compounded annually.

  b) $2979.69 was repaid for a loan of $2000 at 8% per year, compounded monthly.

  c) $1097.84 was repaid for a loan of $850 at 6.5% per year, compounded semi-annually.

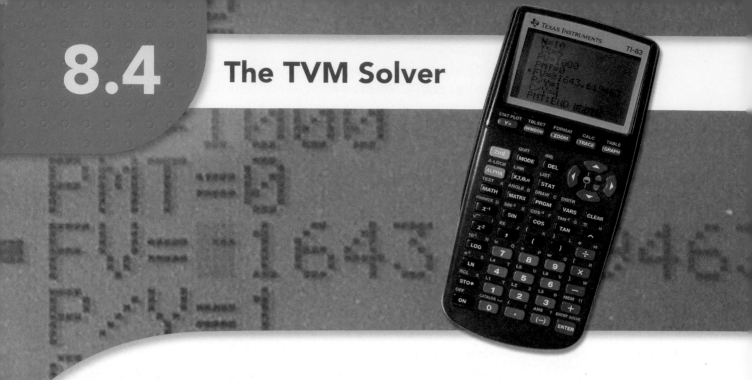

8.4 The TVM Solver

TVM Solver

- a feature of the TI-83 Plus/84 Plus calculators that is used for financial calculations

A graphing calculator can be used to make calculations using the compound interest formula, $FV = PV(1 + i)^n$. The Time–Value–Money **(TVM) Solver** allows you to enter the value of each variable and solve for the remaining unknown value with a simple keystroke.

```
N = number of years
I% = interest rate per year as a percent
PV = present value or principal
PMT = size of the periodic payment
FV = future value or amount
P/Y = number of payments per year
C/Y = compounding periods per year
PMT: END BEGIN  payment at the
                beginning or end of
                each payment interval
```

When entering the interest rate in the TVM Solver, express it as a percent, not as a decimal.

Investigate 1

Tools

- graphing calculator

Future Investment

Samir invested $500 at 6% per year, compounded quarterly. What will the investment be worth after three years?

1. To access the TVM Solver, press [APPS] **1:Finance**, then **1:TVM Solver…**.

2. Set up the values.
   N = Enter the number of years.
   I% = Enter the annual interest rate as a percent.
   PV = Enter the principal.
   PMT = Enter 0. When there are no regular payments, always set PMT = 0.

FV = Enter 0 (a temporary value).

P/Y = Enter 1. When there are no regular payments, always set P/Y = 1.

C/Y = Enter the number of compounding periods per year.

PMT: Choose END.

Technology Tip

The future value, FV, is shown as a negative number because it is money you cannot use right now. When a value is positive, it represents money you are receiving.

3. Use the arrow keys to move the cursor to **FV**. Press [ALPHA] [SOLVE].

4. What was Samir's investment worth after three years?

Investigate 2   Discount Investment

An investment will be worth $4000 in four years. If the interest rate is 5% per year, compounded monthly, what is the present value of the investment?

1. Access the TVM Solver and set up the values. Use **PV** = 0 and enter the appropriate value for **FV**.

2. Move the cursor to **PV** and press [ALPHA] [SOLVE].

3. What is the present value of this investment?

4. How much interest will be paid at the end of four years?

Key Concepts

- The TVM Solver on a graphing calculator can be used to solve problems involving compound interest. Enter the known values, and enter 0 for the unknown value. With your cursor at the location of the unknown value, press [ALPHA] [SOLVE].

- The TVM Solver uses the compound interest formula $A = P(1 + i)^n$. When PV or FV are displayed as negative numbers, they represent money you cannot use right now.

Discuss the Concepts

D1. What values should you enter in each line of the TVM Solver for each problem? Do not evaluate.

    a) $3000 is borrowed for two years at 5% per year, compounded monthly

    b) $5000 is due in three years, discounted at 9% per year, compounded semi-annually

Practise

For help with questions 1 to 3, refer to Investigate 1.

1. Determine the amount of a $2000 investment after five years if interest is 6% per year, compounded semi-annually.

2. Ginny borrowed $1000, at 8.4% per year, compounded monthly. How much must she repay at the end of two years?

3. Chin Lee invests $7500 today, at 5.5% per year, compounded semi-annually. After how many years will he have enough to buy a $9000 motorcycle?

For help with questions 4 and 5, refer to Investigate 2.

4. Eduardo wants to invest enough money today to have $5000 in three years, for a down payment on a car. How much should Eduardo invest today, at 5% per year, compounded quarterly?

5. A no-interest $5000 loan is due in four years. If the creditor were to sell the loan to another creditor, discounted at 9% per year, compounded monthly, how much would the new creditor pay?

Apply B

6. Maria deposited $1000 into an account paying interest at 4.2% per year, compounded monthly. How long will it take for the money to grow to $1500?

7. Keenan invested $2000 in a term deposit that pays 6% per year, compounded semi-annually.

   a) How long will it take for Keenan's investment to double in value?

   b) Would a $10 000 investment double in value in the same length of time? Explain.

8. **a)** What interest rate, compounded quarterly, is needed for a $2000 investment to increase to $3000 after five years?

   b) Would the same interest rate double a $5000 investment after five years? Explain.

9. What interest rate, compounded semi-annually, will double the value of a $3000 investment after

   a) three years?

   b) four years?

   c) five years?

10. Which will reach a value of $5000 faster: $3000 invested at 6% per year, compounded monthly, or $3500 invested at 6.5% per year, compounded semi-annually?

11. Which will double faster: money invested at 8% per year, compounded semi-annually, or at 7.5% per year, compounded quarterly? Justify your answer.

12. You want to be a millionaire by the time you are 55 years old. If you invest $20 000 on your eighteenth birthday at 8% per year, compounded semi-annually, will you meet your goal? If not, what interest rate would you require?

13. How much money would you need to invest on your eighteenth birthday at 8% per year, compounded semi-annually, to be a millionaire by the time you are 60 years old? 65 years old?

14. Rosalind owns a savings bond that will pay her $10 000 when it matures in five years. She needs money now for college tuition, and her cousin is willing to buy the bond at a suitable discount. Current bank rates vary from 3.5% to 5.5% per year, for various savings bonds.

 a) What is the minimum fair discount price for the bond?

 b) What is the maximum fair discount price for the bond?

Extend **C** •

15. Use the TVM Solver to compare the amounts of interest paid on a $600 investment, after four years, at different interest rates and different compounding periods. Describe the method you used.

16. The TVM Solver can be used to determine interest rates. Reed owns a bond that will pay $1200 when it matures in four years. Naomi offered to buy the bond today for $1000. Use a TVM Solver to determine the annual interest rate that Naomi is offering, if interest is compounded semi-annually.

17. Use the TVM Solver to determine the interest rates, compounded semi-annually, quarterly, and monthly, that would give the same interest after one year as 10% per year, simple interest. Describe the method you used.

Effects of Changing the Conditions on Investments and Loans

Banks, paycheque advance companies, loan companies, and stores lend money to their customers at varying interest rates, compounding periods, and terms. It is important for consumers to understand how changing the conditions of a loan will affect the amount they will have to repay. This is also true for changing the conditions of an investment.

$ PayDay Loans

Jasper Williams
181 Upper Beach Rd
Hometown, ON
M7H 3N2

Cash Advance

C O N T R A C T

PayDay Loans Made Simple!

We will pay you your paycheque, less 10%.

You agree to sign over your cheque to us when received from your employer.

Investigate

Tools

- graphing calculator

Investments

Ken deposited $500 into an investment fund that has historically earned 11.3% per year, compounded annually. He intends to leave the money in the fund for at least four years.

1. **a)** Assuming the same rate of return, how much will Ken's investment be worth in four years?

   b) Predict the value of Ken's investment in four years if the rate of return is doubled.

   c) Verify your prediction using technology. Describe the results.

2. **Reflect** Describe how doubling the interest rate affects the value of an investment. Does the amount or the total interest paid double? Explain.

3. a) Predict the value of the investment if Ken doubles the amount of time he keeps his money in the fund.

b) Verify your prediction using technology. Describe the results.

4. Reflect Describe how doubling the amount of time money is invested affects the value of an investment. Does the amount or the total interest paid double? Explain.

Example 1

Use Technology to Compare Different Compounding Periods

Anna has $2000 available to invest at 12% per year, compounded annually. She will need the money in six to eight years to finance her children's education.

a) Use a graphing calculator, graph $A = 2000(1.12)^n$.

b) Use the **CALC** feature to determine the value of A for
    i) $n = 6$ **ii)** $n = 7$ **iii)** $n = 8$

c) Describe the shape of the graph in part a). What happens when you change the total length of time the money is invested?

Solution

a)

  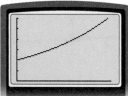

b) i)

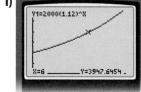

When $n = 6$, the amount is $3947.65.

ii)

When $n = 7$, the amount is $4421.36.

iii)

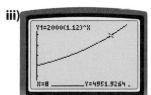

When $n = 8$, the amount is $4951.93.

c) The graph gets steeper from left to right.
Growth between the sixth and seventh years:
$4421.36 − $3947.65 = $473.72
Growth between the seventh and eighth years:
$4951.93 − $4421.36 = $530.56
As the total length of time increases, the investment grows by an increasing amount each year.

Example 2

Future Investment

Tyler wants to have $5000 in four years time. How much would Tyler need to invest today at 4% per year, compounded quarterly? at 4.5% per year, compounded quarterly?

Solution

Method 1: Use a TVM Solver

For 4%, enter the following information in the TVM Solver.

Move the cursor to **PV** and press [ALPHA] [SOLVE].

PV = 4264.11

For 4.5%, enter the following information in the TVM Solver.

Move the cursor to **PV** and press [ALPHA] [SOLVE].

PV = 4180.55

Tyler would have to invest $4264.11 at 4%, or $4180.55 at 4.5%.

Technology Tip
For the TVM Solver:
$A = $ FV
$P = $ PV
$n = $ N

Method 2: Use a Scientific Calculator

For 4%:

$i = 0.04 \div 4$
$\quad = 0.01$
$n = 4 \times 4$
$\quad = 16$
$A = 5000$
$P = 5000(1 + 0.01)^{-16}$
$\quad = 4264.11$ 　　　　　5000 ⎡ × ⎤ 1.01 ⎡ y^x ⎤ ⎡ ± ⎤ 16 ⎡ = ⎤

For 4.5%:
$i = 0.045 \div 4$
$\quad = 0.011\ 25$
$n = 4 \times 4$
$\quad = 16$
$A = 5000$
$P = 5000(1 + 0.011\ 25)^{-16}$
$\quad = 4180.55$ 　　　　　5000 ⎡ × ⎤ 1.01125 ⎡ y^x ⎤ ⎡ ± ⎤ 16 ⎡ = ⎤

Tyler would have to invest $4264.11 at 4%, or $4180.55 at 4.5%.

Technology Tip
Calculators vary. You may need to enter ⎡ y^x ⎤ 16 ⎡ ± ⎤ to get the negative exponent.

Key Concepts

- When changing any conditions of an investment or loan, the amount or principal will also change.

- Doubling an interest rate or term more than doubles the total interest. This is due to the effects of compounding.

- The more frequent the compounding period, the greater the effects of any changes to the investment or loan.

Discuss the Concepts

D1. Erin has $1200 to invest. Determine, without calculating, which rate would provide a greater amount of interest after three years:
  - 5% per year, compounded quarterly
  - 5% per year, compounded semi-annually

  Explain your answer.

D2. A $3000 debt is due to be repaid in four years. When attempting to sell the debt, the creditor received a smaller principal value with a higher interest rate. Should the creditor have been surprised? Explain.

Practise

For help with questions 1 and 2, refer to Example 1.

1. For a $1500 investment, at 7% per year, compounded semi-annually, use a graph to compare the final amounts and total interest after

   a) three years

   b) four years

   c) five years

2. Compare the graphs of $A = 1000(1.03)^n$ and $A = 1000(1.05)^n$. How does changing the compound interest rate from 3% per year to 5% per year affect the shape of the graph? What does this mean in terms of the value of the investment?

For help with question 3, refer to the Investigate.

3. A $675 investment earns interest at 3.4% per year, compounded semi-annually, for five years. How will the interest and the amount be affected if you double

   a) the interest rate?

   b) the total length of time?

For help with question 4, refer to Example 2.

4. Nobuko hopes to have $3000 in two years to buy a home theatre system. Use technology to find the amounts she would need to invest to reach her goal at

   a) 4% per year, compounded semi-annually

   b) 5% per year, compounded semi-annually

Apply

5. Renée has $3400 to invest for three years at 6% per year. She is wondering how much the compounding period affects the amount. Investigate what happens to Renée's investment for compounding periods that are annual, semi-annual, quarterly, and monthly. Describe the results.

6. Terry is confused about the various compounding periods offered by his bank. If he deposits $6000 into an investment account for one year at 5% per year, how much more interest will he earn by compounding

   a) semi-annually instead of annually?

   b) quarterly instead of annually?

   c) monthly instead of annually?

7. Raheela plans to purchase a new car in three years and hopes to have $18 000 at that time.

　a) Determine the principal that Raheela needs to invest today to have $18 000 after three years
　　 i) at 4.5% per year, compounded monthly
　　 ii) at 4.5% per year, compounded semi-annually

　b) Which principal is less? Why?

8. Barb plans to invest $10 000 in a term deposit for two years. She has three choices.
　A 6.8% per year, simple interest
　B 6.2% per year, compounded semi-annually
　C 6.0% per year, compounded quarterly

　Which plan should she choose? Why?

9. Jayeed recently inherited $8000. He plans to use half the money now and invest the other half for at least three years. He has narrowed the investment down to three choices.
　A 3.25% per year, simple interest, cashable any time
　B 3.0% per year, compounded monthly, cashable after two years
　C 3.5% per year, compounded semi-annually, cashable after four years

　a) Which plan earns the most interest after four years? Does that mean it is the best option? Justify your response.

　b) Jayeed decides he will use the investment to make a down payment on a car in two and a half years. Which plan should he choose? Why?

10. A paycheque advance company will give you money for your paycheque two weeks before you receive it, provided you show evidence of a regular paycheque from your employer.

　a) For a $1200 paycheque, how much money would Jasper receive?

　b) What annual interest rate, compounded weekly, is Jasper paying for this loan?

11. The Kwans' business has been successful. They wish to invest $25 000 at 5% per year, compounded semi-annually, and a further $25 000 at 4.8% per year, compounded monthly. Each investment will be for 10 years.

a) Calculate the difference in interest earned by the two investments.

b) Write a short paragraph explaining the difference in the interest earned.

12. a) How much needs to be invested today to have $10 000 after five years
  i) at 6% per year, compounded monthly?
  ii) at 6% per year, compounded semi-annually?

b) Which principal is greater? Why?

13. Interest rates vary depending on the size of the investment and the term. Visit your local bank and find out its current interest rates for different principal investments in guaranteed investment certificates (GICs) for specific periods of time. Copy the table, then use your research to complete the table.

Principal ($)	Term (years)	Interest Rate (%)	Compounding Period	Amount ($)
500	1		monthly	
500	3		quarterly	
1 000	5		semi-annually	
2 000	1		annually	
5 000	5		monthly	
10 000	2		quarterly	
10 000	5		semi-annually	
10 000	5		annually	

Achievement Check

14. a) Suppose you need $10 000 in five years to repay some college expenses. Compare the amounts you would need to invest in these three options to reach your goal.
  A A bond that pays interest at 7% per year, compounded monthly.
  B An investment fund that pays interest at 8% per year, compounded semi-annually.
  C A term deposit account that pays interest at 6.5% per year, compounded daily.

b) Suppose you invest $7000 now. What yearly interest rate, compounded annually, is necessary to have enough to repay the expenses from part a)?

15. On the birth of their son Jamison, the Turleys invested $5000 at 4.9% per year, compounded annually. On Jamison's fifth birthday, the investment matured and his parents reinvested the amount at 5.1% per year, compounded semi-annually, for five years. On his tenth birthday, his parents reinvested the amount at 5.3% per year, compounded quarterly, for five more years. How much more interest did the Turleys earn than if they had invested the $5000 for 15 years at 4.8% per year, compounded monthly?

16. Executives at a company have decided to acquire a corporate jet for company use. They can purchase the aircraft for $2 000 000, and resell it after 10 years for $1 500 000. Interest lost on the money used for the purchase is estimated at 5% per year, compounded semi-annually. Alternatively, they can lease the aircraft for $200 000 per year.

a) Calculate the cost of purchasing the aircraft, keeping it for 10 years, and then reselling it. Include the cost of lost interest on the money used for the purchase.

b) Calculate the cost of leasing the aircraft for 10 years.

Literacy Connect

c) Write a short paragraph advising the president of the company on which plan should be adopted.

17. Jessica plans to invest $4000 for five years, at which time she wants to have at least $6000. What interest rate, rounded to two decimal places, does she require, if the investment is compounded

a) annually?

b) semi-annually?

c) quarterly?

d) monthly?

Math **Connect**
The effective annual interest rate is the equivalent annual interest rate when compounding occurs more often than once a year.

18. Susan received a credit card bill for $2122.67 at the end of December. She decided to wait until the end of January to pay the bill. At the end of January she received a bill for $2159.82 even though she had made no further purchases. Use a TVM Solver to determine the effective annual interest rate, compounded monthly.

8.1 Simple and Compound Interest, pages 422–429

1. Show the growth of a $2000 investment, at both 5% per year simple interest and 5% per year, compounded annually, for six years, using a table and a graph.

2. Use tables and graphs to compare the amounts after four years for a $1500 investment at

   a) 3% per year, compounded annually

   b) 3.5% per year, compounded annually

   c) 4% per year, compounded annually

3. The graph shows the growth of a $2000 investment at 6% per year, compounded annually.

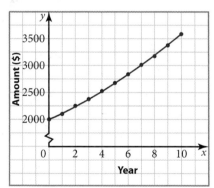

   a) How much is the investment worth after five years?

   b) Estimate the time it would take for the investment to double in value.

   c) How would the graph change if the interest rate were 4% per year, compounded annually? Justify your response.

8.2 Compound Interest, pages 430–435

4. Substitute the values into the formula $A = P(1 + i)^n$. Do not evaluate.

   a) a $600 investment at 7% per year, compounded semi-annually, for three years

   b) a $4000 loan at 9% per year, compounded quarterly, for five years

   c) a $6000 loan at 8.4% per year, compounded monthly, for three years

   d) a $1200 investment at 4.5% per year, compounded semi-annually, for two years

5. Bill made two investments.

   A $5000 at 5.5% per year, compounded quarterly, for four years

   B $2500 at 5.8% per year, compounded semi-annually, for four years

   a) Which investment earned him more money?

   b) What is the total interest earned on his investments?

6. Barbara borrowed $2300 at 10% per year, compounded quarterly.

   a) How much must she repay after five years?

   b) How much of the amount she repays is interest?

8.3 Present Value, pages 436–441

7. Neaz wants to invest enough money today so that his son will have $4800 toward his expenses when he goes to college in five years. If the annual interest rate is 5.7% per year, compounded monthly, how much should Neaz invest?

8. Suppose you owe a sum of $10 000 due in six years. Your creditor is willing to accept early payment of the loan by discounting it at 9.6% per year, compounded monthly. How much should your creditor be willing to accept to pay off the loan today?

9. Jai wants to buy a car. Which is the better deal, with interest rates at 5% per year, compounded semi-annually?
- **Plan A**: $16 250 cash now
- **Plan B**: $1000 down plus $15 500 in one year
- **Plan C**: $500 down plus $16 000 in one year

8.4 The TVM Solver, pages 442–445

10. Copy and complete the table. Use a TVM Solver.

Present Value ($)	Future Value ($)	Term (years)	Compounding Period	Annual Interest Rate (%)
8 000	12 000	5	monthly	
6 000	13 000	10	semi-annually	
1 340	2 000		quarterly	6
100 000	1 000 000		semi-annually	8
4 000		3	monthly	3
	25 000	8	quarterly	5.5

11. A $1000 investment earns interest at 4% per year, compounded quarterly.
- **a)** How long will it take to double the value of the investment?
- **b)** Would other investments double in the same length of time? Explain.

8.5 Effects of Changing the Conditions on Investments and Loans, pages 446–453

12. For a $3000 investment, at 6% per year, compounded quarterly, use a graph to compare the final amounts after each time period.
- **a)** one year   **b)** two years
- **c)** three years

13. You deposit $2000 into an investment account for two years at 7% per year. How much will you earn if interest is compounded
- **a)** annually?
- **b)** semi-annually?
- **c)** quarterly?
- **d)** monthly?

14. Marlon can purchase a company car for his real estate business for $30 000. He expects to sell the car for $12 000 after five years. Interest lost on the money used for the purchase is estimated at 6% per year, compounded quarterly. Alternatively, Marlon can lease the car for $4000 per year.
- **a)** Calculate the cost of purchasing the car, keeping it for five years, and then selling it. Include the cost of lost interest on the money used for the purchase.
- **b)** Calculate the cost of leasing the car for five years.
- **c)** Which plan is a better deal for Marlon? How much more would he pay with the other plan?

For questions 1 to 4, choose the best answer.

1. Which statement is false when comparing simple and compound interest?

   A Simple interest is paid on the principal value but compound interest is paid on an accumulating value.

   B Compound interest is always greater than simple interest.

   C Simple interest is an example of linear growth and compound interest is an example of exponential growth.

   D Compound interest grows faster than simple interest after the first interest period, if the yearly interest rates are equal.

2. When money is invested at 5% per year, compounded semi-annually, for five years,

   A $n = 5$ and $i = 0.05$

   B $n = 5$ and $i = 0.025$

   C $n = 10$ and $i = 0.025$

   D $n = 10$ and $i = 0.05$

3. When changing the compounding period on an investment, which statement is true?

   A More frequent compounding results in a greater amount of interest.

   B More frequent compounding results in the same amount of interest.

   C More frequent compounding results in a lesser amount of interest.

   D More frequent compounding changes both the principal and amount, so there is no consistent result.

4. Which formulas are not correct?

   A $P = A(1 + i)^n$

   B $A = P(1 + i)^n$

   C $P = A(1 + i)^{-n}$

   D $P = A(1 - i)^n$

5. Show the growth of an $1000 investment, at 7% per year, simple interest, and at 7% per year, compounded annually, for 10 years. Use a table and a graph.

6. A credit card company charges interest at 18.5% per year, compounded monthly. Andrea has an unpaid balance of $768.42. If she does not pay off her balance and makes no further purchases, how much will she owe after

   a) one month?

   b) three months?

7. Brenda and Al have $5000 to invest at 6% per year, compounded quarterly. How long would it take for their investment to grow to $8000?

8. Erik needs to borrow $2000. Which loan should he take?

   A $2000 for three years at 10% per year, compounded semi-annually

   B $2000 for three years at 9.2% per year, compounded quarterly

   Justify your response.

9. If $4000 is invested for 10 years, what annual interest rate, compounded semi-annually, would double the money?

Chapter Problem Wrap-Up

In Section 8.1, you illustrated the growth of money the Kwans set aside to begin a business. In Section 8.3, you determined how much the Kwans needed to set aside to have money for business growth. In Section 8.5, you explained the effects of two compounding periods on their investments.

The Kwans are ready to sell their business for $250 000. They will invest the proceeds from the sale, along with the amounts of their investments in Section 8.5. Research current interest rates and provide a plan for the Kwans to invest their money in six different ways. Each investment should mature in a different year, over the next 10 years. Write a report for the Kwans and

include the details of their investments, as well as showing the growth of their investments each year until they mature.

10. Jeeva is 10 years old. His parents have decided to invest some money for his education, so that he will have $15 000 at age 18 when he goes to college. If the investment can earn 6.6% per year, compounded monthly, how much will his parents need to invest?

11. Use words, numbers, and graphs to illustrate the differences among investing $1000 for five years, at 4.5% per year, compounded

   a) annually   b) semi-annually
   c) quarterly   d) monthly

12. A perpetuity is an investment that continues forever, paying out the interest but leaving the principal untouched. The interest rate depends on the economy at the time. A school sets up a scholarship perpetuity with a donation of $50 000. The recipient receives a scholarship worth the amount of the interest earned in that year. The interest rates for the last five years are shown in the table.

Annual Interest Rate (%)	Compounding Period	Scholarship Amount ($)
8	semi-annually	
7.5	quarterly	
5.5	semi-annually	
7	semi-annually	
9	annually	

a) Find the amount of each scholarship.

b) What yearly interest rate, compounded annually, is necessary to guarantee a scholarship of at least $5000?

9 Personal Finance

Good financial sense will help you to achieve your personal goals. In this chapter, you will investigate the world of finance: banks and financial institutions, investing, and credit cards.

For many young adults, buying a vehicle is one of their first major purchases. Later in this chapter, you will look at the financial implications of obtaining and operating a vehicle.

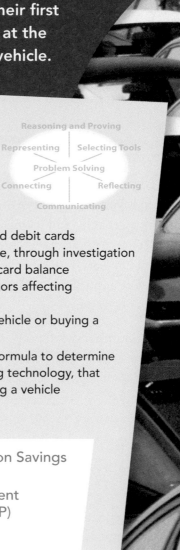

In this chapter, you will

- gather, interpret, and compare information about
  - the various savings alternatives commonly available from financial institutions, the related costs, and possible ways of reducing the costs
  - investment alternatives, and compare the alternatives by considering the risk and the rate of return
  - the costs and incentives associated with various credit cards and debit cards
  - current credit card interest rates and regulations, and determine, through investigation using technology, the effects of delayed payments on a credit card balance
  - procedures and costs involved in insuring a vehicle and the factors affecting insurance rates
  - the procedures and costs involved in buying or leasing a new vehicle or buying a used vehicle
- solve problems involving applications of the compound interest formula to determine the cost of making a purchase on credit and solve problems using technology, that involve the fixed costs and variable costs of owning and operating a vehicle

Reasoning and Proving

Representing | Selecting Tools

Problem Solving

Connecting | Reflecting

Communicating

Key Terms

depreciation

fixed cost

growth rate

Guaranteed Investment Certificate (GIC)

mutual fund

Registered Education Savings Plan (RESP)

Registered Retirement Savings Plan (RRSP)

variable cost

After completing a two-year college course in business management-financial service at Humber College, Sonia took a job as a bank teller. Within a year she was promoted. In her new role as a personal banking officer, Sonia prepares, evaluates, and processes loan applications. Understanding and applying formulas are important skills in her job.

Prerequisite Skills

Decimals

1. Use a calculator to evaluate.

   a) 6.3×2.1

   b) 7×3.04

   c) $10\,000(0.06)(9)$

   d) $500(0.02)(6.5)$

   e) $450 + 450(0.075)(0.25)$

   f) $6750 + 6750(0.035)$

2. Evaluate.

   a) $0.08 \div 2$ **b)** $0.055 \div 4$

   c) $0.072 \div 3$ **d)** $0.06 \div 4$

   e) $0.085 \div 10$ **f)** $0.09 \div 12$

Percents

3. Convert each percent to a decimal.

   a) 16% **b)** 7%

   c) 4.9% **d)** 0.9%

   e) -2.85% **f)** 28.8%

4. Estimate each value. Explain your thinking.

   a) 8% of 750 **b)** 8.5% of 5000

   c) 11% of 1900 **d)** 2.4% of 1800

   e) 0.9% of $25\,000$ **f)** 2.5% of $10\,000$

5. Evaluate without the aid of a calculator.

   a) 10% of 3500 **b)** 5% of 3500

   c) 1% of 160 **d)** 2% of 160

   e) 25% of $10\,000$ **f)** 2.5% of $10\,000$

6. Evaluate. Express your answer as a decimal.

   a) $8\% \div 4$ **b)** $9.6\% \div 3$

   c) $4.8\% \div 12$ **d)** $6\% \div 4$

   e) $18\% \div 12$ **f)** $11.2\% \div 4$

   g) $17.5\% \div 2$ **h)** $15.9\% \div 12$

Exponents

7. Evaluate without the aid of a calculator.

   a) 2^4 **b)** 3^3

   c) $(1.2)^2$ **d)** 1^{50}

   e) $(0.5)^3$ **f)** 0^{365}

8. Evaluate with the aid of a calculator.

   a) $(1.9)^4$ **b)** $(2.95)^3$

   c) $(1.25)^2$ **d)** $(0.9)^{50}$

   e) $(0.55)^3$ **f)** $(0.07)^3$

Compound Interest

9. For each annual rate, r, determine i, the interest rate per compounding period. Round answers to four decimal places, where necessary.

	r (%)	Compounding Frequency	i
a)	9	monthly	
b)	16.9	quarterly	
c)	−4.65	semi-annually	
d)	1.8	quarterly	
e)	0.5	monthly	
f)	28.8	daily	

10. Determine n, the number of compounding periods, for each situation.

   a) quarterly compounding for three years

   b) monthly compounding for five years

   c) semi-annual compounding for four years

   d) daily compounding for six months

   e) daily compounding for two years

   f) monthly compounding for 45 years

11. Find the future value of an investment, FV, for each investment, PV. Use the compound interest formula, $FV = PV(1 + i)^n$, where i is the interest rate per compounding period and n is the number of compounding periods over the life of the investment.

   a) $2000 at 3% compounded annually for seven years

   b) $1000 at 9% compounded monthly for three years

   c) $500 at 4.8% compounded quarterly for one year

   d) $300 at 20% compounded daily for the month of September

12. Use a TVM Solver to evaluate each part of question 11.

Chapter Problem

Rhys is 16 years old and in grade 11. Like many teens, he goes to school, has a part-time job, and has other things he likes to do. He also has goals: to buy a car or a truck, to buy golf clubs, to go skydiving, to travel, to graduate high school. Fortunately, his parents taught him early about money—what it is, how it works, and how to use it to achieve his goals. In this chapter, you will see how some of these goals can be achieved.

Savings Alternatives

In order to achieve your financial goals, you will need to save money. If you are thinking of buying a car, saving for college, or getting your own place, understanding savings alternatives will help you get closer to meeting your goals.

Investigate

Tools

- computers with Internet access

Optional

- literature from financial institutions about available accounts

Savings Accounts From Financial Institutions

You can save your money in many places.

1. Copy and complete the table to compare the interest rate earned on $1000 deposited in savings accounts from three financial institutions (for example, a bank, a credit union, and an Internet bank).

Financial Institution	Name of Savings Account	Interest Rate the Account Pays	Interest Earned in One Month on $1000

2. Some institutions charge fees to customers for providing different services while some do not. Research the fees, if any, associated with each account chosen in question 1. Then copy and complete the table.

Financial Institution	Name of Savings Account	Fees for Routine Transactions	Fees for Making 10 Regular Transactions During One Month

3. Which account, from which institution, do you prefer? Explain why.

Example 1

Interest Earned on Accounts

Jodie received $530 from family members for her birthday. She plans to buy a car in the near future and she is putting all of the birthday money toward the purchase. On June 1, she opened a savings account and deposited the $530. The account pays an annual interest rate of 0.5% compounded daily.

 a) How much interest will Jodie earn in one month (30 days)?

 b) How much interest will Jodie earn in six months (183 days)?

Solution

Method 1: Use the Compound Interest Formula

 a) FV represents the future value of the investment, PV represents the present value of the investment, i represents the interest rate per period, and n represents the number of compounding periods.

$$PV = 530, n = 30, i = \frac{0.005}{365}.$$

$FV = PV(1 + i)^n$

$\quad = 530\left(1 + \dfrac{0.005}{365}\right)^{30}$

$\quad = 530.22$

Remember, i is the annual interest rate, r, divided by the number of compounding periods in a year.

Interest earned $= 530.22 - 530.00$

$\qquad\qquad\qquad = 0.22$

In one month (30 days), Jodie earned 22¢ in interest.

 b) $FV = PV(1 + i)^n$

$\quad = 530\left(1 + \dfrac{0.005}{365}\right)^{183}$

$\quad = 531.33$

Interest earned $= 531.33 - 530.00$

$\qquad\qquad\qquad = 1.33$

In six months, Jodie earned $1.33 in interest.

Method 2: Use a TVM Solver

 a) Determine the value of each TVM Solver variable.

$$PV = 530, n = 30, i = \frac{0.005}{365}$$

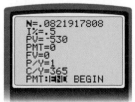

Remember that N is measured in years. 30 days is $\dfrac{30}{365}$ of a year. I% is the **annual** interest rate. PV is a negative value because the investment is money that you cannot use right now.

Move the cursor to FV and press ALPHA then ENTER to determine the future value of Jodie's investment.

```
N=.0821917808
I%=.5
PV=-530
PMT=0
■FV=530.2178515
P/Y=1
C/Y=365
PMT:END BEGIN
```

Interest earned = $530.22 − $530.00   Interest earned is the difference between the future and present values.

Jodie earned 22¢ in interest in one month.

b) To determine the value of her investment in six months, change N to $\frac{183}{365}$ and determine FV.

```
N=.501369863
I%=.5
PV=-530
PMT=0
■FV=531.3302877
P/Y=1
C/Y=365
PMT:END BEGIN
```

There are 183 days in a six-month period.

Interest earned = $531.33 − $530.00
In six months, Jodie earned $1.33 in interest.

Example 1

Determine Service Charges

Hun's bank charges $5.95 for up to 10 transactions per month plus 75¢ for each additional transaction. In November, he made eight transactions; in December, he made 23 transactions. Determine the service charges deducted from Hun's account balance each month.

Solution

In November, Hun is charged $5.95, even though he made only eight transactions.

For December, Hun is charged $5.95 for the first 10 transactions and 75¢ for each of the remaining 13 transactions.

Service charge = 5.95 + (13 × 0.75)
         = 15.70

Hun is charged $15.70 for December's transactions.

Practise

For help with questions 1 and 2, refer to Example 1.

1. Use a TVM Solver to determine the future value of each amount deposited into a daily interest savings account.

   a) $2000 in an account that pays 1% interest per year for the month of April

   b) $3000 in an account that pays 1.5% interest per year for the months of July and August

   c) $1500 in an account that pays 0.25% interest per year for the months of October, November, and December

   d) $400 in an account for one year that pays 2.5% interest per year

   e) $500 in an account for one day that pays 1.75% interest per year

   f) $2500 in an account for one week that pays 1% interest per year

2. Evaluate each part of question 1 using the compound interest formula.

For help with questions 3 and 4, refer to Example 2.

3. A bank charges $6.95 for up to 12 transactions per month plus 75¢ for each additional transaction. Determine the fee for each number of transactions during the month of March.

   a) 14   **b)** 9   **c)** 21

   d) 0   **e)** 18   **f)** 26

4. Another financial institution charges $9.95 for the first 20 transactions per month plus $0.95 for each additional transaction. Determine the service charge for each number of transactions from question 3.

5. Use your answers from questions 3 and 4. Given your current banking needs, which account would serve you better? Explain.

Apply **B** •

6. Sabbi has $600 in a savings account. This account pays 3.25% interest per year, compounded daily. His financial institution does not charge a fee for transactions on his account. Use a TVM Solver.

   a) How much interest will Sabbi earn in the month of April?

   b) How much interest will he earn in one year?

   c) Explain why the answer to part b) is not equal to the answer to part a) multiplied by 12.

For questions 7 to 9, refer to the table.

Banking Option 1	Banking Option 2	Banking Option 3
$9.75 per month for the first 10 transactions; $1.25 for each additional transaction	$14.75 per month for the first 25 transactions; $1.25 for each additional transaction	$24.95 per month for an unlimited number of transactions

Literacy **Connect**

An insurance premium is the amount charged by an insurance company to insure a driver and vehicle.

7. In a typical month, Jack uses an automated bank machine (ABM) twice a week to withdraw cash from his chequing account. Each month, his car payment and his car insurance premium are automatically deducted from his account.

   a) How many transactions does Jack make in a typical month?

   b) Which banking option might be best for Jack?

   c) Calculate the total cost and the cost per transaction for each option.

   d) Suggest a way that Jack could reduce the banking fees that he pays each month.

Literacy **Connect**

Bi-weekly means occurring every two weeks.

Bi-monthly means occurring every two months.

Semi-monthly means occurring twice a month.

8. Alexa is paid bi-weekly by cheque. She usually uses her debit card two or three times per week.

   a) Which banking option might be best for Alexa? Explain.

   b) On October 1, when she went on-line to do her banking, Alexa noticed bank charge debits from her account by her bank for $9.75 and $7.50. Which banking option does Alexa currently use? Explain.

   c) How many transactions were made in Alexa's account last month? Explain.

   d) Calculate the total cost and the cost per transaction for Alexa last month.

9. Ling rarely carries cash. She prefers to use her debit card. She is paid weekly. Her pay is automatically deposited into her chequing account. Ling uses her debit card for everything from buying groceries to eating in restaurants. Ling estimates that she uses her debit card 15 times per week. She writes cheques occasionally.

   a) In a typical month, estimate the number of transactions Ling makes.

   b) Which banking option do you think that she uses? Why?

   c) Calculate the cost per transaction using your answer to part a).

   d) A friend suggests that Ling use a credit card for all her purchases instead of her debit card. Explain why you think her friend made this suggestion.

Chapter Problem

10. When Rhys was 15 years old, he got his first part-time job at a coffee shop. At that time he opened two savings accounts. He learned to "pay himself first." That is, after his pay was deposited into his first savings account, Rhys transferred 10% of his pay to his second account. This account was for long-term savings and investments.

   a) His first paycheque amount was $312.73. How much money did he transfer to his second account?

   b) How much remained in his first account?

   c) The second account paid 3.5% annual interest with daily compounding and had no service charges. Use a TVM Solver to calculate how much interest he would earn in 14 days.

   d) After two weeks, Rhys received his second paycheque for $286.91. How much did he transfer to his second account?

   e) How much money was now in his second account? (Assume that the interest earned in part c) had NOT yet been deposited into his account by the bank.)

   f) How much interest would he earn in the next 14 days?

   g) Estimate the total amount Rhys would have saved in this account in one year.

Extend

11. Rhys's father says that calling a savings account a "savings account" is misleading. It should really be called a "spending account." He says that if you really want to save you should get your money out of a bank account and invest it. What does Rhys's father mean by this statement? Use what you have learned in this section and your own research to help you explain.

9.2 Investment Alternatives

Mr. and Mrs. Johnson are concerned with their children's future. They initiate this discussion:

"OK, you're going to school, you're working, and you've got some money now. One day—I know, it's a long time from now—you may want to buy a house, go on a cruise, or retire with a million dollars, no, two million dollars. How can you create financial independence for yourself and your kids? Yes, I said your kids!"

How can learning about investments now help you in the future?

Investigate

Tools

- computers with Internet access

Optional

- printed materials from investment companies

mutual fund

- type of investment where people pool their money together to buy stocks, bonds, and other assets
- managed by an investment company that charges a fee

Mutual Funds

A **mutual fund** is one type of investment opportunity. To find information on a variety of mutual funds, go to *www.mcgrawhill.ca/links/ foundations11* and follow the links.

1. Choose four to six mutual funds. Look at the one-year rate of return for each fund.

   a) Which fund has the greatest **growth rate**? What is the growth rate?

   b) Which fund has the least growth rate? What is the growth rate?

   c) Explain why investing in a mutual fund might be considered risky.

2. How do the five-year or 10-year rates of return compare for the same funds?

3. Use the compound interest formula or a TVM Solver to calculate the approximate value of $1000 invested 10 years ago in these funds.

Example 1

growth rate

- the percent by which an investment increases (or decreases) in value over a given time

A One-Time Investment

A mutual fund has an average annual rate of return of 12.45%. The investment company charges 2% per year as a fee for managing the account. Suppose $1000 is invested for three years. Calculate the approximate value of the investment, assuming annual compounding. The future value of the investment will be an approximation since all conditions of the investment may not be known.

Solution

Method 1: Use the Compound Interest Formula

$PV = 1000, i = 0.1045, n = 3$

$$FV = PV(1 + i)^n$$
$$= 1000(1 + 0.1045)^3$$
$$= 1000(1.1045)^3$$
$$= 1347.40$$

The actual rate of interest earned is 12.45% – 2%, or 10.45%. So $i = 0.1045$.

The value of the investment is approximately $1347.40 after three years.

Method 2: Use a TVM Solver

$PV = 1000, i = 0.1045, n = 3$

I% is determined by the growth rate 12.45% minus the management fee of 2%.

Find the future value of the investment, FV.

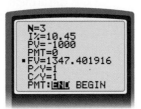

The value of the investment is approximately $1347.40 after three years.

Example 2

Literacy **Connect**

Risk is the uncertainty or the likelihood that an investment will decrease in value.

An Investment That Decreases in Value

Investing often carries an element of risk. Some investments increase in value while some decrease in value. A mutual fund has an average annual rate of return of -5.29%. If the investment company's fees for managing the account are 2% per year, calculate the

approximate value of a $1000 investment after two years, assuming annual compounding. The value of the investment will be an approximation since all conditions of the investment may not be known.

Solution

Method 1: Use the Compound Interest Formula

$PV = 1000$, $i = 0.0729$, $n = 2$

$$\begin{aligned} FV &= PV(1 + i)^n \\ &= 1000(1 - 0.0729)^2 \\ &= 1000(0.9271)^2 \\ &= 859.51 \end{aligned}$$

i is determined by converting $-5.29\% - 2\% = -7.29\%$ to a decimal, which is -0.0729.

The value of the investment is approximately $859.51 after two years.

Method 2: Use a TVM Solver

$PV = 1000$, $i = 0.0729$, $n = 2$

I% is determined by the rate of return of -5.29% minus the management fee of 2%.

Find the future value of the investment, FV.

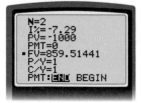

The value of the investment is approximately $859.51 after two years.

Example 3

Regular Investments

Many people set up an investment, such as a **Registered Retirement Savings Plan (RRSP)**, as a series of small, regular investments. Suppose you invest $200 per month from age 16 until your retirement at age 65. Assume the investment averages a 7% annual rate of return, compounded monthly. How much money will you have upon retirement?

Solution

N is now the number of payments. Monthly payments for 49 years is 12 × 49 = 588.

PV is the starting value of the investment, which is zero.

PMT is the value of each payment (i.e., investment), which is $200. It is negative since it is, for the time being, money out of your pocket.

FV is the future value of the investment. This is the variable that you solve for.

P/Y is the number of payments per year, which, in this case, is 12.

C/Y is the number of compounding periods per year, which, in this case, is 12.

PMT: END/BEGIN Set the payment to the END of each month.

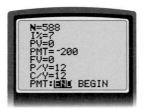

Find the future value of the investment, *FV*.

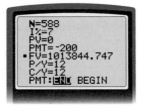

The future value is $1 013 844.75. By age 65, you will have an investment worth more than one million dollars!

Key Concepts

- All investments carry some level of risk. Generally, the greater the risk, the greater the potential return (or loss). Some investments increase in value while others lose value.

- One way to accumulate wealth is to invest regularly over a long period of time. This takes advantage of the power of compound interest.

Discuss the Concepts

D1. How can starting your investments when you are young benefit you when you are much older?

D2. Explain why some investments carry a degree of risk or uncertainty.

D3. How comfortable are you with financial risk? What risks do you take?

Practise **A**

1. Express each percent as a decimal.

a) 6%	**b)** 8%	**c)** 10%
d) 0.5%	**e)** 3.25%	**f)** 4.9%
g) −2.6%	**h)** 5.95%	**i)** 5.06%

2. Copy and complete the table.

	r (%)	Compounding Frequency	i
a)	9.0	monthly	
b)		quarterly	0.04
c)	−4.6	semi-annually	
d)	1.8		0.0045
e)	0.5	monthly	
f)	12.8		0.032

For help with questions 3 and 4, refer to Example 1.

3. Use the compound interest formula to determine the future value of each three-year investment. Assume interest is compounded annually and that each investment has a 2% management fee.

a) $1000 in a fund that averages 6.08% growth per year.

b) $5000 in an investment that averages 18.42% growth per year.

c) $2000 in a mutual fund that averages 2.27% growth per year.

4. Evaluate each part of question 3 using a TVM Solver.

5. Calculate the interest earned for each part of question 3.

For help with question 6, refer to Example 2.

6. One year ago, Jozef invested $2500 in a mutual fund that decreased in value by 4.92%. The fund has a 1.5% management fee. Determine the value of Jozef's investment at the end of one year.

For help with question 7, refer to Example 3.

7. When Meghdad was 17, he began investing $2000 per year in a no-fee investment that paid 3.8% interest per year, compounded monthly. Determine the value of Meghdad's investment after five years.

Apply B

8. a) Hafeeza invested $2000 in a mutual fund that increased in value in its first year by 1.92%. If there was a 2.5% management fee, determine the value of her investment after one year.

   b) Hafeeza decided to leave her money in the same fund. The next year, the fund had a rate of return of 8.83%. Determine the value of her investment at the end of the second year.

   c) Over a 10-year period, Hafeeza's original $2000 investment averaged 7.3% growth. After subtracting the annual management fees, what was the value of her investment?

Literacy Connect

Guaranteed Investment Certificate (GIC)
- a type of investment sold to individuals by banks or trust companies
- usually, GICs pay interest at a fixed rate and cannot be cashed before a specified date

9. To learn about **GICs**, go to *www.mcgrawhill.ca/links/foundations11* and follow the links.

   a) What does "GIC" mean? What is a GIC?

   b) Is a GIC a high-risk or a low-risk investment? Explain.

   c) Find the current annual interest rate paid for a 30-day GIC and calculate how much interest would be paid on a $1000 investment.

10. Pietra invested $1000 in a seven-year GIC that pays 4.10% annual interest compounded annually.

   a) Determine the value of the investment after one year.

   b) Determine the value of the GIC after two years.

   c) Express the future value of this investment as an exponential relation.

   d) Use the relation in part c) to determine the value of the GIC at the end of seven years.

   e) Graph the relation for the seven years.

11. a) Discuss with a partner. In your opinion, is each of the following investments low-risk, medium-risk, or high-risk? Explain your thinking.

   i) opening a savings account

   ii) buying units of a mutual fund

   iii) buying shares in an oil company

   iv) buying a GIC from a bank

   v) buying a hectare of land

   vi) investing in a friend's invention

   vii) buying shares in a bank

b) From the list in part a), which investment might provide the greatest return in the shortest time? Which investment might provide the greatest loss in the shortest time?

12. Kyoko just turned 30 and gave birth to a baby girl. She knows that when her daughter finishes high school, a post-secondary education will cost much more than it does today. Kyoko plans to put $10 per week into her daughter's **Registered Education Savings Plan** (RESP). In addition, the federal government will contribute 20% of the investor's RESP contribution each year up to a maximum of $400 per year.

a) How much will Kyoko have invested by her daughter's first birthday?

b) If Kyoko's investment earns 3.85% interest compounded annually in the first year, how much interest will it earn?

c) How much will the federal government contribute to the fund?

d) How much money will be in the fund after one year?

Registered Education Savings Plan (RESP)

• an investment set up to save for a child's education. The income from the plan grows tax-free.

Chapter Problem

13. After working at a coffee shop for 10 months, Rhys quit to accept a job at a grocery store that pays $2/h more. His new job pays weekly and he is now able to save about $25 per week. He buys his first GIC and is planning to make his first RRSP contribution in the near future.

a) If Rhys does no other investing in his life other than $25 per week from now until he is 65 years of age (a total of 49 years), how much money will he have if his investments average a 7% annual rate of return? Assume monthly compounding.

b) How much money will Rhys have invested over the 49 years?

c) How much interest will he have earned?

d) Rhys says that when he retires he will have "ten times more" than your answer to part a). If he continues to save 10% of his pay, explain why he might be correct.

14. Johanna bought an $800, three-year GIC with a variable rate. In the first year, the GIC pays 3.85% annual interest. In the second year, it pays 4.05% annual interest, and in the third year it pays 4.2% annual interest. All interest is compounded monthly. Calculate the value of the GIC at the end of the three years.

Achievement Check

15. A simple method for calculating the percent that should be invested in moderate- to high-risk investments is the Age Balance Indicator (ABI).

ABI = 90 − investor's age

For example, a 20-year-old investor should invest no more than 70% (90 − 20 = 70) of the investment amount in riskier investments. A 50-year-old should invest no more that 40%.

a) Using this method, the younger you are, the more risk you should take. Is this always true?

b) The ABI does not consider your current financial situation. What other factors are not considered?

c) Produce a scale for considering how risky the following investments are: blue chip stock, GICs, savings account at a bank, volatile stock, mutual funds, Canada Savings Bonds

d) "Generally, the higher the potential rate of return, the more risk an investor takes." This statement, taken with the ABI, says that the younger you are, the higher your potential rate of return. Do you agree or disagree?

Extend Ⓒ

16. Keisha has $1200 in a savings account. She is in grade 11. She is saving for her first year of college, which is two years away. While she wants her money to grow in value, she is not willing to risk having her savings lose value.

a) Given the investment alternatives explored in this section, what investments would you suggest Keisha choose? Research current interest rates to support your decision.

b) Under your plan, determine the value of Keisha's $1200 after two years.

c) Keisha's part-time job allows her to save $250 per month. Determine the value of 24 months of Keisha's savings if she uses the same investment plan that you chose in part a).

d) What is the total amount of money that Keisha will have after two years?

Good, bad, convenient, dangerous, safer than cash, scary, and *expensive* are common words that people use when describing their relationship with credit cards. All of the adjectives are right—depending on how the cards are used. In this section, you will begin to discover the good, the bad, and the ugly of using a credit card.

Investigate

Tools

- computers with Internet access

Optional
- printed materials about credit cards

Literacy **Connect**

An overdue balance is an amount that remains unpaid after the due date has passed.

Credit Cards

Choose two credit cards: one issued by a bank or other financial institution and one offered by a retailer (for example, an electronics store, a furniture retailer, or a gasoline retailer). Gather the following information about each card. Record your findings in a table or chart.

To learn about companies, their credit cards, and their policies, go to *www.mcgrawhill.ca/links/foundations11* and follow the links.

1. Is there an annual fee for holding the card? If so, how much is the annual fee?

2. What annual interest rate is charged on an overdue balance?

3. How often is the interest compounded?

4. How many days after the monthly statement is issued is the payment due?

5. How much interest is charged if the balance is paid in full by the due date?

6. Are there any incentives or rewards associated with being a cardholder?

Example 1

Read the Fine Print

The information found on the back of Ahmad's monthly statement for a credit card issued by his bank is shown.

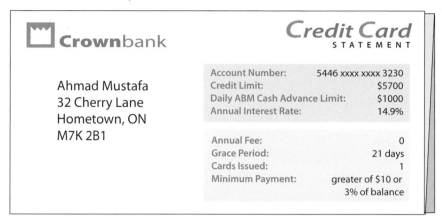

Account Number:	5446 xxxx xxxx 3230
Credit Limit:	$5700
Daily ABM Cash Advance Limit:	$1000
Annual Interest Rate:	14.9%

Annual Fee:	0
Grace Period:	21 days
Cards Issued:	1
Minimum Payment:	greater of $10 or 3% of balance

Ahmad Mustafa
32 Cherry Lane
Hometown, ON
M7K 2B1

a) A statement is issued to Ahmad on the 8th of each month. On what date will the payment be due?

b) On September's statement, Ahmad has a balance of $86.36. Determine his minimum payment.

c) On October's statement, Ahmad has a balance of $462.18. Determine his minimum payment.

d) If it takes three days to process his payment, what is the latest date that Ahmad can pay October's bill and not be overdue?

e) If interest is calculated and compounded daily, determine the daily interest rate. Round your answer to 4 decimal places.

f) Calculate the interest charged on October's bill if it is paid in full five days after the due date. Ahmad paid his September bill in full. He made one new purchase for $462.18 on September 15.

Solution

a) The payment will be due on the 29th of each month.

b) 3% of $86.36 is $2.59, so the minimum payment due is $10.00.

c) 3% of $462.18 is $13.87, so the minimum payment due is $13.87.

d) The bill should be paid no later than the 26th of the month.

If the balance is paid in full on or before the due date, no interest is charged.

e) $\dfrac{14.9\%}{365} = 0.0408\%.$

Remember that *i* equals the annual rate, 14.9%, divided by the number of compounding periods in one year, 365.

f) Unpaid balances are charged interest from the date of the purchase.

The interest charged during the month may exceed the minimum payment, which means that it will take a very, very long time to pay off the debt if only the minimum payment is made each month.

Method 1: Use the Compound Interest Formula

$PV = 462.18$, $i = 0.000\ 408$, $n = 49$

$$
\begin{aligned}
FV &= PV(1 + i)^n \\
&= 462.18(1 + 0.000\ 408)^{49} \\
&= 471.51
\end{aligned}
$$

The bill was paid on November 3. This is five days after October 29 and 49 days after the purchase date.

$$
\begin{aligned}
\text{Interest charged} &= 471.51 - 462.18 \\
&= 9.33
\end{aligned}
$$

Ahmad was charged \$9.33 in interest.

Method 2: Use a TVM Solver

Find the value of FV.

The interest is charged for 49 days, which is $\dfrac{49}{365}$ of a year.

So, $N = \dfrac{49}{365}$, or 0.134 246 575 3.

You are solving for the value of FV.

Move the cursor to the line FV=0 and press $\boxed{\text{ALPHA}}$ then $\boxed{\text{ENTER}}$.

$$
\begin{aligned}
\text{Interest charged} &= 471.52 - 462.18 \\
&= 9.34
\end{aligned}
$$

Ahmad was charged \$9.34 in interest.

Practise

For help with questions 1 to 9, refer to Example 1.

1. Calculate the daily interest rate for each credit card annual interest rate. Express each answer as a percent rounded to 4 decimal places.

   a) 17.9%

   b) 28.8%

   c) 13.9%

   d) 3.9%

2. Use each of the daily interest rates from question 1 and the compound interest formula to determine the future value of an overdue credit card balance of $1500 if interest is charged for 55 days.

3. Refer to question 2. Use a TVM Solver to answer each part of the question.

4. A statement for Kendra's credit card was issued on April 15. Her account offers a grace period of 14 days. It usually takes 3 days for transactions to be processed. Kendra paid her bill on May 19. For how many days will she be charged interest?

To answer questions 5 to 8, refer to Mia's credit card statement.

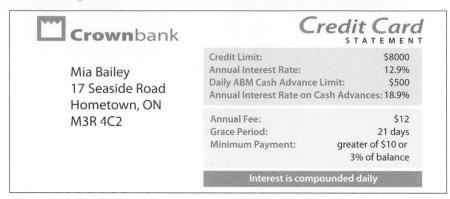

5. A statement is issued to Mia on the 18th of each month.

   a) What is the due date for the January 18 statement?

   b) What is the due date for the February 18 statement?

6. Determine the minimum monthly payment for each.

   a) Mia's December statement has a balance of $289.40.

   b) After using her credit card for all her holiday shopping, Mia's January statement has a balance of $1220.74.

Literacy Connect

7. Explain one advantage and one disadvantage of Mia using her credit card to make all her holiday purchases.

8. Determine each daily interest rate charged on Mia's credit card. Express each answer as a percent and as a decimal rounded to six decimal places.

   a) on cash advances   **b)** on credit card purchases

Chapter Problem

9. Rhys decides to apply for a credit card. His parents have to co-sign his application—that is, they agree to pay the outstanding balance if Rhys cannot or will not pay. On the application, they indicate that they want a spending limit of $250. A portion of Rhys's first credit card statement is shown.

Crownbank		Credit Card STATEMENT
STATEMENT FROM June 25 to July 26		
7/2	The Jeans Factory	48.00
7/7	T-shirt Haus	22.75
7/22	Soccer Unlimited	28.49

Previous Balance:	0.00	New Balance:	
Payments:	0.00	Minimum Due:	
Overdue Balance:	0.00	Statement Date:	July 26
Interest Charged:	0.00	Annual Interest Rate:	16.9%
New Purchases:		Available Credit:	

a) Calculate the amount of the new purchases made this month, and Rhys's new balance.

b) If the minimum payment is $10 or 3% of the balance, whichever is greater, determine Rhys's minimum payment.

c) Determine the due date if payment is due 21 days after the statement date.

d) What are the likely reasons that Rhys's parents asked for a $250 credit limit?

e) Calculate the daily interest rate. Express the answer as a percent and as a decimal rounded to five decimal places.

f) Four days after he received the statement, Rhys went on-line and paid the balance. How much interest was he charged?

Extend

10. Terrell has four credit cards: two issued by banks, one from a gasoline retailer, and one from a furniture store. The table shows his current credit situation.

Credit Card	Balance as of July 1	Annual Interest Rate	Minimum Payment Due
Bank 1	$2527	13.9%	3% of balance
Bank 2	$4318	14.9%	3% of balance
Gasoline Retailer	$227	18.9%	$20
Furniture Retailer	$1308	28.8%	$100

a) Calculate Terrell's current debt.

b) Calculate the total of the minimum payments that he must make this month.

c) Assuming no other purchases are made, calculate the total interest charged on each account for 30 days. All the credit cards compound interest daily.

d) Which credit card should Terrell pay in full first? Why?

e) A credit counsellor advises Terrell to get a personal loan from his bank, pay off all of the credit cards, and then destroy the cards. Using his TVM Solver, he shows the results of his analysis to Terrell.

```
N = 36
I% = 10.50
PV = 8380
PMT(solved) = −272.37
FV = 0
P/Y = 12
C/Y = 12
PMT:END
```

Use the words *monthly payment*, *debt*, and *interest* to explain the meaning of the numbers on the screen in terms of Terrell's monthly payment and how long it will take him to get out of debt.

Obtain a Vehicle

Used cars are less expensive to buy and less expensive to insure. New cars can be bought or leased. Depending on your situation, there are advantages to buying or leasing. The initial costs for obtaining a new vehicle are usually greater than those for obtaining a used vehicle.

Investigate

Tools

- classified advertisements in a newspaper
- used vehicle magazines
- telephone
- telephone book

Optional
- computers with Internet access

Literacy ⟩ **Connect**

A certified vehicle is one that has passed a safety inspection by a mechanic.

A lease is a long-term rental agreement.

Research Vehicles for Sale

Choose one or two vehicles that interest you. Your choices should be realistic for your current financial situation.

1. Use advertisements, phone a local car dealership, or use the Internet to obtain the cost of buying and/or leasing a new vehicle.

    Ask:
    - What features are included? (For example, air conditioning or a CD player.)
    - Are other options available?
    - Is the price quoted with or without taxes?
    - Are there other costs involved in obtaining the vehicle?

2. Use classified advertisements in your local newspaper, local used vehicle magazines, or the Internet to find used models of the vehicles you chose.

    Ask:
    - Is the vehicle certified?
    - Has the vehicle ever been involved in a collision? If so, ask for details.
    - How many kilometres has the car been driven?
    - Is the price negotiable?

Example 1

Buy a New Vehicle

A local dealership is selling a new compact car for $17 995 plus taxes. The dealership offers financing at 4.9% annual interest, compounded monthly, over four years. You have saved $3000 for a down payment. You will finance the rest. What will be your monthly payment?

Solution

First, you need to calculate the after-tax cost of the car. Car dealerships charge PST and GST.

On some calculators, you can enter
17 995 [+] 14 [%] [×] 17 995 [=].
On all calculators, you can enter 17 995 [×] 1.14 [=].
The total cost of the vehicle is $20 514.30.

The amount to be financed is the total cost less the down payment.
Financed amount = $20 514.30 − $3000
                = $17 514.30

Use a TVM Solver or an on-line calculator to determine the monthly payment.

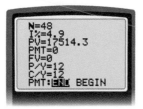

N is the number of payments. Monthly payments for four years is 48 payments.

PV is the amount that was borrowed.

PMT is the value of each payment. It is a negative amount since it is money you cannot use right now.

FV is the future value of the loan after four years have passed, i.e., 0.

P/Y is the number of payments per year. In this case it is 12.

C/Y is the number of compounding periods per year. In this case it is 12.

PMT: END/BEGIN Set the payment to the END of each month.

Find the value of PMT.

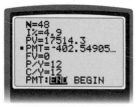

The monthly payment will be $402.55.

Example 2

Total Cost of a Vehicle

Refer to Example 1.

a) Determine the total amount paid for the vehicle.

b) Calculate the total interest paid.

Solution

a) Forty-eight payments of $402.55 need to be made to repay the loan of $17 514.30.

Loan repayment = 402.55 × 48
= 19 322.40

Total cost of car = loan repayment + down payment
= 19 322.40 + 3000
= 22 322.40

The total amount paid for the vehicle is $22 322.40.

b) Interest paid = total amount paid for the car − original price of car
= 22 322.40 − 20 514.30
= 1808.10

The total interest paid is $1808.10.

Example 3

Lease a New Vehicle

Leasing a vehicle is basically entering into a long-term rental agreement. You drive the car but you do not own it. To lease a new car selling for $24 000, a customer agrees to pay a $1000 down payment and to make 48 monthly payments of $369.

a) Calculate the total cost of leasing the vehicle.

b) Calculate the average cost per month over the life of the lease.

Solution

a) Total cost = down payment + monthly payments
= 1000 + (48 × 369)
= 1000 + 17 712
= 18 712

The total cost of leasing the car for four years will be $18 712.

b) 18 712 ÷ 48 = 389.83

The average cost per month, over the life of the lease, is $389.83.

Example 4

Buy a Used Vehicle

A used car will cost much less than a new model of the same car. Sometimes, a used car loan will have a shorter payback period than a loan for a new car. A car is advertised for sale in a local newspaper for $4500.

a) Determine the total cost of the vehicle with 8% PST.

b) Use a TVM Solver or an on-line calculator to determine the monthly payment for a $5000 loan at 8% interest, compounded monthly, for two years.

Solution

a) Cost with tax $= 4500 \times 1.08$
$= 4860$

> Most used vehicles sold privately are subject only to PST.

The total cost of the vehicle, including PST, is $4860.

b)

> N is the number of payments. Monthly payments for two years equals 24 payments.

The monthly payment will be $226.14.

Key Concepts

- Buying or leasing a new vehicle is a big expenditure.
- Often, buying or leasing a new vehicle involves making a down payment.
- A good used car will cost a lot less than a new model of the same car.
- Leasing a new vehicle is basically entering into a long-term rental agreement.

Discuss the Concepts

D1. Talk to 10 students who own vehicles. Where did they get the vehicle (for example, from a parent, a friend, or through a private sale)? Is there a pattern in their answers?

D2. Explain why buying a car is not an investment.

D3. Rolly says, "I think I'll get a motorcycle. It's way cheaper, and I mean more than just the payments." What do you think Rolly means by his last statement?

For help with questions 1 and 2, refer to Example 1.

1. Calculate the after-tax cost of the following new and used vehicles available at a local car dealership.

a) a two-year-old minivan selling for $22 995

b) a new sports car selling for $36 250

c) a five-year-old sports utility vehicle (SUV) selling for $17 999

d) a new compact car selling for $12 995

Use this information for questions 2, 3, and 4.

Three cases of financing a used car are shown. Assume interest is compounded monthly.

a) $4000 borrowed for three years at 9% interest

b) $8500 borrowed for four years at 8.5% interest

c) $15 000 borrowed for five years at 9.25% interest

2. Use a TVM Solver or an on-line calculator to determine the monthly payments for each case.

For help with questions 3 and 4, refer to Example 2.

3. Calculate the total amount paid to the financial institution for each loan.

4. Calculate the total amount of interest paid over the life of each loan.

For help with question 5, refer to Example 3.

5. Calculate the total cost of each new car lease.

a) a car worth $18 000 leasing for $1000 down plus 36 payments of $299

b) a minivan worth $23 500 leasing for 48 payments of $399

c) a luxury sedan worth $72 000 leasing for a $7500 down payment and 39 monthly payments of $899

For help with question 6, refer to Example 4.

6. Vehicles purchased from a private seller (e.g., your neighbour) are not subject to the goods and services tax (GST). Only the provincial sales tax (PST) is charged when you change the vehicle's ownership papers. Calculate the PST due on each used car purchase.

a) a nine-year-old compact car bought from a friend for $2500

b) a 12-year-old mid-size diesel car sold for $4200

c) a 33-year-old camper van with an appraised value of $300

Apply •••

7. Explain why three identical model vehicles of the same age, found in the classified advertisements of a local newspaper, could have three very different prices.

Literacy Connect

8. These words or abbreviations are commonly seen in advertisements for vehicles.

5-spd	auto	obo	PS	170K
AWD	e-test	PB	cert	PW
A/C	FWD	loaded	PL or PDL	'00

Work in a small group. Discuss the meaning of each term. Research the meanings of any terms you do not recognize.

9. To lease a new car worth $30 000, a customer agrees to pay a $1000 down payment and 48 payments of $525.

a) Calculate the total cost of leasing the vehicle.

b) Calculate the average cost per month over the life of the lease.

c) After 48 months, the customer returns the vehicle to the dealership. What options do you think that the customer has at this point?

Chapter Problem

10. Rhys cannot believe the cost for a young male driver to insure his own car, even with a driver-training certificate. Rhys would like to buy a five- or six-year-old pickup truck in two years when he graduates from high school. He has seen the model he wants on a used-vehicle Web site for $6500.

a) Calculate the after-tax cost of a vehicle worth $6500 purchased from a private seller.

b) Rhys decides to open a third savings account. This account has no user fees and pays 3.25% annual interest, compounded daily. How much money will Rhys need to save each week starting now to pay cash for the truck in two years?

c) Until Rhys buys his truck, he agrees to pay his parents the increase in the insurance premium when he is added to the family policy. He will also pay for all of the fuel that he uses. The increase to the family's insurance premium is $760 per year. Rhys estimates that he will spend about $20 per week on fuel. Approximately how much will it cost him to drive his parents' car each month?

11. Leasing an imported sports car requires a $5000 down payment and monthly payments of $695 for four years.

   a) Determine the total amount spent to lease the car.

   b) Calculate the average cost per month over the life of the lease.

- -

Achievement Check

Reasoning and Proving

Representing | Selecting Tools

Problem Solving

Connecting | Reflecting

Communicating

12. A band decides to buy a mini-van to transport their equipment. They find a van at a used vehicle dealership. The dealer paid $5000 for the van and made some needed repairs: he spent $185 for new brakes, replaced all four tires at $125 per tire, replaced a window for $600, and cleaned the van.

   a) If the dealer wants to make a 10% profit on the sale, how much will he charge for the van?

   b) A parent of a band member agrees to lend them money to pay for the van. If she asks for no interest and wants the loan paid back in one year, how much is the monthly payment?

   c) If you are advising the group about the cost of buying the van, what other operating expenses should you point out?

Extend **C** -

13. Research the costs of leasing and buying a new vehicle of your choice.

   a) Compare the initial costs, including the down payments.

   b) Compare the monthly payments.

   c) Compare the total cost over the life of the lease or loan.

   d) Describe two advantages to leasing a new car over buying the car.

   e) Describe two advantages to buying a new car over leasing the car.

14. A local car dealer wants to sell all his current new vehicles before the next year's models are available. He is offering 0.9% financing for 48 months. A small pickup truck is selling for a pre-tax price of $22 180 plus transport and PDI charges of $1100.

   a) Research the meaning of PDI. Explain what it means.

   b) Determine the cost of the truck, after taxes, with transport and PDI charges included.

   c) Determine the monthly payment for a customer who pays a $5000 down payment and finances the rest.

   d) Determine the total amount spent to purchase the vehicle in part c).

   e) As vehicles get older, they lose their value. If the truck loses 15% of its value each year, how much will the truck be worth once the loan is paid in full?

9.5 Operate a Vehicle

Once you obtain a vehicle of your own, the expenses really start to mount. You are now the principal driver so your insurance costs go up—sometimes they go way up! You drive more so your fuel costs go up. In addition, you are making payments on something that is losing value every day that you drive it.

Investigate 1

fixed cost
• an expense that remains the same from one month to the next

variable costs
• an expense that varies in amount or frequency

Operating Expenses

Brianna is in her first year of college. She lives about 10 km from the campus. She just purchased her first car: a five-year-old compact for $5500. Brianna had some money saved for a down payment and borrowed $4000 from her credit union.

With a partner, brainstorm the expenses that Brianna is likely to incur over the next 12 months and then estimate the costs. Separate the costs into **fixed costs** and **variable costs**.

Investigate 2

Tools
■ computers with Internet access

Automobile Insurance

1. Find out about different insurance companies, the cost of car insurance, and the types of coverage you can purchase. Go to *www.mcgrawhill.ca/links/foundations11* and follow the links. Complete an on-line quote for the purchase of a six-year-old compact car with a value of $4000.

2. Make a list of the factors that affect the amount that someone pays to insure himself/herself and the vehicle. Given your situation right now, list the factors that are in your favour for lower insurance costs.

Example 1

Insure a Vehicle

Ralf is 19 and single, and he owns a seven-year-old mid-sized car. He called several insurance agents and the lowest quote he received was $2620/year. There are two payment options: he can pay the insurance premium in full once a year, or he can make monthly payments of $230.

a) Calculate the annual cost if he chooses the monthly instalments.

b) Calculate the difference between the two payment methods.

c) Suggest reasons why Ralf might choose each option.

Solution

a) Total monthly payments $= 230 \times 12$
$$= 2760$$

If Ralf pays monthly, then after a year he will have paid $2760 for insurance.

b) Difference between payments $= 2760 - 2620$
$$= 140$$

The difference between paying once and paying monthly is $140.

c) Choosing the one-time annual payment is less expensive in the long run but choosing the monthly payments allows Ralf to pay smaller amounts, which is more affordable.

Example 2

Calculate Fuel Costs

DeVaughan's truck has a 76-L fuel tank and a fuel efficiency rating of 11.8 L/100 km.

a) Explain what the fuel efficiency rating on DeVaughan's truck means.

b) How far can DeVaughan's truck travel on one tank of fuel?

c) How much fuel would his truck use on a 450-km trip?

d) Explain how to determine the cost of the fuel for the trip in part c).

Literacy **Connect**

Fuel efficiency is a measure of how far a vehicle travels per unit of fuel. Common units of fuel efficiency are litres per 100 km (L/100 km) and miles per gallon (mpg).

Solution

a) Under normal driving conditions, DeVaughan's truck will use approximately 11.8 L of gas to travel 100 km. A vehicle that uses less fuel to travel 100 km is more fuel-efficient.

b) $\dfrac{11.8 \text{ L}}{100 \text{ km}} = \dfrac{76 \text{ L}}{\blacksquare \text{ km}}$ Use a proportion.

$\blacksquare = \dfrac{76 \times 100}{11.8}$

$\blacksquare \doteq 644.07$

DeVaughan's truck can travel approximately 644 km on one tank of gas.

c) $\dfrac{11.8 \text{ L}}{100 \text{ km}} = \dfrac{\blacksquare \text{ L}}{450 \text{ km}}$

$\blacksquare = \dfrac{11.8 \times 450}{100}$

$\blacksquare \doteq 53.1$

DeVaughan's truck will use approximately 53 L of gas for the trip.

d) The cost of the fuel will be 53 times the current price of one litre of gas.

Example 3

Depreciation

A new mid-sized vehicle sells for $21 135. Marizia researched used cars of the same model and found the following information.

Age of Vehicle (years)	Average Selling Price ($)
1	16 000
2	12 750
3	11 000
4	9 800

depreciation
• the amount that the value of an item decreases over time

a) Calculate the **depreciation** of the vehicle during the first year, in dollars.

b) Calculate the depreciation after one year, as a percent of the new vehicle price.

c) Calculate the depreciation after four years, as a percent of the new vehicle price.

Solution

a) Depreciation = new car price − value after one year

$$= 21\ 135 - 16\ 000$$
$$= 5135$$

The vehicle depreciated by $5135 in the first year.

b) Percent depreciation $= \dfrac{\text{actual depreciation}}{\text{new car price}} \times 100$

$$= \frac{5135}{21\ 135} \times 100$$
$$= 24.3$$

5135 [÷] 21 135 [%] [=] 24.3

The vehicle depreciated about 24% after the first year.

c) Actual depreciation $= 21\ 135 - 9800$

$$= 11\ 335$$

Percent depreciation $= \dfrac{11\ 335}{21\ 135} \times 100$

11 335 [÷] 21 135 [%] [=] 53.6

The vehicle depreciated about 54% after the fourth year.

Key Concepts

- Fixed costs are expenses that remain the same from one month to the next; variable costs are expenses that vary in their amount or their frequency.
- Depreciation is the amount by which a vehicle loses value over time.
- One of the major expenses for drivers is insurance. This is especially true for young drivers.

Discuss the Concepts

D1. Why do you think that young male drivers pay more, on average, for car insurance than young female drivers?

D2. Your neighbour owns a 1959 Ford Thunderbird, which is in mint condition and rare. Is this vehicle an expense or an asset? Explain.

For help with questions 1 and 2, refer to Example 1.

Use this information for questions 1 and 2.

Many insurance companies give customers a quote for the cost of insurance for one year. Most companies have payment plans.

Three cases are shown.

a) Vic's insurance company quotes him an annual insurance cost of $1948 or a payment plan of $169 per month.

b) Faith receives an annual insurance quote of $466. The company offers her an option of quarterly instalments of $118.

c) Ramon is 19 and owns a sports car. His insurance company quotes him an annual insurance fee of $3780 and offers him weekly instalments of $74.42.

1. Calculate the difference between the annual fee and the total cost of the instalments in each case.

2. For each case, which payment option would you choose? Explain your choice.

For help with questions 3 and 4, refer to Example 2.

Use this information for questions 3 to 5.

	Vehicle	Tank Size (L)	Fuel Efficiency (L/100 km)
a)	motorcycle	14	1.4
b)	sub-compact car	30	5.9
c)	mid-sized sedan	55	7.8
d)	minivan	75	10.2
e)	full-sized van	92	13.5

3. Use the current price of 1 L of regular gasoline to calculate the cost to fill the tank of each vehicle.

4. Determine the distance that each vehicle can travel on one full tank of gas.

5. In the United States, fuel is sold in gallons. One US gallon is approximately equal to 3.785 L. Determine the number of US gallons required to fill the tank of each vehicle.

6. Categorize each automobile expense as either a fixed expense or a variable expense. Explain your choice.

    a) lease payment

    b) parking fines

    c) insurance

    d) gasoline

    e) depreciation

    f) loan repayment

    g) licence plate sticker

    h) oil changes

    i) bridge tolls

    j) monthly parking permits

For help with questions 7 and 8, refer to Example 3.

7. Calculate the depreciation on each vehicle.

    a) A new car worth $14 595 sells for $12 259 one year later.

    b) An SUV worth $52 999 can be purchased for $43 000 one year later.

    c) A one-year-old minivan can be bought for $18 500. New, it sold for $22 950.

8. Refer to question 7. Calculate the first-year depreciation for each vehicle as a percent of its original selling price. Round your answer to the nearest percent.

Apply **B** ·

9. Maurice spent about $1200 on vehicle maintenance last year. This year he expects to pay 10% more on maintenance. How much should Maurice budget for maintenance this year?

10. Rather than measuring their vehicle's fuel efficiency in litres per 100 km, some drivers choose to use kilometres per litre—the distance the vehicle will travel using 1 L of fuel. Calculate the fuel consumption, in kilometres per litre in each case. Round your answers to one decimal place.

    a) When Rado filled his car's tank last week, it took 47.6 L. His trip odometer read 622 km.

    b) On a weekend vacation, Sharlee used 32.8 L to travel 385 km.

    c) Steve's diesel sedan travelled 1070 km on 54.6 L of diesel.

Chapter Problem

11. A new model of the pickup truck Rhys wants costs $24 500. On average, this model of truck depreciates 21% per year. Rhys plans to buy a truck in two years after he graduates from high school.

a) Determine the value of a one-year-old model of this truck.

b) In two years, Rhys plans to save approximately $6000 for a vehicle. What age of pickup truck should he look for? Show calculations to explain your answer.

12. Many students who live in larger cities choose to purchase a scooter rather than a car. Research the costs of purchasing and operating (insurance, fuel consumption, depreciation, regular maintenance, and repairs) a 125-cc scooter.

Achievement Check

Reasoning and Proving
Representing · Selecting Tools
Problem Solving
Connecting · Reflecting
Communicating

13. The value of an SUV worth $48 000 depreciates by 18% each year.

a) Determine the value of the SUV after five years.

b) Express the depreciated value of the vehicle as an exponential relation. Graph this relation for the first five years.

c) Use the equation from part b) to determine the value of the SUV when it is 10 years old.

d) Explain why the purchase of an SUV should be considered to be an expense rather than an investment.

Extend C

14. During a vacation to South Carolina, Dylan kept these records. The currency exchange rate was 1 US$ = 1.18 CDN$.

Date	Odometer Reading (km)	Distance (km)	Fuel Use (US gallons)	Fuel Use (L)	Fuel Costs (US$)	Fuel Costs (CDN$)	Unit Fuel Cost (CDN$/L)	Fuel Efficiency (km/L)
Mar. 15	236 083	--------	------	------	-------	--------	--------	--------
Mar. 16	236 948		12.7		41.00			
Mar. 17	237 760		12.3		40.00			
Mar. 22	237 897		2.6		8.50			
Mar. 23	238 780		12.5		40.25			
Mar. 24	239 541		----------	42.9	-------	42.85		

a) Copy and complete the table.

b) How many kilometres did Dylan travel during his vacation?

c) Calculate the average fuel consumption for the car in kilometres per litre and in litres per 100 km.

d) Calculate the total amount Dylan spent on fuel in Canadian dollars.

9.1 Savings Alternatives, pages 462–467

1. Mykela's bank charges her $11.50 per month for the first 12 transactions made against her chequing account and $1.25 for each subsequent transaction. Last month, she made 19 transactions.

   a) Calculate Mykela's total bank fees last month.

   b) Describe two things that Mykela could do to reduce her bank fees.

2. A daily interest savings account pays 0.25% interest per year when the balance in the account is under $5000.

   a) Use the compound interest formula to calculate the interest earned on a balance of $425 in a 31-day month.

   b) Use a TVM Solver to answer part a).

3. Calculate the interest earned on $425 in a 31-day month in a daily interest savings account that pays 3.50% interest per year.

9.2 Investment Alternatives, pages 468–475

4. Last year, Gail invested $4000 in a mutual fund. The fund had a one-year rate of return of 14.38%. The investment company charges Gail a 2.25% management fee. Calculate the current value of Gail's investment assuming that interest is paid at the end of the year.

5. Mohammed purchased a five-year GIC that pays 3.65% annual interest compounded annually.

   a) Express the future value of the GIC as an exponential relation.

   b) Use this relation to calculate the future value of the GIC at the end of the five-year period if he invests $2000.

   c) Use a TVM Solver to answer part b).

9.3 Manage Credit Cards, pages 476–481

6. Describe one advantage and one disadvantage of using a credit card.

7. Aiden had the brakes on his car repaired for $344. He charged the debt to his credit card on February 10. When he received his statement, he noticed a due date of March 5. He forgot all about the bill until he received the next month's statement. He paid the bill on April 3. The bank charges 16.9% annual interest compounded daily. How much interest did Aiden's mistake cost him?

9.4 Obtain a Vehicle, pages 482–488

8. You purchase a vehicle from your neighbour. Which tax is charged on the purchase?

9. A four-year lease of a hybrid car requires a $4500 down payment and monthly payments of $399.

   a) Determine the total cost of the lease.

   b) Calculate the average cost per month over the life of the lease.

10. Use a TVM Solver to determine each monthly payment. Assume interest is compounded monthly.

    a) $3000 borrowed for two years at 8.5% annual interest

    b) $10 200 borrowed for five years at 9% annual interest

9.5 Operate a Vehicle, pages 489–495

11. A luxury import dealership claims its vehicles retain 92% of their value each year.

    a) Determine the value of a three-year-old, two-door convertible that sells for $36 000 when new.

    b) Determine the value of a five-year-old, four-door sedan that sells for $87 000 when new.

12. Use the current cost of one litre of regular gasoline.

    a) Calculate the cost of filling a 45-L, mid-sized car.

    b) Calculate the cost of filling a motorcycle that has an 18-L gas tank.

    c) If the motorcycle travels an average of 425 km on one tank of gas, calculate the fuel efficiency in litres per 100 km and in kilometres per litre.

13. Some luxury vehicles have low rates of depreciation: they "hold their value well." The table shows the value of a new luxury sedan and the values of identical models of used vehicles up to three years old.

Age of Car (years)	Estimated Value ($)
new	67 000
1	58 960
2	50 705
3	43 600

    a) Calculate the decrease in value of the car between the first and second years.

    b) Express your answer to part a) as a percent. Round your answer to the nearest percent.

    c) What percent of its original value has the car lost over three years? Round your answer to one decimal place.

    d) Use your answer to part c) to find the average percent rate of depreciation for the three years. Round your answer to one decimal place.

    e) Use your answer to part d) to express the average depreciation of this vehicle as an exponential relation.

    f) Use the relation in part e) to predict the value of the sedan after 10 years.

For questions 1 to 4, choose the best answer.

1. Which annual interest rate will most likely be paid by a bank to customers with money in a savings account?

   A 1.0%   **B** 7.5%

   C 16.9%   **D** 28.8%

2. Which annual interest rate will most likely be charged by a bank to customers with money owing on a credit card account?

   A 1.0%   **B** 7.5%

   C 16.9%   **D** 28.8%

3. Which should not be considered an investment?

   A buying a GIC

   B buying a new car

   C buying shares in an oil company

   D buying a hectare of land

4. Which term is used to describe the amount by which an item loses its value over time?

   A asset

   B investment

   C depreciation

   D deflation

5. Suppose you invest $100 per month from age 16 until your retirement at age 65 and that this investment averages a 6% rate of return, compounded monthly.

   a) How much of your own money will you have invested over the 49 years?

   b) Use a TVM Solver to calculate how much money you will have upon retirement.

   c) How much interest will you earn?

6. Janis is 30 years old and has been making regular RRSP contributions for five years. She has about $14 000 in one mutual fund and about $9000 in another. Last year, the first fund had a 9.72% growth rate, while the second fund experienced a −2.98% rate of return. She pays a yearly 2% management fee for each fund. Assuming that interest is paid at the end of the year, determine the total value of her RRSPs.

7. Leasing a two-seater convertible requires a $2500 down payment and monthly payments of $339 for four years.

   a) Determine the total amount spent to lease the car by the end of the lease.

   b) Calculate the average cost per month over the term of the lease.

8. An eight-cylinder van has an 80-L fuel tank and a fuel efficiency rating of 12.2 L/100 km.

   a) Explain the fuel efficiency rating.

   b) How far can the van travel on one tank of fuel?

   c) How much fuel would the van use on a 425-km trip?

Chapter Problem Wrap-Up

Rhys wants to purchase a pickup truck sooner rather than later. Rhys still works about 25 h per week for $10.25/h. His average net pay each week is $250.

a) Each payday, Rhys transfers 10% to his long-term savings account. On average, how much does he transfer to that account each week?

b) Rhys transfers $120 each week to his third account, which is used for saving for the truck. How much more money will he have after one year than if he transferred $70 each week to this account? This account has no user fees and pays 3.25% annual interest, compounded daily.

c) How much of each week's pay is left for Rhys to use as he wishes?

---

9. Use a chart to organize your work.

a) For each category list the advantages and disadvantages of each option.

Savings:
- chequing account
- savings account

Making Purchases:
- credit card
- debit card

Obtaining a Vehicle:
- purchasing a new vehicle
- purchasing a used vehicle
- leasing a vehicle

b) List the advantages and risks (low, moderate, high) of each investment option.
- GICs
- mutual funds
- RRSPs
- RESPs

c) List the various expenses for obtaining and operating a vehicle. Classify each as a fixed cost or a variable cost. Provide an estimate of each cost.

Chapter 7: Exponents

1. Write as a single power, then evaluate.

a) $6^3 \times 6^2$ **b)** $10^8 \div 10^4$

c) $\left(\dfrac{1}{4}\right)^2 \times \left(\dfrac{1}{4}\right)^3$ **d)** $\dfrac{7^{11}}{7^9}$

e) $(2^5)^2$ **f)** $[(-1)^3]^8$

2. Evaluate. Express your answers as whole numbers or fractions.

a) $(-2)^{-2}$ **b)** 33^0 **c)** 5^{-3}

d) 2^0 **e)** 10^{-3} **f)** 135^{-1}

3. Show that this relation is exponential.

x	0	1	2	3	4	5
y	$\dfrac{2}{3}$	2	6	18	54	162

4. Which model (linear, quadratic, or exponential) would best describe each situation? Why? Match each description with a graph.

a) a runner slowing down by half her speed every 5 s

b) the speed of an airplane speeding up by 10 km/h each second

c) the path of a soccer ball when kicked

d) the population of a town that increases by 2% every year

A 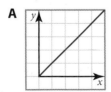   **B**

C   **D**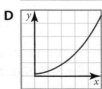

5. A fox population is declining by 1.8% per year. The population can be modelled using the formula $P = 210(0.982)^n$, where P is the population after n years.

a) Use technology to graph this relation.

b) What is the current fox population?

c) What is the expected fox population in 8 years?

6. The half-life of plutonium-238 is 87 years. The expression $1000\left(\dfrac{1}{2}\right)^{\frac{n}{87}}$ is used to calculate the number of milligrams remaining from the original 1 g after n years. Determine the number of milligrams remaining after

a) 6 months   **b)** 25 years   **c)** 500 years

Chapter 8: Compound Interest

7. Use a table and a graph to determine the growth of a $1500 investment for 10 years at

a) 6% per year, simple interest

b) 6% per year, compounded annually

8. Evaluate each expression. Use a scientific calculator and round your answer to two decimal places.

a) $25(1.025)^3$ **b)** $300(1.0175)^{16}$

c) $25(1.025)^{-3}$ **d)** $300(1.0175)^{-16}$

9. A $3000 investment earns interest at 5% per year compounded quarterly for ten years.

  a) What is the value of the investment after one year? two years?

  b) What is the interest earned in the fifth year?

10. Calculate the present value of each amount.

  a) $4000 needed in two years, invested at 5.5% per year compounded annually

  b) $2000 needed in two years, invested at 4% per year compounded semi-annually

  c) $12 500 needed in seven years, invested at 7.5% per year compounded quarterly

11. What interest rate, compounded monthly, will triple the value of an investment after

  a) 12 years?   **b)** 15 years?   **c)** 20 years?

12. Compare the graphs of $A = 500(1.045)^n$ and $A = 500(1.06)^n$. How does changing the compound interest rate from 4.5% to 6% affect the shape of the graph? What does this mean in terms of the value of the investment?

Chapter 9: Personal Finance

13. A bank charges $4.95 for up to ten transactions per month plus 50¢ for each additional transaction. Determine the fee for each number of transactions during the month of April.

  a) 0   **b)** 14   **c)** 2
  d) 20   **e)** 17   **f)** 24

14. Celia bought a $750, three-year GIC. In the first year, the GIC pays 3.5% annual interest. In the second year, it pays 3.8% annual interest. In the third year, it pays 5.25% annual interest. All interest is compounded monthly. Calculate the value of Celia's GIC after three years.

15. Use the compound interest formula to determine the future value of an overdue credit card balance of $652 if interest is compounded daily for 25 days at
  • 16.9% annual interest
  • 18.5% annual interest

16. Calculate the total cost of each new car lease.

  a) a $16 500 car leasing for a $1650 down payment and 36 payments of $349

  b) a $24 990 sedan leasing for monthly payments of $499 for 4 years

17. Veronica's truck has a 68-L fuel tank and a fuel efficiency rating of 12.5 L/100 km.

  a) How far can Veronica's truck travel on one tank of fuel?

  b) How much fuel would her truck use driving from Ottawa to Sudbury (607 km)?

18. Calculate the depreciation on each vehicle.

  a) A $13 895 new car sells for $11 500 one year later.

  b) A one-year-old SUV can be bought for $44 400. New, it sold for $51 699.

Organise Your Personal Finances

Suppose you have finished college and find a job. You earn an annual salary of $32 500.

1. Now that you are working, you have decided to establish a credit rating. You know one way to do this is to apply for (and use) a credit card. Gather information on the credit cards offered by several financial institutions or retailers. Read the small print on the application forms carefully. Credit card interest rates, annual fees, and rewards or special offers vary. Choose one or two credit cards that offer the best deal for you. Explain your choice. Be sure to address these points:
   - What is the minimum annual income needed to apply for the card (if any)?
   - What are the initial and annual fees (if any)?
   - What special features or rewards are offered with the card?
   - What interest rate is charged on an unpaid balance?
   - What happens if you pay the entire balance by the due date?
   - Can you get a cash advance?
   - How is the interest calculated on purchases? on cash advances?
   - What are the security features of the card?
   - What steps should you take if your card is lost or stolen?

2. You have decided to buy or lease a vehicle. Experts recommend that you spend no more than 15% of your income on transportation. Choose a vehicle you like and could afford to own or lease given your income above.

   a) Did you choose to buy a new vehicle, lease a new vehicle, or buy a used vehicle? Explain.

   b) Calculate the cost of buying the vehicle or the conditions of the lease.

   c) Describe how you will finance the purchase or lease, including a payment schedule.

   d) If you choose leasing, how many kilometres can you drive per year without being charged an additional fee?

   e) Set up a monthly budget for the costs of operating the vehicle. Include your calculations and assumptions.

3. Now that you have a regular income, you have decided to "pay yourself first" by saving some of your money. Experts recommend saving a minimum of 10% of your income. Research a variety of investment options. Decide what goals you have for your savings. Choose three investments that would help you reach your goals. Explain your choices. Be sure to address these points:

   - Are your goals long term or short term?
   - For how many years will you be investing your money?
   - What are the interest rates offered by the investments you have chosen?
   - What is the doubling time for your investment choices?

Chapters 1 to 9   Review

Chapter 1: Trigonometry

1. Solve each right triangle.

a)

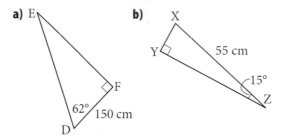

b)

2. A fisherman wants to make sure his boat is anchored safely. He knows that the angle of depression the anchor cable makes with the horizontal when the boat is anchored should be less than 12° to be safe. The boat is 100 m above the seabed and the anchor cable is 440 m long. Is the fisherman safely anchored? Explain.

3. Solve each triangle.

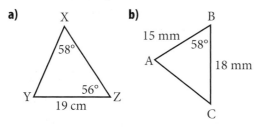

4. A square tarpaulin with a side length of 6 m is secured by rope to create a makeshift tent. The sides of the tarpaulin meet at an angle of 80° as shown. If the sun is directly overhead, what area of shade does the tarpaulin provide, to the nearest square metre?

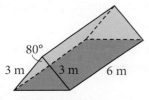

5. Which formula should you use to solve each triangle?

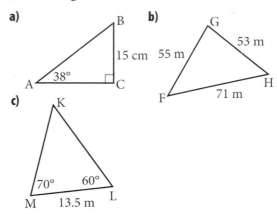

6. Refer to question 5. Solve the triangles.

Chapter 2: Probability

7. A customer service call centre manager decides to start a new training program for her employees if more than 2% of their callers in one day are dissatisfied with their service.

a) The manager surveys 340 callers and finds that none are dissatisfied. She expects 20 more callers. Is it possible that the employees will have to take the training program? Explain your reasoning.

b) If 360 callers were surveyed and 12 were dissatisfied, would the manager start the training program? Show your calculations to justify your answer.

c) The manager decides to repeat the survey the next day. If 33 out of 1000 callers are unsatisfied, and the manager only surveys 100, do you expect she will find the same results as in part b)? Explain your reasoning.

8. A hockey team is about to accept an award at a banquet. There are 18 players on the team; 2 goalies, 6 defencemen, and 10 forwards. A player is randomly selected to accept the award on behalf of the team.

  a) Find the probability that the player selected is a defenceman. Express your answer as a fraction in lowest terms.

  b) Find the probability that the player selected is a goalie or a forward. Express your answer as a fraction in lowest terms. Suggest two possible methods for finding the probability.

  c) If you know for certain that the player selected is not a goalie, find the probability that the player is a defenceman. Express your answer as a decimal.

9. When rolling two dice 40 times and adding the results, an even sum was obtained 10 times.

  a) What is the experimental probability of an even sum? Express your answer as a fraction in lowest terms.

  b) How does this compare to the theoretical probability?

  c) If the dice were rolled 40 more times, would an even sum turn up more frequently to "make up" for the previous rolls? Explain.

  d) Explain how you could use the **randInt(1,2,40)** command to simulate this experiment. Why does this work?

10. A government study has shown that 8 out of 10 collisions involve drivers who are drowsy, using a cell phone, or distracted. In one year, 11% of licensed drivers are involved in a collision.

  a) What is the probability that a driver involved in a collision was not drowsy, using a cell phone, or distracted? Express your answer as a fraction in lowest terms.

  b) What percent of drivers are not involved in a collision in one year?

  c) In one year, what percent of all drivers are involved in a collision and are drowsy, using a cell phone, or distracted at the time?

  d) In one year, what percent of all drivers will be involved in a collision and will not be drowsy, using a cell phone, or distracted at the time?

Chapter 3: One Variable Statistics

11. Choose the best sampling technique for each survey. Explain your choice.

  a) Ms. Donnelly wants to know what speakers would be the most interesting for career day.

  b) A librarian wants to know who is the most popular author.

  c) Byung wants to know how much Ontario college students pay for first-year tuition.

  d) Lynn wants to know what her classmates did over the summer holidays.

12. Identify the bias in each survey. Suggest how it might be removed.

a) A ski resort asks skiers: *What is your favourite winter activity?*

b) A TV show invites the studio audience to ask questions of the guests.

13. Classify each set of data as either discrete or continuous. Which type of graph would best suit each situation? Explain your choice.

a) the number of pets students have at home

b) the time it takes students to complete a 2-km run

14. Give an example of when the median is the best measure of central tendency of a set of data.

15. Find the mean, the median, and the mode of each set of data. Which measure of central tendency best describes the data? Explain.

a) the value of prizes, in dollars: 5, 5, 5, 5, 5, 5, 5, 5, 20, 20, 120

b) the masses of rabbits in a warren, in kilograms: 2.2, 3.7, 3.4, 2.4, 3.0, 3.7, 2.6, 3.5, 2.9, 3.8, 2.7

16. A set of data has a range of 55. The least value in the set of data is 168. What is the greatest value in the set of data?

17. Calculate the variance and the standard deviation for each set of data.

a) 4, 3, 5, 1, 17, 5, 1, 4, 2, 9, 2

b) 35, 44, 37, 41, 41, 36, 37, 40, 29, 38

18. Examine the histogram.

a) Could a circle graph have been used to display the data in the histogram? Explain.

b) What type of distribution is shown?

c) What does the shape of the curve tell you about the sales?

d) List three other facts you can gather from the histogram.

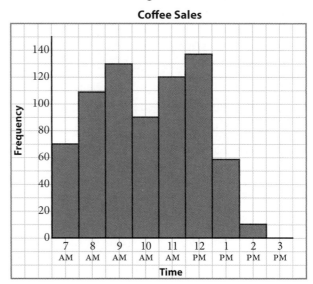

19. Create a set of data that would be modelled using a skewed distribution.

Chapter 4: Quadratic Relations I

20. Write a relation that models each table of values.

a)

x	y
−2	35.0
−1	27.5
0	25.0
1	27.5
2	35.0
3	47.5

b)

x	y
−2	−4
0	−2
2	−4
4	−10
6	−20
8	−34

21. A rock is thrown off a cliff. The path of the rock is modelled by the relation $h = -4.9t^2 + 1.5t + 115$, where h is the rock's vertical distance from the ground, in metres, and t is the time, in seconds.

a) Copy and complete the table of values.

Time (s)	Distance (m)
0	
1	
2	
3	
4	
5	

b) How can you tell that this relationship is quadratic? Give two reasons.

c) Graph this relation.

d) After how many seconds will the rock land?

22. Graph the data given in each table of values. Write a relation in the form of $y = a(x - h)^2$ that models each graph.

a)

x	y
−6	32
−5	18
−4	8
−3	2
−2	0
−1	2

b)

x	y
−1.0	−8.0
0.0	−4.5
1.0	−2.0
2.0	−0.5
3.0	0.0
4.0	−0.5

23. Graph each relation by plotting the vertex and two other points. Then draw a smooth curve through the points.

a) $y = (x + 1)^2 - 1$

b) $y = -0.8(x + 8)^2 - 3$

c) $y = -2(x - 6)^2 + 2$

d) $y = 3(x + 3)^2 - 2$

24. The manager of a local restaurant is trying to decide how much money to spend on advertising. She knows that an increase in advertising spending will increase her profit, up to a point. The situation is modelled by the relation $R = -0.0005(A - 5000)^2 + 12\ 500$, where R is the extra revenue and A is the amount spent on advertising, both in dollars.

a) Create a table of values and graph the relation.

b) What is the vertex of the parabola? What do the coordinates of the vertex represent in this situation?

25. Some types of powerful microphones use a parabolic reflector to direct sound waves into the receiver. One such microphone has a reflector that is 60 mm wide and 27 mm deep.

a) Write a relation to model the parabolic shape of the reflector.

b) Graph your relation.

Chapter 5: Quadratic Relations II

26. Expand and simplify.

   a) $(3x + 7)(8x + 2)$

   b) $(50 - x)(5x + 3)$

   c) $(x + 11)(100x - 10)$

   d) $(8x - 5)(8x + 5)$

27. Write an expression, in simplified form, for the area of this shape.

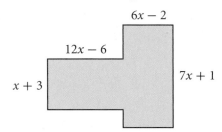

28. For each parabola, write a relation in standard form, $y = ax^2 + bx + c$.

   a) $a = 2$, $b = 6$, y-intercept is 11

   b) $y = 5x^2 + bx + c$, vertex at $(1, 4)$

   c) $a = -3$, passes through $(2, 11)$ and $(0, -5)$

   d) $y = 5x^2 + bx + c$, minimum of 0 when $x = -3$

29. Determine the y-intercept of each relation.

   a) $y = x(x + 12)$

   b) $y = (x - 2.4)(x + 5)$

30. Factor each polynomial.

   a) $x^2 - 17x + 66$ **b)** $x^2 + 8x + 7$

   c) $x^2 - 13x + 40$ **d)** $x^2 - 3x - 18$

   e) $x^2 + 13x$ **f)** $x^2 - 9$

31. Factor each trinomial fully. Expand to check.

   a) $2x^2 - 2x - 4$

   b) $-6x^2 - 12x + 144$

   c) $3x^2 + 3x - 126$

   d) $7x^2 + 42x - 49$

32. Which pairs of expressions are equivalent? How do you know?

   a) $3x^2 - 12x - 63$ $3(3 + x)(x + 7)$

   b) $7x^2 + 42x - 49$ $7(x + 7)(x - 1)$

   c) $4x^2 + 18x + 18$ $4(3 + x)(x + 1.5)$

   d) $-x^2 - x + 2$ $-(x + 1)(x - 2)$

33. Find the zeros of each quadratic relation.

   a) $y = (x + 3)(x - 3)$

   b) $y = 3(x - 14)(x - 1)$

   c) $y = -10x^2$

   d) $y = (x + 4)(x + 4)$

   e) $y = 8(x - 8)(x + 0.5)$

   f) $y = 20x(x - 9)$

34. A toy rocket is pumped full of air and released upward. Its height can be approximated using the relation $h = -10t^2 + 49.8t + 1$, where h is the height above the ground, in metres, and t is the time, in seconds.

   a) One of the zeros of the relation is -0.02. Does this zero mean anything in terms of the situation? Explain.

   b) What is the other zero? What does this zero mean in terms of the situation?

35. a) Write an expression, in simplified form, for the area of grass in this yard.

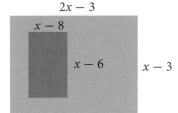
2x − 3
x − 8
x − 6
x − 3

b) The measurements are in metres. For what value of x will the area of grass be 111 m²?

Chapter 6: Geometry in Design

36. Sunflowers have many tiny flowers called florets arranged in a pattern on their heads. These florets create the appearance of many spirals, some opening clockwise and some counter-clockwise. Often the number of spirals in each direction exactly match the data shown in the table.

Sunflower Size	Number of Clockwise Spirals	Number of Counter-Clockwise Spirals
small	21	34
average	34	55
above average	55	89
very large	89	144

a) Calculate the ratio of counter-clockwise spirals to clockwise spirals for each sunflower size. Express each answer as a decimal to five decimal places.

b) What do you notice about these ratios?

c) An underdeveloped sunflower has 13 clockwise spirals. Use your answer in part b) to determine the number of counter-clockwise spirals. Round your answer to the nearest whole number.

37. Patterns are used in the design and manufacture of clothing. What other everyday objects are created from patterns?

38. A new tennis ball package is being designed to have a volume of 1200 cm³. Its height must be three times its diameter. The height and diameter must each be a whole number of centimetres.

a) Determine the minimum height and diameter of the can.

b) Select a suitable scale. Draw a net that can be used to make a scale model of the package.

c) Cut out your net and fold it to make a scale model of the package.

39. A garden designer is creating a layout for a backyard garden. The design must fit into a rectangle measuring 30 ft by 50 ft and each feature must be in the shape of a rectangle. The client would like each feature to be at least 5 ft away from any other feature. Each feature must have the area shown.

Garden Feature	Area (ft²)
flowerbed #1	50
flowerbed #2	150
garden shed	150
fountain	150
garden furniture area	150
pond	100

Design a garden that meets the specifications.

40. An architect wants to build a scale model of a rectangular palace that is to have a length of 310 m, a width of 200 m, and a height of 30 m. Suggest a suitable scale and calculate the dimensions for the model.

Chapter 7: Exponents

41. Write each expression as a single power. Then evaluate the single power.

  a) $4^1 \times 4^4$ **b)** $9^{31} \div 9^{28}$

  c) $\left(\frac{1}{2}\right)^4 \times \left(\frac{1}{2}\right)^3$ **d)** $\dfrac{11^6}{11^3}$

  e) $(3^3)^3$ **f)** $[(-2)^5]^2$

42. In 1957 an earthquake in Alaska measured about 9.0 on the Richter scale. An earthquake with magnitude 6.0 occurred in Japan in early 2007. How many times more intense was the earthquake in Alaska than the one in Japan?

43. Write each expression as a single power, then evaluate. Express your answers as whole numbers or fractions.

  a) $10^{-4} \times 10^3$ **b)** $(4^3)^{-1}$

  c) $\dfrac{5^{-1}}{5^{-3}}$ **d)** $\dfrac{1}{(3^{-1})^5}$

  e) $(-7)^{-4}(-7)^5$ **f)** $\left(\frac{1}{2}\right)^9 \times -\left(\frac{1}{2}\right)^{-10}$

44. a) Write $\dfrac{1}{20^7}$ as a power with a base of 20.

  b) Write 3^{11} as a power with a base of $\frac{1}{3}$.

45. Which relations are exponential? Explain how you know.

A

x	0	1	2	3	4	5
y	6	12	24	48	96	192

B

x	−3	−2	−1	0	1	2
y	1	2	4	8	9	15

C

x	1	2	3	4	5	6
y	125	25	5	1	0.2	0.04

46. a) Sketch the graph of each relation on the same set of axes. Check using a graphing calculator.

  A $y = 3^x$ **B** $y = 2(3^x)$

  C $y = 4(3^x)$ **D** $y = 0.5(3^x)$

  b) Describe the role of a in $y = a(3^x)$.

47. Which statement would best describe the graph?

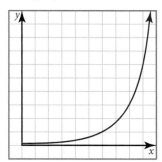

  A the number of pages of a 300-page document printed

  B the population of trout decreases by 5% every 10 years

  C the number of bacteria triples every 2 h

  D the height of a parachutist jumping out of a plane

48. Which model (linear, quadratic, or exponential) would best describe each situation in question 47?

49. A photocopier is set to enlarge an image to 150% of its original size.

   a) If you make a copy of the enlarged image and enlarge it to 150%, what percent of the original is the second image?

   b) How many times would you have to enlarge the image to 150% for it to be at least three times as large as the original? Explain.

50. Cells in a culture are growing by a factor of 2.7 per day. The number of cells in the culture can be estimated using the relation $N = 200(2.7)^d$, where d is the number of days.

   a) Use technology to graph the relation.

   b) How many cells does this culture begin with?

   c) How many cells would there be after 1 day? After 5 days?

51. The half-life of carbon-14 is 5730 years. The relation $C = \left(\frac{1}{2}\right)^{\frac{n}{5730}}$ is used to calculate the concentration, C, in parts per trillion, remaining n years after death. Determine the carbon-14 concentration in each item.

   a) a 1000-year-old wooden cup

   b) a 7500-year-old fly frozen in ice

   c) a 30 000-year-old fossil

Chapter 8: Compound Interest

52. Show the growth of a $4000 investment, at both 7.5% per year, simple interest and 7.5% per year, compounded annually, for five years, using a table and a graph.

53. Determine the value of a $500 investment after three years, at 7% per year, simple interest and 6.75% per year, compounded annually.

54. Evaluate. Use a scientific calculator and round to two decimal places.

   a) $100(1.06)^6$ **b)** $750(1.085)^{10}$

   c) $100(1.06)^{-6}$ **d)** $750(1.085)^{-10}$

55. To make a down payment, Orton borrowed $2400, at 7.5% per year, compounded semi-annually.

   a) How much must he repay after two years?

   b) How much must he repay after two years if he paid $1000 back after the first year?

56. A certain mutual fund has grown by an average of 10.4% per year, compounded annually, over the past eight years. How much would an initial investment of $3500 be worth today?

57. Evaluate. Round to two decimal places.

   a) $2500(1.02)^{-8}$ **b)** $8000(1.03)^{-5}$

58. What principal should be invested today to have $1000 after four years if interest is paid at 5.5% per year, compounded quarterly?

59. Calculate the discounted value of each loan.

a) a $700 debt due in one year, discounted at 6.5% per year, compounded semi-annually

b) a $4000 debt due in three years, discounted at 5.2% per year, compounded quarterly

c) a $2500 debt due in two years, discounted at 6% per year, compounded monthly

d) a $1000 debt due in 18 months, discounted at 8% per year, compounded semi-annually

60. Sandro needs to invest enough money today to have $7000 in three years, for a down payment on a condominium. How much should Sandro invest today, at 6.5% per year, compounded monthly?

61. Kai invests $950 today, at 9.5% per year, compounded semi-annually. After how many years will he have enough money to buy a $1400 scooter?

62. Rose borrowed $2000, at 7.6% per year, compounded quarterly. How much must she repay at the end of one year?

63. Harumi hopes to have $2500 in three years to visit New Zealand. Use technology to compare the amounts she would need to invest at 3.5% per year, compounded semi-annually and at 4% per year, compounded quarterly, to reach her goal.

64. Bethany plans to invest $4000 for two years. She has three choices.

A 5.45% per year simple interest

B 5.3% per year, compounded semi-annually

C 5.2% per year, compounded quarterly

How much interest would Bethany earn with each investment plan?

Chapter 9: Personal Finance

65. Determine the interest earned on each amount deposited in a daily interest savings account.

a) $1600 in an account for May that pays 0.5% per year

b) $350 in an account for May and June that pays 1% per year

c) $2200 in an account for 100 days that pays 0.65% per year

d) $3000 in an account for one year that pays 2.25% per year

e) $4000 in an account for one day that pays 1.75% per year

f) $1250 in an account for one week that pays 1.25% per year

66. Mustafa's credit card charges 17.5% annual interest on regular purchases and 19.5% annual interest on cash advances. Determine the interest due for each situation.

a) a balance of $244.85 for 21 days

b) a $2500 cash advance for 45 days

c) a balance of $642.11 for 3 days

67. When Behrooz started working full-time, he began investing $1500 per year in a no-fee investment that has paid 5.2% per year, compounded quarterly. Determine the value of Behrooz's investment after ten years (before his eleventh deposit).

68. One year ago, Terrant invested $3200 in a mutual fund that decreased in value by 2.74%. Given an annual 1.2% management fee, determine the current value of Terrant's investment.

69. Lisa's credit card requires a minimum payment of the greater of $25 or 5% of the balance. What is her minimum payment for each balance?

    a) $1439.19   **b)** $844.70

    c) $383.68   **d)** $1052.58

70. Bradley's credit card gives a refund of 0.5% on the first $3000 spent on the card, then 1% on further purchases. How much must Bradley spend in one year to recover the $29 annual fee for the credit card?

71. Three cases of financing a used car are shown. Use a TVM Solver or an on-line calculator to determine the monthly payments for each case, assuming monthly compounding.

    a) $5600 borrowed for three years at 8.75% interest

    b) $9000 borrowed for four years at 9% interest

    c) $14 750 borrowed for five years at 9.4% interest

72. Calculate the total amount paid to the financial institution for each loan in question 71.

73. Lang called several insurance agents for quotes on car insurance. The best offers were $2250 annually, monthly payments of $195, and payments of $1150 every 6 months.

    a) Calculate the annual cost of the monthly and semi-annually instalments.

    b) List the options from least to most expensive.

    c) Suggest reasons why Lang might choose each option.

74. Calculate the fuel consumption, in kilometres per litre, for each situation. Round your answers to one decimal place.

    a) Leo kept track of his mileage as a business expense. He travelled 1584 km and used 117.2 L of fuel.

    b) On a road trip, Sheila used 48 L of fuel to travel 600 km.

    c) A fuel-efficient car travelled 1230 km on one tank of fuel. The car used 62 L of gas.

75. Calculate the depreciation on the following vehicles.

    a) A new car worth $16 299 sells for $14 759 one year later.

    b) An SUV worth $56 850 can be purchased for $48 290 one year later.

Technology Appendix

Contents

The Geometer's Sketchpad®, Geometry Software Package

	page		page
Menu Bar	516	Constructing Triangles and Polygons	519
Creating a Sketch	516	Using the Measure Menu	519
Opening an Existing Sketch	516	Constructing and Measuring	
Saving a Sketch	517	Polygon Interiors	520
Closing a Sketch Without Exiting		Dilating and Rotating an Object	520
The Geometer's Sketchpad®	517	Changing Labels of Measures	521
Exiting *The Geometer's Sketchpad*®	517	Using the On-Screen Calculator	521
Setting Preferences	517	Coordinate System and Axes	522
Selecting Points and Objects	518	Creating Graphs	522
Hiding Objects	518	Loading Custom Tools	523

TI-83 Plus And TI-84 Plus Graphing Calculators

	page		page
Keys	524	Finding a Zero or	
Graphing Relations and Equations	524	Maximum/Minimum Value	530
Setting Window Variables	524	Using the Value Operation	531
Setting Up a Table of Values	525	Curves of Best Fit: Quadratic and	
Setting Up the Display	525	Exponential Regression	532
Tracing a Graph	525	Calculations Involving the Sine Law	532
Using Zoom	526	Calculations Involving the Cosine Law	533
Setting the Format	526	Generating Random Numbers	534
Changing the Appearance of a Line	527	THE TVM SOLVER	535
Entering Data Into Lists	527	About the Finance Applications	535
Creating a Scatter Plot	528	Opening the TVM Solver	535
Creating a Histogram	528	What the TVM Solver Variables	
Creating a Box-and-Whisker Plot	529	Represent	535
Line of Best Fit: Linear Regression	529	Investments and Loans (No Regular	
		Payments)	536

TI-89 Titanium Graphing Calculator

	page		page
Accessing the Home Screen	**537**	Collecting Terms with More Than One Variable in Terms	**539**
Clearing the Home Screen	**537**		
Clearing the Command Prompt Line	**537**	Collecting Terms with More Than One Variable in Terms Containing Exponents	**540**
Clearing a Row of Information from the Home Screen or Re-computing a Command	**537**	Expanding Expressions	**540**
		Factoring Expressions	**540**
Clearing out One-Character Variables	**538**	Evaluating an Expression for a Given Value	**541**
Accessing a Catalogue of Commands	**538**		
Collecting Terms with One Variable in Each Term	**538**	Checking the Solution for an Equation	**541**

Microsoft® *Excel* Spreadsheet Software Package

	page
Opening	**542**
GRAPHS	**542**
Circle Graph	**542**
Bar Graph	**543**
Line Graph	**544**

Fathom™ Statistical Software

	page		page
Introduction	**545**	CALCULATE ONE-VARIABLE STATISTICS	**547**
Starting *Fathom*™	**545**		
The Screen	**545**	Measures	**547**
Creating a Case Table	**545**	Sorting Data	**548**
Saving and Opening Collections	**546**	GRAPHS	**548**
Printing, Cutting, and Pasting	**546**	Scatter Plot	**548**
Importing and Exporting	**547**	Histogram	**549**
		Bar Graph	**549**

The Geometer's Sketchpad®, Geometry Software Package

Menu Bar

1 **File** menu—open/save/print sketches
2 **Edit** menu—undo/redo/actions/ set preferences
3 **Display** menu—control appearance of objects in sketch
4 **Construct** menu—construct new geometric objects based on objects in sketch
5 **Transform** menu—apply geometric transformations to selected objects

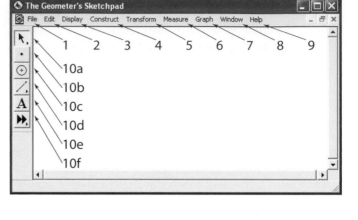

6 **Measure** menu—make various measurements on objects in sketch
7 **Graph** menu—create axes and plot measurements and points
8 **Window** menu—manipulate windows
9 **Help** menu—access the help system, an excellent reference guide
10 **Toolbox**—access tools for creating, marking, and transforming points, circles, and straight objects (segments, lines, and rays); also includes text and information tools
10a **Selection Arrow Tool** (Arrow)—select and transform objects
10b **Point Tool** (Dot)—draw points
10c **Compass Tool** (Circle)—draw circles
10d **Straightedge Tool**—draw line segments, rays, and lines
10e **Text Tool** (Letter A)—label points and write text
10f **Custom Tool** (Double Arrow)—create or use special "custom" tools

Creating a Sketch

- From the **File** menu, choose **New Sketch** to start with a new work area.

Opening an Existing Sketch

- From the **File** menu, choose **Open....** The Open dialogue box will appear.
- Choose the sketch you wish to work on. Then, click on **Open**. OR
- Type in the name of the sketch in the File name: entry box. Then, click on **Open**.

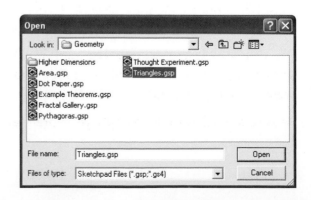

Saving a Sketch

If you are saving for the first time in a new sketch:

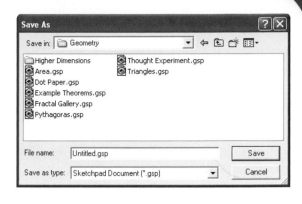

- From the **File** menu, choose **Save As**. The Save As dialogue box will appear.
- You can save the sketch with the name assigned by *The Geometer's Sketchpad*®. Click on **Save**.
  OR
- Press the Backspace or Delete key to clear the name.
- Type in whatever you wish to name the sketch file. Click on **Save**.

If you have already given your file a name:
- Choose **Save** from the **File** menu.

Closing a Sketch Without Exiting *The Geometer's Sketchpad*®

- From the **File** menu, choose **Close**.

Exiting *The Geometer's Sketchpad*®

- From the **File** menu, choose **Exit**.

Setting Preferences

- From the **Edit** menu, choose **Preferences...**.
- Click on the **Units** tab.
- Set the units and precision for angles, distances, and calculated values such as slopes or ratios.

- Click on the **Text** tab.
- If you check the auto-label box For **All New Points**, then *The Geometer's Sketchpad*® will label points as you create them.
- If you check the auto-label box **As Objects Are Measured**, then *The Geometer's Sketchpad*® will label any measurements that you define.

You can also choose whether the auto-labelling functions will apply only to the current sketch, or also to any new sketches that you create.

Be sure to click on **OK** to apply your preferences.

Selecting Points and Objects

- Choose the **Selection Arrow Tool**. The mouse cursor appears as an arrow.

To select a single point:
- Select the point by moving the cursor to the point and clicking on it.

The selected point will now appear as a darker point, similar to a *bull's-eye* ⊙.

To select an object such as a line segment or a circle:
- Move the cursor to a point on the object until it becomes a horizontal arrow.
- Click on the object. The object will change appearance to show it is selected.

To select a number of points or objects:
- Select each object in turn by moving the cursor to the object and clicking on it.

To deselect a point or an object:
- Move the cursor over it, and then click the left mouse button.
- To deselect all selected objects, click in an open area of the workspace.

Hiding Objects

Open a new sketch. Draw several objects such as points and line segments.

To hide a point:
- Select the point.
- From the **Display** menu, choose **Hide Point**.

To hide an object:
- Select another point and a line segment.
- From the **Display** menu, choose **Hide Objects**.

Shortcut: You can hide any selected objects by holding down ⌧CRTL⌧, and typing **H**.

You can make hidden objects reappear by choosing **Show All Hidden** from the **Display** menu.

Constructing Triangles and Polygons

To construct a triangle:
- Choose the **Point Tool**. Draw three points in the workspace.
- Select the points.
- From the **Construct** menu, choose **Segments**.

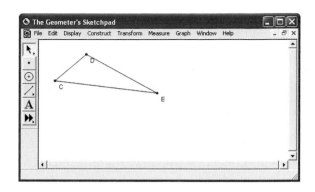

You can construct a polygon with any number of sides.

To construct a quadrilateral:
- Draw four points.
- Deselect all points.
- Select the points in either clockwise or counterclockwise order.
- From the **Construct** menu, choose **Segments**.

Using the Measure Menu

To measure the distance between two points:
- Ensure that nothing is selected.
- Select the two points.
- From the **Measure** menu, choose **Distance**.

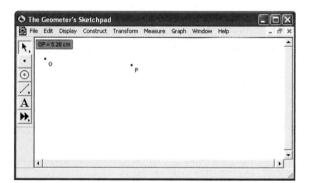

The Geometer's Sketchpad® will display the distance between the points, using the units and accuracy selected in **Preferences...** under the **Edit** menu.

To measure the length of a line segment:
- Ensure that nothing is selected.
- Select the line segment (but not the endpoints).
- From the **Measure** menu, choose **Length**.

To measure an angle:
- Ensure that nothing is selected.
- Select the three points that define the angle in the order Q, R, S. The second point selected must be the vertex of the angle.
- From the **Measure** menu, choose **Angle**.

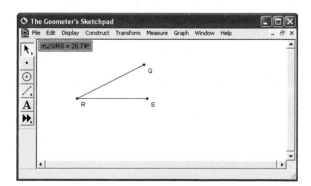

To calculate the ratio of two lengths:
- Select the two lengths to be compared.
- From the **Measure** menu, choose **Ratio**.

Constructing and Measuring Polygon Interiors

The Geometer's Sketchpad® will measure the perimeter and the area of a polygon. However, you must first construct the interior of the polygon.

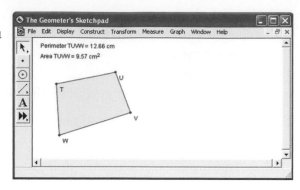

To construct the interior of this quadrilateral:
- Choose the four points of the quadrilateral, in either clockwise or counterclockwise order.
- From the **Construct** menu, choose **Quadrilateral Interior**. The interior of the quadrilateral will change colour.

To measure the perimeter:
- Select the interior of the polygon. It will have a cross-hatched appearance when selected.
- From the **Measure** menu, choose **Perimeter**.

The Geometer's Sketchpad® will display the perimeter of the polygon, using the units and accuracy selected in **Preferences...** under the **Edit** menu.

To measure the area:
- Select the interior of the polygon.
- From the **Measure** menu, choose **Area**.

Dilating and Rotating an Object

To dilate an object:
- Select a point to be the centre of the dilatation. Then, from the **Transform** menu, choose **Mark Center**.
- Select the object(s) to be dilated. From the **Transform** menu, choose **Dilate...**.
- In the Dilate dialogue box, enter the Scale Factor by which you want to dilate the object. Make sure that **Fixed Ratio** is selected. Click on **Dilate**.

To rotate an object:
- Select a point to be the centre of rotation. Then, from the **Transform** menu, choose **Mark Center**.
- Select the object(s) to be rotated. From the **Transform** menu, choose **Rotate...**.
- In the Rotate dialogue box, enter the number of degrees you want to rotate the object. Make sure that **Fixed Angle** is selected. Click on **Rotate**.

Changing Labels of Measures

- Right click on the measure and choose **Label Measurement** (or **Label Distance Measurement** depending on the type of measure) from the drop-down menu.
- Type in the new label.
- Click on **OK**.

Using the On-Screen Calculator

You can use the on-screen calculator to do calculations involving measurements, constants, functions, or other mathematical operations.

- Sketch a right triangle. Select each of the sides. From the **Measure** menu, choose **Length**.
- Click on **OK**. The measurements of the lengths of the sides will appear.

To calculate the perimeter:
- From the **Measure** menu, choose **Calculate**. The on-screen calculator will appear.
- On the workspace, select the first measure.
- On the keyboard, click on +.
- On the workspace, select the second measure.
- On the keyboard, click on +.
- On the workspace, select the third measure.
- Click on **OK**.

The sum of the measures, or perimeter of the triangle, will appear.

To calculate the area:
- From the **Measure** menu, choose **Calculate**.
- Click on 0, ., 5, and *.
- On the workspace, select the base measure.
- Click on *.
- On the workspace, select the height measure.
- Click on **OK**.

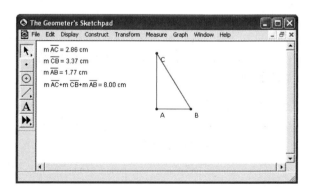

The measure of the area of the triangle will appear.

Coordinate System and Axes

- From the **Graph** menu, choose **Show Grid**.

The default coordinate system has an origin point in the centre of your screen and a unit point at (1, 0). Drag the origin to relocate the coordinate system and drag the unit point to change the scale.

It is useful to show the grid when creating graphs.

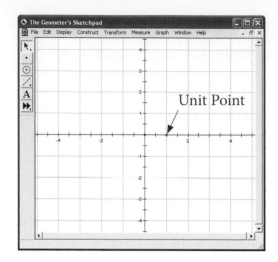

Creating Graphs

To plot a point on an *x-y* grid:
- From the **Graph** menu, choose **Plot Points...**.
- Ensure that Plot A is set to **Rectangular (x, y)**.
- Enter the *x*- and *y*-coordinates of the point.
- Click on **Plot**. A grid will appear with the plotted point. Click on **Done**.

You can plot additional points once you access the Plot Points dialogue box. Enter the coordinates of the next point and click on **Plot**. When you are finished plotting points, click on **Done**.

To graph an equation:
- From the **Graph** menu, choose **Plot New Function**. A calculator screen with the heading **New Function** will appear.
- Using the calculator interface, enter the equation.
- Click on **OK**.

To plot a table of values:
- Select the table of data.
- From the **Graph** menu, choose **Plot Table Data**.

Loading Custom Tools

Before you can use a **Custom Tool**, you must either create your own custom tools, or transfer the sample tools included with *The Geometer's Sketchpad®* program to the **Tool Folder**.

To transfer a sample custom tool:

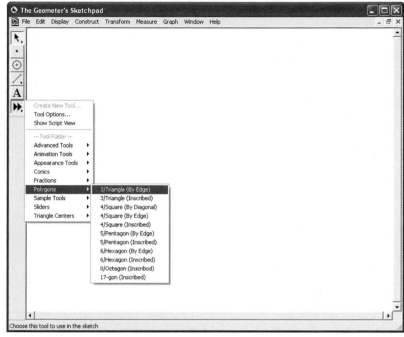

- Open **Windows® Explorer**, and navigate to the **Sketchpad** directory, or whatever directory was used to install *The Geometer's Sketchpad®*.
- Choose **Samples**, and then **Custom Tools**. You will see a list of the custom tools provided with the program.
- Choose the sets of tools you want to use. Then, choose **Copy** from the **Edit** menu.
- Move back up two directory levels to the **Sketchpad** directory, and then choose **Tool Folder**. Choose **Paste** from the **Edit** menu.
- Open *The Geometer's Sketchpad®*. Choose the **Custom Tool**.

You will see the custom tool sets that you copied. Choose one of the tool sets, say **Polygons**. You will see a list of the individual tools available.

TI-83 Plus And TI-84 Plus Graphing Calculators

Keys

The keys on the TI-83 Plus and TI-84 Plus are colour-coded to help you find the various functions.

- The grey keys include the number keys, decimal point, and negative sign. When entering negative values, use the grey [(-)] key, not the blue [-] key.
- The blue keys on the right side are the math operations.
- The blue keys across the top are used when graphing.
- The primary function of each key is printed on the key, in white.
- The secondary function of each key is printed in yellow and is activated by pressing the yellow [2nd] key. For example, to find the square root of a number, press [2nd] [x^2] for [$\sqrt{}$].
- The alpha function of each key is printed in green and is activated by pressing the green [ALPHA] key.

Graphing Relations and Equations

- Press [Y=]. Enter the equation.
- To display the graph, press [GRAPH].

For example, enter $y = \dfrac{3}{5}x^2 - 2$ by pressing

[Y=] [( ] 3 [÷] 5 [ )] [X,T,θ,n] [x^2] [-] 2.
Press [GRAPH].

The graph will be shown using the standard window settings.
To get a better display, press [ZOOM] and select **6:ZStandard**.

Setting Window Variables

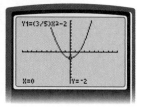

The [WINDOW] key defines the appearance of the graph.
The standard (default) window settings are shown.

To change the window settings:
- Press [WINDOW]. Enter the desired window settings.

In the example shown,
- the minimum x-value is -47
- the maximum x-value is 47
- the scale of the x-axis is 10
- the minimum y-value is -31
- the maximum y-value is 31
- the scale of the y-axis is 10
- the resolution is 1, so equations are graphed at each horizontal pixel

Setting Up a Table of Values

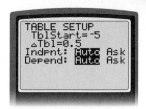

The standard (default) table settings are shown.
This feature allows the X's of the Table to be specified.

To change the Table Set-Up settings
- Press [2nd] [WINDOW]. Enter the desired values.

In the example shown,
- The starting x-value of the table is -5.
- The change in x-values is 0.5.
- Press [2nd] [GRAPH].

The table of values will appear as shown.

Setting Up the Display

The standard (default) graph screen display type is "FULL".
The standard (default) graph screen is shown.

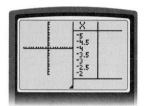

To change to a Graph-Table (G-T) view:
- Press [MODE] [▼] [▼] [▼] [▼]
  [▼] [▼] [►] [►] [ENTER].
- Press [GRAPH].

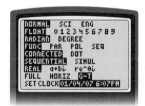

The vertical split-screen will appear as shown.

Tracing a Graph

- Enter a function using [Y=].
- Press [TRACE].
- Press [◄] and [►] to move along the graph.

The x- and y-values are displayed at the bottom of the screen.

If you have more than one graph plotted, use the [▲] and [▼] keys to move the cursor to the graph you wish to trace.

You may want to turn off all STAT PLOTS before you trace a function:
- Press [2nd] [Y=] for [STATPLOT]. Select **4:PlotsOff.**
- Press [ENTER].

Using Zoom

The ZOOM key is used to change the area of the graph that is displayed in the graphing window.

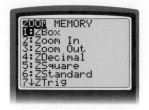

To set the size of the area you want to zoom in on:
- Press [ZOOM]. Select **1:Zbox**. The graph screen will be displayed, and the cursor will be flashing.
- If you cannot see the cursor, use the [►], [◄], [▲], and [▼] keys to move the cursor until you see it.
- Move the cursor to an area on the edge of where you would like a closer view. Press [ENTER] to mark that point as a starting point.
- Press the [►], [◄], [▲], and [▼] keys as needed to move the sides of the box to enclose the area you want to look at.
- Press [ENTER] when you are finished. The area will now appear larger.

To zoom in on an area without identifying a boxed-in area:
- Press [ZOOM]. Select **2:Zoom In**.

To zoom out of an area:
- Press [ZOOM]. Select **3:Zoom Out**.

To display the viewing area where the origin appears in the centre and the x- and y-axes intervals are equally spaced:
- Press [ZOOM]. Select **4:ZDecimal**.

To reset the axes range on your calculator:
- Press [ZOOM]. Select **6:ZStandard**.

To display all data points in a STAT PLOT:
- Press [ZOOM]. Select **9:ZoomStat**.

Setting the Format

To define a graph's appearance:
- Press [2nd] [ZOOM] for [FORMAT] to view the choices available.

The **Default Settings**, shown here, have all the features on the left "turned on."

To use Grid Off/Grid On:
- Select [FORMAT] by pressing [2nd] [ZOOM]. Cursor down and right to **GridOn**.
- Press [ENTER].
- Press [2nd] [ZOOM] for [QUIT].

Changing the Appearance of a Line

The default graph style is a thin, solid line. The line style is displayed to the left of the equation. There are seven options for the appearance of a line.

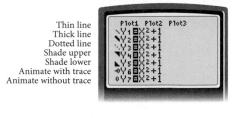

Thin line
Thick line
Dotted line
Shade upper
Shade lower
Animate with trace
Animate without trace

- Press [Y=] and clear any equations there from previous use of the calculator.
- Enter the relation $y = x^2 + 1$ for **Y1**.
- Use the standard window settings.
- Press [GRAPH].

Note the thin, solid line style.

- Press [Y=]. Cursor left to the slanted line.
- Press [ENTER] repeatedly until the thick, solid line shows, as in **Y2** above.
- Press [GRAPH].

Note the thick, solid line.

- For the other treatments, repeat the steps for displaying a thick, solid line until the desired image appears beside Y# on the calculator display.

The graph of **Y3** will appear as a thin, dotted curve.

The graph of **Y4** will be shaded above the curve.

The graph of **Y5** will be shaded below the curve.

The graph of **Y6** will show a flying ball tracing the curve.

The graph of **Y7** will show a flying ball following the curve without leaving a trace.

Entering Data Into Lists

To enter data:

- Press [STAT]. The cursor will highlight the **EDIT** menu.
- Press **1** or [ENTER] to select **1:Edit...**.

This allows you to enter new data, or edit existing data, in lists **L1** to **L6**.

For example, press [STAT], select **1:Edit...**, and then enter six test scores in list **L1**.

- Use the cursor keys to move around the editor screen.
- Complete each data entry by pressing [ENTER].
- Press [2nd] [MODE] for [QUIT] to exit the list editor when the data are entered.

You may need to clear a list before you enter data into it. For example, to clear list **L1**:

- Press [STAT] and select **4:ClrList**.
- Press [2nd] **1** for [L1], and press [ENTER].
  OR

To clear all lists:

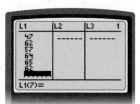

- Press [2nd] [+] for [MEM] to display the **MEMORY** menu.
- Select **4:ClrAllLists**, and then press [ENTER].

Creating a Scatter Plot

To create a scatter plot:
- Enter the two data sets in lists **L1** and **L2**.
- Press 2nd Y= for [STAT PLOT].
- Press **1** or ENTER to select **1:Plot1...**.
- Press ENTER to select **On**.
- Cursor down, and then press ENTER to select the top left graphing option, a scatter plot.
- Cursor down and press 2nd **1** for [L1].
- Cursor down and press 2nd **2** for [L2].
- Cursor down and select a mark style by pressing ENTER.
- Press 2nd MODE for [QUIT] to exit the **STAT PLOTS** editor when the data are entered.

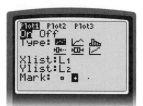

To display the scatter plot:
- Press Y= and use the CLEAR key to remove any graphed equations.
- Press 2nd MODE for [QUIT] to exit the **Y=** editor.
- Press ZOOM and select **9:ZoomStat** to display the scatter plot.

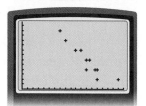

Creating a Histogram

To create a histogram:
- Press 2nd [MEM] **4** and ENTER to clear the lists.
- Press STAT and select **1.Edit**.... Enter the data set in list **L1**.
- Press Y=. Use the CLEAR key to erase any expressions in the list.
- Press 2nd Y= to access the STAT PLOT menu. Select **4:PlotsOff**. Press ENTER.
- Press 2nd [STAT PLOT]. Select **1:Plot1**. Set the plot to **On**, the graph style to Histogram, and the XList to L1.
- Press ZOOM and select **9:ZoomStat**. The histogram will appear.
- Use appropriate window settings and choose a suitable bin width (interval). The histogram will begin at the left bound of your first bin. Then press GRAPH.

For the data set:

154, 175, 166, 138, 161, 171, 165, 188, 139, 137,
144, 154, 186, 191, 177, 173, 164, 154, 186, 173,
151, 164, 174, 154, 138, 156, 146, 176, 194, 151

A suitable bin width is 10 with the graph starting at 130.

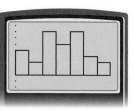

Creating a Box-and-Whisker Plot

To create a box-and-whisker plot:
- Press [Y=] and clear any equations.
- Press [STAT] and select **1.Edit**.... Enter the data set in list **L1**.
- Press [2nd] then [STATPLOT] to access PLOT 1. Turn Plot 1 **On**.
- Cursor down to Type. Turn the second type of Box Plot on as shown.
- Press [GRAPH] to plot the box-and-whisker plot.
- Press [ZOOM] **9:Zoomstat** to see the plot.
- Press the [TRACE] key. Use the cursor to see the median, Q1, and Q3 values for the plot.

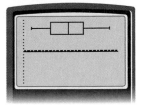

Line of Best Fit: Linear Regression

You can add the line of best fit to a scatter plot by using the LinReg function:
- With the scatter plot displayed, press [STAT]. Cursor over to display the **CALC** menu, and then select **4:LinReg(ax+b)**.
- Press [2nd] **1** for [L1], followed by [,].
- Press [2nd] **2** for [L2], followed by [,].
- Then, press [VARS], cursor over to display the **Y-VARS** menu, select **1:FUNCTION**, and then select **1:Y1**.
- Press [ENTER] to get the LinReg screen, and then press [GRAPH].

The linear regression equation is stored in the **Y=** editor. If you press [Y=], you will see the equation generated by the calculator.

Note: If the diagnostic mode is turned on, you will see values for **r** and r^2 displayed on the LinReg screen. To turn the diagnostic mode off:

- Press [2nd] **0** for [CATALOG].
- Scroll down to **DiagnosticOff**. Press [ENTER] to select this option.
- Press [ENTER] again to turn off the diagnostic mode.

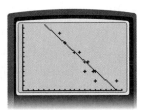

Finding a Zero or Maximum/Minimum Value

There must be at least one equation in the Equation Editor.
- Press [Y=].

The example shows a parabola.

To calculate a zero (x-intercept), maximum, or minimum there <u>must</u> be one seen.
- Press [GRAPH].

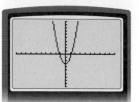

Note: If a zero (x-intercept), maximum, or minimum is not seen adjust the window settings accordingly.

To find a zero:
- Press [2nd] [TRACE] **2**.

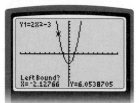

Move to the left side of a zero (x-intercept) by pressing and holding the left cursor key.
- Press [ENTER].

Move to the right side of a zero (x-intercept) by pressing and holding the right cursor key.
- Press [ENTER].

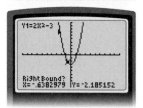

To find the value of a zero (x-intercept) using the calculator's guess:
- Press [ENTER].

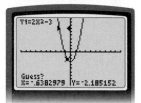

A zero (x-intercept) is shown at the bottom of the screen.

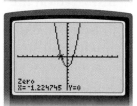

To find a minimum:
- Press [2nd] [TRACE] **3**.

Move to the left side of a minimum by pressing and holding the left cursor key.
- Press [ENTER].

Move to the right side of a minimum by pressing and holding the right cursor key.

- Press ENTER.

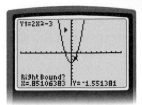

To find the value of a minimum using the calculator's guess:

- Press ENTER.

A minimum is shown at the bottom of the screen. Sometimes the values of X and/or Y are not exact because of the method used by the calculator to determine the values. The value for X, shown, is $-1.938E-6$. This means the number is -1.938×10^{-6}, in scientific notation. Moving the decimal six places to the left will give the number in standard form (0.000 001 938). In this case assume that the X of the minimum is 0 rather than 0.000 001 938. To find a maximum, press 2nd [TRACE] **4**. Follow a similar procedure as above.

Using the Value Operation

To find the corresponding y-value for any x-value for a relation such as $y = x^2 + x - 2$:

- Press Y=. Enter the relation.
- Press ZOOM. Select **6:ZStandard**.
- Press 2nd TRACE to access the **CALCULATE** menu. Select **1:value**.
- Enter a value for x, such as $x = 3$.
- Press ENTER.

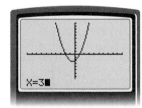

The corresponding y-value, $y = 10$, is displayed.

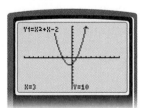

Curves of Best Fit: Quadratic Regression and Exponential Regression

You can add a curve of best fit to a scatter plot by using the **QuadReg** operation to try a quadratic fit, or the **ExpReg** operation to try an exponential fit.

Create a scatter plot using the data shown.

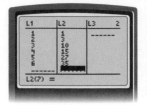 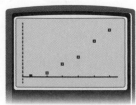

- Press STAT. Cursor over to the **CALC** menu. Then, select **5:QuadReg**.
- Press 2nd 1 for L1, followed by , .
- Press 2nd 2 for L2, followed by , .
- Press VARS. Cursor over to the **Y-VARS** menu. Select **1:Function**, and press ENTER. Select **1:Y1**.
- Press ENTER to obtain the **QuadReg** screen. The equation of the quadratic curve is displayed.

Note: If the diagnostic mode is turned on, you will see values for **r** and r^2 displayed on the **QuadReg** screen. To turn the diagnostic mode off:

- Press 2nd 0 for [CATALOG].
- Scroll down to **DiagnosticOff**. Press ENTER to select this option.
- Press ENTER again to turn off the diagnostic mode.
- Press GRAPH to see the curve of best fit overlaid on the scatter plot.

The quadratic regression equation is stored in the **Y=** editor.

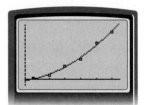

- Press Y= to display the equation generated by the calculator.

If you want to fit an exponential curve, select **0:ExpReg** from the **STAT CALC** menu, rather than **5:QuadReg**.

Calculations Involving the Sine Law

For example, consider $\triangle ABC$. Find the measure of $\angle B$ and the length of side c.

Use the sine law to find the measure of $\angle B$:

$$\sin B = \frac{\sin 28°}{10} \times 12$$

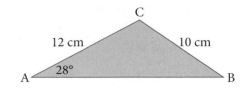

To solve for ∠B:
- Ensure that the **MODE** is set to **Degree**.
- Enter [SIN] 28 [ )] [×] 12 [÷] 10 [ENTER].
- Press [2nd] [SIN]. This will access the [SIN⁻¹] function to calculate the angle.
- Press [2nd] [(−)] for [ANS]. This will insert the answer from the previous calculation.
- Press [ )] and then [ENTER].

The measure of ∠B is about 34°.

Use the sine law to find the length of side c:

$$c = \frac{10 \sin 118°}{\sin 28°}$$

Solve for c:
- Press 10 [×] [SIN] 118 [ )] [÷] [SIN] 28 [ )] [ENTER].

The length of side AB is about 18.8 cm.

Calculations Involving the Cosine Law

Consider △DEF. Find the length of EF and the measure of ∠E.

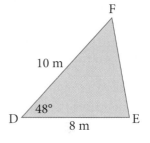

Use the cosine law to find d:
$$d^2 = e^2 + f^2 - 2ef \cos D$$
$$= 10^2 + 8^2 - 2 × 10 × 8 × \cos 48°$$
$$d = \sqrt{10^2 + 8^2 - 2 × 10 × 8 × \cos 48°}$$

To evaluate d:
- Press [2nd] [x^2] for [√].
- Press 10 [x^2] [+] 8 [x^2] [−] 2 [×] 10 [×] 8 [×] [COS] 48 [ )].
- Press [ENTER].

The length of EF is about 7.5 m.

Use the cosine law to find ∠E:
$$e^2 = d^2 + f^2 - 2df \cos E$$
$$10^2 = 7.5^2 + 8^2 - 2 × 7.5 × 8 × \cos E$$
$$10^2 - 7.5^2 - 8^2 = -2 × 7.5 × 8 × \cos E$$
$$\cos E = \frac{10^2 - 7.5^2 - 8^2}{-2 × 7.5 × 8}$$

To solve for ∠E:

- Press $($ 10 x^2 $-$ 7.5 x^2 $-$ 8 x^2 $)$ $÷$
  $($ $(-)$ 2 $×$ 7.5 $×$ 8 $)$.
- Press ENTER.
- Press 2nd COS. This will access the COS⁻¹ function to calculate the angle.
- Press 2nd $(-)$ for [ANS]. This will insert the answer from the previous calculation.
- Press $)$ and then ENTER.

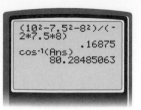

The measure of ∠E is about 80°.

Generating Random Numbers

To avoid generating the same series of random numbers every time, you must insert a random seed.

- Type the month and day of your birthday, followed by the street number of your home, using all digits.
- Press STO▸.
- Press MATH then cursor to **PRB**, and select **1:rand**.
- Press ENTER.

To generate a random number between 0 and 1:

- Press MATH ◂ to select the **PRB** menu.
- Press **1** or ENTER to select **rand**.
- Press ENTER to display a random number between 0 and 1.

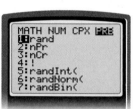

The **MATH PRB** menu also has a function, **randInt(**, which generates an integer in a set range. For example, to obtain a random integer between 5 and 20 inclusive:

- Press MATH ◂ **5** to select **randInt(**.
- Press 5 $,$ 20 $)$ ENTER.

You can also generate sequences of random numbers:

- Press MATH ◂ **1** to select **rand**.
- Press $($ 10 $)$ to perform ten trials.
- Press ENTER to display the ten random numbers on the screen.

You can store a sequence of random numbers in a list. For example, to choose ten random integers between 5 and 20:

- Press MATH ◂ **5** to select **randInt(**.
- Press 5 $,$ 20 $,$ 10 $)$ to perform ten trials in the range 5 to 20.
- Press STO▸, then 2nd **1** for [L1], then ENTER to place the ten random numbers directly into list L1.

The TVM SOLVER

About the Finance Applications

The **TVM Solver** is used to work with annuities (for example, loans and investments with regular payments, and mortgages), and can also be used for non-annuities (for example, loans or investments with no regular payments). **TVM** stands for **T**ime **V**alue of **M**oney.

Opening the TVM Solver

On the TI-83 Plus/TI84 Plus, press 〔APPS〕 1 1.

What the TVM Solver Variables Represent

When There Are Regular Payments:

N	Number of Payments
I%	Annual Interest Rate
PV	Present Value
PMT	Payment
FV	Future Value
P/Y	Number of Payments/Year
C/Y	Number of Compounding Periods/Year
PMT: END BEGIN	Payments at End of Payment Interval

A savings annuity invested at 7%, compounded quarterly, with quarterly deposits of $200, for 3 years is $2645.02.

When There Are No Regular Payments:

N	Number of Years
I%	Annual Interest Rate
PV	Present Value, or Principal
PMT	Always set **PMT=0.00**.
FV	Future Value, or Final Amount
P/Y	Always set **P/Y=1.00**.
C/Y	Number of Compounding Periods/Year
PMT: END BEGIN	END or BEGIN

$1000 invested at 5%, compounded monthly, for 7 years is $1418.04.

Important Points About the TVM Solver
- Set the number of decimal places to 2.
- A value must be entered for each variable.
- Money paid out (cash outflow), such as a loan payment, is negative.
- Money received (cash inflow), such as the final amount of an investment, is positive.
- To quit the **TVM Solver** and return to the Home Screen, press 〔2nd〕 〔MODE〕.

Investments and Loans (No Regular Payments)

Final Amount If you know the principal, or present value, interest rate, compounding frequency, and term of an investment or loan, you can determine its final amount.

For example, to determine the final amount of a **$2500** investment earning 5% interest, **compounded semi-annually**, for **3 years**, follow these steps:

Open the **TVM Solver**, and then, enter the values as shown:

Term is 3 years.
Annual interest rate is 5%.
Principal is $2500.
Final amount is unknown.
2 compounding periods/year

There are no regular payments, so, PMT=0.00 and P/Y=1.00.

To solve for **FV**, cursor to **FV=0.00**, and then, press [ALPHA] [ENTER]:

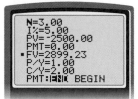

The Final amount is $2899.23.

Present Value, or Principal If you know the final amount, interest rate, compounding frequency, and term of an investment or loan, you can determine its present value, or principal.

For example, to determine the principal of a $6000 debt at 9% interest, compounded quarterly, for 5 years, follow these steps:

Open the **TVM Solver**, and then, enter the values as shown:

Term is 5 years.
Annual interest rate is 9%.
Principal is unknown.
Final amount is $6000.
4 compounding periods/year

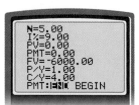

There are no regular payments, so, PMT=0.00 and P/Y=1.00.

To solve for **PV**, cursor to **PV=0.00**, and then, press [ALPHA] [ENTER]:

The principal was $3844.90.

Interest Rate To find the annual interest rate, enter the known values for **N**, **PV**, **FV**, and **C/Y**. Set **I%=0.00**, **PMT=0.00**, and **P/Y=1.00**. Then, cursor to **I%=0.00** and press [ALPHA] [ENTER].

Term To find the term, in years, enter the known values for **I%**, **PV**, **FV**, and **C/Y**. Set **N=0.00**, **PMT=0.00**, and **P/Y=1.00**. Then, cursor to **N=0.00** and press [ALPHA] [ENTER].

TI-89 Titanium Graphing Calculator

Accessing the Home Screen

The standard (default) screen for the TI-89 is shown.

To go to this screen:
- Press [HOME].

Pressing the [HOME] key will always take you back to the home screen.

Clearing the Home Screen

To clear the home screen:
- Press [F1] 8.

Clearing the Command Prompt Line

To clear the command prompt line:
- Press [CLEAR].

Clearing a Row of Information from the Home Screen or Re-computing a Command

In the example, rows of data exist for each command executed.

To go to any row from the home screen:
- Press [▲] the appropriate number of times to highlight a row.

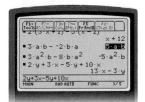

To delete a row from the home screen:
- Press [CLEAR]. Note that the row above has been deleted.

To re-compute a command from any row, highlight the row.
- Press [▲] the appropriate number of times to highlight a row.

- Press [ENTER] [ENTER]. Note the first time you press enter the information is pasted in the command prompt line.

The second time you press enter the command is executed.

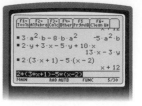

Clearing Out One-Character Variables

A letter may have a stored numerical value. This forces the calculator to compute a numerical answer if operations involving the letter are requested.

In the example, the calculator computed a value of 2 for the expansion of $x(x + 1)$ rather than the algebraic answer, $x^2 + x$, because x had a stored numerical value of 1.

To clear all one-character variables:
- Press [2nd] [F1] [ENTER] [ENTER].

In the example, the calculator provided the algebraic answer.

Accessing a Catalogue of Commands

To access an alphabetic catalogue of commands:
- Press [CATALOG].

To move to a different letter in the list of commands:
- Press [ALPHA] and the first letter of the command desired. Scroll down to the appropriate command and press [ENTER] to paste it to the command prompt line.

Collecting Terms with One Variable in Each Term

In the example, the calculator simplified $2x - 7x$.
To do this:
- Press 2 [X] [−] 7 [X] [ENTER].

In the example, the calculator simplified $3x - 4y + 7x + 8y$.

To do this:
- Press 3 [X] [−] 4 [Y] [+] 7 [X] [+] 8 [Y] [ENTER].

Collecting Terms with More than One Variable in Terms

When there are two variables next to each other there must be a multiplication sign between them otherwise the calculators treat groups of variables as separate items. In other words, the term xy would be treated differently than the term yx. They are not considered like terms unless there were a multiplication sign between both pairs of variables.

In the example, the calculator did not add the like terms of xy and yx until there was a multiplication sign between the variables.

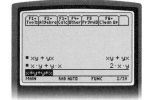

To do this:
- Press [X] [Y] [+] [Y] [X] [ENTER].
- Press [CLEAR] [X] [×] [Y] [+] [Y] [×] [X] [ENTER].

Collecting Terms with More than One Variable in Terms Containing Exponents

In the example, the calculator will collect the like terms $2x^2y^2 - 5y^2x^2$ even though there is no multiplication sign between the variables. This is because the variables are not directly beside each other.

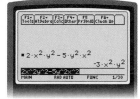

To do this:
- Press 2 [X] [^] 2 [Y] [^] 2 [−] 5 [Y] [^] 2 [X] [^] 2 [ENTER].

In the example, the calculator will not collect the like terms $2xy^2 - 5y^2x$ because the x and y in the first term are side by side.

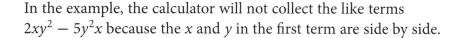

Only when there is a multiplication sign between the x and y in the first term, will the simplified answer be correct.

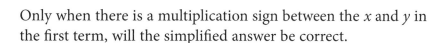

Expanding Expressions

To expand an expression:
- Press F2 3.

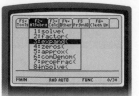

In the example, the calculator expanded $2(x + 3)$.

To do this:
- Press 2 (X + 3)).
  Note the last bracket is essential.

In the example, the calculator expanded $2x(x + 3)$.

To do this:
- Press F2 32 X × (X + 3)).

Note the multiplication sign is necessary to use when multiplying variables together.

In the example, the calculator expanded $(x + 3)(2x - 1)$.

To do this:
- Press F2 3 (X + 3)
  (2 X − 1)).

Note a multiplication sign between brackets is not necessary.

Factoring Expressions

In the example the calculator factored $x^2 + 6x$.

To do this:
- Press F2 2 X ^ 2 + 6 X) ENTER.

In the example the calculator factored $x^2 + 2x - 8$.

To do this:
- Press F2 2 X ^ 2 + 2 X − 8) ENTER.

Evaluating an Expression for a Given Value

You can evaluate an expression for a given value of the variable.

For example, consider the expression $5x + 2$.

To evaluate the expression for $x = 3$:
- Type $5x + 2$ [|] $x = 3$.
- Press [ENTER].

The calculator returns a value of 17.

Checking the Solution for an Equation

You can use a CAS to check whether a given value is the correct solution for an equation.

For example, consider the equation $2x + 1 = -3x - 4$.
Check $x = 1$ and $x = -1$ as possible solutions.

Check $x = 1$:
- Type $2x + 1 = -3x - 4$ [|] $x = 1$.
- Press [ENTER].

Note that the CAS returns a **false** message.
This means that $x = 1$ is not a solution.

Check $x = -1$:
- Type $2x + 1 = -3x - 4$ [|] $x = -1$.
- Press [ENTER].

Note that the CAS returns a **true** message.
This means that $x = 21$ is a solution.

Microsoft® *Excel* Spreadsheet Software Package

Opening

You can access Microsoft® *Excel* from the **Start/Programs** menu or directly from the desktop.

GRAPHS

Circle Graph (Pie Chart)

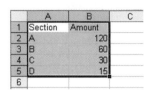

	A	B	C
1	Section	Amount	
2	A	120	
3	B	60	
4	C	30	
5	D	15	
6			

Select the cells that contain the data to be graphed. Then, click on the **Chart Wizard** button, or choose **Chart** from the **Insert** menu, and follow these steps:

Step 1: Select a **Pie Chart type** and **Chart sub-type**. Then, click on **Next**.

Step 2: Make sure the correct cells (**Data range**) and **Series** have been selected.

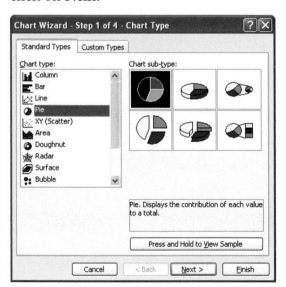

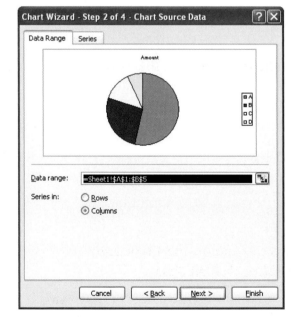

Step 3: Click on the **Titles** tab and enter the **Chart title**. Click on the **Legend** tab and choose the **Placement** of the legend. Click on the **Data Labels** tab and choose the **Data labels** to display. Then, click on **Next**:

Step 4: Choose to locate the chart **As an object in** the worksheet. Then, click on **Finish**:

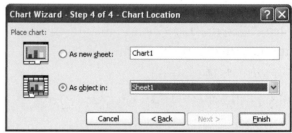

The pie chart will appear on the worksheet.

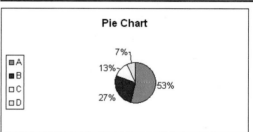

Bar Graph

Step 1: Select a Column chart type and Chart sub-type. Then, click on **Next**.

Step 2: Ensure that the correct cells (**Data range**) and **Series** have been selected. Click on **Next**.

Step 3: Click on the **Titles** tab, and enter the appropriate chart titles. Click on **Next**.

Step 4: Choose to locate the chart as an object in the worksheet. Then, click on **Finish**.

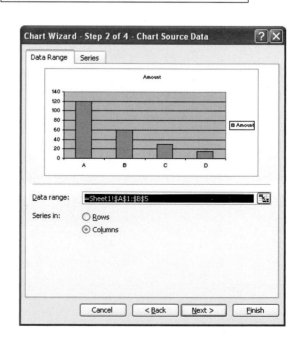

The bar graph will appear on the worksheet.

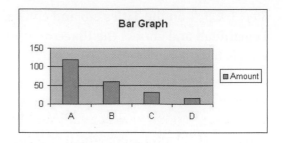

Line Graph

Step 1: Select a Line Chart type and Chart sub-type. Then, click on **Next**.

Step 2: Ensure that the correct cells (**Data range**) and **Series** have been selected. Click on **Next**.

Step 3: Click on the **Titles** tab, and enter the appropriate chart titles. Click on **Next**.

Step 4: Choose to locate the chart as an object in the worksheet. Then, click on **Finish**.

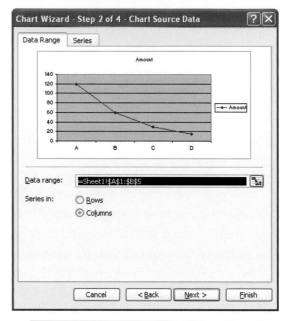

The line graph will appear on the worksheet.

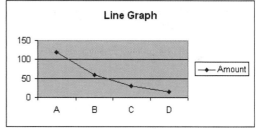

FATHOM™ STATISTICAL SOFTWARE

Introduction

Fathom™ is a dynamic statistics software package. It allows you to enter data, modify views of data, and filter and sort data. This tutorial gives a fast introduction, which will allow you to start working with *Fathom*™ quickly. A complete interactive guide to *Fathom*™ is available on the *Fathom*™ CD-ROM.

Starting *Fathom*™

You can access *Fathom*™ from the Start/Program menu, or directly from the desktop.

The Screen

The *Fathom*™ screen is a working space in which you can place collections, case tables, graphs, and panels for statistical functions. Each panel can be activated by single-clicking on it.
- The menu bar contains all the standard *Fathom*™ functions.
- The tool bar contains icons for key *Fathom*™ objects. You can place new objects in the work space by clicking on any of these icons and dragging to the work space.

Creating a Case Table

Start entering data into *Fathom*™ by creating a case table. For example, to enter height data into a case table:
- Click and drag the **Case Table** icon from the tool bar into the work space.
- Click on the space labelled <**new**>, which is the first attribute heading in the case table. Name this attribute by typing "Height_cm" and (ENTER).
- A cell appears under the Height_cm attribute heading. You can enter the first piece of height data here.
- Press (ENTER) to enter each height and create a new cell for the next height.

Each column in the case table represents a separate "case." Notice that when you entered the attribute heading "Height_cm," a box marked "Collection 1" appeared.

Then, when you entered the first piece of data, a group of gold balls appeared in the box.

Fathom™ organizes data into collections of cases. Each gold ball symbolizes an individual case, which can be a single data point, as here, or a set of several attributes.

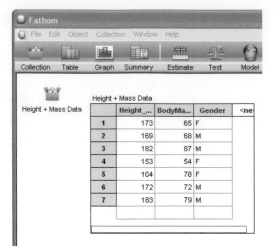

For example, add the attributes BodyMass_kg and Gender to the case table. This allows each case to store an individual's height, mass, and gender.
- Click on the space labelled <**new**>, to the right of the "Height_cm" heading in the case table. Name this attribute by typing "BodyMass_kg" and (ENTER).
- Another <**new**> attribute will appear. Click on this and type "Gender" and (ENTER).
- Enter body mass data in the second column and gender data in the third column.
- Double-click on the heading "Collection 1" and rename the collection by typing "Height + Mass Data" and (ENTER).

Saving and Opening Collections

To save the *Fathom*™ work space:
- Use the **Save** or **Save As...** command from the **File** menu.
- Supply an appropriate name for the collection.

Note that *Fathom*™ files are saved with the postscript ".ftm", and appear in folders with a gold ball icon.

Printing, Cutting, and Pasting

The **Print** command in *Fathom*™, under the **File** menu, prints a copy of the whole work space.

Individual panes in the work space, such as case tables and graphs, can be copied, and pasted into other documents.

Importing and Exporting

Fathom™ has powerful capabilities to import or export data from or to other programs, and to import from the Internet. For more about the commands **Import From File…**, **Import From Url…**, and **Export File…**, found under the File menu, see "Get Data into *Fathom*" in the *Fathom*™ reference manual.

Calculate Single-variable Statistics

Measures

Fathom™ calculates statistics as "measures." For example, to find the mean height for the Height + Mass Data collection:
- Right-click on the Height + Mass Data collection.
- Select **Inspect Collection** from the menu that appears.
- A new pane appears, titled **Inspect Height + Mass Data**. This feature is called the inspector. Click on the **Measures** tab in the inspector to bring up the Measures pane.
- Click on <**new**> and type "meanHeight" and ENTER.
- Double-click in the space under the **Formula** heading.
- A pane called meanHeight formula appears. This is the *Fathom*™ formula editor. Type "mean(". The word "mean" changes colour to show *Fathom*™ recognizes this formula name.
- Now type "Height_cm." The word changes colour to show a recognized attribute name.
- Click on **OK** to exit the formula editor.

In the inspector, the mean of the heights now appears under the Value heading. The formula used appears under the Formula heading. If new data are added, the measure meanHeight is automatically recalculated. Other statistical measures, such as median, range, and standard deviation, can be found.

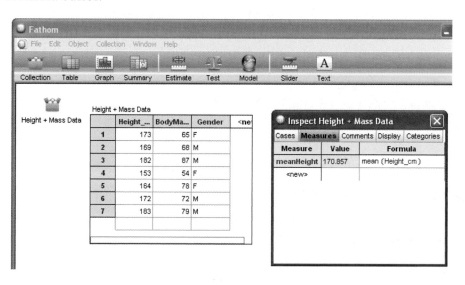

Sorting Data

Cases in a collection can be sorted by any attribute, or by more than one attribute in sequence. For example, to sort the Height + Mass Data collection by gender and then by height:

- Right-click on the Height_cm attribute and select **Sort Ascending** from the menu that appears.
- The data are now sorted by height. Click on **Gender** and select **Sort Ascending**.
- The data are sorted by gender first, since that was the last sort performed. However, the sort by height is preserved within male and female genders.

Height + Mass Data

	Height_...	BodyMa...	Gender	<ne
1	153	54	F	
2	164	78	F	
3	173	65	F	
4	169	68	M	
5	172	72	M	
6	182	87	M	
7	183	79	M	

Graphs

Scatter Plot

To create a scatter plot of body mass versus height:

- Click and drag the **Graph** icon from the tool bar into the work space.
- Click on the Height_cm heading in the case table and drag it to the graph, over the words "Drop an attribute here." The height data will appear along the horizontal axis, with a scale.
- Click on the BodyMass_kg heading and drag it to the vertical axis of the graph. You will see a narrow bold rectangle appear when you are in the right place.
- A scale will appear on the vertical axis, and the data points will be plotted as a scatter graph. Notice that the tab in the top right corner of the graph panel now reads "Scatter Plot."

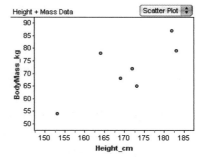

Histogram

To create a histogram of the height data:
- Click and drag the **Graph** icon into the work space.
- Click on the Height_cm heading in the case table and drag it to the horizontal axis of the graph.
- Click on the tab that reads "Dot Plot." A menu of graph types appears. Select Histogram from the menu.
- If using *Fathom™1*, right-click on the graph and select **Show Graph Info** from the menu that appears.
  If using *Fathom™2*, right-click on the graph and select **Inspect Graph**. Then click on the **Properties** tab.

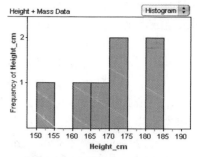

A pane appears below the graph, as shown. Highlight the bin width and type 5. Then, highlight the starting number and type 150. This sets the histogram intervals to start at 150 cm and to be 5 cm wide.

Bar Graph

Fathom™ classifies attributes as continuous (numerical data) and categorical (descriptive data). A bar graph is used for descriptive data. For example, go to the case table, add an attribute called Eyes, and enter an eye colour for each individual.
- Click and drag the **Graph** icon into the work space.
- Click on the Eyes heading in the case table and drag it to the horizontal axis of the graph.

Fathom™ automatically selects a bar graph and counts the frequency of each colour.

Answers

CHAPTER 1

Trigonometry, pages, pages 2–55

Prerequisite Skills, pages 4–5

1. **a)** $x = \pm 6$ **b)** $x = \pm 5$ **c)** $x = \pm 10$
   d) $x = \pm 13$ **e)** $x = \pm 24$
2. **a)** 10 cm   **b)** 12 mm   **c)** 19.2 m
3. 5.8 m
4. **a)** 1:2   **b)** 3:7   **c)** 2:5
5. $10.50
6. **a)** $x = 3$ **b)** $x = 3$ **c)** $x = 20, y = 4$
7. **a)** 1 unit of distance on the map represents 700 000 of the same unit of distance on the earth.
   b) 84 km
   c) 5.7 cm
8. **a)** 3.46   **b)** 19.83   **c)** 9015.98
9. **a)** 7.7   **b)** 26.9   **c)** 0.9
10. **a)** 24°   **b)** 69°   **c)** 36°

1.1 Revisit the Primary Trigonometric Ratios, pages 6–15

1. **a)** opposite: AC or b; adjacent: BC or a; hypotenuse: AB or c
   b) opposite: DE or f; adjacent: EF or d; hypotenuse: DF or e
   c) opposite: XY or z; adjacent: YZ or x; hypotenuse: XZ or y
2. **a)** 0.5000   **b)** 0.7071   **c)** 1.7321
3. **a)** $\angle A \doteq 13.6°$ **b)** $\angle B \doteq 28.8°$ **c)** $\angle C \doteq 51.0°$
4. **a)** 23 m   **b)** 11 m   **c)** 65°
5. **a)** 16.1°   **b)** 73.9°   **c)** 35 cm
6. **a)** 13.5 m   **b)** 12.4 m
7. **a)** 12.9 cm   **b)** 37.8 cm
8. **a)** 45.4 m   **b)** 89.1 m
9. $\angle A = 25°, a \doteq 7.2$ cm, $c \doteq 17.1$ cm
10. 16.8 m
11. 15.5 m
12. 40.5 cm
13. 15 mm
14. 290 cm^2

1.2 Solve Problems Using Trigonometric Ratios, pages 16–23

1. 4°
2. 67 m
3. 59°
4. 1°
5. 5 ft
6. Yes, the angle is 81°.
7. No, the angle is 68°.
8. 477 m
9. 5 km
10. Answers may vary.
11. Lina reversed the opposite and adjacent sides in the fraction; $d \doteq 2065$
12. 27 m
13. 24°
14. 3816 m
15. 121 m
16. 6.7 ft

1.3 The Sine Law, pages 24–33

1. **a)** 41.0 cm   **b)** 64.1 m   **c)** 71.6 cm
2. **a)** 20.9°   **b)** 38.2°
3. **a)** $\angle X = 76°, x \doteq 22.0$ cm, $y \doteq 21.5$ cm
   b) $\angle D \doteq 60.4°, \angle E \doteq 36.6°, d \doteq 21.9$ cm
4. **a)** $\angle A = 62°, b \doteq 17.1$ cm, $c \doteq 26.7$ cm
   b) $\angle E \doteq 22.7°, \angle F \doteq 82.3°, f \doteq 25.6$ m
5. 44 m
6. 8 km
7. The measure of an angle that is opposite one of the known sides.
8. 4 ft
9. from Twillingate: 14 nautical miles; from Fogo: 11 nautical miles
11. 55.8 m
12. Answers may vary.
13. 19.8 cm

1.4 The Cosine Law, pages 34–41

1. **a)** 18.9 cm   **b)** 58.1 mm   **c)** 3.1 m
2. **a)** 53.7°   **b)** 88.0°   **c)** 54.7°
3. $\angle B \doteq 86°, \angle C \doteq 62°, a \doteq 13.5$ m
4. $\angle A \doteq 67°, \angle B \doteq 81°, \angle C \doteq 32°$
5. 9.5 km
6. Either all three sides or two sides and the enclosed angle.
7. 19°
8. 827 m
9. 6.9 km
10. 14.7 m
11. 11.5 m
12. **a)** 86°, 63°, 31°   **b)** no
13. 41°

1.5 Make Decisions Using Trigonometry, pages 42–51

1. **a)** primary trigonometric ratios
   b) cosine law
   c) sine law
   d) primary trigonometric ratios
   e) cosine law
   f) sine law
2. **a)** 64°, 20.5 cm, 22.8 cm
   b) 48.0°, 59.7°, 72.3°
   c) 30°, 12.2 m, 12.8 m
   d) 30°, 60°, 22.5 mm
   e) 47.7°, 80.3°, 48.0 m
   f) 30°, 8.9 cm, 16.7 cm
3. Yes; the green is less than 200 ft away, the shot will make it if there is no wind or error.
4. Yes; the shot will clear the trees if there is no wind or error.
5. Answers may vary.
6. 4.2 km
7. 49.8°, 65.1°, 65.1°
8. 57.7 m
9. **a)** one angle   **b)** one angle   **c)** two sides
10. **a)** 4.4 km   **b)** 66.5°, 51.5°
12. No; the shot will go 0.5 m wide of the net.
13. 53°
14. **a)** 1353.6 m   **b)** 1985.8 m
    c) 1757.2 m   **d)** 12° north of east

Chapter 1 Review, pages 52–53
1. a) $\angle B = 70°$, $a \doteq 11.3$ m, $c \doteq 33.0$ m
   b) $\angle A \doteq 57.1°$, $\angle B \doteq 32.9°$, $a \doteq 29.4$ cm
2. $\angle A \doteq 65.0°$, $\angle B \doteq 25.0°$, $c \doteq 16.6$ cm
3. No; an additional side or angle is needed in order to solve the triangle.
4. 169 m
5. 50.2° east of north
6. No; need to know the measure of at least one angle.
7. $\angle A = 60°$, $a \doteq 13.8$ m, $c \doteq 12.2$ m
8. 4.4 nautical miles
9. 15.5 cm
10. Either all three sides or two sides and the enclosed angle.
11. Answers may vary.
12. 118.3 km
13. $\angle M \doteq 50.0°$, $\angle L \doteq 50.0°$, $\angle K \doteq 80.0°$
14. No; the rafter is too long; answers may vary.
15. 28.4°
16. 3.4 mm
17. cosine law; $\angle R \doteq 43.7°$, $\angle P \doteq 50.1°$, $\angle Q \doteq 86.2°$

Chapter 1 Practice Test, pages 54–55
1.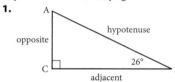
2. $\angle A \doteq 56.3°$, $\angle B \doteq 33.7°$, $c \doteq 6.9$ m
3. No; answers may vary.
4. 3.1°
5. $\angle C = 24°$, $a \doteq 60.5$ m, $b \doteq 59.6$ m
6. 39.2 m
7. $\angle B = 44°$, $\angle C = 68°$, $a = 20$ cm
8. 80.4°
9. $\angle A \doteq 69.0°$, $\angle B \doteq 57.6°$, $\angle C \doteq 53.4°$
10. a) Since $\sin 90° = 1$, the sine law is the same as the primary trigonometric ratio for sine of a right angle; answers may vary.
    b) Yes, since $\cos 90° = 0$, for some triangles it is the same as using the Pythagorean theorem; answers may vary.

CHAPTER 2

Probability, pages 56–97

Prerequisite Skills, pages 58–59
1. a) 0.97   b) 0.4   c) 0.15   d) 0.625
2. a) 0.425   b) 0.3077   c) 0.8333   d) 0.4444
3. a) $\frac{3}{4}$ b) $\frac{4}{25}$ c) $\frac{13}{20}$
   d) $\frac{1}{8}$ e) $\frac{1}{3}$ f) $\frac{1}{1000}$
4. a) $\frac{3}{10}$ b) $\frac{1}{4}$ c) $\frac{4}{5}$
   d) $\frac{9}{20}$ e) $\frac{2}{3}$ f) 1

5. a) $\frac{3}{4}$ b) $\frac{1}{3}$ c) 16   d) $\frac{1}{26}$
6. a) 0.75 or $\frac{3}{4}$ b) $0.\overline{3}$ or $\frac{1}{3}$
   c) 16.0 or 16   d) 0.0385 or $\frac{1}{26}$
7. a) 18   b) 27.7%   c) $\frac{5}{9}$ d) 40%
8. a) bar graph   b) 25   c) van
   d) $\frac{1}{5}$ e) 8%
9. a) 20   b) $\frac{2}{5}$ c) 70%
10. a) 20   b) 8   c) 35%   d) $\frac{17}{20}$

2.1 Probability Experiments, pages 60–67
1. a) $\frac{3}{10}$, 30%, 0.3   b) $\frac{7}{10}$; answers may vary.
2. $\frac{1}{5}$, 20%, 0.2
3. a) 12 times   b) 18 times
   c) $\frac{3}{5}$; answers may vary.
4. a) $\frac{9}{40}$ b) $\frac{19}{40}$ c) $\frac{3}{10}$
5. a) They should be the same height since heads and tails are equally likely; answers may vary.
   b) HT and TH   c) $\frac{19}{40}$ d) $\frac{21}{40}$
6. a) 90%
   b) No, heads and tails are equally likely; answers may vary.
7. a) No, $\frac{8}{240} = 3.3\%$; answers may vary.
   b) Yes; answers may vary.
   c) Yes; answers may vary.
8. a) True; explanations may vary.
   b) True; explanations may vary.
9. a) 1000; answers may vary.
   b) Answers may vary.
10. a) Less than 50%; answers may vary.
    b) Answers may vary.
11. $\frac{4}{9}$; explanations may vary.

2.2 Theoretical Probability, pages 68–75
1. a) $\frac{1}{4}$ b) $\frac{3}{13}$ c) $\frac{10}{13}$
   d) $\frac{1}{26}$ e) 1   f) $\frac{3}{26}$
2. a) $\frac{1}{16}$ b) $\frac{3}{16}$
3. a) $\frac{1}{6}$ b) $\frac{1}{2}$ c) 0   d) $\frac{1}{2}$
4. a) $\frac{2}{5}$ b) $\frac{3}{25}$ c) $\frac{3}{5}$
5. a) $\frac{1}{36}$ b) $\frac{1}{18}$ c) $\frac{13}{18}$
   d) $\frac{1}{6}$ e) $\frac{5}{6}$
6. $\frac{1}{5}$

7. $\frac{1}{12}$; diagrams may vary.

8. a) 14 is impossible; answers may vary.
   b) All possible sums are between 2 and 12; answers may vary.

9. a) 6
   b) i) $\frac{1}{6}$ **ii)** $\frac{1}{3}$ **iii)** $\frac{1}{3}$ **iv)** $\frac{1}{3}$

10. a) $\frac{5}{6}$
   b) P(second die will not match the first die) $= \frac{5}{6}$; answers may vary.
   c) They are the only 2 possible outcomes; answers may vary.

11. a) $\frac{1}{4}$
   b) The dart will not land outside the dartboard; answers may vary.

12. a) $\frac{1}{4}$ **b)** $\frac{3}{4}$; answers may vary.   **c)** 0.625

13. a) $\frac{2}{3}$ **b)** $\frac{2}{3}$
   c) Yes, if Ann is not between Bob and Cathy, then Bob and Cathy are standing beside each other.

14. $\frac{2}{3}$; answers may vary.

2.3 Compare Experimental and Theoretical Probabilities, pages 76–85

1. a) $\frac{1}{4}$ **b)** $\frac{13}{15}$

2. a) $\frac{4}{5}$ **b)** $\frac{1}{2}$
   c) decrease; answers may vary.

3. a) 85%   **b)** 70%

4. a) 1: $\frac{2}{15}$; 2: $\frac{1}{5}$; 3: $\frac{7}{30}$; 4: $\frac{1}{6}$; 5: $\frac{1}{5}$; 6: $\frac{1}{15}$
   b) experimental; answers may vary.

5. a) i) $\frac{1}{3}$ **ii)** $\frac{2}{3}$ **iii)** 0
   b) Too few trials were done to give an accurate experimental probability; answers may vary.

6. a) $\frac{1}{4}$
   b) $\frac{1}{6}$
   c) Yes; answers may vary.
   d) No; answers may vary.

7. a) Use the **rand** command six times, use a number less than 0.25 to represent rain, use a number greater than 0.25 to represent no rain; answers may vary.
   b) Use **randInt(1,4,1)**.

8. a) 2 or 3, since there is a $\frac{1}{4}$ chance of being correct on each question and $\frac{1}{4}$ of 10 is 2.5.
   b) Every time a 1 comes up, record it as a correct answer; answers may vary.

9. a) $\frac{1}{5}$
   b) Answers may vary.

10. a) The average number of correct answers for each trial up to that one; answers may vary.

b) The scatter plot shows the average, on the whole, getting closer and closer to 2.5 as more trials are done. If more trials were done, the graph would likely continue getting closer to 2.5; answers may vary.

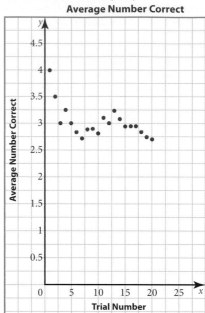

Average Number Correct

11. a) 0.4   **b)** It is larger.
   c) More points are scored for red, so people will aim for it; answers may vary.

12. a) $\frac{3}{10}$ **b)** $\frac{3}{8}$
   c) Some types of fish might be more difficult to catch than others; answers may vary.

14. Theoretically you should break even; answers may vary.

15. a) It is fair; answers may vary.
   b) Answers may vary.
   c) Answers may vary.
   d) Answers may vary.

16. Marucia; answers may vary.

2.4 Interpret Information Involving Probability, pages 86–93

1. a) 25%   **b)** 65%   **c)** 85%

2. a) 62.5%   **b)** 19   **c)** Answers may vary.

3. a) 13   **b)** 89

4. a) 23   **b)** 35

5. a) hits divided by at-bats; answers may vary.
   b) 12
   c) Yes; explanations may vary.

6. a) $\frac{3}{4}$ **b)** 64%   **c)** 16%   **d)** 2 970 000

7. a) 65.5%   **b)** 76%
   c) $\frac{32}{19}$ is greater than $\frac{76}{65.5}$.
   d) These numbers make the increase seem larger than the percents do; answers may vary.

8. a) about 23%
   b) They have the largest populations in the world.
   c) $\frac{5}{26}$

10. a) radio: 35%, television: 60% between 6:00 A.M. and 12:00 midnight, and 50% between 6:00 P.M. and 12:00 midnight

b) No, the content must be broadcast between 6:00 A.M. and 6:00 P.M. on radio, and on television, 60% Canadian content must be broadcast between 6:00 A.M. and 12:00 midnight, and 50% Canadian content between 6:00 P.M. and 12:00 midnight.

c) No, the TV show must meet certain requirements to be considered Canadian: the key producer must be Canadian, the key creative personnel are Canadian, and 75% of service costs and post-production lab costs are paid to Canadians.

d) Answers may vary.

11. a) If the **rand** command produces a number less than 0.3, it rains, otherwise it does not rain; answers may vary.

b) Answers may vary.

c) 49%

Chapter 2 Review, pages 94–95

1. a) $\frac{3}{8}$ **b)** 37.5%   **c)** 0.375

2. a) No, 10 chips is not a large enough sample to determine if all the chips are working; answers may vary.

b) Test chips regularly; answers may vary.

3. a) $\frac{13}{27}$ **b)** $\frac{1}{9}$ **c)** $\frac{2}{9}$ **d)** $\frac{10}{27}$

4. a) $\frac{1}{18}$ **b)** $\frac{17}{18}$ **c)** $\frac{1}{6}$

d) $\frac{1}{3}$ **e)** 1   **f)** $\frac{11}{12}$

5. a)

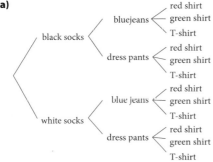

b) i) $\frac{1}{6}$ **ii)** $\frac{1}{2}$ **iii)** $\frac{1}{12}$ **iv)** $\frac{1}{3}$

6. a) 25%   **b)** No; answers may vary.

c) 3; answers may vary.

7. a) $\frac{1}{2}$; answers may vary.   **b)** 0.8

c) If there are extra points awarded for hitting red, then people will aim for it; answers may vary.

8. a) The calculator will generate 10 random integers between 1 and 5; answers may vary.

b) 2; explanations may vary.

9. a) The calculator will generate a random number between 0 and 1; answers may vary.

b) 10; explanations may vary.

10. a) 80%   **b)** 6

11. a) 16   **b)** $\frac{3}{13}$

Chapter 2 Practice Test, pages 96–97

1. C

2. A

3. D

4. false

5. a)

limousine — helicopter, jet
sports car — helicopter, jet
motorcycle — helicopter, jet

b) i) $\frac{1}{6}$ **ii)** $\frac{2}{3}$ **iii)** $\frac{1}{3}$

6. a) 99 936   **b)** 71%

7. a) Divide a spinner into 3 areas, one with half the total area of the spinner, the other with one tenth the total area, and the other with the rest; answers may vary.

b) Any number between 0 and 0.1 can be a loss of $30 000, any number greater than 0.5 can be a gain of $10 000, and any other number would be no loss or gain; answers may vary.

c) Answers may vary.

8. a) red: 40°, blue: 80°, yellow: 240°

b) i) $\frac{1}{9}$ **ii)** $\frac{8}{9}$

c) A result of 1 indicates red, a result of 2 to 3 indicates blue, and a result of 4 to 9 indicates yellow; answers may vary.

d) Answers may vary.

e) $\frac{4}{9}$

CHAPTER 3

One Variable Statistics, pages 98–163

Prerequisite Skills, pages 100–101

1. a) 1, 4, 4, 5, 5, 7, 8, 9, 9, 11, 15, 19

b) 1, 1, 2, 2, 3, 3, 3, 4, 5, 5, 6, 6, 7, 9, 11, 12

c) −11, −5, −3, −3, 0, 1, 1, 4, 5, 5, 7, 8, 12

d) $\frac{3}{16}, \frac{1}{4}, \frac{1}{2}, \frac{5}{8}$

2. a) 41.17   **b)** 10.5   **c)** 70.71   **d)** 59.6   **e)** 4.35

3. a) 11   **b)** 6.86   **c)** 5   **d)** 3.74

4. a) bar graph   **b)** hockey   **c)** curling

d) No, two people like curling, so it is popular among some people; answers may vary.

5. a) entertainment   **b)** $207.40

6. a) broken line graph   **b)** about 18°C

c) about 30°C; answers may vary.

d) The prediction can be checked by recording the average resort temperature for the 17th week and comparing it to the prediction.

7. a) histogram   **b)** 34

3.1 Sampling Techniques, pages 102–109

1. convenience sampling

2. a) combined stratified random sampling and systematic sampling

b) Probably; answers may vary.

c) Choose random numbers to form the teams; answers may vary.

3. a) voluntary-response sampling; answers may vary.

b) stratified random sampling; answers may vary.

c) stratified random sampling; answers may vary.

d) voluntary response sampling or convenience sampling; answers may vary.

4. a) sample: teenagers at local library; population: all students at Zoe's school

b) sample: Enrica and her friends; population: "Canadian Idol" viewers

c) sample: surveyed stores; population: toothpaste sellers

d) sample: people pass Tony; population: all voters

e) sample: people at gym at that time; population: all member of Angelo's gym

f) sample: students in Maya's science class; population: all students in Maya's grade

5. a) Those who do not respond or those the government does not know about; answers may vary.

b) No sampling technique is used, since the government does not need to choose which Canadians to survey. The representative sample is the population. Because the representative sample is so large, it costs too much money and takes too much time to be carried out every year; answers may vary.

c) Yes, since the remaining 3% of the population would probably respond similarly to the 97% that were surveyed; answers may vary.

6. Probably not; it could be a coincidence; answers may vary.

7. a) Ontario high school graduates

b) It would be too expensive and time-consuming to survey them all; answers may vary.

c) Telephone high schools to obtain their graduates' contact information.

d) Cluster sampling; survey every graduate from a few randomly-selected schools; answers may vary.

8. a) simple random sampling

b) No; the number of defective bolts might be changing; answers may vary.

c) He could specify exactly how each bolt is defective; answers may vary.

9. a) Yes; about 10% of each grade is surveyed; answers may vary.

b) Yes; each grade gets a fair representation; answers may vary.

11. a) simple random sampling; the vehicles are chosen randomly.

b) Answers may vary.

c) Very unlikely; there are many possible times between 2 P.M. and midnight, and only a 1 in 20 chance that the same gate would be chosen; answers may vary.

12. a) sample: selected students at the two schools; population: all elementary school students in the school district

b) 20 in grade 4, 25 in grade 5, 30 in grade 6, and 25 in grade 7.

c) 20 in grade 4, 20 in grade 5, 30 in grade 6, and 30 in grade 7.

d) Use a random number generator; answers may vary.

3.2 Collect and Analyse Data, pages 110–117

1. a) Dharma's observations are primary data because she collected information for herself. The cafeteria staff's observations are secondary data because they collected the information for Dharma.

b) Both should be accurate; answers may vary.

2. a) combined voluntary-response sampling and systematic random sampling

b) No; those who returned the survey are probably like-minded people; answers may vary.

c) Answers may vary.

d) Maybe; since the 56% of people responded, it is likely that he will be able to gather reliable information from the survey; answers may vary.

3. a) response bias; only asking football fans and worrying them about relocation; change question to: *Should the provincial and federal governments help build a new stadium?* and ask people outside the game; answers may vary.

b) non-response bias; only the most opinionated people will call in; offer an entry in a contest for a calling as an incentive ; answers may vary.

c) non-response bias; only the most opinionated people will return the survey; offer some incentive for the less opinionated to return the survey, such as an entry in a contest; answers may vary.

d) response bias; the question is clearly biased against the development of the subdivision; change question to: *Are you for or against the decision made by a developer to close this mall in order to build a subdivision?*

4. a) measurement bias

b) Have the question in one type size and alphabetize the options.

5. How do you think the $2000 raised in the last fundraiser should be spent? Randomly selecting a representative sample from each grade; answers may vary.

6. Answers may vary.

7. a) Yes; more people in favour could have called in because they were losing and fewer people opposed could have called in because they were winning.

b) Call and ask others in favour to vote too.

8. Probably; since pilots have nothing to gain or lose by deliberately reporting negatively or positively about air traffic controllers; answers may vary.

9. a) Ask students at your school at random; ask each of your friends to ask ten people the question and then report their responses to you; answers may vary.

b) Primary data; since it is difficult to know whether your friends asked the question without any bias; answers may vary.

10. a) Get honest data; answers may vary.

b) No; Spyware reflects the sample accurately unless someone can block it; answers may vary.

c) telephone-tapping, intercepting e-mails, stealing mail, searching garbage, inappropriate use of medical or banking records

11. It is very vague and might draw a wide range of answers; answers may vary.

12. a) Terence: primary data; Linda: secondary data

b) Terence: the list is objective and comes from a very large sample; because radio listeners enjoyed certain songs does not mean that students at his school will enjoy the same playlist. Linda: the list reflects the music preferences of students in the school; responses might be rushed. Answers may vary.

c) Find a way to combine their data; answers may vary.

13. a) Yes, all four preferred Proteeth.

b) They knew that dentists would prefer a toothpaste that fights cavities, gingivitis, and plaque, so they would prefer Proteeth; answers may vary.

c) Give the dentists several brands of toothpaste that fight cavities, gingivitis, and plaque; survey a greater number of dentists.

15. Answers may vary.

16. Answers may vary.

3.3 Display Data, pages 118–129

1. a) discrete
b) continuous
c) continuous
d) discrete

2. a) Bar graph, since the data is discrete and values are wanted for comparison; answers may vary.
b) Histogram, since the data is continuous; answers may vary.
c) Circle graph, since the data is discrete and part of a total amount; answers may vary.
d) Bar graph, since the data is discrete and values are wanted for comparison; answers may vary.
e) Histogram, since the data is continuous; answers may vary.
f) Circle graph, since the data is discrete and part of a total amount; answers may vary.

3. a) No, since the data is continuous; answers may vary.
b) Yes, though the information about the cities would be gone. Instead, the histogram would display the frequency of each amount of snow in those five cities.

4. The line graph shows continuous data; the circle graph shows discrete data.

5. a)

Score Interval	Tally	Frequency
[30, 40)	||	2
[40, 50)	|	1
[50, 60)	|||	3
[60, 70)	卌	5
[70, 80)	卌 ||	7
[80, 90)	卌	5
[90, 100]	|	1

b)

6.

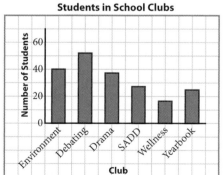

Students in School Clubs

7. Tomas is correct, height is continuous, so a histogram should be used.

8. Answers may vary.

9. Favourite ice-cream flavours; life-spans of a group of salmon tagged in the wild; answers may vary.

10. Answers may vary.

11. a) Discrete; bar graph, since the data is discrete; answers may vary.
b) Discrete; bar graph, since the data is discrete; answers may vary.
c) Continuous; histogram, since the data is continuous; answers may vary.
d) Discrete; bar graph, since the data is discrete; answers may vary.
e) Discrete; bar graph, since the data is discrete; answers may vary.

13. Answers may vary.

14. a)

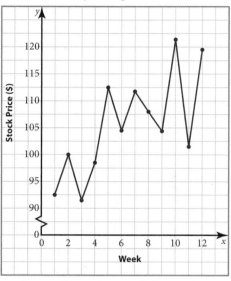

Weekly Closing Stock Price

b) Yes, the price changes dramatically from week to week; answers may vary.

c)

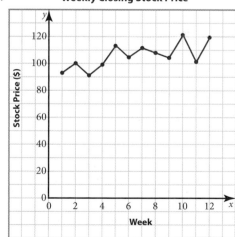

Weekly Closing Stock Price

d) less volatile

e) The second graph so that the stock appears less volatile; the first graph because it makes the stock look unpredictable and unstable.

3.4 Measures of Central Tendency, pages 130–139

1. **a)** mean: 29.3; median: 29; mode: 21 and 38
   b) mean: 63.1; median: 64.5; mode: no mode
2. mean: $31.25; median: $10; mode: $10
3. **a)** mean: 382.2; median: 364; mode: no mode
   b) mean: 403.8; median: 437; mode: no mode
4. **a)** median: [170–175); mode: [165–170); range 35 cm
   b) The median; most values are within 10 cm of it.
5. Shoe size; answers may vary.
6. The mean can get distorted by outliers, but not the median; answers may vary.
7. **a)** mean: 7; median: 7; mode: 7
   b) The mode; because it is the highest bar.
   c) The mode describes the most common shoe size.
8. **a)** mean: 37 000; median: 38 000; mode: 41 000 and 43 000
   b) The median; it describes the average and there are no outliers; answers may vary.
   c) Weather, attractions, location, or the duration of the fair might vary from year to year; answers may vary.
9. **a)** Lionel: mean: 21.3; median: 22; mode: 22
   Jeffrey: mean: 20.9; median: 21; mode: 21
   b) The median best represents Lionel's performance, because he has several outliers; the mean best represents Jeffrey's performance because he was very consistent.
   c) Lionel; all three of his measures of central tendencies higher.
10. **a)**

Position	Hits	At-Bats	Batting Average
1st base	26	71	0.366
2nd base	38	84	0.452
3rd base	25	62	0.403
shortstop	31	67	0.463
catcher	28	70	0.400
pitcher	12	39	0.308
left field	41	88	0.466
centre field	52	88	0.591
right field	47	88	0.534

   b) 0.443   **c)** 0.457
   d) The team's batting average is higher than the mean batting average; not every player has the same number of at-bats; better batters generally have more at-bats.
   e) 0.530   **f)** 0.530
   g) All the fielders have the same number of at-bats; their means have the same denominator.
12. Answers may vary.
13. **a)** $x = 18$ **b)** $x \geq 14$ **c)** $x = 11$ or $x = 8$
14. 164

3.5 Measures of Spread, pages 140–147

1. **a)** 122
   b) first quartile: 107; third quartile: 140
   c) 33
2. **a)** 51   **b)** 30   **c)** 9   **d)** 54
3. 52
4. 102
5. **a)** 12.4 g   **b)** 6 m
   c) 8.9 cm   **d)** 4.2 L
6. **a)** 198.81 cm   **b)** 12.25 kg
   c) $484   **d)** 44.89 mL
7. **a)** variance: 94.5; standard deviation: 9.7
   b) variance: 6.4; standard deviation: 2.5
   c) variance: 4.5; standard deviation: 2.1
   d) variance: 9.8; standard deviation: 3.1

8. There is more variation in the heights of the players on Team Two.
9.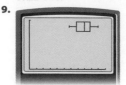
10. Ingrid; she is less likely to have a very low scoring game.
11. **a)** 0.067 cm   **b)** 0   **c)** 0%
    d) Probably not; the failure rate could be 2% or 3% and it likely would not be measured by testing just 10 pistons; answers may vary.
12. range: 21 000; variance: 36 100 000; standard deviation: 6008
14. Answers may vary.

3.6 Common Distributions, pages 148–155

1. **a)** skewed left
   b) bimodal
   c) normal
   d) skewed right
2. **a)** The lengths of hairs on a cat; answers may vary.
   b) The masses of pumpkins in a giant pumpkin contest; answers may vary.
   c) The times for male and female Olympic athletes in the 100 m dash; answers may vary.
3. **a)** bimodal
   b) Girls might be, on the average, better or more focused readers than boys at this age; answers may vary.
4. **a)** To make sure that the mean dress size is close to the mean dress size of its customers; answers may vary.
   b) Yes; to make sure the standard deviation of dresses is similar to the standard deviation of the sizes of customers; answers may vary.
5. **a)** Bimodal, there are many homeowners between 35 and 45 years old, and many between 55 and 65 years old.
   b) To direct campaigning and advertising towards 35 to 45 and 55 to 65 year olds.
   c) mean: about 50; median: about 50
6. **a)** Skewed to the right; lots of highly paid employees; answers may vary.
   b) The mode because it is the greatest measure of central tendency; answers may vary.
   c) The median, since it is less than the mode and the mean; answers may vary.
8. 1360
9. Answers may vary.

Chapter 3 Review, pages 156–157

1. **a)** convenience sampling
   b) voluntary-response sampling
   c) stratified random sampling
2. Survey 60 females and 40 males.
3. Number the people from 1 to 200, then generate 15 random numbers between 1 and 200.
4. *Do you think a carnival should be held for this year's Spirit Week?*
5. **a)** response bias
   b) non-response bias
   c) measurement bias
6. **a)** systematic random sampling
   b) Not everyone will return the survey.

7. a) circle graph, bar graph
b)

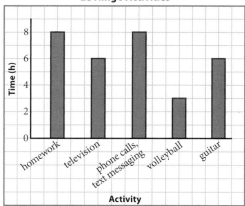

Le Hing's Activities

Le Hing's Activities

- doing homework
- watching television
- making phone calls and text messaging
- playing volleyball
- practising guitar

8. a) 3　　　　**b)** 60%　　　　**c)** It is continuous.
9. a) mean: 59.92; median: 59; mode: 21
b) mean: 7.39; median: 6; mode: 6
c) mean: 72.62; median: 73; mode: no mode
10. a) mean: $83.33; median: $25; mode: $25
b) The mean, since the median and mode only represent one price; answers may vary.
11. a) range: 63; variance: 275; standard deviation: 16.58
b) range: 23; variance: 42; standard deviation: 6.48
12. Answers may vary.
13. a) The mode is near the left or right side of the data; for example, the masses of body-builders; answers may vary.
b) There are two modes in the data, or two peaks in the histogram; for example, the hair length of both men and women; answers may vary.
c) The mode is in the middle, making a perfect normal curve; for example, the scores on a science test.
14. a)

Mark Interval	Tally	Frequency
[30-40)			1
[40-50)	||||	4
[50-60)	|||||		6
[60-70)	||||| |||||	10
[70-80)	||||| ||	7
[80-90)	|||	3
[90-100]			1

b) Yes, the median, mean, and mode are all at the centre, and the graph is almost symmetrically bell-shaped.

Chapter 3 Practice Test, pages 158–159
1. A
2. B
3. C
4. a) primary
b) primary or secondary, depending on the information
c) primary
d) secondary
5. a) response bias, since it is clear that the question is trying to get a positive response; answers may vary.
b) measurement bias, since only a few types of shows are shown, and people may not take the time to fill in the "Other" box, even if their favourite type of show is not sports, reality, or crime drama; answers may vary.
6. a) *Should we allow private-sector investment in our transit system?*
b) *What is your favourite type of television show?*
7. a) 0.1 cm
b) 1.3 cm to 1.7 cm
c) 1.13 cm to 1.17 cm
d) The manufacturing process for nuts may be more accurate and less prone to irregularity than that for washers, or it may be more important for nuts to have a lower standard deviation than for washers; answers may vary.
8. a) range: $31 900; mean: $46 150; median: $42 050; mode: $58 000
b) decrease, since in the first week people go there because it is new. After that, they only go if they really enjoyed it; answers may vary.
9. range: 48 min; variance: 204.8 min; standard deviation: 14.31 min
10. a) bar graph
b) normal distribution

Chapters 1 to 3 Review, pages 160–161
1. $\sin A = \frac{4}{5}$, $\cos A = \frac{3}{5}$, $\tan A = \frac{4}{3}$
2. 115 m
3. a) $b = 50.2$ cm, $c = 50.2$ cm, $\angle C = 86°$
b) $e = 32.3$ cm, $\angle D = 84.7°$, $\angle F = 45.3°$
4. $e = 6.7$ m
5. $\frac{3}{4}$
6. a) $\frac{1}{50}$　**b)** $\frac{1}{10}$　**c)** $\frac{9}{10}$　**d)** $\frac{97}{100}$　**e)** $\frac{1}{10}$
7. a) Green: 60%; Purple: 40%; Red: 0%
b) Green: 36.7%; Purple: 60%; Red: 3.3%
8. a) 20%
b) 12 hits
c) The player may get injured, may get better at getting hits; answers may vary.
9. a) Sample: readers who return the form; population: all readers
b) Sample: his neighbours; population: all people in the town
10. Answers may vary.
a) Not everyone who uses the cafeteria was surveyed so there is a non-response bias; more people can be asked for their opinion so the population is better represented.
b) Students may not volunteer the information resulting in response bias; ask students privately or ask students for proof or progress.
c) The wording of the question will affect responses so there is response bias; ask a simpler question: *Should cell phones be banned from the hallways and cafeteria?*

11. a)

Grade 10 Election Results

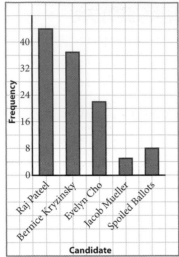

b) Raj Pateel won the vote, there were a total of 116 votes cast, 7% of the ballots were spoiled; answers may vary.

12. a) mean: 2.87, median: 2, mode: 2

b) The mode because it occurs more than twice as often as any other outcome; answers may vary.

13. a) range: 75, variance: 558.59, standard deviation: 23.63

b) range: 8, variance: 4.88, standard deviation: 2.21

14.

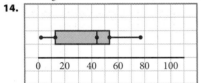

CHAPTER 4

Quadratic Relations I, pages 164–229

Prerequisite Skills, pages 166–167

1. a) 13.1   **b)** −1.7   **c)** −7.7   **d)** −17.1

2. a) −6.5   **b)** 26.1   **c)** −10.5   **d)** −6.7

3. a) 41.4   **b)** −25.2   **c)** −130   **d)** 10.65

4. a) $-2x$ **b)** $7x^2 + 3x + 10$

   c) $8x^2 - 2x$ **d)** $-8x^2 + 2x + 2$

5. a) 0   **b)** 6

   c) 96   **d)** −202

6. a) −18   **b)** 47

   c) −100   **d)** 151

7. a) 192   **b)** −183

   c) −363   **d)** 2284

8. a)

x	y
−2	−10
−1	−7
0	−4
1	−1
2	2

b)

x	y
8	17
12	15
16	13
20	11
24	9

9. a)

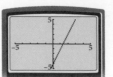

b)

b) a) slope: 3; y-intercept: −4

   b) slope: −0.5; y-intercept: 21

10. a)

x	y	First Differences
3	8	
4	15	7
5	23	8
6	31	8
7	39	8

b)

x	y	First Differences
13	0	
14	1	1
15	4	3
16	9	5
17	16	7

c)

x	y	First Differences
−5	3	
−4	3	0
−3	3	0
−2	3	0
−1	3	0

11. a) slope: $-\frac{1}{2}$; y-intercept: 3

   b) slope: 5; y-intercept: 1

   c) slope: 2; y-intercept: −4

   d) slope: $\frac{2}{5}$; y-intercept: $-3\frac{4}{5}$

12. a) a translation of 4 units down

   b) a translation of 4 units right and 3 units up

   c) a reflection in the vertical line halfway between the pentagons

   d) a rotation about the point (−1.5, 0)

4.1 Modelling With Quadratic Relations, pages 168–179

1. a) quadratic

   b) linear

   c) neither

   d) quadratic

   e) neither

   f) neither

2. a) Not quadratic; the first differences are always −9.

   b) Not quadratic; the second differences are not constant.

   c) Quadratic; the second differences are always 16.

   d) Not quadratic; the second differences are not constant.

3. a) i) Quadratic; the highest power is x^2.

   ii) Not quadratic; there is no x^2 term.

   iii) Quadratic; the highest power is x^2.

   iv) Not quadratic; there is no x^2 term.

   v) Quadratic; the highest power is x^2.

   vi) Not quadratic; there is no x^2 term.

b) i)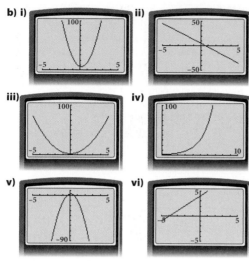

ii)

iii)

iv)

v)

vi)

4. a) minimum: 400 m
b) maximum: 82 m
c) minimum: 0 m

5. a)

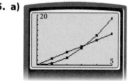

b) Carl's distance-time relationship is quadratic since his graph is a parabola.

6. a)

Time (s)	Height (m)
0	150.0
1	145.1
2	130.4
3	105.9
4	71.6
5	27.5

b) Yes, it is quadratic because of the t^2 term in the relation and because the second differences in the heights are constant, -9.8.

c)

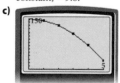

7. a) On Earth:

Time (s)	Height (m)
0	0
1	10.1
2	10.4
3	0.9

On the moon:

Time (s)	Height (m)
0	0
2	26.8
4	47.2
6	61.2
8	68.8
10	70.0
12	64.8
14	53.2
16	35.2
18	10.8

b) Curve A models the motion of the ball on the moon since the ball goes higher and takes longer to land; Curve B models the motion of the ball on Earth.

8. a) four
b) A quadratic relation has a squared variable, and a square has four sides; answers may vary.

9. a)

Length (m)	Width (m)	Perimeter (m)
40	10	$2(40) + 2(10) = 100$
35	15	$2(35) + 2(15) = 100$
30	20	$2(30) + 2(20) = 100$
25	25	$2(25) + 2(25) = 100$
20	30	$2(20) + 2(30) = 100$
15	35	$2(15) + 2(35) = 100$
10	40	$2(10) + 2(40) = 100$

b)

Length (m)	Width (m)	Perimeter (m)	Area (m²)
40	10	$2(40) + 2(10) = 100$	400
35	15	$2(35) + 2(15) = 100$	525
30	20	$2(30) + 2(20) = 100$	600
25	25	$2(25) + 2(25) = 100$	625
20	30	$2(20) + 2(30) = 100$	600
15	35	$2(15) + 2(35) = 100$	525
10	40	$2(10) + 2(40) = 100$	400

c)

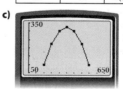

d) 25 m by 25 m

10. a)

Horizontal Distance From Cliff (m)	Vertical Distance From the Base of Cliff (m)
0	11.25
1	11.20
2	11.05
3	10.80
4	10.45
5	10.00
6	9.45
7	8.80
8	8.05
9	7.20
10	6.25
11	5.20
12	4.05
13	2.80
14	1.45
15	0

b)

c) 15 m

12. 13.3 s; 266.7 m

13. Oliver

14. a) No; the second difference is not constant; answers may vary.
b) No; the second difference is not constant; answers may vary.

15. Answers may vary.

4.2 The Quadratic Relation $y = ax^2 + k$, pages 180–193

1. a) $0 < a < 1$ **b)** $a < -1$
c) $0 > a > -1$ **d)** $a > 1$

2. a) positive   **b)** negative
c) positive   **d)** negative

3. a) $k = 3$; vertex: $(0, 3)$
b) $k = -2$; vertex: $(0, -2)$
c) $k = 5$; vertex: $(0, 5)$
d) $k = -7$; vertex: $(0, -7)$

4. a) stretched vertically by a factor of 3
b) translated up by 3 units, has vertex $(0, 3)$
c) reflected in the x-axis and compressed vertically
d) translated down by 12 units, has vertex $(0, -12)$
e) compressed vertically and translated up 13 units, has vertex $(0, 13)$
f) reflected in the x-axis, stretched vertically and translated up 6 units, has vertex $(0, 6)$
g) reflected in the x-axis, compressed vertically and translated down 5 units, has vertex $(0, -5)$
h) stretched vertically and translated down 9 units, has vertex $(0, -9)$

5. a) $0 < a < 1, k > 0$ **b)** $a > 1, k < 0$
c) $a < -1, k < 0$ **d)** $0 > a > -1, k > 0$

6. a) $y = 4x^2 - 6$
b) $y = -0.04x^2 + 5$
c) $y = -\frac{5}{9}x^2 - 3$

7. a) widest: $y = 0.2x^2$ because $0.2 < 5$
farthest from x-axis: $5x^2 + 6$ because $6 > 0$
b) widest: $y = -0.4x^2 - 8$ because $0.4 < 3$
farthest from x-axis: $y = 3x^2 + 9$ because $9 > 8$
c) widest: $y = 2x^2 - 5$ because $2 < 5$
farthest from x-axis: $y = 5x^2 + 7$ because $7 > 5$
d) widest: $y = 0.1x^2$ because $0.1 < 0.25$
farthest from x-axis: $y = 0.25x^2 + 11$ because $11 > 0$
e) widest: $y = 0.03x^2 + 2$ because $0.03 < 0.2$
farthest from x-axis: $y = 0.03x^2 + 2$ because $2 > 1$
f) widest: $y = 0.9x^2 + 6$ because $0.9 < 1$
farthest from x-axis: they are both the same distance from the x-axis since $6 = 6$

8. a) 1.79 m after 0.5 s, 1.15 m after 1 s
b) 1.53 s

9. a)

b) i) 15 m   **ii)** 21.6 m   **iii)** 60 m   **iv)** 72.6 m
c) in the city: 6.6 m; on the highway: 12.6 m. The stopping distance increases by about two times as much when going 10 km/h over the speed limit on the highway.

10. Answer may vary.
a) $(0, 6)$ **b)** -0.06 **c)** $y = -0.06x^2 + 6$

11. a) 19.6 m   **b)** 4.0 s

12. 33.9 m

4.3 The Quadratic Relation $y = a(x - h)^2$, pages 194–203

1. a) $h = 5$; vertex is $(5, 0)$
b) $h = -3$; vertex is $(-3, 0)$
c) $h = -7$; vertex is $(-7, 0)$
d) $h = 2$; vertex is $(2, 0)$

2. a) $a = 1$, so the graph is neither stretched nor compressed; $h = 7$, so the graph is translated 7 units to the right.
b) $a = -1$, so the graph is neither stretched nor compressed, but it is reflected in the x-axis; $h = -3$, so the graph is translated 3 units to the left.
c) $a = 1.5$, so the graph is vertically stretched; $h = -8$, so the graph is translated 8 units to the left.
d) $a = -0.8$, so the graph is vertically compressed and reflected in the x-axis; $h = 2$, so the graph is translated 2 units to the right.
e) $a = 0.1$, so the graph is vertically compressed; $h = 5$, so the graph is translated 5 units to the right.
f) $a = 2$, so the graph is vertically stretched; $h = -1$, so the graph is translated 1 unit to the left.
g) $a = -2$, so the graph is vertically stretched and reflected in the x-axis; $h = 8$, so the graph is translated 8 units to the right.
h) $a = 0.3$, so the graph is vertically compressed; $h = -14$, so the graph is translated 14 units to the left.

3. a) The graph is vertically stretched and translated 7 units to the right, so $a > 1$ and $h = 7$.
b) The graph is vertically compressed, reflected in the x-axis, and translated 5 units to the left, so $0 > a > -1$ and $h = -5$.
c) The graph is neither vertically compressed nor stretched, but it is translated 8 units to the left, so $a = 1$ and $h = -8$.
d) The graph is vertically stretched, reflected in the x-axis and translated 2 units to the right, so $a < -1$ and $h = 2$.

4. a) $y = -2(x - 4)^2$
b) $y = 0.5(x + 5)^2$
5. a) $y = 2(x + 3)^2$; because $3 > 1$
b) $y = -0.2(x - 8)^2$; because $8 > 3$
c) $y = 32(x - 10)^2$; because $10 > 3$
d) $y = 0.85(x + 9)^2$; because $9 > 2$
6. So that a positive h means a translation to the right and a negative h means a translation to the left.
7. a)

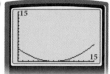

b) 14.07 cm
8. a) -17.07
b) Decrease; if the mountain biker has a greater speed when travelling horizontally, he will have to jump sooner so that he does not overshoot the ramp.
c) -24.14
9. a) $(282, 0)$　　**b)** 0.000 88
c) $y = 0.000\ 88(x - 282)^2$　**d)** 70 m
10. a)

x	$y = (x - 3)^2$	$y = 3 + \sqrt{x}$	$y = 3 - \sqrt{x}$
0	9.00	3.00	3.00
1	4.00	4.00	2.00
2	1.00	4.41	1.59
3	0.00	4.73	1.27
4	1.00	5.00	1.00
5	4.00	5.24	0.76
6	9.00	5.45	0.55
7	16.00	5.65	0.35

b)

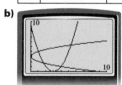

c) They are similar in that they have the same shape, but they are different in that one is a reflection of the other through the line $y = 3$; answers may vary.

4.4 The Quadratic Relation $y = a(x - h)^2 + k$, pages 204–217
1. a) i) $(5, 1)$　　**ii)** positive
b) i) $(-2, -7)$　**ii)** positive
c) i) $(-4, -2)$　**ii)** negative
d) i) $(2, 6)$　　**ii)** negative
e) i) $(-8, 4)$　　**ii)** positive
f) i) $(6, -2)$　　**ii)** negative
g) i) $(2, -5)$　　**ii)** positive
h) i) $(-8, 1)$　　**ii)** negative
2. a) i) $(3, 12)$　　**ii)** upward　　**iii)** stretched
b) i) $(10, -1)$　**ii)** downward　**iii)** compressed
c) i) $(-4, -8)$　**ii)** downward　**iii)** stretched
d) i) $(-20, -5)$　**ii)** downward　**iii)** neither
e) i) $(11, -3)$　**ii)** upward　　**iii)** compressed
f) i) $(-2, 9)$　　**ii)** upward　　**iii)** stretched
g) i) $(-6, 7)$　　**ii)** downward　**iii)** compressed
h) i) $(8, 2)$　　**ii)** upward　　**iii)** stretched
i) i) $(-2, -1)$　**ii)** upward　　**iii)** stretched
j) i) $(4, 6)$　　**ii)** downward　**iii)** compressed

3. a)

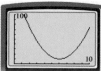

b)

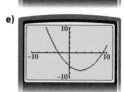

c)

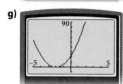

d)

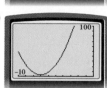

e)

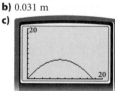

f)

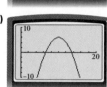

g)

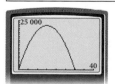

h)

4. a) $(0, 0)$　　　$y = 3x^2$
b) $(7, 3)$　　　$y = 0.375(x - 7)^2 + 3$
c) $(-4, 8)$　　$y = -6(x + 4)^2 + 8$
d) $(-6, 1)$　　$y = 0.5(x + 6)^2 + 1$
5. a) $y = 0.01(x + 2)^2 - 3$
b) $y = -2(x - 8)^2 + 3$
c) $y = 10(x - 5)^2 - 7$
d) $y = -4(x + 3)^2 - 1$
6. a) $(8.7, 7.6)$
b) 0.031 m
c)

d) the football's greatest height above ground
7. a)

Ticket Price, P ($)	Total Revenue, R ($)
0	0
5	12 500
10	20 000
15	22 500
20	20 000
25	12 500
30	0

b) $(15, 22\ 500)$; y-coordinate is the greatest total revenue, x-coordinate is the amount that, when used as the ticket price, results in this total revenue.

8. a) $y = -2.78(x - 30)^2 + 9800$
  b) 9522 m
9. a) 2.3 m
  b) (9.5, 5); when the biker is 9.5 m horizontally from the end of the ramp, the biker's height is 5 m.
  c)

  d) 22.4 m from the ramp
11. Answers may vary.
12. Yes; explanations may vary.
13. a) 1.9 m from the vertex **b)** 2.8 cm from the vertex

4.5 Interpret Graphs of Quadratic Relations, pages 218–225

1. a) −7 **b)** 20 **c)** 2895 **d)** 3.375
  e) −3 **f)** 3.312 **g)** −1.8 **h)** −21
2. a) x-intercepts: −10, 2; y-intercept: −5; minimum: −9; vertex: (−4, −9)
  b) x-intercepts: −2, −6; y-intercept: −6; maximum: 2; vertex: (−4, 2)
  c) x-intercepts: 2, −20; y-intercept: 4; maximum: 12; vertex: (−9, 12)
  d) x-intercepts: −3, 1; y-intercept: −6; minimum: −8; vertex: (−1, −8)
  e) x-intercepts: none; y-intercept: 12; minimum: 3; vertex: (6, 3)
  f) x-intercepts: 2, −10; y-intercept: 10; maximum: 18; vertex: (−4, 18)
3. a) $y = -3(x - 3)^2 + 27$ **b)** $y = -0.5x^2 + 24.5$
  c) $y = -0.1(x - 10)^2 + 10$ **d)** $y = 15x^2$
4. a) 2 s, 169.6 m **b)** 125.5 m
5. a) Smart Car Fortwo

Time, t (s)	Distance, d (m)
0	0
1	1.4
2	5.6
3	12.6
4	22.4
5	35.0

Tesla Roadster

Time, t (s)	Distance, d (m)
0	0
1	6.9
2	27.6
3	62.1
4	110.4
5	172.5

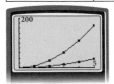

  b) 137.5 m, the coefficients of t^2
  c) first second 1.4 m and 6.9 m; fourth second 9.8 m and 48.3 m; the speed is increasing for each time period.

6. Answers may vary.
7. a) $h = -5(t - 4.5)^2 + 101.25$
  b) 90 m; yes after 6 s, the first time is when the projectile is rising and the second time is when it is falling, explanations may vary.
8. a)

  b) 45° **c)** 75°
  d) the height of the ski ramp
9. 2.7 s

Chapter 4 Review, pages 226–227

1. a) No; the greatest exponent is 1.
  b) Yes; the greatest exponent is 2.
  c) No; the second differences are not constant.
2. a)

Time (s)	Height (m)
0	2.0
0.5	8.3
1.0	12.1
1.5	13.5
2.0	12.4
2.5	8.9
3.0	2.9

  b) about 1.5 s
  c) about 3.1 s
  d) The second differences are constant, when graphed the points in the table form a parabola, and there is a t^2 term.
3. a) no stretch, translated 3.4 units down
  b) reflected in the x-axis, vertically compressed, has not been translated
  c) vertically compressed, translated 15 units up
  d) vertically stretched, translated 3.4 units down
4. Sketches may vary slightly.
5. a) $y = 12x^2 - 100$
  b) $y = -0.02x^2 + 20$
6. a) $y = -8(x - 10)^2$
  b) $y = 0.15(x + 6)^2$
7. a) reflected in the x-axis, vertically compressed, translated 18 units to the right and 15 units up
  b) vertically stretched, translated 1 unit the left and 2 units down
  c) reflected in the x-axis, vertically stretched, translated 9 units to the left and 10.8 units up
  d) vertically compressed, translated 40 units right
8. Sketches may vary slightly.
9. a)

Hourly Rate ($)	Expected Number of Hours per Week	Weekly Revenue ($)
45	42	$1890
50	38	$1900
55	34	$1870
60	30	$1800
65	26	$1690
70	22	$1540

b)

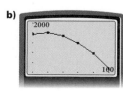

c) $y = -(x - 50)^2 + 1900$
d) $48.75/h

10. a) $y = 0.25(x - 3)^2 - 5$
b) $y = -2.875(x + 4)^2 + 7$

11. Answers may vary.

12. a)

d	0	0.5	1.0	1.5	2.0	2.5	3.0
h	2.15	5.4	7.35	8	7.35	5.4	2.15

b) 2.15 m
c) $y = -2.6(x - 1.5)^2 + 8$

Chapter 4 Practice Test, pages 228–229

1. B
2. C
3. C
4. C
5. B
6. B
7. The first differences increase or decrease by a constant amount and the second differences are a constant.
8. a) vertically compressed, vertex has been translated 8 units to the left
b) reflected in the x-axis, vertically stretched, vertex has been translated 14 units down
c) reflected in the x-axis, vertically stretched, vertex has been translated 7 units to the right and 13 units down
d) vertically compressed, vertex has been translated 20 units to the left and 16 units up
9. a) $y = \dfrac{-1}{49}(x - 35)^2 + 25$
b) about 20 m

10. a)

Number of Layers	Total Number of Pennies
1	1
2	3
3	6
4	10
5	15
6	21
7	28
8	36
9	45
10	55

b) The number of layers squared plus the number of layers, all divided by 2; answers may vary.
c) 14
d) 1275 pennies

11. a) 3 m
b) 4.25 m, 2.5 m
c) no

Chapter 5

Quadratic Relations II, pages 230–291

Prerequisite Skills, pages 232–233

1. a) $18x$ **b)** $135x$
    c) $-88x$ **d)** $4.5x$
2. a) $13x^2 + 4x$ **b)** $-2x + 17$
    c) $10x^2 - 19x + 9$ **d)** $-2x^2 + x - 5$
3. a) $4x + 64$ **b)** $51x + 6x^2$
    c) $-84x^2 + 21x$ **d)** $40x^2 - 50x$
4. a) $8(x + 2) = 8x + 16$ **b)** $3x(x - 8) = 3x^2 - 24x$
5. a)

b)

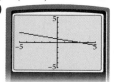

c)

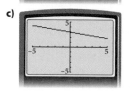

d)

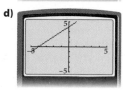

6. a) and d)
7. a) x-intercept: -1.5; y-intercept: 4
    b) x-intercept: -1 and 5; y-intercept: -5
    c) x-intercept: 0 and 6; y-intercept: 0
8. a)

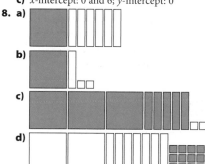

b)

c)

d)

9. a) 40   **b)** 18   **c)** 26   **d)** 11
10. a) 1, 2, 3, 4, 6, 8, 12, 24
    b) 1, 3, 9, 27, 81
    c) 1, 2, 3, 5, 6, 10, 15, 30
    d) 1, 2, 3, 6, 9, 18, -1, -2, -3, -6, -9, -18
11. a) 3 and 7   **b)** 2 and 6   **c)** 2 and 10
    d) 2 and 16   **e)** 2 and 25   **f)** 5 and -4
    g) 8 and -8 **h)** -16 and 4
12. a) $x = 5$ **b)** $x = 13$ **c)** $x = 37$
    d) $x = -13$ **e)** $x = 7$ **f)** $x = 8$
    g) $x = -5$ **h)** $x = -2$
13. a) $3(x + 3)$ **b)** $5(x + 4)$ **c)** $7(x - 5)$
    d) $-8(x + 6)$ **e)** $x(x - 4)$ **f)** $4x(x + 6)$
    g) $-3x(5x - 9)$ **h)** $5(4x^2 - 11)$
14. a) $(x + 1)(x + 2)$ **b)** $(x + 3)(x - 2)$
    c) $(x - 2)(x - 6)$ **d)** $(x + 2)(x + 7)$
    e) $(x - 5)(x + 2)$ **f)** $(x - 1)^2$

5.1 Expand Binomials, pages 234–241

1. a) $2(x + 2)$ **b)** $(x + 1)(x + 2)$
   c) $(2x + 1)(x + 2)$ **d)** $(2x + 1)(3x + 4)$
2. a) $2x + 4$ **b)** $x^2 + 3x + 2$
   c) $2x^2 + 5x + 2$ **d)** $6x^2 + 11x + 4$
3. a) $x^2 + 8x$ **b)** $x^2 + 8x + 7$
   c) $x^2 + 7x + 12$ **d)** $2x^2 + 7x + 3$
   e) $24x^2 + 38x + 10$ **f)** $9x^2 + 12x + 4$
4. a) $12x^2 + 41x + 35$ **b)** $6x^2 + 13x - 44$
   c) $18x^2 + 78x - 60$ **d)** $35x^2 - 46x - 16$
   e) $9 - 64x^2$ **f)** $16x^2 + 72x + 81$
5. a) $2x^2 + 23x + 30$ **b)** $3x^2 + 25x + 50$
   c) $3x^2 - 25x - 132$ **d)** $-20x^2 - 140x + 75$
   e) $4x^2 - 69x + 135$ **f)** $256x^2 + 288x + 81$
6. a) $x^2 - 25$ **b)** $x^2 - 100$
   c) $9x^2 - 49$ **d)** $64x^2 - 25$
   e) $49x^2 - 49$ **f)** $144x^2 - 81$
7. a) $x^2 + 12x + 36$ **b)** $x^2 - 16x + 64$
   c) $16x^2 + 120x + 225$ **d)** $81x^2 - 36x + 4$
   e) $25x^2 - 30x + 9$ **f)** $36x^2 + 144x + 144$
8. Patterns: $(ax + b)(ax - b) = a^2x^2 - b^2$
       $(ax + b)(ax + b) = a^2x^2 + 2abx + b^2$
9. a) i) $6x^2 + 8x - 14$ **ii)** $5x^2 - 13x + 6$ **iii)** $12x^2 - 56x - 55$
   b) i) 946 cm^2 **ii)** 570 cm^2 **iii)** 1001 cm^2
10. a) $2s^2 + 7s - 30$ **b)** 240 m^2
11. $6x^2 + 31x + 23$
12. a) $6x^2 + 19x + 15$ **b)** 111 m^2
   c) smallest base: \$13 500; largest base: \$113 400
13. a) about 0.62
   b) Answers may vary.
14. $46x^2 + 28x + 5$
15. a) $64x + 240$
   b) 432 cm^2; 560 cm^2; 880 cm^2
   c) 21.6¢; 28¢; 44¢
16. a) $3x^3 + 14x^2 + 35x + 18$
   b) $14x^3 - 39x^2 + 26x - 40$
   c) $x^4 + 7x^3 - 18x^2 + 107x + 11$
17. a) $(x + 5)(x + 5)$ **b)** $(x - 9)(x - 9)$
   c) $(x + 12)(x + 12)$ **d)** $(x + 6)(x - 6)$
   e) $(x + 8)(x - 8)$ **f)** $(x + 11)(x - 11)$

5.2 Change Quadratic Relations From Vertex Form to Standard Form, pages 242–247

1. a) $y = x^2 + 12x + 36$ **b)** $y = x^2 - 8x + 16$
   c) $y = x^2 - 30x + 225$ **d)** $y = x^2 - 4x + 4$
   e) $y = x^2 + 18x + 81$ **f)** $y = x^2 - 2x + 1$
2. a) $y = 3x^2 + 54x + 243$ **b)** $y = -2x^2 - 28x - 98$
   c) $y = -8x^2 + 80x - 200$ **d)** $y = 0.5x^2 + 2x + 2$
   e) $y = -0.25x^2 - 4x - 16$
   f) $y = 9.8x^2 - 62.72x + 100.352$
3. a) $y = x^2 - 16x + 67$ **b)** $y = x^2 + 10x + 35$
   c) $y = x^2 + 2x - 12$ **d)** $y = x^2 - 6x + 10$
   e) $y = x^2 + 12x + 29$ **f)** $y = x^2 - 10x + 22$
4. a) $y = 5x^2 - 40x + 92$ **b)** $y = -6x^2 - 108x - 493$
   c) $y = -2x^2 - 28x - 108$ **d)** $y = -8x^2 + 80x - 194$
   e) $y = 2.4x^2 - 24.48x + 68.424$
   f) $y = -1.9x^2 - 10.26x - 18.951$
5. a)
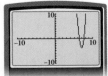
   b)
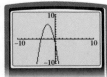

c)
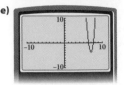
d)

e)
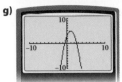
f)

g)
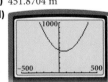
h)
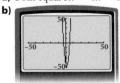

a) and e) are the same; b) and d) are the same; c) and g) are the same; f) and h) are the same.

6. a) $y = 5x^2 - 10x + 12$ **b)** $y = -3x^2 - 30x - 69$
   c) $y = -8x^2 + 160x - 783$ **d)** $y = 12x^2 + 24x + 15$
7. a) 447 **b)** 7 **c)** -181
   d) -20 **e)** -1 **f)** 15.04
8. a) 6; the speed of the racer when the maximum distance is reached.
   b) 50; the maximum distance
   c) $d = -2v^2 + 24v - 22$
   d)
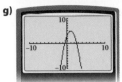

9. a) It shows the y-intercept; but it does not provide any information on the maximum or minimum value of the relation; answers may vary.
   b) It directly shows the vertex of the graph; but not the x- and y-intercepts; answers may vary.
10. a) $h = 0.000\ 549(x - 640)^2 + 227$
   b) $h = 0.000\ 549x^2 - 0.702\ 72x + 451.8704$
   c) 451.8704 m
   d)

11. a) $y = -4.9(t - 2)^2 + 20$ **b)** $y = -4.9t^2 + 19.6t + 0.4$
   c) 19.6 m/s **d)** 20 m
13. a) -1.625 **b)** $y = -1.625(x - 1.8)^2 + 8.0$
   c) 2.735 m
14. a) Both equal $3x^2 - 6x - 45$.
   b)

   c) Answers may vary.

5.3 Factoring Trinomials of the Form $x^2 + bx + c$,
pages 248–255

1. a) 5 and 5   **b)** 4 and 8
   c) -2 and -12 **d)** -2 and -18
   e) 6 and -5 **f)** 3 and -14
   g) 25 and -2 **h)** 8 and -8

2. a) $(x + 3)(x + 12)$ **b)** $(x + 4)(x + 4)$
   c) $(x + 2)(x + 10)$ **d)** $(x + 5)(x + 8)$

3. a) $(x - 2)(x - 11)$ **b)** $(x - 7)(x - 7)$
   c) $(x - 4)(x - 7)$ **d)** $(x - 10)(x - 10)$
   e) $(x - 2)(x + 16)$ **f)** $(x - 3)(x + 16)$
   g) $(x - 5)(x + 4)$ **h)** $(x - 21)(x + 3)$

4. a) $(x + 1)(x + 2)$ **b)** $(x + 1)(x + 6)$
   c) $(x + 2)(x + 6)$ **d)** $(x + 2)(x + 4)$

5. a) $x^2 + 6x + 8 = (x + 2)(x + 4)$
   b) $x^2 + 8x + 7 = (x + 1)(x + 7)$
   c) $x^2 + 8x + 15 = (x + 3)(x + 5)$
   d) $x^2 +10x + 24 = (x + 6)(x + 4)$

6. a) $x(x + 5)$ **b)** $x(x + 22)$
   c) $x(x - 19)$ **d)** $x(x - 15)$
   e) $x(x - 9.8)$ **f)** $x(x + 33.5)$

7. a) $(x + 5)(x - 5)$ **b)** $(x + 10)(x - 10)$
   c) $(x + 11)(x - 11)$ **d)** $(x + 1)(x - 1)$
   e) $(x + 7)(x - 7)$ **f)** $(x + 12)(x - 12)$

8. a) $x(x + 25)$ **b)** $(x + 2)(x + 14)$
   c) $(x + 6)(x - 7)$ **d)** $(x + 8)(x - 8)$
   e) $(x + 4)(x + 9)$ **f)** $(x - 6)(x - 6)$
   g) $(x + 2)(x - 2)$ **h)** $x(x - 32)$

9. a) $(x + 1)(x + 3)$ **b)** not factorable
   c) not factorable   **d)** $(x + 1)(x + 2)$
   e) $(x - 1)(x - 3)$ **f)** $(x + 3)(x - 1)$

10. No two numbers with a product of c have a sum of b; could
not model as a rectangle with algebra tiles; answers may vary.

11. a) $(x + 3)(x - 3)$ **b)** $(x + 10)(x - 10)$

12. a) πx^2 **b)** 25π
   c) $\pi x^2 - 25\pi$ **d)** $\pi(x - 5)(x + 5)$

13. a) $x^2 - 4$ **b)** $\$4800$

14. a) $(x + 2)(x + 5)$
   b) The length is 8 m and the width is 5 m.

15. a) $(x^2 - 1)(x^2 - 25) = (x + 1)(x - 1)(x + 5)(x - 5)$
   b) $(x^2 - 4)(x^2 - 49) = (x + 2)(x - 2)(x + 7)(x - 7)$
   c) $(x^2 - 36)(x^2 - 9) = (x + 6)(x - 6)(x + 3)(x - 3)$

5.4 Factoring Trinomials of the Form $ax^2 + bx + c$,
pages 256–263

1. a) $2(x + 3)(x + 5)$ **b)** $4(x + 6)(x - 1)$
   c) $3(x + 1)(x + 5)$ **d)** $2(x + 4)(x - 3)$
   e) $5(x + 2)(x - 1)$ **f)** $3(x - 2)(x - 2)$

2. a) $7(x - 5)(x - 6)$ **b)** $6(x - 3)(x - 7)$
   c) $-3(x + 4)(x + 6)$ **d)** $10(x - 16)(x + 2)$
   e) $-5(x - 3)(x - 7)$ **f)** $-2(x - 8)(x + 6)$

3. a) $1.2(x - 10)(x + 3)$ **b)** $-2.5(x + 4)(x + 8)$
   c) $3.4(x - 7)(x - 4)$ **d)** $-4.6(x + 6)(x + 6)$

4. a) $5x(x + 4)$ **b)** $3x(x - 7)$
   c) $-7x(x - 7)$ **d)** $-15x(x + 5)$
   e) $8.2x(x + 8)$ **f)** $-4.9x(x - 9)$

5. a) $3(x + 3)(x - 3)$ **b)** $6(x + 4)(x - 4)$
   c) $-3(x + 4)(x - 4)$ **d)** $-8(x + 9)(x - 9)$
   e) $1.2(x + 5)(x - 5)$ **f)** $-4.5(x + 6)(x - 6)$

6. a) $6(x + 4)(x + 4)$ **b)** $5(x + 3)(x - 3)$
   c) $9x(x - 3)$ **d)** $10(x - 8)(x + 3)$
   e) $-4(x + 7)(x - 7)$ **f)** $-2x(x - 9)$
   g) $1.5(x + 6)(x - 3)$ **h)** $-6.2(x + 8)(x - 8)$

7. a)

8. a) S.A. $= \pi r(2h + r)$
   b) about 5184 cm^2
   c) S.A. $= 5\pi r^2$

9. a) S.A. $= \pi r(r + s)$
   b)

Slant Height (cm)	Surface Area (cm^2)
40	$1200\pi \doteq 3770$
45	$1300\pi \doteq 4084$
50	$1400\pi \doteq 4398$
55	$1500\pi \doteq 4712$
60	$1600\pi \doteq 5027$

   c) S.A. $= 4\pi r^2$

10. a) $h = -4.9t\left(t - \dfrac{760}{49}\right)$
   b)

Time (s)	Height Increment (m)	Height (m)
0	0	0
1	71.1	71.1
2	61.3	132.4
3	51.5	183.9
4	41.7	225.6
5	31.9	257.5
6	22.1	279.6
7	12.3	291.9
8	2.5	294.4
9	-7.3	287.1
10	-17.1	270.0

The maximum height is about 295 m.
   c) yes

11. a) main fountain: $h = -4.9t^2 + 19.6t$
     smaller fountain: $h = -4.9t^2 + 14.7t$
   b) main fountain: $h = -4.9t(t - 4)$
     smaller fountain: $h = -4.9t(t - 3)$
   c) main fountain: 19.6 m; smaller fountain: 11.025 m

13. a) $9x^2 - 25$ **b)** $16x^2 - 49$ **c)** $25x^2 - 4$
   Pattern: $(ax + b)(ax - b) = a^2x^2 - b^2$

14. a) $(8x + 3)(8x - 3)$ **b)** $(7x + 6)(7x - 6)$
   c) $(10x + 3)(10x - 3)$

15. a) $(2x + 3)(x + 8)$ **b)** $(2x + 5)(5x + 1)$
   c) $(3x + 1)(4x + 3)$

16. a) Group 1:   Group 2:

   b) They all have x-intercepts.
   c) None have x-intercepts.
   d) Only expressions that can be factored have x-intercepts.

5.5 The x-Intercepts of a Quadratic Relation, pages 264–275

1. a) 8 and -1 **b)** -3

2. a) $x = -4$ and $x = 6$ **b)** no zeros

3. a) $x = 5$ and $x = -3$ **b)** $x = 4$ and $x = 1$
   c) $x = 9$ **d)** $x = 7$ and $x = -6$
   e) $x = -8$ and $x = -2$ **f)** $x = 0$ and $x = -5$

4. a) $x = -2$ and $x = -8$ **b)** $x = 7$ and $x = -5$
   c) $x = 7$ and $x = -1$ **d)** $x = 5$ and $x = -5$
   e) $x = -4$ and $x = -9$ **f)** $x = 7$

5. a) $x = 0$ and $x = 4$ **b)** $x = 25$ and $x = 0$
  c) $x = 9$ and $x = -8$ **d)** $x = -9$
  e) $x = 0$ and $x = 5$ **f)** $x = -6$

6. b) and d) have more than one zero.

7. a) $y = x^2 + 10x + 21; y = (x + 3)(x + 7)$
  b) $y = x^2 - 6x - 27; y = (x - 9)(x + 3)$
  c) $y = -2x^2 - 16x - 24; y = -2(x + 2)(x + 6)$
  d) $y = 6x^2 + 24x + 18; y = 6(x + 1)(x + 3)$
  e) $y = 3x^2 - 24x; y = 3x(x - 8)$
  f) $y = -4x^2 + 40x; y = -4x(x - 10)$

8. a) $h = -1.25d(d - 1.5)$
  b) $d = 0$ and $d = 1.5$; yes
  c)

Horizontal Distance (m)	Height (m)
0	0
0.25	0.39
0.50	0.63
0.75	0.70
1.00	0.63
1.25	0.39
1.50	0

  d) The maximum height is about 0.70 m.
  e)

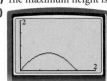

9. a) 1.6 m   **b)** $d = 2$ and $d = -1$
  c) when the skateboarder is 2 m from the ledge
  d)

10. a) $d = 0$ and $d = 2.5$ **b)** 2.5 m
  c) 1.0 m

11. a) $d = 9$ and $d = -4$ **b)** 9 m
  c) No; the maximum height is about 4.2 m.

12. a) $x = -2$ and $x = -5$
  b) $x = \dfrac{15}{4}$ and $x = -\dfrac{5}{4}$
  c) $x = \dfrac{-5 + \sqrt{73}}{4}$ and $x = \dfrac{-5 - \sqrt{73}}{4}$

13. a) no zeros   **b)** has zeros   **c)** no zeros

14. 45°

5.6 Solve Problems Involving Quadratic Relations,
pages 276–285

1. a) $x = 5$ and $x = -4$ **b)** $x = -9$ and $x = -15$
  c) $x = -3$ and $x = -19$ **d)** $x = 8$ and $x = -10$

2. a) $y = (x + 3)(x + 4)$ **b)** $y = (x + 4)(x + 7)$
  c) $y = 3(x + 5)(x + 8)$ **d)** $y = -2(x - 11)(x + 6)$

3. a) $x = -7$ and $x = 4$ **b)** $x = 4$ and $x = -4$
  c) $x = -7$ and $x = 8$ **d)** $x = 7$ and $x = -14$
  e) $x = \sqrt{56}$ and $x = -\sqrt{56}$ **f)** $x = 3$ and $x = -3$
  g) $x = 10$ and $x = -5$ **h)** $x = 8$ and $x = -28$

4. a) $x = 6$ **b)** $x = -3$
  c) $x = 0$ **d)** $x = -5$

5. a) $x = -8$ **b)** $x = 4$
  c) $x = -2$ **d)** $x = -4$
  e) $x = -5$ **f)** $x = 4$

6. a) $y = x^2 + 16x + 48; y = (x + 8)^2 - 16$
  b) $y = x^2 - 8x + 7; y = (x - 4)^2 - 9$
  c) $y = 8x^2 + 32x - 360; y = 8(x + 2)^2 - 392$
  d) $y = -5x^2 - 40x + 240; y = -5(x + 4)^2 + 320$
  e) $y = 6x^2 + 60x; y = 6(x + 5)^2 - 150$
  f) $y = -3x^2 + 24x; y = -3(x - 4)^2 + 48$

7. a)

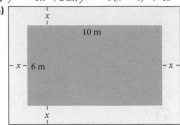

  b) total length: $2x + 10$; total width: $2x + 6$
  c) $4x^2 + 32x + 60$
  d) 5 m

8. a) $10\,000 - 4x^2$ **b)** 30 cm

9. a) $16x^2 + 16x - 96$ **b)** 6 m

10. a) $y = x^2 + 4x - 5; y = 2x^2 + 8x - 10; y = 3x^2 + 12x - 15$;
    answers may vary.
  b) Answers may vary.
  c) $y = 2.5x^2 + 10x - 12.5$

11. a) 72   **b)** 10

12. a) 28   **b)** 15
  c) No; there is no integer solution for $0.5L^2 + 0.5L = 160$.

13. a) at $t = 9$ **b)** 99.225 m
  c) No, it takes longer than 2.5 s to hit the ground.

14. a) $x = 2$ and $x = 14$
  b) (8, 7.2); the longest time the engine will run.
  c)

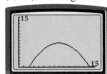

15. a) $h = -0.05d(d - 23)$
  b) 23 m
  c) 6.6125 m

16. a) 2 m   **b)** 7 m

18. 30 m/s; answers may vary.

Chapter 5 Review, pages 286–287

1. a) $x^2 + 13x + 40$ **b)** $14x^2 + 43x - 90$
  c) $x^2 + 26x + 169$ **d)** $x^2 - 49$

2. $16x^2 + 4x - 2$

3. a) $5x^2 + 100x + 507$ **b)** $-0.5x^2 - 8x - 28$
  c) $9x^2 - 144x + 572$ **d)** $2x^2 + 4x - 4$

4. a) 507   **b)** -28
  c) 572   **d)** -4

5. Initial velocity is 29.4 m/s and initial height is 0.9 m; answers
  may vary.

6. a) $x(x + 15)$ **b)** $(x + 5)(x + 8)$
  c) $(x + 5)(x + 5)$ **d)** $(x + 9)(x - 9)$
  e) $(x + 6)(x - 4)$ **f)** $(x - 5)(x - 7)$
  g) $(x + 10)(x - 10)$ **h)** $(x - 12)(x + 1)$

7. a) $(x - 8)(x + 8)$ **b)** 836 cm²

8. a) $4(x + 7)(x + 11)$ **b)** $12x(x + 8)$
   c) $3(x - 9)(x + 5)$ **d)** $-2(x + 6)(x + 6)$
   e) $-8(x + 5)(x - 5)$ **f)** $10(x + 2)(x - 10)$
9. a) $\pi(r + 3)(r - 3)$ **b)** about 679 mm^2
10. a) $x = 0$ and $x = 16$ **b)** $x = 4$ and $x = -4$
   c) $x = -8$ and $x = 4$
11. a) $y = 3x^2 - 6x - 144$; zeros are $x = 8$ and $x = -6$
   b) $y = -4x^2 - 48x - 108$; zeros are $x = -3$ and $x = -9$
12. a) $d = -1$ and $d = 6$
   b) $d = 6$ is the horizontal distance from the kick to landing; $d = -1$ does not have a meaning in this context.
13. a) zeros: -3 and -13; minimum: -25
   b) zeros: 12 and -2; minimum: -245
   c) zeros: -16 and 2; maximum: 162
   d) zeros: -7 and 1; minimum: -96
14. a) $4x^2 + 60x$ **b)** 3 m
15. a) 1.5 m   **b)** 5 m

Chapter 5 Practise Test, pages 288–289

1. D
2. B
3. C
4. B
5. A
6. D
7. C
8. a) $18x^2 - 36x - 80$ **b)** 190 cm^2
9. a) $13x^2 + 182x + 648$ **b)** $-4x^2 + 24x - 20$
   c) $5.6x^2 - 13.44x - 0.136$
10. a) $x = 7$ and $x = -5$ **b)** $x = 4$ and $x = -8$
   c) $x = -2$ and $x = -14$
11. a) 50 m   **b)** 25 m
12. a) 4.2 m   **b)** 3 m   **c)** 4.375 m

CHAPTER 6

Geometry in Design, pages 292–349

Prerequisite Skills, pages 294–295

1. a) rectangle   **b)** parallelogram
   c) circle   **d)** trapezoid
2. a) rectangular prism   **b)** triangular prism
   c) square-based pyramid   **d)** cylinder
3. a) triangle   **b)** square
   c) pentagon   **d)** hexagon
   e) octagon
4. $P = 440$ m; $A = 12\,000$ m^2
5. $P = 45$ cm; $A = 97.5$ cm^2
6. $P = 75$ m; $A = 452$ m^2
7. a) 118 m^2 **b)** 120 m^3
8. 0.7 m^2
9. area $= 534$ m^2; volume $= 942$ m^3
10. $S = 540°$; angle $= 108°$
11. 12 cm by 18 cm
12. 40 ft

6.1 Investigate Geometric Shapes and Figures, pages 296–305

1. D
2. No; the ratio of the two side lengths is about 1.78:1.
3. Answers may vary.

4. Answers may vary.
5. cone, cylinder, square-based pyramid, rectangular prism, triangular prism, triangle, rectangle, square, trapezoid
6. Answers may vary.
7. No; the ratio of the two side lengths is 2:1.
9. Answers may vary.
10. 1.2:1; answers may vary.
11. a) 90°
   b) A triangle with side lengths of 3 units, 4 units, and 5 units is a right triangle.
12. a) scalene, obtuse; answers may vary.
   b) Answers may vary.
13. Red rectangle; the ratio of the sides is 1.6:1.
15. a) 1.545 m
   b) It is the golden ratio.
16. a) 1.4143:1
   b) 1.4141:1
   c) 1.4143:1; it is the same ratio as in part a).
   d) It is 1.4142:1.
17. Answers may vary.

6.2 Perspective and Orthographic Drawings, pages 306–312

1. C
2. 1 cm represents 2 m; length: 24.5 cm, width: 17.5 cm, height: 28.0 cm; answers may vary.
3. B
4. length of 4 cubes, width of 2 cubes, height of 3 cubes
5. Answers may vary.
6. Answers may vary.
7. a)

   b) No, it is impossible to draw so that the farthest left and right tips of the base will be on dots; answers may vary.
8. a) Diagrams may vary.
   b) Diagrams may vary.
   c) They are congruent right triangles; answers may vary.
9. b)

10. All four drawings are valid because you cannot see behind the cubes shown.
11. Answers may vary.
12. Answers may vary.
13.

6.3 Create Nets, Plans, and Patterns, pages 313–326

1. A
2. Diagrams may vary.
3. Diagrams may vary.
4. A pattern because there are several pieces that need to be assembled to make a bookcase; answers may vary.
5. **a)** Answers may vary.
   b) Move the bottom square 1 unit to the left.
6. **a)** Diagrams may vary.   **c)** yes
7. **a)** Diagrams may vary.   **c)** yes
8. **a)** Diagrams may vary.   **b)** about 51.6 m²
   c) about $335
9. Diagrams may vary.
10. Diagrams may vary.
11. **a)** Diagrams may vary.
12. The squares for the walls of the hole keep overlapping other faces.
13. Diagrams may vary.

6.4 Scale Models, pages 327–334

1. 5 in. by 6 in.
2. 85 ft 4 in.
3. Easier to visualize; answers may vary.
4. Half a tennis ball placed on a roll of thick paper; answers may vary.
5.

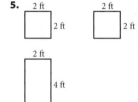

6. Diagrams may vary.
7.

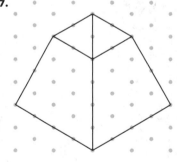

8. **a)** Diagrams may vary.
   c) $40, $38, $32
9. **a)** 9 cm
   b) Diagrams may vary.
10. **a)** Diagrams may vary.
    c) About 26 m³; answers may vary.
    d) About $1949; answers may vary.
11. **a)** The roof of the net will now be made of 6 isosceles triangles.
    b) No change, base remains the same.
12. **a)** Diagrams may vary.
    c) $172 800
13. B
14. Diagrams may vary.

6.5 Solve Problems With Given Constraints, pages 335–345

1. 10 cm
2. 79 m
3. Less material used to make the box, takes up less space; answers may vary.
4. Minimum and maximum space requirements, price; answers may vary.
5. Diagrams may vary.
6. about 2242 m
7. Answers may vary.
8. Answers may vary.
9. **a)**

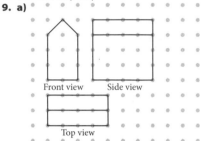

   Front view   Side view

   Top view

   b) Diagrams may vary.   **c)** about $831
10. **a)** diameter: 10 m, height: 8 m
    b) about 327 m³   **c)** about $29 400
12. Diagrams may vary.
13. **a)** Diagrams may vary.
14. Diagrams may vary.

Chapter 6 Review, pages 346–347

1. To ensure the diagonals were equal; answers may vary.
2. The blanket is close to a golden rectangle but is not when folded in half.
3. **b)**

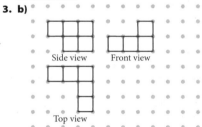

   Side view   Front view

   Top view

4.

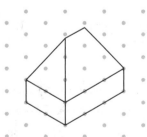

5. Diagrams may vary.
6. Diagrams may vary.
7. Diagrams may vary.
8. wingspan: 84.6 cm; length: 102.6 cm
9. Diagrams may vary.
10. Diagrams may vary.
11. **a)** Side length of hexagon is about 5.55 m.
    b) about $9590

Chapter 6 Practice Test, pages 348–349

1. A

2. B

3. B

4.

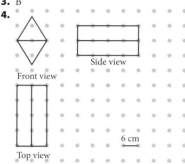

Front view

Side view

Top view

6 cm

5. Diagrams may vary.

6. Diagrams may vary.

7.

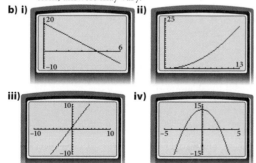

Front view   Side view

Top view

8. Diagrams may vary.

9. a) Diagrams may vary.

 b) about 2196 mL

Chapters 4 to 6 Review, pages 350–351

1. a) i) Not quadratic, the second differences are 0 and the graph is a straight line; answers may vary.

 ii) Quadratic, the second differences are a constant and the graph is a parabola; answers may vary.

 iii) Not quadratic, the graph is a straight line and there is no x^2 term; answers may vary.

 iv) Quadratic, the graph is a parabola and there is an x^2 term; answers may vary.

 b) i) **ii)**

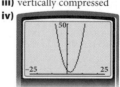

 iii) **iv)**

2. a) The parabola has not been stretched, it opens upward, and the vertex has been translated 4 units to the left of the y-axis.

 b) The parabola has not been stretched, it opens downward, and the vertex has been translated 1 unit to the right of the y-axis.

c) The parabola has been vertically compressed, it opens downward, and the vertex has been translated 7 units to the left of the y-axis.

d) The parabola is vertically stretched, it opens upward, and the vertex has been translated 9 units to the left of the y-axis.

e) The parabola is vertically compressed, it opens upward, and the vertex has been translated 32 units to the left of the y-axis.

f) The parabola is vertically stretched, it opens downward, and the vertex has been translated 18 units to the right of the y-axis.

3. a) i) $(1, 9)$ **ii)** upward   **iii)** not stretched

 iv)

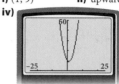

b) i) $(-8, -5)$ **ii)** downward

 iii) vertically stretched

 iv)

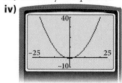

c) i) $(0, -1)$ **ii)** upward

 iii) vertically compressed

 iv)

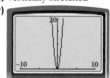

d) i) $(0, 0)$ **ii)** upward

 iii) vertically stretched

 iv)

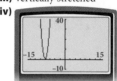

e) i) $(2, 2)$ **ii)** upward

 iii) vertically compressed

 iv)

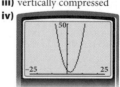

f) i) $(-1, 13)$ **ii)** upward

 iii) vertically stretched

 iv)

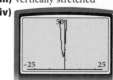

4. a) 6 s, 177.4 m   **b)** 172.5 m
c)

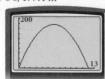

     d) about 12 s

5. a) $30x^2 + 43x + 4$ **b)** $4x^2 + 7x - 30$
    c) $24x^2 - 10x - 4$ **d)** $-4x^2 + 36$
6. a) $4s^2 - 11s + 7$ **b)** 742 m²
7. a) $y = x^2 - 8x + 16.5$ **b)** $y = x^2 + 20x + 97$
    c) $y = 8x^2 + 32x + 59$ **d)** $y = -3.2x^2 + 25.6x - 52$
8. -42
9. a) $(x + 8)(x + 3)$ **b)** $(x + 6)(x - 5)$
    c) $(x - 7)(x - 1)$ **d)** $(x + 4)(x + 4)$
    e) $3(x + 9)(x + 4)$ **f)** $-10(x + 10)(x + 1)$
10. a) Equivalent; explanations may vary.
    b) Not equivalent; explanations may vary.
    c) Equivalent; explanations may vary.
11. a) $5, -4$ **b)** $6, -6$
     c) $7, -5$ **d)** -3
12. a)

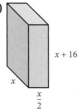

$x + 16$
x
$\dfrac{x}{2}$

     b) $4x^2 + 48x$ **c)** 880 cm²
13. yes

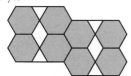

14. b)

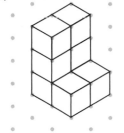

c)

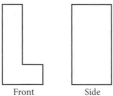

Front   Side   Top

15. a)

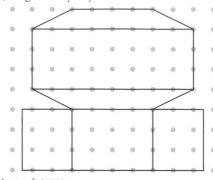

Front   Side
Top

    b) Diagrams may vary.

    c) 48 m²; $1920

CHAPTER 7

Exponents, pages 352–417

Prerequisite Skills, pages 354–355

1. a) 6^2 **b)** 7^4
   c) $(-2)^3$ **d)** 4^8
   e) $\left(\dfrac{1}{4}\right)^5$ **f)** $\left(-\dfrac{4}{5}\right)^2$

2. a) 25   **b)** 343   **c)** 100 000
   d) 9   **e)** -9 **f)** -144
   g) $\dfrac{1}{4}$ **h)** $\dfrac{1}{81}$ **i)** $-\dfrac{1}{125}$

3. a) 2, 5   **b)** 3, -1
   c) $-4, 3$ **d)** $-\dfrac{1}{2}, -\dfrac{2}{3}$

4. Graphs may vary.
5. For each call, the pay increases by $2; answers may vary.
6. a) $A = 78.5$ cm²
   b) $I = \$24$
   c) $V = 125$ m³
   d) $P = 34$ cm
7. Answers may vary.
   a) reflected in the x-axis
   b) right 1 unit, down 2 units
   c) left 3 units, up 2 units

8. Answers may vary.

a)

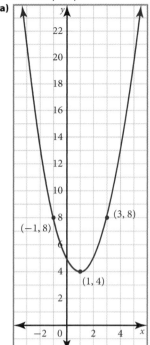

b)

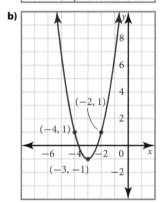

c)

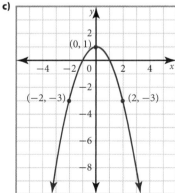

d)

7.1 Exponent Rules, pages 356–363

1. a) $5^4 = 625$ **b)** $2^7 = 128$
c) $(-3)^6 = 729$ **d)** $(-4)^6 = 4096$
e) $\left(\dfrac{1}{4}\right)^5 = \dfrac{1}{1024}$ **f)** $\left(-\dfrac{1}{2}\right)^3 = -\dfrac{1}{8}$

2. a) $6^1 = 6$ **b)** $8^2 = 64$
c) $12^1 = 12$ **d)** $2^4 = 16$
e) $(-2)^3 = -8$ **f)** $(-3)^2 = 9$

3. a) $5^6 = 15\ 625$ **b)** $2^9 = 512$
c) $(-4)^6 = 4096$ **d)** $\left(\dfrac{1}{7}\right)^4 = \dfrac{1}{2401}$
e) $\left(\dfrac{1}{3}\right)^6 = \dfrac{1}{729}$ **f)** $\left(\dfrac{1}{10}\right)^8 = \dfrac{1}{100\ 000\ 000}$

4. a) $36 \times 216 = 7776,\ 6^5 = 7776$
b) $2401 \times 49 = 117\ 649,\ 7^6 = 117\ 649$
c) $59\ 049 \div 729 = 81,\ 9^2 = 81$
d) $\dfrac{2401}{-343} = -7,\ (-7)^1 = -7$
e) $(25)^3 = 15\ 625,\ 5^6 = 15\ 625$
f) $(100\ 000)^2 = 10\ 000\ 000\ 000,\ 10^{10} = 10\ 000\ 000\ 000$
g) $(-512)(-8) = 4096,\ (-8)^4 = 4096$
h) $(-1)^9 = -1,\ (-1)^{99} = -1$

5. a) $9^9 = 387\ 420\ 489$ **b)** $7^8 = 5\ 764\ 801$
c) $(-6)^6 = 46\ 656$ **d)** $24^1 = 24$
e) $9^2 = 81$ **f)** $\left(\dfrac{3}{4}\right)^7 = \dfrac{2187}{16\ 384}$
g) $4^{15} = 1\ 073\ 741\ 824$ **h)** $(-8)^3 = -512$
i) $\left(-\dfrac{5}{7}\right)^4 = \dfrac{625}{2401}$

6. 100
7. 100 000
8. the 4.2 earthquake, $10^{1.4}$ times
9. a) $3^1 \times 3^7,\ 3^3 \times 3^5,\ 3^4 \times 3^4$; answers may vary.
b) $\dfrac{2^5}{2^0},\ \dfrac{2^6}{2^1},\ \dfrac{2^7}{2^2}$; answers may vary.
c) $(7^6)^2,\ (7^3)^4,\ (7^2)^6$; answers may vary.
10. a) yes   **b)** 8^4; answers may vary.
11. a) $\dfrac{1}{36}$ **b)** $\dfrac{1}{216}$
12. a) $\dfrac{1}{4}$ in.^{2} **b)** $\dfrac{1}{16}$ ft^2
13. a) $\dfrac{1}{576}$ ft^2 **b)** 9 in.^{2}

14.

Measurement to be Calculated	Formula	Dimensions Given	Calculated Measurement
Area of a Circle	$A = \pi r^2$	$r = \pi$ cm	31 cm³
Volume of a Cube	$V = s^3$	$s = \frac{1}{2}$ in.	$\frac{1}{8}$ in.³
Volume of a Sphere	$V = \frac{4}{3}\pi r^3$	$r = \frac{1}{8}$ in.	0.0082 in.³
Volume of a Cylinder	$V = \pi r^2 h$	$r = h = 5$ cm	392.7 cm³

15. 216 cm³

16. a) $10^{7.3}$, 19 952 623.15 **b)** $10^{4.8}$, 63 095.73

c) $2^{6.4}$, 84.45 **d)** $\left(\frac{1}{2}\right)^{8.9}$, 0.0021

17. a) $8x^7$ **b)** $-4a^3b^2$
c) $m^{10}n^{15}$ **d)** k^9h^6

7.2 Zero and Negative Exponents, pages 364–371

1. a) 9^{-5} **b)** $\left(\frac{1}{6}\right)^{-3}$

c) $\left(\frac{1}{5}\right)^2$ **d)** 4

2. a) $25, \frac{1}{25}$ **b)** $2, \frac{1}{2}$

c) $256, \frac{1}{256}$ **d)** $1000, \frac{1}{1000}$

e) 1, 1 **f)** $512, \frac{1}{512}$

g) $81, \frac{1}{81}$ **h)** $-8, -\frac{1}{8}$

3. a) 1 **b)** $\frac{1}{8}$ **c)** $\frac{1}{36}$

d) 1 **e)** $\frac{1}{500}$ **f)** $\frac{1}{125}$

g) $\frac{1}{256}$ **h)** $-\frac{1}{1000}$ **i)** 36

j) $\frac{1}{243}$ **k)** 27 **l)** -343

4. Keep dividing 4 from 4^3 to get to 4^{-3}: $4^3 = 64$, $4^2 = 16$,

$4^1 = 4$, $4^0 = 1$, $4^{-1} = \frac{1}{4}$, $4^{-2} = \frac{1}{16}$, $4^{-3} = \frac{1}{64} = \frac{1}{4^{-3}}$;

answers may vary.

5. Fractions are more exact, but whole numbers are easier to compare; answers may vary.

a) 1 **b)** 0.125 **c)** 0.02778
d) 1 **e)** 0.002 **f)** 0.008
g) 0.0039 **h)** -0.001 **i)** 36
j) 0.0041 **k)** 27 **l)** -343

6. a) 8^2 **b)** 5^{-5} **c)** 7^{-2}
d) 12^{-3} **e)** $(-4)^{-1}$ **f)** $(-3)^{-5}$

7. a) 1 **b)** 1 **c)** 1
d) 1 **e)** 1 **f)** 1

8. a) $8^2 = 64$ **b)** $4^3 = 64$

c) $\left(\frac{1}{2}\right)^{12} = \frac{1}{4096}$ **d)** $(-3)^2 = 9$

e) $10^{-6} = \frac{1}{1\,000\,000}$ **f)** $\left(\frac{1}{2}\right)^8 = \frac{1}{256}$

g) $6^{-3} = \frac{1}{216}$ **h)** $5^{-3} = \frac{1}{125}$

i) $4^{-6} = \frac{1}{4096}$ **j)** $\left(\frac{1}{3}\right)^{-3} = 27$

k) $\left(\frac{1}{9}\right)^{-2} = 81$ **l)** $5^{-6} = \frac{1}{15\,625}$

9. a) 8 g **b)** 0.5 g
10. a) 10^3 **b)** $\frac{1}{1000}$, $\left(\frac{1}{10}\right)^3$, 10^{-3}
c) 10^{-6} **d)** 10^{-9}
e) $10^{-3} : 10^{-9}$, 10^6

11. a) 1024 **b)** $\frac{1}{1024}$

c) 1 048 576 **d)** $\frac{1}{1\,073\,741\,824}$

e) $\frac{1}{8}$ **f)** $\frac{1}{8\,796\,093\,022\,208}$

12. a) 1 000 000
b) 10 000
c) $10^{0.5}$

13. a) $\frac{2^a}{2^b}$ **b)** 2^{a-b}
c) 10, multiply the number of vacuums by 10 to double the loudness; answers may vary.

14. a) \$9.44 **b)** \$6168.94
c) \$0.48 **d)** \$84 775.42

15. a) 0.05 g **b)** 0.165 g

16. a) $\frac{2^7}{2^{10}} = 2^{-3}$ **b)** $\frac{3^5}{3^8} = 3^{-3}$

c) $\frac{5^5}{5^4} = 5^1$ **d)** $\frac{7^2}{7^4} = 7^{-2}$

e) $\frac{11^1}{11^3} = 11^{-2}$ **f)** $\frac{2^9}{2^6} = 2^3$

g) $\frac{1}{2^3} \times \frac{1}{2^4} = 2^{-7}$ **h)** $\frac{1}{5^2} \times \frac{1}{5^3} = 5^{-5}$

17. a) 4^4 **b)** 4^{-1} **c)** 4^{-14}
d) 4^4 **e)** 4^{-18} **f)** 4^6

7.3 Investigate Exponential Relationships, pages 372–381

1. The ratio between successive terms is 2, indicating a constant rate of change; answers may vary.
2. b) and d), a) is linear and c) is quadratic; answers may vary.
3. a)

Day	1	2	3	4	5	6	7
Number of Grains of Rice	1	2	4	8	16	32	64

b) The ratio between successive terms is 2, indicating a constant rate of change; answers may vary.
c) 32 768
d) The amount of rice would rise to more than 1 billion grains only halfway through the 64 days; answers may vary.

4. a) Answers may vary.

Distance (cm)	AM Radio Frequency (kHz)
1.0	540
1.3	600
1.7	700
2.2	900
2.6	1200
2.9	1400
3.2	1600

b) Graphs may vary.

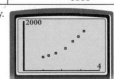

c) Yes, it looks exponential; answers may vary.

5. a) $200 \div 100 \neq 300 \div 200$; answers may vary.

b)

$62.50	$500	$4000	$32 000	$256 000
$125	$1000	$8000	$64 000	$512 000
$250	$2000	$16 000	$128 000	$1 024 000

c) Answers may vary.

6. a) increasingly steep curve upward
b) about 5000, extrapolation
c) about 35 000
d) positive exponential growth

7. a)

Time (h)	Number of Bacteria (1000s)
12	1000
24	2000
36	4000
48	8000
60	16 000
72	32 000
84	64 000
96	128 000
108	256 000
120	512 000
132	1 024 000
144	2 048 000
156	4 096 000
168	8 192 000

b)

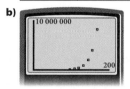

c) 10.5 days

8. a) Decreasing curve then levelling off; answers may vary.
b) 16 min
c) 20°C

9. a) 81%
b) 7, 0.90^7 is the first power of 0.90 less than 0.5; answers may vary.

10. a) It looks very similar to an exponential curve; answers may vary.
b) $180 billion, $1.4 trillion; answers may vary.
c) Answers may vary.

12. a) At every new stage, the end of the branch is broken into two new branches, so the number of branch sections doubles at every stage. Each new branch is half the length of the previous branch. The branches decrease in size exponentially: $1, \frac{1}{2}, \left(\frac{1}{2}\right)^2, \left(\frac{1}{2}\right)^3, \ldots$

b) At every new stage, the white triangles are broken into three white triangles and a shaded triangle, so the number of white triangles triples at every stage. Their size also decreases exponentially: $1, \frac{1}{4}, \left(\frac{1}{4}\right)^2, \left(\frac{1}{4}\right)^3, \ldots$

7.4 Exponential Relations, pages 382–394

1. a) exponential　　**b)** linear
c) exponential　　**d)** quadratic
e) linear

2. a) C　　**b)** A　　**c)** D　　**d)** B

3. a) Graphs may vary.

i)

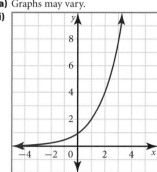

ii)

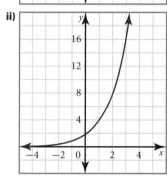

iii)

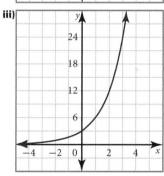

iv)

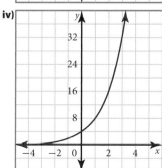

b) The greater the value of a, the faster the graph grows.

4. Answers may vary.

a)

x	−1	0	1	2	3
y = 3^x	$\frac{1}{3}$	1	3	9	27
y = 2(3^x)	$\frac{2}{3}$	2	6	18	54

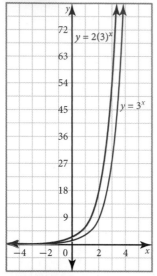

b)

x	−1	0	1	2	3
$y = \left(\frac{1}{2}\right)^x$	2	1	$\frac{1}{2}$	$\frac{1}{4}$	$\frac{1}{8}$
$y = 2\left(\frac{1}{2}\right)^x$	4	2	1	$\frac{1}{2}$	$\frac{1}{4}$

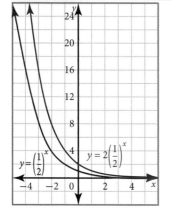

c)

x	−1	0	1	2	3
y = (0.4)^x	2.5	1	0.4	0.16	0.064
y = 0.3(0.4)^x	0.75	0.3	0.12	0.048	0.0192

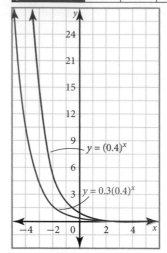

5. Answers may vary.

a)

x	−1	0	1	2	3
y = 2^x	$\frac{1}{2}$	1	2	4	8
y = 2^{3x}	$\frac{1}{8}$	1	8	64	512

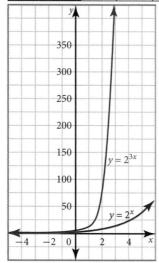

b)

x	−1	0	1	2	3
$y = 10^x$	$\frac{1}{10}$	1	10	100	1000
$y = 10^{\frac{x}{2}}$	0.316	1	3.16	10	31.6

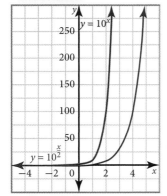

c)

x	−1	0	1	2	3
$y = \left(\frac{1}{2}\right)^x$	2	1	$\frac{1}{2}$	$\frac{1}{4}$	$\frac{1}{8}$
$y = \left(\frac{1}{2}\right)^{\frac{x}{4}}$	1.19	1	0.84	0.707	0.59

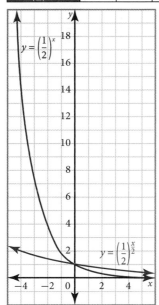

d)

x	−1	0	1	2	3
$y = 2^x$	$\frac{1}{2}$	1	2	4	8
$y = (3)2^{\frac{x}{5}}$	2.61	3	3.45	3.96	4.55

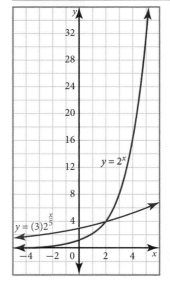

6. a)

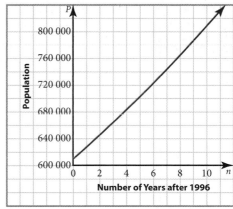

Population Growth in York Region

b) 610 000, population in 1996
c) i) 1 050 079   **ii)** 1 659 082

7. a)

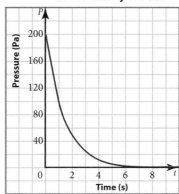

Sound Intesity of a Bell

b) 200, pressure at 0 s
c) i) 100   **ii)** 50

8. a)

Number of years after 1996, n	Population of Toronto, P
1	2 473 966
2	2 488 315
3	2 502 747
4	2 517 263
5	2 531 863
6	2 546 548
7	2 561 318
8	2 576 174
9	2 591 116
10	2 606 144

Number of years after 1996, n	Population of Peel, P
1	907 800
2	937 758
3	968 704
4	1 000 671
5	1 033 693
6	1 067 805
7	1 103 043
8	1 139 443
9	1 177 045
10	1 215 887

Population Growth in Toronto and Peel Region

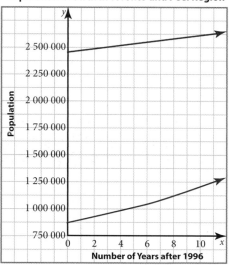

b) the population increases faster when the growth rate is greater

9. a) exponential, because it decreases by the same rate over equal time periods
b) quadratic, because gravity involves quadratics
c) linear, because it increases by the same amount over equal time periods
d) exponential, because it increases by the same rate over equal time periods
e) quadratic, because gravity involves quadratics
f) exponential, because it decreases by the same percent each bounce

10. a) **Sound Intensity Compared to Sound Pressure**

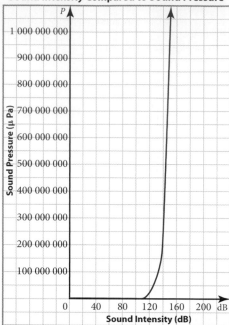

b) $P = 20\ 000$ and $P = 20\ 000\ 000$
c) $P = 2\ 000\ 000\ 000$

11. a) The ratio between successive keys is 1.06, indicating a constant rate of change; answers may vary.
b)

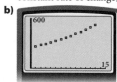

12. a) 1.067; answers may vary.
b) 1.310; answers may vary.
c) 1.105; answers may vary.
d) close to an exponential relationship, because the growth rate is almost the same over equal time periods; answers may vary.
e) about 45 years
f) 2046; answers may vary.

13. a) Each new diagram, a square is added; linear

Diagram 4   Diagram 5

b) Each new diagram, two squares are added; linear

Diagram 4   Diagram 5

c) Each new diagram, a new row is added; quadratic

Diagram 4   Diagram 5

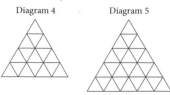

14. a) temperature decreases 9.84°C for every 1000 m, pressure decreases by 12% for every 1000 m

b) the decrease in temperature is linear, the decrease in pressure is exponential

c) there is less atmosphere above as altitude increases; answers may vary.

15. a) add the exponents when multiplying 0.5 by $(0.5)^{x-1}$; answers may vary.

b) $y = 26 \times 0.5^{x-1}$

7.5 Modelling Exponential Growth and Decay, pages 395–405

1. a)

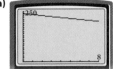

b) 1000   **c)** 3450   **d)** 488 760

2. a)

b) 240   **c)** 201

3. a) 13%

b)

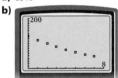

c) 19 h   **d)** 50 h; answers may vary.

4. a) i)

Time (h)	0	1	2	3	4	5	6	7
Mass of Caffeine (mg)	45.6	39.7	34.5	30.0	26.1	22.7	19.8	17.2

ii)

Time (h)	0	1	2	3	4	5	6	7
Mass of Caffeine (mg)	31.0	27.0	23.5	20.4	17.8	15.5	13.4	11.7

b) i)   **ii)**

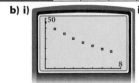 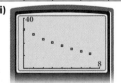

c) can of cola: 11 h; chocolate bar: 9 h

d) Answers may vary.

5. a) 1.25 min   **b)** almost 2 min

c) Yes; answers may vary.   **d)** Answers may vary.

6. a) Yes, because the growth rate is almost the same over equal time periods; answers may vary.

b) about 75%   **c)** 330 s

7. a) increasing

b) 1961 to 1962: 1.1 ppm, 0.34%; 1981 to 1982: 1.05 ppm, 0.31%; 2001 to 2002: 1.99 ppm, 0.53%

c) 1960s: 7.63 ppm, 2.4%; 1970s: 10.76 ppm, 3.3%; 1980s: 14.65 ppm, 4.3%; 1990s: 14.94 ppm, 4.2%

d) Answers may vary.

e) Answers may vary.

8. a)

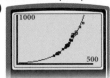

b) Yes, it looks exponential; answers may vary.

c) 1000 g

d) Estimate the mass of a fish given its length; answers may vary.

9. Answers may vary.

11. 7.25 years

12. a) $P = 4\,500\,000\,000(1.02)^t$; P is the population and t is the number of years after 1980

b) 9 000 000 000

c) 3 700 000 000; assuming same rate of increase

7.6 Solve Problems Involving Exponential Growth and Decay, pages 406–413

1. a) 20 min   **b)** 40 000   **c)** 4.7×10^{24}

2. a) 1200 W/cm²   **b)** 960 W/cm²

c) 614.4 W/cm²   **d)** 393.2 W/cm²

3. a) 19.5 mm²   **b)** 9.2 mm²

4. a) 0.25 ppt   **b)** 0.55 ppt   **c)** 0.05 ppt

5. 0.93 ppt

6. a) 10 h

b)

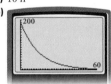

c) 31 h, 56 h

7. a) 4 h

b) i) 16.8 mg/mL   **ii)** 5.2 mg/mL

c) 25 h

8. a) Answers may vary.   **b)** Answers may vary.

9.

Sound Source	Intensity Level (dB)	Relative Intensity
Mosquito buzzing	40	$10^{-12} \times 10^{\frac{40}{10}} = 10^{-8}$ $= 0.000\,000\,01$
Rainfall	50	$10^{-12} \times 10^{\frac{50}{10}} = 10^{-7}$ $= 0.000\,000\,1$
Quiet alarm clock	65	$10^{-12} \times 10^{\frac{65}{10}} = 10^{-5.5}$ $\doteq 0.000\,003$
Loud alarm clock	80	$10^{-12} \times 10^{\frac{80}{10}} = 10^{-4}$ $= 0.0001$
Average factory	90	$10^{-12} \times 10^{\frac{90}{10}} = 10^{-3}$ $= 0.001$
Large orchestra	98	$10^{-12} \times 10^{\frac{98}{10}} = 10^{-2.2}$ $\doteq 0.006$
Car stereo	125	$10^{-12} \times 10^{\frac{125}{10}} = 10^{0.5}$ $\doteq 3.16$

10. a) the number of collisions divided by the number of millions of kilometres driven by all vehicles; answers may vary.
  b) i) 7.6 **ii)** 18.5
11. a) Answers may vary.
  b) Graphs may vary.
  c) Answers may vary.
12. a) Graphs may vary.
  b) Answers may vary.
  c) Answers may vary.
13. a) 286 Bq, 132 Bq **b)** 62 MBq
14. $P = 325(2)^{\frac{n}{15}}$, 1638

Chapter 7 Review, pages 414–415

1. a) $6^5 = 7776$ **b)** $(-2)^6 = 64$
  c) $5^3 = 125$ **d)** $\left(\frac{1}{3}\right)^6 = \frac{1}{729}$
  e) $10^8 = 100\ 000\ 000$ **f)** $(-7)^4 = 2401$
  g) $3^3 = 27$ **h)** $\left(-\frac{1}{2}\right)^5 = -\frac{1}{32}$

2. $\frac{9}{64}$ in.^{2}

3. a) 1 **b)** $\frac{1}{5}$ **c)** $\frac{1}{512}$ **d)** 1
  e) $\frac{9}{4}$ **f)** 64 **g)** $\frac{1}{7}$ **h)** $\frac{1}{9}$
  i) 8 **j)** 5

4. a) exponential
  b) quadratic
  c) linear

5. a) 60 000
  b) 120 000
  c) 122 880 000

6. All graphs pass through (1, 3) and none of them have multiple y-values for the same x-value; $3x$ is the only one with negative values, and $3x^2$ has x-values that share the same y-values; answers may vary.

7. a) Relation of Concentration of Hydrogen Ions to Acidity

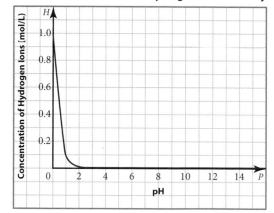

  b) $\dfrac{1}{10\ 000\ 000}$
  c) 0.000 000 025 to 0.000 000 1
  d) 0.000 0025 compared to 0.000 01

8. a)

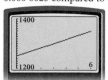

  b) 1250 **c)** 1333

9. a)

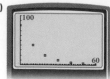

  b) Decay because every 10 s the amplitude is reduced by half; answers may vary.
  c) It has a half-life of 10 s.
  d) 90 s
10. a) 2 h
  b) 500 mg
  c) i) 250 mg **ii)** 62.5 mg
11. a) $50 814 **b)** $66 241 **c)** 4.1%

Chapter 7 Practice Test, pages 416–417

1. a) true **b)** false **c)** false **d)** true
2. a) 243 **b)** 81 **c)** 64 **d)** 1
  e) $\frac{1}{49}$ **f)** 125 **g)** 1 **h)** $\frac{1}{3}$

3. Graphs may vary.
  a) i)

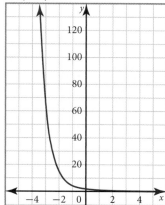

  ii) Exponential decay, because the relation divides by 4 for every x-value.
  b) i)

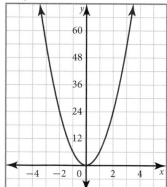

  ii) neither (quadratic)

c) i)

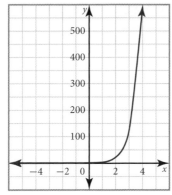

ii) Exponential growth, because the relation multiplies by 5 for every x-value.

d) i)

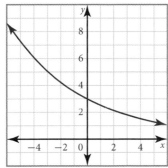

ii) Exponential decay, because the relation divides by 2 for every 4 x-values.

4. a) 3^3 **b)** 3^5 ft^3 **c)** 81

5. If b is positive, then any power of it will be positive; answers may vary.

6. a) Answers may vary.
  b) exponential

7. a)

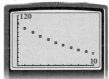

  b) $101.3(0.883)^n$ **c)** 101.3 kPa
  d) 1040 m   **e)** 59.7 kPa

CHAPTER 8

Compound Interest, pages 418–457

Prerequisite Skills, pages 420–421

1. a) 5.16   **b)** 2.1   **c)** 280   **d)** 30.625
  e) 522.5   **f)** 972.1$\overline{6}$ **g)** 742.5   **h)** 1019
2. a) 0.02   **b)** 0.025   **c)** 0.032   **d)** 0.016
  e) 0.005   **f)** 0.021 25   **g)** 0.0025   **h)** 0.0475
3. a) 0.06   **b)** 0.04   **c)** 0.025   **d)** 0.18
  e) 0.185   **f)** 0.1225   **g)** 0.005   **h)** 0.0233
4. a) $20   **b)** $30   **c)** $110   **d)** $24.50
  e) $600   **f)** $112.50   **g)** $2245   **h)** $232.40
5. a) 0.03   **b)** 0.042   **c)** 0.007 75   **d)** 0.013
  e) 0.04   **f)** 0.018   **g)** 0.018 75   **h)** 0.002 75

6. Estimates may vary.
  a) $40   **b)** $500   **c)** $8   **d)** $35
  e) $13   **f)** $12 000
7. a) 1.06   **b)** 1.59   **c)** 238.81   **d)** 6246.02
  e) 0.5   **f)** 0.04   **g)** 0.84   **h)** 0.94
8. a) $50   **b)** $48   **c)** $225   **d)** $1100
9. a) $180   **b)** $86.40   **c)** $49.71   **d)** $450

8.1 Simple and Compound Interest, pages 422–429

1. Simple Interest:

Year	Simple Interest ($)	Amount ($)
0		500.00
1	30	530.00
2	30	560.00
3	30	590.00
4	30	620.00
5	30	650.00

Compound Interest:

Year	A = P(1.06)	Amount ($)
0		500.00
1	500.00(1.06)	530.00
2	530.00(1.06)	561.80
3	561.80(1.06)	595.508
4	595.508(1.06)	631.23848
5	631.23848(1.06)	669.11279

2. Simple Interest:

Year	Simple Interest ($)	Amount ($)
0		800.00
1	64	864.00
2	64	928.00
3	64	992.00
4	64	1056.00
5	64	1120.00
6	64	1184.00
7	64	1248.00
8	64	1312.00
9	64	1376.00
10	64	1440.00

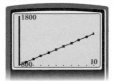

Compound Interest:

Year	A = P(1.08)	Amount ($)
0		800.00
1	800.00(1.08)	864.00
2	864.00(1.08)	933.12
3	933.12(1.08)	1007.7696
4	1007.7696(1.08)	1088.39117
5	1088.39117(1.08)	1175.46246
6	1175.46246(1.08)	1269.49946
7	1269.49946(1.08)	1371.05942
8	1371.05942(1.08)	1480.74417
9	1480.74417(1.08)	1599.20370
10	1599.20370(1.08)	1727.14000

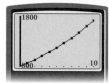

3. Shu Ying's investment after 5 years: $937.50
Shu Jin's investment after 5 years: $957.21

4. a) $1390.00
   b) $1459.14

5. a) $2080; $2163.20; $2249.73
   b) $2100; $2205; $2315.25
   c) $2120; $2247.20; $2382.03

6. $17.81

Simple Interest:

Year	Simple Interest ($)	Amount ($)
0		2000.00
1	108	2108.00
2	108	2216.00
3	108	2324.00

Compound Interest:

Year	A = P(1.054)	Amount ($)
0		2000.00
1	2000(1.054)	2108.00
2	2108(1.054)	2221.832
3	2221.832(1.054)	2341.810 93

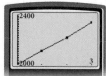

7. a) $7.60
   b) $7.60 in the first year, $7.89 in the second year, and $8.19 in the third year
   c) Simple interest, because it is the same every year.

8. a)

Year	A = P(1.04)	Amount ($)
0		20 000.00
1	20 000(1.04)	20 800.00
2	20 800(1.04)	21 632.00
3	21 632(1.04)	22 497.28
4	22 497.28(1.04)	23 397.1712
5	23 397.1712(1.04)	24 333.058

   b) It grows faster, they would earn $4000 using simple interest; answers may vary.

9. a) about $1125
   b) about 10.4 years
   c) The graph would increase faster and curve more; answers may vary.

10. a)

Year	A = P(1.013)	Population
0		75 600.00
1	75 600(1.013)	76 582.80
2	76 582.8(1.013)	77 578.3764
3	77 578.3764(1.013)	78 586.8953
4	78 586.8953(1.013)	79 608.5249
5	79 608.5249(1.013)	80 643.4358
6	80 643.4358(1.013)	81 691.8004
7	81 691.8004(1.013)	82 753.7938
8	82 753.7938(1.013)	83 829.5931
9	83 829.5931(1.013)	84 919.3779
10	84 919.3779(1.013)	86 023.3298

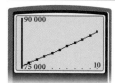

   b) The graph would increase faster and curve more; answers may vary.

11. 3.42% per year, compounded annually

8.2 Compound Interest, pages 430–435

1. a) 530.60 **b)** 245.97 **c)** 1262.48
   d) 3570.62 **e)** 2099.86 **f)** 15 281.42

2. a) $A = 2000(1 + 0.05)^3$
   b) $A = 1000(1 + 0.04)^4$
   c) $A = 50\ 000(1 + 0.03)^{20}$
   d) $A = 750(1 + 0.005)^{12}$

3. a) amount: $1216.65; interest: $216.65
   b) amount: $1265.32; interest: $265.32
   c) amount: $1137.64; interest: $137.64
   d) amount: $1154.64; interest: $154.64

4. a) $1013.84 **b)** $113.84

5. a) $6691.13 **b)** $6719.58 **c)** $6734.28
   d) $6744.25 **e)** $6749.13

6. a) $18 087.26 **b)** $24 325.35

7. $5546.98

8. a) after one year: $5203.02; after two years: $5414.28
   b) $211.26
   c) $290.48
   d) The value of the investment is greater in the ninth year than in the first year, so the interest earned in greater; answers may vary.
9. a) the $2500 investment   **b)** $619.49
10. $132.77
11. Answers may vary.
12. He should take loan B, since it has less interest.
13. a) $4 915 849.32   **b)** $1 915 849.32
14. Markton; 11 452 people
15. $1295.85
17. $7743.48
18. a) 5%   **b)** 6%   **c)** 5%
19. a) $606.28   **b)** $1818.83

8.3 Present Value, pages 436–441
1. a) 1580.63   **b)** 706.43   **c)** 452.64   **d)** 7894.09
   e) 2141.68   **f)** 1126.97
2. a) $3960.47   **b)** $1847.69   **c)** $873.94   **d)** $6729.71
3. a) $1674.97   **b)** $4098.73   **c)** $68 809.18   **d)** $862.30
4. $2000
5. $923.48
6. $4806.37; $15 193.63
7. $26 673.51
8. $2396
9. $45 097.14
10. paying $2399.99 now
11. $9005.01
12. $5060.60
13. a) $28 827.51   **b)** $1172.49
14. a) $3891.33   **b)** $140.37
15. a) $2299.66   **b)** $1210.84   **c)** $1114.15
   d) first situation: $3299.66; second situation: $3210.84; third situation: $3114.15
16. a) 3   **b)** 5   **c)** 4

8.4 The TVM Solver, pages 442–445
1. $2687.83
2. $1182.24
3. 3 years and 6 months
4. $4307.54
5. $3493.07
6. 9 years and 9 months
7. a) 12 years
   b) Yes, any amount would double in the same length of time; answers may vary.
8. a) 8.2%
   b) No, since it did not double the $2000 investment; answers may vary.
9. a) 24.5%   **b)** 18.1%   **c)** 14.35%
10. $3500 invested at 6.5% per year
11. money invested at 8% per year, compounded semi-annually
12. No, the investment will be worth only $364 331.82; 10.9%
13. $37 085.10; $25 053.37
14. a) $7651.34
   b) $8419.73
15. Answers may vary.
16. 4.6%
17. semi-annually: 9.76%; quarterly: 9.65%; monthly: 9.57%

8.5 Effects of Changing the Conditions on Investments and Loans, pages 446–453
1. a) amount: $1843.88; total interest: $343.88
   b) amount: $1975.21; total interest: $475.21
   c) amount: $2115.90; total interest: $615.90
2. The graph of 5% interest increases faster and curves upwards more than the graph of 3% interest; 5% gives more interest than 3%; answers may vary.
3. a) The amount will increase from $798.94 to $942.99 and the interest will increase from $123.94 to $267.99.
   b) The amount will increase from $798.94 to $945.63 and the interest will increase from $123.94 to $270.63.
4. a) $2771.54   **b)** $2717.85
5. The more frequent the compounding periods, the less she needs to invest; answers may vary.
6. a) $3.75   **b)** $5.67   **c)** $6.97
7. a) i) $15 730.86   **ii)** $15 750.44
   b) Compounded monthly because the compounding periods are more frequent; answers may vary.
8. Option A, since it makes the most interest.
   A: $11 360.00; B: $11 298.86; C: $11 264.93
9. a) Plan C; not necessarily the best option, since Jayeed can only use the money after four years; answers may vary.
   b) Plan A, since it earns more interest than plan B, and plan C is not cashable in two and a half years; answers may vary.
10. a) $1080   **b)** 281.3%
11. a) $602.22   **b)** Answers may vary.
12. a) i) $7413.72   **ii)** $7440.94
   b) The second investment has a greater principal because it has less frequent compounding periods.
13. Answers may vary.
15. $372.65
16. a) $1 777 232.88   **b)** $2 000 000
   c) Answers may vary.
17. a) 8.45%   **b)** 8.28%   **c)** 8.19%   **d)** 8.14%
18. 21%

Chapter 8 Review, pages 454–455
1. Simple Interest:

Year	Simple Interest ($)	Amount ($)
0		2000
1	100	2100
2	100	2200
3	100	2300
4	100	2400
5	100	2500
6	100	2600

Compound Interest:

Year	$A = P(1.05)$	Amount ($)
0		2000.00
1	2000(1.05)	2100.00
2	2100(1.05)	2205.00
3	2205(1.05)	2315.25
4	2315.25(1.05)	2431.0125
5	2431.0125(1.05)	2552.56313
6	2552.56313(1.05)	2680.19128

2. a)

Year	A = P(1.03)	Amount ($)
0		1500.00
1	1500(1.03)	1545.00
2	1545(1.03)	1591.35
3	1591.35(1.03)	1639.0905
4	1639.0905(1.03)	1688.26322

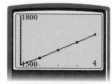

b)

Year	A = P(1.035)	Amount ($)
0		1500.00
1	1500(1.035)	1552.50
2	1552.5(1.035)	1606.8375
3	1606.8375(1.035)	1663.07681
4	1663.07681(1.035)	1721.28450

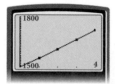

c)

Year	A = P(1.04)	Amount ($)
0		1500.00
1	1500(1.04)	1560.00
2	1560(1.04)	1622.40
3	1622.4(1.04)	1687.296
4	1687.296(1.04)	1754.78784

3. a) about $2700   **b)** about 12 years
   c) The graph would be less steep and would curve upwards more slowly because of the lower interest rate.
4. a) $A = 600(1 + 0.035)^6$ **b)** $A = 4000(1 + 0.0225)^{20}$
   c) $A = 6000(1 + 0.007)^{36}$ **d)** $A = 1200(1 + 0.0225)^4$
5. a) investment A earned him more money
   b) $1863.46
6. a) $3768.82   **b)** $1468.82
7. $3612.10
8. $5634.32
9. Plan C
10.

Present Value ($)	Future Value ($)	Term (years)	Compounding Period	Annual Interest Rate (%)
8000	12 000	5	monthly	8.14
6000	13 000	10	semi-annually	7.88
1340	2000	6.75	quarterly	6
100 000	1 000 000	29.5	semi-annually	8
4000	4376.21	3	monthly	3
16 149.25	25 000	8	quarterly	5.5

11. a) 17 years 6 months
   b) Yes, since doubling does not depend on the principal; answers may vary.

12. a) $3184.09   **b)** $3379.48   **c)** $3586.85
13. a) $289.80   **b)** $295.05   **c)** $297.76   **d)** $299.61
14. a) $28 405.65
   b) $20 000.00
   c) He should lease the car; $8405.65

Chapter 8 Practice Test, pages 456–457
  1. B
  2. C
  3. A
  4. A and D
  5. Simple Interest:

Year	Simple Interest ($)	Amount ($)
0		1000.00
1	70	1070.00
2	70	1140.00
3	70	1210.00
4	70	1280.00
5	70	1350.00
6	70	1420.00
7	70	1490.00
8	70	1560.00
9	70	1630.00
10	70	1700.00

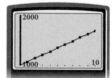

Compound Interest:

Year	A = P(1.07)	Amount ($)
0		1000.00
1	1000.00(1.07)	1070.00
2	1070.00(1.07)	1144.90
3	1144.90 (1.07)	1225.043
4	1225.043 (1.07)	1310.79601
5	1310.79601 (1.07)	1402.55173
6	1402.55173 (1.07)	1500.73035
7	1500.73035 (1.07)	1605.78148
8	1605.78148 (1.07)	1718.18618
9	1718.18618 (1.07)	1838.45921
10	1838.45921 (1.07)	1967.15136

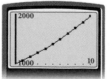

6. a) $780.27   **b)** $804.51
7. 8 years
8. Loan B
9. 7.05%
10. $8859.56
11. a) $1246.18   **b)** $1249.20   **c)** $1250.75   **d)** $1251.80

12. a)

Annual Interest Rate (%)	Compounding Period	Scholarship Amount ($)
8.0	semi-annually	$4080.00
7.5	quarterly	$3856.79
5.5	semi-annually	$2787.81
7.0	semi-annually	$3561.25
9.0	annually	$4500.00

b) 10%

CHAPTER 9

Personal Finance, pages 458–459

Prerequisite Skills, pages 460–461

1. a) 13.23 **b)** 21.28 **c)** 5400
d) 65 **e)** 458.4375 **f)** 6986.25
2. a) 0.04 **b)** 0.013 75 **c)** 0.024
d) 0.015 **e)** 0.0085 **f)** 0.0075
3. a) 0.16 **b)** 0.07 **c)** 0.049
d) 0.009 **e)** −0.0285 **f)** 0.288
4. Answers may vary.
a) 60 **b)** 425 **c)** 209
d) 43.2 **e)** 225 **f)** 250
5. a) 350 **b)** 175 **c)** 1.6
d) 3.2 **e)** 2500 **f)** 250
6. a) 0.02 **b)** 0.032 **c)** 0.004 **d)** 0.015
e) 0.015 **f)** 0.028 **g)** 0.0875 **h)** 0.013 25
7. a) 16 **b)** 27 **c)** 1.44
d) 1 **e)** 0.125 **f)** 0
8. a) 13.0321 **b)** 25.672 375 **c)** 1.5625
d) 0.005 15 **e)** 0.166 375 **f)** 0.000 343
9. a) 0.0075 **b)** 0.04225 **c)** −0.02325
d) 0.0045 **e)** 0.0004 **f)** 0.0008
10. a) 12 **b)** 60 **c)** 8
d) 183 **e)** 730 **f)** 540
11. a) $2459.75 **b)** $1308.65 **c)** $524.44 **d)** $304.97
12. a) $2459.75 **b)** $1308.65 **c)** $524.44 **d)** $304.97

9.1 Saving Alternatives, pages 462–467

1. a) $2001.64 **b)** $3007.65 **c)** $1500.95
d) $410.13 **e)** $500.02 **f)** $2500.48
2. a) $2001.64 **b)** $3007.65 **c)** $1500.95
d) $410.13 **e)** $500.02 **f)** $2500.48
3. a) $8.45 **b)** $6.95 **c)** $13.70
d) $6.95 **e)** $11.45 **f)** $17.45
4. a) $9.95 **b)** $9.95 **c)** $10.90
d) $9.95 **e)** $9.95 **f)** $15.65
5. Answers may vary.
6. a) $1.60 **b)** $19.82
c) The account is earning interest on previously earned interest each new month.
7. a) 11 **b)** Option 1
c) Option 1: $11, $1; Option 2: $14.75, $1.34; Option 3: $24.95, $2.27
d) Withdraw more cash so he makes fewer withdrawals; answers may vary.
8. a) Option 1 **b)** Option 1 **c)** 16 **d)** $17.25, $1.08
9. a) about 65 **b)** Option 3 **c)** about $0.38
d) To make fewer bank transactions; answers may vary.
10. a) $31.27 **b)** $281.46 **c)** $0.04 **d)** $28.69
e) $59.96 **f)** $0.08 **g)** about $800
11. A savings account is for money you are going to use soon; answers may vary.

9.2 Investment Alternatives, pages 468–475

1. a) 0.06 **b)** 0.08 **c)** 0.1
d) 0.005 **e)** 0.0325 **f)** 0.049
g) −0.026 **h)** 0.0595 **i)** 0.0506
2.

	r (%)	Compounding Frequency	i
a)	9.0	monthly	0.0075
b)	16.0	quarterly	0.0400
c)	−4.6	semi-annually	−0.0230
d)	1.8	quarterly	0.0045
e)	0.5	monthly	0.0004
f)	12.8	quarterly	0.0320

3. a) $1127.46 **b)** $7889.56 **c)** $2016.24
4. a) $1127.46 **b)** $7889.56 **c)** $2016.24
5. a) $127.46 **b)** $2889.56 **c)** $16.24
6. $2339.50
7. $11 221.64
8. a) $1988.40 **b)** $2114.27 **c)** $3196.27
9. a) Guaranteed Investment Certificate; A type of risk free investment that lasts a fixed amount of time; answers may vary.
b) Low-risk **c)** Answers may vary.
10. a) $1041 **b)** $1083.68
c) $FV = 1000(1.041)^n$ **d)** $1324.81
e)

11. a) Answers may vary.
i) low-risk **ii)** medium-risk **iii)** high-risk
iv) low-risk **v)** medium-risk **vi)** high-risk
vii) medium-risk
b) Answers may vary.
12. a) $520 **b)** $10.14 **c)** $634.14 **d)** $633.75
13. a) $550 396.54 **b)** $63 700 **c)** $486 696.54
d) He expects to get higher paying jobs.
14. $900.75
16. Answers may vary.

9.3 Manage Credit Cards, pages 476–481

1. a) 0.049% **b)** 0.0789% **c)** 0.0381% **d)** 0.0107%
2. a) $1540.96 **b)** $1566.50 **c)** $1531.76 **d)** $1508.85
3. a) $1541.00 **b)** $1566.50 **c)** $1531.74 **d)** $1508.84
4. 37 days
5. a) February 8 **b)** March 11
6. a) $10 **b)** $36.62
7. advantage: fewer bank transactions; disadvantage: she might buy more than she can afford; answers may vary.
8. a) 0.0518%, 0.000 518 **b)** 0.0353%, 0.000 353
9. a) $99.24 **b)** $10
c) August 17 **d)** Answers may vary.
e) 0.046%, 0.000 46 **f)** $0
10. a) $8380 **b)** $325.35
c) Bank 1: $29.03; Bank 2: $53.19; Gasoline Retailer: $3.55; Furniture Retailer: $31.32
d) Bank 2
e) It will take 36 monthly payments (3 years) of $272.37 to pay off his $8380 debt at 10.5% interest, compounded monthly.

9.4 Obtain a Vehicle, pages 482–488

1. a) $26 214.30 **b)** $41 325
 c) $20 518.86 **d)** $14 814.30
2. a) $127.20 **b)** $209.51 **c)** $313.20
3. a) $4579.20 **b)** $10 056.48 **c)** $18 792
4. a) $579.20 **b)** $1556.48 **c)** $3792
5. a) $11 764 **b)** $19 152 **c)** $42 561
6. a) $200 **b)** $336 **c)** $24
7. different mileage, condition, or damage; answers may vary.
8. 5-speed, automatic, or best offer, power steering, 170 000 km, all-wheel drive, emission test, power brakes, certified, power windows, air conditioning, front-wheel drive, has all extra options, power (door) locks, year 2000 model
9. a) $26 200 **b)** $545.83
 c) buy the car or lease a new car; answers may vary.
10. a) $7020 **b)** $65.35 **c)** $150
11. a) $38 360 **b)** $799.17
13. Answers may vary.
14. a) pre-delivery inspection **b)** $26 539.20
 c) $457.03 **d)** $26 937.44 **e)** $11 578.10

9.5 Operate a Vehicle, pages 489–495

1. a) $80 **b)** $6 **c)** $0.16
2. Answers may vary.
3. Answers may vary.
4. a) 1000 km **b)** 508 km **c)** 705 km
 d) 735 km **e)** 681 km
5. a) 3.7 gallons **b)** 7.9 gallons **c)** 14.5 gallons
 d) 19.8 gallons **e)** 24.3 gallons
6. Answers may vary.
 a) fixed **b)** variable **c)** fixed **d)** variable
 e) variable **f)** fixed **g)** fixed **h)** fixed
 i) variable **j)** fixed
7. a) $2336 **b)** $9999 **c)** $4450
8. a) 16% **b)** 19% **c)** 19%
9. $1320
10. a) 13 km/L **b)** 12 km/L **c)** 20 km/L
11. a) $19 355 **b)** 6
12. Answers may vary.
14. a)

Date	Odometer Reading	Distance (km)	Fuel Use (US gallons)	Fuel Use (L)	Fuel Costs (US$)	Fuel Costs (CDN$)	Unit Fuel Cost (CDN$/L)	Fuel Efficiency (km/L)
Mar. 15	236 083	--------	------	-----	---------	-------	--------	--------
Mar. 16	236 948	865	12.7	48.1	41.00	48.38	1.01	18
Mar. 17	237 760	812	12.3	46.6	40.00	47.20	1.01	17
Mar. 22	237 897	137	2.6	9.8	8.50	10.03	1.02	14
Mar. 23	238 780	883	12.5	47.3	40.25	47.50	1.00	19
Mar. 24	239 541	761	----------	42.9	-------	42.85	1.00	18

 b) 3458 km **c)** 17.8 km/L, 5.6 L/100 km **d)** $195.96

Chapter 9 Review, pages 496–497

1. a) $20.25
 b) Make fewer transactions and use a credit card; answers may vary.
2. a) $0.09 **b)** $0.09
3. $1.27
4. $4485.20
5. a) $FV = PV(1.0365)^n$ **b)** $2392.64 **c)** $2392.64
6. advantage: groups all purchases into one payment; disadvantage: has high interest rates; answers may vary.
7. $8.38

8. PST
9. a) $23 652 **b)** $492.75
10. a) $136.37 **b)** $211.74
11. a) $28 032.77 **b)** $57 340.09
12. a) Answers may vary. **b)** Answers may vary.
 c) 4.2 L/100 km, 23.6 km/L
13. a) $8255 **b)** 14%
 c) 34.9% **d)** 13.3%
 e) $FV = 67\ 000(0.867)^n$ **f)** $16 079.25

Chapter 9 Practice Test, pages 498–499

1. A
2. C
3. B
4. C
5. a) $58 800 **b)** $357 333.44 **c)** $298 533.44
6. $23 632.60
7. a) $18 772 **b)** $391.08
8. a) The van requires 12.2 L of fuel to drive 100 km.
 b) 656 km **c)** 52 L
9. Answers may vary.

Chapters 7 to 9 Review, pages 500–501

1. a) $6^5 = 7776$ **b)** $10^4 = 10\ 000$
 c) $\left(\dfrac{1}{4}\right)^5 = \dfrac{1}{1024}$ **d)** $7^2 = 49$
 e) $2^{10} = 1024$ **f)** $(-1)^{24} = 1$
2. a) $\dfrac{1}{4}$ **b)** 1 **c)** $\dfrac{1}{125}$
 d) 1 **e)** $\dfrac{1}{1000}$ **f)** $\dfrac{1}{135}$
3. Every time the x value increases by 1, the y value is multiplied by 3.
4. a) negative exponential because every 5 s, the speed is divided by 2; B
 b) positive linear because every second, the speed increases by 10; A
 c) quadratic (parabola) because gravity involves a quadratic function; C
 d) positive exponential because every year, the population is multiplied by 1.02; D
5. a)
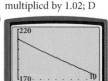
 b) 210
 c) about 182
6. a) 996 mg **b)** 819 mg **c)** 18.6 mg
7.

Years	Simple Interest ($)	Compound Interest ($)
0	1500	1500.00
1	1590	1590.00
2	1680	1685.40
3	1770	1786.52
4	1860	1893.71
5	1950	2007.33
6	2040	2127.77
7	2130	2255.44
8	2220	2390.77
9	2310	2534.22
10	2400	2686.27

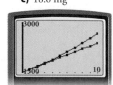

8. a) 26.92   **b)** 395.98   **c)** 23.21   **d)** 227.28

9. a) $3152.84; $3313.46   **b)** $186.44

10. a) $3593.81   **b)** $1847.69   **c)** $7430.48

11. a) 9.2%   **b)** 7.35%   **c)** 5.5%

12. Both graphs start together, but as time increases, the investment at 6% increases faster than the other and increases the gap between them. The 6% investment has greater return than the 4.5% investment.

13. a) $4.95   **b)** $6.95   **c)** $4.95
     d) $9.95   **e)** $8.45   **f)** $11.95

14. $850.10

15. $659.59; $660.31

16. a) $14 214   **b)** $23 952

17. a) 544 km   **b)** 75.875 L

18. a) $2395   **b)** $7299

Chapters 1 to 9 Review, pages 504–513

1. a) $d = 282$ cm, $f = 320$ cm, $\angle E = 28°$
     b) $z = 14$ m, $x = 53$ m, $\angle X = 75°$

2. No; the angle of depression is 13°.

3. a) $z = 18.6$ cm, $y = 24.5$ cm, $\angle Y = 66°$
     b) $b = 16.2$ mm, $\angle A = 70°$, $\angle C = 52°$

4. 23 m²

5. a) trigonometric ratios   **b)** cosine law
     c) sine law

6. a) 19.2 cm, 24.4 cm, 52°   **b)** 47.7°, 82.2°, 50.1°
     c) 15.3 m, 16.6 m, 50°

7. a) Yes; if the last 20 callers are unsatisfied, the percent of unsatisfied callers is greater than 2%.
     b) Yes; $\frac{12}{360} \approx 3.3\%$ **c)** Yes; $\frac{33}{1000} \approx 3.3\%$

8. a) $\frac{1}{3}$
     b) $\frac{2}{3}$. Using part a), $1 - \frac{1}{3} = \frac{2}{3}$. Adding the probabilities, $\frac{2}{18} + \frac{10}{18} = \frac{12}{18} = \frac{2}{3}$
     c) 0.375

9. a) $\frac{1}{4}$
     b) The theoretical probability is $\frac{1}{2}$.
     c) No. The rolls are independent.
     d) Answers will vary.

10. a) $\frac{1}{5}$ **b)** 89%   **c)** 8.8%   **d)** 2.2%

11. a) stratified random sample; answers will vary.
     b) systematic sample; answers will vary.
     c) convenience sample; answers will vary.
     d) simple random sample; answers will vary.

12. a) measurement bias, to remove it they can use participants in many winter activities as a sample; answers will vary.
     b) measurement bias, to remove it they can let viewers call in to ask questions; answers will vary.

13. a) discrete, circle graph or bar graph; answers will vary.
     b) continuous, histogram; answers will vary.

14. test scores; answers will vary.

15. a) mean: 18.2, median: 5, mode: 5; mode, since it is the most likely prize value; answers will vary.
     b) mean: 3.1, median: 3.0, mode: 3.7, mean, since the median and mean are close and there are no outliers; answers will vary.

16. 223

17. a) variance: 19.06, standard deviation: 4.43
     b) variance: 15.36, standard deviation: 3.92

18. a) Answers will vary.
     b) bimodal distribution
     c) the busiest hours are 9:00 A.M. to 10:00 A.M. and 12:00 P.M. to 1:00 P.M.
     d) the least amount of coffee was sold between 2:00 P.M. and 3:00 P.M., more coffee was sold before 11:00 A.M. than after 11:00 A.M., the greatest amount of coffee was sold between 12:00 P.M. and 1:00 P.M.; answers will vary.

19.

Age	5	6	7	8	9	10	11	12
Number of students	3	6	9	4	3	2	2	1

Answers will vary.

20. a) $y = 2.5x^2 + 25$; answers will vary.
     b) $y = -0.5x^2 - 2$; answers will vary.

21. a)

Time (s)	Distance (m)
0	115.0
1	111.6
2	98.4
3	75.4
4	42.6
5	0

     b) The second differences are a constant and there is an x^2 term; answers will vary.

     c)

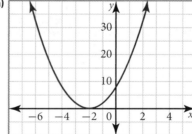

Height of Rock vs Time

     d) 5 s

22. a)

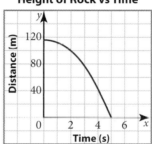

$y = 2(x + 2)^2$

     b)

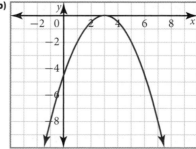

$y = 0.5(x - 3)^2$

23. a)

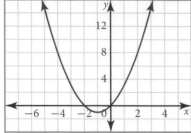

b)

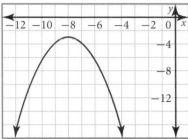

c)

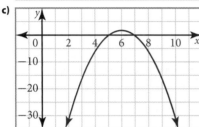

d)

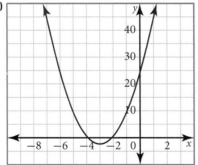

24. a)

Amount Spent on Advertising, A ($)	Extra Revenue, R ($)
0	0
1000	4500
2000	8000
3000	10 500
4000	12 000
5000	12 500
6000	12 000
7000	10 500
8000	8000
9000	4500
10 000	0

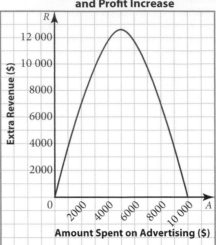

b) (5000, 12 500). The y-coordinate is the greatest profit increase and the x-coordinate is the amount that, when spent on advertising, results in this increase.

25. a) $y = 0.03x^2$; answers will vary.

b)

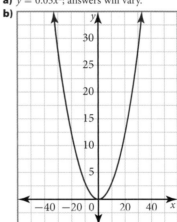

26. a) $24x^2 + 62x + 14$ **b)** $-5x^2 + 247x + 150$
c) $100x^2 + 1090x - 110$ **d)** $64x^2 - 25$

27. $54x^2 + 22x - 20$

28. a) $y = 2x^2 + 6x + 11$ **b)** $y = 5x^2 - 10x + 9$
c) $y = -3x^2 + 14x - 5$ **d)** $y = 5x^2 + 30x + 45$

29. a) 0   **b)** -12

30. a) $(x - 11)(x - 6)$ **b)** $(x + 7)(x + 1)$
c) $(x - 8)(x - 5)$ **d)** $(x + 3)(x - 6)$
e) $x(x + 13)$ **f)** $(x + 3)(x - 3)$

31. a) $2(x + 1)(x - 2)$ **b)** $-6(x + 6)(x - 4)$
c) $3(x + 7)(x - 6)$ **d)** $7(x + 7)(x - 1)$

32. a) not equivalent   **b)** equivalent
c) equivalent   **d)** not equivalent

33. a) $-3, 3$ **b)** 1, 14   **c)** 0
d) -4 **e)** $-0.5, 8$ **f)** 0, 9

34. a) The zero has no meaning because it represents a negative time.
b) $h = -10(t + 0.02)(t - 5)$
c) 5. It is the number of seconds that elapse before the rocket hits the ground.

35. a) $x^2 + 5x - 39$ **b)** 10

36. a) small: 1.690 48, average: 1.617 65, above average: 1.618 18, very large: 1.617 98
   b) They are very close to the golden ratio.
   c) 21 counter-clockwise spirals
37. Quilts, backpacks, wallets, shoes; answers will vary.
38. a) diameter = 8 cm, height = 24 cm
   b) Diagrams will vary.
39. Diagrams will vary.

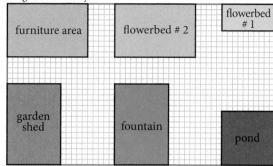

40. 1 cm represents 10 m; 31 cm × 20 cm × 3 cm; answers will vary.
41. a) $4^5 = 1024$ **b)** $9^3 = 729$ **c)** $\left(\frac{1}{2}\right)^7 = \frac{1}{128}$
   d) $11^3 = 1331$ **e)** $3^9 = 19\,683$ **f)** $(-2)^{10} = 1024$
42. 1000 times
43. a) $10^{-1} = \frac{1}{10}$ **b)** $4^{-3} = \frac{1}{64}$ **c)** $5^2 = 25$
   d) $3^5 = 243$ **e)** $(-7)^1 = -7$ **f)** $2^1 = 2$
44. a) 20^{-7} **b)** $\left(\frac{1}{3}\right)^{-11}$
45. A and C; second differences are equal; answers will vary.
46. a)

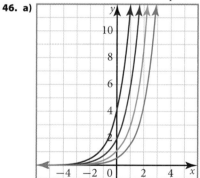

   b) The value a multiplies all the y-values from the original graph by the same amount, making the graph grow faster as a increases, or slower as a decreases.
47. C
48. A: linear increasing; B: exponential decreasing; C: exponential increasing; D: quadratic decreasing
49. a) 225%   **b)** 3 times; it would be a 337.5% enlargement

50. a)

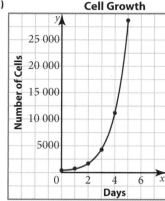

   b) 200   **c)** 520; 28 698
51. a) 88.6%   **b)** 40.4%   **c)** 2.65%
52.

Years	simple interest ($)	compound interest ($)
1	4300	4300
2	4600	4622.50
3	4900	4969.19
4	5200	5341.88
5	5500	5742.52

7.5% Simple and Compound Interest

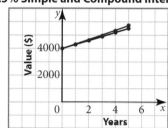

53. $605; $608.24
54. a) 141.85   **b)** 1695.74   **c)** 70.50   **d)** 331.71
55. a) $2780.76   **b)** $1704.36
56. $7723.62
57. a) 2133.73   **b)** 6900.87
58. $803.72
59. a) $656.63   **b)** $3425.68   **c)** $2217.96   **d)** $889.00
60. $5762.87
61. 4.5 years
62. $2156.39
63. $2252.86 at 3.5%; 2218.62 at 4%
64. Plan A: $436; Plan B: $441.15; Plan C: $435.43
65. a) $0.68   **b)** $0.59   **c)** $3.92
   d) $68.26   **e)** $0.19   **f)** $0.30
66. a) $2.48   **b)** $60.81   **c)** $0.92
67. $20 149.78
68. $3073.92
69. a) $71.96   **b)** $42.24   **c)** $25   **d)** $52.63
70. $4400
71. a) $177.43   **b)** $223.97   **c)** $309.06
72. a) $6387.38   **b)** $10 750.29   **c)** $18 543.38
73. a) Monthly: $2340; Semi-annually: $2300
   b) Annual payment, semi-annual payments, monthly payments
   c) monthly and semi-annual payments do not have to be paid all at once, but the annual payment is the cheapest, answers may vary.
74. a) 13.5 km/L   **b)** 12.5 km/L   **c)** 19.8 km/L
75. a) $1540   **b)** $8560

Glossary

A

adjacent side The side that forms one of the arms of the angle being considered in a right triangle, but is not the hypotenuse.

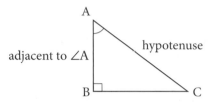

algebraic expression A mathematical phrase made up of numbers and variables.
$3x - 2$, $5m$, and $12xy + x + 14y$

amount The final value of an investment, including the principal and the accumulated interest. Also called the future value.

angle of depression The angle between the horizontal and the line of sight down to an object.

angle of elevation The angle between the horizontal and the line of sight up to an object. Also known as an angle of inclination.

angle of inclination The angle between the horizontal and the line of sight up to an object. Also known as an angle of elevation.

area The number of square units needed to cover a two-dimensional region.

axis of symmetry A vertical line that passes through the vertex of a parabola. The equation of the axis of symmetry is $x = a$, where a is the x-coordinate of the vertex.

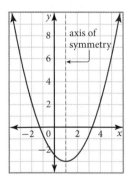

B

bias A survey contains bias if it does not reflect the population. An unrepresentative sample, the wording of the survey questions, and/or the interpretation and presentation of the results.

bimodal distribution A distribution that contains two equally likely measures of central tendency within the data.

binomial A polynomial that has two terms.
$4x^2 + 2$ is a binomial.

box-and-whisker plot A graph representing the first quartile, the median, and the third quartile of a data set with a box. The least and greatest data are represented by lines (whiskers) extending from the box.

C

categorical data Data that are types rather than numbers; for example: colours, types of snack foods, etc.

circumference The perimeter of a circle.

coefficient A number that is multiplied by a variable.
In $y = -2x$, the coefficient of x is -2.

complementary angles Angles whose sum is 90°.

composite figure A figure that is made up of two or more geometric figures.

compound interest The interest paid on the principal and its accumulated interest.

compounding period The length of time for which interest is calculated before being accumulated.

cone A three-dimensional object with a circular base and a curved surface that tapers to a point.

constant term A numerical term which cannot change; that is, it remains constant. In the equation $7x + 3 = -5$, the constant terms are 3 and -5.

constraint A condition that limits the acceptable range of values for a variable.

continuous data Data that can have any numerical value within a finite or infinite interval; for example, the heights of students in your class.

coordinate grid A grid formed by perpendicular number lines. Used for graphing points as ordered pairs.

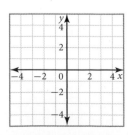

coordinates The numbers in an ordered pair that locate a point on a coordinate grid.

corresponding angles Angles that have the same relative position in a pair of similar triangles. Corresponding angles are equal.

corresponding sides Sides that have the same relative position in a pair of similar triangles. Lengths of corresponding sides are proportional.

cosine law The relationship between the lengths of the three sides and the cosine of an angle in any triangle.

$$a^2 = b^2 + c^2 - 2bc \cos A$$

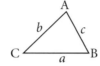

creditor A person or organization that lends money.

cube A prism with six congruent square faces.

curve of best fit A curve that passes through, or as near as possible to, the points on a scatter plot.

cylinder A three-dimensional object with two parallel circular bases.

data Facts or pieces of information.

depreciation The amount that the value of an item decreases over time.

diameter A line segment that passes through the centre of a circle and joins two points on the circumference of the circle.

difference of squares A binomial of the form $x^2 - r^2$. The factors of a difference of squares are $(x - r)(x + r)$.

discrete data Data that are distinct and can be counted; for example, the number of students who like rice.

discount To sell an investment at a value less than its usual price.

distributive property When a polynomial is multiplied by a monomial, the monomial multiplies each term in the polynomial.
$$a(x + y) = ax + ay$$

doubling time Time required for a quantity to double in size, number, or mass.

equation A mathematical statement that two expressions are equal.
$6x - 1 = 4x$ is an equation.

equilateral triangle A triangle with all sides equal and all angles equal.

expand Multiply, often using the distributive property.

experimental probability Determined using the results of an experiment or simulation.
$$P(\text{event}) = \frac{\text{number of successful trials}}{\text{total number of trials}}$$

exponential decay Non-linear growth represented by an exponential relation and a graph with a downward curve.

exponential growth Non-linear growth represented by an exponential relation and a graph with an upward curve.

exponential relation A relation that can be represented by the form $y = a^x$, where a is a positive constant and $a \neq 1$. The ratios of consecutive y-values are constant.

event A set of outcomes with the same result.

first differences The difference between consecutive y-values in a table of values with evenly spaced x-values. First differences are constant for a linear relation.

fixed cost An expense that remains the same from one month to the next.

future value The value of an investment or loan at the end of the term.

G

golden ratio For a rectangle, the ratio of the length to the width is approximately 1.618:1.

golden rectangle A rectangle that is pleasing to the eye. The ratio of the length to the width is approximately 1.618:1.

growth factor The number that is multiplied by the principal when calculating its accumulated value.

growth rate The percent by which an investment increases (or decreases) in value over a given time.

Guaranteed Investment Certificate (GIC) A type of investment sold to individuals by banks or trust companies. Usually, GICs pay interest at a fixed rate and cannot be cashed before a specified date.

 H

half-life The time it takes for a quantity to decay or be reduced to half its initial amount.

height of an object The perpendicular distance from the base of the object to the opposite face or vertex.

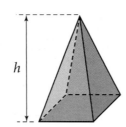

h

hypotenuse The longest side of a right triangle. The side opposite the right angle in a right triangle.

 I

integer A number in the sequence ..., −3, −2, −1, 0, 1, 2, 3, ...

intercept The distance from the origin of a coordinate grid to the point at which the line or curve crosses a given axis.

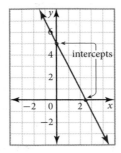

intercepts

intercept form A quadratic relation of the form $y = a(x − r)(x − s)$. The constants, r and s, represent the x-intercepts of the relation.

interquartile range The range of the central half of a set of data when the data are arranged from least to greatest. A measure of how closely data clusters around its mean.

isometric perspective drawing A visual representation of three-dimensional objects in two dimensions.

isosceles triangle A triangle with exactly two equal sides.

 L

legs The two shorter sides of a right triangle. The sides adjacent to the right angle.

like terms Terms that have the same variables raised to the same exponent.
   $4x$ and $−6x$ are like terms.

line of best fit A line that passes through, or as near as possible to, the points on a scatter plot.

linear equation An equation that relates two variables so the ordered pairs that satisfy the equation lie in a straight line on a graph.

linear relation A relation between two variables that appears as a straight line when graphed.

line of symmetry A line that divides a figure into two congruent parts that are reflections of each other in the line.

line segment The part of a line that joins two points.

 M

mathematical model A mathematical description of a real situation. Can be a diagram, a graph, a table of values, a relation, a formula, a physical model, or a computer model.

maximum value The greatest value of a quadratic relation represented by a parabola that opens downward. The y-value at the vertex of a parabola.

mean The sum of values in a set of data divided by the number of values in the set of data.

median The middle value when data is ordered from least to greatest.

minimum value The least value of a quadratic relation represented by a parabola that opens upward. The y-value at the vertex of a parabola.

mode The value or attribute that occurs most often in the set of data.

monomial A polynomial with one term, such as $5x^2$.

mutual fund Type of investment where people pool their money together to buy stocks, bonds, and other assets. Managed by an investment company that charges a fee.

net A two-dimensional pattern that can be folded to make a three-dimensional object. This is a net for a square-based pyramid.

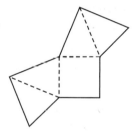

non-linear relation A relation between two variables that does not appear as a straight line when graphed.

normal distribution A bell-shaped distribution that is symmetrical about the mean.

opposite angles The pairs of angles formed on either side when two lines intersect.

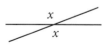

opposite side The side across from the angle being considered. The side that does not form one of the arms of the angle being considered.

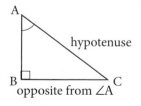

opposite from $\angle A$

order of operations The convention for evaluating expressions with more than one operation: **B**rackets, **E**xponents, **D**ivision, **M**ultiplication, **A**ddition, and **S**ubtraction (BEDMAS).

ordered pairs A pair of numbers used to locate a point on a coordinate grid. The first number indicates the horizontal distance from the y-axis. The second number indicates the vertical distance from the x-axis.

origin The point of intersection of the x- and y-axes on a coordinate grid. The point $(0, 0)$.

orthographic drawing A drawing that uses orthographic projection.

orthographic projection A set of drawings that show up to six views of an object, usually the front, side, and top views.

outcome A possible result of an experiment.

outlier An extreme value in a set of data. A value "far away" from the other values in a set of data.

parabola The graph of a quadratic relation. A symmetrical U-shaped curve.

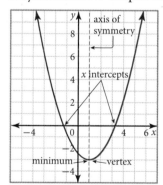

parallel lines Lines in the same plane that do not intersect. Parallel lines have the same slope.

pattern A form, template, or model from which an object can be created.

perfect square trinomial The result of squaring a binomial. A trinomial with identical binomial factors.

perimeter The distance around a closed figure.

perpendicular lines Lines that intersect at right angles.

plan A scale drawing of a structure or object. A design or arrangement scheme.

polynomial An algebraic expression made up of one or more terms, separated by addition or subtraction.

population All individuals or items that belong to a group being studied.

present value The value of an investment or loan on a date before the end of the term.

primary source A person who collects data for their own use.

principal The value of the initial investment or loan.

prism A three-dimensional object with two parallel, congruent polygonal bases. A prism is named by the shape of the base.

proportional Quantities are proportional if they have the same ratio. The side lengths of two triangles are proportional if there is a single value that will multiply each side length of the first triangle to give the side lengths of the second triangle.

pyramid A three-dimensional object with one polygonal base and triangular faces that meet at a common vertex. A pyramid is named by the shape of the base.

Pythagorean theorem In a right triangle, the square of the hypotenuse is equal to the sum of the squares of the legs. For a right triangle with legs a and b and hypotenuse c, $c^2 = a^2 + b^2$.

quadratic equation An expression of the form $ax^2 + bx + c$, where $a \neq 0$.

quadratic relation A relation between two variables that appear as a parabola when graphed. A relation of the form $y = ax^2 + bx + c$, where $a \neq 0$.

quartiles Three values that divide a set of data into four intervals with equal numbers of data.

radius A line segment joining the centre of a circle to a point on the circumference, or the length of this line segment.

range The difference between the greatest and least values in a set of data.

rate of change A change in one quantity relative to the change in another quantity.

ratio A comparison of two quantities measured in the same units.

rectangle A quadrilateral with two pairs of equal opposite sides and four right angles.

rectangular prism A three-dimensional object with three pairs of congruent parallel rectangular faces.

rectangular pyramid A three-dimensional object with a rectangular base and two pairs of congruent triangular faces.

Registered Education Savings Plan (RESP) An investment set up to save for a child's education. The income from the plan grows tax-free.

Registered Retirement Savings Plan (RRSP) An investment that is set up to provide income after retirement. Generally, you are allowed to put money into an RRSP and claim a deduction on your taxes in that year. Contributions accumulate interest tax-free. When the money is taken out of the RRSP, it is taxed as income.

relation An identified pattern, or relationship, between two variables. A relation can be represented by an equation, a graph, a set of ordered pairs, or a table of values.

right angle A 90° angle.

right triangle A triangle that contains one 90° angle.

rise The vertical distance between two points on a line.

run The horizontal distance between two points on a line.

sample A group of individuals or items that are representative of the population from which they are taken.

scale model A model that is an enlargement of a small object or a reduction of a large object.

scatter plot A graph that compares two sets of related data. Shows two-variable data as points plotted on a coordinate grid.

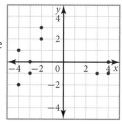

second differences The difference between consecutive first differences. For a quadratic relation, second differences are constant.

secondary source A database or research collected by someone else.

similar triangles Triangles in which the ratios of the lengths of corresponding sides are equal and corresponding angles are equal.

$$\triangle ABC \sim \triangle DEF$$

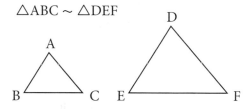

simple interest The money paid on a loan or investment. A percent of the principal.

sine law The relationship between the length of the sides and their opposite angles in any triangle.

$$\frac{a}{\sin A} = \frac{b}{\sin B} = \frac{c}{\sin C}$$

or $\dfrac{\sin A}{a} = \dfrac{\sin B}{b} = \dfrac{\sin C}{c}$

skewed distribution A non-symmetrical distribution of data.

slant height In a pyramid or a cone, the slant height is the least distance from the edge of the base to the vertex.

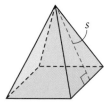

slope A measure of the steepness of a line. Compares the vertical distance to the horizontal distance between two points.

$$\text{slope} = \frac{\text{rise}}{\text{run}}$$

solution The value of the variable that makes an equation true.

sphere A three-dimensional ball-shaped object. Every point on the surface is an equal distance from a fixed point (the centre).

square-based prism A prism with two congruent, parallel square bases and four congruent rectangular faces.

square-based pyramid A pyramid with a square base and four congruent triangular faces.

standard deviation The typical distance of a particular value from the mean. The greater the standard deviation, the greater the spread of the data.

standard form A quadratic relation of the form $y = ax^2 + bx + c$. The constant, c, represents the y-intercept of the relation.

statistics The collection and analysis of numerical information.

supplementary angles Angles whose sum is 180°.

surface area The number of square units needed to cover the surface of a three-dimensional object.

T

table of values A table used to record the coordinates of points in a relation.

x	y
0	1
1	4
2	7
3	10
4	13
5	16

tangent ratio The ratio comparing the length of the side opposite the angle to the length of the side adjacent to the angle in a right triangle.

$$\tan B = \frac{\text{length of side opposite B}}{\text{length of side adjacent to B}}$$

term A number or a variable, or the product of numbers and variables.

tessellation A tiling pattern in which congruent figures cover a plane with no gaps or overlaps.

theorem A mathematical statement that has been proved.

theoretical probability The number of successful outcomes as a fraction of the total number of possible outcomes.

$$P(\text{event}) = \frac{\text{number of successful outcomes}}{\text{total number of possible outcomes}}$$

trial One round of a probability experiment.

triangle A three-sided polygon.

triangular prism A three-dimensional object with two congruent, parallel triangular bases and three rectangular faces.

triangular pyramid A three-dimensional object with a triangular base and three triangular faces.

trigonometry Means *triangle measurement*. Used to calculate lengths of sides and measures of angles in triangles.

trinomial A polynomial with three terms.
$x^2 + 2x + 1$ is a trinomial.

TVM (Time–Value–Money) Solver A feature of the TI-83 Plus/84 Plus calculators that is used for financial calculations.

 V

variable A letter used to represent a value that can change. In the expression $5p + 4$, p is the variable.

variable cost An expense that varies in amount or frequency.

variable term A term that includes a letter or symbol to represent an unknown value. In the equation $7x + 3 = -5$, the variable term is $7x$.

variance The mean of the squares of the deviations from the mean for a set of data.

vertex (of a polygon) A point at which two sides of a polygon meet.

vertex (of a parabola) The point at which the parabola changes from decreasing to increasing or from increasing to decreasing.

vertex form A quadratic relation of the form $y = a(x - h)^2 + k$. The coordinates of the vertex are (h, k).

volume The amount of space occupied by an object. Volume is measured in cubic units.

 X

x-axis The horizontal number line on a coordinate grid.

x-coordinate The first number in an ordered pair, which represents the horizontal distance from the y-axis on a coordinate grid.

x-intercept The x-coordinate of a point at which the graph of a relation crosses the x-axis. The value of x when $y = 0$.

 Y

y-axis The vertical number line on a coordinate grid.

y-coordinate The second number in an ordered pair, which represents the vertical distance from the x-axis on a coordinate grid.

y-intercept The y-coordinate of the point at which the graph of a relation crosses the y-axis. The value of y when $x = 0$.

 Z

zeros The x-intercepts of a quadratic relation. The value(s) of x when $y = 0$.

Index

A

adjacent, 7
amount, 422
    formula, 439
angle of depression, 18, 20
angle of elevation, 17, 20
angle of inclination, 20
area, 294
axis of symmetry, 209, 277, 280

B

bar graph, 118–120
    interpreting, 123
base, 356, 367
bias, 104, 110, 112–113
bimodal distribution, 150–152
binomials
    difference of squares,
        252, 253
    expanding, 234–238,
        248–249
bond, 434
box-and-whisker plot, 140–142

C

calculator
    depreciation, 492
    exponential relations, 409
    trigonometry, 9–11, 19–20,
        26–30, 36–38, 44–47
    vehicle cost, 483
categorical data, 120
certified vehicle, 482
circle graph, 118–120
circumference, 294, 328
clinometer, 16–17
complementary, 12
compound interest, 422, 427,
    472, 463–464, 476–478
    changing conditions,
        446–449
    formulas, 430, 432, 439,
        443, 461
    future value, 422, 430–431,
        442–443, 469–471

monthly payment, 483, 485
present value, 437–438, 443
comparing to simple interest,
    422–427
compounding period, 426, 430
Computer Algebra System
    (CAS)
    expand binomials, 237
constraints, 335, 340
continuous data, 120, 125
cosine law, 34–35
    find measures, 36–37
    formulas, 36, 39
    problem solving, 38, 42–43,
        46–48
credit cards, 476–479
creditor, 438

D

DAL calculator
    trigonometry, 19–20, 26–27,
        37–38, 47
data, 86
depreciation, 491–492
difference of squares, 252, 253
discount, 438
discrete data, 120, 125
doubling time, 394, 408
    formula, 410
down payment, 483, 485

E

event, 60
experimental probability,
    62– 65
    comparing to theoretical,
        76–81
    formula, 62, 65
exponent, 356
    rules, 356–360, 365–366
    zero and negative, 364–367
exponential relations, 373–374,
    376, 389
    comparing to linear,
        quadratic relations, 372–373,
        386–387, 395–397
    decay, 375–376, 397–398
    doubling time, 394, 408
    formulas, 389, 398, 401 410

graphs, 382–384, 389
growth, 375, 376, 388, 398
half-life, 406–408
problem solving, 385,
    398–400, 408–409

F

Fathom™
    histogram, 122
    mean and median, 132
fixed costs, 489, 492
fuel costs, 490–491
fuel efficiency, 490–491
future value, 422, 430–431,
    442–443, 469–471
    formula, 439, 443

G

Geometer's Sketchpad®, *The*
    drawings, 308–309, 312,
        325–326
    golden ratio, 296
    nets, 329–330
    tessellations, 298, 300,
        344–345
    quadratic relations, 183–185,
        195–196, 206, 219, 220
    relations, 173
    trigonometry, 6–7, 24–25,
        34–35
golden ratio, 296–297, 300–301
golden rectangle, 297
grace period, 477
graphing calculator
    bouncing ball, 397–398
    box-and-whisker plot,
        140–141
    compound interest, 425,
        447–448
    exponential relations, 382,
        398–400
    histogram, 121–122, 149
    mean and median, 132
    relations, 172
    quadratic relations, 180–182,
        194–195, 205
    random number generator,
        78–79, 86–88, 103
    regression analysis, 395–397

growth factor, 426, 436–437
growth rate, 468
Guaranteed Investment
    Certificate (GIC), 473

H

half-life, 406–408
    formula, 410
histogram, 121–122, 148–152
    interpreting, 124
hypotenuse, 7

I

insurance, 489–490, 492
insurance premium, 466
intercept form, 264–265, 271
    converting forms, 268–270
interest, *see* compound, simple
    interest
interquartile range, 141–142,
    144
isometric perspective drawings,
    306–308, 310–313

J

lease, 482, 485
linear relations,
    comparing to exponential,
    quadratic relations, 372–373,
    386–387, 395–397

M

mathematical model, 168–169
maximum, 170, 277
measures of central tendency
    (mean, median, mode), 130,
    135
    calculating, 130–133, 135,
    141–143
    choosing best, 133–135
    in distributions, 148–152
measures of spread, 140–145
Microsoft® *Excel*
    bar graph, 119
    circle graph, 120
    mean and median, 132
minimum, 170, 277
mutual fund, 468–470

N

negative exponents, 364–367
net, 318–319, 328–330
    problem solving, 335–340
normal distribution, 148–149,
    151–152

O

opposite, 7
orthographic drawings/
    projections, 306, 309–311,
    313, 320–321
outcome, 60
outlier, 135
overdue balance, 476

P

parabola, 169, 173
    find equations, 210–211,
    221–222, 279–280
    formulas, 189, 199, 211
    graphs, 208–209, 211,
    218–219, 265–267
    transformations, 180–189,
    194–198, 204–207
pattern, 318, 320, 321
perfect square trinomial, 251
perimeter, 294
perspective drawing, *see*
    isometric perspective
    drawing
plan, 318, 320–321, 325–326
polygon
    angles, 295
polynomials
    factoring, 257–259, 267
population, 103–104, 106
power, 356
    rules, 356–360
present value, 437–438
    formula, 443
primary source 111, 113
primary trigonometric ratios,
    see trigonometric ratios
principal, 422, 437
probability, 63, 65, 68
    comparing experimental
    and theoretical, 76–81

experimental, 62–65
experiments, 60–65, 81
theoretical, 69–73
and statistics, 86–89

Q

quadratic relations, 168–173
    axis of symmetry, 209, 277,
    280
    comparing to exponential,
    linear relations, 372–373,
    386–387, 395–397
    converting forms, 242–244,
    268–271, 276–277
    formulas, 189, 196, 199, 211,
    271
    form $y = ax^2 + k$, 180–189
    form $y = a(x - h)^2$, 194–199
    intercept form, 264–265, 271
    problem solving, 218–222,
    243–244, 269–270,
    278–279
    standard form, 242, 244
    vertex form, 204–211
    zeros, 265–267, 280
quartiles, 141–142, 144

R

radioactive decay, 366, 406–407
range, 141, 143, 144
Registered Education Savings
    Plan (RESP), 474
Registered Retirement Savings
    Plan (RRSP), 471
right triangle
    sides, 7
risk, 470, 472

S

sample, 103–104
sampling techniques, 103–106
savings accounts, 462, 465
scale models, 306, 327–331
    problem solving, 335–340
scientific calculator
    present value, 448–449
    trigonometry, 19–20, 26–27,
    36–38, 47
secondary source, 111, 113

service charges, 462, 464–465
simple interest, 422
    formula, 421, 427
    comparing to compound
       interest, 422–427
sine law, 24–25
    find measures, 26–29, 31
    formulas, 26, 31
    problem solving, 30, 42–43,
       45–46, 48
skewed distribution, 150–152
spreadsheet, *see also Fathom™*,
    Microsoft® *Excel*
    compound versus simple
       interest, 423–424
standard deviation, 141,
    143–144
standard form, 242, 244
    converting forms, 242–244,
       268–269
statistics, 86, 89
Statistics Canada, 111
surface area, 258, 261, 294
survey
    designing, 110

T

tessellations, 297–301, 344–345
theoretical probability, 69–73
    comparing to experimental,
       76–81
    formula, 69, 73
tiling pattern, 297
trial, 60
trigonometric ratios, 6–9
    find measures, 9–12, 16–20
    formulas, 8, 13
    problem solving, 20, 42–44,
       48
trinomials
    factoring, 249–253, 256–257,
       259, 265–267
    perfect square, 251
TVM solver, 442–443
    compound interest charged/
       earned, 463–464, 478
    future value, 442–443,
       469–471
    monthly payment, 483, 485
    present value, 443, 448

V

variable costs, 489, 492
variance, 141, 143–144
vehicle expenses
    buying, 482–485
    depreciation, 491–492
    fuel costs, 490–491
    insurance, 489–490, 492
    leasing, 482, 484–485
vertex, 170
vertex form, 204–211
    converting forms, 242–244,
       268–269
volume, 294, 328

X

x-intercepts, 265–267

Z

zeros, 265–267
zero exponents, 364–365, 367

Credits

Photo Credits

t=top; b=bottom; c=centre; l=left; r=right

vi from top "it was just another experiment" by Khaled Mansur/41 in x 83 in/acrylic backpainted on plexi with stainless steel/Photo: Aliyah Guillemette/Courtesy of Maria DeCambra, CP/© Abaca Press [2004] all rights reserved, Tim Garcha/zefa/Corbis, Vasiliki Varvaki/istockphoto.com; **ix b** AP Photo/Aaron Harris/CP, Wolfgang Kaehler/Corbis; **2-3** Jon Gray/Stone/Getty Images; **3 t** David Hiller/Photodisc Green/Getty Images; **5** CP/Jonathan Hayward; **6** Lance Nelson/Stock Photos/zefa/Corbis; **16 t** Brand X Pictures/PunchStock, **c** Tony Freeman/Photo Edit; **18** Wally Stemberger/fotolia.com; **21** Dick Hemingway; **23** NASA/ECN-8611; **24** Adrian Beesley/istockphoto.com; **34** Denis Charlet/AFP/Getty Images; **42** Steve Cole/Getty Images; **45** Dave G. Houser/Corbis; **55** Wolfgang Kaehler/Corbis; **56-57** Barrett & MacKay Photography Inc.; **57 t** U.S. Department of Agriculture; **59** AP Photo/Gary Stewart; **60** Vasiliki Varvaki/istockphoto.com; **68** CP/Chris Haston/© NBC/Courtesy: Everett Collection; **70** First Folio Resource Group Inc.; **76** First Folio Resource Group Inc.; **86** CP/David Boily; **87** AP Photo/Adrian Wyld/CP; **90** CP/Ian Barrett; **97** Tony Bock/Toronto Star; **98-99** Chabrucken/The Image Bank/Getty Images; **99 t** CP/Phototake; **101** Nabil John Elderkin/Stone+/Getty Images; **102** Dick Hemingway; **104** Comstock Select/Corbis; **107** CP/Toronto Star/Vince Talotta; **110** Dick Hemingway; **116** First Folio Resource Group Inc.; **118** Bill Ivy/Ivy Images; **130** David R. Frazier Photolibrary, Inc./Alamy; **140** Adrian Yeo/istockphoto.com; **148** Jack Hollingsworth/Corbis; **159** Mark Richards/Photo Edit; **163** AP Photo/Aaron Harris/CP; **165** Photodisc Collection/Getty Images; **167** Lionel Derimais/Corbis Sygma; **168** CP/© PA Photos Limited [2001] all rights reserved; **169** Roland M. Meisel; **179** Scenics of America/PhotoLink/Getty Images; **180** BananaStock/PunchStock; **193** David Petro; **194** Roland M. Meisel; **203** Roland M. Meisel; **204** Ryan McVay/Getty Images; **215** Xinhua/XINHUA/Corbis; **218** Ruud Taal/epa/Corbis; **224** Courtesy of Vito Palmisano; **229 t** Lawrence M. Sawyer/Getty Images, **c** David Petro; **230-231** Rudy Sulgan/age fotostock/MaXx Images; **231 t** Scott Stulberg/Corbis; **233** John A. Rizzo/Getty Images; **234** Royalty-Free/Corbis; **242** Donald Miralle/Getty Images Sport; **246** Robert Glusic/Getty Images; **247** Larry W. Smith/Getty Images Sport; **248** C. Lee/PhotoLink/Getty Images; **256** Vince Talotta/Toronto Star; **261** Pamela Hodson/istockphoto.com; **264** Robert Sullivan/AFP/Getty Images; **273** Galina Barskaya/istockphoto.com; **274** Sam Emerson/Warner Bros. Entertainment/Getty Images; **276** PhotoLink/Getty Images; **284** Osports.cn/NewSport/Corbis; **289 t** Rudy Sulgan/age fotostock/MaXx Images, **b** C. Borland/PhotoLink/Getty Images; **290** Jerome Prevost/TempSport/Corbis; **291** Con Tanasiuk/Design Pics/Corbis; **292-293** CP/© Abaca Press [2004] all rights reserved; **293 t** "it was just another experiment" by Khaled Mansur/41 in x 83 in/acrylic backpainted on plexi with stainless steel/Photo: Aliyah Guillemette/Courtesy of Maria DeCambra; **295** Tim Garcha/zefa/Corbis; **296 t** Luke Daniek/istockphoto.com, **br** Louvre, Paris, France, Giraudon/The Bridgeman Art Library International; **299** Curt Pickens/istockphoto.com; **300** Luke Daniek/istockphoto.com; **302** Roland M. Meisel; **303** Mark Bond/istockphoto.com; **306** AA World Travel Library/Alamy; **307 both images** First Folio Resource Group Inc.; **310-311** First Folio Resource Group Inc.; **316** M.C. Escher's "Convex and Concave" © 2007 The M.C. Escher Company-Holland. All rights reserved. www.mcecscher.com, Photo credit: Art Resource, NY; **317** Peter Mintz/firstlight.ca; **318** First Folio Resource Group Inc.; **320** Sally and Richard Greenhill/Alamy; **324 both images** First Folio Resource Group Inc.; **325** Sally and Richard Greenhill/Alamy; **327 t** Lee Snider/Photo Images/Corbis, **b** Mark E. Gibson/Corbis; **328** First Folio Resource Group Inc.; **331** CP/Toronto Sun/Alex Urosevic; **333** Roland M. Meisel; **335** Roland M. Meisel; **337** Lowell Georgia/Corbis; **340 both images** Roland M. Meisel; **342** Courtesy of Atomic Energy of Canada Limited; **346-347** Roland M. Meisel; **349** Luke Daniek/istockphoto.com; **352-353** Stocktrek/Pixtal/MaXx Images; **353 t** Tek Image/Science Photo Library; **355** Royalty-Free/Corbis; **356** Koichi Kamoshida/Getty Images News; **362** First Folio Resource Group Inc.; **363** Tony Freeman/Photo Edit; **364** Andrew Syred/Science Photo Library; **372 t** Pete Saloutos/Corbis; **372 b-373** First Folio Resource Group Inc.; **375** Gary S. Chapman/Photographer's Choice/Getty Images; **378** Hemera/MaXx Images; **382** Oleg Prikhodko/istockphoto.com; **395** A. Farnsworth/age fotostock/MaXx Images; **398** Photodisc Collection/Getty Images; **403** Sorin Brinzei/istockphoto.com; **406** Richard T. Nowitz/Corbis; **417** WireImageStock/Masterfile; **418-419** Rudy Sulgan/Corbis; **419 t** Tom Grill/Corbis; **421** David Young-Wolff/Photo Edit; **422** First Folio Resource Group Inc.; **430** Bill Aron/Photo Edit; **436** Rick Friedman/Corbis; **442** First Folio Resource Group Inc.; **446** Ken Brofsky/Getty Images; **457** Ariel Skelley/Corbis; **458-459** Lester Lefkowitz/Corbis; **459 t** Comstock/Corbis; **461** Lon C. Diehl/Photo Edit; **462** Jose Luis Pelaez, Inc./Corbis; **464** Image Source/Corbis; **468** Nancy Ney/Digital Vision; **470** Comstock Images/MaXx Images; **476** Alan Schein Photography/Corbis; **482** Spencer Grant/Photo Edit; **489** David Young-Wolff/Photo Edit; **491** Dennis MacDonald/Photo Edit; **499** Lon C. Diehl/Photo Edit; **502** Comstock/PunchStock; **503 t** McGraw-Hill Companies, Inc./Gary He, photographer, **b** BananaStock/PunchStock.

Illustration Credits

www.mikecarterstudio.com: 164–5, 177

Technical Art

Adam Wood, Kim Hutchinson, and Tom Dart of First Folio Resource Group, Inc.